THE CASE AGAINST MEDIA CONSOLIDATION
Evidence on Concentration, Localism and Diversity

Edited by
Mark N. Cooper

Donald McGannon Center
for Communications Research,
Fordham University

2007

ISBN 0-9-727460-7-2

ACKNOWLEDGMENTS

The papers in this volume were filed as Comments and a Compendium of Research in the Media Ownership proceeding at the Federal Communications Commission.

The following organizations contributed to the preparation of these studies:

Benton Foundation
Brennan Center for Justice at NYU School of Law
Consumer Federation of America
Consumers Union
Ford Foundation
Free Press
Independent Film and Television Alliance
Donald McGannon Communications Research Center
Media and Democracy Coalition
Open Society Institute
Otto Hass Charitable Trust
Social Science Research Council

The opinions expressed in the papers are solely those of the individual authors.

In addition to the authorship of several papers in this volume, the crew at Free Press – Matt Woodbury, Adam Lynn and S. Derek Turner – did yeoman's work in tirelessly and diligently undertaking the tasks that make research possible and readable, i.e. creating data sets, formatting tables and editing text. Ben Byrne of Free Press designed the cover.

CONTENTS

PART VI.
THE IMPACT OF CONSOLIDATION AND
CONGLOMERATION ON LOCALISM AND DIVERSITY

PART VII.
THE CONTEMPORARY TERRAIN OF MEDIA POLICY

PART X:
THE REALITY OF LOCAL MEDIA MARKET STRUCTURE

INTRODUCTION

LARRY A. BLOSSER, BEN SCOTT, JEANNINE KENNEY, GENE
KIMMELMAN, AND GLENN B. MANISHIN

SUMMARY

Consumer Federation of America, Free Press and Consumers Union have produced a *Compendium of Public Interest Research on Media Ownership, Diversity and Localism* in response to the Commission's request for public comment on the continued importance of media ownership rules.[1] Applying a wide lens, we have analyzed and presented the basis of law, economics, and social science that lies at the foundation of the public interest limits on media ownership. Taken together, these multiple and comprehensive studies underscore the essential link between democracy and an open, local, diverse, competitive, and independent media. We urge the Commission to avoid its prior errors and adopt media ownership rules that cultivate localism, encourage a diversity of viewpoints, and preserve a competitive marketplace of ideas for American communities.

This proceeding carries extraordinary consequences for the future of the American mediascape and the health of our political system. The only way democracy can truly work is if there is a free flow of news and information from diverse and independent sources. The public depends upon such open sources to inform itself of pressing political issues at *both* the national and local levels. This is the bedrock principle of the First Amendment that remains as true today as when it was conceived by the Founders.

Changes in technology do not eliminate the need for media ownership limits. Even with the explosion of the Internet and cable channels, most people still rely on their local newspapers and local television stations as the most important sources of local news and information. Those sources thus have disproportionate impact on public opinion. Access to local, independent news sources is already a precious commodity, and further consolidation would be highly problematic. Today, people living in all but a handful of the very largest cities generally have access to only one local newspaper and at most four local television stations producing local news.

Media ownership rules traditionally have protected democracy by keeping sources of news and information diverse and competitive. Attempts to relax these rules require satisfying a very heavy burden of proof – namely,

---

[1] Further Notice of Proposed Rule Making, FCC 06-93 ("NPRM"), Federal Communications Commission ("FCC"), published in the Federal Register on August 9, 2006 (71 Fed. Reg. 45511) by Order, DA 06-1663 (rel. Sept. 18, 2006).

demonstrating that doing so will not implicate fundamental constitutional principles. The compendium of studies accompanying these joint comments show that the vast weight of evidence supports, at a minimum, retaining the newspaper/broadcast cross-ownership and local TV-ownership rules. If further concentration is permitted through relaxation or elimination of these rules, the diversity of local news and information will fall to unacceptably low levels. Cashiering a vibrant marketplace of ideas to suit the interests of a small number of consolidated corporations is simply not in the public interest. American communities can ill afford media concentration that impoverishes the values of localism and gives vertically integrated corporations in horizontally concentrated markets undue influence over the public through control over sources of news and opinion.

Our studies also demonstrate that permitting greater media consolidation directly conflicts with the Commission's statutory obligation, under Section 309(j) of the Communications Act of 1934, to disseminate licenses among a wide variety of businesses, including businesses owned by members of minority groups and women. Racial and ethnic minorities are dramatically underrepresented as media owners. The Commission has a responsibility to broaden, not undermine, the diversity of media owners in order to facilitate a diversity of viewpoint and representation. It cannot fulfill that obligation by simultaneously relaxing media ownership rules. Empirical evidence shows that minority owners better serve their communities, reinforcing the broad principle that the dispersion of ownership to minorities serves the public interest. Our research also shows that relaxing ownership limits undermines the goal of promoting minority ownership.

Perhaps most significantly, our economic analysis of market structures shows unequivocally that the Commission must preserve sensible limits on media ownership. It must prohibit major newspapers from buying up local television stations; and it should not expand the number of TV stations a single company may own in one market. Even in the largest cities in America, the television market is already concentrated. Permitting further mergers will raise concentration levels well above thresholds that would trigger antitrust oversight in any marketplace. The media marketplace must be held to the highest standard in order to protect a diversity of viewpoint.

Our studies of law and social science offer further support for retaining media ownership limits. The Supreme Court has a clear track record on this issue – the FCC's media ownership rules, authorized by Congress, are not only constitutional, they are necessary to preserve and implement First Amendment values. Reasonable media ownership limits can ensure that the public will continue to have access to local news and information, encourage more minority ownership of media outlets, and ensure that diverse viewpoints will get heard.

Finally, our economic and other studies also demonstrate that if the Commission relies upon appropriate local market analysis that correctly defines product and geographic markets, and accounts for the influence of local media outlets, it cannot rationally justify relaxing media ownership rules even in the nation's largest media markets. It is necessary in the public interest to prohibit major newspapers from buying up local television stations and thereby stifling local news production, and also to preserve the existing limits on the number of television stations a single company may own in one market.

Reasonable media ownership limits help ensure that the public will continue to have access to local news and information, encourage more minority ownership of media outlets, and ensure that diverse viewpoints will get heard. An open and robust media is the lifeblood of our democracy because it can serve as a check and balance to government and corporate excess. Thus, there is an essential connection between democracy and a diverse, local, competitive and independent media. We urge the Commission to adopt media ownership rules that encourage a diversity of viewpoints in both ownership of outlets and sources of content, cultivate localism, and preserve competitive outlets. This is the lifeblood of our democratic system and a matter of singular importance to the American people.

THE TASKS BEFORE THE COMMISSION

The ownership rules under review in this proceeding were adopted to promote the diversity of viewpoints presented to the public through newspapers and broadcast stations (both television and radio). The NPRM asks whether the regulations now in force remain "necessary in the public interest" in light of changes in the media marketplace. On each of the three previous occasions when the Commission's efforts to modify its media ownership rules were reviewed by federal appellate courts, the modifications were not affirmed, but rather reversed, remanded or vacated.[2]

In Prometheus, the most recent remand, the Third Circuit was particularly harsh in its criticism of the methodology used by the Commission to evaluate the state of competition in local media markets. The Court declined to uphold the Commission's Cross-Ownership Limits because the Commission failed to provide a reasoned analysis to support the limits that it chose, which led to plainly arbitrary results (such as the Dutchess County, New York local UHF station receiving more weight for diversity and localism

---

[2] *Fox TV Stations v. FCC,* 280 F.3d 1027 (D.C. Cir. 2002); *Sinclair Broadcast Group v. FCC,* 284 F.3d 148 (D.C. Cir. 2002); *Prometheus Radio Project v. FCC,* 373 F.3d 372 (3rd Cir. 2004), *cert denied,* 125 S. Ct. 2903 (2005).

purposes than the New York Times) and employed internally contradictory reasoning.[3]

In these comments and in the attached Compendium of Public Interest Research on Media Ownership, Diversity and Localism, we describe how citizens, including minority groups, use the media as a means of discharging their civic responsibilities as participants in our democratic society. We also present empirical evidence of current media market conditions and the economic forces influencing publishers and mass media producers and distributors. We believe that once the Commission evaluates this information, it will conclude (as we have) that it is necessary in the public interest to prohibit major newspapers from buying up local television stations and thereby stifling local news production, and also to preserve the existing limits on the number of television stations a single company can own in one market. Even in the largest cities in America, the television market is already concentrated.

CONCENTRATION ANALYSIS: A STARTING POINT

In remanding the Cross-Ownership Limits, the *Prometheus* court recognized the legitimacy of concentration analysis as a starting point for the Commission's review. But the court also cautioned that the Commission's statutory public interest mandate, as well as a consistent line of judicial precedent, requires the Commission to examine issues that are beyond the narrower scope of antitrust enforcement.

The Commission ensures that license transfers serve public goals of diversity, competition, and localism, while the antitrust authorities have a different purpose: ensuring that merging companies do not raise prices above competitive levels. *See, e.g.,* Clayton Act, § 7, 15 U.S.C. § 18 (restraining mergers that would lessen competition in a market); Dep't of Justice and Federal Trade Comm'n, Horizontal Merger Guidelines § 0.1 (1997 rev. ed.) ("Merger Guidelines") (seeking to protect consumers by ensuring mergers do not result in anticompetitive prices)."[4]

The logic of the court was sound. There are important differences between markets as defined for antitrust purposes and the "marketplace of ideas." The former is concerned with the ability of a firm (*e.g.,* a producer of "widgets") to maintain a supra-competitive price over a sustained period. But ideas are not widgets. An unfettered media market is not likely to present a full range of diverse and antagonistic views that inform and enlighten the

---

[3] *Prometheus*, 373 F.3d at 408 (3rd Cir. 2004).

[4] *Id.,* at 414.

citizenry. This is particularly true as large firms concentrate their holdings and market power through vertical and horizontal integration.[5]

Media as a product in a concentrated market is not likely to be produced in the service of democratic values, such as an informed electorate and robust debate on issues of public importance, and will not serve all audiences efficiently and fairly. Media producers, especially for broadcast distribution, have a strong incentive to produce content for the "lowest common denominator," i.e., the largest number of consumers, presenting material that serves, and does not offend, prevailing majority tastes.[6] The economic characteristics of media markets lead natural market forces to discriminate against the preferences of minorities – racial, ethnic, and any other relatively small groups whose tastes in media differ from the majority's.

Media is a public good and possesses significant "positive externalities." Like clean air and national defense, benefits accrue to society at large that cannot be captured by the market. For example, investigative journalism uncovering government waste or consumer fraud benefits all citizens—even those who do not read the newspaper or advertise on its pages.

Communications and First Amendment jurisprudence squarely and for decades has supported the proposition that acceptable media policy is about more than economics[7] and requires concern for preservation of a vigorous debate[8] that includes the presentation of a diversity of views[9] on a broad array of issues.[10]

Moreover, in the "marketplace of ideas" there is a need to consider both the potential long-term and short-term (or transitory) effects of

---

[5] *Compendium* Study 17, at 267-269, discusses the available empirical evidence on the tendency toward oligopoly in contemporary media markets. *Compendium* study 3, at 52-58, describes how the contemporary, concentrated commercial mass media fail to provide the broad and positive discourse that democracy needs.

[6] *Compendium* Study 17, at 269-274 reviews the available evidence on the tendency to under serve minorities, while Study 12, at 195-196, presents new evidence. Srudy 11 shows the drastic underrepresentation of minorities and women among owners of TV stations.

[7] *Associated Press v. United States*, 326 U.S. 1, 20 (1945); *Fox Television Stations, Inc., v. FCC*, 280 F.3d 1027, 1047 (D.C. Cir. 2002). *Compendium* Study 3, at 45-52, examines the shows that the reliance on the market to meet society's information needs is a recent theory that is inconsistent with the context and implementation of the First Amendment in the young American republic.

[8] *Red Lion Broadcasting v. FCC*, 395 US 367, 390 (1969) (hereinafter *Red Lion*). *Turner Broadcasting System, Inc. v. FCC*, 512 U.S. 622, 638-39 (1994).

[9] *Associated Press v. United States*, 326 U.S. 1, 20 (1945).

[10] *Red Lion Broadcasting v. FCC*, 395 US 367, 390 (1969). *Compendium* Study 3, at 42-47, reviews First Amendment scholarship that concludes the narrow view of the First Amendment adopted by the Commission is inconsistent with its origin and intent.

concentration.   Long-term effects include censorship, either by the
government or by a private monopoly or oligopoly. But the short-term effects,
though perhaps less obvious, are equally pernicious.[11] The last few days and
weeks prior to a local election or referendum, when voters focus their
attention and make decisions, are particularly crucial times for the
communication of divergent views. This temporal dimension (short voter
attention span, short shelf life/volatility of issue-centric information)
necessitates a more conservative approach when dealing with media
ownership than when addressing other goods and services.

        For all these reasons, the development of the Commission's media
ownership rules should begin, but cannot permissibly end, with
concentration analysis.[12] Other things being equal, a media market with 50
radio stations, 16 TV stations and five newspapers is less likely to be "at risk"
for excessive concentration than a smaller market. However, any index or
quantitative metric should only used as a screening device to identify
transactions needing special scrutiny – a "yellow light" or caution signal. An
index should *never* be used as the basis for giving a transaction an automatic
"green light," because an index may only measure one aspect of "diversity"
(*e.g.*, diversity of ownership), while neglecting or giving too little weight to
other aspects of diversity ("viewpoint diversity" and "source diversity") that
the FCC is obligated to preserve and promote. When one reviews the
language used by the Supreme Court over the course of half a century and the
Courts of Appeals in the last decade,[13] there can be little doubt that the
concern with "undue concentration of economic power"[14] is an important but
nonetheless small part of the broader goal of First Amendment policy[15] to
prevent "an inordinate effect on public opinion,"[16] achieve a "vigorous

---

[11] *Compendium* Study 6, at 87-97, examines the broad impact of television on the
political process and the unique characteristics of elections that heighten the influence
of the media during campaigns. Study 18, at 281-293, discusses the influence of the
media on political processes more generally. Both suggest that the antitrust standard
for economic market power – a significant, non-transitory increase in price – is too
narrow for the broader concerns about influence in the political marketplace.

[12]*Prometheus*, 373 F.3d at 402-403 (3rd Cir. 2004) ("We do not object in principle to the
Commission's reliance on the Department of Justice and Federal Trade Commission's
antitrust formula, the Herfindahl-Hirschmann Index ("HHI"),as its starting point in
measuring diversity in local markets.").

[13] *Compendium* Study 1 provides a thematic review of this history.

[14] *FCC v. Nat'l Citizens Comm. for Broad.*, 436 U.S. 775, 780 (1978).

[15] *See Associated Press*, 326 U.S. at 28 (1945); *Fox*, 280 F.3d at 1047 (D.C.Cir. 2002).

[16] *Sinclair*, 284 F.3d at 148 (D.C. Cir. 2003).

debate"[17] and access to "controversial issues,[18]" and "suitable access to social, political, aesthetic, moral and other ideas and experiences.[19]"

THE PIVOTAL ROLE OF LOCALISM IN THIS PROCEEDING

Far from being rendered irrelevant by the profusion of cable and satellite channels and the Internet, localism is more important than ever in our increasingly diverse society.[20] The late House Speaker, Thomas P. "Tip" O'Neill, once famously remarked "All politics is local." Not only are our representatives to state and federal legislatures elected on a local basis, but many public policy decisions vital to the quality of life and the fabric of our society, including education, land use, law enforcement and emergency services, are made predominantly at the local level.[21]

While the political dimensions of localism are important, the public's need for local news and information transcends politics. Localism also plays a vital role in both our criminal and civil justice systems. Juries are selected locally, and render decisions on issues ranging from simple negligence (the "reasonable person" standard) to obscenity and indecency (the "contemporary community standards" criterion), applying what are fundamentally local standards. Citizen interaction at the local level, in the political, social and cultural spheres, provides the basis for community involvement, identity formation and civic action.[22]

The Commission's own research has demonstrated what Americans have long known intuitively — locally owned broadcast stations provide more local and community news than non-locally owned stations.[23] This is a conclusion the Commission was reticent to concede. An FCC study conducted in early 2004, publicly released only after it was leaked to U.S. Senator Barbara Boxer two years after it was drafted,[24] concluded just that.[25] This is a real-world difference that should inform and drive the decision to hold ownership limits in place to promote localism.

---

[17] *Red Lion*, 395 U.S. at 385 (1969).

[18] *Id.*

[19] *Id.*, at 390.

[20] *Compendium*, Study 4, at 67-71, discusses the increasing diversity of the American population over the past thirty years.

[21] *Compendium* Study 2, at 31-32.

[22] *Compendium* Studies 2, at 32-35, 4, at 63-65.

[23] *Compendium* Study 16, at 239-242, reviews the record and the new evidence.

[24] See Letter from FCC Chairman Kevin Martin to Sen. Boxer, Sept. 18, 2006, available at http://hraunfoss.fcc.gov/edocs_public/attachmatch/DOC-267475A1.pdf

[25] Federal Communications Commission, "*Do Local Owners Deliver More Localism? Some Evidence from Local Broadcast News*," June 2004, http://hraunfoss.fcc.gov/edocs_public/attachmatch/DOC-267448A1.pdf.

TELEVISION AND DAILY NEWSPAPERS DOMINATE LOCAL MEDIA MARKETS

The Commission's *2002 Biennial Review Order* did not cite a single survey asking the key questions: "What media do people rely on most for local news and information?;" and "What media most influence people's opinions about local public affairs?"[26] The answers matter because they are factors in determining the weight of each media outlet in analyzing the impacts of further consolidation, factors the Commission failed to consider in its *2002 Biennial Review Order* and one of the reasons for the *Prometheus* court's remand.

Studies 7 and 8 of the *Compendium* present answers to these questions. In two surveys, conducted in 2004 and 2006, we asked consumers to identify the local news sources that they used most often and those they considered most important. Local newspapers and television are far and away the most important sources, each cited by about one-third of the respondents.[27] Radio and local weeklies were each mentioned by about ten percent of respondents. Our results are consistent with other research, reviewed in Studies 7 and 8, which carefully seeks to identify the sources of news and information that the public uses.

Only a very small percentage of the population (4% first mention, 7% second mention) regards the Internet as a frequently used source of local news and information.[28] Even those who rely on the Internet for local news overwhelmingly go to web sites of traditional media – local newspapers, local TV and national TV – which generally utilize "repurposed" content substantially identical to their traditional distribution formats. Among the 11% of respondents say that the Internet is their most frequent or second most frequent source of local news, the websites of local TV stations and local newspapers account for about half of the sites they visit most frequently.[29] Sites not affiliated with traditional media outlets (blogs, list serves, alternative news sites and others – including aggregators) account for 17% of the sites visited most and second most.

---

[26] *Compendium* Study 7, at 99-101.

[27] *Compendium* Study 7, at 102-106.

[28] *Compendium* Study 8, at 111-119.

[29] As the *Prometheus* court observed: "There is a critical distinction between websites that are independent sources of local news and websites of local newspapers and broadcast stations that merely republish the information already being reported by the newspaper or broadcast station counterpart. The latter do not present an 'independent' viewpoint and thus should not be considered as contributing diversity to local markets. Accordingly, the Commission should have discounted the respondents who primarily rely on these websites from its total number of respondents who indicated that they use the Internet to access local news." *Prometheus*, 373 F.3d at 405-06 (3rd Cir. 2004)

When asked about the credibility of web sites, the overwhelming majority (about 70%) of online news users said that an association between a web site and a traditional source of news would make the website more credible. The evidence on preferences for web sites and the complementarity and linkages between traditional outlets and Internet sites provide support for the *Prometheus* court's criticism of the Commission's treatment of the Internet in developing the Diversity Index.[30]

That the Internet plays a small role in providing news and information about local public affairs should not be surprising when one examines the function of Internet web sites and bloggers, as we have in Study 8, at 121-123. They simply do not undertake the reporting and editing functions that typify journalism as traditionally defined. The *Prometheus* court offered just such a penetrating analysis of the role of the media and its characterization is just as true today as it was three years ago.[31] If we are concerned about the dissemination of information, not just opinion, about local public affairs, traditional local outlets remain the dominant sources.

THE DIVERSITY INDEX: A FLAWED SNAPSHOT OF MEDIA MARKETS

In its most recent Notice, the Commission tentatively concludes, given the fundamental flaws revealed on appeal from its 2002 proceeding, that the Diversity Index "is an inaccurate tool for measuring diversity."[32] The *Prometheus* court accepted the idea that a single index drawn from the general antitrust framework *could* be created, but nevertheless found fault with the Commission's implementation. Indeed, all three courts examining the

---

[30] A separate study conducted by Pew, also summarized in Study 8, focuses on bloggers, Study 8, at 132-134. The results of the Pew study provide further support for the *Prometheus* court's observation that websites of individuals and organizations cannot be viewed as "media outlets" for viewpoint diversity purposes.

[31] *Prometheus*, 373 F.3d at 407 (3rd Cir. 2004) (internal citations omitted). ("In terms of content, 'the media' provides (to different degrees, depending on the outlet) accuracy and depth in local news in a way that an individual posting in a chat room on a particular issue of local concern does not. But more importantly, media outlets have an entirely different character from individual or organizations' websites and thus contribute to diversity in an entirely different way. They provide an aggregator function (bringing news/information to one place) as well as a distillation function (making a judgment as to what is interesting, important, entertaining, *etc.*) Individuals... and entities... may use the Internet to disseminate information and opinions about matters of local concern... but ... are not, themselves... 'media outlets' for viewpoint-diversity purposes. Like many entities, they just happen to use a particular media outlet – the Internet – to disseminate information. Similarly, advertiser-driven websites such as hvnet.com... hardly contribute to viewpoint diversity.")

[32] NPRM at ¶32.

Commission's rules since 2002 that have remanded regulations accepted the proposition that we must count "voices" without regard to their content and substitutability, and adopted the principle that the Commission must fashion an approach that is consistent, logical and rational, leading to a result that reasonably reflects media market reality.

The *Prometheus* court identified three principal problems with the Diversity Index. First, the Commission assumed that all outlets within a media type had equal market shares. Second, it assigned weights to different media types that were both inconsistent and not based on sound empirical measures. Finally, the link the Commission established between the index and the merger approval rule was tenuous at best.[33]

In *Compendium* Studies 19 and 20, we review the critique of the Commission's methodology and follow the *Prometheus* court holding to construct a reasonable measure of market structure. In Studies 25 through 27, we present analyses of approximately 50 markets. We begin in Study 25 with a comparison across ten markets (the same ten markets the Commission reviewed in detail) of the results of the Commission's Diversity Index and an alternative approach — one that seeks to respond to the principal criticisms the *Prometheus* court leveled against the Diversity Index. The weights assigned to each media type are based on the results of a national random sample survey conducted in August 2006. Available industry data on market shares of individual firms were used in place of the Commission's "equal market shares" assumption that the court found counter-intuitive and irrational.

In 2002, Commission's approach yielded unrealistically low estimates of media market concentration. The FCC found only one of the ten markets to be above the concentrated threshold and none above the highly concentrated threshold. However, when audiences of the media outlets are properly factored in, the results are dramatically different: *every* market is above the concentrated threshold and eight of the ten are above the highly concentrated threshold.[34]

In *Compendium* Study 26 we examine the impact of newspaper-TV mergers on the market structure of the ten FCC sample markets. In Study 27, we examine the impact of TV-TV mergers on 15 markets. Our analysis concludes that in every case, the increase in concentration caused by the mergers would exceed the Department of Justice *Merger Guidelines*.

CONCENTRATION OF OWNERSHIP UNDERMINES LOCALISM AND DIVERSITY

Several of the studies included in the *Compendium* document how the deleterious effects on localism and diversity flow from concentration of

---

[33] *See Compendium* Studies 19, at 301-304; and 20, at 307-320.

[34] *Compendium* Studies 25-27, examine over 50 markets.

ownership within local markets,[35] consolidation of media into national chains, and conglomeration across media types.

We review an extensive body of quantitative and qualitative evidence. National chains and conglomerates reduce local-oriented content. The trend in commercial mass media, particularly television, is toward a reduction in news coverage of local issues in the period leading up to elections.[36] Local public affairs programming is notable by its absence on most television stations.[37] Recent studies based on FCC data confirm much of the earlier research. Consolidation and conglomeration give rise to a "largest market share/lowest common denominator" ethic that undercuts stations' ability to deliver culturally diverse programming, locally-oriented programming and public interest programming.[38]

We address in detail the role that ownership plays in the viewpoints presented in mass media outlets. Academic and anecdotal evidence compiled since the Commission's 2002 Biennial Review Order convincingly demonstrates that media ownership matters.[39] The owners of media outlets influence what and how events are covered. Owners may seek to influence policy processes. They may also exhibit "slant" or "bias," and may not serve the needs of all members of the community.[40] Slant or bias affects not only the tone of coverage, but also the quantity of coverage and the subjects on which media outlets choose to editorialize.[41]

We also note the systemic problems that economic pressures induced by concentrated ownership cause in newsrooms. Producing local news, supporting in-depth investigative journalism, and offering extensive coverage of local politics is costly.[42] The economic logic of consolidation is to reduce labor costs by centralizing content production, reducing reporting expenditures, repurposing content across media platforms, and filling the news hole with low-budget content such as coverage of weather, crime, and accidents. Meanwhile, coverage of local politics and elections has reached

---

[35] Studies 4, at 65-71; 6, at 99-103; 10, at 159-168; and 16, at 239-242, review and present qualitative and quantitative evidence that addresses various aspects of the impact of concentration and conglomeration on localism, diversity and the quality of news and information that reach the public. Compendium Studies 15, at, 229-234, and 16, at 247-261, demonstrate that concentration does not improve the quality or increase the quantity of local news and public affairs programming.

[36] Compendium Study 4, at 63-67.

[37] Compendium Studies, 4, at 63-67; and 16, at 242-245.

[38] Compendium Study 17, at 267-274.

[39] Studies 5, at 71-75; and 17, at 267-274, review the literature. Study 16, at 239-242, reviews analyses based on the Commission's data that shows that consolidations, conglomeration and concentration detract from localism and diversity.

[40] Compendium Studies 5, at 77-86; and 17, at 267-274.

[41] Compendium Studies 5, at 86-88; and 17, at 274-280.

[42] Compendium Study 17, at 274-280.

crisis levels of inadequacy. Yet, *Compendium* Study 9 shows that disinvesting in good journalism accelerated the spiral of decline, rather than reversing it.[43]

CONCENTRATED OWNERSHIP: RISKY BUSINESS FOR MEDIA COMPANIES

We examine the economics of today's newspaper and television industries in *Compendium* Study 9. When the Commission voted to relax its cross-ownership rules in 2003, it gave substantial weight to the argument that unless media owners were permitted to engage in consolidation and conglomeration in pursuit of scale economies, local media outlets would be seriously weakened or unable to survive.[44]   But over the past three years, the premise that consolidation and conglomeration are necessary to the economic well-being of media companies has been challenged by reality.

Data derived from recent sales of media properties, as well as evidence from other sources, including trade and academic literature as well as the popular press, show that newspaper and television properties are selling at healthy multiples of cash flow and experiencing profit margins comparable to other media businesses.[45] Large conglomerates and chains — which have emphasized centralization, the realization of synergies and staff cuts — are struggling, but smaller chains and stand-alone properties with a focus on quality news and locally produced content have been thriving.[46]

Consequently, although traditional media outlets face economic challenges today as their audiences and advertisers migrate to the Internet, more conglomeration and consolidation will not solve the problem. Therefore, the Commission should not rely on the spurious claim that more concentration in ownership is the key to local media survival as justification for relaxing media ownership rules. The actual data simply do not support that conclusion. As the *Prometheus* court explained, the Commission has discretion to draw lines, but when it does so must have a quantitative basis in actual evidence, not mere suppositions or anecdotes.[47]

Consolidation and Conglomeration Do Not Yield Improvements in the Quality or Quantity of Local News and Information.

Compendium Studies 15 and 16 offer a critical examination of the record evidence relied upon by the Commission in the *2002 Biennial Review Order* in support of its conclusion that media cross-ownership can enhance

---

[43] *Compendium* Studies 9, at 139-142 and 10, at 159-168.
[44] For example in 2002 *Biennial Review Order* ¶¶ 360, 366.
[45] *Compendium* Study 9, at 139-149.
[46] *Compendium* Studies 9 at 139-149 and 10 at 168-177.
[47] *Prometheus*, 373 F.3d at 407 (3rd Cir. 2004).

quality. Neither of the two studies relied on by the Commission — a study by the Project on Excellence in Journalism and another by the Commission's own Media Ownership Working Group (MOWG) study 7 — provides a valid basis for reaching the stated conclusion.

In paragraph 32 of the current NPRM, the Commission asks for comments on how it should approach cross-ownership limits, including whether the newspaper/broadcast cross-ownership rule and the radio/television cross-ownership rule are necessary in the public interest as a result of competition. We provide a comprehensive answer. although the Commission previously reached, and the *Prometheus* court accepted, the wrong conclusion based on an inadequate evidentiary record, it is not too late to reverse course. There is no credible evidence that consolidation and/or conglomeration have positive effects.[48]   On the contrary, subsequent rigorous empirical evidence shows that newspaper/TV combinations and duopolies do not result in increases in the quantity or quality of local news and information available to the public. The very data on which the Commission relied to lift the newspaper-TV cross-ownership ban, when reanalyzed by its own staff, contradicts its earlier conclusion.[49]

Media Concentration Does Not Increase Diversity or Produce More Innovation

In the *2002 Biennial Review*, the Commission found that concentration of the media is good for consumers.[50]   It did so by relying on two theories: Peter Steiner's argument that concentrated media companies provide greater diversity,[51] and Joseph Schumpeter's theory that monopolists produce more innovation. It is debatable whether these theories, first articulated more than 50 years ago, were ever validly applied to media markets.   But not unsurprisingly, the actual data once again contradict the Commission's earlier presumptions.

Part 7 of the *Compendium* evaluates the question of consumer benefits of diversity and innovation and from media consolidation and concludes that consolidation produces irreparable consumer harms.[52]   It is overwhelmingly clear that they do not apply to 21st century American mass media. Profit-maximizing behavior increases bias. News coverage and political speech tend to be targeted toward the larger and more desirable demographic groups, leaving minority audiences under-served. The phenomena of targeting,

---

[48] *Compendium* Studies 15, at 229-234 and 16, at 239-261.
[49] *Compendium* Study 16, at 239-242.
[50] 2002 *Biennial Review Order* ¶¶ 194, 396, claimed economic efficiencies but the like to the public interest goals is lacking.
[51] 2002 *Biennial Review Order* ¶ 188.
[52] *Compendium* Study 17, at 267-280.

slanting and spinning, particularly in political discourse, have been extensively documented in the literature.[53] Competition matters. There will probably always be partisan media outlets and a natural tendency for media organizations to stake out positions at the extremes. Competition between mass media is important, regardless of whether it reduces bias, or merely exposes conscientious readers and viewers to a wider range of news sources.[54]

MEDIA OWNERSHIP LIMITS PROVIDE A NEEDED COUNTERWEIGHT TO MARKET FORCES TENDING TOWARD EVER-INCREASING CONCENTRATION

The market structures of commercial mass media in the first decade of the 21st century have moved far from atomistic competition in the direction of oligopoly and monopolistic competition. Among the factors contributing to this trend are economies of scale and strong differences in preferences between population groups, which tend to drive commercial mass media to target programming toward larger social groups and under-serve minorities. National chains and media conglomerates have amassed market power sufficient to enable their owners to pursue their political preferences, both through economic power and the owners' control over staffing decisions and editorial policy.[55] Advertisers reinforce the trend by targeting commercial messages to preferred demographics and by avoiding sponsorship of programs that might be viewed by their target audience as controversial or discomforting.[56]

The literature[57] establishes that a more competitive market structure, particularly one characterized by diversity of ownership across geographic, ethnic and gender lines, would increase the diversity of programming. Minority owners have been shown to be more likely to serve the needs of their communities.[58] Public policies promoting ownership diversity are necessary to counteract the loss of diversity resulting from media concentration.[59]

Evidence in the record, summarized in *Compendium* Study 15, demonstrates that had the Commission conducted a proper analysis of the programming market and the impact of concentration of ownership on source diversity, it would have concluded that the restrictions on duopolies and

---

[53] *Compendium* Study 18, at 283-293.
[54] *Compendium* Study 18, at 283-293.
[55] *Compendium* Studies 10 at 168-177, and 17, at 267-274.
[56] *Compendium* Studies 5, 86-88 and 17, at 274-278.
[57] *Compendium* Study 17, at 274-280.
[58] *Compendium* Studies 4, at 63-65, and 12, at 195-196.
[59] *Compendium* Studies 4 at 65-67; and 13, at 201-207. *Compendium* Study 14 presents a case study that shows the vastly different perspectives portrayed by local and national papers of a major event.

triopolies should be much more stringent because the concentration of ownership of outlets undermines diversity by reducing the ability of independent programmers to produce content.

THE COMMISSION MUST CONSIDER THE IMPACT OF ITS OWNERSHIP RULES ON NEW ENTRANTS, INCLUDING WOMEN AND MINORITIES

The *Prometheus* court rebuked the Commission for failing to consider the effects that the repeal of the Failed Station Solicitation Rule would have on potential minority station owners.[60]   As previously noted, Part V of the Compendium concludes that minority-owned full-power television stations are more likely to produce local news content than their non-minority-owned counterparts; similarly we find that minority and female station owners are more likely to focus on the needs of the local community. *Compendium* Study 11, which corrects many flaws in the FCC data on TV licenses held by women and members of minority groups, paints a troubling picture of the small and declining percentage of full-power commercial television stations owned by female and minority owners:

Women comprise 51 percent of the U.S. population, but own a total of only 67 stations, or 4.97 percent of the total.

Minorities comprise 33 percent of the U.S. population, but own a total of only 44 stations, or 3.26 percent of the total.

We find that by standard measures of performance and in comparison to other areas of the economy, broadcast television is one of the worst performing areas of American life when it comes to minority ownership.

In Study 12, we reaffirm the finding that minority owners do a better job of serving their communities.[61] In Study 13 we demonstrate empirically that minority owners tend to thrive in more competitive (less concentrated) markets and that relaxation of media ownership limits in the past have led to less minority ownership, rather than more.[62] Conversely, the likely outcome of further industry consolidation and concentration will be fewer minority-owned stations, in general, and fewer minority-owned stations airing local news content.

The Commission is obligated by statute to eliminate "market entry barriers for entrepreneurs and other small businesses" and to do so by "favoring diversity of media voices."[63] However, the Commission has shown little interest in turning the raw ownership data it gathers from stations on a routine basis via an automated process into useful reports. A thorough and

---

[60] *Prometheus*, 373 F.3d at 431-32 (3rd Cir. 2004).

[61] *Compendium* Study 12, at 195-196.

[62] *Compendium* Study 13, at 207-212.

[63] 47 U.S.C. §257, §309(j).

comprehensive study of the current and historical ownership of all broadcast stations (radio as well as television) should be undertaken by the Commission and the results of the study, as well as the raw data, made available to the public before the Commission considers the adoption of further revisions to its media ownership rules. It is clear that if the Commission wishes to permit further media consolidation, it must explain how that result does not undermine its ability to meet its statutory obligation to promote minority ownership.

LIMITATIONS ON MEDIA OWNERSHIP ARE NEEDED TO PRESERVE AND ENHANCE SOURCE DIVERSITY

In the *2002 Biennial Review Order*, the Commission failed to treat source diversity as a separate goal and it failed to analyze the role and state of source diversity in detail.[64]   It failed to examine the ownership of programming and ignored the evidence in the record that the ownership and control of programming in the television market is concentrated. These errors contributed to the Commission's decision to relax the duopoly rule, tripling the number of markets in which multiple stations could have been owned by a single entity had the rules not been remanded.

Studies 23 and 24 provide a great deal of additional evidence that policy changes in the 1990s undermined source diversity. Study 22 examines the impact of three major policy changes in the early and mid-1990s on the production and distribution of video content, primarily broadcast television programming in America: the repeal of the Financial Interest / Syndication rules and the enactment of both the Cable Act of 1992 and the Telecommunications Act of 1996. It shows that these policy changes led to the formation of a vertically integrated, tight oligopoly in television entertainment and a dramatic shrinkage of the role of independent producers of content. By two widely accepted economic measures of market concentration, the Herfindahl-Hirschman Index (HHI) and the market share of the top four firms (the 4 Firm Concentration Ration or CR-4), the video market has become a concentrated, vertically integrated, tight oligopoly. The policy changes and resulting alterations in market structure and behavior were not limited to the prime time, first-run broadcast sector, however. They also affected the syndication market, cable television and theatrical movies because prime time programming plays a critical role in the overall video entertainment product space.

Study 24 considers how the production and distribution of television and movie content for broadcast and cable TV, as well as theatrical release were affected by the emergence of this vertically integrated tight oligopoly.

---

[64] See Study 22.

This oligopoly engages in a number of predatory business practices that both limit competition from independents and deprive the public of new, fresh voices. They foreclose the market to independents by leveraging their vertical market power and by self-supplying product. They exercise their market power as buyers of content (monopsony power) with two practices that are especially damaging to competition from independent producers. The first is that networks often demand that they be given an equity participation in an independently developed television series in order for it to be placed on the primetime schedule. The second is that basic cable channels owned by members of the oligopoly will not pay license fees that are commensurate with the production values and the scope of licensed rights they demand in independently produced TV movies. Study 24 concludes that, if not amended, these same policy changes could have a major impact upon the ability of independents to offer product through the Internet and other developing digital platforms, including the rapidly approaching digital multicast channels.

LIMITS ON MEDIA OWNERSHIP ARE NEEDED TO PROTECT DIVERSITY, LOCALISM & COMPETITION

As the actual market and audience data analyzed in the *Compendium* demonstrates, today's media marketplace, dominated by a handful of mega-corporations, allows a small number of organized private interests to circumscribe the limits of public debate, to marginalize the views of unprofitable or politically undesirable speakers by denying them access to high-impact mainstream media, and to undermine competition. It is the Commission's responsibility to temper private control over the media system through the adoption of public policies that promote a diversity of voices, expanding the marketplace to include all voices, and safeguarding citizens' ability to deliberate with all viewpoints. Limits on media ownership are necessary, as are policies designed to expand ownership of media outlets and viewpoint diversity.

The *Compendium* provides the Commission with a number of specific proposals for economic methodology for use in its review. We draw special attention to our model of market structure analysis. In the *Compendium* Study 20, we suggest methodology that serves as a useful successor to the failed Diversity Index and which rigorously complies with the *Prometheus* court's remand order. It combines the same general approach to geographic markets employed by the Commission in its earlier review, but also incorporates usage data derived from commercial sources and on survey data that appropriately weight the influence of each type of media. This measure produces a ranking that reflects reality, addresses the court's criticisms, and eliminates the absurd results that the Commission's Diversity Index produced in several markets, including New York. We also recommend that although standard measures of concentration from the Department of Justice and the industrial organization literature are used in the analysis, the Commission should apply a higher standard in recognition of the importance of media to public discourse. However, the attached *Compendium* studies of specific markets find that even using traditional and inadequate antitrust guidelines, *any* mergers of dominant local media violate those guidelines. Using the *Compendium's* proposed methodology, the conclusion that the Commission cannot and must not allow mergers in concentrated media markets becomes inescapable.

In order to properly address the remand from the *Prometheus* court and to uphold its statutory obligations to serve the public interest, the Commission must engage in a thorough review of the available economic and social scientific evidence. This evidentiary record must be vetted and scrutinized to determine its reliability and consequences, and then to fashion the proper course of action.

The *Compendium* provides a robust and well-researched starting point for the Commission's analysis. Moreover, the Commission must expansively and meaningfully involve the public. We strongly support the initiation of public hearings which began in October of 2006, and we trust that these will continue through the coming months. To meet that goal, the Commission must also release a further notice of proposed rulemaking providing the public with detailed proposals for any media ownership rule changes and the opportunity to comment prior to making any rule changes final.

The Commission must also conduct a thorough review of minority and female ownership of broadcast stations prior to issuing any media ownership order. It is to the considerable shame of the Commission that it has neither performed such a study in recent years, nor collected data sufficient to accurately analyze the question. No consolidation should be permitted in any form prior to the completion of a Commission study of minority ownership in radio and television and a justification as to how media consolidation and an expansion of minority ownership of broadcast stations can coexist.

Democracy requires a free flow of information from diverse and independent sources. Most people look to their local newspapers and local television stations for the local news and information they use to inform themselves of pressing political issues. Local news markets are already highly concentrated. The Commission bears a heavy burden of proof to demonstrate that any rule change it makes is in the public interest. The evidence submitted into the record through the *Compendium* makes clear it cannot be met.

The Commission must preserve sensible limits on media ownership. It must prohibit cross-ownership of local dominant newspapers and local television stations, in order to prevent one company from gaining excessive control over one community's news and information. It should not expand the number of TV stations a single company can own in one market. Even in the largest cities in America, the television market is already concentrated. There is no justification in law, economics, or social policy for permitting further media consolidation and inflicting its harmful results on local communities.

Reasonable media ownership limits can ensure that the public will continue to have access to local news and information, encourage more minority ownership of media outlets, promote competition, and ensure that diverse viewpoints will get heard. A diverse, antagonistic and competitive local media is the lifeblood of our democracy because it serves as a check against government and corporate excess and against competitor abuses, and provides multiple sources for local news, information and viewpoints so essential for a well-informed electorate. The courts have recognized there is an essential connection between democracy and a diverse, local, competitive and independent media. As the Commission proceeds, we urge it, too, to recognize and preserve that same principle.

In sum, the Commission should adopt media ownership rules that encourage a diversity of viewpoints, cultivate localism, and preserve competitive outlets. Such rules are vital to our democratic system and a matter of singular importance to the American public.

COMPENDIUM OF PUBLIC INTEREST RESEARCH ON MEDIA OWNERSHIP, DIVERSITY AND LOCALISM

PART I:

LAW AND POLICY

STUDY 1:
SUPREME COURT JURISPRUDENCE SUPPORTS MEDIA OWNERSHIP LIMITS

MARK COOPER

LAW AND POLICY: INTRODUCTION

Three times in the past half-decade Federal Appeals Courts have remanded Federal Communications Commission (FCC) ownership rules for lack of a coherent analytic approach or a sound empirical basis.[1] The first two cases, dealing with individual ownership rules, were decided by the Federal Appeals Court for the District of Columbia. In *Fox* the Court overturned the rule that limited the number of stations a network could own nationwide (the national cap). In *Sinclair* the same Court overturned an FCC rule that limited the number of markets in which one owner could hold two TV broadcast licenses (the duopoly rule).

The third case, heard by the Third Circuit in *Prometheus* was the first to involve the full array of media ownership rules at one time. In addition to the two TV rules that had been overturned earlier, it involved rules that banned the ownership of a TV station and a newspaper in the same market (newspaper-TV cross-ownership and newspaper-radio cross-ownership), as well as several rules affecting radio station ownership. This case was important, not only because it involved many rules, but also because it embodied the first attempt of the Commission to respond to the earlier remands of its rules. This was the first time that the Commission had endeavored to articulate and implement a full fledged empirical methodology for assessing the level of concentration in media markets as a basis for adopting ownership limits and merger policy.

The Third Circuit ruled that the FCC had failed miserably to meet the legal standard, not because the task is too difficult, but because the FCC made inconsistent and contradictory arguments and unfounded, unrealistic assumptions in its analysis.[2] Building on the earlier criticism of the FCC

---

[1] Prometheus Radio Project. v. FCC 373 F.3d 372 (3rd Cir. 2004) (hereafter Prometheus); Fox Television Stations, Inc., v. FCC, 280 F.3d 1027 (D.C. Cir. 2002) (Fox); Sinclair Broadcasting, Inc. v. FCC, 284 F.3d 148 (D.C. Cir. 2002) (hereafter Sinclair).

[2] Frank, Ahnrens. "'Soldier's Ethic' Guides Powell at the FCC." *Washington Post*, October 15, 2003 at E-4, quotes FCC Chairman Michael Powell complaining "The issue is very complex; have you heard the opposition express their criticism in a complex way? No. It's a lot easier to blast the messenger than deal with the substance of the issue."

approach by the D.C. Circuit Court of Appeals, the Court in *Prometheus* provides a comprehensive framework for analyzing media markets and writing rules that will pass legal and constitutional muster.

The terrain of media ownership policy is clear.   Diversity and localism remain focal points of public policy.   Ownership limits are a reasonable approach to promoting both.   Television remains an important medium for news and information and a major influence on the political process because broadcast signals are still extremely scarce.   The standards to promote democratic discourse under the Communications Act are higher than under the antitrust laws.

In order to grasp the framework that the *Prometheus* Court laid out, we must start from the foundation of media policy in First Amendment jurisprudence.   None of the Appeals Court cases have been taken up by the Supreme Court on appeal.   Each of them cited prior Supreme Court rulings on the nature of the media and FCC regulations that were upheld.   In other words, the law is settled, here, notwithstanding repeated attempts by broadcasters to convince the court to break with prior Supreme Court rulings. Thus, the logical way to understand the legal context for this proceeding is to start from *Prometheus*, then to move to *Fox* and *Sinclair*, concluding with the broader body of Supreme Court jurisprudence.

CONTEMPORARY FIRST AMENDMENT JURISPRUDENCE ON MEDIA OWNERSHIP LIMITS

The *Prometheus* Court reiterated the principle that Congress and the FCC can impose limitations on ownership by holders of licenses to broadcast TV and radio signals.   Using the broad language of the Supreme Court, the Third Circuit Court noted the long held view that "diversification of mass media ownership serves the public interest by promoting diversity of program and service viewpoints as well as by preventing undue concentration of economic power."[3]

These two central themes of Supreme Court jurisprudence – promoting diversity and preventing undue concentration and influence – were prominent in the other recent cases as well.   In *Fox* the D.C. Circuit stated that public policies to promote a more diverse media landscape are constitutional, even if they reduce economic efficiency.   The D.C. Appeals Court continues to articulate the proposition that "the Congress could reasonably determine that a more diversified ownership of television stations would likely lead to the presentation of more diverse points of view."[4]   It

---

[3] *Prometheus*, 373 F.3d at 383 (citing *FCC v. Nat'l Citizens Comm. for Broad.*, 436 U.S. 775,(1978)
[4] *Fox*. 280 F.3d at 1047.

went on to outline the logic of ownership limits. "By limiting the number of stations each network (or other entity) owns, the ... Rule ensures that there are more owners than there would otherwise be."[5]

In *Sinclair* the D.C. Circuit concluded that in order to ensure that discourse is balanced it is permissible for policy to prevent undue concentration of economic power and excessive influence. The D.C. Circuit Court in *Sinclair* restated the broad purpose in promoting the public interest when it stated "the greater the diversity of ownership in a particular area, the less chance there is that a single person or group can have an inordinate effect, in a political, editorial, or similar programming sense, on public opinion at the regional level."[6]

These rulings reflect a line of Supreme Court cases running through the middle half of the twentieth century, from roughly 1927 to 1978. In those cases, the Supreme Court articulated a *bold aspiration* for the First Amendment in the age of electronic media.

The unique characteristics of broadcast media were recognized by the Congress early in the century and the airwaves (radio spectrum) were defined as a public resource.[7] Public policies were repeatedly upheld by the Court to ensure that the immense power of the new media be utilized to promote democratic debate and the free flow of information.

The aspiration for the First Amendment was given its modern formulation by Justice Black in 1945 in the seminal case, *Associated Press v. United States*. He concluded that the First Amendment **"rests on the assumption that the widest possible dissemination of information from diverse and antagonistic sources is essential to the welfare of the public."**[8]

In *Associated Press* Judge Learned Hand painted a picture of diversity that was properly complex, noting that a newspaper "serves one of the most vital of all general interests: the dissemination of news from many different sources, and with as many different facets and colors as possible" because "it is only by cross-lights from varying directions that full illumination can be secured."[9]

---

[5] Id.

[6] *Sinclair*, 284 F.3d at 160 .

[7] Bagdikian, Ben, 2000, *The Media Monopoly* (Boston: Beacon Press).; McChesney, Robert, 2000, *Rich Media, Poor Democracy: Communication Politics in Dubious Times* (New York: New Press, 2000); provide history and progressive critiques of the development of this policy.

[8] *Associated Press v. United States*, 326 U.S. 1, 20 (1945) (hereafter Associated Press).

[9] *United States v. Associated Press*, Inc. 52 F.Supp. 362, 372 (S.D.N.Y. 1943).

Since then, the Supreme Court has reaffirmed this view with respect to newspapers and has unflinchingly applied it to all forms of mass media, including broadcast TV[10] and cable TV.[11]

In *Red Lion,* the Court ruled that discourse must be full and open because "[i]t is the right of the viewers and listeners, not the right of the broadcasters, which is paramount...the right of the public to receive suitable access to social, political, aesthetic, moral and other ideas and experiences... [T]he 'public interest' in broadcasting clearly encompasses the presentation of vigorous debate of controversial issues of importance and concern to the public."[12]

In *FCC v. National Citizens Committee for Broadcasting,*[13] a 1978 case, the court upheld limitations on cross-ownership of TV stations and newspapers "on the theory that diversification of mass media ownership serves the public interest by promoting diversity of program and service viewpoints, as well as by preventing undue concentration of economic power."[14]

ECONOMIC EFFICIENCY IS A SECONDARY CONCERN

The D.C. Circuit decision in *Fox* highlighted the trade-off between diversity and efficiency. Economic efficiency is not the only, or even the primary, goal of policy affecting electronic media.

An industry with a larger number of owners may well be less efficient than a more concentrated industry. Both consumer satisfaction and potential operating cost savings may be sacrificed as a result of the Rule. But that is not to say the Rule is unreasonable because the Congress may, in the regulation of broadcasting, constitutionally pursue values other than efficiency – including in particular diversity in programming, for which diversity of ownership is perhaps an aspirational but surely not an irrational proxy. Simply put, it is not unreasonable – and therefore not unconstitutional – for the Congress to prefer having in the aggregate more voices heard.[15]

This underscores a theme articulated by Justice Frankfurter in concurring in *Associated Press,*

A free press is indispensable to the workings of our democratic society. The business of the press, and therefore the business of the Associated Press, is the

---

[10] *Red Lion Broadcasting v. FCC,* 395 U.S. 367 (1969) (hereafter Red Lion); *FCC v. National Citizens Committee for Broadcasting,* 436 U.S. 775 (1978) (hereafter NCCB).

[11] *Turner Broadcasting System, Inc. v. FCC,* 512 U.S. 622, 638-39 (1994) (hereafter *Turner I*); *Time Warner Entertainment Co., L.P. v. FCC,* 240 F.3d 1126 (D.C. Cir. 2001) (hereafter *Time Warner III*).

[12] *Red Lion,* 395 U.S. at 385 (1969).

[13] *NCCB,.*436 U.S. 775 (1978)

[14] *Id.,* at 780.

[15] Fox, 280 F.3d at 1047(D.C. Cir. 2002).

promotion of truth regarding public matters by furnishing the basis for an understanding of them. Truth and understanding are not wares like peanuts and potatoes. And so, the incidence of restraints upon the promotion of truth through denial of access to the basis for understanding calls into play considerations very different from comparable restraints in a cooperative enterprise having merely a commercial aspect.[16]

SPEECH IS THE PRIMARY CONCERN AND BROADCAST VOICES ARE SCARCE

The distinction between the commercial marketplace and the forum for democratic discourse becomes readily apparent when we respond to the advice frequently given by the most ardent advocates of pure economics in the face of complaints about mediocrity in the media – "If you do not like what is on the tube, turn it off." This reply, which we can withstand from a consumer standpoint, is devastating for citizens. It may be perfectly acceptable to force consumers to vote with their dollars and turn off commercial entertainment, but it is not acceptable for citizens to be turned off by substandard civic discourse with no comparable alternative to which they can turn. As Justice Brandeis explained in his concurrence in *Whitney v. California*,

> Those who won our independence believed that the final end of the State was to make men free to develop their faculties; . . . that the greatest menace to freedom is an inert people; that public discussion is a political duty; and that this should be a fundamental principle of American government.[17]

The desire for active participation and the duty to discuss have important implications. Justice Brandeis' admonition against turning citizens into passive 'couch potatoes' reinforces the distinction between citizen and consumer suggested by Justice Frankfuter.[18] It reminds us that citizens must enter the debate not simply as passive consumers (listeners or viewers), but also as active speakers. One goal is to ensure that they are well informed, receiving good, diverse information; but an equal if not higher goal is that citizens must have the opportunity to speak and be heard.[19]

In *Red Lion*, the seminal television case, the Court expressed a similar sentiment, noting that "speech concerning public affairs is more than self-expression; it is the essence of self-government."[20] The desire for active participation and the duty to discuss have important implications. In particular, citizens must enter the debate not simply as listeners or viewers, but also as speakers. One goal is to ensure that they are well informed,

---

[16] *Associated Press v. United States*, 326 U.S. at 28 (1945).

[17] *Whitney v. California*, 274 U.S. 357, 375 (1927).

[18] Sunstein, Cass, *Republic.Com* (Princeton, Princeton University Press, 2001), pp. 46-47.

[19] Id., p. 115.

[20] Red Lion, 395 U.S. at 390 (1969).

receiving good, diverse information. But an even higher goal is to have them engage actively as participants in civic discourse. The First Amendment implications of policies should not only be about how much citizens have to listen to, but also about their opportunities to speak and be heard.

The *Prometheus* Court notes the dilemma that broadcasting poses from the point of view of the speaker's orientation of the First Amendment. Even in a 500-channel world, spectrum, and therefore broadcast voices are scarce from the speakers' point of view. The increase in alternative media does not reverse that fact.

> Even were we not constrained by Supreme Court precedent, we would not accept the Deregulatory Petitioners' contention that the expansion of media outlets rendered the broadcast spectrum less scarce. In *NCCB*, the court referred to the 'physical' scarcity of the spectrum – the fact that many more people would like access to it than can be accommodated. The abundance of non-broadcast voices does not render the broadcast spectrum any less scarce.[21]

The need to license spectrum is one of the bases on which public obligations can be imposed on the holders of licenses. Starting with a 1943 radio case, *National Broadcasting Co. v. United States,*[22] and continuing through the most recent cases, the Supreme Court found that "where there are substantially more individuals who want to broadcast than there are frequencies to allocate, it is idle to posit an unabridgeable First Amendment right to broadcast comparable to the right of every individual to speak, write, or publish."[23]

Opponents of a bold aspiration for the First Amendment would like to see this scarcity as the sole basis for public policy so that they can declare an abundance of cable and satellite channels available and escape their public interest obligations. The claim is wrong because it is a listener/viewer analysis, not a speaker analysis. Even if hundreds of channels are available to citizens as listeners, this does not empower them as speakers. Broadcasting is still a powerful electronic voice granted by government license.

In fact, cable and satellite owners control all of the channels, so they are a single powerful voice. It is not the scarcity of spectrum that matters, but the scarcity of voices. In a nation of almost 300 million people, the number of channels is still far exceeded by the number of persons wishing to broadcast. The number of holders of broadcast licenses and cable franchises is minuscule compared to the total population. The possession of this government granted rights to speak confers an immense advantage on the holder of the license.

---

[21] *Prometheus,* 372 F.3d at 402 (3rd Cir. 2004)..
[22] *National Broadcasting Co. v. United States,* 319 U.S. 190 (1943).
[23] *Red Lion,* 395 U.S. at 388 (1969).

Ownership Plays a Critical Role in Diversity Policy

In *Fox*, the D.C. Circuit noted the connection between ownership and diversity, opining that in attempting to promote "diversity in programming, for which diversity of ownership is perhaps an aspirational but surely not an irrational proxy," it is not unreasonable – and therefore not unconstitutional – for the Congress to prefer having in the aggregate more voices heard.[24]

This proposition has been central to limitations on media ownership by holders of broadcast licenses for well over half a century. Indeed, the Supreme Court upheld ownership limits even before the landmark case in which it articulated the aspiration of the "widest possible dissemination of information from diverse and antagonistic sources." In upholding the ban on cross-ownership of different types of media, the Supreme Court concluded it was "a reasonable means of promoting the public interest in diversified mass communications."[25]

In the recent media ownership order the FCC restated its commitment to this fundamental principle, concluding that

> the balance of the evidence, although not conclusive, appears to support our conclusion that outlet ownership can be presumed to affect the viewpoint expressed on that outlet.... A larger number of independent owners will tend to generate a wider array of viewpoints than would a comparatively smaller number of owners."[26]

Although the FCC expressed some uncertainty about the empirical relationship between ownership and viewpoint diversity, it went on to offer two important additional observations that reinforced its conclusion. The FCC noted that taking a point of view is to be expected, declaring

> we do not pass judgment on the desirability of owners using their outlets for the expression of particular points of view... we have always proceeded from the assumption that they do so and that our rules should encourage diverse ownership precisely because it is likely to result in the expression of a wide range of diverse and antagonistic viewpoints.[27]

This combined with the importance of media outlets in democratic discourse pushes public policy to lean towards policies that take extra precautions in regard to media ownership limits.

---

[24] *Fox*, 280 F.3d at 1047(D.C. Cir. 2002)..

[25] *NCCB*, 436 U.S. at 802 (1978).

[26] Federal Communications Commission, *2002 Biennial Regulatory Review – Review of the Commission's Broadcast Ownership Rules and Other Rules Adopted Pursuant to Section 202 of the Telecommunications Act of 1996*, 18 FCC Rcd 13620, 13711-47 (2003), ¶27. (hereafter Order)

[27] Id., ¶30.

Further, owners of media outlets clearly have the ability to affect public discourse, including political and governmental affairs, through their coverage of news and public affairs. Even if our inquiry were to find that media outlets exhibited no apparent "slant" or viewpoint in their news coverage, media outlets possess significant *potential* power in our system of government.[28]

CONCLUSION

In each of the Appeals Court rulings that have struck down the FCC's media limits the Courts have restated the Supreme Court jurisprudence. The Supreme Court has not taken up any of these decisions. The bold aspiration for the First Amendment, that seeks vigorous debate that draws citizens in and recognizes the powerful voice that a broadcast license conveys to its holder remains firmly in place.

---

[28] Id., ¶28.

STUDY 2:
THE LEGAL AND SOCIAL BASES FOR LOCALISM ARE STRONGER THAN EVER

MARJORIE HEINS AND MARK COOPER

LOCALISM REMAINS CENTRAL TO BROADCASTING

Broadcasting is by its nature a local phenomenon, and serving the diverse needs of local communities has long been an intrinsic part of American broadcast policy. The importance of localism as a core policy goal can be traced to the 1927 Radio Act.[1] Over the years, not only the Federal Communications Commission but the Supreme Court and Congress have recognized the importance of local broadcast stations serving local communities, "'as an outlet for local self-expression.'"[2] As the Supreme Court explained in 1994, "Congress designed this system of allocation to afford each community of appreciable size an over-the-air source of information and an outlet for exchange on matters of local concern. ... [T]he importance of local broadcasting 'can scarcely be exaggerated, for broadcasting is demonstrably a principal source of information and entertainment for a great part of the nation's population.'"[3] Here as elsewhere in U.S. broadcasting policy, "the people as a whole retain their interest in free speech by radio and their collective right to have the medium function consistently with the ends and purposes of the First Amendment. It is the right of the viewers and listeners, not the right of the broadcasters, which is paramount."[4]

More recently, the D.C. Circuit Court in the case of Sinclair *v. The FCC* restated the broad purpose and the local focus in promoting the public interest when it stated "the greater the diversity of ownership in a particular area, the less chance there is that a single person or group can have an inordinate effect, in a political, editorial, or similar programming sense, on public opinion at the regional level."[5]

---

[1] See, e.g., Napoli, Philip. Foundations of Communications Policy: Principles and Process in the Regulation of Electronic Media. Cresskill, NJ: Hampton Press, 2001, p. 203.

[2] United States v. Southwestern Cable, 392 U.S. 157, 174 (1968) (quoting H.R. Rep. No. 1559, 87th Cong.., 2d Sess., 3).

[3] Turner Broadcasting System, Inc. v. FCC, 512 U.S. 622, 663 (1994) (quoting in part U.S. v. Southwestern Cable, 392 U.S. at 177).

[4] Red Lion Broadcasting Co. v. FCC, 395 U.S. 367, 390 (1969).

[5] Sinclair Broadcasting, Inc. v. FCC, 160 F.3d 148 (D.C. Cir. 2002).

The goal of localism is inseparable from the other pillar of American broadcast policy: diversity. Diversity does not just mean programming from different corporate producers; it means diversity in the *content* and *viewpoint* of programming.[6] Thus, ten or even twenty newscasts that all serve up the same superficial, if-it-bleeds-it-leads sound bites do not constitute diversity. Serving local interests is meaningless if the diverse elements in a community – cultural, social, and political – are not represented on the airwaves.[7]

It is important also to define the geographic parameters of localism. The Commission has long equated localism with broadcast markets. But as these markets expand through increased power levels and other technological advances, the needs of local communities get lost. There are more than 80,000 government units in the U.S., including school districts, town districts, and county districts, and what happens at these local levels of governance is not often considered newsworthy to commercial broadcasters operating in large metropolitan areas.

THE FEDERAL SYSTEM DEPENDS ON LOCALISM

While courts have repeatedly affirmed the constitutional and legal basis for policies promoting localism and diversity, the political commitment to these policies is constantly under attack. Moreover, because broadcasters have First Amendment rights, which are affected by policies to promote localism and diversity, it is important that there be an evidentiary basis to conclude that these policies are necessary and actually do promote the public interest.

---

[6] See Red Lion, 395 U.S. at 389-95. .

[7] Huffington, Arianna, "Blog Heaven." The American Prospect, July 1, 2004. See also Leanza, Cheryl. 2004. "Monolith or Mosaic: Can the Federal Communications Commission Legitimately Pursue a Repetition of Local Content at the Expense of Local Diversity?" 53 American U. L. Rev. 597, 603, 610 (faulting the Commission's 2003 media ownership proceedings for ignoring "diversity at the local level"; "[f]uture analysis of this question cannot rightly consider diversity and localism as two separate goals that are analytically distinct"). Evidence that increasing the number of outlets does not necessarily increase diversity can be found in Dejong, A.S. and B. J. Bates 1991. "Channel Diversity in Cable Television." Journal of Broadcasting and Electronic Media 35: 159-66; Grant, A. E. 1994. "The Promise Fulfilled? An Empirical Analysis of Program Diversity on Television." The Journal of Media Economics 7:1: 51-64; Hellman, Heikki and Martin Soramaki, 1994. "Competition and Content in the U.S. Video Market." Journal of Media Economics 7 ; Lin, C. A. 1995. "Diversity of Network Prime-Time Program Formats During the 1980s," Journal of Media Economics 8: 17-28; Kubey, Robert, et al. 1995. "Demographic Diversity on Cable: Have the New Cable Channels Made a Difference in the Representation of Gender, Race, and Age?" Journal of Broadcasting and Electronic Media 39: 459-71.

Localism and diversity remain critically important to our democracy and the commercial mass media have not fulfilled, and are not likely to fulfill, these fundamental goals of communications policy.

In spite of three quarters of a century of Congressional policy to promote localism in the broadcast media and Supreme Court acceptance of these policies, in the recent media ownership proceeding, the chief expert witness for the national broadcast networks declared localism to be an unjustified preoccupation of the Commission that lacks a coherent basis. In his words:

> The Commission's preoccupation with localism is difficult to explain or justify. Why should the government seek to promote local content as opposed to, and especially at the expense of, any other category of ideas? Once can readily imagine categories of ideas more central to the political, social, educational, aesthetic or spiritual lives of Americans. Further, to fasten on any category of ideas readily runs afoul of First Amendment values. In short, a focus on local content or local outlets appears to lack a coherent policy basis.[8]

This statement is wrong on every count. To begin with, a policy of promoting localism does not run afoul of the First Amendment. The Supreme Court has rejected this claim repeatedly over the past seventy-five years. Second, given our federal system, local government is in fact our central political institution. Third, we define many of our social and aesthetic values in local terms. For example, local courts and juries decide a wide range of civil and criminal issues based on what are essentially community understandings of what a "reasonable man" would think or do, depending on local conditions. Having vibrant local media outlets to promote good local government and strong social ties in local communities is an essential part of our democracy.[9]

Congress has adhered to the localism principle. The legal precedent remains strong because the political and social reality of life in America continues to demand strong local media institutions. No matter how strongly

---

[8] Owen, Bruce N. "Statement on Media Ownership Rules." Attachment to Comments of Fox Entertainment Group and Fox Television Stations, Inc., National Broadcasting Company, Inc. and Telemundo Group, Inc., and Viacom, *In the Matter of 2002 Biennial Regulatory Review – Review of the Commission's Broadcast Ownership Rules and Other Rules Adopted Pursuant to Section 202 of the Telecommunications Act of 1996, Cross Ownership of Broadcast Stations and Newspapers, Rules and Policies Concerning Multiple Ownership of Radio Broadcast Stations in Local Markets, Definition of Radio Markets*, MB Docket No. 02-277, MM Dockets 02-235, 01-317, 00-244, 2 January 2003, p. 10.

[9] Alexis de Tocqueville's well known celebration of local associations started with "the permanent associations which are established by law under the names of townships, cities, and counties, a vast number of others are formed and maintained by the agency of private individuals." cited in Terchek, Ronald J. and Thomas C. Conte. (Eds.), *Theories of Democracy* (Lanham, MD: Rowan & Littlefield, 2001), cited in p. 27.

national and international issues affect our society, or how prominent they become, there is much truth to the saying that all politics in America is local. This is because of the fundamental federal structure of our national government.

Even national elections are essentially local. The extreme concentration of the 2004 presidential election in so-called "battleground" states reminds us that we elect the President on a state-by-state basis. We elect Senators on a state-wide basis and our Representatives on the basis of small single-member districts.[10] These are local races.

More importantly, we reserve a host of public policy decisions that are vital to the quality of life and the fabric of our society – police, emergency services, education, land-use – for local units of government. Only defense is solely national policy and even here the national defense has come to rely significantly on the National Guard, which is a state level institution.

Three-quarters or more of spending on education, police, and parks and recreation is accounted for by state and local governments, mostly at the local level. About two-thirds of all government spending on community development and natural resources are spent by state and local governments, equally divided between state and local.[11] Personal transfer payments – social and income security and welfare – are also largely federal, but income security and welfare too have many state and local variations.

SOCIAL BASES OF LOCALISM

A host of social processes are grounded in the local community. The primary referent for identity and community has traditionally been, and remains, significantly local.[12] A primary focus on political participation and mobilization captures the most critical aspect for media policy. There are both sociological and psychological reasons why local ties support participation.

Being embedded in networks where one can influence or be influenced by action is psychologically gratifying and a spur to action. Social identity is defined, and political activity is instigated, on the basis of group

---

[10] Keyssar, Alexander. *The Right to Vote*. New York: Basic Books, 2000.

[11] U.S. Census Bureau, *Statistical Abstract of the United States: 2002* (Washington, D.C.: U.S. Department of Commerce, 2002), Tables 414-416, 453.

[12] Rifkin, Jeremy. *The Age of Access*. New York, Jeremy P. Tarcher/Putnam, 2000, pp. 7-9. Dewey, John. *The Public and its Problems*. Athens, Ohio: Swallow Press, 1954; Sirianni, Carmen and Lewis Friedland. *Civic Innovation in America: Community Empowerment, Public Policy, and the Movement for Civic Renewal*. Berkeley: University of California Press, 2001, especially Chapter 5.

identity and affiliation.[13] Groups are defined by the permeability and permanence of their boundaries and their location in the social hierarchy.[14] The social context helps to determine which organizations and messages are effective.   Some contexts provide greater credibility and opportunities to persuade voters.   Segmentation, separation, or sorting of organizations facilitates the garnering of commitment and support and makes message management easier.

The salience of the organization's identity to the members is defined by several factors – the clarity and strength of the shared understanding of the organization's location in society and the motivation to act on that shared social identity are paramount.   Sociological theories stress the importance of the interaction between the members of the organization to create solidarity.[15] Intervening social processes affect participation[16] since "frequent discussion of politics and the partisan composition of an individual's network influence participation."[17]

"For a community, frequent cooperation by its members leads to tighter social linkages and increased trust in one another – a 'virtuous circle' of participation and trust."[18] Repetition[19] and connection between the speaker

---

[13] Hechter, Michael. 2004. "From Class to Culture." American Journal of Sociology 110:2; Wright, Stephen C., Donald M. Taylor and Fathali M. Moghaddam. 1990. Responding to Membership in a Disadvantaged Group: From Acceptance to Collective Protest. Journal of Personality and Social Psychology 58.

[14] Id.

[15] The impact of conversational networks in church and work settings on participation is to a significant degree mediated by the different viewpoints that individuals are exposed to when they discuss politics in these settings." Scheufele, Dietram A., et al. 2004. Social Structure and Citizenship: Examining the Impacts of Social Setting, Network Heterogeneity, and Informational Variables on Political. Political Communication 21: 315; Mutz, Diana C. 2002. "Cross-Cutting Social Networks: Testing Democratic Theory in Practice." American Political Science Review 96.

[16] Huckefeldt, Robert and John Sprague. Citizens, Politics, and Social Communication: Information Influence in an Election Campaign. New York: Cambridge University Press, 1995; McLeod, Jack M., Dietram A. Scheufele and Patricia Moy. 1999. Community, Communications, and Participation: The Role of Mass Media and Interpersonal Discussion in Local Political Participation. Political Communication 16; Scheufele, Dietram A., Matthew C. Nisbet and Dominique Brossard. 2003. Pathways to Participation? Religion, Communication Contexts and Mass Media, International Journal of Public Opinion Research 15.

[17] Scheufele, et al. 2004. p. 317; Knoke, David. 1990. "Networks of Political Action: Toward Theory Construction." Social Forces 68; Knoke, David. Organizing for Collective Action: The Political Economies of Associations. New York: Aldine de Gruyter, 1990b.

[18] Scheufele, et al., 2004: 318; Brehm, John and Wendy Rahn. 1997. Individual Level Evidence for the Causes and Consequences of Social Capital. American Journal of Political Science; Putnam, Robert D. Making Democracy Work: Civic Traditions in Modern Italy. Princeton: Princeton University Press; Scheufele, Dietram A. and Dhavan V.

and listener make messages more effective.   Personal familiarity, positive feelings and respect for the speaker increase thought about the message and its overall persuasiveness.[20]   Face-to-face interactions are particularly well suited to benefit from these conditions for persuasion.[21]

From a practical point of view, for example, getting out the vote thrives on local connections.[22]   Knowledge of the local area and local individuals are vastly superior as resources for mobilizing participation. The sociability of the political participation – working together, voting together – provides social reinforcement, trust and psychological gratification.

Local media that focus on local issues, cultures, and interests are a critical part of this equation. As law professor and media scholar Edwin Baker points out, for the media to meet the diverse needs of the public, they must

> perform several tasks. First, the press should provide individuals and organized groups with information that indicates when their interests are at stake. Second, the media should help mobilize people to participate and promote their divergent interests... Third, for pluralist democracy to work information about popular demands must flow properly - that is, given the practical gap between citizens and policymakers, the press should make policymakers aware of the content and strength of people's demands.[23]

Shah. 2000. Personality Strength and Social Capital: The Role of Dispositional and Informational Variables in the Production of Civic Participation. *Communication Research* 27.

[19]   Weiss, R. F. and B. Pasamanick. 1964.   Number of Exposures To Persuasive Communication in The Instrumental Conditioning of Attitudes. *Journal of Social Psychology* 63; Verba, Sidney, Lehman Schlozman and Henry Brady. *Voice and Equality: Civic Volunteerism in American Politics*. Cambridge: Harvard University Press, 1995.

20 Scheufele, Dietram A., Matthew C. Nisbet. Dominique Brossard, and Erik C. Nisbet. 2004. Social Structure and Citizenship: Examining the Impact of Social Setting, Network Heterogeity, and Informational Variables on Political Participation. *Political Communications* 21, Huckfeldt, R., Johnson E. and J. Sprague. 2002.   Political Environments, Political Dynamics and the Survival of Disagreement. *Journal of Politics* 62.

[21] Niven, 2004; Green, Donald P. and Alan S. Gerber. 2000. *Getting Out the Vote in Youth Vote: Results for Randomized Field Experiments*. New Haven: Institution for Social and Policy Studies, Yale University; Green, Donald P. and Alan S. Gerber. 2001. The Effect of a Nonpartisan Get Out the Vote Drive: An Experimental Study of Leafleting. *Journal of Politics* 62:3; Kilgard, 1999; Reams and Ray, 1993; Jason, 1984.

[22] Hanson, John Mark. "The Majoritarian Impulse and the Declining Significance of Place." in Gerald M. Pomper and Marc D. Weiner. (Eds.), *The Future of American Democratic Politics*. New Brunswick: Rutgers University Press, 2003.

[23] Baker, C. Edwin. "Giving Up on Democracy: The Legal Regulation of Media Ownership." Attachment C, Comments of Consumers Union, Consumer Federation of America, Civil Rights Forum, Center for Digital Democracy, Leadership Conference on Civil Rights and Media Access Project. *In the Matter of Cross Ownership of Broadcast*

The broadcast media cannot fulfill this critical role if they are not rooted in local communities. Broadcast television has an immense impact because of its key role in the social and psychological processes of democratic discourse. Broadcast television is a primary source of information, particularly for local issues.[24] Television is also the premier medium for advertising[25] and efforts to influence public opinion.[26] Visual images are particularly powerful in conveying messages.[27] The dictates of the television

---

Station and Newspaper/Radio Cross-Ownership Waiver Policy: Order and Notice of Proposed Rulemaking, MM Docket No. 01-235, 96-197, December 3, 2001, p. 16 (hereafter, CFA/CU Comments).

[24] Cooper, Mark. "When Law and Social Science Go Hand in Glove." in Philip Napoli (Eds.), *Media Diversity: Meaning and Measurement*. Mahwah, NJ: Lawrence Earlbaum, 2006.

[25] Hansen Glenn J. and William Benoit, 2002. Presidential Television Advertising and Public Policy Priorities, 1952 –2002. *Communications Studies* 53: 285; Patterson, Thomas E. and R.D McClure, *The Unseeing Eye: The Myth of Television Power in National Politics.* New York: Putnam, 1976; Kern, M. *30 Second Politics: Political Advertising in the Eighties.* New York: Praeger, 1988; Brians, C. L. and M. P. Wattenberg, Campaign Issue Knowledge and Salience: Comparing Reception for TV Commercials, TV News, and Newspapers. *American Journal of Political Science* 40: 172-93, 1996.

[26] Kim, Sei-Hill, Dietram A. Scheufele and James Shanahan. 2002. Think About It This Way: Attribute Agenda Setting Function of the Press and the Public's Evaluation of a Local Issue. *Journalism and Mass Communications Quarterly* 79:7, 2002; Chaffee, Steven and Stacy Frank. 1996. How Americans Get Their Political Information: Print versus Broadcast News. *The Annals of the American Academy of Political and Social Science* 546; McLeod, Jack M., Dietram A. Scheufele, and Patricia Moy. 1999. Community, Communications, and Participation: The Role of Mass Media and Interpersonal Discussion in Local Political Participation. *Political Communication* 16. For a fuller explanation of the impact of television, see the separate Comments of the Consumer Federation of America and Consumers Union filed in this NOI.

[27] Domke, David, David Perlmutter and Meg Spratt. 2002. The Primes of Our Times? An Examination of the 'Power' of Visual Images. *Journalism*3:2: 131-59. The authors present a detailed social psychological and even neurological discussion of the reasons why and ways in which visual images have a greater impact, but the politically oriented research that they cite as consistent with their findings include Krosnick, J. A. and D. R. Kinder. 1990. "Altering the Foundation of Support for the President Through Priming." *American Political Science Review* 84: 497-512; Pan Z. and G. M. Kosicki, "Priming and Media Impact on the Evaluation of the President's Performance," 24 *Communications Research* 3-30, 1997; Just, M.R., A. N. Crigler and W. R. Neuman. Cognitive and Affective Dimensions of Political Conceptualization. in A. N. Crigler (eds.), *The Psychology of Political Communications*. Ann Arbor: University of Michigan Press, 1996.

news production process also affect the process of issue formation and debate.[28]

CONCLUSION

Localism is intrinsically related to diversity in media sources, media outlets, media institutions, and the actual content of media programming. In this section, we describe these various forms of diversity and emphasize why all are needed to advance the fundamental goal of communications policy – to provide the widest possible public access to and participation in a rich and vibrant marketplace of ideas.

Diversity and antagonism in civic discourse are neither easy to achieve nor easy to measure. Opponents of policies to enrich civic discourse complain that the imprecision of the outcome makes it difficult, if not impossible, to measure success. This merely reflects the fact that the goal of having an informed citizenry is inherently qualitative and complex. Most social and psychological relationships have numerous highly intertwined causes; there is no reason that knowledge and participation in public policy formation should be otherwise.

---

[28] Graber, Doris. *Mass Media and American Politics*. Washington, D.C.: Congressional Quarterly, 1997; Gans, Herbert J. *Democracy and the News*. Oxford: Oxford University Press, 2003.

STUDY 3:
A BROAD, POSITIVE VIEW OF THE FIRST AMENDMENT

BEN SCOTT

INTRODUCTION

The bold aspiration for the First Amendment that we have articulated in earlier studies has a direct link to a more fundamental debate over the nature of the First Amendment. The narrow, negative view advocated by the broadcasters, and adopted by the Federal Communications Commission (FCC), stands in sharp contrast to the broad positive view taken by the Supreme Court. The view taken of the First Amendment deeply influences the policy that is pursued in consideration of limits on media ownership.

In the FCC's analysis of the cross-ownership regulations outlined in the 2003 Rule & Order (R&O),[1] we believe that fundamental attributes of public First Amendment rights were not sufficiently considered, if indeed they were brought to the attention of the Commission at all. There is an unquestioned assumption that the First Amendment's role in this proceeding is merely to negatively prohibit any abridgement of any one speaker, as opposed to a positive responsibility to expand the diversity of voices from all speakers. It is of critical importance that the Commission now take up a serious intellectual inquiry into the constitutional basis that supports its interpretation of which policies best serve the goals of the First Amendment.

The absence from the ruling of these essential ideas concerning the public's constitutional rights provided by the free press contributes to a general misunderstanding of the historical development of commercial journalism in the United States and its relationship to citizenship and public service. To correct this problem, these comments will question the Commission's assumptions about constitutional rights and make broad arguments that point to profoundly different policy goals and ends. It is of necessity an historical argument. An accurate account of the composition of the First Amendment in the early Republic and its implications for the history of journalism point to radically different conclusions with regard to the standards and thresholds of public service, diversity, localism, and competition than those espoused by the Commission in its Rule and Order.

These conclusions require a thoroughgoing reevaluation of the analytical, constitutional, economic and legal premises upon which the 2003

---

[1] Federal Communications Commission, 2002 Biennial Regulatory Review – Review of the Commission's Broadcast Ownership Rules and Other Rules Adopted Pursuant to Section 202 of the Telecommunications Act of 1996, 18 FCC Rcd 13620, 13711-47 (2003),

ruling is based and upon which the current proceeding is conducted. In short, policies that favor the dominant market interests in the local news media are not commensurate with either the public interest needs of a locality or the First Amendment responsibilities of the government. The mechanism of market-based regulation in the media system is a poor solution for the protection of First Amendment rights. Survival of the fittest in oligopoly markets is hardly a recipe for providing a free, fair, and comprehensive public debate. We require here a positive view of the First Amendment which goes beyond simply guarding the speech rights of any given speaker. Protecting the free speech of the few does not provide it for the many — on the contrary, it may well impede it. This follows from a fundamental contradiction between the goals of democracy and those of market competition. Markets logically produce winners and losers and function most efficiently when inequality between players is wide. Democracy functions best when all speakers have the opportunity to be heard and inequality in debate is narrow. An analysis of public rights to a free press as conceived by the Founding Fathers and the first generations of American government bears out this argument. The history of journalism further reinforces the point by persuasively demonstrating that regulation through the marketplace is a relatively new phenomenon in American journalism that has been disputed from its inception as neither free nor commensurate with First Amendment ideals.

In an effort to specify our concerns as much as possible, we shall respond to instances in the 2003 ruling that we believe require reconsideration in light of a more comprehensive review of historical and theoretical analyses. Listed below are three statements from the R&O that we feel capture the concepts we wish to address. In particular, we would like to draw attention to principles supporting the Commission's understanding of the marketplace of ideas, the market as the arbiter of public political communication, the First Amendment, and the relationship of these ideas to the history of commercial journalism.

¶ 352 "Nor it is particularly troubling that media properties do not always, or even frequently, avail themselves to others who may hold contrary opinions. Nothing requires them to do so, nor is it necessarily healthy for public debate to pretend as though all ideas are of equal value entitled to equal airing….Indeed, the very notion of a marketplace of ideas presupposes that some ideas will attract a following and achieve wide currency, while others quietly recede having failed to conquer the hearts and minds of the citizenry. Our Constitution forbids government action to pre-select the winners in this competition or to guarantee the circulation of any particular set of ideas."

¶ 353 "Nor is it troubling that media properties may allow their news and editorial decisions to be driven by "the bottom line." Again, the need and desire to produce revenue, to control costs, to survive and thrive in the marketplace is a time honored tradition in the American media. Indeed, it was not until newspaper publishers learned to market their papers as tools of commerce that the press became a force in the public debate that lead to the framing of our Constitution."

¶ 354 "In short, to assert that cross-owned properties will be engaged in profit maximizing behavior or that they will provide an outlet for viewpoints reflective of their owner's interests is merely to state truisms, neither of which warrants government intrusion into precious territory bounded off by the First Amendment. To the contrary, we are engaged in this exercise precisely because we seek to encourage the airing of diverse and antagonistic viewpoints. It would be odd indeed if our rules were structured to inhibit the expression of viewpoints or to promote only an accepted set of ideas."

These statements all appear in the R&O in the section concerning cross-media ownership. We feel that this is the most important rule at issue, and so we have chosen to focus our discussion here. Further, within these statements are clearly displayed the positions and assumptions guiding the Commission with regard to the First Amendment, the nature and history of commercial journalism, and the marketplace of ideas.

From ¶352, it appears to us that the Commission interprets the First Amendment as primarily, if not exclusively a negative right—i.e. the government will protect free speech from being abridged, but it has no responsibility to promote diversity. From ¶353, it appears to us that the Commission understands the First Amendment to have been conceived and shaped in an explicit environment of commercial media operating in a self-defined marketplace of ideas. Moreover, the implication is that the Founders understood the media system in this way, a smaller and yet formally similar version of the system we currently have. It is this ongoing system of commercial journalism that the Commission refers to as the "time honored tradition" of the American media marketplace.

Finally, from ¶354, we understand the Commission to be arguing that the market is the primary, exclusive, and best mechanism to govern the output of the public media system. By promoting efficiency in the marketplace, the Commission appears to believe that it is promoting the degree of diversity, localism, and competition demanded by the public through their patterns of consumption. By removing regulation and allowing the fittest voices to survive in the media market, the Commission states that it has most firmly guaranteed that the government plays no role in either inhibiting or promoting any particular viewpoint.

In the following, we argue that these understandings of the marketplace of ideas, the First Amendment, the circumstances of the Founders, and the history of journalism are seriously flawed and lead to unjustified conclusions. We will argue that the commercial mass media system is not a time honored tradition of American journalism dating from the 18th century, but rather a more recent development. Further, we will demonstrate that the Founders certainly did not understand commercial journalism and the marketplace of ideas in the way that we do now. Finally, we will couch all of these arguments in a discussion of the First Amendment which asserts an alternative understanding of its principles which we believe are a more appropriate reading of the legacy of the Bill of Rights – a positive view of the First Amendment. It is this positive view which should guide the Commission's analysis of public interest limits on media ownership.

THE NARROW, NEGATIVE VIEW OF THE FIRST AMENDMENT

The Well-Oiled Marketplace Assumption

The starting point for developing a balanced view of how the First Amendment should guide communications policy is a deconstruction of the prevailing concept of negative rights and the concomitant conception of the relationship between the press, its public, and their common government. [Here we should understand press to refer to the media system as a whole]. The pillars around which these relationships are built are the First Amendment and the marketplace of ideas.

The conventional position on the relationship between the press, the public, and the government mirrors the model of laissez-faire economics. The press is seen as a marketplace of information providers dependent upon consumer interest to survive and flourish. The public is seen as a group of political consumers each in search of the best presentation and interpretation of facts and ideas to assist in his or her political decision making on public affairs, i.e. how they should vote every two to four years (or increasingly, whether they should bother), and which social and political institutions warrant support and which antipathy. The press provides the raw materials for debate, and each viewpoint is given a fair hearing. The public readership follows and engages the battle in a "marketplace of ideas" by selecting and advocating particular positions. The result is the truth, or what the majority of the public has ordained as the people's opinion of the truth. This informed consensus then forms the foundation of representative democracy, the sentiment that elects officials and guides the formulation of public policy between elections.

Conventional wisdom provides that the system is a well-oiled machine. The role of the government is merely to make sure none of the voices in the marketplace of ideas are prevented from speaking. The public is served by a large array of media channels, all of which are dependent for market success on their degree of relevance to public interest. From this vantage point, the best any good regulator can do is stay out of the way and let the competition of ideas provide for a free and fair public debate and ultimately a truthful representation of public opinion. Any government intervention merely amounts to a politically motivated intent to suppress and influence developments in the public sphere. This simplistic but powerful model of the mass media and the government's First Amendment responsibilities begins to fall apart under scrutiny.

A marketplace works best when it is unfettered, guided only by the invisible hand of efficiency and competition. The government's role, in this view, is to stay out of the conditions of production and see to it that the health of the marketplace is nurtured and perpetuated. Any degradation of public service is due to market inefficiency and can be corrected through economic measures. In this model, the marketplace of ideas is conflated with the marketplace for media content. Citizens are treated as consumers. The primary concern is what an individual may buy in the media marketplace, not what public services are offered by the media system to the citizenry. When consumer and civic behavior are blended into a single set of marketplace transactions between political ideas (where public interest is determined competitively rather than deliberatively), the FCC has made a very specific move in conceiving the nature of the relationship between press, public, and government.

Beneath this portrait of the current administration of the media marketplace and the government's regulatory apparatus lies the First Amendment. Every understanding of the interrelationship between press/public/government assumes an interpretation of the freedom of speech and the press. These liberties have historically proven hard to define. The understanding of how free speech and a free press should be deployed in society has always been influenced by the current assumptions of contemporary policy makers about history, legal theory, and democracy's relationship with media. Despite these historical vagaries, the core values of press and speech freedom are woven into the fabric of the American political system.

The model of the press regulator as marketplace facilitator rests on a solid base of case law that has consistently focused on First Amendment rights as negative freedom, i.e. the freedom from interference, which applies primarily to the individual. It is a legal philosophy of the mold shaped by John Milton, John Locke, and John Stuart Mill. The central premise is that the absolute protection of every individual's political speech will naturally provide for a free and full public debate—as no one with a mind to speak will be prevented from doing so and the rational merits of each individual statement will determine its fate. Conventionally, the portrait of constitutional thinking about the First Amendment ends there, although there is much more to consider.

This concept of free speech for the individual has fed and been fed by the popular conflation of the market and American democracy as interlocking (if not interchangeable) ideals. Competition in the marketplace, the de facto impropriety of government interference, and blind faith in the natural forces of an unencumbered market system to yield only the best outcomes—these are values that have come to stand astride Adam Smith's economic legacy as well as Thomas Jefferson's political tradition of free speech.

The Reality of Contemporary Commercial Mass Media

However, we make a grave mistake when we unreflectively assume a fit between 18th century political thought and 21st century media economics. The relationship between democracy and media markets has changed over time, and the ideal of negative speech rights in the marketplace of ideas has been used to paper over the obvious economic conditions that now inhibit the diversity of viewpoints the public requires. The ideals of the freedom of the press become shibboleths that mask dysfunction when the marketplace of ideas is neither fair nor diverse. There is nothing in the Constitutional tradition of the marketplace of ideas that would suffer the dominant market power of the firms that controls our media system today. The notion that we have a media system that gives equal treatment to all voices is no longer defensible.

Conceptually, the highly concentrated, oligopoly markets for the mass mediation of modern political communication has been squashed into a town-meeting hall in colonial Massachusetts. This is a gross misrepresentation of Jefferson's political thinking, the historical development of free speech rights, and the structure of the modern political economy. The Founders could not have conceived the media in the form it currently holds, and they would almost certainly have framed the debate over the free press in different ways had they the slightest notion of what was to come. Nonetheless, the historical resonance of the "marketplace of ideas" as a political philosophy associated with the Founding Fathers and the judicial edicts of the First Amendment titans of the libertarian bench—most notably Justices Holmes and Black—has caused these ideas to seep into the political culture as dogmatic constitutional interpretations. Moreover, the contemporary political rhetoric merging the market and democratic government has blended with this tradition to produce a powerful bloc of blind support for libertarian speech and press rights. Despite the depth of entrenched fortification beneath these doctrines, they are badly flawed. We have essentially applied a political philosophy of the free press designed to accommodate one historical period and its media economics and applied it into a totally different future context without considering the ensuing problems. In this uncritical ideological zone, the idea of the government as the market facilitator makes perfect sense. In practice, the American public urgently deserves a thoroughgoing review of how the legacy of the First Amendment can regain its position as the champion of viewpoint diversity rather than the handmaiden of the marketplace.

THE BROAD, POSITIVE VIEW OF THE FIRST AMENDMENT

What do we mean by First Amendment rights? The key analytical problem here is to identify the central purpose of the Amendment. What rights and liberties follow from forbidding Congress to interfere with speech? What are the conditions sufficient to provide free speech and which are merely necessary?

Our belief is that the conventional wisdom about the First Amendment mistakes a necessary condition for a sufficient one in the guarantee of free speech rights, and in so doing elides the very foundation of its intention and importance. More specifically, negative freedom (the absolute protection of individual speakers from interference) has pushed out positive freedom (the provision of a public sphere in which the public has a right to hear all speakers) as the central right protected by the law. It is necessary for all individuals to have the right to speak freely, but that is not sufficient to guarantee that the public may hear all voices. A prohibition on interference does not account for the social, economic, and political conditions in society which structurally impede certain voices while amplifying others. Whereas an active responsibility to provide for free speech would demand that public power remove these obstructing conditions whenever possible. "Freedom from" has distracted us from "freedom for".

Among the most damaging results of this misunderstanding have been further misconceptions embedded in the primary one. For example, the protection from public censorship (government power), a necessary condition for complete negative freedom but not a sufficient one (as there are substantial forms of private power which have the power to censor), has also been mistaken for a sufficient condition for complete negative freedom of speech. And worst of all, the positive freedom which guarantees to promote and sustain the structure of public hearings has been dismissed as neither a necessary nor a sufficient condition, but rather an automatic result of negative freedom. In its most widely understood form, then, the First Amendment means merely the protection of individual speech from government interference. By this reasoning, private entities may lawfully disrupt the public's ability to hear the full spectrum of social speakers by self-interestedly gate-keeping the primary forums for public speech.

The over-commitment to a negative view of the First Amendment to the exclusion of a positive view stems from a simplification of history. By this reading, the Founding Fathers inaugurated the great experiment in self-government by breaking with the traditions of English common law which protected speakers and printers from prior restraint, but prosecuted them subsequently if their utterances were found objectionable. American law would protect all speech from prior restraint and from subsequent prosecution, the idea being that the benefits of completely free speech would outweigh the damages of the occasional libel and pernicious falsehood. These libertarian thinkers recognized that a free society depended upon free, fair, and open discussion in the public sphere in order to formulate a well deliberated public opinion to guide representatives in the government. A law which expressly prohibited Congressional interference with public speech would make this public sphere of deliberation sacrosanct.

However, recent historical inquiry has shown the 18th century roots of the libertarian tradition to be questionable. There is evidence to suggest that the libertarian tradition was not particularly prevalent among the Founders. Moreover there is evidence to suggest that they understood and valued positive freedom with an equal, if not greater passion than negative freedom. The unearthing of an alternative tradition of First Amendment thinking among the Founders has begun to topple the theoretical scaffolding holding up much of more contemporary libertarian legal and social thinking on the issue. The alternative tradition allows for a profoundly different understanding of the First Amendment with impressive implications.

To begin with, no one knows exactly what the Founders had in mind when they drafted the First Amendment. Like much of the Constitution, the Framers were blessed, in Leonard Levy's apt phrase, with a "genius for studied imprecision."[2] In other words, there is good reason to believe they did not precisely commit to one interpretation or another because they expected subsequent generations to require room for maneuver. The documented context of the writing of the First Amendment is murky and leaves few clues. It is not at all clear what they thought, and it seems most likely that they were not all that sure themselves. In such a case, it would seem critical for historians to explore the record to search for alternative or complementary understandings of the First Amendment to broaden our perception of original intent as well as its historical legacy.

In his recent study of the period, legal scholar Akhil Reed Amar argues that "[t]he essence of the Bill of Rights was more structural than not, and more majoritarian than counter."[3] Or in other words, the first ten amendments to the Constitution were less about protecting minority rights — less a foundation for a libertarian tradition — than they were a positive plan for promoting majoritarian rights. He argues that even though the Bill of Rights has traditionally been read as a list of inalienable rights guarding minorities from the tyranny of the majority, its original intent was quite different. He makes a powerful case that structural concerns, i.e. those dealing with the sanctity of the public's collective right to self-government, were foremost in the minds of the Founders, not the inalienable rights of individuals. The great concern was protecting the public and the means of self-government from they tyranny of ruling elites. This majority protection,

---

[2] Leonard W. Levy. *Emergence of a Free Press.* New York: Oxford University Press, 1985, p. 348.

[3] Akhil Reed Amar, *The Bill of Rights.* (New Haven: Yale University Press, 1998), xiii.

he argues, was the driving principle behind the Bill of Rights in its original historical setting.

With regard to the First Amendment, this means that the freedom of expression should be broadly conceived as the protection of the public's right to hear all points of view in a free, fair, and full sphere of deliberation. It is only secondarily an edict protecting the speech of all individual speakers. Minority rights to expression are thus a function of the majoritarian principle. By prohibiting the power of government from interfering with public speech in general, the structural integrity of the public sphere would be preserved. This is not to say that the Founders would have countenanced private power (economic, political or religious) disrupting the public sphere. Quite simply, in the late 18th century the only power strong enough to curb the freedom of expression in the public sphere was the government. If a law was created to forbid that interference, the possibility of minority power corrupting self-government would be thwarted.[4] The Founders saw the dire necessity of keeping the public informed, engaged, and active in political society. Jefferson's warning of the consequences of a de-politicized public resonates with the primary threat of elite usurpation of power: "If once they [the people] become inattentive to the public affairs," he wrote his friend Edward Carrington, "you and I, and Congress and Assemblies, Judges and Governors, shall all become wolves."[5]

If the First Amendment is seen as a law protecting majoritarian rights to self-government through free expression, the idea that it is limited to the prohibition of government interference with individual speech is clearly inadequate. For example, if the integrity of the public sphere were to be threatened by a private power, the First Amendment would have jurisdiction. Or if the public sphere could be promoted, maintained, or empowered through government action, this also would fall under First Amendment principles. The law forbids the government from abridging free expression, but it says nothing about a prohibition on government promotion of free expression. Moreover, a majoritarian interpretation implies that it is not only *not* forbidden, but that it is positively obliged.[6]

---

[4] Amar, 18-21. Amar argues that it was the 14th Amendment which turned the tide of First Amendment thinking into a libertarian camp. This is a persuasive claim, but it does not change the original intent of majoritarian rights nor the validity of the theoretical tradition, which hails from it.

[5] Adrienne Koch and William Peden, ed. *The Life and Selected Writings of Thomas Jefferson.* New York: Modern Library, 1944, 412. Quote taken from a letter to Edward Carrington, January 16, 1787.

[6] Amar, 41. Amar also suggests that Article IV of the Constitution supports this position.

The Historical Context of the First Amendment

Recent scholarship on the character of the press in Revolutionary America grants us a very important insight with regard to the public sphere and the freedom of expression. Newspapers at the founding of the nation functioned like a town meeting on paper, to be circulated throughout educated society.[7] This notion is very helpful in the assessment of what early Americans perceived that the press ought to be. Recalling that the revolution and the nascent republican policies of the government greatly expanded the press system and its role in public life, we can expect that the institution experienced a kind of social redefinition as more people came into frequent contact with it. As might be expected, the society thought of the new in terms of the old, i.e. the burgeoning press was conceived in relation to a well-understood form of public political communication, public meetings in the town hall. It was to be a forum for deliberative democracy located between civil society and the state wherein all citizens (defined quite strictly in the 18th century) could contribute as anonymous equals (free of the biases and encumbrances of economic fortunes and social entanglements) to the crafting of public policy which aimed at producing the common good. The idea of a rational discourse among citizens who have discarded their personal interests to collectively pursue the common good pervaded the thinking of the Revolutionary generation—even if such an ideal could never actually manifest itself. Thus there is a strong, idealistic foundation for understanding the free press as the majoritarian, structural right to participate in this forum which draws on this burgeoning self-conception of the Founders. "Printers thought of their newspapers as the infrastructure to the public sphere and presented them as common carriers for the information and deliberations of a rational citizenry."[8]

Far from using the newspapers as "tools of commerce" to engage the political sphere, as the R&O interprets this historical period (¶353), the media system of the early Republic was explicitly non-commercial and explicitly public, political, and regulated by the state. Colonial newspapers were begun as quasi-governmental organs: they characterized themselves as "public prints" and often bore the phrase "Printed by Authority" on their mastheads. Their printer/editors were often postmasters, and a major source of income for colonial printers was printing the laws and other government documents.[9] In the years leading up to the Revolution, and in the period that followed printers understood themselves as part of a movement and as having a

---

[7] Kevin Barnhurst and John Nerone, *The Form of News: A History* (New York: Guilford Press, 2001).

[8] Barnhurst and Nerone 46-48, quotation on 48.

[9] Charles E. Clark. The public prints: the newspaper in Anglo-American culture, 1665-1740. New York: Oxford University Press, 1994.

special responsibility to represent the public. Both printers and political leaders viewed the press as the structure of the public sphere, as providing a neutral forum for public deliberation. They contrasted the "liberty of the press" with "licentiousness," by which they meant the pursuit of private political or commercial goals at the expense of the common good. They understood that licentiousness would undermine the republic.[10]

Indeed, the press of the early Republic was overwhelmingly political and explicitly driven by public resources and guidelines. Public policy, both official and unofficial, supported the press. Officially, local, state, and national governments all subsidized the press by paying for the printing of the laws and other public documents.[11] Later, one of the first official acts of the federal Congress was to pass postal legislation which included heavy subsidies for newspapers.[12]

Meanwhile, unofficially, politicians subsidized printers to support their political positions and candidacies.[13] As a result of the integration of the press into the political and governmental system, the press in the US grew far faster than market forces would have allowed. The press in turn became an engine of growth for other sectors of the economy. Until the second half of the nineteenth century, the press understood itself as political more than commercial.[14]

Although printers were often canny entrepreneurs, they were simultaneously citizens and political leaders. Moreover, they understood commerce and politics to be in tension, and insisted on moral and ethical guidelines to prevent their commercial interests from overcoming the common good. Until the second half of the nineteenth century, the First Amendment guarantees of freedom of speech and press were understood to be limited by the concerns of the public good and the health of the public sphere. The press did not come to be understood as a singular institution in a common commercial marketplace until the mid-nineteenth century.

---

[10] Stephen Botein. 1975. "Meer Mechanicks' and an Open Press: The Business and Political Strategies of Colonial Printers." *Perspectives in American History* IX: 127-225; Stephen Botein, "Printers and the American Revolution." in Bernard Bailyn and John B. Hench, (eds.) *The Press & the American Revolution*. Worcester: American Antiquarian Society, 1980; Leonard Levy. *Emergence of a Free Press*. New York: Oxford University Press, 1985; John Nerone. *Violence against the Press: Policing the Public Sphere in US History* New York: Oxford University Press, 1994.

[11] For more on this, see Culver Smith. The press, politics, and patronage : the American government's use of newspapers. 1789-1875. Athens: University of Georgia Press, 1977.

[12] Richard R. John. *Spreading the News*. Cambridge: Harvard University Press, 1995.

[13] Jeffrey L. Pasley. "The tyranny of printers": newspaper politics in the early American republic. Charlottesville: University Press of Virginia, 2001.

[14] Barnhurst and Nerone, chapters 1-4.

Saul Cornell, in his study of the Constitutional debates, gives special emphasis to the relationships between the press and the public sphere. "Not only was the debate over the Constitution an important phase in the evolution of the public sphere in America, but the contest over it focused unprecedented attention on the politics of the public sphere itself."[15] The ideal of free and full public access to a rational debate over the common good — stripped so far as possible from the pursuit of private advantage — emerges in the writings of many of the early republic's best editorialists (who of course wrote anonymously in keeping with the spirit of the public sphere). Cornell notes that Philadelphia editorialist, "Centinel" (probably Samuel Bryan) "envisioned the public sphere of print as an important means of cementing the nation together. Print afforded a means of achieving social cohesion without a strong coercive authority."[16] Far from an economic marketplace, the press in its finest form would embody its function as the basis for deliberative self-government. Of course, there were a handful of papers that published scandal and pitched their content at sales rather than service. These were a substantial minority with small influence. Jefferson blasted these papers, referring to them as "polluted vehicles."[17]

We can see these understandings in action in the postal policy of the new federal government which reflected the Founders commitment to the right of the citizenry to as a wide a circulation of public information as possible. Richard John describes what he calls the "educational rationale for postal policy" adopted into the Post Office Act of 1792. Essentially, it was the intent of the Framers to create a postal system that best facilitated the distribution of public information to the citizens active in the self-governing of the society. Were it not for considerations of local markets and delivery guarantees, newspapers would likely have been distributed for free as a matter of principle. Lawmakers certainly considered it before opting to grant newspapers full access to the postal system with extremely favorable rates. These low rates ensured the feasibility of wide distribution and resulted in a huge expansion of the press system. The policy acted as a public subsidy for the promotion and circulation of public information for the purposes of cultivating the values of self-government.[18]

The Postal Act represented a government regulation designed to promote majoritarian rights to free speech by expanding and enriching the public sphere. Similarly the Founders supported public libraries and educational institutions. The public right to have access to, and the capacity to

---

[15] Saul Cornell. *The Other Founders*. Chapel Hill: University of North Carolina Press, 1999, p. 21.

[16] Cornell, 104.

[17] Koch and Peden, 581. These lines are taken from a letter to John Norvell, June 11, 1807.

[18] John, 30-37.

know, the truth were a critical part of the Enlightenment understanding of the public sphere.[19]   The government could certainly sponsor a free press, i.e. make laws to positively enhance it, even as, conversely, it could not negatively curtail it.

The expansion of the press system after the Revolution elevated newspapers into "the matrix of the function of popular government and the protection of civil liberties."[20] That is, public opinion embraced the free circulation of public information and the freedom of expression as an important part of governmental society. Newspapers were evolving into the 4th Estate, "an informal or extra constitutional fourth branch that functioned as part of the intricate system of checks and balances that exposed public mismanagement   and   kept   power   fragmented,   manageable,   and accountable."[21] The importance of public engagement and participation in the ongoing debates in the press was not only a central legal right but a functional, practicable goal.

The number of papers in proportion to the number of eligible voters (defined rather strictly in those days) was impressive, and access for speakers and readers alike was not a problem. Jefferson eloquently summarizes the principles at stake: "The basis of our governments being the opinion of people," he wrote, "the very first object should be to keep that right; and were it left to me to decide whether we should have a government without newspapers, or newspapers without government, I should not hesitate a moment to prefer the latter. But I should mean that every man should receive those papers, and be capable of reading them."[22] This is an oft-quoted passage; but its final sentence, often omitted, warrants special attention here. The implication is that it is not enough to negatively protect the press system. It must be actively promoted to ensure universal distribution of all public information to all citizens. In other words, the public's right to hear all voices and properly digest their messages is the central platform of a democracy.

In the history of the First Amendment, then, the key question is not where and when strict libertarian concepts of free expression were adopted, nor where the boundaries of the public sphere or the 4th Estate were drawn. The important conclusion is that this arena of public discourse was of central importance to the Framers of a democratic experiment. The structural integrity of the press system, the institutions of town hall meetings and public assemblies, and the ability of anyone with an opinion to set up a soap box on a street corner were all generally recognized as the true meaning behind the

---

[19] Smith, 44-46.

[20] Levy, 273. See also Barnhurst and Nerone, 43-5.

[21] Levy, 273. See also John Nerone. *The Culture of the Press in the Early Republic* (New York: Garland Publishing,1989), 19.

[22] Koch and Peden, ed., 411-12. Quote taken from a letter to Edward Carrington, January 16, 1787.

freedom of expression. The important thing for them was not the specifics of protecting each individual speaker, but rather ensuring that the system as a whole remained operational and effective in the dissemination of all ideas to all citizens. This analysis highlights the contention that for the Framers of the freedom of the press, the structural issues were more important than the individual ones.

THE CONTEMPORARY LOGIC OF A POSITIVE VIEW OF THE FIRST AMENDMENT

Given this review of history which qualifies and revises traditional accounts of First Amendment origins, it follows that the development of legal and theoretical ideas about the freedom of the press should also reflect a different logic. The theoretical postulate which we may take from the identification of majoritarian rights as primary to individual rights can be directly mapped onto the idea that positive freedom or affirmative freedom assumes and precedes negative freedom or prohibitive freedom. That is to say, the protection and sustenance of the majority's right to a free, fair and full public sphere is not guaranteed simply by prohibiting government from interfering with individual speech.

First Amendment scholar Zechariah Chafee eloquently explained why negative freedoms are insufficient: "To us this policy is too exclusively negative. For example, what is the use of telling an unpopular speaker that he will incur no criminal penalties by his proposed address, so long as every hall owner in the city declines to rent him space for his meeting and there are no vacant lots available?" Chafee argues that the public must make available to all willing speakers the means to speak their mind, "for otherwise the subjects that most need to be discussed will be the very subjects that will be ruled out as unsuitable for discussion...We must do more than remove the discouragements to open discussion. We must exert ourselves to supply active encouragements."[23]

In a more recent treatment of this negative/positive freedom debate, Owen Fiss distinguished two primary treatments of the First Amendment, the "autonomy principle" and the" public debate principle." The "autonomy principle" is the libertarian tradition which holds that individual speech rights, properly protected, will automatically yield a full and free public debate if left unencumbered. The "public debate principle" is the majoritarian tradition which denies that autonomy is fully instrumental in providing for the public's rights and authorizes an active state to cultivate and promote the structural conditions of an "uninhibited, robust, and wide-open" public

---

[23] Zechariah Chafee. *Free Speech in the United States* (Cambridge: Harvard University Press, 1941), p. 559.

debate, to quote from Justice Brennan's ruling in *New York Times Co. v. Sullivan* (1964).[24]

The positive freedom which obliges the state to make laws that aid rather than abridge free expression rejects the adequacy of purely negative rights. Moreover, it recognizes the corollary responsibilities of the state that are not questioned as "infringements" on First Amendment freedoms though they unquestionably aid in its promotion. Alexander Meiklejohn's position on this distinction is worth quoting at length:

> "First, let it be noted that, by those words [the text of the First Amendment], Congress is not debarred from all action upon freedom of speech. Legislation which abridges that freedom is forbidden, but not legislation to enlarge and enrich it. The freedom of mind which befits members of a self-governing society is not a given and fixed part of human nature. It can be increased and established by learning, by teaching, by the unhindered flow of accurate information, by giving men health and vigor and security, by bringing them together in activities of communication and mutual understanding. And the federal legislature is not forbidden to engage in that positive enterprise of cultivating the general intelligence upon which the success of self-government so obviously depends. On the contrary, in that positive field the Congress of the United States has a heavy and basic responsibility to promote the freedom of speech."[25]

In this interpretation, flouting the legitimacy of affirmative government action in the realm of public speech on the grounds that it violates the speech rights of individuals misunderstands the priority of majority over minority rights and the structural basis of the First Amendment.

Paul Stern defines the Meiklejohnian "political interpretation of speech" further, writing "that our protection of free speech is grounded in its function of sustaining a framework of unconstrained public discourse in which agents can deliberately define their purposes by reciprocally weighing the merits of opposing positions."[26] The "framework" must retain its structural integrity, must adhere to the "public debate principle" of Owen Fiss, because it is the foundation of deliberative self-government. Without it, democracy falls apart, and public power devolves to private speakers whose liberties are permitted to corrupt the majoritarian right to a full public sphere.

To the extent that private speech (or more to the point, private control of the systems of communication) does not serve or contradicts a public function, it is not protected by the First Amendment, and in some cases must be actively resisted to preserve the forms of speech which are constitutionally

---

[24] Owen M. Fiss. "Why the State?" *Harvard Law Review* 100, no. 4 (1987): 785.

[25] Alexander Meiklejohn, *Political Freedom* (New York: Harpers, 1960), pp. 19-20.

[26] Paul G. Stern. "A Pluralistic Reading of the First Amendment and Its Relation to Public Discourse." *Yale Law Journal* 99, no. 4 (1990): 925.

mandated. This resistance does not come in the form of suppressing speech, but rather in the form of empowering more speech to match the advantage gained by a disproportionately amplified private speaker in the public sphere.

This is an absolutely central point with regard to the modern press. Gone are the days when the town meeting and the community forum could stand for the public debate. The mass media is the general arena of deliberation. The press, once conceived as a part of the public sphere and a player in the public debate, has become the mediator of that debate as well as its primary player. When that mediator, using its accumulated economic power, volume and control, begins to advocate from a position of private interest, the principles of the First Amendment's structural protections, its majoritarian rights, are weakened.

CONTEMPORARY COMMERCIAL MASS MEDIA

Moving out into the realm of the political culture, if the intent of a media channel is not primarily to serve the public, but rather to sell papers, increase ratings, scoop rivals, or deliver up content which draws the audiences most desirable for sale to advertisers—or more controversially, if the intent is to push a particular political position or omit a particularly political position—the majoritarian principles of the First Amendment are undermined.

We are not arguing that the government should take an overly intrusive hand in the editorial rooms of commercial media, but rather that the commercial media system itself is at odds with the principles of the First Amendment in important ways. Either the government must take a hand in expanding speech to include that which is excluded by the private masters of the public debate, or it must regulate the structural administration of the public sphere to facilitate entry into the marketplace of underrepresented voices. More to the point, we can no longer be satisfied with a definition of the First Amendment that rests exclusively with the forms of negative freedom universally applied.

Arguing that the press has turned away from its public mission does not mean that it should be muzzled or censored. It means that the media must bear the burden of regulation due a system of public debate institutionalized into a commercial system for private gain. The public rights stripped out by market forces must be reinstated by public policy. The spirit of the First Amendment would indicate that the solution lies in re-publicizing the public sphere. Private control of the system and its major voices can only be countered by the public protection of the system through the advocacy and subsidy of more speech, specifically from those speakers who are not permitted or able to gain access to the current media.

Congress and the FCC have the responsibility to positively protect the right to public speech by ensuring a free, full, fair, and deliberative space for public debate. William Hocking described his proposals to "provide presumptive but not prescriptive routes" to a satisfactory public sphere as "means to freedom" not obstructions to it.[27] Therefore, they must open up the media to ensure that all opinions may be heard. That this cannot easily be done in a commercial system does not make it less necessary. As famously put by the Hutchins Commission in 1947 whose report reads just as relevantly today as it did half a century ago: "Freedom of the press means freedom from and freedom for...The freedom of the press can remain a right of those who publish only if it incorporates into itself the right of the citizen and the public interest."[28]

Given the importance of the structure of the media system to the guarantee of the First Amendment, we must investigate the structure of the commercial marketplace of ideas. There are major problems with mapping an exchange model of marketplace competition onto the public sphere of political communication.

The concept of the marketplace of ideas did not exist in the 18th century. The Founders had another structural model in mind: the public sphere. It sounds a lot like the marketplace of ideas, but there are key differences. To get at these differences, we must understand early American thinking on organized power and free expression. In the libertarian tradition of First Amendment thought, the prohibition of organized public power from activity in the arena of public speech is the foundation of the right. Perhaps because of this beginning, this tradition has rarely considered other forms of organized power which might threaten the public's right to free expression, such as privately organized power. It seems a logical move to make, but it has not often been made in mainstream legal theory. Yet we should take note that the Founders argued against public power not to explicitly exempt private power, but because no privately organized power then existed that had the capacity to topple free and full public debate.

Of course, in modern times, this is no longer the case. There are many seats of privately organized power with the ability to topple free expression. But the theory of the structure of public speech has not taken this fully into account. In large part, this is because the marketplace of ideas has replaced the public sphere as the ideal type at the center of theory on the First Amendment. The public sphere demands protection from all organized power, internal and external. No minority interests may control the system of communication and no voice within the public sphere should have a

---

[27] William Ernest Hocking. *Freedom of the Press.* Chicago: University of Chicago Press, 1947, p. 96.
[28] Robert M. Hutchins. *A Free and Responsible Press.* Chicago: University of Chicago Press, 1947, p. 18.

structural advantage over another. In the marketplace of ideas, it is only the external intervention of public power which is prohibited. No restrictions are placed on internal private power. Hence the private censor may replace the public censor without breaking the rules.

This strikes us as a bitter irony. Essentially, the zeal of the First Amendment defenders of the private right to uninhibited speech has led directly to the ability of minority speakers to distort the marketplace of ideas, box out unwanted speakers in the most mainstream channels to which everyone has access, and defend their actions as inalienable constitutional rights. It is the direct result of the conflation of individual, negative speech rights with the marketplace model—to the exclusion of public, affirmative speech rights and the ideal of the public sphere. In today's media marketplace, dominated by a handful of mega-corporations, a group of organized private interests can gate-keep the marketplace, determine the parameters of public debate, and marginalize unprofitable or politically undesirable speakers by denying them access to the high-impact, mainstream media. The marketplace has no rules and no theoretical problems with a homogenous bloc of political communication in the center of public communication, banishing the bulk of diversity to low traffic media like small circulation print publications and little known websites. When we grant absolute freedom to private media operators to do as they choose with their channels, we give them the constitutional right to ignore their constitutional duty—to give all public ideas a public hearing. Why should we fear public tyranny and embrace its private form? Owen Fiss laments precisely: "Autonomy provides the proponents of deregulation with a constitutional platform that is ill-deserved."[29]

There have been occasional legal attempts to recognize and rectify this state of affairs. For example, in *Associated Press v. United States* (1945), the Supreme Court ruled that AP could not withhold news from public media channels who wished to take advantage of the wire service. Justice Black writing for the Court ruled: "Freedom of the press from governmental interference under the First Amendment does not sanction repression of that freedom by private interests."[30]   Justice Frankfurter affirmed this sentiment: "A public interest so essential to the vitality of our democratic government may be defeated by private restraints no less than by public ownership."[31] This is a clear vindication of public over private rights to freedom of expression, affirmative structural rights trumping negative individual rights. By implication, any private media organization's actions (despite falling

---

[29] Fiss, 790. Perhaps the best statement of this irony is in Jerome A. Barron. 1967. "Access to the Press--a New First Amendment Right." *Harvard Law Review* 80:8: 1641-78.

[30] Quoted in Barron, 1654.

[31] Quoted in Hocking, 172

under First Amendment protection) which infringe upon the full and free public debate are subject to public regulation by virtue of the higher law of public rights to a free and full debate.

Scholars have subsequently wondered with astonishment how a precedent failed to be set in this case to protect the public interest from private appropriation.[32] The much cited Hutchins Commission Report (1947) on the press is replete with instances and warnings about the contradiction of preventing government from hindering the press even while endorsing the very same tyranny in the form of private media companies with a stranglehold on the marketplace.

The Hutchins Commission reflected on new broadcast technology, market forces, and the nature of the modern press and came to ominous conclusions. Essentially, the public importance of the press was increasing as the mass media increased the range and depth of market penetration. Yet the nature of mass communication meant fewer speakers and vastly fewer operators of the major media due to the apparent necessity of economies of scale in these industries. Further, the vast majority of the speakers were engaged in commercial service, not public service, rendering the public interest a distant second as a priority.[33]

In large part, this should not have been surprising, as the common knowledge about freedom of the press allowed for absolute freedom for media channels and the guaranteed provision of public service through the invisible hand of the marketplace. Without overturning, or at least troubling, these two pillars of First Amendment orthodoxy, no progress would be made. The Hutchins Commission came to precisely this conclusion—although their recommendations fell far short of implementing their critique in any meaningful way. "Since the consumer is no longer free not to consume, and can get what he requires only through existing press organs," the Commissioners wrote, "protection of the freedom of the issuer is no longer sufficient to protect automatically either the consumer or the community. The general policy of laissez faire in this field must be reconsidered."[34]

Reconsidered in reference to what, we might ask? The expansive definition of First Amendment rights has historical roots, legal theory, and political currency to back it up. The "polluted vehicles" of the early republic have become the polluted system of modern times. Gone is even the pretense of the public sphere as the Founders envisioned it.[35] A few points of summary

[32] See for example, Hocking, 172 and Lee C. Bollinger. *Images of a Free Press.* Chicago: University of Chicago Press, 1991, p. 111.

[33] See Bollinger, 28-29; Hutchins, 1.

[34] Hutchins, 125.

[35] See for example, C. Wright Mills. *The Power Elite.* New York: Oxford University Press, 1956.; Jerome Barron. 1967. "Access to the Press--a New First Amendment Right." *Harvard Law Review* 80:8: 1641-78; Edward Herman and Noam Chomsky. *Manufacturing Consent.* New York: Pantheon Books, 2002 [1988].; Robert W.

will suffice to connect the major arguments with the current discussion on the history, theory, and political conceptions of the First Amendment.

CRITIQUE OF MARKET-PRIMARY IN FEDERAL POLICY

Essentially, there is a dangerous fallacy in assuming that the marketplace of ideas is commensurate with the public sphere of deliberative democracy. The idea that a laissez-faire regulatory scheme that cedes all control of mass mediated public debate to commercial media concerns will somehow magically yield a representative sample of public ideas and interests is bankrupt. Perhaps one could equate the two in a town hall meeting in an 18th century Massachusetts farming community whose citizens had access to a dozen different mainstream newspapers of varying partisan stripes; but no longer. Not only does the current system invite corruption and the distortion of public representation for private gain, it absolutely ignores the imperative at the foundation of the First Amendment that the freedom of the press is the public right not only to contribute to the public debate, but also to consume and consider a free and representative variety of public opinion. The market will naturally favor some voices over others, some topics over others, and transform citizens into political consumers. This process has proceeded blithely apace for so long that we appear to have forgotten our roots. In this context, we note that the very apathy of disillusion is now held up as proof of satisfied customers, or rather, citizens.

The critique follows two central tracks. First, as media firms consolidate and concentrate ownership in the marketplace, the number of voices in the public sphere diminishes. This phenomenon is the direct result of federal deregulation based on libertarian, free market conceptions of First Amendment duties. Diversity gives way to homogenized content calculated for the economic and political benefit of minority interests at the expense of the majority. Market power is based on the idea of reducing competition, streamlining production, leveraging pre-existing market advantages, and selling for the maximum price what may be produced for the minimum cost. Any public benefit that accrues from this process is largely incidental. The market is simply a poor mechanism for arbitrating public debates. Jerome Barron's savage explanation is a handy blueprint: "There is inequality in the power to communicate ideas just as there is inequality in economic bargaining power; to recognize the latter and deny the former is quixotic. The 'marketplace of ideas' view has rested on the assumption that protecting the

---

McChesney. *Rich Media, Poor Democracy.* New York: New Press, 2000; Leonard Downie Jr. and Robert G. Kaiser. *The News About the News.* New York: Alfred A. Knopf, 2002; and Robert W. McChesney and John Nichols. *Our Media, Not Theirs.* New York: Seven Stories, 2002.

right of expression is equivalent to providing for it."[36] The failure of that postulate to deliver is manifest in the continued de-politicization of modern society and the deep-seated problems we face from under-representation of minority viewpoints in the mainstream media.

The second track of the critique addresses a product of this system and represents its most visible form: the content of the media system. At the most basic level, mainstream media has homogenized to an unprecedented extent. Standardized fare is cheaper to produce and more easily manipulated politically than a diverse marketplace. Moreover, even if a political motive is not immediately apparent, the drive to place profit before public service inevitably produces content that satisfies the minimum threshold of the lowest common denominator of public taste.

The First Amendment is not meant to sanctify the marketplace of ideas, it is meant to ensure to every citizen "the fullest possible participation" in the working through of social problems. "When a free man is voting, it is not enough that the truth is known by someone else, by some scholar or administrator or legislator. The voters must have it, all of them. The primary purpose of the First Amendment is, then, that all the citizens shall, so far as possible, understand the issues which bear upon our common life. That is why no idea, no opinion, no doubt, no belief, no counter belief, no relevant information, may be kept from them."[37]

It is consent and consensus through informed debate, not competition and submission through Darwinian dogfights, which is sought by the public spirited intent of the Constitution and the affirmative freedom of expression provided for the American public. The social contract is not an invitation to a Machiavellian power struggle but a commitment to the common good. Federal regulation that ignores this reality and commits itself to the service of market forces is doing the public a profound disservice. As Jerome Barron puts it: "As a constitutional theory for the communication of ideas, laissez faire is manifestly irrelevant."[38] The era when the First Amendment could be seen primarily as a defender of personal liberties in an unfettered public sphere is long gone (if it ever existed). The only way to claim the public right to a deliberative discussion about common affairs with guaranteed access for all citizens is to temper the private control over the media system with public policies that promote a diversity of voices. The only way to reinstall an affirmative right to the structural integrity of public communications systems is to expose the marketplace as an inadequate method of producing fair treatment for all.

In a marketplace, individual rights (property rights) have precedence over public rights (assets commonly held). In a public sphere, the reverse is

---

[36] Barron, 1647-8.
[37] Meiklejohn, 73-75.
[38] Barron, 1656.

true. Though the manifestations of this debate are complex, the basic questions are very simple. To which victor go the spoils of public policy? The private interest or the common good?

CONCLUSION

We set out to describe and critique the status quo of libertarian First Amendment thinking which lies at the base of the FCC's R&O on media ownership and to offer an alternative set of possibilities. The overarching conclusion is that this paradigm does exist, is easily within reach, and requires only the will of public consideration to find purchase in a regulatory regime. It is neither esoteric nor impractical, but draws from relatively common sense approaches to history, legal traditions, and public policy.

The public interest was always the primary concern. The Founders understanding and discussion of these legal rights are sometimes easy to misread, not because their reasoning is unclear, but because the historical situation in which it was applied is so different from our own. Proceeding with the intent of untangling the specificities of historical moments, we begin to see that the balance of public and private interests in the First Amendment corresponds to a balance of negative and affirmative liberties. The prohibition on government power to abridge speech does not prohibit, and in fact obliges, a complementary policy of support and enhancement of the public sphere. From this position, we may then see the inadequacy of the marketplace to achieve the ideals the Founders intended and which we aspire to sustain. On the contrary, the marketplace of ideas, when taken to its modern context of oligopoly commercial mass media, produces a scenario which tends toward the exact opposite of the public rights the Founders intended and democratic society demands.

The Commission should base its rules governing the public interest limits on media ownership on an affirmative, majoritarian view of the First Amendment. The consumer media marketplace is no substitute for the citizens' public sphere. Public policy should seek to expand the marketplace to include all voices, to protect the common good in the public sphere to deliberate with all viewpoints. The private power to interfere with these common rights must not be ignored, but must be vigilantly curtailed. Limits on media ownership should be maintained and policies undertaken to expand ownership of media outlets and viewpoint diversity.

PART II:
THE PILLARS OF MEDIA OWNERSHIP
LIMITS REMAIN FIRM:
THE CONTINUING IMPORTANCE OF LOCALISM,
MEDIA OWNERSHIP AND TELEVISION

STUDY 4
LOCALISM AND DIVERSITY

MARJORIE HEINS AND MARK COOPER

THE CONTINUING IMPORTANCE OF LOCALISM

The important role of the media in informing citizens about local affairs is well documented.[1] The link between localism and de-concentration of the media seems obvious. Changes in electronic media distribution technologies have not significantly altered this fundamental relationship.[2]

Waldfogel finds important localism effects operating in the media that support this view. He finds that the preference externality operates in non-prime time programming because it is subject to greater local control and therefore can be more responsive to local market conditions.[3] Concentration of national and local markets into national chains reinforces the tendencies of media owners to ignore local needs.[4]

---

[1] Kim, Sei-Hill, Dietram A. Scheufele and James Shanahan. 2002. Think About It This Way: Attribute Agenda Setting Function of the Press and the Public's Evaluation of a Local Issue, *Journalism and Mass Communications Quarterly* 79: p. 7; Chaffee, Steven and Stacy Frank. 1996. How Americans Get Their Political Information: Print versus Broadcast News. *The Annals of the American Academy of Political and Social Science* 546; McLeod, Jack M., Dietram A. Scheufele, and Patricia Moy 1999. Community, Communications, and Participation: The Role of Mass Media and Interpersonal Discussion in Local Political Participation. *Political Communication* 16.

[2] Krotoszynski, Ronald J., Jr. and A. Richard M. Blaiklock. 2000. Enhancing the Spectrum: Media Power, Democracy, and the Marketplace of Ideas *University of Illinois Law Review* 813: 866:"The Commission historically has placed a high value on local control of broadcasting on the theory that local control would result in the provision of programming that better meets the needs of the community of license..."A quick perusal of cable programming practices demonstrates the veracity of the proposition. With the exception of PEG channels and leased-access channels, cable programming presents very little programming responsive to the needs, wants, and desires of local communities. If you want the prized hog competition at the state fair covered live, you need a local media presence. Elections for city, county and even state officers might go uncovered if left to the networks or national cable news channels. Although alternative sources of information exist, including the Internet and local newspapers, most Americans continue to rely upon local and network television for their news programming. With respect to local news, local broadcasters are effectively the only game in town."

[3] Waldfogel, 2001b, p. 13; Waldfogel, 2001a, p. 9.

[4] Krotoszynski and Blaiklock, pp. 871...875-876: "The Commission's efforts to preserve localism as a feature of the broadcast media will be effectively thwarted if large,

Waldfogel's findings on localism, derived from the basic economics of the media, cut across each of the major products.

> The local data indicate, to a greater extent than the national prime time or cable data, both the distance between black and white preferences and the fact that local programming, far more than national programming, caters to those preferences.[5]

While the economics of television give rise to strong concerns about localism,[6] Waldfogel sees indications of similar localism effects in newspaper markets as well, supporting the conclusion that "content origin matters." He describes localism's effect on behavior in the findings of a study on the entry of a national newspaper into local markets as follows:

> How does national news media affect local news sources and local political participation?
>
> Preliminary results- Increased circulation of national daily affects:
>
> Local paper circulation – reduces targeted audience readership
>
> Local paper positioning – toward local content
>
> Local political participation – reduces voting, less so in presidential years.

Gee and Waldfogel have recently examined the impact of localism on voter turnout by studying the effect of the availability of Spanish language television on Hispanic voting. This ties the media directly to the most important political outcome – participation.

---

corporate entities are permitted to amass large station holdings and use central programming techniques to achieve economies of scale and scope... "Common ownership of media outlets is not conducive to competition in news and other local content programming. Consolidated news departments, like consolidated marketing departments, are a common feature of multiple station groups. Divided control of media outlets within a community creates a healthy competition among news and programming sources."

[5] Waldfogel, 2001b, p. 13.

[6] Krotoszynski and Blaiklock, pp. 866: "Given economies of scale, it might be inefficient to cover the hog competition at the state fair. Perhaps Jerry Springer or Montel Williams would generate higher ratings or cost less to broadcast. From a purely economic point of view, covering a debate between candidates for local office might be a complete disaster. Many local television and radio stations nevertheless provide such coverage on a voluntary basis. Perhaps local commercial television broadcasters do not provide such coverage solely out of the goodness of their hearts or a keen sense of civic responsibility. Nevertheless, the fact remains that a national television channel generally would not cover the lieutenant governor's race in South Dakota absent the most extraordinary and unlikely of circumstances."

Many questions about localism in media remain unanswered. But it is clear from the results of this study that at least one aspect of localism – the availability of local news – is important....

Television bears a mixed relationship with political participation. Historically, the spread of television has been linked with declining political participation. But it is important to distinguish the message and the medium. Television carries both local and national news. The spread of television, like other national information sources, can attract people away form local products and local affairs. But television can also include local content, chiefly local news, and we find that the availability of Spanish-language local television news significantly boosts Hispanic voter turnout.[7]

CONCENTRATION, CONSOLIDATION AND CONGLOMERATION UNDERMINE LOCALISM AND DIVERSITY

Several recent studies based on FCC data show that localism and diversity are harmed by concentration of local markets, consolidation into chains and conglomeration across media types.[8] These studies confirm much earlier research.[9] The dictates of mass audiences create a largest market share/lowest common denominator ethic that undercuts the ability to deliver culturally diverse programming,[10] locally-oriented programming,[11] and public

---

[7] Oberholzer-Gee, Felix and Joel Waldfogel. "Media Markets and Localism: Does Local News en Espanol Boost Hispanic Voter Turnout?" *Rethinking the Discourse on Race: A Symposium on How the Lack of Racial Diversity in the Media Affects Social Justice and Policy*, April 28-29, 2006, pp. 13-14.

[8] Anonymous, Do Local Owners Deliver More Localism? Some Evidence from Local Broadcast News (Federal Communication Commission, draft dated June 17, 2004), p. 14; Alexander, Peter J. and Brendan M/Cunningham. 2004. Diversity in Broadcast Television: An Empirical Study of Local News. International Journal of Media Management 6; Alexander, Peter J. and Brendan M. Cunningham. Same Story, Different Channel: Braodcast News and Information. (October 4, 2004).

[9] Waldfogel, Television; Waldfogel and George; Waldfogel. Comments on Consolidation and Localism.

[10] Stone, V. A. 1987. "Deregulation Felt Mainly in Large-Market Radio and Independent TV," Communicator, April: 12; Aufderheide, P. 1990. "After the Fairness Doctrine: Controversial Broadcast Programming and the Public Interest." Journal of Communication, pp. 50-51; McKean, M. L. and V. A. Stone 1991. Why Stations Don't Do News RTNDA Communicator June: 23-24; Stone, V. A., "New Staffs Change Little in Radio, Take Cuts in Major Markets TV, RTNDA Communicator, 1988; Slattery, K. L. and E. A. Kakanen. 1994. Sensationalism Versus Public Affairs Content of Local TV News: Pennsylvania Revisited. Journal of Broadcasting and Electronic Media, 1994; Bernstein, J. M. and S. Lacy. 1992. "Contextual Coverage of Government by Local Television News." Journalism Quarterly 69:2: 329-341; Carroll, R. L. 1989. "Market Size and TV News Values." Journalism Quarterly 66: 49-56; Scott, D. K. and R. H. Gopbetz. 1992. "Hard News/Soft News Content of the National Broadcast Networks:

interest programming.[12]   News and public affairs programming are particularly vulnerable to these economic pressures.[13] As market forces grow, these types of programming are reduced.[14] Unfortunately, the coverage that disappears tends to deal with schools, localized government affairs, and other community-strengthening materials that enable people to live more secure and educated lives.[15]

1972-1987." Journalism Quarterly 69:2: 406-412; Ferrall, V. E. 1992. "The Impact of Television Deregulation" Journal of Communications; pp. 21... 28... 30.

[11] Slattery, Karen L., Ernest A. Hakanen and Mark Doremus. 1996. "The Expression of Localism: Local TV News Coverage in the New Video Marketplace." Journal of Broadcasting and Electronic Media 40; Carroll, Raymond L. and C.A. Tuggle. 1997. "The World Outside: Local TV News Treatment of Imported News." Journalism and Mass Communications Quarterly Spring; Fairchild, Charles. 1999. "Deterritorializing Radio: Deregulation and the Continuing Triumph of the Corporatist Perspective in the USA." Media, Culture & Society 21; Layton, Charles and Jennifer Dorroh. 2002 "Sad State." American Journalism Review June; Olson, Kathryn. 1994. "Exploiting the Tension between the New Media's "Objective" and Adversarial Roles: The Role Imbalance Attach and its Use of the Implied Audience." Communications Quarterly 42:1: 40-41; Stavitsky, A. G. 1994. "The Changing Conception of Localism in U.S. Public Radio." Journal of Broadcasting and Electronic Media.

[12] Bagdikian, Media Monopoly, pp. 182...188; Clarke, P. and E. Fredin. 1978. "Newspapers, Television, and Political Reasoning." Public Opinion Quarterly Summer; Pfau, M. 1990. "A Channel Approach to Television Influence." Journal of Broadcasting and Electronic Media 34: 17-36; Cundy, D. T., "Political Commercials and Candidate Image." in Lynda Lee Kaid (eds.), New Perspectives in Political Advertising. Carbondale, IL: Southern Illinois University Press, 1986; O'Keefe, G. J. 1980. "Political Malaise and Reliance on the Media" Journalism Quarterly 57:1: 133-128; Becker, S. and H. C. Choi. 1987. Media Use, Issue/Image Discrimination. Communications Research 14: 267-290; Robinson, J. P. and D. K. Davis. 1990. Television News and the Informed Public: An Information Process Approach. Journal of Communication 40:3: 106-119.; Voakes, Paul S., Jack Kapfer, David Kurpius, and David Shano-yeon Chern. 1996. Diversity in the News: A Conceptual and Methodological Framework. Journalism and Mass Communications Quarterly, Autumn 1996; Bishop, Ronald and Ernest A. Hakanen. 2002. In the Public Interest? The State of Local Television Programming Fifteen Years After Deregulation. Journal of Communications Inquiry 26.

[13] McManus, J. H. 1992. "What Kind of a Commodity is News?" Communications Research, 19:6:787-805.

[14] Bagdikian, pp. 220-221; Paletz, D. L. and R. M. Entmen. Media, Power, Politics. New York: Free Press, 1981; Postman, Neil, Amusing Ourselves to Death: Public Discourse in the Age of Show Business. New York: Penguin Press, 1985.; Lacy, Stephen. 1992. "The Financial Commitment Approaches to News Media Competition." Journal of Media Economics 5:2: 5-21.

[15] Bass, Jack. "Newspaper Monopoly." in Gene Roberts, Thomas Kunkel, and Charles Clayton (eds.), Leaving Readers Behind. Fayetteville: University of Arkansas Press, 2001; Gish, Pat and Tom Gish, We Still Scream: The Perils and Pleasures of Running a

The central fact that all of these discussions share is that market forces provide neither adequate incentives to produce the high quality media product, nor adequate incentives to distribute sufficient amounts of diverse content necessary to meet consumer and citizen needs.

THE LACK OF LOCALISM AND DIVERSITY IN THE COMMERCIAL MASS MEDIA

The growing impact of homogenization in the TV industry, stimulated by the lifting of both national ownership limits and restrictions on vertical integration, is unmistakable.[16] Local programming has been restricted or eliminated.[17] Stories of local importance are driven out of the high-visibility hours or off the air.[18] Pooled news services reduce the ability of local

---

Small-Town Newspaper. and Shipp, F. R. "Excuses, Excuses: How Editors and Reporters Justify Ignoring Stories." in William Serrin (eds.), The Business of Journalism. New York: New Press, 2000. Complaints about the failure to cover larger national and international stories also abound (see Phillips, Peter and Project Censored, Censored 2003. New York: Seven Stories, 2002; Borjesson, Kristina. Into the BUZZSAW. Amherst, New York: Prometheus Books, 2002.

[16] McChesney, Robert. The Problem of the Media. New York: Monthly Review Press, 2004; Ben H. Bagdikian. The New Media Monopoly. Boston: Beacon Press, 2004; Meyer, Thomas. Media Democracy. Cambridge: Polity Press, 2002; Meyerowitz, J. 1985. No Sense of Place: The Effect of Electronic Media on Social Behavior. New York: Oxford; Kunkel, Thomas and Gene Roberts. 2001. The Age of Corporate Newspapering, Leaving Readers Behind. American Journalism Review May. On coverage of the 1996 Telecommunications Act see, Gilens, Martin and Craig Hertzman. "Corporate Ownership and News Bias: Newspaper Coverage of the 1996 Telecommunications Act." paper delivered at the Annual Meeting of the American Political Science Association, August, 1997, p. 8; Network Affiliated Stations Alliance. "Petition for Inquiry into Network Practices" Federal Communications Commission, 8 March 2001).

[17] Layton, Charles, 1999. "What do Readers Really Want?" American Journalism Review March. reprinted in Gene Roberts and Thomas Kunkel, Breach of Faith: A Crisis of Coverage in the Age of Corporate Newspapering. Fayetteville: University of Arkansas Press, 2002; McConnell, Bill and Susanne Ault. "Fox TV's Strategy: Two by Two, Duopolies are Key to the Company's Goal of Becoming a Major Local Presence." Broadcasting and Cable, July 30, 2001; Trigoboff, Dan, "Chri-Craft. Fox Moves In: The Duopoly Marriage in Three Markets Comes with Some Consolidation." Broadcasting and Cable, August 6, 2001; Trigoboff, Dan. "Rios Heads KCOP News." Broadcasting and Cable, October 14, 2002; Beam, Randal A. 1995. "What it Means to Be a Market-Oriented Newspaper." Newspaper Research Journal 16, Beam, Randall A. 2002. "Size of Corporate Parent Drives Market Orientation." Newspaper Research Journal 23; Vane, Sharyn. 2002. "Taking Care of Business." American Journalism Review March; Neiman Reports. 1999. The Business of News, the News About Business, Summer.

[18] E.g., Lacy, Stephen, David C. Coulson and Hugh J. Martin. 2004. Ownership Barriers to Entry in Non-metropolitan Daily Newspaper Markets. Journalism & Mass Communications Quarterly 81, Summer; Wimmer, K. A. 1988. "Deregulation and the

stations to present local stories and eventually erode the capability to produce them.[19]

A recent study from the Project for Excellence in Journalism affirms these conclusions. Among its findings were that smaller station groups overall tended to produce higher quality newscasts than stations owned by larger companies—by a significant margin; and that network affiliated stations tended to produce higher quality newscasts than network owned and operated stations—also by a large margin. The Project concluded that "overall, the data strongly suggest regulatory changes that encourage heavy concentration of ownership in local television by a few large corporations will erode the quality of news Americans receive."[20]

Additional evidence gathered by the Commission demonstrates how the current structure of media ownership ill-serves the intertwined goals of localism and diversity. [21] Martin Kaplan described a survey of more than 10,000 late news broadcasts that aired during the seven weeks before the 2002 election in the top fifty U.S. markets. Campaign ads outnumbered campaign news stories by nearly 4:1. Almost 60% of the broadcasts contained no election coverage. Nearly half the coverage that did exist focused on horserace or strategy, not issues. Stations owned by large media corporations carried a lower percentage of local campaign news than the national average. Stations owned by small or medium-sized companies carried a consistently higher percentage of local news.

Updating this research in October 2004, Kaplan found similarly troubling patterns in the 2004 election. In battleground states, campaign ads have outnumbered campaign stories during local news shows – six minutes to three minutes. In non-battleground states, campaign ads occupied about 1.5 minutes, while election news stories took up just over two minutes. Even more troubling for localism, the presidential race received far more attention than local races. While 80 percent of the news stories were devoted to the presidential campaign, only 5 percent were devoted to local elections. Even

Future of Pluralism in the Mass Media: The Prospects for Positive Policy Reform." *Mass Communications Review*

[19] Alger, Dean. *MEGAMEDIA: How Giant Corporations Dominate Mass Media, Distort Competition and Endanger Democracy.* Lanham, MD: Rowan and Littlefield, 1998.

Chapter 6, *The Media and Politics* NY: Harcourt Brace College, 2nd edition, 1996; Media Studies Center Survey, University of Connecticut, Jan. 18, 1999; Public Interest." *Journal of Communication,* 40.Auletta, Ken. 1998. "The State of the American Newspaper." *American Journalism Review* June; Rabasca, Lisa. 2001. "Benefits, Costs and Convergence." *Presstime* June: p. 3.

[20] Project for Excellence in Journalism. Does Ownership Matter in Local Television News: A Five-Year Study of Ownership and Quality. Executive Summary,17 February 2003.

[21] Kaplan, Martin. Testimony. FCC Broadcast Localism Hearing. Monterey, CA. 21 July 2004, www.localnewsarchive.org.

where senators were running, the presidential election got 75 percent of the news coverage – 68 percent in those states where the senate races are considered a toss-up. Campaign issues (as opposed to campaign strategy and the horserace) were covered in 42 percent of the stories about local elections, but 29 percent of the stories covering the presidential election.[22] Doing the math, we find that about one-quarter of the campaign stories on the local news covered issues in the presidential campaign, but only about one-fiftieth covered local campaign issues.

A recent re-analysis of FCC data on TV news found an average of 24 hours of local public affairs programming and an average of 19.93 hours combined local news and local public affairs programming during a one-month period.[23] That is, separating public affairs from news, TV stations averaged less than ¼ hour of local public affairs programming in a month. New analysis also indicates a broad failure of commercial TV stations to present local public affairs programming.[24] In a two week sample period, only 41 percent of the commercial stations aired any local public affairs programming. In sharp contrast, over 90 percent of public stations aired such programming. Commercial stations aired just 45 minutes of such programming in the two week period. Local stations owned by the major national networks aired just over 37 minutes of local public affairs shows, while independently owned stations aired 110 minutes.[25] Public (noncommercial) stations aired over 6 hours.

The Public Interest Coalition recently presented specific examples of how radio industry consolidation has eviscerated localism and diversity in news reporting:

---

[22] Interim Report Local TV News Ignores Local and State Campaigns (Lear Center Local News Archive, Oct. 21, 2004),
http://www.learcenter.org/pdf/LCLNAInterim2004.pdf
[23] Napoli, Philip. 2003. Television Station Ownership and Local News and Public Affairs Programming: An Expanded Analysis of FCC Data. paper presented at Annual Meeting of International Communication Ass'n, May: 13-14, re-analyzing data in Thomas C. Spavins, Loretta Denison, Scott Roberts and Jane Frenette. The Measurement of Local Television News and Public Affairs Programs. Washington, D.C.: Federal Communications Commission, 2002.
[24] Yan, Michael and Philip Napoli, "Market Structure, Stations Ownership, and Local Public Affairs Programming on Local Broadcast Television," paper presented at the Telecommunications Policy Research Conference, October 2004.
[25] The finding of greater responsiveness of local media to local needs in program variety has been well documented in recent years in a series of studies of "preference externalities." see Waldfogel, 2001b; Joel Waldfoge and Siegelman, 2000; Waldfogel and George, 2000; See also "Survey Shows Solid Growth in TV News and Staffing." *RTNDA Communicator*, September 2004, p. 6 (only 759 TV stations in the U.S. offer any local news at all).

Radio personalities pretend to discuss local news, make commentary on local events, and critique local nightlife and hot spots, all without ever setting foot within a thousand miles of the transmitter. ... Clear Channel audiences in Toledo and Lima, Ohio receive newscasts produced in Columbus. And Corpus Christi residents heard news of a hurricane from a Clear Channel bureau located at least a hundred miles away. ... Most disturbingly, national group owners have practiced deceptions to make programming appear local while in fact distributing a national service. ... References to time, date and location are stripped from guest interviews so that they can appear to be "live" when aired in distant locales. Listeners are urged to "call in" to pre-recorded shows.[26]

In essence, the radio industry, which has been subject to the most unfettered process of national consolidation, demonstrates how local content can be homogenized off the air.[27] The industry is focused on "perfecting the art of seeming local" without actually being local.[28]

In the cultural realm, the situation is equally disturbing. A survey by the Future of Music Coalition in 2002 reported that virtually every radio music format is now controlled by an oligopoly. Consolidated control combined with shorter play lists means "few opportunities for musicians to get on the radio," and "deprives citizens of the opportunity to hear a wide range of music." Supposedly distinct formats have as much as 76% overlap in content, even though listeners say they want to hear longer play lists, more variety, and more local musicians.[29]

Additional evidence of the parlous state of local broadcasting comes from research on how well the mass media are serving racial and ethnic minorities. Greater concentration has resulted in less diversity of ownership, and diversity of ownership – across geographic, ethnic and gender lines – is correlated with diversity of programming. Studies by Joel Waldfogel and others show that overall African-American and Hispanic audiences are

---

[26] Comments of the Alliance for Better Campaigns *et al.* in *Digital Audio Broadcasting Systems*, MM Docket No. 99-325 (June 16, 2004), pp. 20-21, and sources cited. See also Leon Lazaroff. "Media Firm Accused of Dodging FCC Rules." *Chicago Tribune* 16 Oct. 2004, http://www.freepress.net/news/5009 (Sinclair Broadcasting, which owns more TV stations than any other company, uses "distance-casting" from company headquarters to broadcast local news, sports, and weather).

[27] Fairchild, Charles. 1999. "Deterritorializing Radio: Deregulation and the Continuing Triumph of the Corporatist Perspective in America." *Media, Culture and Society* 21: 557-559; Bachman, Kathy. "Music Outlets Tune in More News Reports." *MediaWeek*, 29 October 2001.

[28] Wilde Anne Mathews. "A Giant Radio Chain is Perfecting the Art of Seeming Local." *Wall Street Journal*, 25 February 2002, p. A1; Staples, Brent. "The Trouble with Corporate Radio: The Day the Protest Music Died." *The New York Times, 20* February 2003 p. A30.

[29] Future of Music Coalition. *Radio Deregulation: Has It Served Citizens and Musicians?* (Ric Dube and Gillian Thomson, eds.) (18 Nov. 2002), pp. 3-5.

under-served, and that communities without African-American-oriented media have lower rates of African-American participation in elections.[30] That is, minority owners are more likely to present minority points of view just as females are more likely to present a female point of view, in the speakers, formats and content they put forward.

DEMOGRAPHIC CHANGE AND THE INCREASING NEED FOR DIVERSITY AND LOCALISM

While it is certainly true that there is a great deal more information available to more educated citizens today than thirty years ago, it is also true that they need more information. Over the past 30 years, the makeup of the population that the media serves has grown in size and diversity. Mobility, globalization of the economy, internationalization of communications, and social fragmentation place greater demands on the communications network to enable citizens to be informed about increasingly complex issues, to express their opinions more effectively in civic discourse and to remain connected to their communities.

Counting the number of outlets without reference to the population they serve or the issues they must deal with ignores the needs of the citizenry for information. It also ignores the growing mismatch between huge corporate conglomerates that produce and distribute news and individual citizens that consume it.

The broad parameters of change in American society over the past three decades have been so profound that we can safely conclude that a much more diverse set of media institutions and outlets is needed to disseminate information. We focus on the past three decades because many of the rules

---

[30] Oberholzer-Gee, Felix and Joel Waldfogel. Electoral Acceleration: The Effect of Minority Population on Minority Voter Turnout. *NBER Working Paper 8252.* Cambridge, MA: National Bureau of Economic Research, 2001. Available from http://papers.nber.org/papers/w8252.pdf; Siegelman and Waldfogel, "Race and Radio: Preference Externalities, Minority Ownership, and the Provision of Programming to Minorities." *Advertising & Differentiated Products* 73:10 (Michael R. Baye & Bon P. Nelson eds., 2001). See also *Whose Spectrum is it, Anyway? A Historical Study of Market Entry Barriers, Discrimination, and Changes in Broadcast and Wireless Licensing.* study prepared for the FCC by the Ivy Planning Group, Dec. 2000, http://www.fcc.gov/opportunity/meb_study/historical_study.pdf; Christine Bachen, *et al.,* 1999. *Diversity of Programming in the Broadcast Spectrum: Is There a Link Between Owner Race or Ethnicity and News and Public Affairs Programming?* (study prepared for the FCC), http://www.fcc.gov/opportunity/meb_study/content_ownership_study.pdf; Christopher Yoo. Architectural Censorship and the FCC *Vanderbilt U. Law School Public Law & Legal Theory Working Paper No. 04-10,* undated, http://ssrn.com/abstract=555821.

governing the structure of media ownership were adopted in the early 1970s. For the purposes of this analysis, we start with the household as the consumption unit (see Exhibit 1). TV markets are defined in terms of households. The bulk of newspaper distribution is home delivery.

The number of households has increased by 67 percent in the past two decades. This is twice as fast as the increase in the population. This reflects a dramatic change in the composition of households units. The number of married families has declined, while single parent households have increased sharply.

Exhibit 1: Growing Diversity of the U.S. Population: Gender, Race and Marital Status

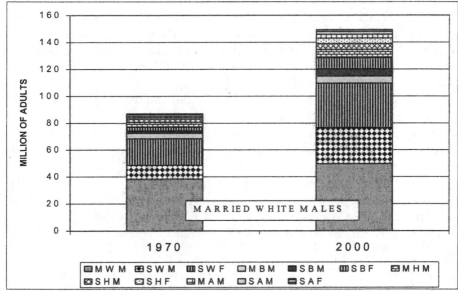

Sources: U.S. Bureau of the Census, Statistical Abstract of the United States: (Washington, D.C.:U.S. Department of Commerce, various years), 2001 -Table 59, 1986 – p. 35. Hispanic percentage assumed constant between 1970 and 1980.

At the same time, there has been a dramatic change in the racial and ethnic make-up of the population. The share of Hispanics and Asian/Pacific Islanders has doubled. Combining these two trends produces a stunning increase in the diversity of the population. While the population has become increasingly diverse, it has been drawn more tightly into a more complex world. In 1970, exports and imports equaled about eight percent of gross national product. In 2000, the figure was twenty percent. Global financial markets, in which the U.S. is the leading actor, have grown dramatically. In 1970, the goods and services produced by the U. S. economy equaled about fifteen percent of global financial transactions. By 2000, they equaled only two percent.

The increase in diversity is even larger when measured at a local level (see Exhibit 2). It shows a measure of the racial/ethnic diversity within each state. It uses five categories,

> White non-Hispanic,
> Hispanic,
> Black,
> Asian and Pacific Islander, and
> American Indian, Eskimo and Aleut.

Exhibit 2: Increasing Population Diversity in States: HHI

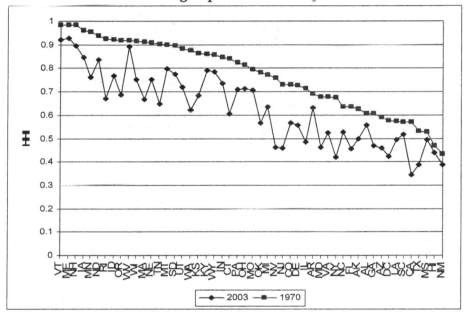

Source: U.S. Bureau of the Census, Population Division, Historical Census Statistics on Population Totals by Race, 1790 to 1990, and Hispanic Origin, 1970 to 1990, for the United States, Regions, Divisions, and States, Working Paper No. 56 for 1970, database for 2003.

To describe the racial/ethnic diversity of the population we calculate the Herfindahl Hirschmann Index. The HHI takes the share of each group in the total, squares it, and sums across all groups. If everyone in a state fit in the same group, the HHI would be 1. If the population were evenly divided across all five groups, the HHI would be .2 ($.2^2 + .2^2 + .2^2 + .2^2 + .2^2 = .2$). Thus, the lower the HHI the more diverse the population. The great differences in population across the states are clear, even in 1970.

Several states were almost perfectly homogenous, with an HHI almost equal to 1, while several others were much more heterogeneous, with an HHI equal to .5. At the same time, there has clearly been an increase in heterogeneity in the past three decades. The number of states with an HHI of .5 or less has increased from 1 to 15. On average, the HHI declined by 30 percent.

The HHI can be converted to a standard measure of diversity used by biologists to describe the distribution of species or families in a population. This measure relies on the reciprocal of the HHI (1/HHI). Dividing the reciprocal of the HHI by the number of categories yields a measure of the Equitability or Evenness Index (see Exhibit 3). If the population were evenly spread across the groups, the Evenness Index would be equal to 1. If the population were entirely concentrated in one group, it would be .2 (because there are five groups). We observe small changes in evenness at the extremes (low heterogeneity and high heterogeneity) and large changes in the middle. The increases vary from a low of .01 to a high of .17. Overall, the index increased from .28 in 1970 to .4 in 2003, a 43% increase.

Exhibit 3: Evenness Index of Population in States

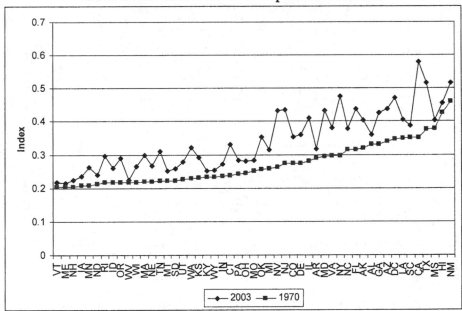

Source: *U.S. Bureau of the Census, Population Division, Historical Census Statistics on Population Totals by Race, 1790 to 1990, and Hispanic Origin, 1970 to 1990, for the United States, Regions, Divisions, and States, Working Paper No. 56 for 1970, database for 2003.*

Another way to measure the diversity in a population that has been used in the analysis of media is subtract the HHI from 1, this yields a statistic called Simpson's D (D= 1- HHI). This has a useful interpretation.

The diversity value obtained is equivalent to the probability that two of the objects of classification (the elements), chosen at random, would be in a different category. If all of the objects are in one category, then the probability is 0, as is the diversity measure; if all of the objects are in different categories, the Simpson's D is 1.0, which corresponds to the probability that all the objects are in different categories.[31]

Exhibit 4 shows the results of this calculation. Of course, the pattern is the same as for the earlier calculation. There is a wide dispersion of diversity across the states and diversity increased over the period. On a weighted average basis, the probability that any two people chosen randomly from any given state would be members of the same group increased from just under 29 percent in 1970 to just under 46 percent in 2003. Measured at the state level, the average American in 2003 lived in a state that was 60 percent more diverse than the state in which the average American lived in 1970.

Exhibit 4: Increasing Population Diversity in States: Simpson's D

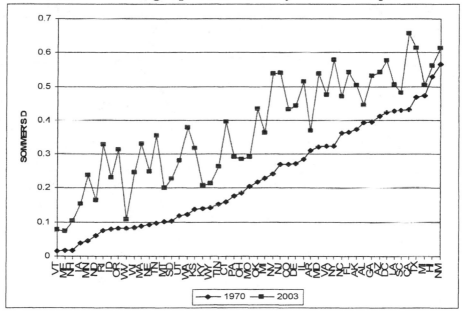

Source: U.S. Bureau of the Census, Population Division, Historical Census Statistics on Population Totals by Race, 1790 to 1990, and Hispanic Origin, 1970 to 1990, for the United States, Regions, Divisions, and States, Working Paper No. 56 for 1970, database for 2003.

---

[31] McDonald, Daniel G. and Shu Fang Lin. 2004. "The Effect of New Networks on U.S. Television Diversity." *Journal of Media Economics* 17: 2.

STUDY 5
MEDIA OWNERSHIP AND VIEWPOINT

MARK COOPER

OWNERSHIP POINT OF VIEW REMAINS AN IMPORTANT CONCERN IN THE MEDIA

With the incessant and fierce debate and finger pointing about bias in the media, there would seem to be little reason for the FCC to doubt the fact that media outlets have a point of view, whether or not it rises to the level of slant or bias. The evidence in the record did not justify the FCC's hesitation on this point and evidence continues to mount to suggest that media outlets definitely have a point of view. To the extent that the FCC cited uncertainty about the relationship between ownership and points of view to make policy, as in the cross-ownership rulemaking,[1] it erred.

The FCC cited one poorly done study that argued there is no relationship between ownership and viewpoint, but acknowledged that the flaws in the research were substantial.[2]   On the other side it acknowledged several academic studies cited by the Consumer Federation of America (CFA) that demonstrated the connection between ownership and viewpoint, one a case study of a major piece of legislation, the second a statistical study of campaign coverage.[3] This point is so central to the undertaking of media ownership limits, we feel compelled to revisit the issue here to erase any doubt that the connection between ownership and viewpoint is real and must be the basis for policy.

---

[1] Federal Communications Commission. *2002 Biennial Regulatory Review – Review of the Commission's Broadcast Ownership Rules and Other Rules Adopted Pursuant to Section 202 of the Telecommunications Act of 1996,* 18 FCC Rcd 13620, 13711-47 (2003), ¶361.

[2] The FCC's minimal effort to address the issue of bias, Pritchard, David. September, 2002. Viewpoint Diversity in Cross-Owned Newspapers and Television Stations: A Study of News Coverage of the 2000 Presidential Campaign. Federal Communications Commission, involved a very small number of observations and no effort to introduce a comparison group. It found that half of the newspapers and television stations that were cross-owned shared a bias. On re-examination, Baker, Dean. December 2002. Democracy Unhinged: More Media Concentration Means Less Public Discourse, A Critique of the FCC Studies on Media Ownership Washington, DC: Department of Professional Employees, AFL-CIO, p. 6, concluded that "seven of the ten combinations had a common slant, and only three had a different slant in their coverage." This is a remarkably high bias and, in our view, only underscores the problem of ownership across the media.

[3] Order, ¶34.

It is interesting to note that the episode of charge and counter of bias that CFA put in the record was the early stages of finger pointing in an ongoing episode that has been cited in a number of recent academic articles as the animus to bring a more rigorous approach to the subject.[4] The very dispute CFA cited is the origin of a cottage industry of both anecdotal accounts and academic scholarship that demonstrates how central viewpoint is to the media landscape.[5] We recall that analysis because it links to so much more detailed evidence on the importance of ownership and viewpoint that has come to light since.

BIAS-BASHING (BY THE MOST PROMINENT AMERICAN JOURNALISTIC ICONS)

The "biases" of owners are frequently known, as a flap about Rupert Murdoch's news operations at Fox television attests. The close political connection between Fox's Roger Ailes and the Republican Party was underscored by his admission that he had sent a public policy memo to the Bush Administration.[6] The response from Fox to these "charges" of bias were explained in a 2002 best seller by Bernard Goldberg says mountains about the slanting of TV news and commentary across the board.

> This is how Roger Ailes… explained it in a *New York Times Magazine* piece in June 2001: "There are more conservatives *on* Fox. But we are *not* a conservative network. That disparity says far more about the competition." In other words, if Fox is alleged to have a conservative bias, that's only because there are so few

---

[4] Shiffer, Adam, J. 2006. "Assesing Partisan Bias in Political News : The Case(s) of Local Senate Election Coverage." *Political Communications* 23; Lee, Tien-Tsung. 2005. "The Liberal Media Myth Revisited: An Examination of Factors Influencing Perception of Media Bias" *Journal of Broadcasting and Electronic Media* 49:1; Gentzow, Matthew and John M Shapiro, *Media Bias and Reputation*, (2004); Mullainathan, Sendhil and Andrei Shleifer. 2004. The Market for News. *American Economic Review* 95.

[5] The CFA discussion launched from Goldberg, Bernard, *Bias: A CBS Insider Exposes How the Media Distort the News*. Washington, D.C.: Regnery, 2002. The set of popular press books cited in literature includes this as the earliest and then adds Coulter, Ann. *Slander: Liberal Lies about the American Right*. New York: Three Rivers Press, 2003, on the conservative side and Alterman, Eric. *What Liberal Media? The Truth About Bias and the News* New York: Basic, 2003 and Franken, Al. *Lies and the Lying Liars Who Tell Them: A Fair and Balanced Look at the Right*. New York: EP Dutton, 2003.

[6] The story "broke" in the *Washington Post* with the publication of a segment of Bob Woodward's *Bush At War*. New York: Simon and Schuster, 2002, p. 207, which Ailes disputed (see Grove, Lloyd, "The Reliable Source," *Washington Post*, 19 November 19 2002). The incident reinforced the perception of Fox News as "The Most Biased Name in News: Fox Channel's Extraordinary Right-wing Tilt." Ackerman, Seth. *The Most Biased Name in News*. (FAIR, August 2002), a bias that is embodied in the "format, guests, expertise, topic and in-house analysts." *Cable News Wars: Interviews* (PBS, Online Newshour, March 2002), p. 2.

conservative voices on the air at ABC, CBS, NBC, CNN and MSNBC. There certainly *is* a conservative "attitude" at Fox, a conservative sensibility.[7]

The affinity between the network and the Republican Party had a historical base. In a paper entitled "The Fox News Effect: Media Bias and Voting" Della Vigna and Kaplan have "analyzed the entry of Fox News."

> Between October 1996 and November 2000, the conservative Fox News Channel was introduced in the cable programming of 20 percent of US towns... We investigate if Republicans gained vote share in towns where Fox New entered. We find a significant effect of the introduction of Fox News on the vote share in Presidential elections between 1996 and 2000. Fox News also affected the Republican vote share in the Senate and voter turnout.[8]

They go on to note "the effect was smaller in towns with more cable channels which is consistent with the moderating effect of competition."[9] The effect was also smaller in more homogeneous environments – "In addition, Fox had a smaller effect in rural areas and in Republican congressional district, possibly because in these town the share of non-Republicans at risk of being convinces was smaller."[10] Both of these effects – competition and heterogeneity – play an important role in the academic research on bias as discussed below.

Goldberg ends his discussion of bias in the TV media, which begins with and focuses on an op-ed piece about liberal bias in the TV media he had published in the *Wall Street Journal*, with a discussion of bias in the print media in a second op-ed on the editorial pages of the *Wall Street Journal*.

> Consider this: In 1996 after I wrote about liberal bias on this very page, Dan [Rather] was furious and during a phone conversation he indicated that picking the *Wall Street Journal* to air my views was especially appalling given the conservative views of the paper's editorial page. "What do you consider the *New York Times*?" I asked him, since he had written op-eds for that paper. "Middle of the road," he said.

> I couldn't believe he was serious. The *Times* is a newspaper that has taken the liberal side of every important social issue of our time, which is fine with me. But if you see the *New York Times* editorial page as middle of the road, one thing is clear: You don't have a clue.[11]

---

[7] Goldberg, Bernard. *Bias*. Washington, DC: Regnery, 2002, p. 190.

[8] Della Vigna, Stefan and Ethan Kaplan. "The Fox News Effect: Media Bias and Voting." *NBER Working Paper 12169*. Cambridge, MA: National Bureau of Economic Research, 2006, p. i.

[9] Id., p. 1.

[10] Id., p.2-3.

[11] Goldberg, 2002. p. 222, citing "On Media Bias, Network Stars Are Rather Clueless," *Wall Street Journal*, 24 May, 2001.

There are many who would debate the "liberal" bias of the *New York Times*, but it is clear that there is little love lost between the *New York Times* and Mr. Ailes and Fox's supporters. Within a week of the revelation of Mr. Ailes' memo to the White House, the *New York Times* chastised Ailes in an editorial, pointing out that giving advice to the President would be fine, were Mr. Ailes still in the business of advising political candidates, but as a top executive of a news organization he should know better than to offer private counsel to Mr. Bush.

> Mr. Ailes' action seems especially hypocritical for someone who has spent years trumpeting the fairness of Fox and the partisanship of just about everybody in the news business. Fox's promotional slogan is: "We report, you decide." But the news channel has a Republican tilt and a conservative agenda.[137]

The academic evidence on the slant of the *New York Times* is mixed. One study examined the prominence of issues given emphasis during presidential years from 1946 to 1997, controlling for the party of the incumbent president. Prior to 1960,

> the *New York Times* gives more emphasis to topics that are owned by the Democratic Party (civil rights, health care, labor and social welfare), when the incumbent President is a Republican. This is consistent with the hypothesis that the *New York Times* has a Democratic partisanship, with some "watchdog" aspects, in that during the presidential campaign it gives more emphasis to issues over which the (Republican) incumbent is weak. In the post-1960 period the *Times* displays a more symmetric type of watchdog behavior, just because during presidential campaigns it gives more coverage to the typically Republican issue of Defense when the incumbent President is a Democrat, and less so when the incumbent is a Republican.[12]

This analysis reminds us that slant may consist of a number of factors, the most commonly studied of which are tone and frequency of reporting, with tone being more difficult to measure than frequency.

The friction between the *New York Times* and *Fox*, can be understood in light of the results of a study entitled "A Measure of Media Bias."[13] The study used ADA rankings of members of Congress to estimate the "conservative/liberal" bias of the newspapers and think tank reports that the Congressmen cited in their statements. *Times* and *Fox* were at the opposite ends of the spectrum on every measure. *Fox* was about 15 points more conservative than the mean and the *New York Times* being about 15 points above it on the preferred measure of bias, which was an adjusted measure of

---

[12] Puglisi, Ricardo. *Being the New York Times*. Political Economy and Public Policy Series, Suntory Centre, April 2006.
[13] Groseclose, Timothy and Jeff Milyo. 2005. "A Measure of Media Bias." *Quarterly Journal of Economics* 120.

the number of sentences devoted to think tanks. This points to another important measure of point of view – the amount of space devoted to an issue.

In the dispute that played out in the press, Paul Krugman (certainly a Democrat, if not a liberal) writing in the *New York Times*, repeated Al Gore's complaint that the "liberal media" had gone very conservative.

> This week Al Gore said the obvious. "The media is kind of weird these days on politics," he told The New York Observer, "and there are some major institutional voices that are, truthfully speaking, part and parcel of the Republican Party.
>
> The reaction from most journalists in the "liberal Media" was embarrassed silence. I don't quite understand why, but there are some things that you're not supposed to say, precisely because they are so clearly true.[14]

The treatment of the Gore campaign by the press is the subject of a Kennedy School of Government Case study that seeks to qualitatively examine some of the major stories that played prominent roles in the campaign,[15] which also cites a quantitative study by the Committee of Concerned Journalists and the Project for Excellence in Journalism.[16] Both suggest that there was something to the complaint. One of the interesting observations that has implications for understanding the structural causes of bias is the concern that

> the meta-narrative tended to "trump the reporters' judgment," making it "difficult for an individual reporter to write a story that differs from the popular meta-narratives." For another, it led to problems with "what to do with facts that betray the meta-narrative."[17]

Michael Kelly, a conservative columnist, could not let the Gore/Krugman complaint pass without comment.[18] He cites about a dozen "major surveys on the political beliefs and voting patterns of mainstream print and broadcast journalists" from 1962 to 2001, which show about a three-to-one ratio (46 to 15) of liberals to conservatives. He answers the rhetorical question, "Does a (still) largely liberal news media (still) exhibit a largely liberal bias?" with a resounding "Sure."[19] He cites S. Robert Lichter, president of the independent Center for Media and Public Affairs, who observes that,

[14] Krugman, Paul. "In Media Res." *New York Times*, 29 November 2002, p. A39.

[15] Scott, Ester. Al Gore and the "Embellishment" Issue:Press Coverage of the Gore Presidential Campaign. *Kennedy School of Government Case Program*, c15-02-1679.0, October 2003.

[16] *The Last Lap: How the Press Covered the Final Stages of the Campaign*, 31 October 2000.

[17] Scott, p. 26, citing *The Last Lap*.

[18] Kelly, Michael. "Left Everlasting." *The Washington Post*, 11 December 2002, p. A33.

[19] Kelly, Michael. "Left Everlasting (Cont'd)." *The Washington Post*, 18 December 2002, p. A35.

[J]ournalists tell the truth – but like everyone else, they tell the truth *as they see it*. Even the most conscientious journalists cannot overcome the subjectivity inherent in their profession, which is expressed through such everyday decisions as whether a topic or source is trustworthy.[20]

A study by Lee documents the flip side of this statement.[21] Just as journalists tell the truth *as they see it*, consumers hear the truth as they see it. According to this study,

People are more likely to believe the media cannot be trusted if they are male and conservative, disagree that most people are honest, but believe that honest people cannot be elected to high office. Cynicism at both the personal and political levels is the strongest predictor of a media bias perception, according to the Life Style data. Further, according to the NES data, media distrust is predicted by being conservative and Republican, partisanship extremity, and political cynicism.[22]

An Annenberg study found the "Public and Press Differ about Partisan Bias, Accuracy and Press Freedom."[23] Eighty six percent of journalists think news organizations get their facts straight, compared to 45 percent of the public. Only 16 percent of journalists think it is "a good thing if some news organizations have a decidedly political point of view in their coverage of news," compared to 45 percent of the public.

The attitudes the audience brings into the media market, called priors in the academic literature, and the incentives journalists have, both play a part in the expanding analysis of media bias.

The important and unavoidable lesson is that editorial preferences are deeply embedded in commercial mass media not only on the editorial pages, but also on the news pages. In a sense, this is the essence of the concept of antagonism. Rather than claim that many outlets owned by a single entity will present a neutral, objective, or balanced picture, public policy should recognize that diversity and antagonism of viewpoints comes from diversity of ownership. Indeed, Lichter entered the fray with a letter to the editor pointing out,

In some cases, the coverage of social and political issues clearly coincides with the perspectives of journalists. But such correspondence is not guaranteed, and it cannot be reliably predicted to operate in particular instances.[141]

---

[20] Id.
[21] Lee, pp. 51-52.
[22] Id., p. 51.
[23] May 24, 2005.

Systematic Empirical Evidence

There is a growing body of research that demonstrates the tendency of media outlets to take a point of view. The CFA analysis put forward two different types of analysis. The first was quantitative assessments. CFA cited an article from the June 2002 *American Political Science Review* that makes it clear that ownership (embodied in the editorial position of the outlet) matters in reporting the news.[24]

One of the essential elements of an impartial press in the United States is the "wall of separation" between the editorial pages and the pages devoted to the news. While the political beliefs of newspaper owners and editors are clearly articulated on opinion pages, their views are not supposed to infiltrate the reporting of the news. The analysis presented in this paper raises questions about this claim. We examine newspaper coverage of more than 60 Senatorial campaigns across three election years and find that information on news pages is slanted in favor of the candidates endorsed on the newspaper's editorial pages. We find that the coverage of incumbent Senators is most affected by the newspaper's endorsement. We explore the consequences of "slanted" news coverage by showing that voters evaluate endorsed candidates more favorably than candidates who fail to secure an editorial endorsement. The impact of the endorsement decision on voters' evaluations is most powerful in races receiving a great deal of press attention and among citizens who read their local newspapers on a daily basis.[25]

This article provided a methodology that was followed by others. Druckman and Parkin use the same approach to content analysis to evaluate relative slant focusing on a single senate race and tied the reporting to electoral behavior.[26]

Combining comprehensive content analysis of the newspapers with an Election Day exit poll, we assess the slant of campaign coverage and its effect on voters. We find compelling evidence that editorial slant influences voter's decisions. Our results raise serious questions about the media's place in democratic process.[27]

In short, slant in the media affected voting.

---

[24] Kahn, Kim Fridkin and Patrick J. Kenny. 2002. The Slant of News: How Editorial Endorsements Influence Campaign Coverage and Citizens' Views of Candidates. *American Political Science Review* 96: 381.

[25] Additional sources cited in support of this proposition include Page, Benjamin I. *Who Deliberates*. Chicago: University of Chicago Press, 1996; Rowse, Edward. *Slanted News: A Case Study of the Nixon and Stevenson Fund Stories*. Boston: Beacon, 1957.

[26] Druckman, James N. and Michael Parkin. 2005. The Impact of Media Bias: How Editorial Slant Affects Voters. *Journal of Politics*, 67:4.

[27] Id., p. 1030

Systematic studies of coverage of local issues found that "objectivity violations in all 20 stories were classified as serving the self-interest of the news organization or its parent corporation."[28] Additional studies in this vein have documented the extent and impact of point of view in a variety of types of media and covering a wide range of subjects. Shiffer distinguishes between partisan bias and structural bias and finds both in the coverage of 95 senatorial campaigns.[29] Structural bias is defined as follows: "some things are selected to be reported rather than other things *because* of the character of the medium or because of the incentives that apply to commercial news programming instead of partisan prejudices held by newsmen."[30] Moreover, some of the structural factors may be non-ideological ownership factors, such as the case of market forces where newspapers slant the news to "reflect the ideology of their states."[31]

The dynamics of the newsroom relationships between editors and reporters create a tendency to produce stories that are unbalanced.

> While partisan balance may have existed over the course of the entire coverage, individual stories were seldom balanced. In fact, the viewer had only a one in four chance of seeing an approximately balanced story, while 40 percent of the time the viewer was likely to see a story that was structurally imbalanced in every measured way. But this research also indicates that this would vary depending on the station and the day the viewer was watching.[32]

Slant or bias is measured not only in the tone of coverage, but also in the quantity of coverage or the subjects on which media outlets choose to editorialize. Thus, Hallock found that a change in ownership, from a local family to a chain, resulted in "reduced emphasis on local issues."[33] Maguire found a change in ownership resulting in a change in the quality and quantity of coverage, with local stories suffering most in the shift from local family ownership to large chain ownership.[34]

The study of slant in reporting has been applied to a number of topics beyond campaign coverage and endorsements, with a consistent finding of

---

[28] McManus, J. 1991. How Objective is Local Television News? *Mass Communications Review* 18:3:21-30.

[29] Shiffer, Adam, J. 2006. "Assesing Partisan Bias in Political News: The Case(s) of Local Senate Election Coverage." *Political Communications* 23.

[30] Id,, p. 29.

[31] Id., p. 31.

[32] Carter, Sue, Frederick Fico, and Joycelyn A. McCabe. 2002. Partisan and Structural Balance in Local Television Election Coverage. *Journalism and Mass Communications Quarterly* 79.

[33] Hallock, Steve. 2005. "Acquisition by Gannett Changes Paper's Editorials." *Newspaper Research Journal* 25: 2.

[34] Maguire, Miles. 2005. "Change in Ownership Affect Quality of Oshkosh Paper." *Newspaper Research Journal* 26: 4

bias. The topics include coverage of the president,[35] economic events,[36] important political issues,[37] and calling states on election night.[38]

The second type of studies picks a single issue and examines how it was handled in the media. The example CFA chose was particularly relevant, a study of the reporting of coverage of the Telecommunications Act of 1996, in which the media had a direct stake. This study by James Snider and Benjamin Page looked at the decision to allow TV stations to have additional digital spectrum without paying for it, while other parts of the spectrum were being auctioned for other commercial uses.[39] The editorial positions of media corporations that owned newspapers and had significant TV station ownership (at least 20% of revenues from that source) were compared to the editorial stands on the spectrum give-away/auction issue of newspapers owned by companies having little or no TV station ownership. The findings were striking:

> The results on editorials are very strong and highly significant [statistically]; in fact, among newspapers that editorialized on the subject, every one whose owners got little TV revenue editorialized against the spectrum 'giveaway,' whereas every one with high TV revenues editorialized in favor of giving broadcasters free use of spectrum.[40]

CFA provided other examples of self-interested action by media owners in several case studies of cross-owned papers including examples in of promotion of projects or local initiatives in which the owner had a stake[41]

---

[35] Groeling, Tim and Samuel Kernell. 2005. Is Network News Coverage of the President Biased? *Journal of Politics* 60:4

[36] Lott, John R., and Kevin A. Hassett. *Is Newspaper Coverage of Economic Events Politically Biased?* Washington, D.C.: American Enterprise Institute, 2004; Dyck, Alexander and Luigi Zingales. 2003. The Media and Asset Prices. *University of Chicago, NBER & CEPR.*

[37] Ansolabehere, Stephen, Erik C. Snowberg, and James M. Snyder, Jr. 2005. Unrepresentative Information: The Case of Newspaper Reporting on Campaign Finance Reform. *Public Opinion Quarterly* 69: 2

[38] Mixon, J. Wilson, Amit Sen, and E. Frank Stephenson. 2004. Are the Networks Baised? 'Calling States in the 2000 Presidential Election. *Public Choice* 118.

[39] Snider, James H., and Benjamin I. Page. 1997. "Does Media Ownership Affect Media Stands? The Case of the Telecommunications Act of 1996." Paper delivered at the *Annual Meeting of the Midwest Political Science Association*, April.

[40] Id., pp. 7-8.

[41] Consumer Federation of America, Consumers Union, Center for Digital Democracy and the Media Access Project, "Initial Comments" *In the Matter of 2002 Biennical Regulatory Review of the Commission's Broadcast Ownership Rules and Other Rules Adopeted Pursuant to Section 202 of the Telecommunications Act of 1996, Cross-ownership of Broadcast Stations and Newspapers, Rules and Policies Concerning Multiple Ownership of Radio Broadcast Stations in Local Markets and Definition of Radio Markets,* Docket Nos. MB 02-277, MM 01-235, MM 01-317' and MM 00-244, January 2, 2003, pp.231-234.

and cases in which criticism of the co-owned outlet was dampened or eliminated.[42]   The 2004 election produced a bevy of incidents that were debated as examples of slant, driven by the point of view of the outlet owner. Among the most prominent were Sinclair's on-again, off-again airing of "Stolen Honor,"[43] and the effort of a broadcaster to donate free air time to one candidate as a personal contribution.[44]

Theory Links Concentration to Bias

The intense study of bias in the media has spawned a second development of note – the development of theoretical models to explain the persistence of bias. The theoretical approach has sought to understand the structural conditions of media bias. There are both supply-side and demand-side theories of why viewpoints permeate the media space.

The supply-side theories of bias are the most familiar. They launch from a variety of factors – the ideological beliefs of owners/editors,[45] the career interests of journalists,[46] or the economic interests of advertisers.[47] Here we focus on the implications of this research on consolidation and competition in media markets. The theory supports the concern about consolidation. While these are theoretical papers, they cite empirical research that comports with and therefore validates their models.

An examination of potential merger impact reached the following conclusion:

> The cleanest result about the effect of mergers on the *amount* of persuasion... says that if, in then no-merger equilibrium, both outlets are owned by the same type, and if there will in fact be a merger when mergers are permitted, then total persuasion (all of the type preferred by owners) will increase. That is, if

[42] Id., pp. 227, 230

[43] For a flavor of the controversy, contrast the editorial in the *Wall Street Journal*, Sinclair and a Double Standard, October 13,2004 to the *Boston Globe, Sinclair's Slander*, October 15, 2004. It should come as no surprise that this became bound up in more than Presidential politics, as Legg Masson's *Telecom & Media Insider* pointed out that "Sinclair Move Risks Backfiring by Complicating Company's (and Industry's) Deregulatory Agenda," October 15, 2004.

[44] Pappas Communications in Los Angeles. The FCC required the time be considered a personal contribution.

[45] Bagdikian, Ben. *The Media Monopoly*. Boston: Beacon, 2000; McChesey, etc.

[46] Dyck and Zingales.

[47] Ellman, Mathew and Fabrizio Germano. 2004. What Do Papers Sell? *UPF Economics and Business Working Paper No. 800*; Reuter, J. and Zitzwitz. 2006. Do Ads Influence Editors? Advertising and Bias in the Financial Media. *Quarterly Journal of Economics* 121; Hamilton, James T. *All the News That's Fit to Sell*. Princeton: Princeton University Press, 2003; Baker, C. Edwin. *Advertising and a Democratic Press*. Princeton: Princeton University Press, 1994.

there is a dominant media ideology when mergers are prohibited, and if permitting mergers will actually lead to a merger, then the dominant ideology will become stronger.[48]

An examination of how competition would impact reporting bias caused by advertisers reached the following conclusion:

First and foremost, it shows how media competition can prevent harmful effect of advertising on news reporting.[49]

An examination of reporting on company financial performance reached the following conclusion:

Interestingly, we find that media spin tends to follow the spin promoted by the company. This is more so the fewer alternative source of information about a company are available, the more demand for information there is, and the less reputable a newspaper is.[50]

The demand-side theories are less familiar. On the demand side, one approach is to ask whether pandering is profitable, or more delicately put whether outlets "cater to the prejudices of their readers."[51] The motivation is to maximize profits by telling readers what they want to hear. The conclusion is that "on topics where reader beliefs diverge (such as politically divisive issues), newspapers segment the market and slant toward extreme positions."[52] "Powerful forces motivate news providers to slant and increase bias, rather than clear up confusion," so "greater competition typically results in more aggressive catering to such prejudices as competitors strive to divide the market."[53] In the presence of heterogeneous, conscientious readers, however, "the biases of individual media sources tend to offset each other, so the beliefs of the conscientious reader become more accurate than they are with homogeneous readers.... Greater partisanship and bias of individual media outlets may result in a more accurate picture being presented to a conscientious reader."[54] Heterogeneity interacts with competition in this view to produce the outcome.

---

[48] Balan, David J., Patrick DeGraba, and Abraham L. Widkelgren. 2003. Media Merges and the Ideological Content of Programming. *Bureau of Economics FTC* .

[49] Ellman and Germano, p. 25.

[50] Dyck and Zingales, p. 1.

[51] Mullainathan, Sendhil and Andrei Shleifer. 2004. The Market for News. *American Economic Review* 95, p. 1.

[52] Id., p. 1.

[53] Id., p. 6...20.

[54] Id. p. 5

Others start from the demand side proposition that "firms will tend to distort information to make it conform with consumers' prior beliefs"[55] but factor in supply side considerations.

> When a media firm is concerned with maintaining a reputation for accuracy, this force tends to produce slanting towards the preexisting beliefs of the firm's customers. Even if the firm believes that the truth contradicts these beliefs, it will be reluctant to report contradictory evidence because consumers may infer that the firm has inaccurate information. The more priors favor a given position, the less likely the firm becomes to print a story contradicting that position.[56]

This is the problem of coping with the meta-narrative identified by the Project on Excellence in Journalism's analysis of the reporting on the 2000 campaign.

The key dynamic in this model, at the level of firms, is that as the likelihood of *ex-post* feedback about the state of the world improves, the amount of bias occurring in equilibrium decreases."[57]   In this view, "independently owned outlets can provide a check on each others' coverage and thereby limit equilibrium bias, an effect that is absent if the outlets are jointly owned."[58]

Competition may discipline media outlets, or advertisers on the supply-side. It may provide conscientious readers a richer field in which to form opinions. It may do all of these things. In any case, these models fit within the paradigm articulated in Supreme Court jurisprudence that relies on the "cross-lights" of "diverse and antagonistic sources." Owners have significant control over the color, direction and intensity of the lights that are shined on public policy issues.

---

[55] Gentzkow, Matthew and Jesse M. Shapiro. "Media Bias and Reputation." University of Chicago, Graduate School of Business and NBER, 14 September 2005, p. 3.
[56] Id., pp. 3-4.
[57] Id., p. 4.
[58] Id. p. 33.

STUDY 6:
TELEVISION REMAINS A DOMINANT MEDIUM IN DEMOCRATIC DISCOURSE

Mark Cooper

Media Influence and Policy

If a cottage industry has grown up around the study of bias in the media in the past few years, a full blown industrial sector has existed for a couple of decades in the study of the importance of media, in general, and television, in particular, in the policy and political process.

Writing in 2000, Mille and Krosnick pointed out that

> During the last two decades, however, it has become clear that the media do indeed shape public opinion. Not only have investigations used improved methods to document persuasion, but new media effects have been identified as well, including agenda setting and news media priming. Agenda setting occurs when extensive media attention to an issue increases its perceived national importance. Priming occurs when media attention to an issue causes people to place special weight on it when constructing evaluations of overall presidential job performance.[1]

Walgrave and Aelst note that the ability of the media to influence public opinion has been studied and varies in two broadly different situation – "routine times" and during elections.[2] Exhibit 1 summarizes the finding of 19 major studies they identified dealing with the media's impact during routine times. It distinguishes the level of impact, time period of the study and nation of the study. The most recent studies show strong impacts. The issues covered in the studies that find strong effects in recent years involve the major policy concerns of the past couple of decades including economic issues like jobs, taxes, inflation and economic growth, public health, crime, education, foreign affairs, and environmental issues like global warming.

The branch of the literature that focuses on politics and political campaigns is even larger and generally just as strong in its findings. Not only is "Mass media coverage... generally believed to affect public opinion indirectly through phenomena such as agenda setting and priming," but

---

[1] Miller, Joanne and Jon A. Krosnick. 2000. News Media Impact on the Ingredients of Presidential Evaluations: Politically Knowledgeable Citizens are Guided by Trusted Sources. *American Journal of Political Science* 44:2: 295.

[2] Walgrave, Stefann and Peter Van Aelst. 2006. The Contingency of the Mass Media's Political Agenda Setting Power: Toward a Preliminary Theory. *Journal of Communications* 56.

there is growing evidence that "media coverage directly influences the vote intention of campaign deciders."[3]

Exhibit 1: Media Impact Studies

		Prior to 1990's	1990 to 1995	1996 to present
Impact - All Nations	None	1	0	0
	Hardly any	2	2	0
	Weak	0	2	4
	Strong/ Considerable	3	3	6
Impact - United States	None	1	0	0
	Hardly any	2	0	0
	Weak	0	2	0
	Strong/ Considerable	3	3	4

Source Walgrave, Stefann and Peter Van Aelst. 2006. The Contingency of the Mass Media's Political Agenda Setting Power: Toward a Preliminary Theory. Journal of Communications 56.

Walgrave and Aelst argue that "the short campaign period of several weeks before Election Day is fundamentally different from routine periods: the behavior of political actors, their reaction on media coverage, and even the dynamic of media coverage itself follow different logics in both periods."[4] They argue that the forceful efforts of political parties and candidates who "have daily press briefings, stage their own (pseudo) events, incessantly flood the media with press releases, and continuously make provocative statements… make it more difficult for the media to set the political agenda."[5]

---

[3] Fournier, Patrick, Richard Nadeau, Anre Blais, Elisabeth Gidengil and Neil Nevitte. 2004. Time-of-voting Decision and Susceptibility to Campaign Effects. Electoral Studies 23:4: 12. The more recent studies that the authors cite in support of the direct effect include , Miller, J. M. and J. A. Krosnick. "News Media Impact on the Ingredients of Presidential Evaluations: A Program of Research on the Priming Hypothesis." In D.C. Mutz, P.M. Sniderman, and R.A. Brody. Political Persuasion and Attitude Change. Ann Arbor: University of Michigan Press, 1996; and Zaller, J. "The Myth of Mass Media Impact Revived: New Support for a Discredited Idea." In D.C. Mutz, P.M. Sniderman, and R.A. Brody, Political Persuasion and Attitude Change. Ann Arbor: University of Michigan Press, 1996

[4] Walgrave and Aelst, 2006, p. 96.

[5] Id., p. 97.

They add that "the media devote more attention to politics," and that the media is "more balanced in election times."[6] They add that media can affect the outcome by

> following the agenda of party A more closely than that of party B, give more attention to issue X than to issue Y. The agenda setting power of journalist in election times lies more in their discretion to include or exclude information of political actors than in their autonomous selection of issues. To be sure, besides agenda setting, the media can influence politics in many other ways during the campaign.

The different ways in which the media may influence the political process, depending on the context is underscored by recent findings from a study of primaries. Barker and Lawrence argue that "given that nomination campaigns are one-party contests, journalists may be less paranoid regarding accusations of partisan or ideological favoritism, which may lead to more interpretive coverage."[7] They argue that the importance ideological differences, which are strong factors in most studies of media influence, are diminished in one party primaries, so voters are more "receptive to other cues."[8] Sequential votes also allow the media to play up "momentum" as a factor to influence public opinion. They find "considerable support for a direct effects model of influence, in that news consumption is predictive of perceived value congruence."[9] They also found that "bombastic, unabashedly biased 'new media' can have a significant impact over the attitudes of *even those consumers who are predisposed to disagree with the message source.*"[10] The "new media" they have in mind, is talk radio. We observe the mix of partisan and general media that interacted in the discussion of bias in Study 5.

THE DOMINANT ROLE OF TELEVISION

The importance of TV rests on more than its role as an important source of information, as discussed earlier. TV has come to dominate mass media in political discourse[11] by influencing on attitudes and behaviors,[12]

---

[6] Id., pp. 97-98.

[7] Barker, David, C. and Adam B. Lawrence. 2006. Media Favoritism and Presidential Nominations: Reviving the Direct Effects Model. *Political Communications* 23: 42.

[8] Id., p. 42.

[9] Id., p. 48.

[10] Id., p. 48.

[11] Albarran, Alan B. and John W. Dimmick. 1993. An Assessment of Utility and Competitive Superiority in the Video Entertainment Industries. *Journal of Media Economics* 6; Bennett, W. Lance and Regina G. Lawrence. 1995. News Icons and the Mainstreaming of Social Change. *Journal of Communications* 45; McLeod, Douglas M. 1995. "Communicating Deviance: The Effects of Television News Coverage of Social Protests." *Journal of Broadcasting & Electronic Media* 39; Dimmick, John B. 1997. "The

especially in election campaigns. Television and radio have long been recognized as occupying different product spaces[13] although radio's role may yet be changing.[14] Generally, radio is seen as having less of an impact than television.[15] The difference between TV and radio may be in citizen exposure to political advertising on TV, while radio talk shows have a different, more intimate impact.[16]   Still, broadcast does not compete effectively with newspapers in the news function.[17]

Theory of the Niche and Spending on Mass Media: The Case of the Video Revolution." *Journal of Media Economics* 10; Sparks, Glenn G., Marianne Pellechia, and Chris Irvine. 1998. Does Television News About UFOs Affect Viewers' UFO Beliefs?: An Experimental Investigation. *Communication Quarterly* 46; Walma, Julliete H., Tom H. A. Van Der Voort. 2001. The Impact of Television, Print, and Audio on Children's Recall of the News. *Human Communication Research* 26.

[12] Wilkins, Karin Gwinn. 2000. "The Role of Media in Public Disengagement from Political Life." *Journal of Broadcasting & Electronic Media* 44.

[13] Clarke, Pere and Eric Fredin. 1978. Newspapers, Television and Political Reasoning. *Public Opinion Quarterly* Summer; Robinson, John P. and Mark R. Levy. 1996. New Media Use and the Informed Public: A 1990s Update. *Journal of Communications* Spring

[14] The role of radio talk shows is the new development. Johnson, Thomas J., Mahmoud A. M. Braima, and Jayanthi Sothirajah. 1999. Doing the Traditional Media Sidestep: Comparing Effects of the Internet and Other Nontraditional Media with Traditional Media in the 1996 Presidential Campaign. *Journalism & Mass Communication Quarterly* 76, find that nontraditional media do not have an impact on a variety of measures of knowledge and perceptions about the 1996 presidential campaign and to the extent they do, it was specifically radio talk shows, influencing views of Clinton negatively (see also Moy, Patricia, Michael Pfau, and LeeAnn Kahlor. 1999. Media Use and Public Confidence in Democratic Institutions. *Journal of Broadcasting & Electronic Media* 43).

[15] Berkowitz, D., and D. Pritchard. 1989. Political Knowledge and Communication Resources. *Journalism Quarterly* 66; Chaffee, Steven H. Xinshu Zhao and Glenn Leshner. 1994. Political Knowledge and the Campaign Media of 1992. *Communications Research* 21, Spring; Drew, Dan and David Weaver. 1991. Voter Learning in the 1988 Presidential Election: Did the Media Matter? *Journalism Quarterly* 68.

[16] Johnson, Braima and Sothirajah, 2000, juxtapose the earlier finding of a lack of influence for radio with more recent findings that radio talk shows have an impact. See also, Johnson, Braima and Sothirajah, 1999, and Stamm, K., M Johnson and B. Martin. 1997. Differences Among Newspapers, Television and Radio in their Contribution to Knowledge of the Contract with America. *Journalism and Mass Communications Quarterly* 74.

[17] Stepp, Carl Sessions. 2001. "Whatever Happened to Competition." *American Journalism Review* June."Wasn't it television and radio that were going to kill newspapers? "I don't really consider them competition in that old-school way," stresses Florida Sun-Sentinel editor Earl Maucker. "They reach a different kind of audience with a different kind of news...Publisher Gremillion, a former TV executive himself, seconds the point, "I don't believe people are watching TV as a substitute for reading the newspaper..." ...Many newspapers are increasingly writing off local TV

The ascendance of television as the premier political medium can be seen in a number of recent studies. For example, in the Baker and Lawrence study that found both a direct effect of media on voting and a partisan media effect, the general "nonpolitical news exposure factor score" that was used in the analysis was overwhelmingly defined by television, with local news networks the most important. [18] Local network news had a factor loading of .91; national network news had a factor loading of .57, and politics in newspapers has a loading of .17. Of course, this was a national issue, played out sequentially in state primaries, so that it is likely to get attention in all the media.

Similarly, a study of the 2004 presidential election found that "attention to television news, televised debates, and now Internet news are important predictors, or at least correlates, of voter learning of candidate issue positions and voter interest in the election campaign." [19] The effect of TV news attention on campaign interest was almost as large as exposure to the Presidential debates and over three times as large as attention to newspapers or the Internet. Reviewing a number of studies, they conclude that television news viewing has the largest and most consistent effects on various measures of engagement with the presidential election. [20]

Similarly, the influence of broadcast television on the New Hampshire primary, which plays a pivotal role in selecting presidential candidates, has been well documented. One recent study "found powerful network news effects, particularly with respect to "horse race" reports on which candidate gained and fell back but also with respect to televised evaluations of more substantive matter such as character and issue positions." [21] There remains a debate over which media has the greatest

---

news as a serious threat, treating local stations instead as potential partners who can help spread the newspapers' brand name to new and bigger audiences."
[18] Baker and Lawrence, 2006, p. 59.
[19] Drew and David, 2006, p. 25.
[20] Id., pp. 26-27, citing Jun, Son Youn and Kim, Sung Tae. 1995. "Do the Media Matter to voters? Analysis of Presidential Campaigns, 1984-1996." Paper presented to the *Political Communication Division of the International Communication Association*, Washington, D.C.; Zhao, Xinshu and Steven Chaffee. 1995. Campaign Advertisements versus Television as Sources of Political Issue Information. *Public Opinion Quarterly* Spring 59; Chaffee, Steven H. Xinshu Zhao and Glenn Leshner. 1994. Political Knowledge and the Campaign Media of 1992. *Communications Research* 21, Spring; Weaver, David and Dan Drew. 1995. Voter Learning in the 1992 Presidential Election: Did the 'Nontraditional' Media and Debates Matter? *Journalism & Mass Communication Quarterly* 72, Spring; Sotirovic and Jack M. McLeod. "Knowledge as Understanding: The Information Processing Approach to Political Learning." in Lynda L. Kaid (eds.), *Handbook of Political Communications Research*. Mahwah: NJ, Erlbaum, 2004.
[21] Farnsworth, Stephen J. and S. Robert Lichter. 2003. The 2000 New Hampshire Democratic Primary and Network News. *American Behavioral Scientist* 46:5: 588. The

impact and whether different types of media have different effects,[22] but there is general agreement that television has a significant influence on public opinion and perception of issues. For example, Romer, Jamieson, and Aday, in a study more recent than the 19 reviewed by Walgrave and Aelst, found "strong support for the television-exposure hypothesis."[23] Riffe, in a study of perception of environmental risk, which also post-dates the Walgrave and Aelst note that that "respondents who most frequently read and view media reports about the environment are more likely to rate their own environmental risks as higher,"[24] although in this study, newspapers had a slightly larger effect than television.

Gentzkow has looked at the impact of the spread of television on elections. He argued that as television displaced newspapers and radio, it had the effect of lowering voter turn out.

> The estimated effect is significantly negative, accounting for between a quarter and a half of the total decline in turnout since 1950. I argue that substitution away from other media with more political coverage provides a plausible mechanism for linking television to voting. As evidence from this, I show that the entry of television in a market coincide with sharp drops in consumption of

---

authors cite support for the importance of television in the New Hampshire Primary Moore, D.W. 1984. "The Death of Politics in New Hampshire." *Public Opinion* 7; Farnsworth, Stephen J. and S. Robert Lichter. 1999. No Small Town Poll: Network Coverage of the 1992 New Hampshire Primary. *Harvard International Journal of Press/Politics*, 4; Buhr, T. "What Voters Know About Candidates and How they Learn It: The 1996 New Hampshire Republican Primary as a Case Study in W.G. Mayer (Eds.), *In Pursuit of the White House 2000: How We Choose Our Presidential Nominees*, Chatham: NJ, Chatham House, 2001; and Farnsworth, Stephen J. and S. Robert Lichter. 2002. The 1996 New Hampshire Republican Primary and Network News. *Politics and Policy* 30.

[22] Sotirovic, Mira. 2003. "How Individual Explain Social Problems The Influences of Media Use." *Journal of Communications* March, p. 122 finds "active processing of national television public affairs content increases, while active processing of newspaper public affairs content decreases the likelihood of individualistic explanations" of crime and welfare. The authors cite Iyengar, S. *Is Anyone Responsible*. Chicago: University of Chicago Press, 1991 and Mcleaod, J. M., S. Sun, A. Chi, and Z. Pan. 1990. "Metaphor and Media." *Association for Education in Journalism*, August, as demonstrating the differential impact of media types.

[23] Romer, Daniel, Kathleen Hall Jamieson, and Sean Aday. 2003. Television News and the Cultivation of Fear of Crime. *Journal of Communications* March 2003, p. 99. The frame the issue as follows (p. 88): "Why has the public persisted in believing that violent crime is a widespread national problem in the U.S. despite declining trends in crime and the fact that crime is concentrated in urban locations?...The results indicate that across a wide spectrum of the population and independent of local crime rates, viewing local television news is related to increased fear of and concern about crime.

[24] Riffe, Dan. 2006. "Frequent Media Users See High Environmental Risks." *Newspaper Research Journal* 27:1: 48.

newspapers and radio, and in political knowledge as measured by election surveys. I also show that both the information and turnout effects were largest in off-year congressional elections, which receive extensive coverage in newspapers but little or no coverage on television.[25]

Interestingly, using a similar data set on the introduction of television, Gentzkow and Shapiro do not find a generally negative effect of preschool television exposure on standardized test scores latter in life.[26] This suggests that it is not the medium, but the message that matters. The failure to devote attention to coverage of politics is the key, Waldfogel and George have reached a similar conclusion with respect to national newspaper outlets.[27] As national outlets siphon readers away from local outlets, turnout in local elections declines much more than turnout in national elections (which are covered in national outlets).

Framing and Agenda Setting

The broadcast media play a special role in influencing the agenda of public policy issues and the public's perception of those issues.[28] The agenda setting and influence of perception that takes place during election campaigns frames issues.[29] There is a fierce struggle, a dance, between candidates and

[25] Gentzkow, Matthew. "Television and Voter Turnout." University of Chicago Graduate School of Business, 28 October 2005,p. 1.

[26] Gentzkow, Matthew and Jesse M. Shapiro. 2006. Does Television Rot Your Brain? New Evidence From the Coleman Study. NBER Working Paper 12021, February.

[27] Waldfogel, Joel. Who Benefits Whom in Local Television Markets? Philadelphia: The Wharton School, November 2001.

[28] Kim, Sei-Hill, Dietram A. Scheufele and James Shanahan. 2002. Think About It This Way: Attribute Agenda Setting Function of the Press and the Public's Evaluation of a Local Issue. Journalism and Mass Communications Quarterly 79:7 Chaffee, Steven and Stacy Frank. 1996. How Americans Get Their Political Information: Print versus Broadcast News. The Annals of the American Academy of Political and Social Science 546; McLeod, Jack M., Dietram A. Scheufele, and Patricia Moy. 1999. Community, Communications, and Participation: The Role of Mass Media and Interpersonal Discussion in Local Political Participation. Political Communication 16; Scheufele, Dietram A. 2000. "Agenda-setting, Priming and Framing Revisited: Another Look at Cognitive Effects of Political Communications." Mass Communications & Society 3; and Macomb, Maxwell. 1972. The Agenda-Setting Function of Mass Media. Public Opinion Quarterly 36.

[29] Valentino, Nicholas A., Vincent L. Hutchings and Ismail K. White. 2002. Cues that Matter: How Political Ads Prime Racial Issues During Campaigns. American Political Science Review 96: 75; Edsall, Thomas B. and Mary D. and Edsall. Chain Reaction: The Impact of Race, Rights and Taxes on American Politics. New York: Norton, 1991; Jamieson, Kathleen Hall. Dirty Politics: Deception, Distraction and Democracy. New York: Oxford University Press, 1992; Gilens, Martin. 1996. "Race Coding and White Opposition to Welfare," American Political Science Review 90; Mendelberg, Tali,

the media over the agenda of the campaign, because setting the agenda has an impact on how people perceive the candidates and vote.[30] The most intense agenda setting battles have frequently revolved around issues like crime[31] and race. Studies have shown that subtle race cues in campaign communications may activate racial attitudes, thereby altering the foundations of mass political decision-making.[32] While race may be a particularly prominent case of influence over attitudes and agenda-setting, the media plays a powerful role across a broad range of issues.[33]

"Executing Hortons: Racial Crime in the 1988 Presidential Campaign," *Public Opinion Quarterly,* 61, 1997, *The Race Card: Campaign Strategy, Implicit Messages and the Norms of Equality.* Princeton: Princeton University Press, 2001; Valentino, Nicholas A. 1999. "Crime News and the Priming of Racial Attitudes During the Evaluation of the President." *Public Opinion Quarterly* 63.

[30] Tedesco, John, C. "Issue and Strategy Agenda Setting in the 2004 Presidential Election: Exploring the Candidate-Journalist Relationship." *Journalism Studies* 6:2;Norton, Michael I. and George R. Goethais. 2004. Spin (and Pitch) Doctors: Campaign Strategies in Televised Debates. *Political Behavior* 26:3; Granato, Jim and M.C. Sunny Wong. 2004. Political Campaign Advertising Dynamics. *Political Research Quarterly* 57; Damore, David. 200. "The Dynamics of Issue Ownership I Presidential Campaigns." *Political Research Quarterly,* 57:3; Herrson, Paul, S. and Kelly D. Patterson. "Agenda Setting and Campaign Advertising in Congressional Elections." in James A. Thurber, Candace Nelson (eds.), *Crowded Airwaves: Campaign Advertising in Elections.* Washington D.C.: Brookings, 2000.

[31] Holian, David B. 2004. "He's Stealing My Issues! Clinton's Crime Rhetoric and the Dynamics of Issue Ownership." *Political Behavior* 26:2.

[32] The references cited in support of this proposition include Mendelberg, 2001; Coltrane, Scott and Melinda Messineo. 1990. The Perpetuation of Subtle Prejudice: Race and Gender Imagery in the 1990's Television Advertising. *Sex Roles* 42; Entman, Robert M., and Andrew Rojecki. *The Black Image in the White Mind: Media and Race in America.* Chicago: University of Chicago Press, 2000; Gray, Herman. *Watching Race Television and the Struggle for Blackness.* Chicago: University of Chicago Press, 1995; Dixon, Travis, L. and Daniel Linz. 2000. Overrepresentation and Underrepresentation of African Americans and Latinos as Lawbreakers on Television News. *Communications Research* 50; Gilliam, Franklin D. Jr. and Shanto Iyengar. 2000. "Prime Suspects: The Influence of Local Television News on the Viewing Public." *American Journal of Political Science* 44; Peffley, Mark, Todd Shields and Bruce Williams. 1996. The Intersection of Race and Television. *Political Communications* 13.

[33] Kim, Sheufele and Shanahan, p. 381. Graber, Doris. *Mass Media and American Politics.* Washington, DC: Congressional Quarterly, 1997;Paletz, David L. *The Media in American Politics: Contents and Consequences.* New York: Longman, 1999; Just, Marion, R., Ann N. Crigler, Dean F. Alger, Timothy E. Cook, Montague Kern, and Darrell M. West. *Crosstalk: Citizens, Candidates and the Media in a Presidential Campaign.* Chicago: University of Chicago Press, 1996; Kahn, Kim F. and Patrick J. Kenney. *The Spectacle of U.S. Senate Campaign.* Chicago: University of Chicago Press, 1999; Iyengar, Shanto and Donald R. Kinder. *News That Matters: Television and American Opinion.* Chicago:

The importance of visual images in *priming* the audience has been affirmed, while the understanding of the mechanisms through which the effect operates grows.

Findings suggest that visual news images (a) influence people's information processing in ways that can be understood only by taking into account individual's predispositions and values, and (b) at the same time appear to have a particular ability to trigger consideration that spread through one's mental framework to other evaluations.[34]

The special role of television in providing information and influencing elections is well recognized. Research attention now focuses on how television affects election campaigns and public opinion. "[V]oters do learn about candidates and their position on issues (policy) from candidate advertising."[35]

Advertising

The impact of television is pervasive throughout all elections.[36]

Television has become society's primary source of information, and local television news is more likely to be used by viewers than national news

University of Chicago Press, 1987; McCombs, Maxwell E. and Donald Shaw. 1972. The Agenda-Setting Function of the Mass Media. *Public Opinion Quarterly* 36.

[34] Domke, David, David Perlmutter and Meg Spratt. 2002. The Primes of Our Times? An Examination of the 'Power' of Visual Images. *Journalism* 3: 131. The authors present a detailed social psychological and even neurological discussion of the reasons why and ways in which visual images have a greater impact, but the politically oriented research that they cite as consistent with their findings include Krosnick, J. A. and D. R. Kinder. 1990. Altering the Foundation of Support for the President Through Priming. *American Political Science Review* 84; Pan, Z. and G. M. Kosicki. 1997. Priming and Media Impact on the Evaluation the President's Performance. *Communications Research* 24; Just, M. R., A. N. Crigler and W. R. Neuman. "Cognitive and Affective Dimensions of Political Conceptualization." in A. N. Crigler (eds.), *The Psychology of Political Communications*. Ann Arbor: University of Michigan Press, 1996; Iyengar and Kinder.

[35] Hansen, Glenn J. and William Benoit. 2002. Presidential Television Advertising and Public Policy Priorities, 1952 –2002. *Communications Studies* 53: 285. The studies cited in support of this proposition include Patterson, T. E., and McClure, R. D. *The Unseeing Eye: The Myth of Television Power in National Politics.* New York: Putnam Books, 1976; Kern, M. *30 Second Politics: Political Advertising in the Eighties.* New York: Praeger, 1988; Brians, C. L. and M. P. Wattenberg. 1996. Campaigns Issue Knowledge and Salience: Comparing Reception for TV Commercials, TV News, and Newspapers. *American Journal of Political Science* 40.

[36] Brazeal, LeAnn M, and William L. Benoit. 2001. A Functional Analysis of Congressional Television Spots. *Communications Quarterly* 49: 346-437.

broadcasts. Therefore, how such election news is relayed on local television is increasingly important in our political system.

Candidates and campaign consultants believe that television advertising is pivotal to winning a state-level campaign...

Research confirms that television spots influence election outcomes at all levels.[37]

The impact of television is not only in news coverage, but also, and perhaps even more importantly, in advertising and the interaction between advertising and news. TV in general, and network TV in particular, has become the premier vehicle for political advertising. The differential impact of television advertising is clear.

Clearly, television is a unique communications medium unlike any other, including print, radio, and traditional public address. Unlike most other media, television incorporates a significant nonverbal component, which not only serves to suppress the importance of content but also requires little deliberative message processing...

A number of empirical studies have concluded that reliance on information from television leads to less understanding of policy issues than newspapers. Studies also indicate that when people use television for political news, they emerge less informed than those of equal education and political interest who avoid the medium.[38]

Certainly the huge amounts spent on TV advertising by candidates attests to its importance. The audience that is most susceptible to advertising and news coverage by this account is precisely the audience on which general elections focus – the undecided middle – thereby justifying the spending. Whereas candidates must focus on the committed, active party base in primaries, they must shift their attention to the less aware, less committed middle of the political spectrum to get elected.[39]

---

[37] Carter, Fico and McCabe, 2002, p. 42.. In support of this statement the authors cite Joslyn, R. 1981. "The Impact of Campaign Spot Advertising Ads." *Journalism Quarterly* 7; Mulder, R. 1979. "The Effects of Televised Political Ads in the 1995 Chicago Mayoral Election." *Journalism Quarterly* 56; and Pfau, M. and H. C. Kenski. *Attack Politics.* New York: Praeger, 1990.

[38] Sinclair, Jon R. 1995. "Reforming Television's Role in American Political Campaigns: Rationale for the Elimination of Paid Political Advertisements." *Communications and the Law* March.

Gwiasda, Gregory W. 2001. "Network News Coverage of Campaign Advertisements: Media's Ability to Reinforce Campaign Messages." *American Politics Research* 29: 461 Kaid, L. L., et al. 1993. Television News and Presidential Campaigns: The Legitimation of Televised Political Advertising. *Social Science Quarterly* 74; Ansolaehere, S and S. Iyengar. 1995. "Riding the Waive and Claiming Ownership Over Issues: The Joint Effect of Advertising and News Coverage in Campaigns." *Public Opinion Quarterly* 58;

TELEVISION AND THE POLITICAL PROCESS

There is yet a more fundamental manner in which television affects political dialogue. Many media critics across the political spectrum have argued that hyper commercialism, combined with the expansion of media outlets, deeply affects the news reporting process, particularly as it relates to politics. The media ownership proceeding does not directly address the question of hyper commercialism. However, media ownership rules should be cognizant of the underlying forces that affect the media. We believe that the negative effect that media processes have on political discourse reinforces the case for diversity of institutions and sources. Hyper commercialism will not go away with a more concentrated media market, but its negative effects will be heightened if the market becomes more concentrated and institutional diversity withers.

The News Production Cycle of Commercial Mass Media

On the one hand, there are more television outlets needing to fill more space than ever before.[40] On the other hand, these outlets need to attract more viewers than ever to be profitable. The media's schedule and perpetual news cycle become the driving force, emphasizing speed, simplicity and routinization.[41] The news production process is transformed.

> The problems stem largely from the very nature of commercially supplied news in a big country. News organizations are responsible for supplying an always-new product to large numbers of people, regularly and on time. As a result, news must be mass-produced, virtually requiring an industrial process that takes place on a kind of assembly line.[42]

Lemert, James B. William R. Elliott, and James M. Bernstein. *News Verdicts, the Debates, and Presidential Campaigns.* New York: Praeger, 1991; Hansen and Benoit, p. 284. While Zaller, J. R. *The Nature and Origins of Mass Opinion.* New York: Cambridge University Press, 1998 is cited as the origin of the hypothesis on effect, the author does note that Joslyn, M. and S. Cecolli. 1996. "Attentiveness to Television News and Opinion Change in the Fall of 1992 Election Campaign." *Political Behavior* 18, find that the most attentive are most influenced. Benoit, William L. and Glenn Hansen. 2002. Issue Adaptation of Presidential Television Spots and Debates to Primary and General Audiences. *Communications Research Reports* 19.

[40] Kovach, Bill and Tom Rosenstiel. *Warp Speed: America in the Age of Mixed Media.* New York: The Century Foundation Press, 1999.

[41] Gans, Herbert J. *Democracy and the News.* Oxford: Oxford University Press, 2003, p. 50; Kovach and Rosentsteil, 1999, p. 6.

[42] Gans, 2003, p. 49.

The tight schedules and competition for attention put their stamp on the newsgathering and reporting process.[43]   Reporting becomes highly condensed and selective.[44] Planned events and personalities are the easiest to cover. Short pieces require extreme simplification. Stories become stylized so they can be easily conveyed. Time pressures create a tendency to not only run quickly with a story but to uncritically pass through manufactured news.[45] Entertainment and aesthetic values dictate the nature of the picture and getting good video images becomes a critical need.[46] Staging gives the news the predictability it needs, but results in typecasting and posing.[47]

Competition drives news outlets to seek blockbuster scoops and to play the big story more intensely and longer, to hold the larger audiences that have been attracted.[48]   The search to find and maintain the audience's attention drives the media towards exaggeration and emotionalism at the expense of analysis.

Four types of news are ideally suited to perform this function. Celebrity personalities become a centerpiece because of the easy point of focus on highly visible individuals.[49] Scandal attracts audiences so the personal travails of prominent figures in titillating circumstances are grist for the media mill, attracting attention without threatening the audience. This news may not be happy, but it fills the preference for happy news because it involves someone else's troubles of no direct relevance to public policy or the public's welfare. The horse race and hoopla – the game frame – is another easy way to frame the news and to produce constant updating of who is ahead.[50] Who wins and loses is much easier to portray than the complexity of what is at stake. Verbal duels[51] and loud, often one-sided arguments find audiences more easily than reasoned, balanced debates.[52] Talk show pundits

[43] Street, John. *Mass Media, Politics and Democracy.* New York: Palgrave, 2001, pp. 36-52.
[44] Graber, Doris A. 2003. "The Rocky Road to New Paradigms: Modernizing News and Citizenship Standards." *Political Communication 20*,113-114.
[45] Kovach and Rosentsteil, 1999, p. 21, 44.
[46] Meyer, Thomas. *Media Democracy.* Cambridge: Polity Press, 2002, p. 32-35.
[47] Meyer, 2002, p. 67; Graber, 2003, p. 112-114; Jones, Nicholas. *Soundbites and Spindoctors: How Politicians Manipulate the Media – and Visa Versa.* London: Cassel, 1995.
[48] Kovach and Rosentsteil, 1999, p. 7-8.
[49] Street, 2001, p. 47-49; Meyerowitz, J. *No Sense of Place: The Effect of Electronic Media on Social Behavior.* New York: Oxford, 1985.
[50] Street, 2001, p. 47; Graber, p. 111-112; Gitlin, T. "Bits and Blips: Chunk News, Savvy Talk and the Bifurcation of American Politics." in P. Dahlgren and C. Sparks (eds.), *Communications and Citizenship: Journalism and the Public Sphere.* London: Routledge, 1991, p. 119-136.
[51] Meyer, 2002, p. 35; Kovach and Rosenstiel, 1999, p. Ch. 7; Street, 2001, p. 44
[52] Barker, David, C. *Rushed to Judgment.* New York: Columbia University Press, 2002.

grab attention with extreme positions, usually negative attacks on targets that are not in the room to defend themselves.

The Impact on Journalism and Politics

Both journalism and politics suffer as a result of this process. Pressures to submit to heavy profit-maximizing strategies that foster financial gain at the expense of journalistic values prevail. As a result, "There has been an enormous increase in expenditure on public relations by both government and business... these powerful institutions subsidize the cost of gathering and processing the news in order to influence positively the way they are reported."[53]

Politicians conform and cater to the demands of the media, while they leverage their ability to manipulate their public image. The politicians acquiesce in a Faustian bargain. "In exchange for their 'tactical' submission to the media rules, political actors gain a well-founded expectation that they will be invited to help shape the way the media portray them."[54] Their interaction with the media becomes a form of extracted publicity as photo-ops and other premeditated activities that place them in the most favorable theatrical light serve their interests. Political entities submit to the media's dictatorship over the depiction of parties and personalities, "in which both politics and the media recognize only images of themselves, thereby losing sight of the real world."[55]

Journalism degenerates into a dance[56] between reporters and political handlers in which the spinmeisters have the upper hand. Spinmeisters become gatekeepers who can punish or reward with access to politicians and who control the scheduling of events. They can stonewall some or give exclusives to others. As a result, "top-down news turns journalists into messengers of the very political, governmental, and other leaders who are... felt to be untrustworthy and unresponsive by significant numbers of poll respondents."[57] The media produces a blend of news and free advertising for the candidates.[58] As with all advertising, the point may be to give a misimpression rather than convey accurate information. Hence, journalistic

---

[53] Levine, Peter. "Can the Internet Rescue Democracy? Toward an On-Line Commons." In Ronald Hayuk and Kevin Mattson (eds.), *Democracy's Moment: Reforming the American Political System for the 21st Century*. Lanham, ME: Rowman and Littlefield, 2002, P. 124.

[54] Meyer, 2002, p. 58.

[55] Meyer, 2002, p. 133; Gans, 2003, p. 47-48.

[56] Sparrow, Bartholomew H. *Uncertain Guardians: The News Media as A Political Institution*. Baltimore: Johns Hopkins University Press, 1999: 28-38.

[57] Gans, 2003, p. 49.

[58] Meyer, 2002, p. 53; Dorner, A. *Politainment*. Frankfurt/Main: Surhkamp, 2001.

values are marred.[59] Dependence on well-connected sources and pressures to get a story out first short-circuit the application of traditional standards of reporting. Discourse degenerates into a stream of stage-managed, entertainment-oriented, issueless politics.[60]

The watchdog function is short-circuited by close relationships.[61] This awards too much attention to too few political figures and views and sets the stage for politicians to manage their public identities through manipulation of the media's tendencies. Parties and ordinary group affiliations recede, as individuals and lead institutions become the center of attention.

The fashion in which stories are selected and the time-frame within which these stories are developed, in accordance with mass media's pursuit of big headlines and profits, have undercut politicians' ability to realize legitimate political agendas.[62] Instead, parties and political players shape their decisions and actions within the framework of how the media will present them.[63]

Without an ongoing dialogue of the conditions that enable the reported events to take place, the public cannot adequately formulate opinions; hence, they cannot act or mobilize in an educated manner. Public involvement in policy formation suffers not only because of the shift in focus fostered by the media, but also because of the short time-frame demanded by the media. The recognition of the news as being reported 'outside of time' highlights the troubling difference between the media's timeline and the timeline necessary for political agendas to be carried out.[64]

The critical elements of responsibility, causality and connectedness between events are lost. "Abbreviating the time interval normally demanded by the political process down to what the media's production schedule permits means abridging the entire process by deleting the procedural components that qualify it as democratic."[65] Insisting that politicians' rush to get their views to their constituents before they can be swayed in an opposing direction further truncates debate.[66] The rapid-fire sequence of simple, emotional snapshots staged to increase popularity replaces discourse as the basis of politics.

---

[59] Graber, 2003, p. 88.

[60] Gans, 2003, p. 50-51.

[61] Curran, James. *Media and Power*. London: Routledge, 2002, p. 150.

[62] Street, 2001, p. 57-58, 83, 90.

[63] Gans, 2003, p. 83; Cook; Cook, Timothy E. *Governing with the New: The News Media as a Political Institution*. Chicago: University of Chicago Press, 1998

[64] Meyer, 2002, p. 24.

[65] Meyer, 2002, p. 106.

[66] Meyer, 2002, p. 104.

Implications

Institutional diversity can play an important role. To most media analysts in our democracy, institutions play a critical role in mediating between individuals and the political process. Some draw the link between the institution and the investigative role.

> Democratic governance requires a free press not just in the sense of a diversity of expression. It requires the *institution* of a free press. It requires media with the financial wherewithal and political independence to engage in sustained investigative journalism, to expose the errors and excesses of government and other powerful political and economic actors…

> Our best hope for democratic governance in this world is far messier than the ideal republic of yeomen. It requires mediating institutions and associations, private and public concentrations of wealth and power, and varied mechanisms to maintain multiple balances of power within government, within civil society, and between government and civil society.

> One of the central benefits of promoting deconcentrated and diverse media markets is to provide a self-checking function on the media. The media needs to be accountable to the public, but that function cannot, as a general matter, be provided by government action in our political system. It can best be provided by the media itself, as long as there is vigorous antagonism between sources of news and information.

Institutional diversity reflects the special expertise and culture of certain media, such as the newspaper tradition of in-depth investigative journalism. Institutional diversity is grounded in the watchdog function.[67] The quality of investigative reporting and the accessibility of different types of institutions to leaders and the public are promoted by institutional diversity. Institutional diversity involves different structures of media presentation (different business models, journalistic culture and tradition) and these institutions often involve different independent owners and viewpoints across media. To promote institutional diversity, like other forms of diversity, the institutions must be independently owned. Yet even in independently owned conglomerates, the journalistic ethic can be overwhelmed. Institutional diversity is impacted by conglomeration.

---

[67] Baker, C. Edwin. *Media, Markets and Democracy*. Cambridge: Cambridge University Press, 2001, p. 85: argues as follows: "To perform these, different societal subgroups need their own media. Admittedly, these subgroups (or their members) may not *necessarily* need to own or control their own independent media. Avenues of regular and effective media access might suffice. Still, much greater confidence that the media will serve the democratic needs of these groups would be justified if ownership or control was so distributed."

Institutional diversity is also extremely important for the broader public policy issue of noncommercial sources of news.

CONCLUSION

The extreme importance of television as a source of information for citizens and influence on public opinion and voting behavior has been demonstrated strongly over the past decade in the social science literature. Study 7, documents that the public still relies on television as its primary source of news and information. The loop has been closed by adding the link between media and politics to the link between media ownership and point of view. The dramatic interaction between political campaigns, political process and the media underscores the critical importance of media policy.

PART III:
LOCAL TELEVISION STATIONS AND DAILY NEWSPAPERS REMAIN THE DOMINANT SOURCES OF LOCAL NEWS

STUDY 7
MEDIA USAGE:
TRADITIONAL OUTLETS STILL DOMINATE
LOCAL NEWS AND INFORMATION

MARK COOPER

CORRECTING THE FLAWS IN THE FCC APPROACH

In establishing new standards for when a local broadcaster may own newspapers in a community, the FCC highlighted the need to understand what media people actually use the most[1] to obtain local news and information,[2] to ensure that its rules accurately reflect the influence of each medium in local markets. Unfortunately, the Commission never conducted or found a survey that asked the most important question: which media people *rely on most* for **local** news and information. This unfortunate lack of data was a correctible error that the FCC chose to ignore.

Therefore, in January of 2004, a national random sample survey was conducted to assess the relative importance of media sources for news and information about national and local events.[3] The survey was designed in part to address the critical methodological flaw in the FCC's analysis of media sources[4] which was conducted as one of the Media Ownership Working

---

[1] Federal Communications Commission. 2003. 2002 Biennial Regulatory Review – Review of the Commission's Broadcast Ownership Rules and Other Rules Adopted Pursuant to Section 202 of the Telecommunications Act of 1996, 18 FCC Rcd 13620, 13711-47¶409. (hereafter Order). "We have concluded that various media are substitutes in providing viewpoint diversity, but we have no reason to believe that all media are of equal importance. Indeed the responses to the survey make it clear that some media are more important than others, suggesting a need to assign relative weights to the various media,"

[2] Order, at ¶32, "Although all content in visual and aural media have the potential to express viewpoints, we find that viewpoint diversity is most easily measured through news and public affairs programming. Not only is news programming more easily measured than other types of content containing viewpoints, but it relates most directly to the Commission's core policy objective of facilitating robust democratic discourse in the media. Accordingly, we have sought in this proceeding to measure how certain ownership structures affect news output."

[3] The survey instrument was administered by the Opinion Research Corporation as part of their Caravan Survey, which consisted of a national sample of 1011 respondents.

[4] Cooper, Mark. 2003. *Abracadabra! Hocus Pocus! Making Media Market Power Disappear with the FCC's Diversity Index*. Washington, D.C.: Consumer Federation of America, Consumers Union.

Group (MOWG) projects.[5]   In our surveys, we correct this and other major errors in the FCC's survey approach to media weights.[6]

Distinguishing Between Local and National News and Information

In its effort to identify the most important sources of news, the FCC asked a question that combined both national and local news. "What single source do you use most often for local or national news and current affairs?" This, of course, destroys the possibility of using this question to specifically assess the importance of local media. Instead, the FCC fell back on a much weaker question about local sources of news. "What source, if any, have you used in the past 7 days for local news and current affairs?"[7] This question does not necessarily tell us anything about what people use or rely upon the most for local news and information in the broad sense. It belittles the importance of the local news question by not only shrinking the scope of consideration for respondents ("in the past 7 days"), but also by being itself dismissive of the question altogether ("What source, if any…").

We corrected this problem in our surveys. In the first survey we used the identical wording of the FCC, but we ask separate questions about national and local sources of news. To distinguish the national from the local object of the question, we gave examples. Furthermore, because the criticism of the FCC approach stems in part from its reliance on a "weak" question about frequency of use that failed to directly address the importance of sources, we asked a second question about each source that was intended to pinpoint the importance of the sources in determining public opinion.[8]

---

[5] Nielsen Media Research. 2002. "Consumer Survey On Media Usage." *Media Ownership Working Group Study* No. 8, September.

[6] More technical and detailed discussions of the survey flaws addressed in this paper as well as other technical flaws in the FCC approach can be found in Cooper, Mark N. 2003. *Media Ownership and Democracy in the Digital Information Age*. Palo Alto: Center for Internet and Society, Chapters 7 and 8.

[7] The FCC also asked the question in an unbalanced manner. That is, it directly asked all the respondents who mention a given media in response to the first question, whether they had gotten any news from each of the other sources. The fewer the respondents who gave a medium in response to the first question, the greater the number who were directly prompted about it on the second round. The FCC then gave equal weights to the first and second responses. This has the effect of artificially increasing the weight of the lesser sources (since more people are prompted) especially when the question is about weak exposure to a source.

[8] Moy Patricia, Marcos Torres, Keiko Tanaka, and Michael R. McCluskey. 2005. Knowledge or Trust? Investigating Linkages between Media Reliance and Participation. *Communications Research* 32:1, p. 62 note that in describing "the construct of media dependency and its operationalization… reliance [is] grounded in intensity (whether and how much an audience member relies on a particular medium for a

Handling Multiple Responses

The FCC compounded the problem by mishandling the responses to its weak question. This was an open-ended question in which respondents were allowed multiple responses. Sources they mention first clearly came to their minds. One might infer that what they recall reflects the importance of the sources to them. Unfortunately, the FCC did not simply accept these responses. It followed up with a prompted question directed only at those who did not mention a specific source. The FCC asked those people who failed to mention a source whether they had used it. The FCC then combined the answers to the two questions, giving them equal weight. This approach was certain to overweight the less prevalent and important sources by asking many more people about those sources a second time with a prompted question.

In order to accommodate multiple sources of information, we adopted the approach used by the Pew Research Center for People and the Press.[9] The Interviewer reads a list of potential sources and records the sources cited first and second as most frequent and as most important. The resulting list of questions is as follow:

Now thinking about national issues, like the Presidential election or the war in Iraq, what single source do you use most often for news and information?

And what do you use second most often?

Which single source is most important in determining your opinion about national issues?

And what source is second most important?

Now thinking about local issues, like the a city council election or school, police and fire department services, what single source do you use most often for news and information?

And what do you use second most often?

Which single source is most important in determining your opinion about local issues?

And what source is second most important?

---

specific political issue) and exposure as frequency (how often an individual watches or reads about politics)." They cite Miller, M.M. and S.D. Reese. 1982. Media Dependency as Interaction: Effects of Exposure and Reliance on Political Activity and Efficacy. *Communications Research* 9.

[9] Pew Research Center Survey. 2004. "Perception of Partisan Bias Seen as Growing — Especially by Democrats." 11 Jan. Available from http://people-press.org/reports/display.php3?ReportID=200.

Identifying Media Types

The FCC survey also failed to properly distinguish between the different types of TV delivery. The FCC asked about broadcasting v. cable, but with over 80% of all households subscribing to cable or satellite and receiving the broadcast networks in the subscription, the broadcast/cable distinction becomes confusing. The FCC acknowledged that it had problems with the responses to these questions on its survey instrument, noting that

> [a]lthough the responses to one survey question in MOWG [Media Ownership Working Group] study No. 8 suggests that cable is a significant source of local news and current affairs, other data from the study casts some doubt on this result... Our experience suggests that the local cable news response is too high."[10]

The problem was their failure to distinguish national from local sources.

In our first survey, we used a question similar to the FCC that distinguished cable from broadcast, allowing the national v. local issues to cut through the confusion. Having shown that the public does distinguish between national and local TV sources of news and information, when given separate questions, as discussed below, we changed the wording in the second survey to reflect the underlying distinction – national v. local TV and daily newspapers. This follows the Pew wording in TV choices. The choice sets for media sources in the two surveys are as follows:

Broadcast TV channels	Local TV news
Cable or satellite news channels	National TV news
A daily newspaper	A local daily newspaper
	A national daily newspaper
A local weekly newspaper	A local weekly newspaper
Radio	Radio
The Internet	The Internet
Magazines	Magazines
OTHER [SPECIFY]	OTHER [SPECIFY]
NONE	NONE
DON'T KNOW	DON'T KNOW
REFUSED	REFUSED

The ultimate goal of this exercise is to produce the most highly refined and cautious estimate of local sources of news. Ultimately, in our analysis of local media market structure, we base our media weights on local

---

10 Order, ¶¶413-414.

TV, local dailies, local weeklies, and radio, which are the dominant sources of local news by far, but we also treat national news outlets and the Internet as additional news sources.   However, as the results show, they have little weight in local news.

TRADITIONAL SOURCES OF LOCAL NEWS DIFFER DRAMATICALLY FROM SOURCES OF NATIONAL NEWS

We begin the analysis by reviewing the evidence that was at the core of the remanded rules.   We then bring in the results of our most recent survey.

The 2002-2004 Surveys

To begin the analysis, we compare our wording and approach to the Dec. 19, 2003 – Jan. 4, 2004 survey results obtained by The Pew Research Center for The People & The Press.

For national issues the results for both the first mentions and the total mentions are very similar in the two surveys.   For national news, television (cable plus broadcast) dominates in both surveys, getting the first mention over 60% of the time (see Exhibit 1).   Newspapers are next, with first mentions in the mid-teens.   Radio and the Internet garner approximately 10%, sometimes slightly less.

In both surveys, newspapers move up as a percentage of total mentions, to the mid-twenties, while TV declines to around or slightly below 50%.   Throughout this analysis, whenever we show the sum of first and second mentions, we present them as a percentage of the total mentions.   This is essentially what the FCC did by creating an index that summed to 100%. Radio and the Internet remain at around 10%.

In fact, these national results have been quite stable for over a decade (see Exhibit 2).   Over the course of the past dozen years, the Internet appears to have reduced newspapers, radio and other sources by a few percentage points.

Exhibit 1: National Sources of News – CFA Compared to Pew

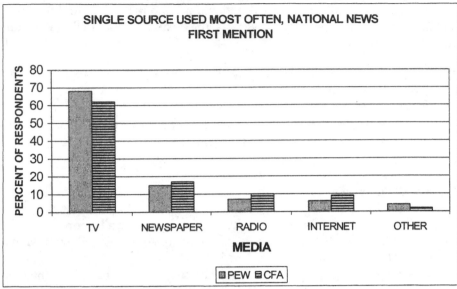

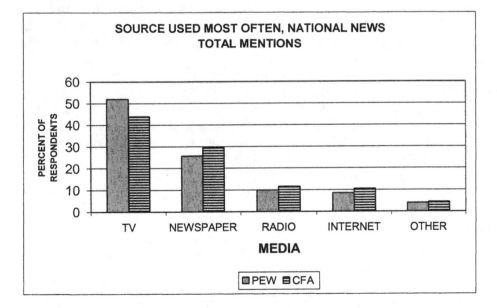

Source: *Consumer Federation of America/Consumers Union Poll, January 2004; Pew Research Center for the People & the Press. 2003. "Cable and Internet Loom Large in Fragmented Political News Universe." Pew Research Center. 11 January 200, 3The Pew Research Center For The People & The Press, Cable and Internet Loom Large in Fragmented Political News Universe, January 11, 2003.*

Exhibit 2: Trends of Most Used Media: Early in Presidential Election Years

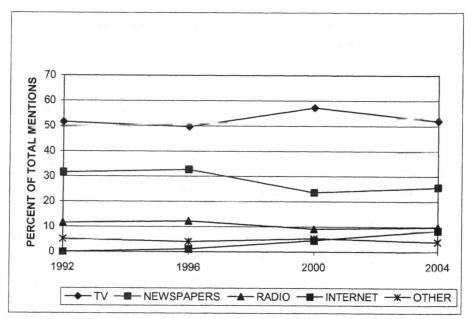

Source: Sources: Graber, Doris A., Graber, Doris. Processing Politics. Chicago: University of Chicago Press, 2001Processing Politics: Learning from Television in the Internet Age (Chicago: University of Chicago Press, 2001), p. 3; Nielsen Media Research. 2002. "Consumer Survey On Media Usage." Media Ownership Working Group Study No. 8, September Nielsen, Consumer Survey on Media Usage (Federal Communications Commission, Media Ownership Working Group, September 2002). Pew Research Center for the People & the Press. 2003. "Cable and Internet Loom Large in Fragmented Political News Universe." Pew Research Center. 11 January 2003The Pew Research Center For The People & The Press, Cable and Internet Loom Large in Fragmented Political News Universe, January 11, 2003; Source: Consumer Federation of America/Consumers Union Poll., January 2004 Pew Research Center For The People & The Press. 2003. "Cable and Internet Loom Large in Fragmented Political News Universe." Pew Research Center. 11 January 2003; The Pew Research Center For The People & The Press, Cable and Internet Loom Large in Fragmented Political News Universe, January 11, 2003.

However, a careful analysis of major sources for local news and information tells a very different story (see Exhibit 3). Our survey shows that the difference between sources of national and local news is quite dramatic and consistent with widely recognized patterns of media usage.

Newspapers are a much more important source of local news. Local newspapers (dailies plus weeklies) are the first mentions of 57% of the respondents compared to only 15% for national news. Television drops from 62% (for national news) to 27% (for local news). Note, however, that broadcast television remains quite important. The Internet drops from 10%

(for national news) to 2% (for local news). Radio is constant at just under 10% for both national and local news.

Exhibit 3: 2004 Survey, Frequency of Use and Importance of Sources of
Local and National News and Information
(% of Respondents)

| | | FIRST MENTION | | TOTAL MENTIONS | |
		Local	National	Local	National
MOST OFTEN USED	Dailies	35	14	30	21
	Weeklies	22	3	20	6
	Broadcast	21	27	24	23
	Cable	6	35	9	25
	Internet	2	10	4	12
	Radio	7	9	13	11
	Magazines	0	1	0	2
MOST IMPORTANT	Dailies	34	16	29	22
	Weeklies	18	3	17	6
	Broadcast	21	24	24	20
	Cable	6	30	10	23
	Internet	3	10	5	9
	Radio	8	9	14	10
	Magazines	0	2	0	1

Source: Consumer Federation of America/Consumers Union Poll. January 2004Consumer Federation of America/Consumers Union Survey, Poll, January 2004.

For total mentions we found the same pattern. Newspapers are much more frequently mentioned for local news, TV and the Internet less so. Broadcast TV is cited at roughly the same level for both local and national news. Radio is relatively constant.

The results for the responses to the question asking about "the most important news source" track the results for the responses to "the most often used news source" quite closely. For national news, TV is most frequently cited, followed by newspapers, radio and the Internet. Note that television is somewhat less likely to be cited as important (54% of first mentions) than most used (62% of first mentions). For local news, the pattern of first mentions is almost identical to that for most used. Broadcast television is the second most often cited source on influence. It is relatively constant across local and national.

The ability of respondents to distinguish between different media for different types of news is reinforced by their nuanced responses to the television question.   The cable/broadcast difference is critical for understanding the role of the media in civic discourse. Repeated claims about the abundance of programming available affected the framework in which media ownership rules were written by the FCC. Our survey shows that the FCC's references to an abundance of national entertainment channels – "hundreds of choices" – are largely irrelevant to the Commission's central obligation to promote diversity and competition in local sources of news and information.

Approximately 35% of respondents listed cable as their first mention for national news, but only 6% listed it as their first mention for local news. In contrast, broadcast TV was given as the first mention for national news by 27% of the respondents and 21% mentioned it first for local news. This is consistent with the evidence in the FCC's media ownership record that cable does not provide a significant independent source of local news, while broadcast remains a very significant source of local news.

The 2005-2006 Surveys

The results of the 2006 survey parallel those of the 2004 survey closely (see Exhibit 4). For example, the sum of TV in the national question on first mentions is 59 percent, compared to 62 percent in the earlier survey. There is also a sharp difference between the source and importance of different media types depending on the type of news being addressed. TV plays a much more prominent role in national news, primarily because of national TV. The main impact of changing the wording of the questions appears to have been to increase the relative importance of local TV, perhaps because of the earlier wording of "broadcasting" or "cable and satellite" did not clearly identify local TV.

Local newspapers have a much larger role in local news, as in the earlier survey. Dailies were 35 percent of first mentions for local in 2004; they are 37 percent in 2006.

Local dailies and weeklies have a much smaller role in national issues than in local issues. The reliance on and importance of local daily newspapers is about the same in the 2006 survey as they were in the 2004 survey. The reliance and importance of weekly newspapers and their importance is much lower in the 2006 survey.

The other major finding from the prior earlier survey that is replicated here is that the Internet is a much less frequent or important source of local news than national news. These results will be examined in detail in the section on the Internet.

**Exhibit 4: 2006 Survey, Frequency of Use and Importance of Sources of
Local and National News and Information
(% of Respondents)**

		FIRST MENTION		TOTAL MENTIONS	
		Local	National	Local	National
	Local Dailies	37	10	31	16
	National Dailies	1	3	1	5
	Local Weeklies	12	31	11	4
MOST	National TV	2	38	4	30
OFTEN	Local TV	33	21	33	20
USED	Internet	3	14	5	14
	Radio	6	10	12	10
	Magazines	0	14	1	3
	Other	2	1	2	1
	Local Dailies	34	12	29	16
	National Dailies	2	5	2	5
	Local Weeklies	10	2	10	3
MOST	National TV	6	35	6	30
IMPORTANT	Local TV	30	14	31	17
	Internet	4	13	6	13
	Radio	8	10	12	11
	Magazines	1	2	1	3
	Other	2	1	2	1

Source: *Consumer Group Survey, August 2006.*

While there is great similarity in the overall mentions of more
frequent and most important sources of news, it should be noted that there
are differences at the individual level, as predicted by the political science
literature, which sheds some light on the local sources. Exhibit 5 shows the
sources cited as most important within each medium that was cited as most
frequent. The diagonals show the consistent responses. For example, 44
percent of the respondents who said local TV was their most frequent source
of news on national issues also said local TV was the most important source.

The results for importance of the media track those for frequency of
use quite closely in the aggregate (see Exhibit 5). The sources rank in the
same order as for use and the percentages are similar. It is also notable that
the dailies are cited as the most used and most important source of local
news, surpassing TV by 4 % for both use and importance, but that TV gets
many more second mentions. Similarly, local weeklies exceed radio in first
mentions, but radio gets more second mentions.

Exhibit 5: Most Frequent Source Compared to Most Important Source (Percent of Respondents)

MOST IMPORTANT		Local TV	National TV	Radio	Internet	Magazines	Local Daily	National Daily	Local Weekly	Other	Total
								MOST FREQUENTLY USED			
National Issues	Local TV	44	28	5	4	2	9	2	3	0	100
	National TV	6	64	4	6	1	7	4	2	1	100
	Radio	3	7	65	8	2	4	2	1	2	100
	The Internet	2	12	2	64	2	6	5	1	1	100
	Magazines	13	27	0	0	33	0	0	0	0	100
	Local Daily	6	16	6	3	2	53	6	4	1	100
	National Daily	5	10	6	3	6	15	48	2	0	100
	Local Weekly	39	13	4	9	0	4	4	13	4	100
	Other	11	29	11	0	0	0	6	0	28	100
	Off Diagonal Avg.	11	18	5	4	2	6	4	2	1	-
Local Issues	Local TV	59	6	6	4	1	17	1	4	6	100
	National TV	42	29	6	0	2	13	4	2	0	100
	Radio	22	2	43	5	1	12	3	7	2	100
	The Internet	30	2	8	39	0	6	5	1	1	100
	Magazines	50	13	0	13	0	25	0	0	0	100
	Local Daily	14	4	4	3	0	65	2	4	2	100
	National Daily	6	11	0	0	0	39	39	6	0	100
	Local Weekly	15	5	5	3	0	15	4	51	1	100
	Other	0	16	3	0	0	10	0	3	42	100
	Off Diagonal Avg.	22	7	4	4	1	17	2	6	2	-

Source: Consumer Group Survey, August 2006.

In contrast, 59 percent of those who said local TV is their most frequent source of local news also said it was the most important. For newspapers, 53% of those who said national newspapers were the most frequent source of national news also said they were the most important. For local news, 65% of those who said local newspapers were the most frequent source also said they were the most important.

The diagonals are substantial, especially for the TV and newspapers. However, note that the diagonals are larger for national issues than for local issues primarily because local TV and local dailies get a lot more off diagonal mentions.   For example, 42% of those who said national TV was the most frequent source of local news said local TV was the most important source. For newspapers, 39% of those who said national papers were the most frequent source of local news said local papers were the most important.

The four traditional sources – local TV, local dailies and weeklies and radio – dominate the local news landscape mentioned by 88 % of the respondents as the most frequently used source and 72 % for second most frequent. They are cited as most important by 82 % of the respondents and second most important by 71 %. Local newspapers and local TV are about equal, each accounting for about one-third of the mentions. Radio and local weeklies are about equal, each accounting for about 10 % of mentions.

The Internet is at best a supplement for local news and information that is relied upon by a very small percentage of the population (4 % first mention, 7 % second mention).

- Even those who rely on the Internet, overwhelmingly go to web sites of traditional media, local TV and daily newspapers and national TV.

- Among the 11% of respondents who say that the Internet is their first or second most frequent source of news, the websites of local TV and daily newspapers account for about half (51%) of the primary sites they visit most frequently. Sites not affiliated with a traditional media outlet (blogs, list serves, alternative news sites and others, including aggregators) account for only 17% of the sites visited most and second most.

A recent survey by the Radio-Television News Directors Foundation (RTNDF) reaches similar conclusions to the surveys discussed above. Unfortunately, it does not distinguish between national and local news. However, it finds that local TV news and local newspapers are "people's major sources of news."

---

[11] Radio-Television News Directors Foundation. *2006 Future of News Survey.* September 2006.
[12] Id., p. 7

Exhibit 6 compares the percentage of people who identified a medium as a major source of news in the RTNDF study to who identified it as the most important source in our survey. The RTNDF gave respondents three choices, we allowed only two. We also distinguished local from national news, which the RTNDF did not. We include the average of the responses to the local and national questions in our survey to the RTNDF results. The rank order of the source is identical and the importance of distinguishing national from local news is underscored.

Exhibit 6: Comparison of RTNDF and Consumer Group Surveys on Major, Most Important Sources of News

Source of News	RTNDF 3 Choices	Consumer Groups, Most or Second Most National	Local	Average
Local TV	66	39	61	50
Local Newspaper	28	31	57	44
National TV	28	57	8	33
Local Radio	15	20	22	21
Internet	11	28	10	19
National Newspaper	4	8	2	5

Sources: Radio-Television News Directors Foundation, 2006 Future of News Survey, September 2006; Consumer Group Survey, August 2006.

STUDY 8:
THE INTERNET AND LOCAL NEWS AND INFORMATION

MARK COOPER

THE INTERNET AS A SOURCE OF NEWS AND INFORMATION

In both of our surveys we have noted that the Internet is cited much less frequently as a source of local news and information than for national news.   The impact of the Internet on the dissemination of news and information was a central issue in the Court case.   The Court drove home the critical factor that diversity comes from independent sources of information, something the Internet, which carries very little independent news, hardly provides.

> There is a critical distinction between websites that are independent sources of local news and websites of local newspapers and broadcast stations that merely republish the information already being reported by the newspaper or broadcast station counterpart.   The latter do not present an "independent" viewpoint and thus should not be considered as contributing diversity to local markets.[1]

The distinction between local and national sources was also emphasized in the Internet discussion.

> The Commission does not cite, nor does the record contain, persuasive evidence that there is a significant presence of independent local news sites on the Internet... And the examples the Commission does cite – the Drudge Report and Salon.com – have a national, not local, news focus.[a]
>
> [a] Moreover, the Drudge Report is an "aggregator" of news stories from other news outlets' websites and, as such, is not itself normally a "source" of news, national or local.[2]

These survey results provide strong support for the Court's lengthy discussion of the Internet.   They confirm that the Internet is not a major source of local news, a fact that was repeatedly demonstrated in the FCC proceeding, but ignored by the FCC when it created its Diversity Index.   We examined this in detail.

---

[1] *Prometheus Radio Project v. FCC*, 373 U.S. 372, 406 (3rd Cir. 2004).

[2] *Id.*, at 406, n.34.

The 2002-2004 Surveys

While the Internet is much more likely to be a source of national news, that is only true of younger respondents (see Exhibit 1). We find that the Internet is about three times as likely to be cited as a source of national news by younger respondents as by the remainder of respondents – about three times as often. A contemporaneous <u>national news for younger respondents</u>. However, the Internet drops off dramatically as a source of local news even among this younger age group (see Exhibit 2). The percentage of respondents age 18-24 who mentioned the Internet first drops from 23% for national news to 3% for local news.

Exhibit 1: Internet Use for National News Varies Strongly By Age Group

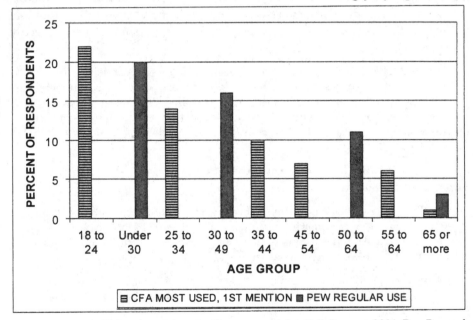

Source: *Consumer Federation of America/Consumers Union Poll. January 2004; Pew Research Center For the People & the Press. 2003. "Cable and Internet Loom Large in Fragmented Political News Universe." Pew Research Center. 11 January 2003.The Pew Research Center for the People & the Press, Cable and Internet Loom Large in Fragmented Political News Universe, January 11, 2003.*

Exhibit 2: Internet Use for Local News is Low Across Age Groups

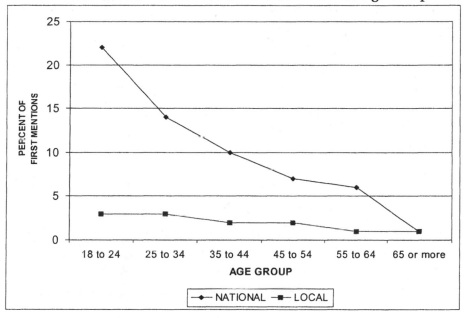

Source: Consumer Federation of America/Consumers Union Poll, January 2004.

The 2005-2006 Surveys

The 2006 survey shows a similar pattern (see Exhibit 3). The Internet plays a much larger role on national issues and younger respondents exhibit a much greater reliance on the Internet for national than local news. For the local issues, there is little difference between the age groups because there is not much local information on the Internet.

When they go online, respondents tend to go to the web sites of traditional media. National media are very strong on national issues (see Exhibit 4). For those who go on the Internet for information, web sites of traditional sources still dominate, especially for local issues. Even those who rely on the Internet as their first or second most frequent source of local information overwhelmingly go to web sites of traditional media, local TV and daily newspapers and national TV. Among the 11% of respondents who say that the Internet is their first or second most frequent source of news, the websites of local TV and daily newspapers account for almost half (51%) of the primary sites they visit most frequently. Sites not affiliated with a traditional media outlet (blogs, list serves, alternative news sites and others, including aggregators) account for only 17% of the sites visited most and second most.

Exhibit 3: Internet Usage by News Type, Frequency of Use and Age Group

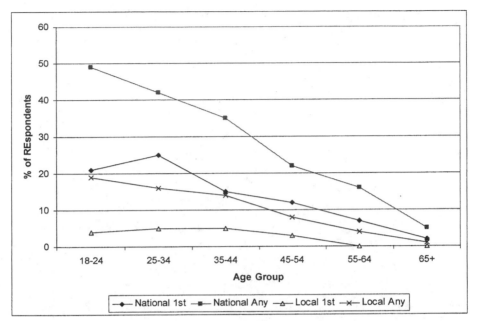

Source: Consumer Group Survey, August 2006

The Pew analysis shows that although people have expanded their use of online distribution, the source data remains the same.   Almost everyone relies on the traditional outlets – TV, newspapers, radio. When people go online, they are much more likely to go to the website of a traditional media outlet.   While aggregation service or portals are also popular online, these portals simply redistribute stories from other sources. They are not independent sources of news. The genuine alternatives, blogs, alternative news sites and list serves, have a much lower level of usage.

The bottom line for Pew is striking.

The web serves mostly as a supplement to other sources rather than a primary source of news. Those who use the web for news still spend more time getting news from other sources than they do getting news online. In addition, web news consumers emphasize speed and convenience over detail. Of the 23% who got news on the internet yesterday, only a minority visited newspaper web sites.   Instead, websites that include quick updates or major headlines, such as MSNBC, Yahoo, and CNN, dominate the web-news landscape.

Exhibit 4: Where Users Frequently Get News Online
(Percent of those who Get News Online; Usage: Pew is Yesterday, CFA is 1st Mention Most Often)

Type of Site		All Online Users				Heavy Users			
		Pew	CFA			Pew Broadband	CFA 1st or 2nd Mention		
			National	Local 1	2		National	Local 1	2
Traditional Media	National TV	16	56	19	36	21	52	26	55
	Local TV	8	5	15	17	21	3	27	14
	National Daily	6	7	2	4	8	7	3	13
	Local Daily	9	3	15	12	11	6	25	20
	Radio	2	3	2	3	3	2	2	7
New Media	Portal/Other	14	13	10	27	17	15	10	39
	Int'l News Site	3	6	1	2	3	6	3	8
	Alternate News	2	4	1	2	2	6	3	3
	List serves	2	3	1	1	2	5	2	1

Sources: Horrigan, John B. "For Many Home Broadband Users, the Internet is a Primary News Source." Pew Internet and American Life Project, 22 March 2006Horrigan, John B., For Many Home Broadband Users, the Internet is a Primary News Source, Pew Internet and American Life Project, March 22, 2006, p. 12; Consumer Group Survey, August 2006.

The rise of the internet has also not increased the overall news consumption of the American public. The percentage of Americans who skip the news entirely on a typical day has not declined since the 1990s. Nor are Americans spending any more time with the news than they did a decade ago, when their choices were much more limited.[3]

Exhibit 5 demonstrates the basis for this conclusion in dramatic fashion. It shows the frequency with which respondents use offline traditional and online sources, as well as the destinations to which they go online. Traditional offline outlets still are still vastly more important and the online outlets of those sources dominate the online destinations.

Exhibit 5: Traditional Media Still Dominate As the Source of News

Do your ever get news or information from...?
Did you happen to get news or information from this source YESTERDAY?

		Percent of Respondents	
		EVER	YESTERDAY
OFFLINE:	Traditional Outlet (National or local TV, Newspaper or Radio)	100%	95.4%
	Web site of a Traditional Outlet	43.1%	16.5%
ONLINE:	Web portals (Google news, Yahoo news)	25.4%	10.5%
	Alternative web site (Blog, Alternative News, List serve)	10.2%	3.7%

Source: Pew Internet and American Life Project. 2005. RDD Tracking Study, Nov/Dec. Pew Internet and American Life Project Nov/Dec 2005 RDD Tracking Study

Recognizing that portals are not independent sources of news, but simply aggregate existing source, which are generally from traditional sources, there is very little independent content accessed. To the extent that portals make sources that would not have been available in the offline world available, they do increase availability. However, for local news the amount of such content is slim.

The Belo Survey

A survey of online users conducted by the Dallas Morning News strongly reinforces these observations (Exhibit 6). First, web sites affiliated with traditional news organizations are the overwhelming favorites for online news users. Almost 9 out of 10 respondents give the web site of a local TV station or newspaper as the preferred destination. Web portals garner only 3 %, while the other/don't know category garners 7 %. The younger respondents, who are generally considered the most web savvy, exhibit the same tendencies.

---

[3] Kohut, Andrew, et. al. "Maturing Internet New Audience – Broader than Deep." The Pew Research Center for the People & the Press, 20 July 2006, p. 2.

**Exhibit 6: Web Sites Affiliated With Traditional News Organizations
Are the Preferred Source for Local News**
(Internet web site would go to first for details about local news story)

Age	Local		National		News Magazine	Portal	DK/ Other
	TV	Paper	TV	Paper			
15-25	43	41	6	2	1	3	4
26-34	48	39	3	0	0	2	8
35-34	55	29	2	1	0	5	8
45-54	59	29	1	1	0	3	7
55-64	61	21	4	1	0	5	9
65+	68	16	6	0	3	4	3

*Source: Belo Interactive. Online Credibility Survey. 9-19 July 2004 Belo Interactive,
Online Credibility Survey, conducted July 9-19, 2004.*

Second, respondents were asked about their interest in news about
various topics (see Exhibit 7). The strongest interest was expressed in news

Exhibit 7: Interest in News about Various Topics

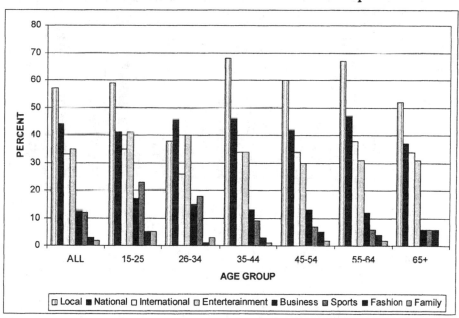

*Sources and Notes: Belo Interactive. Online Credibility Survey. 9-19
July 2004lo Interactive, Online Credibility Survey, June 2004.
Interest in News about: Where you live = Local, from Around the Country = National, from
Around the World = International, In Entertainment and Personalities = Entertainment,
About Business and Careers = Business, In Sports = Sports, About Fashion, Lifestyles &
Health = Fashion, In Relationships, Family and Friends = Family;*

"about where you live." It was the only category that exceeded 50 % saying (~57%) this news is very important; second was national news (~44). International news and entertainment news were generally cited by 30 to 40% of respondents. The other types of news have much lower percentages. Only in the 26-34 age group did national news have a higher percentage of respondents saying it was very important. This is primarily because of a lack of interest in local (not a heightened interest in national) news.

Third, in this survey newspapers have a huge advantage in credibility over other sources (see Exhibit 8). The Internet is generally second in credibility in this survey, interestingly, with much lower levels of credibility among the younger respondents. The respondents were also asked about the impact of an association

Exhibit 8: Newspapers Have an Advantage in Credibility (Which Medium Provides the Most Credible Information?)

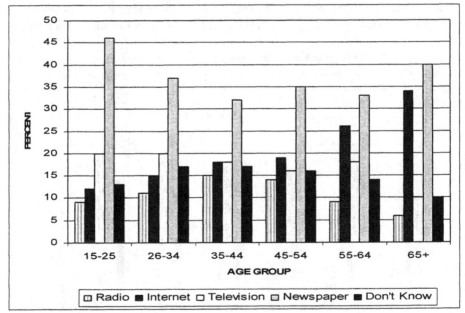

Source: Belo Interactive. Online Credibility Survey. 9-19 July 2004Belo Interactive, Online Credibility Survey, June 2004.

between a web site and a traditional source of news (see Exhibit 9). The overwhelming majority of respondents (about 70%) said this would make the web site more credible. Interestingly, the younger respondents were more likely to respond in the affirmative than the older respondents.

This evidence on the preferences for web sites and the complementarity and linkages between traditional outlets and Internet sites supports the *Prometheus* Court's reasoning on the treatment of the Internet in the determination of the Diversity Index.

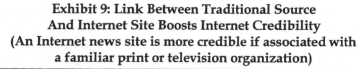

Exhibit 9: Link Between Traditional Source
And Internet Site Boosts Internet Credibility
(An Internet news site is more credible if associated with
a familiar print or television organization)

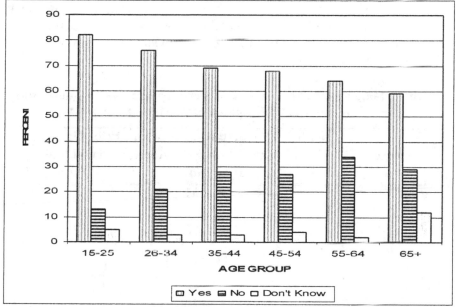

Source: Belo Interactive. Online Credibility Survey. 9-19 July 2004Belo Interactive, Online Credibility Survey, June 2004.

A NOTE ON WORDING AND SEQUENCING OF THE SOURCE AND INTERNET QUESTIONS

The analysis presented in this study and the study on Internet use for national and local information is based on the sequence of questions described in Study 7. That is, we asked people where they go for national and international news and information first and which sources influence their opinion, national and international news second. Then we asked the questions about local news and information. The distinction between the subjects – national vs. local is important because the media ownership proceeding is focused on local news. We also asked the question about where people go on the Internet for news and information for anyone who had the Internet at home. We provided a list of independent sources and did not include pure aggregators. This, too, is consistent with the framework of the

Court ruling.   To the extent that respondents only go to aggregator sites, they would have said "other."

To examine the impact of these choices on the analysis, we asked the questions in a different way one a different date of another national random sample survey.   We did not ask the national/international questions first, we asked only those who said they went online for news (as opposed to everyone who has the Internet) and we included the aggregators in the list of web sites that were visited.   The respondents move in the direction that would be expected (see Exhibit 10).   Without being asked about national and international news and information first, more respondents say they go to national sites for local news.

Exhibit 10: Major Sources of News: Different Approaches to Questioning (Percent of Total Respondents and Mentions)

Source	With Prior Question About National News		Without Prior Question About National News	
	1st	1st or 2nd	1st	1st or 2nd
Local TV	33	61	33	59
National TV	2	8	10	23
National Daily	1	2	2	5
Local Daily	37	57	26	46
Local Weekly	12	21	14	14
Radio	7	22	10	24
Internet	3	10	8	21

Source: Consumer Group Survey, August 2006, September 2006.

Turning to the web sites that those who go online for news visit, we find that the local sites have the largest increase – reflecting the fact that the national news question was not asked first (see Exhibit 11).   National dailies increase.   Given the option of aggregators, a larger number of respondents say they went to those sites first.   Combining aggregators and other, we observe an increase from 5 percent of the total population to 7 percent on first mentions and a 7 to 13 for first or second mentions.

This difference would have little impact on the general conclusions about the frequency and importance of various media outlets, certainly with respect to the role of the Internet.   Because the percentage of respondents who give the Internet as a source is so small, the shift between traditional sources and aggregators would have little effect on the overall media map that was drawn.

Exhibit 11:
Different Approaches to Questions Result
in Small Differences in Responses
(Percent of Total Respondents and Mentions)

Website Visited	All Internet at Home/ Aggregators not Identifie		Internet News Users/ Aggregators Identified	
	1st	1st or 2nd	1st	1st or 2nd
National TV	12	19	9	14
Local TV	13	22	2	4
National Daily	1	4	1	3
Local Daily	10	18	3	5
Radio	3	5	1	2
Other/Portals	5	7	7	13
Blogs	0	1	1	2
Alternative News	1	1	1	1
International News	1	2	1	2
List Serves	1	1	0	2

Source: Consumer Group Survey, August 2006, September 2006.

THE INTERNET AND JOURNALISM

Media Functions in the Production and Dissemination of News and Information

Although the Internet has provided an expanded arena for discussion, the traditional mass media still dominate the gathering, editing and dissemination of information about local events and public affairs. The Court gave a nuanced framework for analyzing the importance and impact of alternative media.

The other Internet issue that receives a great deal of attention is the relationship between the Internet as a news medium and the production of news and information. The *Prometheus* court did not use the term blogs, but it addressed the heart of the issue with a lengthy and nuanced discussion of the unique characteristics of the "information" that is the object of First Amendment policy in the case. The role of the media in creating and protecting the integrity of this information is substantial.

In terms of content, "the media" provides (to different degrees, depending on the outlet) accuracy and depth in local news in a way that an individual posting in a chat room on a particular issue of local concern does not. But more importantly, media outlets have an entirely different character from individual or organizations' websites and thus contribute to diversity in an entirely different way. They provide an aggregator function (bringing news/information to one place) as well as a distillation function (making a judgment as to what is interesting, important, entertaining, *etc.*) Individuals... and entities... may use the Internet to disseminate information and opinions about matters of local concern... but ... are not, themselves... "media outlets" for viewpoint-diversity purposes. Like many entities, they just happen to use a particular media outlet – the Internet – to disseminate information. Similarly, advertiser-driven websites such as hvnet.com... hardly contribute to viewpoint diversity."[331]

The Court's view of the difference between the Internet as a distribution medium and the production of news and information is right on and can be linked directly to recent analyses of alternative media (see Exhibit 12). If we distinguish three functions – reporting, editing and response – and three different ways of implementing each function – not doing it, using a closed approach , or using an open approach – we can classify the various types of media. We then get into the debate about whether the new media are providing the functions of the old. They give a great deal of response, but not that much reporting and editing.

Blogging

Our surveys did not address this issue, except in asking whether respondent used blogs as primary or secondary sources of information. For national news, fewer than 3% of all respondents (5% of those who get online news) mentioned blogs as a first or source of information. For local news only 1% of all (2% of those who get online news) mentioned blogs as a first or second source.

Pew conducted a recent study[332] that addresses some of these issues and they support the view of the *Prometheus Court*. From the point of view of what, why and how they blog, there is clearly a difference between media/journalism as defined by the court and blogging.

The predominant reasons for blogging, stated by about half of the bloggers, are self-expression and sharing of personal experiences. Next most frequent reasons about (one-third) are to stay in touch with friends and family. In fact, about half the bloggers believe most of their readers are people they know. This is an extension of the water cooler and backyard fence aspect of civic discourse.

---

[331] *Prometheus* , 372 F.3d at 407 (3rd Cir. 2004)..

[332] Lenhart, Amanda and Susan Fox. "Bloggers: A Protrait of the Internet's New Storytellers." Washington, D.C.: Pew Internet & American Life Project, 19 July 2006.

"Three in four bloggers (77%) told us that expressing themselves creatively was a reason that they blog."[333] Other major reasons given were to document personal experiences (76%), share practical knowledge (64%) motivate people to action (61%) and keep in touch with family and friends (60%).

"The largest percentage of bloggers... (37%) say that "my life and personal experiences"[334] was the main topic. Next was political and government (11%), followed by entertainment (7%), sports (6%) news and current events (5%), and business (5%).

About one-third of bloggers define themselves as journalists, but only about one third-of bloggers responding to the survey say they often "spend extra time trying to verify facts," and just over one-third include links to original source material. Only 15% say they "quote other people/media directly."

In sum, on both the demand side (where people go for news) and on the supply-side, what bloggers do, it seems clear that blogging does not meet the *Prometheus* Court's definition. This is not to say that blogging does not provide valuable communications and networking functions, it is just not local news and information for the vast majority of citizens.

---

[333] Id., p. 7.
[334] Id., p. 9.

Exhibit 12:
The Emerging News Media Space

REPORTING ↓	EDITING: NONE			EDITING: CLOSED	EDITING: OPEN	
RESPONSE:	NONE	CLOSED	OPEN	NONE	CLOSED	OPEN
NONE	GOOGLE NEWS	CHAT GROUP	PUNDITRY BLOG	GROUP BLOG		
CLOSED	HOMEPAGE, PODCAST		WITNESS BLOG W/ FEEDBACK	TRADITIONAL MEDIA		
OPEN	METABLOG			MEDIA CHANNEL	SLASHDOT	INDYMEDIA, WIKIPEDIA, GATHER

MEDIA/JOURNALISM with all three functions present

Categories adapted from Bruns, Alex. *Gatewatching*. New York: Peter Lang Publishing, 2005 Bruns, Alex, *Gatewatching* (New York: Peter Lang Publishing, 2005) and Rogers, Richard. *Information Politics on the Web*. Cambridge: MIT Press, 2004.Rogers, Richard, *Information Politics on the Web* (Cambridge: MIT Press, 2004)

PART IV:
CONCERNS ABOUT THE IMPACT OF
NEWSPAPER-TV COMBINATIONS
ON PRINT JOURNALISM

STUDY 9:
LOCAL MEDIA AND THE FAILURE OF THE CONSOLIDATION/ CONGLOMERATION MODEL

MARK COOPER

SETTING THE STAGE

In the upcoming media ownership proceedings at the Federal Communications Commission (FCC), Big Media will sing a song of gloom and doom about the economics of the media business. As they have done in the past, they are likely to insist that consolidation between outlets and conglomeration across media sectors are necessary to save the media industry from ruin.

Even though mergers reduce diversity of ownership, Big Media often claims that mergers preserve outlets or improve their quality, which is better than losing the independent voice altogether or having it be weak. They will demand that rules limiting their ability to buy up media properties be eliminated or dramatically curtailed.

Recent trends in media markets suggest that they cannot make this case. Local TV stations and newspapers are still very healthy businesses. While they may not generate the kinds of returns that oil companies enjoy or hedge funds seek, they are, in fact, quite profitable compared to typical businesses in America and buyers have been proving that by paying handsome prides for these properties.

The most "startling" aspect of the recent events in the newspaper and TV sectors is the message being sent by the prices recently paid to acquire newspaper and TV station properties.

> There is some good news in the unrest... If the sale price of Knight Ridder – $4.5 billion – was a referendum on the health of the industry, the answer was positive. The price was higher than most expected and acknowledges the fact that many newspapers still enjoy profit margins of about 20 percent – higher than that of most businesses.[1]

> Despite weak station-group stocks, broadcast properties themselves are fetching surprisingly high prices. Deals for many of Emmis Broadcasting's

---

[1] Ahrens, Frank. "A Push Toward Private Control of Newspapers." *Washington Post 17* June 2006, D3.

stations closed recently at startling values. The planned sale of broadcaster Liberty Corps. to Raycom is only slightly less impressive.[2]

A June 17, 2006 article by Frank Ahrens in the *Washington Post* goes even farther to draw a dramatic lesson from recent events. "The recent breakup of the Knight Ridder Inc. newspaper chain has helped to spark interest around the country in returning papers to local or private ownership after decades of expansion by corporate media conglomerates."[3] The issues Ahrens sees raised by these recent trends in the newspaper business feed directly into the issues that are at the core of the media ownership proceeding:

> Now after two decades of circulation decline that have led to strife in boardrooms, some of the very precepts that stabilized the business – newspapers should be publicly held companies, local ownership is limiting, and bigger is better – are being repudiated.[4]

The failure of the consolidation/conglomeration strategy should certainly not be taken to mean that the local media industries do not have problems; it just means that consolidation/conglomeration is not a solution to the problems it faces. The real challenge facing traditional media outlets like newspapers and local broadcast stations is that audiences are migrating to the web and advertising dollars are following them there. Consolidation of the traditional, physical, push media does not address this issue. Rather, the business of journalism, print and video, must develop strategies for online distribution.   Physical world consolidation is neither a sufficient condition, nor even a helpful step in meeting this larger long term challenge. One part of the solution highlighted by recent developments is a change in ownership – "With private ownership, shareholders are off your back. A helpful thing as newspapers take risks to follow their readers to the Internet and beyond."[5]

Demonstrating that the economic conditions do not call for consolidation or conglomeration is critically important in the ownership proceeding because the public policy of promoting diversity and localism in the media sets a presumption against consolidation and conglomeration. As a nation, we prefer a less concentrated, more institutionally diverse media for the sake of healthy democratic discourse. This preference has been enacted into law by the Congress, implemented by the FCC and found constitutional by the Supreme Court. It now appears that policies to promote diversity and localism are not in conflict with the fundamental economics of the industry.

---

[2] Higgins, John M. "Nice Price: Despite Recent Deal Snags, the Station Market is Still Relatively Strong." *Broadcasting and Cable*, 20 February 2006, p. 6.

[3] Ahrens, 2006, p. D1.

[4] Id.

[5] Id.

As a result, restrictions and bans on consolidation and conglomeration make perfect public policy sense.

NEWSPAPERS

Two factors seem to be fueling the ongoing turmoil in the newspaper industry. On one side is the failure of the consolidation/conglomeration approach of the past couple of decades to produce the returns that *Wall Street* seems to demand. In the case of Knight Ridder, "the upheaval started last fall, when a major shareholder of the venerable Knight Ridder chain began urging the board to breakup the company, saying shareholders were not getting the best value for their stock."[6] After Knight Ridder was successfully sold, turmoil broke out at an even larger conglomerate, The Tribune, when the second largest shareholder "accused management of pursuing a failed strategy of melding local TV stations and newspapers and failing to keep pace with the industry."[7] The financially successful sale of the Knight Ridder papers and the boardroom melodrama at the Tribune have put the issue in the headlines. The Tribune's "content conglomerate" strategy has failed, not because the individual businesses are unhealthy, but because conglomeration is not a solution to the problem the industry faces.

Thus, on the other side is the continuing strong performance of many of the basic newspaper assets. The sale of the Knight Ridder chain to McClatchy, which surprised some, and the immediate resale of twelve papers to small or mid-sized chains and individuals suggest that the newspaper business is moving away from the conglomerate "content" model that seemed fashionable a few years ago. What we observe is that people who want to be in the newspaper business are finding that they can make money in the newspaper business, especially if they figure out how to effectively distribute the product online. Circulation is down, but readership may not be[8], and advertisers are beginning to figure out about the new opportunities being presented online by local newspapers.

McClatchy sold its recently acquired Knight Ridder papers in markets it did not choose to enter for between 9.5 and 11.1 times cash flow.[9] Those are

---

[6] Id.

[7] Siklos, Richard and Katherine Q. Seelye. "At Tribune a Call for a Split." *New York Times*, 15 June 2006, C1.

[8] The *Philadelphia Inquirer* and *The Wall Street Journal* both claim increasing readership due to online readers. (See von Hoffman, Nicholas. "Anybody Want to Buy a Newspaper?" *The Nation*, 2 December 2005.)

[9] Dirks, Van Essent & Murray. "McClatchy will be #2 – Acquisition is Largest in Total Circulation." 1st Quarter Update. 31 March 2006; Saba, Jennifer. "It's Official: McClatchy Sells 5 KR Papers – to 4 Companies." *Editor & Publisher*, 7 June 2006; Theses numbers were a little lower than other deals as noted in Levingston, Steven and

considered healthy numbers in the industry.   Indeed, they are the very same numbers that we observe in cable systems and no one suggests that the cable business is on the brink of ruin.

Even at the troubled Tribune Company, the newspaper business is quite profitable.

> While the company does not break out the margin for individual papers, analysts estimate that the profit margin at the Times could have been as high as 20 percent last year. That is lower than those at other Tribune properties but higher than those of many Fortune 500 companies.[10]

The Project on Excellence in Journalism hypothesized in *The State of the News Media: 2005* that "the species of newspaper that may be most threatened is the big-city metro paper that came to dominate in the latter part of the 20th century."[11] The problem is what I have called the wheelbarrow problem.[12] Trying to cover a large geographic area, the physical paper simply becomes too large to give enough detail – either in reporting or advertising – to meet the needs of individuals at different ends of the region. There is so much to cover that consumers would have to carry their papers around in wheelbarrows. As the Project on Excellence in Journalism put it:

> The top three national newspapers in the U.S. suffered no circulation losses in 2005. The losses at small newspapers, in turn, appeared to be modest. It was the big-city metros that suffered the biggest circulation drops and imposed the largest cutback in staff. Those big papers are trying to cover far-flung suburbs and national and regional news all at the same time – trying to be one-stop news outlets for large audiences.[13]

Ahrens recently noted this pattern of turmoil in the industry as well.

> And even though big-city newspapers are losing circulations, many small and mid-size newspapers are growing. It was those Knight Ridder papers that caught McClatchy's eye...

> The smaller papers are growing because, unlike in large media markets, they are either the only or the dominant advertising vehicle in town. It is an

---

Terence O'Hara. "McClatchy's Paper Chase." *Washington Post,* 14 March 2006, p. D1, "Knight Ridder Sold for 9.5 times free cash flow, making the purchase price, on a cash-flow basis, cheaper than any other major newspaper deal of the past five years. Recent deals have priced newspapers at 12 to 14 times their free cash flow."

[10] Siklos, Richard and Katharine Q. Seelye. "Fitfully Blending Papers and TV." *New York Times,* 19 June 2006, p. C4.

[11] Project on Excellence in Journalism. 2006. "Overview." *The State of the News Media: 2005,* p. 3 (hereafter PEJ).

[12] Cooper, Mark N. *Media Ownership and Democracy in the Digital Information Age.* Palo Alto: Center for Internet and Society, 2003, pp. 127-129.

[13] PEJ, 2006, p. 3.

advantage that large papers, such as the Philadelphia Inquirer, cannot match, as advertisers have more ways to reach consumers there.[14]

For the big-city papers, the challenges come from "niche publications serving smaller communities and targeted audiences,"[15] as well as online revenues. The Tribune's flagship paper – the Los Angeles Times – exhibits the problem in the extreme.   "Los Angeles County is made up of 88 independent cities, a sprawling region that is difficult for any one news organization to cover in depth. It has also absorbed a huge influx of people who do not speak English."[16]

Yet, McClatchy held onto four large newspapers and the price fetched by the Philadelphia newspapers it flipped was about $1,000 per subscriber, a figure equal to that which Fox paid for DirectTV. When the subject of breaking up the Tribune Company comes up, the price mentioned for the L.A. Times is about the same. In short, the stand alone newspaper business model appears to be making a comeback.

William Dean Singleton, CEO of privately held MediaNews Group Inc., which bought four of the papers McClatchy flipped to become the fourth largest newspaper chain in the country, wadded into the middle of the Tribune turmoil by comparing the price he was paying for newspapers to the cost of Tribune's plans to buy back its stock--an effort to pump up its stock price.

They're buying back their stock for 7.9 times cash flow or something? That's a good buy. I'm out paying 12 times [cash flow] to buy newspaper assets. I wish I could buy them for 7.9, but I can't."

Singleton's perfectly happy to keep buying papers on the cheap while others disparage the future of print. It's "still a very, very, very profitable piece of what we do and will be doing for a long time," he said, citing the installation of new presses at four of his papers as testimonial to his confidence[17].

Singleton's lament about having to pay higher prices for newspaper properties actually extends to the whole Knight Ridder deal. As an article in the Washington Post pointed out when the sale to McClatchy was concluded,

Knight Ridder sold for 9.5 times free cash flow, making the purchase price, on a cash flow basis, cheaper than any other major newspaper deal of the past five years. Recent deals have priced newspapers at 12 to 14 times their free cash flow.[18]

---

[14] Ahrens, 2006, p. D3.

[15] Id.

[16] Siklos and Seelye, 2006, p. C4.

[17] Rosenthal, Phil. 'Singleton Sold on Newspapers." *Chicago Tribune*, 21 June 2006.

[18] Levingston, Steven and Terence O'Hara. "McClatchy's Paper Chase: Family Owned Chain to By Knight, Plans to Sell off 12 Dailies." *Washington Post*, 14 March 2006, D1.

The ability of McClatchy to flip the papers at prices much closer to the industry average suggests that it was either the size of the chain that was put up for sale that was the problem or the quality of management at the Knight Ridder chain.[19] The industry in general commands higher multiples.

Importantly, it is not only the economic benefits of conglomeration that have not panned out; the claims of journalistic benefits have also proven elusive. John Morgan is cited in the Ahrens article as a "newspaper analyst," who

> has become converted to the return-to-private thinking, which he said has its journalistic benefits.
>
> The fact is, Wall Street is so short-nosed and so dedicated to maximizing return on investment to the exclusion of almost everything else, you're going to have situations where, basically, you have a lot of public shareholders who have interests that are inimical to good journalism.[20]

Ahren's warns that the impact of the shift will be complex.

> But lest a generation of newspaper journalists – who have watched corporate parents slash costs through layoffs, budget cuts, bureau closings and the like – gets dewy-eyed over the prospect of local, private ownership, Singleton warned: I don't think there's a lot of difference between performing well to please your shareholders or performing well to please your bankers.[21]

The theme is clear. Consolidation and conglomeration bring sharp reductions in staff but fail to produce economic benefits. This opens the door for smaller chains and those dedicated to print journalism to move the industry in a different direction, a vision they are backing up by purchasing assets at healthy prices. The bottom line for the Knight Ridder-McClatchy deal is striking. McClatchy bought Knight Ridder for 9.5 times cash flow and sold a dozen papers, considered to be the least attractive properties from McClatchy's point of view for 11 times cash flow to more than half a dozen owners.

LOCAL TELEVISION

The television sector exhibits a set of characteristics that parallel the developments in the newspaper business to a remarkable degree. The range of prices for newspapers given above suggests a healthy economic situation while the local broadcast market is in even better shape. As an article in *Editor and Publisher* quoting Tom Buono of BIA Financial Network noted just prior to the release of the proposed ownership rules in May 2003, "The reality

---

[19] Id.
[20] Ahrens, 2006, p. D3.
[21] Id.

is, broadcasting in general is selling for a few multiples [of cash flow] higher than newspapers... If newspapers are going for multiples of 8 to 12, it's more like 10 to 14 for TV, and radio is even higher."[22]

At exactly the time that McClatchy's purchase and resale of the Knight Ridder papers caught the attention of the newspaper trade press, a similar series of events startled the TV market. In an article headlined "Nice Price," *Broadcasting and Cable* recounted a series of TV station sales:

> One media investment banker pegs the $987 million Liberty Corp. sale at 13 times cash flow. Emmis has cut four deals totalling $659 million for stations at 13-16 times annual cash flow...

> And the high-priced deals were generally not troubled situations where the buyer was betting on a significant turnaround.[23]

> Underlying these high prices is a highly profitable business.

> So how do buyers justify their high prices? The first attraction is that stations generate lots of cash flow, with margins often hitting 40%-50% (By comparison, strong newspapers generate 20% margins). Those earnings are relatively predictable, so lenders allow high leverage. That helps enhance return on investment.

Drama was not lacking in the TV sector. While the drama was playing out in the boardroom of the Tribune Company, Univision, the number one Spanish language broadcaster and the fifth largest broadcast network in the U.S., was up for sale by its private owners. The owners had set a high target price and only two groups of bidders came forward, one of which had trouble holding its team together, which garnered headlines. In the end, the price settled at a very handsome $12 billion.

> At $11 billion or $36 a share, Univision is not getting the $40 a share it had originally signaled that it was hoping for when it put itself up for sale in February. But the price remains one of the highest multiples paid for a media company in recent memory.[24]

> Univision yesterday confirmed its planned sale to a consortium of private-equity investors who will pay $12.3 billion and assume $1.4 billion in debt.[25]

The basic profitability analysis and the challenges noted for newspapers are similar in the local TV business. The Project on Excellence in Journalism describes local TV broadcasting as follows: "The industry is still

---

[22] Fitzgerald, Mark and Todd Shields. "After June 2, Papers May Make Broadcast News." *Editor and Publisher*, 27 May 2003, p. 4.

[23] Higgins, 2006, p. 6.

[24] Sorkin, Andrew Ross. "Univision Considering Better Bid." *New York Times*, 27 June 2006, p. C11.

[25] Jordan, Miriam, Dennis K. Berman and John Lyons. "Investor Group Snags Univision: Televisa Fumes." *Wall Street Journal*, 28 June 2006, p. B1.

enormously profitable. Pre-tax profit margins of 40% to 50% are not uncommon."[26] A recent article in the *Wall Street Journal* noted that "it is still not unusual for a big-city station to have profit margins of more than 40%. Even stations in mid-size markets can achieve margins that exceed 30%." [27] In fact, small market prices were strong. For example, Disney CEO Bob Iger, when asked about beefing up its small station group, responded, "Every time we've looked at potential acquisitions in that space, we felt that the prices being paid were just a little bit too high."[28] The strong value of these TV properties was affirmed when Media General sold four properties in mid-sized markets for an average of 15 times cash flow.[29]

The *Wall Street Journal* does note that "Local Stations Struggle to Adapt as Web Grabs Viewers."[30] The trigger to the challenge is largely a failure of national networks not local stations. It is a combination of cable and satellite fragmenting the big national audiences, national networks failing to produce hits that attract eyeballs, and advertisers moving online. The successful response, suggested by the case study of WOOD in Grand Rapids Michigan, involves the same elements suggested by the newspaper business – a focus on journalism and the development of effective online models.[31]

Interestingly, although advertising revenues at local stations are down, the production and distribution of local news remains an extremely profitable undertaking. The claim that entertainment had to save the news, which was the mantra in the past media ownership proceeding, has been turned on its head. News is now leading entertainment as a profit center for local TV stations.

Developing online news distribution channels that generate revenue appears to be the way to go. As the Wall *Street Journal* noted: "News represents 50% of income at WOOD, which is typical in the industry. (Local prime-time ad sales make up another 40%, with daytime sales accounting for the balance)." "Most important, according to Ms. Kniowski, has been a shift in emphasis from feature-type stories to harder news. The station has largely abandoned what she calls "touchy feely" stories – such as local firefighters saving a cute kitten from a rooftop."[32]

---

[26] Project on Excellence in Journalism. 2006. "Local TV." *The State of the News Media: 2005*, p. 1.

[27] Barnes, Brooks. "Local TV Stations Struggle to Adapt as Web Grabs Viewers, Revenue." *Wall Street Journal*, 12 June 2006, p. A11.

[28] Higgins, 2006, p. 6.

[29] Romano, Allison. "Media General Wraps Sales." *Broadcasting and Cable*, 1 August 2006. The markets rank an average of 105 in a total 210 Designated Market Areas.

[30] Barnes, 2006, p. A11.

[31] Id.

[32] Id.

The attractiveness of local news has penetrated through the industry, with expanding coverage. "News is typically good business. Unlike syndication, where stations often split ad time with the distributor, affiliates keep all the ad time in news. And some advertisers, such as political campaigns, are most interested in buying time during the news."[33]

Paralleling the Tribune's difficulty making cross-media conglomeration pay off are Sinclair's troubles with centralized, chain TV news.

> Four years ago, Sinclair Broadcasting Group launched a highly controversial centralized news operation that it said would allow its stations to affordably broadcast local news. Today, the station owner is giving the experiment a vote of no confidence, shutting down half a dozen newscasts at various stations and overhauling its News Central service.[34]

Sinclair's problem was simple: TV news is local and "using centralized news, critics say, stripped stations of their localism...Too much of the news came from a place where none of the viewers lived... Viewers were told these were local newscasts, but it did not pass the small test."[35] Ironically, "Sinclair says it will continue to supply its stations with its controversial editorials, called *The Point*..." The segments have been another flashpoint in local markets, derided by media activists as ultra-conservative and not reflective of local issues and sensibilities. "We will continue to provide a point of view... It's very important to our company." [36]

While local stations have discovered that sticking to the news business is good business, the national networks seem to be heading in a different direction – "to adopt the formula that worked so well in prime time: not too many negative stories, with attractive people delivering the news in a more compelling way." [37] This raises concerns among some, who see the TV news business better supported by focusing on the news.

> But if their news operations push the entertainment element too far, they will chase away a blue-chip audience that values substance more than style. While the audience for the evening news cast is aging and declining in size, it's still substantial, and the shows all generate tens of million in revenues....

---

[33] Romano, Allison. "Late News Get Earlier." *Broadcasting and Cable,* 12 June 2006.

[34] Romano, Allison. "Sinclair Rethinks News Mission." *Broadcasting and Cable,* 20 March 2005, p. 16.

[35] Id.

[36] Id.

[37] Robins, J. Max. "News Investment Pays Off." *Broadcasting and Cable,* 12 September 2005, p. 8.

The takeaway from all this: Successful news organizations know clearly who they are and what their mission is – and they execute it, especially when it matters most.[38]

THE BOTTOM LINE

Thus, in both the TV and newspaper sectors, companies "generally continue to enjoy fat, if flat profit margins."[39]   Exhibit 1 summarizes the financial numbers that have been cited in recent press accounts of acquisitions.

Exhibit 1: Financial Ratios in the Major Mass Media

	Cash Flow Multiples in Recent M&A Activity	Stock Market Prices as a Cash Flow Multiple
Newspapers	9.5 to 14	7.9
Local TV Stations	10.6 to 16.1	7 to 8
Cable Systems	9.4 to 11.1	8.5

Sources: Levingston, Steven and Terence O'Hara. "McClatchy's Paper Chase: Family Owned Chain to by Knight, Plans to Sell off 12 Dailies." Washington Post, 14 March 2006, p. D1.

While there is some consternation in the trade press over the divergence between the cash flow multiples paid in mergers and acquisitions and the cash flow multiples implicit in stock price, this appears to be a routine feature of the market for these types of assets.   Consider the following discussion from an extremely popular text, Harold Vogel's *Entertainment Industry Economics*, dealing with the economics of these industries.   Taken together, these articles give a comprehensive picture of the media markets.

> We can approximate the value of a broadcast (and similarly… a cable) property in the following manner: Assign a multiple of cash flow, say in the range of eight to twelve times, a higher or lower figure depending on prevailing interest rates and similar recent transaction prices. Then subtract from the product of the assumed multiple times the cash flow an amount representing "net debt…"   To then arrive at a per share estimate, divide the resulting difference by the number of shares outstanding…Such calculations focus attention on the difference in the value of broadcast and cable properties as measured by the going multiple of cash flow (i.e., the so-called private market value) and the value of the underlying publicly traded shares. A wide divergence will, of course, enhance takeover prospects.

---

[38] Id.
[39] Levingston and O'Hara, 2006, p. D1.

Just as in broadcasting properties, however, private market values, which include an implicit control premium, are normally much higher than are seen in public market trading of shares...

Publishing companies, like those in other media-related industries, are valued primarily on comparisons of cash-flow generation capabilities.   As in broadcasting or cable, a multiple of projected cash-flow... is determined by taking into consideration the multiples of similar, recently traded properties...

The value thus derived would then (as described for cable...) be further adjusted for net debt and for the estimated worth of off balance sheet items to arrive at the private market value of the property. This is the price that a rational investor might pay to take control of the property and its cash flows. But, in addition, this price estimate may also be used as a basis for measuring the relative investment attractiveness of publicly traded shares, which normally sell at a significant discount to the private market value estimate.a/

a/ Discounts to private value might be as much as 40%, and EBDITA multiples will, in publishing, typically range from six to ten times projections – with the long run historical average ratio of total market value to EBITDA for newspaper publishers at approximately 8.2.[40]

These quotes capture all of the key elements in the financial terrain of the newspaper and TV (as well as the cable) markets described in the trade press in recent months. The multiples observed are in the higher range of those used, as demonstrated by Vogel. The discounts of publicly traded stocks to private market valuations are at the levels identified.   In short, these media properties are profitable properties that command "nice prices" when they are sold.

THE REVENUE CHALLENGE

"Fat but flat" is not enough for the analysts.   So, they ask the television business, 'Where does earnings growth come from?" insisting that four revenue streams are necessary.   In addition to advertising, there are retransmission consent, digital channels and the Internet.[41]

In the newspaper business, "The central economic question in journalism continues to be how long it will take online journalism to become a major economic engine, and if it will ever be as big as print or television."[42] The attention is now focused on Internet distribution of content produced in the newsrooms of the traditional media.

---

[40] Vogel, Harold. *Entertainment Industry Economics: A Guide for Financial Analysis, 6th Edition.* Cambridge: Cambridge University Press, 2004, pp. 252...285...324...327.
[41] Higgins, 2006, p. 6.
[42] PEJ, 2006, Overview, p. 4.

Finally, newspapers are starting to see the Internet as central to their future. In 2005, newspaper Internet advertising revenue topped $2 billion for the first time, a 31 percent increase over 2004....

Although "convergence" across newspapers, TV and radio has been a cherished industry buzzword for years, the portfolio approach focuses primarily on the Internet and print rather than on traditional radio and television... Federal Communications Commission rules bar newspapers from owning broadcast stations in the same market... and even if they could, TV and radio face the same competitive pressures and declining audiences that newspapers do. Instead, many newspapers are enthusiastically adding new audio and video options to their web sites, from newscasts to stories to commentary.[43]

Ms. Kniowski is going after classified clients of the areas dominant newspaper, the Grand Rapids Press, which is owned by Advance Publications Inc. "We've got to figure out how to take money away from them," she says. With the emergence of low-cost digital video, she hopes the station's Web site might someday sell video ads for something as mundane as pedigreed puppies.

"That ad in their newspaper or on their Web site? That should be video and it should be bought from us."[44]

Exhibit 2 shows a recent estimate of online advertising revenues, growing at over 30 percent per year. In the battle between newspapers and TV stations, newspapers have gotten out to a huge lead. Expectations are for these numbers to continue to grow at very high rates.

While convergence of offline and online distribution of content receives a great deal of attention, cross-ownership of traditional TV and newspaper properties has receded. Even in 2003, as the lifting of the ban loomed, two fundamental concerns were being raised, which presaged the developments of recent months – the economic performance of converged properties was not stellar and the core competences of the media are quite different.

Perhaps the biggest impediment, however, is the perception that the results that grand fathered newspapers are getting from broadcast convergence have so far been, if not a bust, then underwhelming.[45]

Newspapers are fundamentally about news while radio makes money "by playing music, which has nothing to do with the business of the newspaper."[46]

---

[43] Smolkin, Rachel. 2006. "Adapt or Die." *American Journalism Review* June/July, p. 2.
[44] Barnes, 2006, p. A11.
[45] Fitzgerald and Moses, 2003, pp. 11, 17.
[46] Moses, Lucia. "Radio Reception May Be Fading." *Editor and Publisher*, 23 June 2003, p. 12.

Exhibit 2: Online Advertising Revenue

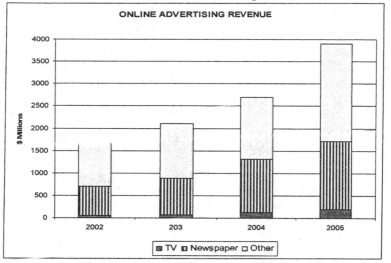

Source: Romano, Allison. "Bring it Online." Broadcasting and Cable, 12 December 2005, p. 9, citing Bollen & Associates.

Moreover, some fear development of "a kind of 'cross-ownership compulsion' that pressures pure-play newspaper companies to get into broadcast convergence, whether they want to or not."[47] How this pressure would play out, is uncertain.   Some who have experience with cross-ownership, such as Gil Thelen, publisher of the *Tampa Tribune*, suggest "if there is pressure it will be on non-converged media that will find it harder to retain employees who want to learn multimedia." Ultimately, a fundamental problem arises because in many of these markets there is only one newspaper. The result can be a very distorted market. "More often, the obstacle is that the major newspaper is aligned with a rival TV affiliate."[48]   In short, the economic gain of complementaries is uncertain, at best, while the public policy costs are clear.

ACADEMIC RESEARCH CONFIRMS THE REALITY

While the realization that huge conglomerates may not be the answer has recently burst into the popular press, the academic press has long charted the two elements that seem to be roiling the media industries.

---

[47] Fitzgerald, Mark and Lucia Moses. "At the Crossroads." *Editor and Publisher*, 23 June 2003, p. 11.
[48] Romano, Allison. "Newspapers and Stations try Cross-Pollination." *Broadcasting and Cable*, 25 July 2005, p. 16.

On the one hand, the failure of conglomerates to generate positive results was noted in a broad comparison of various types of cross media mergers under the title "Mergers and Acquisitions in the Media Industries: Were Failures Really Unforeseeable?"

> Over the last two decades, mergers and acquisitions (M&A) have become the most preferred strategic tool of firms in the media industry. As still claimed by analysts and managers, M&A deals are expected to generate economic efficiency, especially through size effects (economies of scale and scope and other synergies). However, it seems that the hopes placed in these synergies are generally disappointed. Indeed, among a sample of 11 media firms for fiscal years 1998 and 1999, it appears a firm's size and a simultaneous presence in many businesses of the media industries do not improve economic performance, nor does the possession of complementary assets. The existence of economies of scale and scope, or at least the ability of firms to implement them, has still to be proved.[49]

A half a dozen years later, the benefits of consolidation and conglomeration remain unproven. Stockholders seeking short term gains have run out of patience, triggering turmoil in the industry.

On the other hand, the unique type of profitability that typifies the newspaper business has been noted in the academic literature as well. As a recent study titled "Ownership Structure of Publicly Traded Newspaper Companies and Their Financial Performance" concluded

> There are characteristics of the newspaper industry that may make it more appealing to these relatively passive institutional investors. In general, the financial performance of newspapers is less volatile than is true of many other industries. Profit margins are high, and the ability to ride out economic downturns is good. Investment in the newspaper product itself has resulted in solid long-term revenue growth, which may serve to reduce pressures of short-term results regardless of the type of investors in the firm.[50]

Questions about the investor style and the complexity of motives have also been identified in the academic literature. Whether or not one thinks that "Wall Street Made Me Do It,"[51] as one article put it, there would

---

[49] Peltier, Stephanie, "Mergers and Acquisitions in the Media Industries: Were Failures Predictable," *Journal of Media Economics*, 17(4), 2004, p. 261.

[50] An, Soontae, Hyun Seung Jin and Todd Simon. 2006. Ownership Structure of Public Traded Newspaper Companies and Their Financial Performance. *Journal of Media Economics* 19:2: 131, citing Soloski, John. "Taking Stock Redux: Corporate Ownership and Journalism of Publicly Traded Newspaper Companies." In Robert Picard (eds.), *Corporate Governance of Media Companies* Jonkoping, Sweden: Jonkoping International Business Press, 2005.

[51] Maguire, Miles. 2003. "Wall Street Made Me Do It: A Preliminary Analysis of the Major Institutional Investors in U.S. Newspaper Companies." *Journal of Media Economics* 16:4.

appear to be opportunities to match investors and journalistic values, as McClatchy seems to have done.

> Furthermore, it appears that it may be possible to identify institutional investors who have longer time horizons than others, suggesting it is possible for newspaper companies to attempt to modify their shareholder base in a way that would allow more room for maneuver in pursuing a public service agenda. At the same time, however, newspaper companies should be mindful that a stated objective of long-term investing does not necessarily signify that an institutional investor will adopt a hands-off approach or be willing to subordinate financial objectives to journalistic ones.[52]

The Knight Ridder chain "modified its shareholder base," while the debate at the Tribune Company is about a similarly radical change. Indeed, there are apparently numerous individuals and groups that are "Yearning to Put Papers Back in Local Hands."[53]

The academic literature not only supports the notion of the profitability of the newspaper business, it also finds that investment in the newsroom increases circulation[54] and profits[55] in part by improving the quality of journalism.[56]

> These data indicate that newsroom investment would have been good business for these 1450 dailies. Newspaper managers who continue to cut newsroom investment to preserve higher profits might indeed be eating their seed corn... If the results of this study were found to be applicable to the newspaper industry, the failure to invest in the newsroom could be a form of slow-motion suicide, where a company's disinvestment gradually alienates core readers and reduces the attractiveness of newspapers as advertising outlets. This scenario would explain studies that indicate Thomson newspapers ran themselves out

---

[52] Id., p. 262

[53] Holson, Laura M. "Yearning to Put Papers Back in Local Hands: In Several Cities, a Push for Dailies Free of Absentee Corporate Owners." *New York Times,* 1 July 2006, p. B1.

[54] Choo, Sooyoung, Esther Thorson and Stephen Lacy. 2004. The Relationship Between Newspaper Newsroom Investment and Circulation: A study of 27 'Quality' Dailies. *Newspaper Research Journal* 25, Fall; St. Cyr, Charles, Stephen Lacy and Susana Guzman-Ortega. 2005. Circulation Increases Follow Investment in Newsrooms. *Newspaper Research Journal* 26, Fall.

[55] Rosensteil, Tom and Amy Mitchell. 2004. The Impact of Investing in Newsroom Resources. *Newspaper Research Journal* 25, Winter.

[56] Moses, Lucia. "Profiting From Experience." *Editor and Publisher,* 3 February 2003. Meyer, Philip. 2004. "The Influence Model and Newspaper Business." *Newspaper Research Journal* 25, Winter; Overholser, Geneva. 2004. "Good Journalism and Business: An Industry Perspective." *Newspaper Research Journal* 25, Winter.

of business and that public newspapers tend to draw more weekly competition.[57]

The literature also suggests a strong conclusion about competition. Competition drives investment, improves quality and lowers costs.

Economic theory and research provide evidence that intense competition among newspapers will result in increased newsroom budgets, changes in content and decreases in advertising cost per thousand... It appears that competition helps newspapers in the long run. The response to competitors helps to maintain content quality and keep prices down."[58]

Moreover, although Dean Singleton surmises that there is little difference in the behavior of privately and publicly held newspapers, the academic literature suggests otherwise. Privately held papers invest more in quality to achieve higher circulation.

Research indicates that privately owned dailies are likely to spend more on their newsrooms than are publicly held dailies with large profit margins. This results from the need for high-profit publicly held companies to produce high short-run profit margins that satisfy the demands of the stock market. This higher spending suggests that privately owned dailies are more likely to have higher quality than high profit public papers, which helps to keep more readers satisfied and reduces the likelihood that readers will turn to weeklies to get their news.[59]

Given recent developments in the industry and the long standing academic research on investment, competition and quality, we would not expect to see research results that show significant benefits to journalism from cross-media ownership. In fact, the literature is all over the map, reflecting the uncertainties about cross-media operations.

First, much analysis confuses multimedia journalism, the effort to distribute stories on more than one medium; conglomeration, the merger of two traditional media types such as TV and newspapers; and coordinated

---

[57] Chen, Rene, Esther Thorson and Stephen Lacy. 2005. The Impact of Newsroom Investment on Newspaper Revenues and Profits: Small and Medium Newspapers, 1998-2002. *Journalism and Mass Communications Quarterly* 82:3: Autumn, p. 627. The reference to Morton is Morton, John, "When Newspapers Eat their Seed Corn," *American Journalism Review*, November 1995. The reference to Thomson is Lacy, Stephan and Hugh J. Martin. 1998. Profits Up, Circulation Down for Thomson Papers in the 80s. *Newspaper Research Journal* 19, Fall. The reference to inviting competition is Lacy, Stephen, David C. Coulson and Hugh J. Martin. 2004. Ownership Barriers to Entry in Non-metropolitan Daily Newspaper Markets. *Journalism & Mass Communications Quarterly* 81, Summer.

[58] Lacy Stephen and Hugh J. Martin. 2004. Competition, Circulation and Advertising. *Newspaper Research Journal* 25, Winter, pp. 32-33.

[59] Lacy, Coulson, Martin, 2004, p. 332.

joint production of news for distribution across media outlets of various types. Definitions are all over the map, too.[60]

Second, much of the research is qualitative, focusing on how journalists and editors feel about convergence,[61] rather than measuring what it actually does to or for the production of news.

Third, partnerships have not advanced very far[62] or yielded clear benefits in terms of either financial improvement[63] or journalism quality.[64] Two trends that are clear are that cross promotion takes up a significant amount of air time and television seems to be the larger beneficiary.

THE CONTINUING SOAP OPERA AT THE TRIBUNE COMPANY

The drama surrounding the Tribune Company has not reached its conclusion, but the soap opera offers lessons.

The newspaper business is a profitable business. "Across the industry, profits are actually better than the bad headlines suggest."[65] Even the *Los Angeles Times*, the focal point of mush of the drama at the Tribune Company "enjoys a profit margin of about 20%, lower than that of its parent's flagship Chicago Tribune, but higher than many metro papers."[66] To put this in perspective, the Scripps Newspapers "cash-flow margins – 28.9 percent in the second quarter – were among the highest in the industry."[67]

---

[60] Gordon, Richard. "Convergence Defined." *USC Annenberg Online Journalism Review* posted 13 Nov. 2003; Dailey, Larry, Lori Demo and Mary Spillman. 2005. Most TV/Newspapers Partners At Cross-Promotion Stage. *Newspaper Research Journal* 26, Fall; Dueze, Mark. 2004. "What is Multimedia Journalism." *Journalism Studies* 3:2.

[61] Lowrey, Wilson. 2005. "Commitment to Newspaper-TV Partnering: A Test of the Impact of Institutional Isomorphism." *Journalism and Mass Communications Quarterly* 82: Autumn; Dupagne, Michel and Bruce Garrison. 2006. The Meaning and Influence of Convergence: A Qualitative Case Study of Newsroom Work at the Tampa News Center. *Journalism Studies* 7:2. Singer, Jane B. 2004. "Strange Bedfellows: The Diffusion of Convergence in Four News Organizations." *Journalism Studies* 5:1.

[62] Dailey, Larry, Lori Demo and Mary Spillman, "Most TV/Newspapers Partners At Cross-Promotion Stage," *Newspaper Research Journal,* 26: Fall, 2005.

[63] Glasser, Mark, "Business Side of Convergence Has Myths, Some Real Benefits," *USC Annenberg Online Journalism Review,* May 19, 2005.

[64] Ketterer, Stan, Tom Weir, J. Stevens Smethers and James Back, "Case Study Shows Limited Benefits of Convergence," *Newspaper Research Journal,* 25: Summer, 2004; "Partnerships and Public Service: Normative Issues for Journalists in Converged Newsrooms," *Journal of Mass Media Ethics,* 21:1, 2006.

[65] Siklos, Richard. 2005. "How Did Newspapers Land in This Mess?" *New York Times,* October 1, p. BU4.

[66] Ellison, Sara. 2006. "Tribune Faces Pressure to Sell Los Angeles Paper," *Wall Street Journal,* September 18, p. A10.

[67] Fabrikant, Gerldine. 2006. "Successful Scripps Seeks Next Food Network," *New York Times,* August 14, 2006, p. C3.

The public and private valuations of the newspaper assets differ sharply, as has frequently been the case in the industry. As one major investor in the Tribune put it "the fact that the value of the assets exceeds the current stock price is indisputable."[68]

There are many who believe that eating your seed corn by cutting staff is not the way to proceed. The Chandler's had raised this point in their initial call for a break up of the company. In an open letter to the board, the family invoked the tradition of the newspaper and said further cost cuts would damage its quality."[69] The editor and the publisher of the Tribune took this position in resisting the demand from corporate headquarters to make more cuts at the *Los Angeles Times*. Their sentiment was expressed in an article that reported on a letter from civic leaders.

> The Los Angeles Times quoted Mr. Baquet [the Editor of the paper] on the possibility of making further job cuts. "I am not averse to making further job cuts," he told the paper. "But you can go too far, and I don't plan to do that. I just have a difference of opinion with the owners Tribune about what the size of the staff should be. To make substantial reductions would significantly damage the quality of the paper."
>
> For an editor to public defy management over budget cuts isn't unheard of. More remarkable was that Mr. Baquet's publisher, Mr. Johnson, joined him in resisting the push for cuts. The article quoted Mr. Johnson saying he agreed with Mr. Baquet that "newspapers can't cut their way into the future. We have to carefully balance economic reality with serving our readers."[70]

The idea was expressed by others as well. "An Editor at the paper said the article was prompted by a letter on Tuesday from 20 civic leaders, who called on Tribune to put more money into the paper or consider selling it".[71] The publisher was ultimately forced to resign, although the editor stayed on.[72]

The civic leaders point to the important local role of the newspaper as their motivation for writing.

> "People don't like policy issues here," said Brendan Huffman, president of the Valley Industry and Commerce Association. "But the fact is that we are the

---

[68] Seelye, Katherine Q. and Jennifer Steinhaur. 2006. "At Los Angeles Times, A Civil Executive Rebellion," *The New York Times*, September 21, p. C12.

[69] Id., p. A10.

[70] Id., p. A10.

[71] Seelye, Katherine Q. 2006. "Los Angeles times Editor Openly Defies Owner's Call for Job Cuts," *New York Times*, September 15, p. C3.

[72] Kurtz, Howard, 2006, "Tribune Co. Ousts Publisher at L.A. Times: Jeffrey Johnson Had Fought Budget Cuts," *Washington Post*, October 6.

world's 17th largest economy and it is very important to cover these stories and educate the population."[73]

There were a number of people and groups who stepped forward with offers to buy the paper, affirming the interest in stand alone newspaper businesses.

While those who seek to buy the paper outright agree with the business leaders about the paper's coverage, they see themselves as the solution. The potential buyers include three billionaires: David Geffen, the music mogul, Eli Board, the philanthropist, and Ronald Burkle, the supermarket tycoon.[74]

Interestingly, there are both commercial and non-commercial models on the table, all of which emphasize that "the paper needs to be locally owned."[75]

Obviously, conglomeration is no panacea for the newspaper business. In fact, the challenge repeatedly identified in the analysis of the Tribune situation is the Internet. "But revenue growth is difficult to come by amid a bumpy transition to the Internet, where there are myriad rivals for information and advertising that were once chiefly the purview of print newspapers."[76]

For nearly a century, newspapers were unrivaled in their ability to deliver news and advertising. News staffs grew fat as hiring decision were made on coverage needs rather than bottom lines.

Now, as newspapers lose readers and advertising to other media and struggle to transition to Internet and other digital forms of delivery, while attempting to maintain profit margins of more than 20 percent and mollify Wall Street's need for growth, cuts in jobs and newsroom budgets are coming fast and deep.[77]

The "bumpy transition" to the Internet is different at different newspapers (see Exhibit 3). Studies 7 and 8 show that people who go online visit the web sites of traditional sources. Efforts to measure online newspaper readership are blossoming and the results are most interesting from the point of view of the troubled chains (Knight Ridder and Tribune) identified in this analysis. Scarborough Research analyzed online readership in the top 25 markets. The 26 dailies in those markets account for around four-fifths of the average circulation of all dailies in America. The study includes the flagship papers

---

[73] Seelye, Katherine Q. and Jennifer Steinhaur. 2006. "At Los Angeles Times, A Civil Executive Rebellion," *The New York Times*, September 21, p. C12.
[74] Id., p. C12.
[75] Id., p. C12.
[76] Siklos, 2005, p. BU4.
[77] Ahrens, Frank. "Tribune Empire Could Crumble." *Washington Post*, 26 September 2006, p. D5.

of the two troubled chains. It also includes the largest cross-owned papers in the country.

On average, the online readership (exclusive and duplicative) equals 20 percent of the total readership of the paper. In other words, for every four subscribers to the physical paper, there is one online reader. The flagship papers of the troubled chains are all below the average. The Los Angeles Times ranks dead last. If the L.A. Times were performing as well online as the two leaders (the Cleveland Plain Dealer and the Tampa Tribune) it would have 750,000 more online readers. Even at the national average, it would have over a quarter of a million more online readers.

That cross-ownership is no panacea for the Internet problem is also clear in these estimates. On average, the cross-owned papers in these markets are not performing as well as the other papers. While there are a couple papers among the leaders, more are at the bottom of the list.

CONCLUSION

Given the failure of conglomeration/consolidation and the shift in focus to the Internet, Frank Ahrens writes that "As FCC Digs Into Ownership, Big Media No Longer Cares,"

> Since 2003, the media giants have greatly expanded their presence on the Internet, buying successful web sites or redoubling their own efforts. The continued roll out of high-speed Internet, the improvement in online content and an explosion of handheld devices have combined to give Big Media much greater reach and potentially greater influence than it would have had, were companies allowed to buy a few more television stations each.[78]

But, if Big Media no longer cares, should public policy? The answer is an emphatic Yes. For the first time in a generation, the prospect of increasing competition in local news is real; allowing cross-ownership mergers would invariably stifle and mute that competition. The typical media market in America (the middle decile for example) has one dominant newspaper with a market share of about two-thirds of the market. The leading TV station has a market share close to one-third of the TV market. A merger between the two creates a dominant media first that overshadows any other rivals in the market. Moreover, the local news websites to which individuals go for local news and information are overwhelmingly the sites of the local newspapers and the local TV stations.[79] A merger between the two would extend the concentration of local sources to the Internet.

---

[78] Ahrens, Frank. "As FCC Digs Into Ownership, Big Media No Longer Cares." *Washington Post*, 29 June 2006, D1.
[79] Pew Internet and American Life Project. 2005. RDD Tracking Study, Nov/Dec.

Exhibit 3: Internet Performance of Major Newspapers

Paper	Circulation	Online Readers			Percent of Total Readers			Cross-Owned	Troubled Chain
		Unique	Duplicate	Total	Unique	Duplicate	Total		
Cleveland Plain Dealer	1,297,880	449,958	165,892	615,850	23.5	8.7	32.2		
Tampa Tribune	749,087	162,747	192,069	354,816	14.7	17.4	32.1	Y	
New York Times	3,060,475	366,540	981,043	1,347,583	8.3	22.3	30.6		
Boston Globe	1,541,869	197,453	469,175	666,628	8.9	21.2	30.2		
Washington Post	2,174,630	140,521	778,502	919,023	4.5	25.2	29.7		
Atlanta Constitution	1,647,410	224,484	428,687	653,171	9.8	18.6	28.4	Y	
San Diego Union-Trib.	1,078,469	80,882	260,447	341,329	5.7	18	24		
Arizona Republic	1,485,880	119,501	324,920	444,421	6.2	16.8	23		
San Francisco Chronicle	1,513,263	147,692	297,111	444,803	7.5	15.2	22.7		
Seattle Times	1,225,545	114,814	236,077	350,891	7.3	15	22.3		
Sacramento Bee	966,296	42,508	204,399	246,907	3.5	16.8	20.4		
Star Tribune	1,605,472	85,929	303,891	389,820	4.3	15.2	19.5		
Houston Chronicle	1,897,254	100,408	282,312	382,720	4.4	12.4	16.8		
Orlando Sentinel	1,053,952	46,920	164,069	210,989	3.7	13	16.7		
Baltimore Sun	1,064,219	45,138	157,881	203,019	3.6	12.5	16		Y
Oregonian	1,137,490	38,696	176,242	214,938	2.9	13	15.9		
Chicago Tribune	2,820,701	135,070	397,766	532,836	4	11.9	15.9	Y	Y
Detroit News	1,858,169	99,212	247,274	346,486	4.5	11.2	15.7		
Pittsburgh Post	943,544	28,826	143,248	172,074	2.6	12.8	15.4		
St. Louis Post Dispatch	1,255,472	62,615	163,358	225,973	4.2	11	15.3		
Miami Herald	1,162,424	45,320	162,522	207,842	3.3	11.9	15.2	Y	Y
Dallas Morning News	1,798,163	71,730	249,410	321,140	3.4	11.8	15.2	Y	
Philadelphia Enquirer	1,968,063	108,511	196,606	305,117	4.8	8.6	13.4	Y	Y
Denver Post	1,465,403	39,911	180,385	220,296	2.4	10.7	13.1		
St. Petersburg Times	1,016,950	40,309	101,911	142,220	3.5	8.8	12.3		
Los Angeles Times	4,257,507	163,941	429,786	593,727	3.4	8.6	12.3	Y	Y
Total	42,045,584	3,159,636	7,694,983	10,854,619	6	14.5	20.5		
Non-Cross-Owned	28,124,412	2,236,843	5,509,823	7,746,666	6.2	15.4	21.6		
Cross-owned	13,921,172	922,793	2,185,160	3,107,953	5.4	12.8	18.3		
Troubled Chains	11,272,914	497,980	1,344,561	1,842,541	3.8	10.3	14		

Source: Scarborough Research, A New Story Lead for the Newspaper Industry, August 2006.

The most interesting development flowing from digital convergence has been an outbreak of competition in local news markets between newspapers and television stations.   Although both television and newspapers produce news, the form and format of production and the manner in which they are consumed are so different that they are not generally seen as competing products, either by antitrust authorities or by consumers.   The cross elasticity of demand is low.[1] With both sets of entities now targeting online distribution as a growth area, they may lock horns in a manner they have not in the past.

For now the power of a hometown newspaper's brand is a big draw online.   "The newspapers have a little leg up, but we are extremely competitive," says Rich Harris, executive VP/general Manager of digital media and strategic marketing for NBC Universal's TV-station group."[2]

The failure of conglomeration to produce results, the shift toward private ownership and smaller newspaper chains, and the growing focus on online distribution challenge the notion that newspaper-TV cross-ownership is necessary to save either industry from economic ruin.   In light of this, the policy that prefers a larger number of owners, in general, and the independence of the two most important sources of local news and information, in particular, cannot be said to impose a burden on either industry.

More importantly, the evidence suggests that local newspapers and TV stations are about to come into competition through their Internet web sites in a manner that has not typified the local news market in the past.   It would be utter folly to allow this burgeoning competition to be squelched by cross-media mergers.

Structural rules, like the ban on cross-ownership, are intended to alter behavior, precisely because it constrains the conduct of market participants.   As practiced in antitrust cases and industrial policy, the goal of structural limitations is to promote economic efficiency.   In the case of the cross ownership ban, the goal is to promote a more diverse forum for democratic discourse and to promote localism in the media.   What this analysis shows is that the economic costs of achieving this goal through a ban on cross-ownership are small, if any at all, while the benefits in promoting diversity and competition are large.

---

[1] Cooper, Mark N. *Media Ownership and Democracy in the Digital Information Age*.   Palo Alto: Center for Internet and Society, 2003, pp. 124-126.

[2] Romano, Allison. "Bring it Online." Broadcasting and Cable, 12 December 2005, p. 8.

STUDY 10
CONCERNS ABOUT PRINT JOURNALISM AND CROSS-OWNERSHIP

MARK COOPER AND STEVE COOPER

THE STRUGGLE OVER THE ESSENCE OF PRINT JOURNALISM

The collapse of the conglomerate model, the tension between Wall Street's and Main Street's concerns, and the public versus private ownership debate underscore a long standing debate over the media in general and newspapers in particular.

> The underlying theme in Tribune's unraveling is that in a time of technological transition, the two publics that are served by many of the nation's newspapers are no longer getting along so well. One is the public market – that is, Wall Street – which cares only about an attractive return on its investment. The other is the so-called public good that newspapers serve by professionally gathering and reporting for their communities.[1]

Some argue that the tensions can be handled, with distant management that appreciates the local roots of the business.

> While journalists measure the success of newspapers by Pulitzer Prizes, investors usually do not. That said, one of the company's 21 newspapers, the Rocky Mountain News, has won four Pulitzer prizes since 2000; the company's papers won five Pulitzers between 1980 and 1999.

> John Temple, the editor and publisher of the Rocky Mountain News and director of content for Scripps's newspapers, said the company supported the role of the local newspaper. "Ken Lowe gives individuals like me the independence and authority to do the right thing," he said. "Our mantra has been to do what is right for our community.[2]

Others suggest that it is a business that requires a different point of view, but to the same effect.

> Mr. Geffen has told friends the paper could be expensive but that he was prepared to pour hundreds of millions of dollars into it. He has said he would buy the paper with his own money and would be happy with a 5 percent return on investment; far below what the Los Angeles Times has said is a 20 percent profit margin now.

---

[1] Siklos, Richard.. "How Did Newspapers Land in This Mess?" *New York Times*, 1 October 2005, p. BU4.
[2] Fabrikant, Geraldine. "Successful Scripps Seeks Next Food Network." *New York Times*, 14 August 2006, p. C3.

Mr. Geffen's principle goal, he has said, is increasing the size of the staff, greatly improving the paper's electronic operations and increasing the coverage of real estate and automobiles, areas of great interest to Angelenos.[3]

While the latter may seem "Quiixotic," there is clearly a theme in the current debate and in the literature that sees this as a way to go. The question becomes how public policy can promote the outcome.

The FCC does not regulate newspapers, but it certainly can consider the impact of newspaper-TV combinations on the overall media environment, which includes newspapers. The cross ownership situations will almost certainly not involve local owners. They will most likely be the largest of the corporate entities, certainly in the newspaper space. This will reinforce or preserve tendencies that have been harmful to democratic discourse. There are also unique impacts that cross-ownership situations have on print journalism.

THE UNIQUE IMPACT OF NEWSPAPER-TELEVISION MERGERS

There is a complex relationship between newspapers and TV. On the supply-side, the antagonism between TV and newspapers is an important element of promoting civic discourse. At the same time, the operation of newspaper newsrooms produces many stories, especially local, that become an input for TV news. Without the much more intensive and in-depth news gathering of papers, the news product space will be reduced. On the demand side, we observe that newspapers and television are complements. Consumers seek in-depth follow-up of the news headlines that they encounter in broadcast. We want to preserve the antagonism and independent resources that newspapers bring.

To the extent that FCC regulation of the media subject to its authority has the consequence of deconcentrating the production of local news and preserving the antagonism between the print and broadcast media, it should do so. An avenue of integration that would be particularly destructive of the journalistic values in our society or destructive of the competitive and symbiotic relationship between newspapers and broadcast that disciplines the broadcast media should be a source of serious concern to the Commission.

Thus the Commission can legitimately enquire into the impact on civic discourse of conglomeration, concentration and integration in each of the media. Several recent books about newspapers paint an extremely troubling picture. Many analysts believe that the health of both American journalism and the newspaper industry will depend on their ability to successfully achieve three things: diluting what has become an increasingly

[3] Seelye, Katherine Q. and Jennifer Steinhaur. 2006. "At Los Angeles Times, A Civil Executive Rebellion." *The New York Times*, 21 September 2006, p. C12.

over-concentrated marketplace; better managing the balance between providing informative, influential news coverage and sustaining a profitable newspaper; and recommitting ourselves to, as Leonard Downie, Jr. and Robert G. Kaiser of *The Washington Post* put it, "independent, aggressive journalism [which] strengthens American democracy, improves the lives of its citizens, checks the abuses of powerful people, supports the weakest members of society," and, ultimately, "connects us all to one another."[4] Put more simply by Bartholomew Sparrow, quoting former journalist Harold Evans, "[T]he challenge before the American media 'is not to stay in business – it is to stay in journalism'."[5] The suggestion here is that the challenge for newspapers that are drawn into cross ownership situations in which democracy has an important stake is to stay in print journalism.

There are three direct ways in which removal of the ban on cross-ownership would affect print journalism. There is also the concern that the pattern of conglomeration and cross-media ownership in the newspaper industry and the potential for a substantial increase in these developments will result in a qualitatively new type of problem: the potential for fundamental, institutional conflicts of interest.

> The flurry of debate over media consolidation masks an equally, if not more disturbing trend: the conflict of interest inherent in diversified cross-ownership of newsgathering institutions by multinational concerns. A media market in which *The Washington Post* and *Newsweek* join in "strategic alliances" with NBC, Microsoft Corp. helps underwrite the salaries of reporters for MSNBC, and America Online helps capitalize CNN expands the potential for conflict of interest far beyond the individual to the institutional level. Indeed, the cross-ownership and content sharing that typifies American mass media today raises legitimate questions about whether journalists working on such far-flung conglomerates can avoid conflicts of interest on the institutional level, and about what such conflicts do to the notion of an independent press...

> Institutional conflict of interest extends the conflict inherent in a commercial press... beyond the immediate concerns of the journalist or even the news organization for which he or she works.[6]

---

[4] Downie Jr., Leonard and Robert G. Kaiser. *The News About the News*. New York: Alfred A. Knopf, 2002, p. 13.
[5] Sparrow, Bartholomew H. *Uncertain Guardians: The News Media as A Political Institution*. Baltimore: Johns Hopkins University Press, 1999, p. 103.
[6] Davis, Charles and Stephanie Craft. 2000. New Media Synergy: Emergence of Institutional Conflict of Interest. *Journal of Mass Media Ethics* 15, pp. 222-223.

PRESSURE FROM CONCENTRATION, VERTICAL INTEGRATION AND CONGLOMERATION ON JOURNALISTIC VALUES

The prospect of mergers between TV stations and newspapers raises concerns about vertical integration conglomeration and horizontal concentration (see Figure III-1).[7] Such a merger is said to be vertical if the news production output of the newspaper operation would become input for the TV distribution activity. It is a conglomerate merger if the new entity spans two separate markets: the print news and the video news market. Both of these changes would have negative effects on the journalistic endeavor of the newspaper.

- The dictates of video delivery would alter the nature of reporting and commitments to investigative journalism.

- The conglomeration in larger enterprises would reduce the journalistic activity to a profit center that is driven by the larger economic goals of the parent.

- Combining the two activities within one entity diminishes the antagonism between print and video media.

The purely horizontal aspect of these mergers also poses a problem. The basic activity of gathering news as an input for distribution is very similar in the print and television media. To the extent large entities control a substantial part of the production of news in an area, these mergers can create market power.

Diminishing Journalistic Values

Consider the contrast between journalistic values and the image presented by Tribune Company executives describing how the Chicago Tribune and Chicago television station WGN, among other media properties, view their business:

> Tribune had a story to tell – and it was just the story Wall Street wanted to hear.
>
> In charts and appendices, they showed a company that owns four newspapers—and 16 TV stations (with shared ownership of two others); four radio stations; three local cable news channels; a lucrative educational book division; a producer and syndicator of TV programming, including Geraldo

---

[7] See Consumers Union, et al. 2002. "Reply Comments of Consumers Union, Consumer Federation of America, Media Access Project and Center For Digital Democracy." *In the Matter of Cross-Ownership of Broadcast Stations and Newspaper Newspaper/Radio Cross-Ownership Waiver Policy*, MM Dockets No. 01-235, 96-197, February 15, 2003.

Rivera's daytime talk show; a partnership in the new WB television network; the Chicago Cubs; and new-media investments worth more than $600 million, including a $10 million investment in Baring Communications Equity Fund, with dozens of Asian offices hunting out media investments.

...There was an internal logic and consistent language to their talk: Tribune, said the four men, was a "content company" with a powerful "brand." Among and between its divisions, there was a "synergy."

...It was a well-scripted, well-rehearsed performance, thorough and thoroughly upbeat. And the word "journalism" was never uttered, once.

...Even apart from TV and new media – at the Tribune papers themselves – the editor in chief rarely presides at the daily page one meeting. The editor's gaze is fixed on the future, on new-zoned sections, multimedia desks, meetings with the business side, focus group research on extending the brand, or opening new beachheads in affluent suburbs. "I am not the editor of a newspaper," says Howard Tyner, 54, whose official resume identifies him as vice president and editor of the Chicago Tribune. "I am the manager of a content company. That's what I do. I don't do newspapers alone. We gather content."[8]

We have seen that the economic synergies are elusive, at best. When the two largest sources of news and information – television and newspaper – come under the same ownership roof, there is special cause for concern about business pressures that could undermine the forum for democratic discourse.

Reducing Antagonism and the Watchdog Role

Except where there is meaningful competition between local newspapers, I believe that lifting the newspaper/broadcast cross-ownership ban would significantly undercut the watchdog role that newspapers play over broadcasters and thereby undermine, particularly in the realm of political speech, Congress' goal of ensuring a vigorous exchange of views.

Industry commenters in FCC proceedings have made an important aspect of the case for us. Their repeated statements that joint ventures are not effective means for capturing economic efficiencies underscore the important role of antagonism. In other words, they claim that independent entities in joint ventures are too difficult to keep in line.

Tash sees advantages to partnering, including the ability for both companies to maintain separate and independent voices.

"Anything you do ends up being in partners' interest rather than being forced through common ownership," Tash says. "If it's common ownership, you might add up the pluses and minuses and decide it's a net-plus, even if it's a net-minus for one partner. In this relationship, it has to be a net plus for both.

---

[8] Auletta, Ken. 1998. "The State of the American Newspaper." *American Journalism Review* June.

Tash admits that partnerships with other media companies can be tricky. "You can't rely on orders from a common owner to work through issues that arise."[9]

It is exactly that antagonism that the forum for civic discourse needs, but would lose with cross-ownership. In Tampa, Florida, Media General, Inc. owns both the *Tampa Tribune* newspaper and WFLA-TV. The decision to co-locate the two media outlets led to a loss of editorial and journalistic integrity even before the actual move:

> Others wonder how the cozy, inbred relationship between the newsrooms might affect their coverage of each other. *Tribune* TV writer Walter Belcher offered a chilling example, saying editors forced him to lay off criticism of WFLA for nearly a year prior to the opening of the News Center [which housed the *Tribune* and WFLA news operations in the same space to facilitate their integration], supposedly to avoid ill will between the staffs. "I told them that maybe I should just stop writing about TV altogether," Belcher says with a laugh. "I eventually went back to [covering WFLA] in February, but I still felt like I had to be careful and explain some things more clearly."[10]

Unfortunately, such chilling of free speech in a newsroom is no laughing matter. Nor is it the only example in which Belcher's coverage of WFLA came under scrutiny from joint management. Belcher's coverage was compromised further when managers at WFLA requested that he not write about speculation that a reporter would be leaving the station to follow her husband, a former WFLA reporter who moved to another station in Alabama.

A. H. Belo Corporation (Belo), owner of the *Dallas Morning News* and WFAA-TV, had a similar experience, with a decision that the *Morning News* should cease any TV criticism in order to stay away from critical reporting about its sister station.

> Then there is a question of how the *Morning News* would cover the station. Because the two share Belo as a parent, the newspaper has often been criticized as being too soft on its sibling. But now that the two were officially partners, the News decided it could no longer cover WFAA objectively. Rather than exclude the one station from its coverage, the *News* halted all TV criticism.[11]

Not only was the *Morning News*'s coverage of WFAA-TV stifled because of the co-ownership, an important media critic for the entire market was also lost. If joint corporate ownership of a newspaper and television station can lead to coverage being dropped to maintain positive internal relations, what other types of coverage could be jettisoned to protect corporate interests?

---

[9] Rabasca, Lisa. 2001. "Benefits, Costs and Convergence." *Presstime* June, p. 3.

[10] Strupp, Joe. "Three Point Play." *Editor and Publisher*, 21 August 2000, p. 23.

[11] Moses, Lucia. "TV or not TV? Few Newspapers are Camera Shy, But Sometimes Two Into One Just Doesn't Go." *Editor and Publisher*, 21 August 2000, p. 22.

Consolidating News Production

The driving force behind the push for cross ownership demonstrates that the supply of news involves the production of a single product. A substantial part of the economies that are sought is driven by a desire to use reporters in both activities, to repurpose or repackage their output. It is the reporter producing copy that is the central activity of both TV and newspaper newsrooms. On the supply side it starts as one product.

Media giants like Gannett Co.,[12] Times Mirror Co., [13] and Hearst[14] that are pushing hard for cross-ownership would find another vehicle to consolidate dailies and weeklies and to slash staffs and pages. Now the TV station would be pulled into this process. In the interest of monopolizing a region or cutting costs, the newspaper goliaths ignore the needs of the local people – intense, focused coverage of local schools, community activities, and community concerns such as crime and local development.

Tampa again provides a case in point. There is no doubt that the economic goal is to combine the production of news. Economic convergence just needs to overcome the cultural and professional differences that characterize the newsrooms. As a key player in the most vigorous effort to create convergence put it "The single greatest challenge we have is to overcome our [work] cultural differences."[15]

Those pushing convergence from the newspaper side are even more adamant about ridding the operation of the journalistic ethic.

"An ongoing concern is how to integrate the entrepreneur into a traditional culture," Thelen [the Tampa Tribune's executive editor and vice chairman] says. "This will be a challenge for the company to adjust to. We want to place a high value on experimental risk taking, rather than on the tried and true journalism story."[16]

Reporters caught in the convergence frenzy clearly bristle under the heavy-handed efforts to merge the media.

---

[12] Roberts, Gene, Thomas Kunkel, and Charles Clayton. "Leaving Readers Behind." In Roberts, Gene, Thomas Kunkel, and Charles Clayton (eds.), *Leaving Readers Behind.* Fayetteville: University of Arkansas Press, 2001, p. 5.

[13] Roberts, Kunkel and Layton, 2001, p. 9; Rowse, Arthur E. *Drive-By Journalism.* Monroe, ME: Common Courage Press, 2000, pp. 24-25.

[14] Bass, Jack. "Newspaper Monopoly" in Gene Roberts, Thomas Kunkel, and Charles Clayton (eds.), *Leaving Readers Behind.* Fayetteville: University of Arkansas Press, 2001, pp. 113, 116.

[15] Tompkins, Al and Aly Colon. "NAB 200: The Convergence Marketplace." *Broadcasting and Cable,* 10 April 2000, p. 48, quoting WFLA News Director Bradley.

[16] Colon, Aly. "The Multimedia Newsroom." *Columbia Journalism Review,* June 2000, p. 26.

But Kathleen Gallagher, a Milwaukee Journal Sentinel investment writer, who often does live 45-second interviews from the newsroom, finds the TV piece "disconcerting." [TV anchors] spend all this time thinking about their product and how they present themselves, and you're interrupting the writing of your story to do [the interview] quickly.[17]

"The last newspaper story I wrote, I wrote on my own time," says veteran WFLA reporter Lance Williams. "But the fun part of it is there are no restrictions on my story. It is hard to write a minute and thirty-second story. But writing for the newspaper is freeing.

"My brain was mush by the end," says Barron, who normally runs WFLA's Sarasota bureau. "There were times when I sat down to write a script for TV and would start putting in attribution like it was a newspaper story."[18]

With a 110,000-daily-circulation lead over the competition, Brown says the Times still beats the Tribune with basic, hard-core journalism. "I think [convergence] creates a serious distraction, potentially, in how they cover the news," he says. "There is a risk of dilution."[19]

However, whatever happens, the Tampa convergence experience raises at least two concerns. If journalists spend time contributing to each other's media, when will they have time to gather the news? And more important, will similar media convergence mean that fewer voices produce the news or perhaps, some voices will be lost.[20]

The problem is not limited to Tampa or Milwaukee. Lewis Friedland outlines several processes that have starved local news reporting of resources and cautions that

To allow further linkages between these two, already powerful movements towards concentration would further damage the already fragile environments of local news.

What would be the almost certain, immediate effect of allowing newspaper-television cross ownership? The most obvious effect would be a constriction of the supply of local news and a concomitant restriction in the supply of local news sources.[21]

While the general impact of triggering a merger trend will have negative impacts on journalistic values, it is important to note that there are ways in which combinations pose special threats to the preservation of journalistic principles. While mergers tend to starve the journalistic values of

---

[17] Rabasca, 2001, p. 2.
[18] Strupp, 2000, p. 21.
[19] Id., p. 22.
[20] Tompkins and Colon, 2000, p. 53.
[21] Friedland, Lewis. "Statement" Attached to "Reply Comments of Consumer Federation, et al." Cross Ownership of Broadcast Stations and Newspapers, MM Docket No. 01-235, 15 February 2002.

the enterprise of resources, in the drive to produce profits for the merged entity, the multitasking[22] and cross selling[23] that typifies combination mergers pose a special threat. They are intended specifically to homogenize the media.

Moreover, because professional lines are breached, it is quite problematic to define activities and preserve professional ethics.

The alliance between the *Chicago Tribune* and Tribune-owned WGN channel 9 led the American Federation of Television and Radio Artists (AFTRA) to file a grievance against the station after a WGN reporter (an AFTRA member) was asked to write for the newspaper without additional compensation. "I think that with the consolidation of the media, it's a real danger," says Eileen Willenborg, executive director of AFTRA's Chicago chapter. She raises another issue as well. 'You can't spread professionals so thin and still have a professional product." *Tribune* executives declined comment.[24]

As staff began to work more closely, they discovered a disparity in the pay levels between television reporters and newspaper reporters. Religion writer Bearden used to get extra pay for filing TV stories in addition to her newspaper stories. With convergence, the extra pay will dry up. *Tribune* managers say they know they will have to address the pay issue if newspaper staffers routinely appear on television.

And then there is the issue of workload. Reporters and photojournalists worry the marriage will mean more work without more money.[25]

Along with concerns about journalistic quality and time management come the question of compensation of reporters, who perform crossover work, as well as redefining job descriptions and hiring rules for incoming reporters. So far, no staffers have received extra pay for going beyond their regular workload, and many say they would like to see the issue settled before convergence becomes more routine.[26]

These pressures and problems emerge in all mergers. They are heightened because the "fear is that corporate bean counters see convergence simply as a way to 'thin the herd' of reporters rather than using the huge reporting teams fielded by papers to greatly broaden the scope of broadcast stories."[27]

---

[22] Rabasca, 2001, p. 4.

[23] Id., p. 4; Tompkins and Colon, 2000, p. 50; Mitchell, Bill. "Media Collaborations." *Broadcasting and Cable*, 10 April 2000.

[24] Moses, 2000, p. 23.

[25] Tompkins and Colon, 2000, p. 50.

[26] Strupp, 2000, p. 22.

[27] McConnell, Bill. "The National Acquirers: Whether Better for News or Fatter Profits, Media Companies Want in on TV/Newspaper Cross-Ownership." *Broadcasting and Cable*, 10 December 2001.

TRENDS WITHIN PRINT JOURNALISM

The FCC also should recognize that cross-ownership may reinforce disturbing trends in the newspaper market. The economic "logic" of pursuing profits through conglomeration, concentration and national integration is potent, but the Commission's job is to consider the impact of those economic trends on the quality of civic discourse. It cannot pay homage to pure economics but ignore the end point to which reliance on pure economics will drive civic discourse.

At the simplest and most general level, the extent to which newspapers have experienced the trends more in the past may be an indication of what will happen in other media. Indeed, given the developments in radio during the rapid acceleration of integration of stations into national chains unleashed by the 1996 Telecommunications Act, the general impact of these trends on civic discourse seems clear and should be a major source of concern to the Commission.

Concentration Eliminates Diversity

In *Taking Stock*, Gilbert Cranberg, Randall Bezanson and John Soloski argue that if any one thing is to blame for the deterioration of American newspapers it is the over-concentration of the marketplace.[28] The efforts of the large newspaper corporations to monopolize regions and their respective voices has lead to an entirely profit-driven business model that has in turn de-prioritized product quality and debilitated most news operations' ability to fully serve a free press.[29] Companies like Gannett and Knight Ridder, two of seventeen dominant chains, have taken control of dozens of newspapers, buying out hundreds of competitors, and reducing citizens' access to probing, helpful information that is vital to daily life. Many of the public companies have begun to seek advantages from grouping papers into dominant metropolitan and regional chains and then combining many aspects of the news operations, sharing news among all of the nominally separate papers. This is a strategy of vertical integration through control over content.[30]

---

[28] Cranberg, Gilbert, Randall Bezanson, and John Soloski. *Taking Stock: Journalism and the Publicly Traded Newspaper Company*. Ames: Iowa State Press, 2001.

[29] Cranberg, Bezanson and Soloski, cite Roberts, Gene. 1996. "Corporatism vs. Journalism." *The Press-Enterprise Lecture Series* 31, 12 February; for recent discussions see also Dugger, Ronald. "The Corporate Domination of Journalism." in William Serrin (ed.), *The Business of Journalism*. New York: New Press, 2000; Sparrow, 1999, Chapter 4.

[30] Cranberg, Bezanson and Soloski, 2001, p. 11.

This has an immediate and negative impact on any given local news consumer, for he is fed a generic dose of coverage that does not likely inform him of what is going on in his neighborhood. In Wisconsin, for instance, Gannett purchased Thompson's central holdings (eight dailies and six weeklies) to add to the two it already owned there, effectively monopolizing the area.[31]   Suddenly, thousands of subscribers lost their essential local coverage.

Similar cases can be found all over the country.[32] CNHI bought eight Thompson dailies in Indiana, adding to the four it already owned there. CNHI and Gannett now account for 40% of Indiana's daily circulation. The consequences of this are clear: fewer voices and perspectives are provided and the ability of the people to "make judgments on the issues of the time," something central to the American Society of Newspaper Editors' *Statement of Purpose*, is hindered.[33]

The statistics at this point are staggering. Chains own 80 percent of America's newspapers and the aforementioned content-sharing has become one of the biggest hurdles.[34] In the Southeast, Knight Ridder shared content between three of its papers, *The Charlotte Observer*, *The State* (Columbia, SC) and *The Sun News* (Myrtle Beach, SC), which are at least one hundred miles away from each other and span two states. The likelihood of coverage being pertinent to individual readers in districts this far apart is virtually nil. In Baltimore, Times Mirror Co. bought a Patuxent chain of thirteen weeklies in the Baltimore suburbs even though it owns *The Baltimore Sun*. If any of those thirteen weeklies were offering opposing viewpoints to the *Baltimore Sun*, the purchase cut citizens' access to this competing dialogue. In monopolizing these local of ideas, the newspaper corporations demonstrate that they are not committed to upholding their position as the "broadly democratic and broadly representative source of information in our democratic society."[35]

Family operated papers are also being swallowed up by the corporate papers who toss fists full of money at them.[36] In Hartford, Times Mirror Co. bought *The Hartford Advocate*, a weekly created for the sole purpose of competing with the Times Mirror-owned *Hartford Courant*, the dominant

---

[31] Bass, 2001, p. 111.

[32] Id.

[33] Cranberg, Bezanson and Soloski, 2001, p. 86.

[34] Downie and Kaiser, 2002, p. 68.

[35] Id., p. 13.

[36] From this we can easily conclude that "the owners most likely to encourage their editors' ambitions, give them adequate resources and support aggressive, intelligent journalism are companies controlled by a single family" (Downie and Kaiser, 2002, p. 76).

daily.[37] In Montana, Lee Enterprises bought *The Hungry Horse Tribune* and *The Whitefish Pilot* and began running identical editorials as if the two communities had the same concerns.[38] In Westchester County, NY, Gannett combined ten papers it owned and created one, *The Journal News*, sacrificing successful, respected papers such as *The Tarrytown Daily News*.[39]

Profit at the Expense of Journalism

The frightening reality of this corporate expansion is that these companies, over the past few decades, have shown a declining interest in journalism and an overwhelming interest in profit-maximizing business practices. This 'business over news' attitude has countless drawbacks that have manifested themselves in various forms at hundreds of now-weakened newspapers.

Before identifying the specific ills, it is important to understand the corporate structures and mandates that have undermined America's newspapers' goals. Cranberg, Bezanson and Soloski note that "news has become secondary, even incidental, to markets and revenues and margins and advertisers and consumer preferences."[40] This list of motivating factors sums up where the newspaper chains' allegiances lie. This is due, in large part, to the make-up of the corporate boards that run the newspaper companies. "They draw heavily from industry, finance and law for outside directors."[41] *Taking Stock* research indicates that "of the 131 outside directors on the boards of the 17 dominant chains, only 17 (13 percent) have had experience on the editorial side of a news organization."[42] Furthermore, seven companies "have *no* outside directors with a newspaper background" and "a half-dozen only have one."[43] Without dedicated newspaper people involved in the highest level of management, the publicly owned (and traded) newspaper becomes a stock market entity like any other, and the product, news, becomes an expendable commodity that is "altered to fit tastes" and used to drive shareholder value up, without regard for journalistic integrity.[44]

While *Taking Stock* does concede that "some editors may still dominate corporate conversations about what constitutes news and how to

---

[37] Bissinger, Buzz. "The End of Innocence." in Roberts, Gene, Thomas Kunkel and Charles Layton (eds.), *Leaving Readers Behind*. Fayetteville: University of Arkansas Press: 2001, p. 83.

[38] Bissinger, 2001, p. 103.

[39] Roberts, Kunkel and Layton, 2001, p. 5.

[40] Id., p. 2.

[41] Cranberg, Bezanson and Soloski, 2001, p. 42.

[42] Id.

[43] Id.

[44] Id., p. 108.

deploy news gatherers," it cautions that "most no longer make such determinations singly or without elaborately justifying the effects on the bottom line."[45] In surveying CEOs of some of these companies, they find a common commitment to shareholders and stock value, not news and readers. William Burleigh of Scripps Howard points to a "suitable return" as his obligation, while Robert Jelenic of Journal Register Co. says his "mandate from the board is to produce longtime shareholder value."[46] The simple omission of news and readers as motivation speaks on how these papers are run, assembled and presented to the public – as money-making machines that subvert their "primary purpose of gathering and distributing news and opinion [in order] to serve the general welfare."[47]

Editors at papers big and small describe the stress caused by major newspaper corporations bearing down on their news operations, enforcing a bottom line principle, and, ultimately, infringing on their editorial role and the newspaper's output. *Taking Stock* cites an editor survey in which ninety percent of editors interviewed affirmed that they felt pressure from the bottom line, many adding that they felt "resignation" and "resentment" because of this pressure.[48] Geneva Overholser, former editor of *The Des Moines Register*, conducted a study for the American Journalism Review and found that "ownership by public corporations has fundamentally and permanently transformed the role of editor," noting that of the seventy-seven editors surveyed, "half of them said they spent a third or more of their time on "matters other than news."[49] *The News About the News* explains that editors who once "spent their days working with reporters...now spend more of their time in meetings with the paper's business-side executives, plotting marketing strategies or cost-cutting campaigns."[50]

The result of the 'business over news' attitude has been the deterioration of the American newspaper. *The Philadelphia Inquirer*, for example, became one of the nation's strongest papers while Gene Roberts was its editor. When Knight Ridder bought the daily, it began slashing staff and putting tremendous pressure on Roberts to increase profits. Roberts soon had enough of the corporate newspaper model and retired with the *Inquirer's* daily circulation at 520,000 and its Sunday circulation at 978,000. Eleven years later, the paper's circulation had plummeted to 365,000 daily and 732,000 Sunday.[51] Surprisingly, Knight Ridder's profit margins rose to just under 20

---

[45] Id., p. 78.

[46] Id., p. 64.

[47] Id., p. 86.

[48] Cranberg, Bezanson and Soloski, 2001, p. 89; Neiman Reports. 1999. *The Business of News, the News About Business,* Summer.

[49] Downie and Kaiser, 2002, p. 93.

[50] Id., p. 68; Neiman Reports, 1999.

[51] Downie and Kaiser, 2002, p. 81.

percent during that time, epitomizing what has become an industry trend: "publicly traded newspaper companies have seen significant growth in their cash flow, despite modest growth in revenues."[52] Hence, although subscription rates are dropping because the quality of the papers is dropping, the chains are still profiting.

This pattern has been repeated at the L.A. Times, providing more fuel for the debate over whether cuts cause subscriber declines or *visa versa* "The size of the Times editorial staff has shrunk from 1,200 five years ago to 940 now, and Times staffers say the executives in Chicago would like to reduce that to about 800. Times circulation has dropped from 1.1 million in 1999 to 852,000 this year."[53]

In order to accomplish this, the major corporations often hire analysts to determine how much of their newsroom staff and resources they can cut. At *The Winston-Salem Journal* in North Carolina, a newspaper owned by Richmond's Media General, a consulting firm (DeWolff, Boberg & Associates) was brought in to analyze how efficiently the paper's staff was operating. After making the reporters keep "precise diaries on how they spent their time over three weeks, DeWolff, Boberg produced a "grid" describing how much time various journalistic endeavors should take.[54] Based on the placement of a story within the paper, the analysis suggested how much time should be spent working the story (down to the tenth of an hour), whether or not a press release should be used, how many and which types of sources should be used and, of course, how long the story should be. It took three months for the editors to convince the owners that "creative work like journalism cannot be governed by such arbitrary formulas."[55] Nonetheless, Media General laid off twenty percent of its workforce by the time DeWolff, Boberg had completed their consultation.

Knight Ridder had a similar outlook for the San Jose Mercury News whose publisher, Jay T. Harris, revealed that "the drive for ever-increasing profits [was] pulling quality down." What eventually drove Harris away from the paper were Knight Ridder's demands that the paper reach "a specific profit margin, an exact percentage figure" that would give them a suitable return. Harris could no longer stomach Knight Ridder's lack of regard for the paper's journalistic responsibilities and left.[56]

Instances of staff cutting by corporate companies have piled up over the past two decades. When Gannett bought *The Asbury Park Press* (boosting its and Newhouse's combined share of New Jersey's circulation to a

---

[52] Cranberg, Bezanson, Soloski, 2001, p. 38

[53] Kurtz, Howard. "Tribune Co. Ousts Publisher at L.A. Times: Jeffrey Johnson Had Fought Budget Cuts." *Washington Post,* 6 October 2006, p. C7.

[54] Downie and Kaiser, 2002, p. 97.

[55] Id.

[56] Id., p. 109.

whopping 73 percent) it immediately liquidated a fourth of the newsroom staff, from 240 people to 185.[57] Next, the news hole was reduced, bleeding out niche local coverage that was vital to a highly subdivided area with many townships and districts. The *Press* had trained itself to adequately serve its varied readership, setting up localized bureaus and printing five zoned editions. Gannett swiftly dropped the *Press* to four zoned editions and in a final swipe at the newsroom staff; the chain increased workloads and took away overtime pay.

The *Press* is one of hundreds of papers wrestling with these new terms of competition, terms that "have little or nothing to do with news quality."[58]   MediaNews acquired the *Long Beach Press-Telegram* and immediately cut 128 jobs. Knight Ridder acquired the *Monterey County Herald* and dropped 28 employees on day one. The Journal Register Co. bought the *Times-Herald* (Norristown, PA) and subsequently fired 25 people. Their op-ed page was dropped, the mayor stopped subscribing and within one year the paper was completely detached from Norristown's immediate needs. Time and again, economic pressures have swelled, undermining "traditional journalistic standards and values" and proving that "there is no obvious way to simultaneously shrink a newspaper and make it better."[59]

Happy News

The corporate paper takeovers of the past two decades have also resulted in the 'softening' of news to appease advertisers who want buoyant, happy readers perusing their ads. Avoiding content that some advertisers find boring (mainly government, especially state and local government news) or unlikely to give readers the zest they need to buy, has become commonplace as the papers remove hard news sections to add "reader-friendly" content, as Gannett calls it. Their aforementioned *Asbury Park Press* reporters were told that "there will be no bad news in the "Day in the Life stories," and "no aggressive reporting or attempts to expose problems or wrongdoing."[60] Gannett's *Courier-Journal* in Rockford, Illinois was criticized in an evaluation by former editor Mark Silverman for emphasizing "hard-news subjects" and suggested the paper consider "more how-to stories, stories that show how a person or a group of people accomplished something, question-and-answer columns, 'ask the experts' call-in hot lines, and even first-person stories by readers."[61]   These are examples of the "prevailing ethos" at Gannett and other corporate newspaper companies – soft news is

---

[57] Neiman Reports, 1999, p. 143.
[58] Cranberg, Bezanson, and Soloski, 2001, p. 13.
[59] Downie and Kaiser, 2002, p. 69.
[60] Id., p. 87.
[61] Id., p. 91.

easy and inexpensive to cover; it is devoid of controversy and is therefore safe; and, most importantly, it makes advertisers happy.

The dilemma here is not that the chain-owned newspapers are adding content. That, in theory, is a good thing. But, in order to make room under the shrunken budgets, other content has to be cut, and it almost always comes out of the hard-news bin. This means that Gannett can easily and profitably remove hard-news reporters at the *Asbury Park Press*, load up on AP story releases, shrink hard-news story length, and add low-cost sections like "Whatever," a teen beat section, and "Critters," a pet section which includes pet obituaries that cost readers at least 50 and sometimes 300 dollars to print.[62] To compensate, the chains do a significant amount of the cutting in the state government bureaus. In 1998, "only 513 reporters" nationwide were covering all state governments full-time. *Breach of Faith* points out that, disturbingly, over 3000 media credentials were issued for that year's Super Bowl.[63]

The corporate departure from state government coverage has come with little or no regard for journalistic integrity or the benefits the public receives from this coverage. Bureaus at hundreds of papers across the country have been slashed. The *Journal-Constitution*, in Atlanta, used to house one of the most prolific state government bureaus in the nation, boasting twelve esteemed reporters. When Cox bought the paper, it was left with three statehouse reporters. Shortly thereafter, the *Journal-Constitution* had slanted, one-sided coverage that did not have the resources to inform itself adequately and, in turn, inform the public sufficiently. When the reporter crunch received bad press, Cox doubled its number of statehouse reporters to six.

In Montana, the *Great Falls Tribune* earned a great reputation for state government coverage, only to have Gannett buy the paper and attempt to shut down the entire bureau in order to rely strictly on the Associated Press. The editors talked new president Chris Jensen out of it, only to find copies of the paper on their desks with "Gs" "marked on any story he considered too governmental.[64] The editor's copy and budget were being cut, to the point where law books that were vital to reporting were no longer being ordered.

Former Georgia Governor Zell Miller's concern is that the turnover of the statehouse reporters and their relative youth and mobility detract from the coverage, coverage that is already being hampered. "They don't have a long view of the leaders," he said. "They don't have context. There's no

---

[62] Id., p. 91.
[63] Roberts, Kunkel and Clayton, 2001, p. 10.
[64] Walton, Mary and Charles Layton. "Missing the Story at the Statehouse." in Roberts, Gene and Thomas Kunkel (eds.), *Breach of Faith: A Crisis of Coverage in the Age of Corporate Newspapering.* Fayetteville: University of Arkansas Press, 2002, p. 14.

historical perspective whatsoever."[65]   Reaching this low-point in state reporting is the function of nearly two decades of corporate ownership demoralizing the veteran reporters, forcing them to leave for papers where they can truly pursue their journalistic endeavors and substituting young, inexperienced reporters who need jobs – the kind of staff that will do what you tell them.   As this cycle permeates the rest of the newsroom, as other departments are slashed, it will become increasingly difficult for chain-owned papers to serve as a free press.

While the phenomenon is most prevalent in smaller markets, it also afflicts some of the largest newspapers, including *USA Today*,[66] *The Washington Post*[67] and the *New York Times*.[68] In order to maintain advertiser relationships, coverage has to be undermined. These instances make it seem as though advertisers have as much say about what is being reported as the reporters do. This is certainly not a healthy journalistic environment.

Under Serving Commercially Unattractive Audiences

Putting circulation quality over circulation quantity is the other major tactic the corporate papers use to cut cost and boost profits. This means that newspapers determine the value of a region with respect to its attractiveness to advertisers. The advertisers are not interested in pitching their products to economic and social groups that they do not normally attract or who fall into unwanted demographics. So, they put pressure on the papers to get their ads to the "right" people for the smallest price.

According to *Taking Stock*, "the practice of cutting circulation has increased in the past two decades, with papers halting circulation to areas where readers don't interest advertisers."[69] The result of this is that the lowest circulation penetration is found "in areas with high concentrations of both

---

[65] Id., p. 21.

[66] Rowse, 2000, p. 163.

[67] According to Rowse, 2000, p. 49, in 1994, *The Washington Post* ran a huge story urging the approval of GATT without admitting that it was a subsidiary of American Personnel Communications and stood to profit $1.3 billion if GATT went through. Similarly, p. 159, the *Post* runs ads for the Nuclear Energy Institute, a large supplier of advertising revenue, and neglected to run a story about a report by Public Citizen which said 90 percent of nuclear reactors had been operating in violation of government safety rules.

[68] According to Street, John. *Mass Media, Politics and Democracy*. New York: Palgrave, 2001, p. 141, "*The New York Times* changed an article about Tiffany's, a huge advertiser, and accompanied it by a bland editorial, to avoid damaging their relationship with the company." Similarly, Rowse, 2000, p. 162, notes that Chrysler, an enormous source of ad revenue for whomever it deals with, demands to see the content in the pages accompanying its ads to ensure that it is 'positive' and 'light.'

[69] Cranberg, Bezanson and Soloski, 2001, p. 93.

low income and minority populations."[70] This leaves the minority and low-income populations under served by the press, with fewer opportunities to access the valuable daily news and entertainment that people in higher "quality" socioeconomic groups are supplied with.

Furthermore, "competition for socioeconomically defined market segments increasingly takes the form of altering the subject matter and shape of news content, delivering the types and forms of information that persons in the socioeconomically defined market prefer."[71] This means that not only are the chain papers physically not getting copies to certain social groups (their tactics will be highlighted momentarily), they are slanting the news they do print to please the readers that the advertisers want pleased. At this point, the low income and minority populations are doubly deserted. The financial motivations of the corporate owners strip the newsrooms of their ability to justly report and inform, and prohibit us from celebrating, mourning, and co-existing fruitfully as a culture.

The "deliberate industry strategy to pursue a more upscale readership" has been exposed by researchers at the University of Iowa's school of journalism by surveying directors at the largest 90 U.S. dailies. The research states:

> Interviews...made it evident that lower-income neighborhoods were being disadvantaged by such tactics as requiring payment in advance, refusing to deliver to public housing, door-to-door sales efforts only on days of the month when government checks were due, and denial of discounts. Combined with "aggressive pricing"- that is, charging more – the practices amount to writing off a whole class of potential readers.[72]

These tendencies are reinforced by a relative absence of minorities from newsrooms. Vanessa Williams weaves together the relationship between communities, journalists, news organizations, reporting and democracy that I have highlighted throughout this analysis.

> Black and white and red all over: the continued struggle to integrate American newsrooms. It's a play on an old riddle. In this case, the black and white refer to race, although I might add that in recent years the industry, faced with the rapidly changing demographics of the country, must also be concerned with Asians, Hispanics, and Native Americans. The red refers to the heated emotions that color this struggle: frustration, embarrassment, anger.

> What does this have to do with the news product? Everything. News organizations' continued inability to integrate African-Americans and other journalists of color into their newsrooms and to more accurately and fairly represent racial and ethnic communities threatens the credibility and viability of daily general-circulation newspapers. How can a newspaper claim to be a

---

[70] Id., p. 96.
[71] Id., p. 10.
[72] Id., p. 95.

journal of record for a given city or region if it routinely ignores or misrepresents large segments of the population in the geographic area it covers?...

Our greatest concern about the industry's failure to grasp the gravity of its diversity deficit should be the potential harm to society. Many Americans continue to operate out of misinformation and misunderstanding when it comes to perceptions and relationships between racial groups, between religious groups, between men and women, straight and gay people, young and old people, middle-class and working-class people. The press, by failing to provide more accurate, thorough, and balanced coverage of our increasingly diverse communities, has abdicated its responsibility to foster an exchange of information and perspectives that is necessary in a democracy.[73]

The unique "market failures" discussed in the previous chapter provide the basis for public policy intervention to ensure robust civic discourse. That is, if we were only concerned about the traditional market failures described in the previous section, we might rely on antitrust policy, perhaps with a more rigorous set of structural screens and a heightened concern for vertical/conglomerate issues. However, the unique market failures demand much more public policy intervention to promote such civic discourse.

When entities merge, everyone in the market loses an independent voice, while a small segment of the market gains better coverage. In fact, depending on the distribution of preferences, the least well-served in the market may become even less well-served, if the merged entity drives out sources that are targeted to the needs of minorities and atypical groups. This is particularly true when a national entity buys out a local entity. When the merger crosses institutional lines, it may result in an equally severe loss of institutional diversity.

---

[73] Williams, Vanessa. "Black and White and Red All Over: The Ongoing Struggle to Integrate America's Newsrooms." in William Serrin (eds.), *The Business of Journalism*. New York: New York Press, 2000, p. 100.

PART V:

RACIAL AND GENDER DIVERSITY

STUDY 11:
OUT OF THE PICTURE,
THE LACK OF RACIAL AND GENDER DIVERSITY
IN TV STATION OWNERSHIP

S. Derek Turner

Introduction

In 2003, the Federal Communications Commission implemented a series of policies that promised to completely alter the mass media marketplace.[1] The proposed rule-changes were met with an unprecedented public and congressional backlash[2], and were ultimately overturned by the courts.[3] Three years later, the FCC is poised to once again force rule changes upon an unwilling public. In July 2006, the FCC issued a *Further Notice of Proposed Rulemaking*, soliciting public comment on the issues raised on remand by the Third U.S. Circuit Court of Appeals in its *Prometheus v. FCC* decision.[4]

---

[1] Federal Communication Commission. 2003. In the Matter of 2002 Biennial Regulatory Review – Review of the Commission's Broadcast Ownership Rules and Other Rules Adopted Pursuant to Section 202 of the Telecommunications Act of 1996; Cross-Ownership of Broadcast Stations and Newspapers; Rules and Policies Concerning Multiple Ownership of Radio Broadcast Stations in Local Markets; Definition of Radio Markets; Definition of Radio Markets for Areas Not Located in an Arbitron Survey, MB Docket Nos. 02-277. 01-235, 01-317, 00-244, 03-130, FCC 03-127. Herein referred to as "2003 Order."

[2] Ben Scott. 2004. "The Politics and Policy of Media Ownership." American University Law Review Vol. 53: 3, February.

[3] Prometheus Radio Project, et al. v. F.C.C., 373 F.3d 372 (2004) (herein referred to as "Prometheus"), stay modified on rehearing, No. 03-3388 (3d Cir. Sept. 3, 2004), cert. denied, 73 U.S.L.W. 3466 (U.S. June 13, 2005).

[4] Federal Communications Commission. 2006. Further Notice of Proposed Rulemaking, in the Matter of 2006 Quadrennial Regulatory Review – Review of the Commission's Broadcast Ownership Rules and Other Rules Adopted Pursuant to Section 202 of the Telecommunications Act of 1996; 2002 Biennial Regulatory Review – Review of the Commission's Broadcast Ownership Rules and Other Rules Adopted Pursuant to Section 202 of the Telecommunications Act of 1996; Cross-Ownership of Broadcast Stations and Newspapers; Rules and Policies Concerning Multiple Ownership of Radio Broadcast Stations in Local Markets; Definition of Radio Markets, MB Docket Nos. 06-121; 02-277 ; 01-235; 01-317; 00-244, FCC-06-93; Herein referred to as "Further Notice"

A key issue before the Commission is how the rule changes will impact female and minority ownership of broadcast radio and television outlets. This report provides the first complete and accurate assessment and analysis of female and minority full-power commercial broadcast television ownership. The purpose of this study is to provide the public, Congress, and the FCC itself with a complete understanding of the state of minority and female television ownership, as well as the potential effects of proposed rule changes on female and minority ownership.

MINORITY AND FEMALE TV OWNERSHIP: A SORRY HISTORY

Historically, women and minorities have been under-represented in broadcast ownership due to a host of factors — including the unfortunate fact that some of these licenses were originally awarded decades ago when the nation lived under a segregationist regime. The FCC, beginning with its 1978 *Statement of Policy on Minority Ownership of Broadcasting Facilities*, has repeatedly pledged to remedy this sorry history.[5]

Congress also has recognized the poor state of female and minority ownership. The Telecommunications Act of 1996 contains specific language aimed at increasing female and minority ownership of broadcast licenses and other important communications mediums.[6] The Act requires the FCC to eliminate "market entry barriers for entrepreneurs and other small businesses" and to do so by "favoring diversity of media voices."[7] The Act also directs the Commission when awarding licenses to avoid "excessive concentration of licenses" by "disseminating licenses among a wide variety of applicants, including small businesses, rural telephone companies, and businesses owned by members of minority groups and women."[8]

---

[5] Federal Communications Commission. 1978. *Statement of Policy on Minority Ownership of Broadcasting Facilities*, 68 FCC 2d, 979, 980 n. 8.

[6] 47 U.S.C.§257, §309(j)

[7] Section 257 is contained within Title II of the Communications Act and thus does not directly encompass broadcast services. However, the Commission has interpreted some aspects of the language of §257 to apply to broadcast licensing. In 1998, the Commission stated: "While telecommunications and information services are not defined by the 1996 Act to encompass broadcasting, Section 257(b) directs the Commission to 'promote the policies and purposes of this Act favoring diversity of media voices' in carrying out its responsibilities under Section 257 and, in its Policy Statement implementing Section 257, the Commission discussed market entry barriers in the mass media services." See Federal Communications Commission 98-281, *Report and Order: In the Matter of 1998 Biennial Regulatory Review -- Streamlining of Mass Media Applications Rules, and Processes -- Policies and Rules Regarding Minority and Female Ownership of Mass Media Facilities*, MM Docket No. 98-43, November 25, 1998, herein after referred to as *the Form 323 Report and Order*.

[8] 47 U.S.C.§309(j)

The FCC initially appeared to take this mandate seriously. In 1997, the Commission completed a proceeding, as required by the 1996 Act, which identified barriers to entry for small businesses (which has been interpreted to include minority- and female-owned entities) and set forth the agency's plan for eliminating these barriers.[9] Unfortunately, subsequent triennial reports have lacked substance.[10]

In 1998, the Commission further demonstrated its seriousness by taking a crucial first step to determine the actual state of female and minority ownership of broadcast radio and television stations. That year, the FCC began requiring all licensees of full-power commercial stations to report the gender and race/ethnicity of all owners with an attributable interest in the license.[11] In the *Form 323 Report and Order*, the Commission stated:[12]

> Our revised Annual Ownership Report form will provide us with annual information on the state and progress of minority and female ownership and enable both Congress and the Commission to assess the need for, and success of, programs to foster opportunities for minorities and females to own broadcast facilities.

Other than this monitoring effort, the FCC has done very little to promote female and minority broadcast ownership (and the follow-up on this monitoring has been abysmal). In its 1999 Order that allowed television duopolies, the Commission paid lip-service to concerns about the policy change's effect on minority and female ownership, but still went forward with rule changes that allowed increased market concentration.[13] In 2004, the Commission sought input into how it could better implement Section 257 of

---

[9] Federal Communications Commission. *In the Matter of Section 257 Proceeding to Identify and Eliminate Market Entry Barriers for Small Businesses, Report*, GN Docket No. 96-113, 12 FCC Rcd 16802 (1997).

[10] In his dissenting statement on the 2004 Section 257 report, Commissioner Michael Copps described the report as a "a slapdash cataloging of miscellaneous Commission actions over the past three years that fails to comply with the requirements of Section 257."

[11] 47 C.F.R. 73.3615

[12] Federal Communications Commission. 1998. *Report and Order, In the Matter of 1998 Biennial Regulatory Review Streamlining of Mass Media Applications, Rules, and Processes Policies and Rules Regarding Minority and Female Ownership of Mass Media Facilities*, MM Docket Nos. 98-43; 94-149, FCC 98-281.

[13] Federal Communications Commission. 1999. Report and Order, In the Matter of Review of the Commission's Regulations Governing Television Broadcasting Television Satellite Stations Review of Policy and Rules, MM Docket Nos. 87-8. 91-221, FCC 99-209.

the 1996 Act. But this proceeding remains open, and the current chairman has shown no sign of interest in completing this important matter.[14]

In the 2003 Order implementing Powell's rule changes, the FCC assured the public that ownership diversity was a key policy goal underlying its approach to ownership regulation.[15] However, the *Third Circuit* found otherwise, stating that "repealing its only regulatory provision that promoted minority television station ownership without considering the repeal's effect on minority ownership is also inconsistent with the Commission's obligation to make the broadcast spectrum available to all people 'without discrimination on the basis of race.' "[16]

THE FCC SHOWS NO CONCERN FOR TRACKING MINORITY AND FEMALE OWNERSHIP

The 2006 *Further Notice* seeks public comment on the issue of minority and female ownership. But before considering the potential effects of policy changes on female/minority ownership, we must first know the *current* state of ownership and evaluate the effects of previous policy changes. No one should be in a better position to answer these questions than the Commission itself. The FCC possesses gender and race/ethnicity information on every single broadcast entity and knows exactly when licenses changed hands.

However, the FCC has no accurate picture of the current state of female and minority ownership, and shows no sign of taking the matter seriously. Though the Commission has gathered gender/race/ethnicity data for the past seven years, it has shown little interest in the responsible dissemination of the information contained within the Form 323 filings.

This lack of interest or concern is made evident by the FCC's own Form 323 summary reports. Station owners began reporting gender/race/ethnicity information in 1999, and the FCC released its first "summary report" in January 2003 (for reporting in 2001).[17] A second summary followed in 2004 (for reporting in 2003).[18] The most recent report

---

[14] Federal Communications Commission, Media Bureau. "Media Bureau Seeks Comment on Ways to Further Section 257 Mandate and to Build on Earlier Studies" DA 04-1690, MB Docket No. 04-228, 15 June 2004.

[15] See *2003 Order*, "Encouraging minority and female ownership historically has been an important Commission objective, and we reaffirm that goal here."

[16] See *Prometheus*, 373 F.3d at 421, n58 (3rd Cir. 2004).

[17] Though this data summary is not directly displayed on the FCC's ownership data page (http://www.fcc.gov/ownership/data.html), it can be downloaded at http://www.fcc.gov/ownership/ownminor.pdf and http://www.fcc.gov/ownership/ownfemal.pdf

[18] Though this data summary is not directly displayed on the FCC's ownership data page (http://www.fcc.gov/ownership/data.html), it can be downloaded at

was issued in June 2006 (for the 2004-2005 period).[19] However, calling these publications "summary reports" is somewhat misleading, as they are merely a listing of each minority or female-owned station's Form 323 response and not aggregated in any manner. No information on the stations not owned by women or minorities is given.

Closer examination of these summary reports reveals significant problems. Some station owners listed in the 2003 summary are missing from the 2004 report but reappear in the 2006 summary, despite the fact that ownership had not changed during the interim period. Certain stations have ownership interests that add up to greater than 100 percent. In some instances, the type of station facility (AM, FM or TV) is not specified.

But the most alarming problems are ones of omission. Not a single station owned by Radio One is listed, even though the company is the largest minority-owned radio broadcaster in the United States. Stations owned by Granite Broadcasting, the largest minority-owned television broadcaster, are also missing from the FCC's summary reports. However, examination of the individual Form 323 filings for these stations shows that they are indeed minority-owned. Why aren't they in the FCC's summary?

The answer likely lies in how the larger-group stations report ownership information, and how the FCC harvests the information for their summary reports. Most of the licenses of those stations missed by the FCC are "owned" by intermediate entities, which are in some cases, many degrees separated from the "actual" owner. Some stations file more than 20 Form 323 forms (one for each holding entity), with the true owners listed on only one of the filed forms. And in many cases, the actual ownership information is attached as an exhibit and not listed on the actual form. Thus the FCC, which tabulates the information for their summaries by harvesting these electronic forms via an automated process, misses stations that file in this convoluted and confusing manner.[20]

Sources inside the Media Bureau indicate that there is little oversight of Form 323 fillings and the summary reports produced from them.[21] This lack of concern is made evident not only by the poor quality of the summary reports, but by the significant number of improperly filed forms. Station

---

http://www.fcc.gov/ownership/owner_minor_2003.pdf   and
http://www.fcc.gov/ownership/owner_female_2003.pdf
[19]   http://www.fcc.gov/ownership/owner_minor_2004-2005.pdf   and
http://www.fcc.gov/ownership/owner_female_2004-2005.pdf

[20] Indeed, the average number of stations owned by each unique female/minority owner who appears on the FCC Form 323 summary is 1.4, versus 2.5 for female/minority owners who should, but do not appear in the FCC's summary. This difference is weakly statistically significant (one-sided p-value of 0.039).

[21] Byerly, Carolyn M. "Questioning Media Access: Analysis of FCC Women and Minority Ownership Data." Department of Journalism, Howard University.

owners who listed themselves as one race in a certain year are listed as a completely different race in later years; race and gender information is left blank; names are misspelled; attribution of ownership in other stations is not listed as required; and some stations fail to file every two years as required by law.[22]

This obvious lack of concern is truly troubling given the Commission's stated commitment and legal obligation to foster improved female and minority broadcast ownership. The FCC has both the raw data and the resources to adequately address the issues raised by the *Third Circuit* regarding minority ownership but chooses instead to ignore this issue and rely on public commentators to do its job.

Due to limited resources, this study is limited to full-power commercial broadcast television stations. We hope that the results of this study and the flaws in the current FCC summary reports will inspire the Commission to undertake a similar analysis of the more than 11,000 commercial radio stations. Furthermore, we hope that the Commission will undertake a longitudinal analysis to determine the effects of current policies on female and minority ownership of all broadcast stations.

METHODOLOGY

The universe of full-power commercial television stations was determined using the FCC's CDBS Public Access Database.[23] Each individual station's Form 323 ownership filing was then reviewed, with ownership information assigned using the most recent filings (in most cases, the most recent filings were from 2004-2006).[24]

"Ownership" was defined as the gender or race of owners with voting interest that exceeded 50 percent alone or in the aggregate. If no single gender or race met these criteria, then stations were assigned "no controlling interest status." This status most often was assigned to publicly traded

---

[22] Numerous examples of these types of errors were noted. For example, Christina M. Coonce, the female American Indian/Alaska Native co-owner of WNYB was listed as "white" in the station's 1999 Form 323 filing but as American Indian/Alaska Native in later filings. In a 1999 filing for KBJR, the African-American owner of Granite Broadcasting, W. Don Cornwell, is listed as "W Don Ornwell" and as a white male.

[23] The list was gathered on July 18th 2006. In addition to stations listed by the FCC as "licensed", each station that had "construction permit-off-air" or "licensed and silent" status was examined to determine if the station was currently on the air, and if so, were added to the list of licensed stations.

[24] This review was conducted from July 18th to August 3rd. Ownership reported herein is considered current as of June 2006, as stations are required to file an updated Form 323 report within 30 days of a change in ownership structure, in addition to their biennial filing.

corporations where listed entities did not form a majority of the voting interest. Information concerning stations that are operating under local marketing agreements (LMAs) was obtained from contracts that were filed with individual Form 323 filings. Data from the National Telecommunications and Information Administration's 1998 and 2000 *Minority Commercial Broadcast Ownership* reports were verified and updated with information from the CDBS database, as well as other publicly available sources and interviews with station representatives.

Stations broadcasting on channels 2-13 were assigned VHF status, while stations broadcasting on channels 14-69 were assigned UHF status. Information about the network affiliation and local news content of each station was determined by viewing station Web sites, checking local programming listings or contacting the station.[25] The above data were merged with demographic data at the state and Designated Market Area levels, using information from the U.S. Census Bureau and BIA Financial. Statistical analysis methods such as ANOVA, t-tests, and OLS and probit models were employed to examine the statistical significance of market-level ownership and market-level demographics, as well as differences in ownership concentration. Significance levels are highlighted in each figure.

MINORITY AND FEMALE TV OWNERSHIP

There are currently 1,349 full-power commercial television stations in the United States. Sixty-seven — or 4.97 percent — of the stations are owned by women.   Forty-four of the 1,349 stations, or 3.26 percent, are minority-owned. Of these stations, 18 have black or African-American owners, accounting for 1.33 percent of all stations. Nine of these stations were controlled by a single entity, Granite Broadcasting. Hispanic or Latino owners controlled 15 stations, or 1.11 percent of the total. American Indian or Alaska Native owners control five stations, or 0.37 percent, while Asian owners control six stations, or 0.44 percent. There are no stations in the United States owned by Native Hawaiian or Pacific Islanders (see Exhibit 1).

By comparison, non-Hispanic White owners controlled 1,033 stations, or 76.6 percent of the total stations. The bulk of the remaining stations were owned by entities with no single race/ethnicity accounting for greater than 50 percent of the voting interest (or where the proper information was not given). In most cases, the 264 stations designated as having "no controlling interest" are owned by large publicly traded corporations such as Clear

---

[25] Stations were deemed to air local news if they aired at least one local news broadcast during the programming week, regardless of whether or not the station itself actually produced the newscast.   Thus stations airing repurposed or repackaged news broadcasts are still counted as airing local news.

Channel, whose voting stock is disbursed among a wide population of shareholders.

Exhibit 1: Full-Power Commercial Television Ownership
By Gender & Race/Ethnicity

Category	Owner	Number of Stations	Percent of All Commercial Full Power TV Stations
Gender	Female	67	4.97
	Male	948	70.27
	No Controling Interest	327	24.24
	Unknown	7	0.52
Race/Ethnicity	Amer. Ind./AK Nat.	5	0.37
	Asian	6	0.44
	Black or Afric. Amer.	18	1.33
	Hispanic or Latino	15	1.11
	Nat. Haw/Pac. Isl.	0	0.00
	All Minority	44	3.26
	White	1,033	76.58
	No Controling Interest	264	19.57
	Unknown	8	0.59
	Total Universe	1,349	

Source: Form 323 filings; Free Press research

Seven stations, or 0.52 percent, are controlled by entities whose race/ethnicity and gender status could not be determined, and an additional station (WATM-TV) is controlled by an owner whose race/ethnicity status could not be determined.

Of the 1,349 total full-power commercial broadcast television stations, 576 are VHF stations, operating on channels 2-13. The remaining 773 are UHF stations, which operate on channels 14-69. UHF stations usually have a smaller audience and broadcast at a lower power than their VHF counterparts.

The FCC uses a "discount rule" to measure the nationwide audience reach of UHF stations, giving them half the potential audience reach compared to VHF stations. Consequently, VHF station licenses are considered more valuable than UHF licenses and the bulk of stations operating in this region are affiliated with the traditional "big four" networks of ABC, CBS, NBC and Fox. More than 92 percent of VHF stations are affiliated with these networks.

Women own 30 of the 576 VHF stations, or 5.21 percent. The remaining 37 female-owned stations are UHF stations, or 4.79 percent of UHF stations. There are 12 minority-owned VHF stations, accounting for 2.08 percent of the total. The remaining 32 minority-owned stations make up 4.14 percent of UHF stations.

The already low-level of minority broadcast television ownership is even lower in the more valuable VHF market. African-Americans own six

VHF stations, or 1.04 percent of the total. Latinos control three VHF stations, or 0.52 percent. There are two American Indian/Alaska Native-owned VHF stations and just one Asian-owned VHF station, accounting for 0.35 and 0.17 percent, respectively.

The data above encompass all stations where females and/or minorities control greater than 50 percent of the voting interest in the entity that ultimately owns the station license. However, some stations are operating under Local Marketing Agreements, or LMAs. Under an LMA, the official owner has little or no input in the station's daily operation, which is directed by the owner of another station in the same market. LMAs have been widely criticized by industry observers and members of the FCC for being little more than a scheme to avoid FCC ownership limits.[26] For example, the six stations controlled by Carolyn C. Smith of Cunningham broadcasting are all operated by Sinclair under LMA's in markets where Sinclair would otherwise be in violation of the current duopoly rule. Carolyn Smith is the mother of Sinclair CEO David Smith, which along with the LMA relationship suggests that Cunningham is merely a front for Sinclair.

Free Press identified two minority-owned stations and eight female-owned stations that are under the *de facto* control of male or non-minority owners.[27] When these stations are removed from the total tally, the level of female ownership drops to 4.37 percent of all full-power commercial stations, while minority ownership falls to 3.11 percent of all stations.

No Controlling Interest but No Diversity at the Top

There were 264 stations with "no controlling interest" held by a single race, or 19.6 percent of all stations. But only one of these 264 stations — Atlanta's WTBS, which is owned by Time Warner — has a minority CEO.

There were 327 stations with "no controlling interest" by gender, or 24.24% of all stations. Of these 327 stations, only two stations (KJNP and WEHT) have a female CEO or president.

---

[26] See, for example, Findlay, Prentiss. "Group Says Stations Not Independent." *Charleston Post and Courier*, 20 December 2004; see also Schmelzer, Paul. "The Death of Local News." *Alternet*, 23 April 2003.

[27] In addition to the six Cunningham stations, the other two female-owned stations operated under an LMA are WZVN (operated by Waterman Broadcasting) and WNYB (owned by Christina Coonce, but under the *de facto* control of Tri-State Christian Television, controlled by Mrs. Coonce's husband, Garth). The two minority owned stations operated under LMA's are KFWD (operated by Belo) and KVIQ (operated by the Eureka Group).

FEMALE AND MINORITY BROADCAST TV OWNERSHIP DOES NOT MATCH THEIR PROPORTIONS OF THE GENERAL POPULATION OR OTHER ECONOMIC SECTORS

Women make up half of the U.S. population, yet own less than one twentieth of the full-power commercial television stations. Minorities account for nearly 33 percent of the U.S. population but own just 3 percent of the television stations.

Given the long history of prejudice and economic discrimination against women and minorities, it is not too surprising that broadcast ownership is below these groups' respective proportions of the general population. However, the level of female and minority broadcast TV ownership is also very low when compared to other sectors of the economy, and even the information sector as a whole. In industries like transportation and health care, female and minority ownership is some five to 10 times higher than in the broadcast television industry (see Exhibit 2).[28]

This disparity is even more telling when considering individual race and ethnic groups. In sectors such as transportation and health care, all minority groups own businesses at or near their proportion of the general population. But in the TV broadcast sector, the two largest groups — African-Americans and Latinos — barely own 1 percent of stations (see Exhibit 3).

Also note that while the level of minority broadcast TV ownership has decreased in recent years, the percentage of minority ownership in the economy as a whole has increased, from 14.6 percent in 1997 to 17.9 percent in 2002.[29]

CONCLUSIONS

As the FCC considers how to respond to the remand of the 2003 Powell Commission media ownership rules, it must pay close attention to the Third Circuit's strong language regarding the Commission's failure to adequately justify its rule changes in regards to female and minority ownership. It is not sound policymaking to assert that diversity, localism, and female/minority ownership are important goals, but then ignore the effects that rule changes have on these goals. Furthermore, it is a failure of responsibility to gather valuable information on ownership but then to do nothing with the data. And it is inexcusable to continue to release data summaries the Commission knows to be flawed.

---

[28] U.S. Census Bureau. 2005. *Economic Census*, data collected in 2002.
[29] Data for non-farm sectors from 1997 and 2002; data for broadcast TV sector from 1998, 2000, and 2006.

Exhibit 2: Female & Minority Business Ownership by Sector

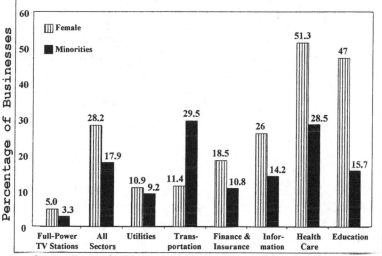

Source: Form 323 Filings; U.S. Census Bureau; Free Press Research

Exhibit 3: Minority Business Ownership
by Race/Ethnicity & Sector

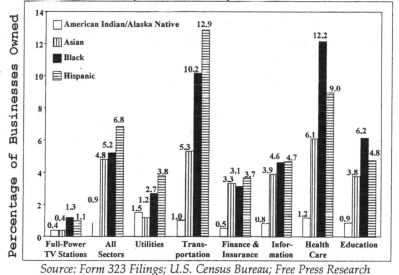

Source: Form 323 Filings; U.S. Census Bureau; Free Press Research

The findings of this study are a crucial first step toward understanding the true state of female and minority broadcast ownership, and the effects of regulatory policy on these owners. But this study was focused on the narrower universe of full-power commercial television, and says nothing about radio. It could be argued that radio is the more important medium, since there are 10 times as many outlets and the price of entry for female and minorities is comparatively low. The FCC's form 323 summaries seem to show a decline in female and minority radio ownership, but given their flaws a more thorough census is needed. The Commission should conduct this work and pay close attention to the changes in ownership over time.

The FCC should not proceed with any rulemaking before it has thoroughly studied the issue of female and minority broadcast ownership. Furthermore, we feel that the results of our study demonstrate that any policy changes that allow for increased concentration in television markets will certainly lead to a decrease in the already low number of female and minority-owned TV stations and minority-owned local TV news outlets. Enacting regulations that lead to such outcomes directly contradicts the Commission's statutory and legal obligations under the 1996 Telecommunications Act. Instead, the Commission should consider proactive policies that protect and promote female and minority ownership.

The Commission also should take the following actions:

The FCC Media Bureau should conduct a comprehensive study of every licensed broadcast radio and television station to determine the true level of female and minority ownership.

- The study should examine the level of ownership at both the national level and at the DMA and Arbitron market levels.

- The study should be longitudinal, examining the changes since 1999, when the Commission began gathering gender and race/ethnicity ownership information.

- The study should focus on station format and content, particularly paying attention to local news production.

- The results of the study, as well as the raw data, should be made available to the public.

The FCC should revise and simplify the public display of individual Form 323 station filings.

- A citizen searching for the owner of a local station should easily be able to ascertain the true identity of a station owner.

- The practice of station licenses being held by layers and layers of wholly owned entities should be thoroughly examined by the Commission.

- Broadcast licenses are awarded for temporary use of the public airwaves, and the identities of the owners should be clearly stated on a single form.

The Commission should expand the universe of stations that are required to file Form 323.

- Currently, no owners of Class-A or low-power stations are required to file ownership information with the FCC. However, the Commission states that these classes of stations are important entry points for female and minority owners. To validate this hypothesis, the Commission should extend the obligation of filing Form 323 to these stations.

- Currently all non-commercial educational broadcasters file Form 323-E, which does not solicit information about the gender, race, and ethnicities of station owners. The Commission should require their owners to disclose this information.

STUDY 12:
REACHING AND SERVING THE COMMUNITY

S. DEREK TURNER

One of the clear findings of previous research, as described in Studies 4 and 5, is that minority communities are underserved and that minority owners strive to serve their communities. The concern about a lack of minority owners is compounded by the interaction of these two effects. Minority ownership could address the tendency of the commercial mass media to under serve these groups. The data set we compiled on minority ownership addresses two aspect of this issue and reinforces those findings.

OWNERSHIP, NETWORK AFFILIATION AND LOCAL NEWS PRODUCTION

The stations affiliated with the so-called "big four" networks — ABC, CBS, NBC and Fox — are consistently the top-rated stations in each market and are usually found on the lucrative VHF portion of the dial. These stations also produce the highest-rated local news content and thus command most of the local advertising revenue. Nearly 92 percent of VHF stations air local news content, compared to 47 percent of UHF stations. And over 96 percent of big-four affiliated VHF stations air local news content, compared to 81 percent of big-four-affiliated UHF stations.

Ownership of a big-four-affiliated station almost certainly guarantees a significant audience share and a news operation. However, minorities own just 13 of the 847 big-four-affiliated stations, or 1.5 percent (and just 1.3 percent of the big-four-affiliated VHF stations).

The difference in ownership patterns is stark when comparing the types of stations owned by minorities and non-minorities. Of the 1,305 non-minority owned stations, 834 are big four affiliated, or 64 percent. However, only 13 of the 44 minority-owned stations are affiliated with the big four networks, or 29.5 percent.

But the situation is reversed for independent stations unaffiliated with a big four network, the secondary English-language networks UPN, WB (and their successors CW and MYNTV) and Ion, or the Spanish-Language networks Telefutura, Telemundo and Univision. Just 161 of the 1,305 non-minority owned stations are independent, or 12.3 percent. However, 18 of the 41 minority-owned stations are independent, or 41 percent.

The fact that minority owners control so few big-four stations suggests that the percentage of minority-owned stations airing local news is likely to be lower than their non-minority counterparts. This is true: 41

percent of minority-owned stations air local news versus 67 percent of non-minority owned stations.

But that's not the whole story. Minority-owned big four stations are just as likely to air local news as their non-minority owned counterparts (92 versus 90 percent). Two-thirds of the minority-owned Spanish-language-network-affiliated stations air local news, versus half of the non-minority owned Spanish-language-network affiliates. And over 23 percent of the minority-owned independent stations air local news versus just 15 percent of the non-minority-owned independent stations.   These data indicate that minority owners are just as capable of serving their local communities as their non-minority counterparts.

Another way to illustrate this point is to examine the 892 full-power commercial television stations that air local news. Of the 874 non-minority owned stations that air local news, only 24 are independent stations, or just 2.7 percent. However, 22 percent of the minority-owned stations that air local news are independent stations. So even though minority owners are largely kept out of the lucrative big four affiliated market, they still manage to produce local news content at levels higher than non-minority independent station owners.

MINORITY OWNERSHIP OF TV STATIONS IS LOW EVEN IN MARKETS WITH LARGE MINORITY POPULATIONS

Because full-power broadcast television stations are geographically limited in their market reach, information about minority ownership at the local level is more telling than the national aggregate. The traditional geographic boundary used for analysis of television markets at the local level is the Designated Market Area, or DMA.

Like ownership at the national level, minorities are vastly underrepresented at the DMA level, even in areas where minorities are the majority. Minority-owned stations are present in 36 of the nation's 210 DMAs. Examination of individual race/ethnic groups shows very little overlap between minority-owned stations. American Indian or Alaska Native-owned stations are in four of the 210 DMAs. Asian-owned stations are present in six of the 210 DMAs. Black- or African-American owned stations are in 17 of the 210 DMAs, while Hispanic- or Latino-owned stations are present in 10 of the nation's 210 DMAs. Non-minority owned stations are present in every single DMA. DMA coverage is slightly better for women-owners, but still far below that of men. Female-owned stations were present in 51 of the nation's 210 DMAs.

In 18 DMAs minorities make up the majority of the population living within the market. However seven of these DMAs have no minority-owned stations. The remaining 11 minority-majority populated DMAs all have very low levels of minority-ownership, some 3 to 10 times below the level of minority population living within each market.

Hispanics or Latinos are the only minority group that formed a plurality or majority of the population within a sizeable number of DMAs. Only six of the 16 markets with a plurality or majority of the population made up of Latinos had stations owned by Latinos. However, even in these six markets, the level of Hispanic or Latino-ownership was 3 to 8 times below the proportion of the Latino population living there.

While there is only one DMA where African-Americans constitute a majority of the population (Greenwood-Greenville, MS), there are 59 markets where the African-American proportion of the population is at or above the nationwide level. However, black-owned stations are present in just five of these 59 markets. Figure 20 shows the 10 markets with the highest percentages of African Americans living within each market. Only one of these markets contains an African American-owned station, WRBJ in Jackson, Mississippi.

There are no African-American-owned full power commercial TV stations in many cities with considerable African-American populations, such as Atlanta, New Orleans, New York City and Washington, D.C. Other than Jackson, Mississippi, Detroit is the only city with a large African-American population that has a black-owned TV station. This station is owned by Granite and may change hands by the end of the year.

Honolulu is the only DMA where Asians constitute a majority of the population, and there is one Asian-owned station in this market. In the 17 markets where the Asian proportion of the population is at or above its nationwide level, there are only 2 Asian-owned stations.

Data for American Indian or Alaska Native population was not available at the DMA level. However, there are no American Indian/Alaska Native owners in the states with the highest American Indian and Alaska Native populations (New Mexico and Alaska). Three of the five American Indian/Alaska Native-owned stations are located in Oklahoma and owned by David Griffin, a broadcaster whose family has operated KWTV since 1953. The other two are in the Seattle, Washington and Buffalo, New York markets (KHCV and WNYB).

HISPANIC-OWNED STATIONS ARE LOCATED IN MARKETS WITH LARGE HISPANIC POPULATIONS BUT BLACK-OWNED STATIONS ARE NOT

Though there are many markets with high Hispanic and Latino populations that have no Latino-owned stations, Hispanic or Latino-owned stations are more likely to be in markets with higher levels of Latino population. This phenomenon is also true for Asian-owned stations, driven primarily by the single Asian-owned station in Hawaii (see Exhibit 1).[1]

However, black-owned stations are not more likely to be in markets with bigger African-American populations. These findings suggest that language, particularly Spanish, is an important factor underlying ownership. These findings also suggest that due to difficulties with capital access and other institutional barriers to ownership, African-American owners may be purchasing stations where they can — in certain smaller, less lucrative Midwestern markets. However, perhaps due to the legacy of racism in the South, African-American owners haven't been able to operate in the smaller Southern markets. While having African-American owners anywhere is desirable, it is troubling that African-American owners do not operate in African-American communities, where they would add a valuable perspective to the coverage of local news and community affairs.

Exhibit 1: Minority Population in Markets with Minority-Owned Full-Power Commercial TV Stations

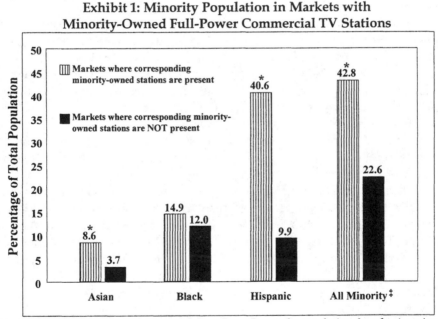

Source: Form 323 filings; BIA Financial; Free Press Research; population data for American Indian/Alaska Native at DMA-level was not available, * = difference is statistically significant at p<0.005; ‡ = this category only encompasses the race/ethnicities shown in this figure

---

[1] These data were calculated using 210 observations, one for each DMA. Each DMA was scored for the presence of a minority-owned station, an American Indian/Alaska Native-owned station, an Asian-owned station, and a black or African American-owned station. When calculating the population percentages, each market was weighted by the total population within each market, though the figures are not very different (and remain significant) without weighting.

THE NATIONAL REACH OF MINORITY-OWNED STATIONS

Another way to look into the connection between minority-owned stations and minority audiences is to determine the national reach of minority-owned stations — that is, how many minority households are living where there is a minority-owned station? As mentioned above, minority-owned stations are present in 36 of the nation's 210 DMAs. These stations reach approximately 21 percent of all U.S. TV households, but just 30 percent of all minority TV households. To contrast, non-minority owned stations reach over 98 percent of all U.S. TV households.

These figures were calculated using the FCC's UHF discount rule, which attributes just half of a market's audience to UHF stations. Without the UHF discount, minority-owned stations reach 38 percent of all U.S. TV households and 54 percent of all minority TV households, while non-minority owned stations reach 100 percent of U.S. TV homes (see Exhibit 2).

Exhibit 2: National Population Reach
of Minority-Owned Full-Power Commercial TV Stations

Station Owned by Race/Ethnicity	Percent of All U.S. TV Households Reached		Pct. of All Minority TV HH Reached		Percent of Asian TV Households Reached		Pct. of Black/Afr. Amer. TV HH Reached		Pct. of Hisp./Latino TV HH Reached	
	With UHF Discount	Without UHF Discount	With UHF Discount	Without UHF Discount	With UHF Discount	Without UHF Discount	With UHF Discount	Without UHF Discount	With UHF Discount	Without UHF Discount
Amer. Ind./AK Nat.	2.1	3.2								
Asian	5.3	9			10	19.1				
Black	7.3	13.3					8.7	16.8		
Hispanic or Latino	6.9	12.1							21.8	37.3
Nat. Haw/Pac. Isl.	0	0								
All Minority	21.5	37.6	29.7	53.6						
Non-Minority	98.1	100								

Source: Form 323 filings; BIA Financial; Free Press research

Perhaps more telling is the percentage of each minority group reached by each associated minority-owned station group. Under the UHF discount, Asian-owned stations reach only 10 percent of U.S. Asian TV households, while African American-owned stations reach just 8.7 percent of African American TV households. Latinos fare better than other minorities in this measure (primarily due to the Los Angeles market), with Latino-owned stations reaching 21.8 percent of all Latino TV households.

These findings provide greater context to the overall national ownership numbers. Not only is minority ownership low, but minority owners are reaching just a small portion of the minority audience. It is quite troubling that up to 91 percent of African-American households are not served by an African-American broadcaster. Even more troubling is the potential outcome of media consolidation on these few minority-owned stations. If just a handful were lost to consolidation, these already anemic numbers would fall even further.

STUDY 13:
THE LINK BETWEEN AND CONCENTRATION OF MEDIA MARKETS AND A LACK OF RACIAL DIVERSITY IN TV STATION OWNERSHIP

S. Derek Turner and Mark Cooper

Introduction

The previous two studies show the dramatic under representation of minorities and women among broadcast license holders and the impact this has on the ability of minority and female owners to reach their communities. This under representation and under serving of these communities is a longstanding historical problem. What role does concentration of ownership play in this problem? This study shows that relaxation of ownership limits and increases in media concentration negatively affect minority ownership. Public policies that allow concentration ownership make matters worse.

Historical Comparison: Minority Ownership of Full-Power Commercial TV Stations Has Decreased Since 1998

This study represents the first complete census of all licensed full-power commercial broadcast television stations operating in the United States. There was one other attempt to ascertain the level of female broadcast TV ownership, a 1982 study commissioned by the FCC.[1] However, that study determined the gender ownership for just a sample of stations, not the full universe.

Since 1990, the National Telecommunications and Information Administration (NTIA) has administered the Minority Telecommunications Development Program (MTDP), a program first initiated during the Carter administration to increase minority ownership of radio and television broadcasting stations as well as other telecommunications businesses. From 1990 to 2000, the NTIA released several reports that estimated the total number of minority-owned radio and television stations.

The agency has not conducted any further research into this matter since their last report was issued in December 2000, and officials have indicated that they do not intend to issue any further reports. When asked

---

[1] ELRA Group Inc. *Female Ownership of Broadcast Stations.* prepared for the Federal Communications Commission, May 1982.

about plans for future studies by the National Association of Hispanic Journalists, the NTIA directed the group to the flawed FCC summaries of Form 323 data.[2]

Because of the differing methodologies, direct comparisons between this study and earlier NTIA reports are not valid. At the time NTIA conducted its studies, it did not have the full ownership information that is now available from individual Form 323 filings. To compile their list of minority-owners, the NTIA relied on word of mouth and membership information from various minority broadcast trade associations. While this effort provided a fairly complete assessment of minority broadcast ownership, it was not a full census of all broadcast stations. The agency has indicated that its results were not comprehensive, and that future work based on Form 323 filings would provide a more complete picture of minority ownership.[3]

Using the NTIA's 1998 list, the list of current minority owners, ownership information from the FCC and interviews with station representatives, Free Press identified nine stations that were missed by the NTIA in its 1998 report, for a total of 40 stations. A similar effort was applied to correct the 2000 NTIA report, but it was less precise because the NTIA omitted the names of minority-owned stations and owners in that survey. However, Free Press did identify 35 total stations that were minority-owned in 2000 (see Exhibit 1). While these corrected data provide a more complete assessment of the historical trend in minority television ownership, they do not represent a rigorous census of all stations.

---

[2] National Telecommunications and Information Administration. *Letter from NTIA to Ms. Veronica Villafane, President, National Association of Hispanic Journalists,* April 27, 2006.
Available at http://www.nahj.org/nahjnews/articles/2006/april/NTIAResponseLetter.pdf.
"Presently, NTIA has no plans to conduct a minority ownership study. You may find of interest, however, data on female and minority ownership from the Federal Communications Commission's ownership reports filed in calendar year 2003. The data are available on the Commission's website. ..."
[3] See the 2000 NTIA report, which states: "MTDP acknowledges that despite its best efforts, non-sampling error likely occurred because of an inability to identify all of the nation's minority commercial broadcasters. Such error may be reduced in the future as a result of the FCC's recent requirement that owners disclose on their biennial reports information about the participation of minorities and women in station ownership. ... In establishing the requirement, the Commission noted the difficulty NTIA faces in obtaining complete and accurate information from broadcast owners. It concluded that NTIA's data would complement, but not substitute for, information the Commission gathered, because as the licensing authority, it is 'appropriately and uniquely situated to collect information on the gender and race of the attributable interests of its licensees.' "

Exhibit 1: Minority Full-Power Commercial Television Ownership Since 1998 By Gender & Race/Ethnicity

Race/Ethnicity	Historical Data for 50 U.S. States & DC				Current Ownership for 50 U.S. States & DC	
	Corrected 1998 NTIA Data		Corrected 2000 NTIA Data		2006 Free Press Census	
	Number of Stations	Percent of All Commercial Full Power TV Stations	Number of Stations	Percent of All Commercial Full Power TV Stations	Number of Stations	Percent of All Commercial Full Power TV Stations
Amer. Ind./AK Nat.	2	0.17	3	0.23	5	0.37
Asian	3	0.25	3	0.23	6	0.44
Black	25	2.07	21	1.63	18	1.33
Hispanic or Latino	10	0.83	8	0.62	15	1.11
Nat. Haw/Pac. Isl.	0	0.00	0	0.00	0	0.00
All Minority	40	3.31	35	2.72	44	3.26
White	n/a		n/a		1,033	76.58
No Controling	n/a		n/a		264	19.57
Unknown	n/a		n/a		8	0.59
Total Universe	1,209		1,288		1,349	

Source: Form 323 Filings; NTIA; Free Press research

However, these data clearly show there has been no improvement in the level of minority broadcast television ownership since 1998, despite the fact that the total universe of stations has increased by approximately 12 percent. Furthermore, there has been a marked decrease in the total number of black or African-American owned stations — dropping nearly 30 percent since 1998.

OWNERSHIP CONCENTRATION: FEMALE AND MINORITY OWNERS CONTROL FEWER STATIONS PER OWNER THAN MALE AND WHITE OWNERS

White male and large corporate station owners tend to own far more stations than their minority and female counterparts. The average number of stations owned per unique non-minority owner is 5.4, while male owners controlled an average of 4.8 stations each. However, the average number of stations owned per unique owner is 1.9 for minorities and 2.3 for women.

While the average number of stations owned by a unique minority owner is 1.9, for Latinos it is even lower, at and average of 1.3 stations per unique owner. This reflects the fact that the largest Latino group owner controls just three stations, compared with the largest white male group owner, Ion (formerly Paxson), which controls 57 stations.

There are a total of 269 unique owners, and 140 of these control more than one station. Over 54 percent of white male owners control more than one station, compared to 32 percent of minority owners.

These differences have a practical importance on several levels. First, given that the median minority or female owner controls just a single station, these operations are more likely to better serve their local communities than stations controlled by large group owners. This is confirmed by a recently surfaced 2004 FCC study which demonstrated that locally owned and operated stations aired more local news content than their conglomerate counterparts, devoting an additional 20 to 25% of each half hour broadcast to local news coverage.[4] Second, minority and female station owners are more likely than their white male counterparts to feel the negative effects of increased consolidation. Women and minority owners will find it more difficult to compete with the large group owners for programming and advertising dollars.

TRACKING OWNERSHIP: FCC RULES CHANGES LED TO THE SALE OF MINORITY-OWNED STATIONS

Using the corrected list of minority-owned TV stations from the 1998 NTIA report, Free Press tracked the ownership of the 40 stations that were minority owned as of that year, investigating the effects of two key policy changes that occurred in the late 1990's: the increase in the national ownership cap from 25 percent to 35 percent and the 1999 FCC Order that allowed local television duopolies. Free Press identified 17 minority-owned stations that were sold to non-minority owners after 1998. Nine of these seventeen sales would not have been permitted under the old national ownership cap and duopoly rules (see Exhibit 2).[5] Had these stations not been sold, minority ownership would be 20 percent higher than the current level. Furthermore, 7 of the 8 station sales that would have been permissible under the old national cap and duopoly rules were sales to large station group owners, and may not have occurred if not for the pressures of increased industry consolidation.

---

[4] "Do Local Owners Deliver More Localism? Some Evidence from Local Broadcast News." *Federal Communications Commission Working Paper*, 17 June 2004.

[5] 22 of the 40 minority-owned stations (in 1998) have changed owners since 1998. In addition to the 17 stations listed above, one was sold by a Latino to a Latino (KRCA), one was sold by a Latino to a Latino-owned company that later became non-Latino majority controlled (KLDO sold by Panorama to Entravision), two were held by companies that later became non-minority controlled (KTMW and KSMS), and one station's status could not be determined (there is no record in the CDBS of Albuquerque station KDB-TV). KTVJ and WHSL are only partial station sales, as Roberts Broadcasting retained 50% of the voting interest in these two stations. Since 1998, there has been a loss of 22 minority owned stations and a gain of 26 minority owned stations.

Exhibit 2:
Sales of Minority Full-Power Commercial Television Stations: Stations that were Minority Owned in 1998

Station	Owner in 1998	Race/Ethnicity	Year of Sale	Purchaser	Would have Been Permitted under 25% Cap?	Would have Been Permited under Duopoly Ban?
KCMY	Ponce-Nicasio	Hispanic/Latino	2000	Paxson	No	Yes
KEYE	Granite Broadcasting	African American	1999	CBS	No	No
KLTV	TV 3 INC.	African American	2000	Cosmos (Raycom)	Yes	Yes
KNTV	Granite Broadcasting	African American	2002	NBC Universal	No	No
KPST	Golden Link TV Inc.	African American	2002	Univision	Yes	No
KTRE	TV 3 INC.	African American	2000	Cosmos (Raycom)	Yes	Yes
KTVJ	Roberts Broadcasting	African American	2003	Univision	Yes	Yes
KUPX	Roberts Broadcasting	African American	1999	Paxson	No	Yes
WATL	Qwest	African American	2000	Tribune	No	Yes
WGTW	Brunson Comm.	African American	2004	Trinity Broadcasting	Yes	Yes
WHPX	Roberts Broadcasting	African American	1999	Paxson	No	Yes
WHSL	Roberts Broadcasting	African American	2003	Univision	Yes	Yes
WLBT	TV 3 INC.	African American	2000	Cosmos (Raycom)	Yes	Yes
WNOL	Qwest	African American	2000	Tribune	No	No
WPTA	Granite Broadcasting	African American	2005	Malara	Yes	Yes
WPTT	WPTT Inc.	African American	2000	Sinclair	Yes	No
WTMW	Urban Broadcasting Corp.	African American	2002	Univision	Yes	Yes

Source: Form 323 Filings; NTIA; Free Press research

Granite Broadcasting, the largest minority station owner in 1998 (and today) controlled 10 stations in 1998. Since then, the company has sold three stations (KNTV to NBC-Universal in 2002; KEYE to CBS in 1999, and WPTA to Malara Broadcasting in 2005) and acquired two stations (KRII in 2000, and WISE in 2005).[6] Granite could not have sold its stations to NBC and CBS under the national ownership cap limits that were in effect prior to 1996. Furthermore, the sale of California's KNTV would have been prohibited before the FCC allowed market duopolies in 1999, as NBC also owns the local Telemundo affiliate KSTS in the Bay Area.

African-American-owned Roberts Broadcasting controlled four stations in 1998. Two of these stations were sold to Paxson (WHPX and KUPX, both in 1999) in deals that would not have been permitted under pre-1996 national ownership caps. The other two stations owned by Roberts Broadcasting in 1998 (KTVJ and WHSL, now KTFD and WRBU) remain partially owned by the company, but Univision now holds a 50 percent interest in each of these stations and controls all aspects of their day-to-day operations. The Roberts brothers have since acquired two new station licenses (by constructing new stations), WZRB in Columbia South Carolina, and WRBJ in Jackson Mississippi. These are the only two African American owned stations in the South.

---

[6] In addition, Granite is currently in the process of acquiring Binghamton New York CBS station WBNG, and selling San Francisco WB station KBWB, thus the current station count for Granite is nine, reflecting ownership as of August 3rd, and after these station sales close.

Quincy Jones, the legendary African-American music producer, owned two stations in 1998 — WATL in Atlanta and WNOL-TV in New Orleans. In 1999, the Tribune Company purchased both of Jones' stations as a part of their merger with Mr. Jones' company, Qwest. These sales wouldn't have been allowed under the pre-1996 ownership limits. And WNOL could not have been sold under the pre-1999 duopoly rules, as Tribune also owns the New Orleans ABC affiliate, WGNO-TV.[7]

In 1998, WGTW was the only station in the country owned by an African-American woman, Dorothy Brunson, who acquired the station license in 1988 after winning the license of failed station WKBS-TV at auction. But by 2004, Brunson found it difficult to acquire syndicated programming and sold the station to Trinity Broadcasting.[8]

Other minority-owned stations were sold to large conglomerates due in part to FCC rule changes that allowed for increased consolidation. Pittsburgh station WPMY (formerly WPPT) was sold to Sinclair by African-American owner Eddie Edwards in 2000, after the FCC allowed duopolies. (Sinclair also owns the local Fox affiliate WPGH-TV.). Another African-American owner, Eddie Whitehead sold KPST (now KFSF) in 2001 to Univision, creating a duopoly in San Jose. Carmen Briggs, a Latino woman, sold KCMY (now KSPX) to Paxson in June 2000 in a deal that exceeded the pre-1996 national ownership limits.

But perhaps the most notable loss of a minority-owned station since 1998 was Jackson Mississippi's WLBT and two other stations owned by Frank Melton, KTRE and KLTV. WLBT is one of only two stations to have had its license revoked by the FCC. WLBT violated the Fairness Doctrine via its flagrant, pro-segregationist activities in the 1950s and 1960s – which included selling airtime to the Ku Klux Klan. After being stripped of its license in 1971, WLBT came under the control of the African-American-owned group Communications Improvement, which sold the station in 1980 to TV3 Inc., a group owned by Melton, an African-American. Melton helped improve the station's news operations and took over first place in the ratings. However, by 2000, Melton felt he could no longer compete with the large corporate station owners for programming and advertising revenue, and sold all three stations to Cosmos Broadcasting, now called Raycom Media, the 14th-largest broadcast owner in the nation.[9]

The case of WLBT and the other minority-owned stations put up for sale makes it clear that increased consolidation has a measurable effect on

[7] Schneider, Michael. "Tribune to Acquire Qwest, Creating Big Easy Duopoly." *Daily Variety*, 10 November 1999.

[8] "Changing Hands." *Broadcasting and Cable*, 30 August 2004.

[9] Mills, Kay. 2004. "Changing Channels: The Civil Rights Case That Transformed Television." *Prologue Magazine*, Vol. 36, No. 3, Fall.

minority ownership. Small-station owners find it increasingly difficult to compete against large companies in the acquisition of both programming and advertising clients. Too many station owners find the financial pressures of consolidation too hard to resist.

MINORITY-OWNED STATIONS CAN THRIVE IN LESS CONCENTRATED MARKETS

Minority-owned stations tend to be, on average, in the larger (by both number of stations and population) television markets, or Designated Market Areas.[10] Given that the larger markets tend to be less concentrated, it is not surprising that markets with minority owned stations are less concentrated than those without these stations.[11]

But even if the size of the market and the level of minority population in the market are held constant, markets with minority owners are *significantly* less concentrated than markets without minority owners. And when these factors are held constant, markets with a minority-owned VHF station airing local news are also *significantly* less concentrated than markets without a minority-owned VHF station airing local news.

Furthermore, when market size and level of minority population is held constant, the markets that saw the addition of new minority owned stations since 1998 are *significantly* less concentrated than markets that did not gain new minority owners.[12]

Another way of examining this issue is to look at the probability that an individual station will be minority owned, given the particular characteristics of each market or station. Under this analytical frame, we still find that even when holding market and station characteristics constant, as a

---

[10] The simple pairwise correlation between DMA rank (lowest number being the highest ranked) and the presence of a minority-owned station is highly significant, and shows that the rank of a market with a minority-owned station is on average 71, versus 112 for a station without a minority owner.

[11] HHI, or the Herfindahl-Hirschman Index, is a measure of the amount of competition within a market, in this case the local broadcast TV market. The higher the HHI, the more concentrated the market. Markets with a minority owner present have a total day HHI of 2,511 versus 3,800 for markets without a minority owner (this is statistically significant at a p-value of less than 0.0005). The DOJ considers markets with HHIs over 1,800 to be highly concentrated. Of the 210 DMA's, 202 have HHIs above 1,800 (the mean HHI is nearly 3,579, with the median value at 2,900). As expected, the largest markets have HHI's lower than the smaller markets, but even the largest markets remain highly concentrated (the mean and median HHI for the top ten markets is 1,958 and 1,926 respectively; the mean and median HHI for the top 50 markets is 2,236 and 2,289 respectively; for the bottom 50 markets the values are 5,710 and 5,226 respectively).

[12] In total, there was a loss of 22 minority owned stations since 1998, and a gain of 26. See Appendix B for details.

market becomes more concentrated, a station is significantly less likely to be minority-owned or be a minority-owned station that airs local news. Similarly, holding market characteristics constant, as a market becomes more concentrated, the probability that a particular market will have a minority-owned station, a minority-owned news station, or have added a minority-owned station since 1998, are all significantly lower.

MARKET CONCENTRATION AND MINORITY OWNERSHIP

To examine the relationship between minority-ownership of full-power commercial television stations and television market concentration, several econometric models were constructed.   The first set of models examines the effect that the presence of a minority owned station in a market has on market concentration.   In order to control for market-specific effects, two control variables were used: market rank and the percent of minority population within a given market. This approach is also used to examine the relationship between minority-owned news stations and market concentration. These models are specified as:

$$HHItotalday = \alpha + \beta_1(minorityown)_i + \beta_2\ (marketrank)_i + \beta_3\ (pctminor)_i + \varepsilon_i$$
$$HHItotalday = \alpha + \beta_1(minorownnews)_i + \beta_2\ (marketrank)_i + \beta_3\ (pctminor)_i + \varepsilon_i$$
$$HHItotalday = \alpha + \beta_1(minorownVHFnews)_i + \beta_2\ (marketrank)_i + \beta_3\ (pctminor)_i + \varepsilon_i$$
$$HHItotalday = \alpha + \beta_1(addminorown)_i + \beta_2\ (marketrank)_i + \beta_3\ (pctminor)_i + \varepsilon_i$$

Where;

HHItotalday = the HHI for a particular market, based upon station audience share.
minorityown = dummy variable for the presence of a minority-owned station in a given market.
marketrank = the Nielsen market rank for the 2005-2006 period.
pctminor = the percentage of a market's population that is of minority racial or ethnic status.
minorownnews = dummy variable for the presence of a minority-owned local news station
minorownVHFnews = dummy variable for the presence of a minority-owned VHF news station.
addminorown = dummy variable for a market that added a minority-owned station after 1998.

The results are presented below in Exhibit 3, 4, 5 and 6. These models suggest that the presence of a minority owned station, a minority owned VHF news station, or a new minority-owned station, is negatively associated with market concentration.

Exhibit 3

Dependent Variable = HHI total day

	OLS	Robust Regr.
	Coeff.	Coeff.
	Beta-Value	
	(sig.)	(sig.)
	(sig. w/ rob.err.)	
Minority-owned Station	-435.6969 -0.087587 (0.112) (0.016)^	-285.4295 (0.030)^
Market Rank	19.76933 0.639241 (0.000)# (0.000)#	9.177394 (0.000)#
Percent Minority Population	-2.17345 -0.020914 (0.702) (0.684)	-1.67478 (0.538)
constant	1616.35 (0.000)# (0.000)#	2192.86 (0.000)#
N = 210	R² = 0.4533 adjusted-R² = 0.4453	R² = 0.4518 adjusted-R² = 0.4439

* = sig. at 10% level; ^ = sig. at 5% level; # = sig. at 1% level

Exhibit 4

Dependent Variable = HHI total day

	OLS	Robust Regr.
	Coeff.	Coeff.
	Beta-Value	
	(sig.)	(sig.)
	(sig. w/ rob.err.)	
Minority-owned Station w/ Local News	-376.4767 -0.0532756 (0.318) (0.163)	-338.3842 (0.065)*
Market Rank	20.06072 0.6486625 (0.000)# (0.000)#	9.460458 (0.000)#
Percent Minority Population	-3.441814 -0.0331188 (0.540) (0.511)	-2.178654 (0.423)
constant	1568.00 (0.000)# (0.000)#	2159.54 (0.000)#
N = 210	R² = 0.4492 adjusted-R² = 0.4412	R² = 0.4497 adjusted-R² = 0.4417

* = sig. at 10% level; ^ = sig. at 5% level; # = sig. at 1% le

Source: Form 323 Filings; BIA Financial; Free Press Research

	Exhibit 5				Exhibit 6	
	Dependent Variable = HHI total day				**Dependent Variable = HHI total day**	

	OLS	Robust Regr.			OLS	Robust Regr.
	Coeff.	Coeff.			Coeff.	Coeff.
	Beta-Value				Beta-Value	
	(sig.)	(sig.)			(sig.)	(sig.)
	(sig. w/ rob.err.)				(sig. w/ rob.err.)	
Minority-owned VHF Station w/ Local News	-998.0537	-580.4603		Added a Minority-Owned Station After 1998	-575.9534	-272.949
	-0.0886898				-0.0940821	
	(0.089)*	(0.037)^			(0.077)*	(0.088)*
	(0.023)^				(0.014)^	
Market Rank	20.14959	9.264841		Market Rank	20..13091	9.698766
	0.6515361				0.6509321	
	(0.000)#	(0.000)#			(0.000)#	(0.000)#
	(0.000)#				(0.000)#	
Percent Minority Population	-5.329496	-4.73582		Percent Minority Population	-2.18187	-1.668853
	-0.051283				-0.020995	
	(0.338)	(0.074)*			(0.699)	(0.547)
	(0.298)				(0.678)	
constant	1600.73	2214.84		constant	1564.03	2130.40
	(0.000)#	(0.000)#			(0.000)#	(0.000)#
	(0.000)#				(0.000)#	
N = 210	$R^2 = 0.4543$	$R^2 = 0.4522$		N = 210	$R^2 = 0.4549$	$R^2 = 0.4478$
	adjusted-R^2 = 0.4463	adjusted-R^2 = 0.4442			adjusted-R^2 = 0.4469	adjusted-R^2 = 0.4398

* = sig. at 10% level; ^ = sig. at 5% level; # = sig. at 1% level   * = sig. at 10% level; ^ = sig. at 5% level; # = sig. at 1% le

Source: Form 323 Filings; BIA Financial; Free Press Research

While this is an interesting and important finding, it may be more appropriate to treat minority ownership as a *dependent* variable, and examine the *probability* that a given station (or market) will be minority-owned (or contain a minority-owned station) given the characteristics of a market, including the market concentration.

These probability models are generally specified as:

$minorownsta = \alpha + \beta_1(HHItotday)_i + \beta_2(mktrank)_i + \beta_3(pctminor)_i + \beta_4(VHF)_i + \beta_5(bigfour)_i + \varepsilon_i$

$minornewssta = \alpha + \beta_1(HHItotday)_i + \beta_2(mktrank)_i + \beta_3(pctminor)_i + \beta_4(VHF)_i + \beta_5(bigfour)_i + \varepsilon_i$

$minorownmkt = \alpha + \beta_1(HHItotday)_i + \beta_2(mktrank)_i + \beta_3(pctminor)_i + \varepsilon_i$

$minornewsmkt = \alpha + \beta_1(HHItotday)_i + \beta_2(mktrank)_i + \beta_3(pctminor)_i + \varepsilon_i$

$addminorown = \alpha + \beta_1(HHItotday)_i + \beta_2(mktrank)_i + \beta_3(pctminor)_i + \varepsilon_i$

Where

minorownsta = *dummy variable for a minority-owned station.*
minornewssta = *dummy variable for a minority-owned station that airs local news.*
minorownmkt = *dummy variable for a market with a minority-owned station.*
minornewsmkt = *dummy variable for a market with a minority-owned station that airs local news.*
addminorown = *dummy variable for a market that added a minority-owned station after 1998.*
HHItotalday = *the HHI for a particular market, based upon station audience share.*
mktrank = *the Nielsen market rank for the 2005-2006 period.*
pctminor = *the percentage of a market's population that is of minority racial or ethnic status.*
VHF = *dummy variable for a station operating on channel 2-13.*
bigfour = *dummy variable for a station that is affiliated with one of the big four networks.*

Each probability model was investigated as a linear OLS model, and as a WLS (robust) linear model. But given the limitations of linear models in the case of a dummy dependent variable, these probabilities were also examined using Probit, and Logit binary response models.

The results are presented below in Exhibits 7, 8, 9, 10 and 11. These results suggest that the probability that a given station is minority-owned is significantly lower in more concentrated markets, even if market and station characteristics are held constant. Furthermore, a given station is less likely to be a minority-owned local news station in more concentrated markets. This result is also seen when examining the probability that a *market* will have a minority-owned station or a minority-owned local news station. Furthermore, less concentrated markets were more likely to have added a minority-owned station after 1998, even after controlling for market rank and minority population.

These findings are very robust to model specification type, and are extremely important, for they suggest that minority-owners thrive in more competitive markets, regardless of market or station characteristics. Also, minority production of local news is more likely to occur in a competitive market versus markets with less competition, regardless of market or station characteristics.

The magnitude of the effect of market concentration is quite large. For example, the predicted probability of a market having a minority-owned station at the median concentration level is approximately 17 percent (under the robust-standard error Probit model). If that concentration increases by one-half of one standard deviation (a 940 unit increase in HHI), then the predicted probability of a market having a minority-owned station drops by two-thirds, to about 6 percent. Likewise, for an individual station, the predicted probability of being minority-owned at the median market HHI is about 2.1 percent (under the robust-standard error Probit model). An increase of one-half of one standard deviation in HHI also leads to a large drop in the predicted probability, falling to just 0.8 percent.

These findings suggest that the likely outcome of further industry consolidation and concentration will be fewer minority-owned stations and minority-owned stations airing local news content. This has tremendous implications for the current ownership proceeding at the FCC. One unambiguous consequence of further industry consolidation and concentration will be to diminish both the number of minority-owned stations and the already low number of minority-owned stations airing local news content. The FCC should seriously consider the effects on minority owners and viewers before it moves to enact policies that will lead to increased market concentration.

Indeed, as shown above, previous pro-consolidation policies enacted by the FCC in the late 1990's had a significant impact on minority ownership, indirectly or directly contributing to a loss of 40 percent of the stations that were minority owned as of 1998.

CONCLUSION

This study has shown that public policy relaxing limits ownership concentration not only fails to promote minority ownership but actually undermines it at three levels. First, the trend since rules were relaxed in the mid-1990s shows a decline in minority ownership, despite an increase in the number of overall stations. Second, examination of the stations that were sold since that change in policy shows that many sales of minority owned stations to non-minorities were made possible directly by that change. There may have been indirect effects as well, since many of the sales that took place could have taken place prior to the change in policy, but did not. The pressures to consolidate unleashed by the relaxation of the previous limits may have pushed minority owners, who have little prospect of keeping up the trend, to sell out. Third, econometric evidence supports the proposition at the macro level that this micro-level data would suggest – greater concentration is associated with lower levels of minority ownership.

Exhibit 7
Dependent Variable = station owned by a minority (dummy)

	OLS	Probit
	Coeff. Beta-Value (sig.) (sig. w/ rob.err.)	Coeff. dF/dx (sig.) (sig. w/ rob.err.)
HHI total day	-0.000011 -0.072878 (0.041)^ (0.002)#	-0.0003752 0.0000194 (0.012)^ (0.006)#
Market Rank	0.0002288 0.073232 (0.052)* (0.058)*	0.0045539 0.0002351 (0.013)^ (0.007)#
Percent Minority Population in Market	0.0007315 0.073532 (0.009)# (0.035)^	0.0071797 0.0003707 (0.056)* (0.061)*
VHF Station	0.0024051 0.006697 (0.834) (0.833)	-0.0002628 -0.0000136 (0.999) (0.999)
Big Four Station	-0.0453484 -0.123403 (0.000)# (0.003)#	-0.5981723 -0.0374242 (0.001)# (0.004)#
constant	0.05546 (0.001)# (0.000)#	-1.09931 (0.003)# (0.001)#
N = 1349	R² = 0.0244 adjusted-R² = 0.0208	pseudo R² = 0.089

* = significant at 10% level; ^ = significant at 5% level; # = significant at 1% level

Exhibit 8
Dependent Variable = minority owned station airing local news (dummy)

	OLS	Probit
	Coeff. Beta-Value (sig.) (sig. w/ rob.err.)	Coeff. dF/dx (sig.) (sig. w/ rob.err.)
HHI total day	-0.00000607 -0.0641 (0.075)* (0.036)^	-0.0004846 -0.0000109 (0.028)^ (0.071)*
Market Rank	0.0000443 0.022658 (0.553) (0.560)	0.0028309 0.0000639 (0.237) (0.221)
Percent Minority Population in Market	0.0002696 0.04391 (0.128) (0.276)	0.0063395 0.0001431 (0.219) (0.316)
VHF Station	-0.0056394 -0.025007 (0.437) (0.443)	-0.1849883 -0.004069 (0.419) (0.221)
Big Four Station	0.0112352 0.048685 (0.159) (0.168)	0.3827043 0.0079049 (0.141) (0.114)
constant	0.0152167 (0.153) (0.086)*	(1.54) (0.006)# (0.021)^
N = 1349	R² = 0.0056 adjusted-R² = 0.0019	pseudo R² = 0.059

* = significant at 10% level; ^ = significant at 5% level; # = significant at 1% level

Source: Form 323 Filings; BIA Financial; Free Press Research

Exhibit 9			Exhibit 10		
Dependent Variable = market with a minority-owned station (dummy)			Dependent Variable = market with a minority-owned station airing local news		

	OLS	Probit		OLS	Probit
	Coeff.	Coeff.		Coeff.	Coeff.
	Beta-Value	dF/dx		Beta-Value	dF/dx
	(sig.)	(sig.)		(sig.)	(sig.)
	(sig. w/ rob.err.)	(sig. w/ rob.err.)		(sig. w/ rob.err.)	(sig. w/ rob.err.)
HHI total day	-0.0000281	-0.0006441	HHI total day	-0.0000128	-0.0007912
	-0.1398196	-0.0000977		-0.0906995	-0.000359
	(0.112)	(0.003)#		(0.318)	(0.017)**
	(0.041)^	(0.001)#		(0.210)	(0.038)^
Market Rank	-0.0006912	0.001169	Market Rank	-0.0004261	0.0012612
	-0.1111809	0.0001773		-0.0973687	0.0000572
	(0.210)	(0.660)		(0.289)	(0.705)
	(0.247)	(0.652)		(0.313)	(0.721)
Percent Minority Population in Market	0.0046665	0.0183777	Percent Minority Population in Market	0.0021154	0.0119873
	0.2233715	0.0027868		0.1438456	0.000544
	(0.001)#	(0.003)#		(0.040)^	(0.101)
	(0.003)#	(0.002)#		(0.132)	(0.185)
constant	0.24043	0.3792889	constant	0.1197049	0.344887
	(0.001)#	(0.479)		(0.020)^	(0.665)
	(0.001)#	(0.462)		(0.025)^	(0.727)
N = 210	R² = 0.1273 adjusted-R² = 0.1146	pseudo R² = 0.1898	N = 210	R² = 0.0623 adjusted-R² = 0.0486	pseudo R² = 0.1768

* = significant at 10% level; ^ = significant at 5% level;
\# = significant at 1% level

* = significant at 10% level; ^ = significant at 5%
level; \# = significant at 1% level

Source: Form 323 Filings; BIA Financial; Free Press Research

Exhibit 11

Dependent Variable = added minority owned
station in market after 1998 (dummy)

	OLS	Probit
	Coeff.	Coeff.
	Beta-Value	dF/dx
	(sig.)	(sig.)
	(sig. w/ rob.err.)	(sig. w/ rob.err.)
HHI total day	-0.0000262	-0.0005219
	-0.1604588	-0.0000598
	(0.077)*	(0.016)^
	(0.035)^	(0.005)#
Market Rank	0.0002054	0.0039963
	0.0406665	0.0004577
	(0.656)	(0.162)
	(0.697)	(0.159)
Percent Minority Population in Market	0.0034945	0.0168858
	0.2058482	0.0019338
	(0.003)#	(0.010)#
	(0.023)^	(0.007)#
constant	0.09863	-0.5118781
	(0.095)*	(0.346)
	(0.066)*	(0.290)
N = 210	R^2 = 0.0703 adjusted-R^2 = 0.0568	pseudo R^2 = 0.1351

* = significant at 10% level; ^ = significant at 5% level; # =

Source: Form 323 Filings; BIA Fina ncial; Free Press Research

STUDY 14:
A CASE STUDY OF WHY LOCAL REPORTING MATTERS:
THE RACIAL FRAMING OF THE RESPONSE TO KATRINA IN PHOTOJOURNALISM IN LOCAL AND NATIONAL NEWSPAPERS

MARK COOPER AND STEVE COOPER

OVERVIEW

This study examines the framing of the response to hurricane Katrina in local and national newspapers as part of a broader study of the importance of localism in media markets. It replicates an earlier study by Gandy and Lee, adding a comparison of the coverage in local and national papers as well as key control variables (such as the locale depicted in the photo and the action of each individual in each photo).

Gandy and Lee studied the photojournalism record presented in the *New York Times* and *The Washington Post* with a concern that "American photojournalists followed a traditional template used by the Western press when it covers periodic disasters in the Third World. Observers suggest that many of the images of the disaster in New Orleans looked very similar to the images of American doctors and marines rescuing the starving desperate victims." But Gandy and Lee did not have extensive data on the underlying "reality" of the events in New Orleans. This Study uses the photojournalism record of the hometown papers as a baseline – *the Times Picayune* and *the Sun Herald*, both of which won Pulitzer Prizes for their coverage.

We find that the national papers simplified the situation and exaggerated the role of victims. Corroborating Gandy and Lee, we find that out-of-town newspapers depicted many more passive black victims in New Orleans and one of the papers reported many more negative actions by Blacks. At the same time, we find a uniform absence of Black rescuers across all papers, particularly in National Guard Units, that raises questions about the racial make-up of these units and their deployment, beyond the issue of photojournalism.

The findings underscore the importance of local sources of news. Even though distribution through a new medium such as the Internet may make sources more readily available, it is the original local reporting that is the key. Out-of-town newspapers simply do not report many of the stories that truly matter "where you live" (although the Katrina story was too big not to cover) or do not do so in a manner that reflects the local reality.

FRAMING RACIAL ROLES IN PHOTOJOURNALISM

Social and political bases of localism (demonstrated in Study 4), clear public preference for traditional, local sources of news and information, and media usage patterns underscore the continuing importance of local news outlets (demonstrated in Study 5), even as distribution of local content moves online. The fact that myriad outlets can be accessed online does not mean that numerous sources dealing with a specific local area are available. In other words, even though distribution through a new medium such as the Internet may make a local source more readily available in an area, it is the original local reporting that is the key. Out-of-town newspapers simply do not report many of the stories that matter "where you live." Even when they do, there is a difference. The local angle on the local story is important, even when it becomes a big enough story to be covered by out-of-town papers.

This Study substantiates that assertion by analyzing the coverage of one of the biggest local stories of the past year, the impact of hurricane Katrina on the Gulf Coast. A recent paper by Gandy and Lee presented an analysis of the photographic record of the impact of Hurricane Katrina on the Gulf coast.[527] It analyzed all of the photographs published by the *New York Times* and the *Washington Post* in the first week after Katrina came ashore. This Study compares the reporting in local newspapers to that of the national papers.

Gandy and Lee asked what "specific news templates were relied upon in presenting the story of Katrina and the victims and heroes she brought to the fore." They are particularly concerned that "American photojournalists followed a traditional template used by the Western press when it covers periodic disasters in the Third World," suggesting that "many of the images of the disaster in New Orleans looked very similar to the images of American doctors and marines rescuing the starving desperate victims."

Gandy and Lee chose the *New York Times* and the *Washington Post* "because these papers are read by the nation's opinion leaders, and because they are generally believed to set the agenda for other major news media in the US." These are prominent national papers.

At the same time, Gandy and Lee hypothesized that there might be a difference in how the papers reported since "the *Times* is a national newspaper with readers outside of New York representing 40% of its total,

---

[527] Gandy, Oscar. "Thinking About Race, Ideology and Structure in the Presentation of Disastrous Events: The Case of Katrina." *Rethinking the Discourse on Race*. St. John's University School of Law, 28 April 2006 and Lee, Chul-joo and Oscar H. Gandy. Others' Disaster: How American Newspapers covered Hurricane Katrina (Methods, Results and Discussion). *Rethinking the Discourse on Race*. St. John's University School of Law, 28 April 2006.

while the national readership of the Washington Post accounts for only 10%." Because the population of the Washington metro area is 60 percent African American, versus 27 percent for the New York area and 10 percent nationwide, Gandy and Lee hypothesized that "the framing of stories in the Post should be more favorable to African Americans than images appearing in the Times."

The analysis was confined to the first week after Katrina came ashore (August 30 to September 7). "Given that our primary focus is on representational differences among Katrina rescuers and victims, the very first week of the crisis cycle was most appropriate for our analysis."

While there were some differences between the two papers, the major findings of the study were as follows:

- Both presented a photojournalistic record that was heavily laden with Black victims (NYT = 78%; WP = 72%),

- who were overwhelmingly passive, compared to White victims (NYT = 88% of White victims active v. 12% of Black victims; WP = 82% of White victims active v. 18% of Black).

- Black rescuers were scarce in both (NYT = 3%; WP = 20%)

- And there were virtually no images of Blacks rescuing Whites (NYT = 0; WP = 2%).

Although Gandy and Lee did not code positive and negative actions of victims into their basic analytic frame, they did note that a "substantial portion of Katrina photos published by both NYT (i.e. 6 out of 16 [38%]) and the WP (6 out of 20 [30%]) that represent Black victims as active also suggest that these Black people were engaging in socially undesirable activities."

While the image that Gandy and Lee found fit their hypothesis of a "Third World" view of disaster relief, they were confronted with the challenge that the photos and the data they produced may have actually represented the underlying reality of the situation. They countered by citing some evidence that the victims were more evenly divided between Blacks and Whites (51% to 45%) than the photos portrayed and offered a hypothesis that the racial makeup of the rescuers was likely to be more mixed than presented in the photos, although no evidence was offered in support.

The Gandy and Lee paper focused on the audience of out-of-town, national newspapers for another one of its hypotheses. The *Washington Post* did present images that were somewhat more favorable to Blacks than the *New York Times*, but Gandy and Lee are correct to focus on the fact that the overall image in both papers was negative, as they define it.

Gandy and Lee did not test what we believe could be a more salient feature of the photojournalism approach that would dictate the framing of the Katrina response. The *New York Times* and the *Washington Post* are both national newspapers distant from the event. But how did local newspapers depict it? Did the local papers of record present a different picture than the national, out-of-town papers? We set out to compare the depiction of the two.

METHOD

For the same time period, August 30 to September 7, we gathered the photojournalism record from four papers, adding two local papers, The *New Orleans Times-Picayune* and The Gulfport-Biloxi *Sun Herald*, to the same two national papers.

New Orleans Times Picayune = TP

Gulfport-Biloxi Sun Herald   = SH

Washington Post   = WP

New York Times   = NYT

We applied the same coding scheme to the photo record in both national and local papers. Gandy and Lee coded each photo on four dimensions:

Race: Black or White

Role: Rescuer or Victim

Setting: Alone v. Multiple People

Action: Passive v. Active (Positive or Negative)

Gandy and Lee coded the overall action frame of each picture, which in the case of many pictures involves a judgment call about what the picture portrayed. We chose to code each individual in each picture to preserve and represent detail. We defined the Alone v. Multiple People paradigm in the "Setting" dimension to describe whether a victim was in the presence of a rescuer ("multiple people") and vice versa. So, for instance, 3 victims in a photograph containing no rescuers are coded as "alone."

Also, because we are comparing home town, local papers, and out-of-town, national papers, it is important to control for what locale was being captured in the photo. There were three different locales depicted in the pictures – New Orleans, the Mississippi Coast, and other cities to which people had been evacuated. Most of the evacuees were from New Orleans. The reality in each location was different.

RESULTS

The survey of the papers produced 528 pictures with 1223 individuals (See Exhibit 1). The home town papers focused on their local area, with scattered images from other locales, while the out-of-town papers covered all areas, although New Orleans was the dominant locale in each by far. Observed differences in the overall action frame depicted in national and local papers could reflect differences in the locales represented.

Exhibit 1: The Database

Newspaper	Photos	Individuals	Locations (% of Individuals)			
			N.O.	Miss.	Other	Total
Times Picayune	123	308	93%	1%	6%	100%
Sun Herald	166	327	12	84	4	100
Washington Post	159	364	53	24	23	100
New York Times	80	224	68	15	18	100

There is a sharp difference in the racial make-up of New Orleans and Biloxi, which is reflected in the race of the victims (see Exhibit 2). New Orleans is two-thirds Black and black victims predominate. Biloxi is two-thirds White and White victims predominate.

Exhibit 2: The Racial Makeup of the Impact Area Populations and Victims Depicted

	Population (%) (% of Total)		Victims in Hometown Papers (% of Victim Images)	
	N.O.	Biloxi	N.O.	Biloxi
White/Other	33%	81%	38%	67%
Black	67	19	62	33
Total	100	100	100	100

When we compare the pictures of the two locales offered by the hometown and out-of-town papers, we find a clear difference. The out-of-town papers accentuate the main victim frames (see Exhibit 3). In New Orleans, where Blacks were the predominant victims in the hometown paper, the out of town papers exaggerate the presence of Black victims. In Biloxi, where Whites were the predominant victims in the hometown paper, the out-of-town papers exaggerate the presence of white victims.

Exhibit 3: Victim Images in Hometown and Out-of-Town Papers
(% of Total Locale Images)

	New Orleans			Mississippi		
	TP	WP	NYT	SH	WP	NYT
White	20	14*	11**	46	59**	76**
Black	43	61**	53*	23	15+	12+

+ p < .10, * p < .05, ** p < .01

The reality depicted in the *Times Picayune* on a picture-by-picture basis was much more complex than in the national papers (see Exhibit 4). About half of the pictures in the *Times Picayune* included uniform action frames. That is, every individual in the photo fell into the same one of the 48 categories used to classify individuals. This percentage was much higher for the other papers – almost 90 percent in the Sun Herald, over 80 percent in the Washington Post, and about 75 percent in the New York Times. The Times Picayune was much more likely to have ties – photos in which two or three categories were equally represented in a given picture. The TP was also somewhat more likely to have plurality photos in which multiple categories were represented but one predominated. Based on this analysis, from the point of view of New Orleans, we suggest that the out-of-town papers simplified the situation.

Exhibit 4: The Complexity of Individual Pictures

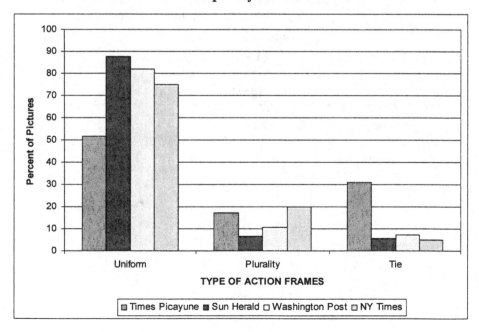

Because of this underlying complexity, we chose not to categorize each picture. Rather, we conducted the analysis at the level of the individuals depicted.

Our analysis focuses on New Orleans because it was the center of national attention and, as a result, the number of photos in the national press of other areas was too small for detailed analysis.

Our examination of the Gandy and Lee hypothesis provides support for several of the main points, although introducing a baseline with the Times Picayune and controlling for the locales of the photos makes the differences somewhat smaller (see Exhibit 5). Out of town newspapers were more likely to depict blacks as victims who were alone and passive. They were more likely to depict whites actively rescuing blacks and less likely to depict whites actively rescuing whites.

There were no instances of negative White images in any of the papers. One of the out-of-town papers (WP) depicted a higher percentage of Blacks engaging in actions that were coded as negative.

Other characteristics of the action frames pointed out by Gandy and Lee are in evidence as well, but they cannot be attributed to framing choices by the national media, since they are in evidence in all three papers. They may point to other social issues, however. Across all papers there are few black rescuers in the photos. White rescuers outnumber black rescuers by 3 or 4 to one, in a region of the country where the ratio of whites to blacks in the population is close to 1 or 1.5 to 1. Based on uniforms, this appears to be There were no instances of negative White images in any of the papers. One of the out-of-town papers (WP) depicted a higher percentage of Blacks engaging in actions that were coded as negative.

Other characteristics of the action frames pointed out by Gandy and Lee are in evidence as well, but they cannot be attributed to framing choices by the national media, since they are in evidence in all three papers. They may point to other social issues, however. Across all papers there are few black rescuers in the photos. White rescuers outnumber black rescuers by 3 or 4 to one, in a region of the country where the ratio of whites to blacks in the population is close to 1 or 1.5 to 1. Based on uniforms, this appears to be particularly true of the National Guard. The racial make-up of the National Guard, more specifically the units deployed for disaster relief, must be examined to unravel this mystery. Is the National Guard segregated? Were units selectively deployed? Are predominantly black or mixed racial units deployed in Iraq? Is there a difference in the military occupational specialties (MOS) of black and white units?

**Exhibit 5: The Key Action Frames in the Gandy & Lee Hypothesis
(Photos of New Orleans Only)**

		CFA Coding Coding individuals in photos of New Orleans Locale			Gundy & Lee Photos coded all locales	
		TP	WP	NYT	WP	NYT
White Victims	Alone	6	5	5	18	19
	Alone - Passive	6	6	5	7	8
	Alone - Negative	0	0	0	0	0
Black Victims	Alone	30	42**	33	44	48
	Alone - Passive	15	24*	18	30	26
	Alone - Negative	4	10**	5	4	3
White Rescuers	All	29	18**	29	38	35
	Rescuing Blacks	11	14	17*	20	17
	Rescuing Whites	8	2**	0**	8	3
Black Rescuers	All	8	8	7	2	8
	Rescuing Blacks	3	1	1	1	3
	Rescuing Whites	4	5	3	0	1

+ p < .10, * p < .05, ** p < .01

CONCLUSION

It may be a little harsh to say that the out-of-town papers simplified, exaggerated and distorted the image of the Katrina disaster in New Orleans, but that was the direction in which their photojournalism tended, when compared to the hometown paper of record. The negative image of Blacks was distorted, but not as severely as suggested by the Gandy and Lee discussion that did not have a baseline reality. Adding such a baseline, defined in this analysis as the presentation depicted in the hometown paper, moderates the effect, but reinforces the conclusion because important controls were added.

The fact that our approach found smaller differences does not mean that the Gandy and Lee approach was wrong. It was just different. Two primary sources of the differences are in their coding of pictures, as opposed to individuals.

Cases where we found a plurality of one type of action in a picture would be coded strictly as that type of picture in the Gandy and Lee approach. This eliminates from the analysis the actions of non-plural individuals, which magnifies the differences between our numbers and Gandy and Lee's. To the extent that passive Blacks were the plurality, which is likely, it would accentuate this action frame. If the impact of the frame is the overall theme of the picture, then counting each individual separately might be said to underestimate the effects of framing.

Second, evacuees were overwhelmingly Blacks from New Orleans. As evacuees, they were likely to be in passive situations. The fact that the national papers included many more photos of evacuees drove their presentation in the direction questioned by Gandy and Lee. For our analysis, which was focused on a home-town vs. out-of-town comparison, we dropped the pictures of evacuees who had already reached their destination. But evacuees *were* part of the national story. In this sense, the fact that the differences hold up with our approach makes the Gandy and Lee argument stronger, since we have controlled for alternative explanations.

More important, from the point of view of this analysis, are the clear differences between hometown and out-of-town representation of the events. This difference, and the fact that the *Times Picayune* and the *Sun Herald* both won Pulitzer Prizes for their coverage of the events, further reminds us of the importance of local newspapers.

PART VI:
THE IMPACT OF CONSOLIDATION AND CONGLOMERATION ON LOCALISM AND DIVERSITY POLICY

STUDY 15:
CONSOLIDATION AND CONGLOMERATION DIMINISH DIVERSITY AND DO NOT PROMOTE THE PUBLIC INTEREST: REVIEW OF THE HEARING RECORD

Mark Cooper

INTRODUCTION

The cornerstone of the effort to relax the ownership limits is the claim by the FCC that consolidation and/or conglomeration can promote the goals of the Communications Act. Although the court accepted the claim,[1] the record evidence is extremely thin. In fact, there is no evidence in the record that achieve routine levels of statistical significance to show that consolidation and/or conglomeration contribute to any of the goals of the Act. Subsequent, rigorous empirical evidence shows that newspaper TV combinations and duopolies do not increase the quantity or quality of local news and information available. The FCC concluded and the Court accepted the wrong conclusion. Since the new rules have been suspended, there will be no harm if the FCC reverses its conclusion under the quadrennial review and returns to the standard in place prior to 2003.

Here it is critical to appreciate the standard that should be applied. Given the recognition that "the widest possible dissemination of information from diverse and antagonistic sources" and the close association of points of view with ownership, the loss of an independently owned outlet is a significant harm to democratic discourse. Moreover, newspapers and television are the dominant source of local news and information by far. The gain from consolidation and conglomeration that eliminates independent voices from the forum for democratic discourse must be very large to offset the loss of a major independent voice. Neither the record evidence nor subsequent research demonstrates such a substantial gain.

This paper reviews the record evidence, which the FCC failed to cite in its order. The next two papers bring new evidence to bear on this critically important issue.

---

[1] Prometheus Radio Project, et al. v. FCC 373 (2004) (Prometheus); p. 52.

CLAIMED BENEFITS OF CROSS-OWNERSHIP ARE NOT DEMONSTRATED IN THE RECORD

Project for Excellence in Journalism

The FCC's order claiming that cross-ownership can enhance quality rests on two studies – its own Media Ownership Working Group (MOWG) study 7 and a study by the Project on Excellence in Journalism.[2] Following the FCC's record, the court cited these two studies the relevant paragraphs in the order. Neither of the studies provides a valid basis for reaching the stated conclusion.

The PEJ study was dismissed by the Commission as follows: "Whether or not the PEJ study is unbiased, its result appear statistically insignificant, the underlying data have not been made available, and therefore, cannot be considered reliable or convincing evidence."[3] Having dismissed the study as fundamentally flawed, the FCC cautioned, when it cited the study in the cross-ownership discussion that " We use PEJ's filing here solely as a source of anecdotal evidence, not as a statistical study, and do not base our conclusions regarding the newspaper/broadcast cross-ownership rule upon it."[4] The irony of the Commission even mentioning a study it had so brutally criticized is magnified by the fact that in original and the reply comments the PEJ reached exactly the opposite conclusion that the FCC did,

> The closest the PEJ Study comes to what the FCC might or might not do is this rather general observation: "The data strongly suggest regulatory changes that encourage heavy concentration of ownership in local television by a few large corporations will erode the quality of news Americans receive."[5]

Two of the four areas of analysis in the PEJ of cross-owned properties contradicted the claims of the FCC – rating trends and enterprise. In fact, the only difference between cross-owned and non-cross-owned stations that even

---

[2] Project for Excellence in Journalism, Economists Inc's "Critique of the Recent Study on Media Ownership" A Response by the Project for Excellence in Journalism, March 18, 2003, p.1.

[3] Federal Communications Commission, 2002 Biennial Regulatory Review – Review of the Commission's Broadcast Ownership Rules and Other Rules Adopted Pursuant to Section 202 of the Telecommunications Act of 1996, 18 FCC Rcd 13620, 13711-47 (2003), (hereafter Order), ¶573.

[4] Order, ¶345, footnote 766.

[5] Reply Comment, "Economists Inc.'s 'Critique' of the Recent Study on Media Ownership: A Response by the Project for Excellence in Journalism," Federal Communications Commission, 2002 Biennial Regulatory Review – Review of the Commission's Broadcast Ownership Rules and Other Rules Adopted Pursuant to Section 202 of the Telecommunications Act of 1996, March 18, 2003, p. 1.

approached statistical significance was the trend of declining rating (Chi sq – 5.16, p < .10), which points in the opposite direction from the FCC conclusion.

Commission Studies

Thus,

the Commission principally relied on the findings of its MOWG study that newspaper-owned television stations provided almost 50% more local news and public affairs programming stations, 21.9 hours per week.... The Commission also found corresponding advantages in quality of local coverage provided by newspaper-owned stations, as shown by ratings (measuring consumer approval) and industry awards (measuring critical approval).

Neither the Commission in the order nor the Court in its ruling noted CFA's criticism of this conclusion. Indeed, the Court states, "But the Citizens Petitioners do not suggest that a study entirely focused on intramarket combinations would have different results."[6] Actually, in the record we suggested exactly that.

In order to make meaningful inferences about the effects of cross ownership, one must compare apples to apples. Cross-owned stations are highly ranked stations in large markets. Without proper controls – i.e. comparing them to small market low ranked stations – leads on to make false claims for the benefits of cross-ownership that are properly attributable to station rank and market size.

The primary numerical evidence on which the FCC relied was not presented as statistically significant (no statistical tests were applied). The Newspaper Association of America, whose comments the FCC cited, simply reworked the same data. Both failed to introduce proper controls or apply statistical tests.

Exhibit 1 presents the flaw in the FCC/NAA analysis in graphic terms. It shows the market size (i.e. rank of the DMA) on the X-axis. It shows the total hours of local news on the Y-axis. In the market ranked equal to those where we find cross-owned stations, there is little difference in the production of news.

Exhibit 2 shows the mean number of hours of news. The exhibit shows news programming of four types of stations in each market: those with the most hours in the market; the highest ranked station, the second rank station and the cross-owned station. Three of the six cross-owned stations had the most hours in their market; all six of the cross-owned stations were ranked first. The non-cross-owned stations with the most hours have a higher average number of hours than the cross-owned stations. The non-cross owned stations that had the highest ratings had a higher average number of

---

[6] Promethreus, p. 50.

Exhibit 1: News Production, Market Size, Market Rank and Cross-Ownership

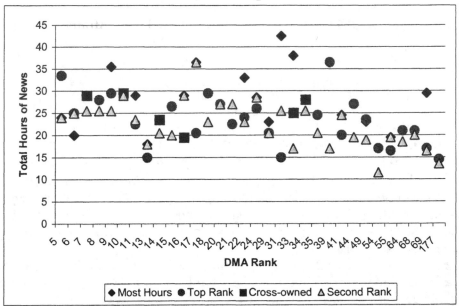

Source: Spavins, Thomas C., et al, "The Measurement of Local Television News and Public Affairs Programs," Appendices B and C.

hours than the cross-owned stations. Any apparent advantage of cross-owned stations is a function of comparing them to much lower ranked station in smaller markets. There is no way to infer that cross-ownership will result in an increase of news produced.

Exhibit 2: Hours of News Supplied by Station Rank and Market Size

		Most Hours	Top-Rated Stations	Second-Rated Stations
All DMA's	Non-Cross-Owned	32.5	28.9	22.5
	Cross-Owned	27.5	27.5	
Top 34 DMA's	Non-Cross-Owned	35.6	28.5	24.7
	Cross-Owned	27.5	27.5	

Source: Calculated from Spavins, Thomas C., et al, "The Measurement of Local Television News and Public Affairs Programs," Appendices B and C.

The above analysis focuses on the output of stations, rather than the output of markets. Looking at the total quantity of news in markets with cross owned stations, we observe that two of the six markets with cross owned stations were on the trend line of all stations as calculated in Exhibit 3. There were two well above the line. There were two somewhat below it.

Exhibit 3: Total Hours of Local News and Public Affairs
(Markets With Cross Owned Stations compared to trend line)

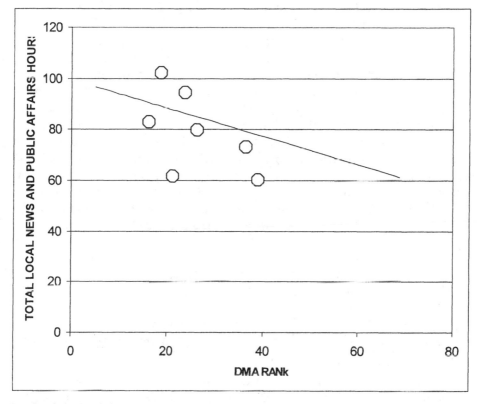

Source: Calculated from Spavins, Thomas C., et al, "The Measurement of Local Television News and Public Affairs Programs," Appendix A.

There were three close to it. The bold claims that concentration and cross ownership are good for news output is not supported by this data. At best there is a small difference between stations in newspaper/broadcast combinations and duopolies. Whatever small increases in quality and/or quantity come with very large losses in media ownership diversity.

The second type of data offered in support of the proposition that cross-ownership improves local news was to count awards for local news programs. A number of problems in the approach were pointed out in the record. Putting those problems aside, the data poses similar problems. The evidence does not support the claim to benefits of concentration and cross ownership, when market size and station rank. The networks contend that the journalistic awards received by cross-owned stations indicate that such stations are "better off" than non-cross-owned stations. Looking at a cross-owned situation in the same market, however, it is difficult to conclude that the stations are better or worse (See Exhibit 4). We observe many that are better and many that are worse. The inconclusiveness of the award data above is demonstrated by the following observations. In the aggregate, cross-owned stations may be more likely to win awards, but the statistical validity of the conclusion and the representativeness of the sample are suspect. When viewed on a market-by-market basis, the data is not convincing. There were nine markets with cross-owned stations in which awards were made. In four markets, the cross-owned stations won all of the awards. They tended to be among the top two highest ranked stations. The non-cross-owned stations that won awards in markets where cross-owned stations exist were ranked considerably lower in terms of viewership. On average, they were ranked (between third and fourth) in their markets, compared to the cross-owned stations that won (which were ranked second on average). In five markets where awards were won, the cross-owned station won none, they tended to lower ranked. The cross-owned stations that did not win awards were ranked about fourth on average. Generally, the non-cross owned stations did more with less.

CLAIMS THAT OTHER FACTORS 'MITIGATE' THE HARM OF CROSS-OWNERSHIP ARE UNSUPPORTED

The FCC tried to brush aside the clear negative impact of cross-media mergers with the claim that ownership does not matter, as summarized by the court,

> First, it found that "[c]ommonly-owned newspapers and broadcast stations do not necessarily speak with a single, monolithic voice." Given conflicting evidence in the record on whether ownership influences viewpoint, the Commission reasonably concluded that it did not have enough confidence in the proposition that commonly owned outlets have a uniform bias to warrant sustaining the cross-ownership ban.[7]

The record evidence to which the Commission points is yet another study that lacks statistical validity and, upon close reading does not support the Commission's position.[8] As demonstrated in *Study 5: Media Ownership and Viewpoint*, the link between ownership and point of view is well demonstrated in the academic literature and this single fatally flawed cannot stand as a basis for doubt of that proposition.

---

[7] *Prometheus*, pp. 51-52.
[8] Ownership Order, ¶ 362.

The second basis for claiming that cross-ownership will do no harm involved other sources of news. As the Court noted, "the Commission found that diverse viewpoints from other media sources in local markets (such as cable and the Internet) compensate for viewpoints lost to newspaper/broadcast consolidation."[9] Ironically, the FCC ended up not counting cable as an independent source of news, so it is hard to understand how it could simultaneously count and not count. The Court accepted the argument to discount cable, but found the same reasoning applied to the Internet –

> we affirm the Commission's reasoned decision to discount cable. But we think that the same rationale also applies to the Internet. Therefore, it s decision to count the Internet as a source of viewpoint diversity, while discounting cable, was not rational.[10]

Additional evidence summarized in Studies 7 and 8 shows that the Internet has not become a significant independent source of local news and information. Television and newspapers remain the dominant sources of such information.

Beyond the flawed statistical studies of cross-owned stations, the FCC provides a lengthy recounting of self-serving claims by broadcasters that they would do more if they could buy newspapers.   The claim of synergies allowing improvement in operations is not supported by independent evidence, untainted by the economic interest of the commentors in the record evidence, or elsewhere. As noted, to the extent that any conclusions have statistical validity in the PEJ study, they contradict the claim. Moreover, the academic literature on synergistic benefits of cross-media conglomeration shows that they are non-existent as described in Studies 9 and 10.

Thus, the record evidence did not support the Commission's decision to abandon the prohibition on cross-ownership and subsequent evidence contradicts that decision. Moreover, it should be noted that the Commission did not propose to poke a small hole in the cross-ownership ban. Rather, it proposed a blanket, no-questions asked safe harbor that would allow cross media mergers in over four-fifths of the media markets in the country.[11]

THE LOCAL TELEVISION OWNERSHIP RULE

As with the cross-ownership rule, the Commission concludes that "Anecdotal and empirical evidence in the record demonstrates post-combination increases in the amount of local news and public affairs

---

[9] Prometheus, p. 52.
[10] Prometheus, p. 62.
[11] The Commission never published a full list of which markets would be subject to which limitations under the cross media limits test. This is our estimate of the impact.

programming offered by commonly owned stations."[12]   As in the case of cross-ownership, the order fails to take note of the CFA analysis that demonstrated the empirical evidence was not statistically valid.   As in the case of cross-ownership, subsequent, statistically valid analysis contradicts the Commission's conclusion.

The networks ignore the importance of ownership and instead present information to the Commission demonstrating that the quantity of news is increasing and therefore implying that the quality of the news is being preserved. Lengthy tables are provided to show that the networks have increased the number of hours devoted to news. The networks claim that duopolies enable them to do so, but the evidence does not support this conclusion (see Exhibit 4). Increases in news coverage are equal in duopoly and non-duopoly markets. More importantly, the loss of independent hours of news exceeds the gain in the total hours of news. In other words, we get a little more quantity at a severe cost to quality (independent hours of news). Conversely, the ban on duopolies promotes diversity of viewpoints (measured by ownership) without detracting from the quantity of news.

Exhibit 4: Television News Awards

	Non-Cross Owned	Cross Owned
4 Or More Awards	12	0
3 Awards	8	2
2 Awards	14	4
1 Award	23	2

Sources: Spavins, Thomas C., et al, "The Measurement of Local Television News and Public Affairs Programs," Appendices B and C.

Appendix B to the broadcast networks comments, which presents an econometric analysis, is consistent with these findings.   It finds a small increase in the *probability* that a station will cover news (from 66.5 to 74.5 percent), but no statistically significant differences in the amount of news. Because the networks disregard ownership, the study did not examine the loss of independent news.   Also the network-sponsored econometric study cannot address the question of causality. It did not inquire as to whether the duopolists added news after a duopoly was created, or merely bought stations that already produce news.

An examination of the detailed data provided by FOX and NBC shows that they did not add news to any stations that did not already carry it

---

[12] Order, ¶169.

and, in one case; they eliminated the news on a duopoly station. Thus, Appendix B to the Network filing has mistakenly ascribed a positive effect to duopolies where none exists. In terms of news carriage, the networks were not able to show a positive effect in the amount of news carried, and completely ignored the negative effect of the loss of an independent news voice (see Exhibit 5).

A similar conclusion emerges from the study prepared for Sinclair by Robert Crandall.[13] Using a standard of statistical significance that is rarely seen in the academic social science literature (10 percent), Crandall concludes that duopolies result in a slight decrease in advertising rates. The decrease is extremely small, just .3 percent. In other words, according to Crandall, prohibiting duopolies (which preserves a valuable independent TV voice) imposes a statistically insignificant and quantitatively minuscule economic cost.

Exhibit 5: The Costs of Duopoly Far Exceed the Benefits

	Duopoly			Non-Duopoly	
	# of Markets	Change in Hours of News	Lost Hours of Independen News	# of Markets	Change in Hours of News
Fox	9	+1.7	-2.5	16	+1.9
NBC	6	+4.4	-12.0	10	+3.9
Total/Average	15	+2.8	-6.3	26	+2.7

Source:
a/ Viacom data does not provide sufficient detail to conduct the lost hours analysis.
b/ Fox shows much larger gains for non-duopolies when it goes back to its pre-acquisition of stations, which in many cases is a decade or more ago. Use of this data would make non-duopolies appear even more valuable. This analysis uses changes since 11/2000.

CONCLUSION

Thus, we believe that the record evidence did not support the conclusions reached by the FCC. Although the Court accepted some of the propositions underlying the decision to relax the ownership limits, it found the implementation of relaxed rules so faulty that actual changes in the rules were stayed. The weakness of the record evidence we have described in this paper demonstrates two points. First, to the extent that the *Prometheus* Court accepted the erroneous reasoning of the FCC, it was mistaken. Second, to the extent that the erroneous conclusions about the relationship between ownership and the policy goals led the FCC to seek broad relaxation of the

[13] Crandall, Robert W., The Economic Impact of Providing Service to Multiple Local Braodcast Stations Within a Single Geographic Market," Sinclair, Exhibit1.

rules it went too far.   Both observations are important.   Developments and analysis since the court decision reinforce our conclusion and these two observations.

STUDY 16
CONSOLIDATION AND CONGLOMERATION DIMINISH DIVERSITY AND DO NOT PROMOTE THE PUBLIC INTEREST: NEW EVIDENCE

MARK COOPER AND S. DEREK TURNER

Since the Court ruling, a great deal of evidence has come to light that contradicts the FCC's order. Most importantly, a significant part of that evidence is directly related to the evidence that was entered into the proceeding and formed the basis for the Media Ownership Order. In other words, the fabric of the order was rotten to the core and the remnants that passed judicial review should be discarded. The FCC has opened the door to this very proposition by incorporating all of the prior evidence into this proceeding, rather than starting afresh.

THE PEJ DATA

The plot involving the PEJ studied thickened dramatically in recent weeks when it was revealed that subsequent to the Court ruling the Commission obtained the PEJ data set, applied the statistical controls that were lacking in the original study, and found that the **PEJ data contradicts the FCC's conclusion.** In short, having incorrectly cited the PEJ study as supporting the lifting of the ban on newspaper TV cross ownership, the FCC then proved using the very same data that it had erred in doing so. The direct contradiction between what the FCC said and what the FCC did applies to every aspect of the proceeding. Not only does concentration harm localism, but various form of conglomeration and consolidation do as well.

Studies addressing two different output measures were developed from the PEJ database. One output measure was the quantity of local news. The second output measure was the diversity of the output of local and national news. Essentially, the database counted the number of minutes devoted to different types of stories. The localism measures are straightforward counts– the number of total news seconds, the number of local news seconds and the number of local-on-location news seconds.

The diversity measure is more controversial. The primary variable used was actually much more a measure of variety than diversity. If one station devoted 30 second each to two different stories, both were counted as contributing to variety. However, if two stations devoted 30 seconds each to the same story, that was not counted as contributing to diversity at all. Only if a station that "duplicated" the coverage of a story devoted more time to it, did it count as diversity and only the incremental time counted. "[I]f any two or more local news stations broadcasts cover the same story on the same day only the second beyond the collective average of the respective overlapping broadcasts are counted as adding to diversity."[1] This is at odds with the fundamental definition of diversity as the Supreme Court interprets it. "Antagonistic" reporting of the same events is essential to creating the "cross-lights" that reveal truth. This measure severely undercounts that essential concept. Nevertheless, it too contradicts the FCC's conclusions.

In some specifications, a more appropriate measure of diversity was used. This "total DMA diversity" "counts the total time devoted to all unique stories covered."[2] This measure of diversity produced even more robust results confirming the negative effect of concentration on diversity.

The primary finding of the localism study was that local ownership matters in the production of local news.

> The estimates presented in Section 4 suggest that local ownership may have significant implications for local content. In particular, local ownership appears to increase total, local and local on-location news seconds. Moreover, the increase in total new seconds from local ownership appears to be almost entirely driven by an increase in local news.[3]

> Owned-and-operated broadcast television stations produce less local news, but do not air significantly less total news or local on-location news. Therefore, it appears that owned and operated stations substitute non-local news for local news (that is not on location). This might indicate substitution of network feeds for no-on-location content.[4]

Consolidation in the national television market does not improve the performance of the broadcast station owners. This finding emerges in both the localism and diversity studies.

> As a local owner acquires television stations in more DMAs, they produce less total news. The large (albeit statistically insignificant) point estimates from the local news and on-location local news regression indicate that the decrease in total news may be primarily driven by decreases in local and local on-location news seconds.[5]

> In short, our estimate suggests that increasing concentration appears to diminish diversity in local broadcast news both at the firm and market level.

---

[1] Alexander, Peter J. and Brendan M. Cunningham, *Same Story, Different Channel: Broadcast News and Information* (October 4, 2004).

[2] Id. p. 15.

[3] Anonymous, *Do Local Owners Deliver More Localism? Some Evidence from Local Broadcast News* (Federal Communication Commission, draft dated June 17, 2004), p. 14.

[4] Id., p. 15.

[5] Id. P. 15.

This result is robust to the measure of diversity used in estimation and emerges after controlling for possible endogeneity in market structure.[6]

Conglomeration across media types does not improve the performance of the broadcast station owners.

While newspaper ownership is not a significant factor, a local television station owner who owns a within-DMA radio station appears to produce significantly less local news, possibly because they substitute local radio news for local television news.[7]

Our theoretical research suggests that media variety allows consumer to insure against the idiosyncratic nature of information from particular sources. Moreover, the empirical evidence we have assembled suggests that concentrated media markets exhibit more homogeneity in the information conveyed to consumers. Such concentration can, therefore, inhibit the ability of individuals to derive a more stable payoff from media consumption.

This finding implies that regulatory policy designed to protect and encourage competition simultaneously helps satisfy a second policy objective: diversity.[8]

Specifically, using the relative station-level diversity metric, we find that when the structure of the market becomes more concentrated, relative diversity of local news content is diminished. Importantly, this result is not robust to an instrumental variables specification. However, using the total market diversity metric, HHI is significant in OLS and robust to instrumental variable transformation. Since the total market diversity metric is arguably superior to the incremental metric as a measure of overall diversity, this result is useful – it suggests that total diversity within a DMA is sensitive to the level of concentration. Since we find that market structure plays an equally important role in determining product variety in national broadcasts, we are fairly confident of this finding.[9]

The final sentence of the above citation indicates that the negative impact of concentration on diversity in local news also occurs for nation news, even though the weak definition of diversity is used: "In particular, we find that concentration displays a negative and significant relationship with national news broadcast variety."[10]

One can hardly imagine a more stunning contradiction of the FCC's claim that ownership and concentration do not matter. However, these studies go to the general relationship between ownership, concentration and the policy outputs that Congress is concerned about: localism and diversity.

---

[6] Alexander, Peter J. and Brendan M/Cunningham, "Diversity in Broadcast Television: An Empirical Study of Local News," *International Journal of Media Management* 6:177
[7] Id., p. 14
[8] Alexander, Peter J. and Brendan M. Cunningham,
[9] Alexander and Cunningham, Same Story, p. 24.
[10] Id., p. 20.

These finding are crucial since the FCC relied on general concerns about these relationship to relax the limits on ownership. But what about the specific policies – duopolies and newspaper cross ownership, which are at issue in this proceeding? The PEJ database used to examine the general relationships does not contain enough observations to examine these policies. However, other databases have been constructed to do so.

DUOPOLIES

In a series of studies Yan and Napoli have shown that duopolies are not associated with the provision of larger amounts of local news or public affairs programming.[11]   Using a sample of TV stations and a two-week constructed random sample of local news and public affairs programming, Napoli and Yan have shown that duopolies do not provide more local news and public affairs programming. In the appendix to this paper, their approach to assessing the impact of ownership characteristics is extended to cross-ownership between newspapers and TV stations. They conclude that there is no statically significant difference in the quantity of local news or public affairs programming cross-ownership does not increase the amount of news or public affairs programming provided.

In a study of local public affairs programming, Napoli and Yan fill an important gap in the analysis. They reach exactly the same conclusion that the updated PEJ analyses of local news did.

Perhaps the most interesting are the findings regarding the effect of the station ownership characteristics. First, if there is nay result that has been consistent throughout the models, it is the negative effects of TP$, the ownership by one of the big four broadcast networks. Coupled with the marginally significant positive effect of local ownership, these findings suggest that (big four) network ownership has hampered the provision of local public affairs programming.

Equally interesting is the lack of significant effect of duopoly ownership found in this study. In relaxing the multiple ownership rules in 1999, the FCC argued that the new rules would lead to increased local news and public affairs programming in the local market by emphasizing the economic efficiencies and public service benefits to be gained from combined resources under common ownership of stations. However, these programming benefits have not

---

[11] Yan, Michael and Philip Napoli, "Market Structure, Station Ownership, and Local Public Affairs Programming on Local Broadcast Television," Telecommunications Policy Research Conference, October 2004; Yan Michael Zhaoxu and Yong Jin Park, "Duopoly Ownership and Local Informational Programming on Television: An Empirical Analysis," Telecommunications Policy Research Conference, September 2005; Napoli, Philip, *Market Conditions and Public Affairs Programming: Implications for Digital Television Policy* (Washington, D.C.: Benton Foundation, N.D.).

materialized. More damaging to the FCC's reasoning, the study also found that a station's public affair programming decision was not affected by its financial resources (as measured by a station's 2002 revenues).

Together, the findings regarding local ownership, network ownership and duopoly call into question the underlying rationale of the FCC's current policies toward more relaxed national and multiple ownership rules (particularly in terms of economies of scale contributing to greater production of such programming).[12]

Ironically, Yan and Napoli went on to caution that "[a]t the very least, the results presented in this study suggest that it would be premature for the Commission to ignore the question of ownership in its ongoing localism inquiry."[13]   We now know that the FCC has not ignored the role of ownership, but when it found that the evidence contradicted its Order, it suppressed the evidence.[14]

Yan and Park revisited the issue of the effect of duopolies on public affairs programming and local news by expanding the data set and adopting a different methodology. The original Yan and Napoli study pulled a random sample of stations for the randomly constructed two weeks of programming. This turns up a number of duopoly stations, but not necessarily matched comparisons for those stations in their own market. Yan and Park expanded the data set to include a set of matched comparisons for the duopoly situations (while relying on the same randomly constructed two week sample of programming. Using a quasi-experimental design, they compared duopoly and non-duopoly stations within duopoly markets, as well as non non-duopoly stations in non-duopoly markets. They also added a before and after component, testing whether the introduction of duopolies affected the output of stations.   Thus, there are three types of stations in their design – duopoly (DD), non-duopoly in duopoly markets (DN), and non-duopoly stations in non-duopoly markets (NN).

Across the board, the findings did not support the claims that allowing duopolies would increase the production of either local news or public affairs.

Looking at the market level, during the two-week sample period in 2003, the stations in duopoly markets aired an average of 29.2 hours of local news programming, while those in non-duopoly markets did 29.8 hours. The difference is not statistically significant. One of our research questions asks whether or not duopoly markets, as a whole provide more local news programming than non-duopoly markets.   The answer, according to our findings here is no. Stations in duopoly markets do not broadcast more local

---

[12] Yan and Napoli, p. 16

[13] Oid.,p. 16.

[14] Dunbar, John. "Lawyer Says FCC Ordered Study Destroyed", *Associated Press*, September 14th 2006.

news programming than those in non-duopoly markets. The same conclusion also applies to the 1997 data. Note, however, stations in both type of markets has significantly increased their local programming from 1997 to 2003. There is no interaction effect between market type and the time trend. In other words, stations in duopoly markets did not increase their local news programming more than those in non-duopoly markets...

One of our key research hypotheses is whether or not stations increase their local informational programming after joining a common ownership... The duopoly stations (DD) did increase their local news programming form 18.5 hours in 1997 to 22.6 hours in 2003. However, so did two other types of stations (DN and NN). We tested for the interaction effect between station type and the time trend and found no such effect. Therefore, the duopoly stations did not enjoy a greater increase that the other types of stations.[15]

It is worth recalling that this is exactly the conclusion we reached in our reply comments in the earlier proceeding, when we examined the data introduced by the networks. The evidentiary basis for relaxing the rule based on the quantity of news never existed, as described more fully in *Study 15: Consolidation and Conglomeration Diminish Diversity and Do Not Promote the Public Interest: A Review of the Hearing Record in the Media Ownership Proceeding.* Yan and Park bring a larger data base and a rigorous research design to bear on the question.

Turning to the different types of stations, the duopoly stations (DD) broadcast significantly fewer hours of local news programming in 2003 than their non-duopoly counterparts in the same market (DN). They also contributed less time to local news than non-duopoly stations from markets that has no common television ownership, although the difference was not significant.[16]

This is exactly the result shown in *Study 15: Consolidation and Conglomeration Diminish Diversity and Do Not Promote the Public Interest: A review of the Hearing Record in the Media Ownership Proceeding,* Exhibit 2, with respect to cross-ownership. That exhibit is based on the FCC's own data. Again, the hearing record did not support the conclusion reached and the more recent data confirms that conclusion.

Yan and Park explored the claim that weaker stations in the duopoly would be helped by the combination to do a better job of providing local news. Again, they found no such effect.

One strong argument for the relaxation of the television multiple ownership rules is that joint ownership can benefits the weaker station in a combination disproportionately.... [T]he significant increases in local new programming experienced by the three types of stations were all attributable to the major

---

[15] Yan and Park, pp. 11-12.
[16] Id., pp. 11-12.

stations.   For example, major DD stations increased their local news programming by eight hours and major NN stations did by 10.3 hours. On the contrary, the minor stations did not show any significant increases in their local news programming at all.   Thus there is no evidence that joint ownership induces minor stations to produce more local news programming.[17]

Yan and Park also analyzed this set of questions for the provision of local public affairs programming. They reach the same conclusion.

At the market level, stations in duopoly markets broadcast slightly more local public affairs programming than their counterparts in non-duopoly markets in both 1997 and 2003, but the differences were not statistically significant. In addition, there were no significant changes in local public affairs programming for the two types of markets across the years. If anything, the changes form 1997 to 2003 were negative.

At the station level, duopoly stations broadcast the least amount of local public affairs programming in both years. Note, however, none of these changes was statistically significant.   Looking at the provision of local public affairs programming by the major and minor stations, neither the major stations nor the minor stations increased their local public affairs programming once becoming duopolies. Again, the changes were on the declining side.[18]

NEW EVIDENCE ON CROSS-OWNERSHIP

We applied the approaches used by Napoli and Yan for duopolies to the cross-ownership issue by obtaining the identical programming information for all cross-owned stations in the U.S. and merging the data with the random sample of stations.   We then conducted both a matched comparison analysis and a multiple linear regression analysis. We find that cross-ownership is not associated with the provision of larger amounts of local news or public affairs programming.

Matched Comparison Results

Yan and Park added non-duopoly stations in duopoly and non-duopoly markets to the database for purposes of the duopoly analysis. We added the 27 cross-owned stations to the database and sought the best matches available in the original database. This turned up 14 markets in which there were cross-owned and non-cross-owned stations (see Exhibit 1).

The cross-owned stations tended to be much higher ranked. Nevertheless, the difference between cross-owned and non-cross-owed stations was not significant (see Exhibit 2).   Adding in station rank as a covariate yields the same result. Station rank is significantly related to local

---

[17] Id., p. 13.
[18] Id. p. 13.

news production in the expected direction, the lower the rank the less the output. Given the small number and lack of good matches, we focus out attention on the multiple regression approach.

Exhibit 1: Matched Comparisons

Cross-Owned Market	Station	Channel	Network	Share	Rank	Owner
New York	WNYW	5	Fox	5.25	5	Fox Television
Los Angeles	KTLA	5	WB	6	6	Tribune Bcstg Co.
Chicago	WGN	9	WB	8	4	Tribune Bcstg Co.
Dallas-Ft. Worth	WFAA	8	ABC	12	1	Belo Corp
Miami-Ft. Laud.	WDZL	39	WB	5.5	5	Tribune Bcstg Co
Cincinnati	WCPO	9	ABC	11.75	2	Scripps Howard Bcstg
Miwaukee, WI	WTMJ	4	NBC	16.25	1	Journal Comm
Columbus, OH	WBNS	10	CBS	16.25	1	Dispatch Printing Co
Dayton, OH	WHIO	7	CBS	18.25	1	Cox Broadcasting
Pudacah	WPSD	6	NBC	14.75	2	Paxton media
Waco	KCEN	6	NBC	12.25	2	Frank Mayborn Enterp
Baton Rouge	WBRZ	2	ABC	13	2	Manship Stations
Fargo-Valley City	WDAY	6	ABC	13.75	2	Forum Publishing Co
Columbus-Tupelo	WCBI	4	CBS	15.25	2	Morris Multimedia
Average				12.02	2.6	

Non-Cross-Owned Market	Station	Channel	Network	Share	Rank	Owner
New York	WCBS	2	CBS	8.25	3	CBS/Viacom
Los Angeles	KCAL	9	IND	4.75	7	CBS/Viacom
Chicago	WBBM	2	CBS	7	5	CBS/Viacom
Dallas-Ft. Worth	KDFW	4	Fox	9	3	Fox Television
Miami-Ft. Laud.	WFOR	4	CBS	9	1	CBS/Viacom
Cincinnati	WSTR	64	WB	4.75	5	Sinclair Bcst
Miwaukee, WI	WITI	6	Fox	11.5	2	Fox Television
Columbus, OH	WCMH	4	NBC	13.75	2	NBC/GE
Dayton, OH	WDTN	2	ABC	7.75	3	LIN Television Corp
Pudacah	WDKA	49	WB	2	5	Lucci, Paul T.
Waco	KWKT	44	Fox	6.75	4	Comm Corp of America
Baton Rouge	WAFB	9	CBS	21.5	1	Raycom Media
Fargo-Valley City	KXJB	4	CBS	13.5	3	Catamount Bcst Group
Columbus-Tupelo	WLOV	27	Fox	6	3	Lingard Bcstg Corp
Average				8.96	3.6	

Exhibit 2: Analysis of Matched Comparisons

	Local News		Local Public Affairs	
	Beta (signif.)	Beta (signif.)	Beta (signif.)	Beta (signif.)
Cross-Ownership	0.260 (0.181)	0.174 (0.355)	0.286 (0.141)	0.261 (0.194)
Station Rank		-0.369 (0.050)**		-0.103 (0.604)

** = significant at the 5% level

Multiple Regression Results

Yan's most recent analysis, *Newspaper/Television Cross-Ownership and Local News and Public Affairs Programming on Television Stations: An Empirical Analysis*, reaches similar conclusions. "The Regression analysis of the study controlled for [market factors] and its results shows that cross-ownership did not have any significant relationship with the amount of local news and public affairs programming aired by the samples stations during the sample period."[19]

Because the policies affect cross-ownership and duopolies, as well as the fact that likely market impacts are different, we did several additional analyses of the data and specified the multiple regression models somewhat differently.

This paper uses the same dataset and reaches the same conclusion, while taking a somewhat different approach to specifying the model. Napoli and Yan specified a mix of station and market variables that predict the quantity of local news provided.

The three most important control variable in the Napoli and Yan analysis were the type of license (VHF-UHF), whether the station was an affiliate of one of the big four networks (ABC, CBS, NBC, Fox) and the revenue of the station. For a number of reasons we build a basic model that does not include these variables.

The nature of the license has ceased to be relevant in the current media environment. With cable distribution of video signals, the VHF-UHF distinction is not longer relevant. With over 80 percent of households receiving their video signals over cable, the "strength" of the signal no longer

---

[19] Yan, Michael Zhaoxu. 2006. "Newspaper/Television Cross-Ownership and Local News and Public Affairs Programming on Television Stations: An Empirical Analysis", A report commissioned by the Donald McGannon Communication Research Center at Fordham University, under a grant from the Benton Foundation, October 3rd.

matters. To the extent that the VHF-UHF distinction was important in the analysis, it was a proxy for other historical characteristics of the station. Therefore, in the place of the VHF-UHF variable, we use the age of the station.

There is one characteristic of the license that is relevant, the city of the license. A broadcaster has a must-carry right in a specific geographic area, and the location of the license is fixed. To capture this, we include market rank along with the other market characteristics Napoli and Yan included.

For the purposes of the original duopoly analysis, the inclusion of whether a station was affiliated with one of the Big 4 networks or one of the Top 4 networks was appropriate. By definition, the formation of a duopoly affects the affiliation of the acquired station. Moreover, public policy prevented mergers between the top four stations in the market; it largely held constant the issue of Big 4 and Top 4. In the case of cross-ownership policy, the FCC did not have this stipulation. It is possible that a combination merger would change a station's affiliation and rank. It is unlikely that two affiliates of one of the Big 4 network will compete head-to-head in a market. The most likely outcome is that affiliation will not change. There is a small chance that the identity of the Big 4 stations might change. Nevertheless, we drop this characteristic as a control variable, but examine it as a policy relevant intervening variable.

The make-up of the Top 4 could be affected by a cross-ownership combination. However, this variable was not statistically significant in either the duopoly or the cross-ownership analyses conducted by Napoli and Yan, so we drop it from the analysis altogether.

Station revenue may be more policy relevant in the cross-ownership analysis than the duopoly analysis. The hope for combinations of a newspaper and a TV station is that would shift revenue shares between stations. In reality, that hope has not generally been achieved. Nevertheless, we drop this variable as a control variable, but examine it as a policy relevant intervening variable.

The models used were generally specified as follows:

$news\_l = \alpha + \beta_1(type)_i + \beta_2(rank)_i + \beta_3(yrstd)_i + \beta_{4\text{-}8}[market\ controls]_i + \beta_9(big4)_i + \beta_{10}(rev\_s)_i + \varepsilon_i$

$pa\_l = \alpha + \beta_1(type)_i + \beta_2(rank)_i + \beta_3(yrstd)_i + \beta_{4\text{-}8}[market\ controls]_i + \beta_9(big4)_i + \beta_{10}(rev\_s)_i + \varepsilon_i$

$presence = \alpha + \beta_1(type)_i + \beta_2(rank)_i + \beta_3(yrstd)_i + \beta_{4\text{-}8}[market\ controls]_i + \beta_9(big4)_i + \beta_{10}(rev\_s)_i + \varepsilon_i$

$pa\_l\_dum = \alpha + \beta_1(type)_i + \beta_2(rank)_i + \beta_3(yrstd)_i + \beta_{4\text{-}8}[market\ controls]_i + \beta_9(big4)_i + \beta_{10}(rev\_s)_i + \varepsilon_i$

Where,

$news\_l$ = *seconds of local news*
pa_l = *seconds of local public affairs*
$presence$ = *dummy variable for presence of local news*

pa_l_dum = dummy variable for presence of local public affairs programming
type = dummy variable for cross-owned station
rank = DMA market rank
yrstd = year station was stared (expressed in ### format; i.e. 1954 = 54, 2002 = 102)
big4 = dummy variable for ABC, CBS, Fox, or NBC affiliated stations
rev_s = station revenues
market controls =
ptv_m = number of public television stations in market
cable_m = percentage of households in market subscribing to cable
tvhh3 = number of television households in market, 2003 (thousands)
ptvview = percentage of public television viewing in a station's market
othview = percentage of non-broadcast television viewing in a station's market

Each model is examined in a parsimonious manner, investigating the added effects of the market control variables as well as the big-four and station revenue variables. For the examination of seconds of local news, OLS and Robust regression models were used. However, the presence of a significant number of stations with zero seconds of public affairs programming created methodological problems. To adequately deal with this corner-solution scenario, Tobit models were used. Dummy variables for the presence of any local news or local public affairs programming were created, and investigated using Probit and linear probability models. However, the fact that every single cross-owned station in the sample aired local news precluded the use of a Probit model. Thus, a Tobit model was employed for the variable *presence* when investigating the effect of cross-ownership.

Results examining the effect of cross-ownership are listed below in Exhibits 3-6.

Market rank and age of station are statistically significant and large predictors of the amount of news produced. The direction of the relationship is as expected. The larger the market, the greater the amount of news produced. The older the station, the greater the amount of news produced. The coefficient on the cross-ownership variable – type – is not statistically significant. None of the other variables is statistically significant either. Moreover, controlling for the age of the station and the market in which it is located, measured by the market rank, renders the relationship between cross-ownership and the amount of news statistically insignificant.

When we reintroduce the two station characteristics as intervening variables, we find that their coefficients are significant and they increase the amount for variance explained significantly. Age of station and rank remain statistically significant, and the other variables remain statistically not significant.

Exhibit 3: Effect of Cross-Ownership on Amount of Local News

Dependent Variable = Local News (news_l)

	OLS	Robust Regr.	OLS	Robust Regr.	OLS	Robust Regr.	OLS	Robust Regr.
	Coeff. Beta (signif.) (sig. w/ rob.err.)	Coeff. (signif.)	Coeff. Beta (signif.) (sig. w/ rob.err.)	Coeff. (signif.)	Coeff. Beta (signif.) (sig. w/ rob.err.)	Coeff. (signif.)	Coeff. Beta (signif.) (sig. w/ rob.err.)	Coeff. (signif.)
type	215.8334 0.0487 (0.242) (0.227)	260.4077 (0.141)	177.2227 0.0411 (0.309) (0.275)	196.9035 (0.252)	271.1242 0.0584 (0.171) (0.112)	285.1201 (0.134)	147.1774 0.3258 (0.424) (0.361)	138.1575 (0.455)
rank	-3.3992 -0.1427 (0.000)# (0.001)#	-4.4174 (0.000)#	-4.4286 -0.1856 0.000 (0.000)#	-4.5500 (0.000)#	-6.4700 -0.2733 (0.000)# (0.000)#	-7.5943 (0.000)#	-6.5111 -0.2744 (0.000)# (0.000)#	-7.0793 (0.000)#
yrstd	-56.4422 -0.7473 (0.000)# (0.000)#	-59.7830 (0.000)#	-40.8849 -0.5239 (0.000)# (0.000)#	-44.0963 (0.000)#	-56.7719 -0.7534 (0.000)# (0.000)#	-60.8676 (0.000)#	-39.5891 -0.5084 (0.000)# (0.000)#	-42.9163 (0.000)#
ptv_m					-37.0583 -0.0416 (0.426) (0.398)	-28.0980 (0.529)	-44.2822 -0.0507 (0.306) (0.289)	-50.7322 (0.243)
cable_m					-2.8679 -0.0199 (0.662) (0.633)	1.0278 (0.871)	-4.6495 -0.0324 (0.449) (0.413)	-3.5764 (0.562)
TVHH3					-0.0974 -0.0907 (0.129) (0.107)	-0.1105 (0.073)*	-0.1333 -0.1261 (0.073)* (0.176)	-0.1579 (0.035)^
ptvview					78.3121 0.0799 (0.133) (0.118)	51.3614 (0.305)	70.3505 0.0707 (0.173) (0.164)	50.8090 (0.326)
othview					16.6757 0.1202 (0.115) (0.093)*	13.1793 (0.194)	14.3041 0.0995 (0.167) (0.158)	9.8062 (0.345)
big4			922.7512 0.30525 (0.000)# (0.000)#	842.6817 (0.000)#			806.4215 0.2678 (0.000)# (0.000)#	733.2874 (0.000)#
rev_s			4.2781 0.1217 (0.020)^ (0.071)*	4.8365 (0.008)#			7.8520 0.2248 (0.001)# (0.004)#	8.1873 (0.001)#
cons.	5761.28 (0.000)# (0.000)#	6027.08 (0.000)#	4003.67 (0.000)# (0.000)#	4303.58 (0.000)#	5387.15 (0.000)# (0.000)#	5656.76 (0.000)#	3754.44 (0.000)# (0.000)#	4278.80 (0.000)#
	$R^2 =$ 0.6139	$R^2 =$ 0.6666	$R^2 =$ 0.6743	$R^2 =$ 0.670	$R^2 =$ 0.6248	$R^2 =$ 0.6795	$R^2 =$ 0.6870	$R^2 =$ 0.7021
	adj-$R^2 =$ 0.61	adj-$R^2 =$ 0.66	adj-$R^2 =$ 0.67	adj-$R^2 =$ 0.69	adj-$R^2 =$ 0.61	adj-$R^2 =$ 0.67	adj-$R^2 =$ 0.67	adj-$R^2 =$ 0.69

* = significant at 10% level; ^ = significant at 5% level; #= significant at 1% level

Exhibit 4: Effect of Cross-Ownership on Presence of Local News

Dependent Variable = Presence of Local News (presence); dummy

	OLS	Tobit	OLS	Tobit	OLS	Tobit	OLS	Tobit
	Coeff. Beta (signif.) (sig. w/ rob.err.)	Coeff. (signif.)	Coeff. Beta (signif.) (sig. w/ rob.err.)	Coeff. (signif.)	Coeff. Beta (signif.) (sig. w/ rob.err.)	Coeff. (signif.)	Coeff. Beta (signif.) (sig. w/ rob.err.)	Coeff. (signif.)
type	0.0399 0.0293 (0.594) (0.193)	0.0469 (0.617)	0.0450 0.0347 (0.537) (0.145)	0.0536 (0.548)	0.0339 0.0237 (0.672) (0.367)	0.0385 (0.700)	0.0491 0.0361 (0.525) (0.175)	0.0582 (0.535)
rank	0.0006 0.0830 (0.114) (0.114)	0.0008 (0.109)	0.0003 0.0386 (0.552) (0.580)	0.0004 (0.486)	0.0010 0.1302 (0.199) (0.184)	0.0013 (0.169)	0.0006 0.0829 (0.410) (0.399)	0.0009 (0.332)
yrstd	-0.0130 -0.5591 (0.000)# (0.000)#	-0.0163 (0.000)#	-0.0087 -0.372 (0.000)# (0.000)#	-0.0105 (0.000)#	-0.0131 -0.5613 (0.000)# (0.000)#	-0.0164 (0.000)#	-0.0090 -0.3841 (0.000)# (0.000)#	-0.0110 (0.000)#
ptv_m					0.0040 0.0146 (0.831) (0.833)	0.0040 (0.868)	0.0030 0.0112 (0.870) (0.880)	0.0024 (0.914)
cable_m					0.0018 0.0404 (0.499) (0.469)	0.0026 (0.444)	0.0011 0.0249 (0.676) (0.647)	0.0016 (0.627)
TVHH3					0.0000 0.03 (0.701) (0.687)	0.0000 (0.672)	0.0000 0.1463 (0.134) (0.201)	0.0000 (0.096)*
ptvview					0.0684 0.2261 (0.001)# (0.001)#	0.0888 (0.001)#	0.0626 0.2084 (0.004)# (0.004)#	0.0796 (0.003)#
othview					0.0060 0.1393 (0.164) (0.146)	0.0073 (0.180)	0.0059 0.1357 (0.175) (0.213)	0.0070 (0.194)
big4			0.2491 0.2745 (0.000)# (0.000)#	0.3218 (0.000)#			0.2870 0.316 (0.000)# (0.000)#	0.3763 (0.000)#
rev_s			0.0007 0.0675 (0.352) (0.188)	0.0009 (0.317)			-0.0005 -0.0454 (0.623) (0.600)	-0.0007 -0.561
cons.	1.6232 (0.000)# (0.000)#	1.7826 (0.000)#	1.1606 (0.000)# (0.000)#	1.1679 (0.000)#	1.0310 (0.000)# (0.000)#	1.0192 (0.002)#	0.6222 (0.029)^ (0.035)^	0.4940 (0.159)
	R² = 0.3257 adj-R² = 0.3176	pseudo-R² = 0.22	R² = 0.3660 adj-R² = 0.3525	pseudo-R² = 0.26	R² = 0.3537 adj-R² = 0.3323	pseudo-R² = 0.24	R² = 0.3935 adj-R² = 0.3668	pseudo-R² = 0.29

* = significant at 10% level; ^ = significant at 5% level; #= significant at 1% level

Exhibit 5: Effect of Cross-Ownership on Amount of Local Public Affairs

Dependent Variable = Local Public Affairs (pa_L)

	OLS	Tobit	OLS	Tobit	OLS	Tobit	OLS	Tobit
	Coeff. Beta (signif.) (sig. w/ rob.err.)	Coeff. (signif.)	Coeff. Beta (signif.) (sig. w/ rob.err.)	Coeff. (signif.)	Coeff. Beta (signif.) (sig. w/ rob.err.)	Coeff. (signif.)	Coeff. Beta (signif.) (sig. w/ rob.err.)	Coeff. (signif.)
type	49.5981 0.1234 (0.064)* (0.340)	66.8353 (0.209)	53.6855 0.1406 (0.045)^ (0.354)	63.4730 (0.225)	66.2041 0.1563 (0.023)^ (0.293)	95.9423 (0.092)*	67.8651 0.1688 (0.019)^ (0.313)	87.1508 (0.114)
rank	-0.1050 -0.0486 (0.443) (0.367)	-0.5670 (0.054)*	-0.1747 -0.0827 (0.305) (0.140)	-0.5530 (0.119)	-0.0936 -0.0433 (0.726) (0.634)	-0.5354 (0.337)	-0.0982 -0.0465 (0.714) (0.602)	-0.5136 (0.344)
yrstd	0.0800 0.0117 (0.859) (0.841)	-0.6657 (0.480)	-0.4040 -0.0585 (0.511) (0.319)	-1.1980 (0.356)	0.0642 0.0093 (0.888) (0.876)	-0.7042 (0.455)	-0.4343 -0.0627 (0.488) (0.321)	-1.1797 (0.365)
ptv_m					1.6545 0.0203 (0.808) (0.757)	2.8854 (0.837)	2.2493 0.0289 (0.739) (0.671)	2.9902 (0.825)
cable_m					1.0336 0.0786 (0.283) (0.329)	1.5667 (0.424)	0.9344 0.0732 (0.329) (0.406)	1.0281 (0.587)
TVHH3					-0.0102 -0.1039 (0.278) (0.166)	-0.0164 (0.393)	-0.0082 -0.0867 (0.480) (0.295)	-0.0253 (0.290)
ptvview					4.9906 0.0558 (0.513) (0.332)	16.7731 (0.293)	5.1017 0.0576 (0.525) (0.372)	16.4382 (0.309)
othview					-0.1186 -0.0094 (0.939) (0.932)	0.6661 (0.839)	-0.1434 -0.0112 (0.929) (0.922)	0.7367 (0.823)
big4			-8.7317 -0.0326 (0.687) (0.466)	-29.7960 (0.506)			-12.4751 -0.0465 (0.591) (0.307)	-46.7730 (0.327)
rev_s			-0.2480 -0.0797 (0.375) (0.433)	-0.0717 (0.894)			-0.1995 -0.0641 (0.581) (0.633)	0.2778 (0.695)
cons.	47.6583 (0.173) (0.102)	11.6291 (0.872)	96.1495 (0.094)* (0.008)#	75.6433 (0.532)	-21.4236 (0.818) (0.729)	####### (0.440)	29.4862 (0.779) (0.633)	4.6388 (0.623)
	R^2 = 0.0182 adj-R^2 = 0.0063	pseudo- R^2 = 0.00	R^2 = 0.0258 adj-R^2 = 0.0050	pseudo- R^2 = 0.01	R^2 = 0.0324 adj-R^2 = 0.0002	pseudo- R^2 = 0.01	R^2 = 0.0389 adj-R^2 = - 0.0034	pseudo- R^2 = 0.01

* = significant at 10% level; ^ = significant at 5% level; #= significant at 1% level

Exhibit 6: Effect of Cross-Ownership on Presence of Public Affairs

Dependent Variable = Presence of Local Public Affairs (pa_L_dum); dummy

	OLS	Probit	OLS	Probit	OLS	Probit	OLS	Probit
	Coeff. Beta (signif.) (sig. w/ rob.err.)	Coeff. (signif.) (sig. w/ rob.err.)	Coeff. Beta (signif.) (sig. w/ rob.err.)	Coeff. (signif.) (sig. w/ rob.err.)	Coeff. Beta (signif.) (sig. w/ rob.err.)	Coeff. (signif.) (sig. w/ rob.err.)	Coeff. Beta (signif.) (sig. w/ rob.err.)	Coeff. (signif.) (sig. w/ rob.err.)
type	0.0263 0.0164 (0.802) (0.803)	0.0662 (0.808) (0.806)	-0.0124 -0.0079 (0.909) (0.908)	-0.0260 (0.927) (0.927)	0.0480 0.0286 (0.673) (0.684)	0.1215 (0.677) (0.682)	0.0061 0.0037 (0.958) (0.959)	0.0171 (0.955) (0.955)
rank	-0.0015 -0.1737 (0.006)# (0.005)#	-0.0040 (0.006)# (0.007)#	-0.0010 -0.1156 (0.146) (0.146)	-0.0026 (0.154) (0.164)	-0.0014 -0.1581 (0.198) (0.202)	-0.0036 (0.188) (0.196)	-0.0012 -0.1379 (0.270) (0.271)	-0.0032 (0.259) (0.263)
yrstd	-0.0028 -0.1019 (0.118) (0.124)	-0.0073 (0.115) (0.121)	-0.0019 -0.0657 (0.453) (0.452)	-0.0051 (0.435) (0.443)	-0.0028 -0.1031 (0.119) (0.124)	-0.0075 (0.111) (0.115)	-0.0015 -0.0542 (0.542) (0.536)	-0.0043 (0.518) (0.518)
ptv_m					0.0015 0.0045 (0.957) (0.957)	0.0042 (0.952) (0.952)	-0.0009 -0.0029 (0.973) (0.973)	-0.0022 (0.976) (0.976)
cable_m					0.0011 0.021 (0.773) (0.776)	0.0025 (0.796) (0.798)	-0.0005 -0.01 (0.892) (0.893)	-0.0017 (0.867) (0.869)
TVHH3					-0.0000 -0.0139 (0.884) (0.884)	-0.0000 (0.866) (0.866)	-0.0001 -0.1386 (0.252) (0.221)	0.0002 (0.237) (0.235)
ptvview					0.0342 0.0965 (0.255) (0.239)	0.0900 (0.255) (0.245)	0.0321 0.0885 (0.322) (0.305)	0.0849 (0.321) (0.305)
othview					0.0023 0.0455 (0.707) (0.696)	0.0060 (0.708) (0.703)	0.0020 0.039 (0.753) (0.752)	0.0057 (0.737) (0.738)
big4			-0.0669 -0.0608 (0.446) (0.439)	-0.1898 (0.415) (0.413)			-0.1018 -0.0929 (0.277) (0.270)	-0.2866 (0.245) (0.239)
rev_s			0.0015 0.1202 (0.174) (0.151)	0.0026 (0.189) (0.201)			0.0025 0.1999 (0.082)* (0.039)**	0.0071 (0.087)* (0.065)*
cons.	0.7271 (0.000)# (0.000)#	0.6025 (0.094)* (0.098)*	0.6473 (0.006)# (0.005)#	0.4133 (0.503) (0.510)	0.4649 (0.203) (0.167)	-0.0613 (0.950) (0.946)	0.5621 (0.186) (0.166)	0.2048 (0.856) (0.852)
	R² = 0.0440 adj-R² = 0.0325	pseudo-R² = 0.03	R² = 0.0557 adj-R² = 0.0357	pseudo-R² = 0.04	R² = 0.0503 adj-R² = 0.0188	pseudo-R² = 0.04	R² = 0.0674 adj-R² = 0.0264	pseudo-R² = 0.05

* = significant at 10% level; ^ = significant at 5% level; #= significant at 1% level

In Yan's October 2006 study, he finds that cross-ownership has a statistically significant positive effect on the presence of local news.

However, Yan cautions against over-interpreting this finding, stating "cross-owned stations were more likely to be in the business of providing local news, though evidence of a causal relationship would require examining whether and how stations' provision of local informational programming changed after they became part of a newspaper/television combination." Indeed, this result is more likely attributed to the fact that most of the cross-owned stations in the sample were grandfathered prior to 1975, and all but one of the non-grandfathered cross-owned stations aired news prior to the formation of the cross-ownership relation.

In our model of the effect of cross-ownership on the presence of local news, we find that cross-ownership is not significant. The difference in this result and Yan's October 2006 result is likely due to the presence of the station age control variable in our model, which may capture the effect of the established news status of the grandfathered combinations.

The results also indicate that cross-ownership has no effect on the production or amount of local public affairs programming. While the OLS results indicate significance, the OLS model is not appropriate for this data set, given the fact that 57 percent of stations in the sample aired zero seconds of public affairs programming. The Tobit model appropriately deals with this corner-solution scenario, and demonstrates that cross-ownership has no effect on the amount of public affairs programming.

The evidence clearly supports the conclusion that there is no direct relationship between cross ownership and the amount of local news or public affairs programming. We do not find much of a case for an indirect effect either. Controlling for all the other variables, the relationship between cross-ownership and the potential intervening variables, Big 4 and Station Revenue is not significant. In the Probit model that includes only Market Rank and Station Age, as control variables for predictors of cross-ownership, Big 4 is not related to cross-ownership in a statistically significant way, but Station Revenue is. However, the magnitude of the indirect effect would be small (at the mean revenue the probability of cross-ownership is about 7 percent; at one standard deviation above this mean revenue the probability of cross-ownership is approximately 10 percent). These models do not explain much of the variance in cross-ownership (see Exhibit 7).

Exhibit 7: Indirect Effect of Cross-Ownership

Dependent Variable = Cross-Owned (type); dummy

	OLS	Probit	OLS	Probit	OLS	Probit	OLS	Probit
	Coeff. Beta (signif.) (sig. w/ rob.err.)	Coeff. (signif.) (sig. w/ rob.err.)	Coeff. Beta (signif.) (sig. w/ rob.err.)	Coeff. (signif.) (sig. w/ rob.err.)	Coeff. Beta (signif.) (sig. w/ rob.err.)	Coeff. (signif.) (sig. w/ rob.err.)	Coeff. Beta (signif.) (sig. w/ rob.err.)	Coeff. (signif.) (sig. w/ rob.err.)
rank	-0.0005 -0.1009 (0.094)^ (0.070)*	-0.0034 (0.131) (0.128)	0.0003 0.0564 (0.453) (0.330)	0.0005 (0.866) (0.835)	0.0004 0.0704 (0.545) (0.504)	0.0015 (0.720) (0.683)	0.0006 0.1223 (0.298) (0.229)	0.0026 (0.540) (0.465)
yrstd	-0.0051 -0.2974 (0.000)# (0.000)#	-0.0416 (0.000)# (0.000)#	-0.0035 -0.1948 (0.018)^ (0.011)^	-0.0348 (0.005)# (0.007)#	-0.0043 -0.2631 (0.000)# (0.000)#	-0.0379 (0.000)# (0.000)#	-0.0028 -0.1627 (0.051)* (0.039)^	-0.0311 (0.015)^ (0.017)^
ptv_m					0.0029 0.0148 (0.851) (0.837)	0.0098 (0.926) (0.910)	0.0018 0.0095 (0.906) (0.899)	0.0145 (0.891) (0.872)
cable_m					-0.0008 -0.0248 (0.719) (0.714)	0.0000 (1.000) (1.000)	-0.0010 -0.0303 (0.663) (0.651)	-0.0019 (0.899) (0.895)
TVHH3					0.0001 0.2513 (0.005)# (0.029)^	0.0002 (0.156) (0.079)*	0.0000 0.0646 (0.570) (0.537)	0.0000 (0.885) (0.858)
ptvview					-0.0026 -0.0123 (0.878) (0.845)	-0.0099 (0.942) (0.934)	-0.0082 -0.0372 (0.658) (0.588)	-0.0306 (0.823) (0.793)
othview					-0.0013 -0.0438 (0.703) (0.617)	-0.0177 (0.513) (0.423)	-0.0025 -0.0799 (0.494) (0.370)	-0.0191 (0.479) (0.366)
big4			-0.0425 -0.0607 (0.422) (0.310)	-0.1859 (0.629) (0.592)			-0.0344 -0.0516 (0.521) (0.372)	-0.1455 (0.744) (0.707)
rev_s			0.0024 0.2904 (0.000)# (0.011)^	0.0062 (0.087)* (0.056)*			0.0023 0.3025 (0.005)# (0.025)^	0.0067 (0.216) (0.142)
cons.	0.5007 (0.000)# (0.000)#	1.5620 (0.010)# (0.007)#	0.3013 (0.031)^ (0.021)^	0.8216 (0.439) (0.418)	0.4303 (0.036)^ (0.035)^	1.5997 (0.318) (0.329)	0.4022 (0.097)* (0.106)	1.3923 (0.430) (0.488)
	R² = 0.1012		R² = 0.1468		R² = 0.1390		R² = 0.1675	
	adj-R² = 0.0940	pseudo-R² = 0.18	adj-R² = 0.1324	pseudo-R² = 0.19	adj-R² = 0.1141	pseudo-R² = 0.21	adj-R² = 0.1347	pseudo-R² = 0.21

* = significant at 10% level; ^ = significant at 5% level; #= signi

Although we have argued that the Napoli and Yan approach in the duopoly analysis was appropriate, given the policy and the different intentions and effects of duopolies compared to cross-ownership mergers, we have applied our approach to the duopoly variable as well. We have run this analysis on the same set of stations as in the original random sample (i.e. we do not include the cross-owned stations). The results are similar.

The models were generally specified as follows:

$news\_l = \alpha + \beta_1(duo\_s)_i + \beta_2(rank)_i + \beta_3(yrstd)_i + \beta_{4-8}[market\ controls]_i + \beta_9(big4)_i + \beta_{10}(rev\_s)_i + \varepsilon_i$

$pa\_l = \alpha + \beta_1(duo\_s)_i + \beta_2(rank)_i + \beta_3(yrstd)_i + \beta_{4-8}[market\ controls]_i + \beta_9(big4)_i + \beta_{10}(rev\_s)_i + \varepsilon_i$

$presence = \alpha + \beta_1(duo\_s)_i + \beta_2(rank)_i + \beta_3(yrstd)_i + \beta_{4-8}[market\ controls]_i + \beta_9(big4)_i + \beta_{10}(rev\_s)_i + \varepsilon_i$

$pa\_l\_dum = \alpha + \beta_1(duo\_s)_i + \beta_2(rank)_i + \beta_3(yrstd)_i + \beta_{4-8}[market\ controls]_i + \beta_9(big4)_i + \beta_{10}(rev\_s)_i + \varepsilon_i$

Where all variables are as described above, and duo_s = dummy variable for a duopoly station.

Results are presented below in Exhibits 8 - 12.

Market Rank and Age of the station are statistically significant predictors of the amount of news; the coefficient on the duopoly variable is not significant. Again, we find that controlling for station age and market rank alone renders the relationship between duopoly status and the amount of news statistically insignificant. Including the station characteristic variables as controls, explains more variance and we find a statistically significant coefficient on both Big 4 and Stations Revenue, as Napoli and Yan did. The coefficient on duopoly was not statistically significant. Duopolies did not produce more public affairs than non-duopolies, and none of the other variables was significant (with the exception that more hours of public television viewing in a market may have a small positive effect on the amount of public affairs programming produced). There is also no indication that duopoly has a significant indirect effect on news or public affairs (see Exhibit 12).

Exhibit 8: Effect of Duopoly on Amount of Local News

Dependent Variable = Local News (news_l)

	OLS	Robust Regr.	OLS	Robust Regr.	OLS	Robust Regr.	OLS	Robust Regr.
	Coeff. Beta (signif.) (sig. w/ rob.err.)	Coeff. (signif.)	Coeff. Beta (signif.) (sig. w/ rob.err.)	Coeff. (signif.)	Coeff. Beta (signif.) (sig. w/ rob.err.)	Coeff. (signif.)	Coeff. Beta (signif.) (sig. w/ rob.err.)	Coeff. (signif.)
duo_s	47.2502 0.0134 (0.766) (0.764)	60.1555 (0.695)	-94.7219 -0.0269 (0.543) (0.485)	-84.7684 (0.581)	37.1831 0.0105 (0.817) (0.816)	42.6029 (0.784)	-98.8102 -0.0281 (0.529) (0.477)	-89.9843 (0.568)
rank	-3.0978 -0.1343 (0.003)# (0.005)#	-3.9614 (0.000)#	-3.7037 -0.1596 (0.002)# (0.007)#	-4.0146 (0.001)#	-4.9345 -0.2138 (0.013)# (0.011)^	-5.8849 (0.002)#	-5.3018 -0.2285 (0.005)# (0.007)#	-5.1603 (0.007)#
yrstd	-56.0540 -0.7571 (0.000)# (0.000)#	-59.1702 (0.000)#	-39.0480 -0.5106 (0.000)# (0.000)#	-41.4465 (0.000)#	-56.1126 -0.7579 (0.000)# (0.000)#	-60.0116 (0.000)#	-38.6411 -0.5053 (0.000)# (0.000)#	-41.3690 (0.000)#
ptv_m					-13.3065 -0.0144 (0.786) (0.776)	-5.2560 (0.912)	-20.3582 -0.0223 (0.657) (0.646)	-29.1731 (0.527)
cable_m					-0.0924 -0.0007 (0.989) (0.988)	4.2627 (0.525)	-1.5653 -0.0111 (0.810) (0.794)	-0.2542 (0.969)
TVHH3					-0.0639 -0.0497 (0.422) (0.342)	-0.0770 (0.317)	-0.0586 -0.0457 (0.478) (0.515)	0.0256 (0.757)
ptvview					61.7453 0.0652 (0.256) (0.243)	32.5192 (0.536)	53.8708 0.0557 (0.320) (0.329)	22.9439 (0.673)
othview					12.7453 0.0951 (0.245) (0.215)	8.5656 (0.418)	11.9771 0.0856 (0.265) (0.258)	6.1826 (0.567)
big4			850.5913 0.2915 (0.000)# (0.000)#	774.2783 (0.000)#			827.5520 0.2836 (0.000)# (0.000)#	759.6710 (0.000)#
rev_s			7.1231 0.1628 (0.004)# (0.035)^	8.5707 (0.000)#			7.8426 0.1793 (0.005)# (0.010)#	8.7902 (0.000)#
cons.	5701.791 (0.000)# (0.000)#	5939.448 (0.000)#	3829.314 (0.000)# (0.000)#	4032.907 (0.000)#	5175.460 (0.000)# (0.000)#	5428.314 (0.000)#	3420.335 (0.000)# (0.000)#	3866.614 (0.000)#
	R^2 = 0.5924	R^2 = 0.6382	R^2 = 0.6606	R^2 = 0.6848	R^2 = 0.5978	R^2 = 0.6504	R^2 = 0.6650	R^2 = 0.6813
	adj-R^2 = 0.5869	adj-R^2 = 0.6333	adj-R^2 = 0.6524	adj-R^2 = 0.6773	adj-R^2 = 0.5830	adj-R^2 = 0.6375	adj-R^2 = 0.6485	adj-R^2 = 0.6656

* = significant at 10% level; ^ = significant at 5% level; # = significant at 1% level

Exhibit 9: Effect of Duopoly on Presence of Local News

Dependent Variable = Presence of Local News (presence); dummy

	OLS	Probit	OLS	Probit	OLS	Probit	OLS	Probit
	Coeff. Beta (signif.) (sig. w/ rob..err.)	Coeff. (signif.) (sig. w/ rob..err.)	Coeff. Beta (signif.) (sig. w/ rob.err.)	Coeff. (signif.) (sig. w/ rob.err.)	Coeff. Beta (signif.) (sig. w/ rob.err.)	Coeff. (signif.) (sig. w/ rob.err.)	Coeff. Beta (signif.) (sig. w/ rob.err.)	Coeff. (signif.) (sig. w/ rob.err.)
duo_s	0.0950 / 0.0822 / (0.160) / (0.159)	0.2160 / (0.460) / (0.419)	0.0820 / 0.0728 / (0.231) / (0.191)	0.0276 / (0.939) / (0.925)	0.0845 / 0.0731 / (0.209) / (0.199)	0.2547 / (0.425) / (0.369)	0.0892 / 0.0791 / (0.188) / (0.136)	0.1051 / (0.782) / (0.734)
rank	0.0008 / 0.1097 / (0.061)* / (0.064)*	0.0026 / (0.185) / (0.174)	0.0004 / 0.0561 / (0.432) / (0.462)	0.0016 / (0.530) / (0.528)	0.0013 / 0.1660 / (0.131) / (0.113)	0.0052 / (0.216) / (0.223)	0.0007 / 0.0963 / (0.379) / (0.354)	0.0030 / (0.519) / (0.511)
yrstd	-0.0134 / -0.5537 / (0.000)# / (0.000)#	-0.0558 / (0.000)# / (0.000)#	-0.0091 / -0.3731 / (0.000)# / (0.000)#	-0.0367 / (0.000)# / (0.000)#	-0.0135 / -0.5563 / (0.000)# / (0.000)#	-0.0627 / (0.000)# / (0.000)#	-0.0095 / -0.386 / (0.000)# / (0.000)#	-0.0432 / (0.000)# / (0.000)#
ptv_m					0.0052 / 0.0170 / (0.801) / (0.8037)	0.0496 / (0.628) / (0.667)	0.0045 / 0.0154 / (0.821) / (0.834)	0.0518 / (0.633) / (0.681)
cable_m					0.0012 / 0.0260 / (0.677) / (0.655)	0.0023 / (0.874) / (0.869)	0.0006 / 0.0122 / (0.845) / (0.829)	0.0015 / (0.926) / (0.919)
TVHH3					0.0000 / 0.0543 / (0.491) / (0.524)	0.0001 / (0.405) / (0.396)	0.0001 / 0.1362 / (0.118) / (0.182)	0.0002 / (0.348) / (0.329)
ptvview					0.0668 / 0.2151 / (0.004)# / (0.003)#	0.3727 / (0.002)# / (0.000)#	0.0636 / 0.2053 / (0.007)# / (0.006)#	0.3589 / (0.006)# / (0.002)#
othview					0.0059 / 0.1338 / (0.199) / (0.163)	0.0369 / (0.132) / (0.122)	0.0068 / 0.1527 / (0.140) / (0.164)	0.0384 / (0.131) / (0.133)
big4			0.2632 / 0.2816 / (0.000)# / (0.001)#	0.7724 / (0.007)# / (0.004)#			0.3047 / 0.3259 / (0.000)# / (0.000)#	0.9198 / (0.003)# / (0.001)#
rev_s			0.0005 / 0.0356 / (0.643) / (0.470)	0.0190 / (0.195) / (0.154)			-0.0008 / -0.0553 / (0.512) / (0.406)	0.0133 / (0.390) / (0.279)
cons.	1.6222 / (0.000)# / (0.000)#	4.7556 / (0.000)# / (0.000)#	1.1594 / (0.000)# / (0.000)#	2.7011 / (0.007)# / (0.005)#	1.0591 / (0.000)# / (0.000)#	2.1985 / (0.120) / (0.079)*	0.5956 / (0.056)* / (0.063)*	0.1701 / (0.921) / (0.907)
	R² = 0.3159 adj-R² = 0.3066	pseudo-R² = 0.32	R² = 0.3601 adj-R² = 0.3448	pseudo-R² = 0.37	R² = 0.3463 adj-R² = 0.3222	pseudo-R² = 0.37	R² = 0.3924 adj-R² = 0.3625	pseudo-R² = 0.41

* = significant at 10% level; ^ = significant at 5% level; # = significant at 1% level

Exhibit 10: Effect of Duopoly on Amount of Local Public Affairs

Dependent Variable = Local Public Affairs (pa_L)

	OLS	Tobit	OLS	Tobit	OLS	Tobit	OLS	Tobit
	Coeff. Beta (signif.) (sig. w/ rob.err.)	Coeff. (signif.)	Coeff. Beta (signif.) (sig. w/ rob.err.)	Coeff. (signif.)	Coeff. Beta (signif.) (sig. w/ rob.err.)	Coeff. (signif.)	Coeff. Beta (signif.) (sig. w/ rob.err.)	Coeff. (signif.)
duo_s	-23.4194 -0.0921 (0.189) (0.068)*	-10.8811 (0.772)	-23.0500 -0.0984 (0.180) (0.120)	-11.3927 (0.750)	-25.6711 -0.1009 (0.154) (0.055)*	-12.0988 (0.746)	-23.9611 -0.1023 (0.176) (0.110)	-11.7233 (0.741)
rank	-0.2296 -0.1380 (0.049)^ (0.054)*	-0.5984 (0.023)^	-0.1738 -0.1124 (0.201) (0.173)	-0.4482 (0.128)	-0.2938 -0.1766 (0.186) (0.047)^	-0.7666 (0.116)	-0.2407 -0.1557 (0.257) (0.093)*	-0.6601 (0.144)
yrstd	0.1192 0.0223 (0.737) (0.769)	-0.4453 (0.564)	-0.0477 -0.0086 (0.927) (0.911)	-0.4636 (0.655)	0.0994 0.0186 (0.782) (0.811)	-0.4789 (0.533)	-0.0404 -0.0079 (0.933) (0.921)	-0.4542 (0.661)
ptv_m					2.3746 0.0355 (0.665) (0.637)	2.8380 (0.810)	2.8977 0.0477 (0.575) (0.556)	2.8452 (0.792)
cable_m					0.2843 0.0278 (0.714) (0.637)	0.5546 (0.737)	0.0403 0.0043 (0.956) (0.949)	-0.0396 (0.979)
TVHH3					-0.0035 -0.038 (0.692) (0.548)	-0.0124 (0.527)	-0.0066 -0.0775 (0.477) (0.414)	-0.0199 (0.334)
ptvview					8.9048 0.1304 (0.143) (0.055)^	22.8678 (0.083)*	8.8942 0.138 (0.146) (0.076)*	21.9220 (0.087)*
othview					1.2823 0.1326 (0.295) (0.185)	2.8700 (0.289)	1.1501 0.1234 (0.342) (0.288)	2.8023 (0.279)
big4			-12.7449 -0.0656 (0.454) (0.443)	-24.5039 (0.508)			-13.6608 -0.0703 (0.441) (0.233)	-32.3613 (0.395)
rev_s			0.2074 0.0711 (0.452) (0.443)	0.4254 (0.437)			0.2248 0.0771 (0.466) (0.519)	0.5704 (0.356)
cons.	58.645 (0.037)^ (0.046)^	26.777 (0.658)	68.708 (0.120) (0.043)^	34.246 (0.723)	-38.113 (0.610) (0.540)	-180.196 (0.280)	-4.292 (0.958) (0.940)	-117.315 (0.502)
	R² = 0.0201 adj-R² = 0.0069	pseudo-R² = 0.00	R² = 0.0287 adj-R² = 0.0053	pseudo-R² = 0.01	R² = 0.0331 adj-R² = - 0.0025	pseudo-R2 = 0.01	R² = 0.0422 adj-R² = - 0.0050	pseudo-R² = 0.01

* = significant at 10% level; ^ = significant at 5% level; # = significant at 1% level

Exhibit 11: Effect of Duopoly on Presence of Local Public Affairs

Dependent Variable = Presence of Local Public Affairs (pa_L_dum); dummy

	OLS	Probit	OLS	Probit	OLS	Probit	OLS	Probit
	Coeff. Beta (signif.) (sig. w/ rob..err.)	Coeff. (signif.) (sig. w/ rob..err.)	Coeff. Beta (signif.) (sig. w/ rob.err.)	Coeff. (signif.) (sig. w/ rob.err.)	Coeff. Beta (signif.) (sig. w/ rob.err.)	Coeff. (signif.) (sig. w/ rob.err.)	Coeff. Beta (signif.) (sig. w/ rob.err.)	Coeff. (signif.) (sig. w/ rob.err.)
duo_s	0.1022 0.0788 (0.257) (0.256)	0.2590 (0.271) (0.263)	0.0916 0.0702 (0.343) (0.353)	0.2341 (0.350) (0.352)	0.0976 0.0749 (0.283) (0.289)	0.2543 (0.282) (0.277)	0.0874 0.0670 (0.368) (0.375)	0.2258 (0.372) (0.370)
rank	-0.0012 -0.1423 (0.040)^ (0.038)^	-0.0032 (0.039)^ (0.042)^	-0.0009 (0.218) (0.221)	-0.0024 (0.220) (0.233)	-0.0016 -0.1857 (0.159) (0.158)	-0.0043 (0.150) (0.154)	-0.0015 -0.1758 (0.195) (0.198)	-0.0041 (0.182) (0.187)
yrstd	-0.0027 -0.099 (0.134) (0.140)	-0.0071 (0.132) (0.139)	-0.0011 -0.04 (0.664) (0.654)	-0.0030 (0.667) (0.663)	-0.0027 -0.0994 (0.135) (0.143)	-0.0073 (0.126) (0.132)	-0.0008 -0.0297 (0.749) (0.739)	-0.0025 (0.727) (0.721)
ptv_m					-0.0018 -0.0053 (0.948) (0.948)	-0.0052 (0.943) (0.944)	-0.0056 -0.0167 (0.843) (0.845)	-0.0144 (0.847) (0.850)
cable_m					0.0014 0.0274 (0.715) (0.717)	0.0035 (0.735) (0.737)	-0.0002 -0.0047 (0.951) (0.952)	-0.0010 (0.927) (0.927)
TVHH3					-0.0000 -0.0724 (0.445) (0.432)	-0.0001 (0.439) (0.437)	-0.0001 -0.1159 (0.281) (0.244)	-0.0002 (0.268) (0.282)
ptvview					0.0500 0.1429 (0.105) (0.100)*	0.1346 (0.098)* (0.095)*	0.0519 0.1444 (0.123) (0.110)	0.1397 (0.117) (0.107)
othview					0.0046 0.0938 (0.453) (0.452)	0.0128 (0.435) (0.438)	0.0055 0.1059 (0.408) (0.411)	0.0152 (0.387) (0.394)
big4			-0.0192 -0.0177 (0.838) (0.840)	-0.0524 (0.831) (0.835)			-0.0390 -0.036 (0.689) (0.685)	-0.1199 (0.641) (0.637)
rev_s			0.0016 0.0975 (0.297) (0.234)	0.0043 (0.313) (0.286)			0.0021 0.1311 (0.210) (0.141)	0.0060 (0.212) (0.182)
cons.	0.6821 (0.000)# (0.000)#	0.4873 (0.190) (0.194)	0.5394 (0.027)^ (0.020)^	0.1096 (0.867) (0.862)	0.3172 (0.402) (0.374)	-0.4736 (0.639) (0.623)	0.2684 (0.546) (0.523)	-0.5858 (0.623) (0.610)
	R² = 0.0425 adj-R² = 0.0295	pseudo-R² = 0.03	R² = 0.0506 adj-R² = 0.0278	pseudo-R² = 0.04	R² = 0.0568 adj-R² = 0.0220	pseudo-R² = 0.04	R² = 0.0684 adj-R² = 0.0225	pseudo-R² = 0.05

* = significant at 10% level; ^ = significant at 5% level; # = significant at 1% level

Exhibit 12: Indirect Effect of Duopoly

Dependent Variable = Duopoly (duo_s); dummy

	OLS	Probit	OLS	Probit	OLS	Probit	OLS	Probit
	Coeff. Beta (signif.) (sig. w/ rob..err.)	Coeff. (signif.) (sig. w/ rob..err.)	Coeff. Beta (signif.) (sig. w/ rob.err.)	Coeff. (signif.) (sig. w/ rob.err.)	Coeff. Beta (signif.) (sig. w/ rob.err.)	Coeff. (signif.) (sig. w/ rob.err.)	Coeff. Beta (signif.) (sig. w/ rob.err.)	Coeff. (signif.) (sig. w/ rob.err.)
rank	-0.0020 -0.3043 (0.000)# (0.000)#	-0.0103 (0.000)# (0.000)#	-0.0016 -0.2368 (0.003)# (0.001)#	-0.0122 (0.001)# (0.000)#	-0.0022 -0.3403 (0.007)# (0.001)#	-0.0148 (0.003)# (0.000)#	-0.0017 -0.2565 (0.043)^ (0.015)^	-0.0145 (0.009)# (0.005)#
yrstd	0.0008 0.0405 (0.526) (0.491)	0.0049 (0.407) (0.355)	0.0040 0.1822 (0.034)^ (0.012)^	0.0220 (0.031)^ (0.016)^	0.0007 0.0344 (0.593) (0.559)	0.0044 (0.465) (0.405)	0.0040 0.1833 (0.035)^ (0.016)^	0.0221 (0.032)^ (0.022)^
ptv_m					0.0154 0.0587 (0.456) (0.439)	0.0434 (0.637) (0.613)	0.0153 0.059 (0.456) (0.451)	0.0688 (0.489) (0.475)
cable_m					0.0007 0.0163 (0.824) (0.817)	0.0007 (0.956) (0.956)	-0.0004 -0.0109 (0.880) (0.874)	0.0011 (0.940) (0.938)
TVHH3					0.0000 0.0175 (0.850) (0.883)	-0.0000 (0.761) (0.783)	-0.0000 -0.0976 (0.335) (0.282)	-0.0002 (0.155) (0.120)
ptvview					0.0110 0.0409 (0.632) (0.650)	0.0403 (0.696) (0.738)	-0.0014 -0.0052 (0.952) (0.945)	-0.0906 (0.486) (0.465)
othview					0.0050 0.1315 (0.278) (0.297)	0.0326 (0.166) (0.264)	-0.0000 -0.0004 (0.997) (0.996)	-0.0141 (0.638) (0.578)
blg4			0.0249 0.03 (0.711) (0.736)	0.3617 (0.267) (0.292)			0.0104 0.0125 (0.883) (0.893)	0.2619 (0.438) (0.459)
rev_s			0.0032 0.2561 (0.003)# (0.038)^	0.0083 (0.062)* (0.088)*			0.0036 0.288 (0.003)# (0.040)^	0.0108 (0.029)^ (0.060)*
constant	0.2676 (0.011)^ (0.009)#	-0.6544 (0.147) (0.138)	-0.0619 (0.723) (0.685)	-2.2336 (0.017)^ (0.009)#	-0.0628 (0.824) (0.850)	-2.1522 (0.081)* (0.173)	-0.0217 (0.946) (0.944)	-1.2552 (0.459) (0.457)
	$R^2 =$ 0.0941 adj-$R^2 =$ 0.0860	$R^2 =$ 0.1211	$R^2 =$ 0.1633 adj-$R^2 =$ 0.1473	$R^2 =$ 0.2020	$R^2 =$ 0.1045 adj-$R^2 =$ 0.0757	$R^2 =$ 0.1389	$R^2 =$ 0.1683 adj-$R^2 =$ 0.1316	$R^2 =$ 0.2163

* = significant at 10% level; ^ = significant at 5% level; # = signi

PART VII:

THE CONTEMPORARY TERRAIN OF MEDIA POLICY

STUDY 17:
THE CHALLENGE OF CONTEMPORARY COMMERCIAL MASS MEDIA ECONOMICS TO DEMOCRATIC DISCOURSE

Mark Cooper

Introduction

The legal discussion in Studies 1, 2, and 3 sets out the public policy issues by emphasizing the ways in which civic discourse transcends mere economics to include diversity and localism, both of which are vital to democratic discourse. The discussion of point of view, bias or slant, in Study 5 demonstrates the link between ownership and diversity. The discussion of bias arrives at the conclusion that competition is critical to promoting vibrant democratic discourse. This section takes the argument one step farther. It demonstrates why the economic characteristics of mass media production results in "market failure" at the start of the 21st century. In other words, the problem is not that 'good' economics makes for 'bad' civic discourse. In fact, vigorous, atomistic competition is generally considered supportive of democracy, although not, in itself sufficient to deliver the media democracy needs, as discussed in Study 3. The problem is that the structural tendencies of contemporary media markets make for 'bad' economics that reinforce the tendency of failure in the forum for democratic discourse. The tendency of ownership structures to deviate from competitive markets is an economic problem that becomes a challenge for democratic discourse because owners can combine economic influence with their privileged position in the forum for democratic discourse to exercise undue influence over public opinion to the detriment of citizens and democratic discourse.

Competition and Democracy

Economists stress that vigorously competitive markets are compatible with democratic processes. There are political reasons to prefer atomistically competitive markets. Scherer and Ross, among the most prominent analysts of industrial organization, note that analysis should begin with the political implications of economic institutions.[1] Specifically, they ask, "Why is a

---

[1]Scherer, F. Michael and David Ross. *Industrial Market Structure and Economic Performance.* New York: Houghton Mifflin Company, 1990, p. 18: "We begin with the political arguments, not merely because they are sufficiently transparent to be treated

competitive market system held in such high esteem by statesmen and economists alike? Why is competition the ideal in a market economy, and what is wrong with monopoly?" They provide a series of answers, starting from the decentralized, objective processes that typify atomistically competitive markets that check the power of large entities.

> One of the most important arguments is that the atomistic structure of buyers and sellers required for competition decentralizes and disperses power. The resource allocation and income distribution problem is solved through the almost mechanical interaction of supply and demand forces on the market, and not through the conscious exercise of power held in private hands (for example, under monopoly) or government hands (that is, under state enterprise or government regulation). Limiting the power of both government bodies and private individuals to make decisions that shape people's lives and fortunes was a fundamental goal of the men who wrote the U.S. Constitution.[2]

Other economic characteristics of atomistically competitive markets that converge with democratic principles are the autonomy and freedom of entry that such markets imply.

> A closely related benefit is the fact that competitive market processes solve the economic problem *impersonally*, and not through the personal control of entrepreneurs and bureaucrats...

> [Another] political merit of a competitive market is its freedom of opportunity. When the no-barriers-to-entry condition of perfect competition is satisfied, individuals are free to choose whatever trade or profession they prefer, limited only by their own talent and skill and by their ability to raise the (presumably modest) amount of capital required.[3]

Thus, atomistic competition promotes individualistic, impersonal decisions with freedom of opportunity and relatively low resource requirements for entry. These are ideal for populist forms of democracy.[4]

---

briefly, but also because when all is said and done, they, and not the economists' abstruse models, have tipped the balance of social consensus toward competition."

[2] Id., p. 18.
[3] Id., p. 18.
[4] Lessig, Lawrence. *Code and Other Laws of Cyberspace.* New York: Basic Books, 1999, pp. 166-167: "Relative anonymity, decentralized distribution, multiple points of access, no necessary tie to geography, no simple system to identify content, tools of encryption – all these features and consequences of the Internet protocol make it difficult to control speech in cyberspace. The architecture of cyberspace is the real protector of speech there; it is the real "First Amendment in cyberspace," and this First Amendment is no local ordinance... "The architecture of the Internet, as it is right now, is perhaps the most important model of free speech since the founding. This model has implications far beyond e-mail and web pages."

Lawrence Lessig points out that at the time of the framing of the Constitution the press had a very atomistic character.

> The "press" in 1791 was not the *New York Times* or the *Wall Street Journal*. It did not comprise large organizations of private interests, with millions of readers associated with each organization. Rather, the press then was much like the Internet today. The cost of a printing press was low, the readership was slight, and anyone (within reason) could become a publisher – and in fact an extraordinary number did.[5]

The problem in contemporary mass media markets is that they have moved quite far from the competitive form of organization. In fact, the pursuit of efficiency through economies of scale and network effects has pushed many contemporary industries toward oligopoly or monopoly. This is a source of concern and requires vigilant solutions in all commercial markets. Efficiency that results from large economies of scale also leads to small numbers of competitors and can degenerate into inefficient abuse of monopoly power.[6] In media markets, where the impact reverberates so powerfully in the forum for democratic discourse, these tendencies must be prevented from imposing the graver condition of distorting civic discourse.

MARKET FAILURE IN MEDIA MARKETS

It has long been recognized that the contemporary technologies and the cost structure of commercial mass media production are not conducive to vigorous, atomistic competition. Print and broadcast media have unique economic characteristics.[7] To the extent that economics is a consideration, economic competition in commercial mass media markets cannot assure diversity and antagonism.[8] The conceptual underpinnings of the argument

---

[5] Lessig, 1999, p. 183.

[6] Cooper, Mark N. 2001. "Antitrust as Consumer Protection in the New Economy: Lessons from the Microsoft Case." *Hasting Law Journal* 52, April.

[7] Berry, Steven T. and Joel Waldfogel. 1999. Public Radio in the United States: Does it Correct Market Failure or Cannibalize Commercial Stations? *Journal of Public Economics* 71, point out free entry may not accomplish the economic goals set out for it either. There is evidence of the anticompetitive behaviors expected to be associated with reductions in competition, such as price increases and excess profits. Wirth, M. O. 1984. "The Effects of Market Structure on Television News Pricing." *Journal of Broadcasting* 28: 215-24; Simon, J., W. J. Primeaux and E. Rice. 1986. "The Price Effects of Monopoly Ownership in Newspapers." *Antitrust Bulletin* Spring; Rubinovitz, R. 1991. "Market Power and Price Increases for Basic Cable Service Since Deregulation." *Economic Analysis Regulatory Group, Department of Justice*, 6 August 1991 Bates, B. J. 1993. "Station Trafficking in Radio: The Impact of Deregulation." *Journal of Broadcasting and Electronic Media* 37:1: 21-30.

[8] Ray, W. B. *FCC: The Ups and Downs of Radio-TV Regulation*. Iowa: Iowa State University Press, 1990; Wat W. 1996. "The Supreme Court Defines the Forum for

are well known to media market analysts.[9]   On the supply-side, media markets exhibit high first copy costs or high fixed costs.[10] On the demand-side, media market products are in some important respects non-substitutable or exhibit strong group-specific preferences.[11]

The "welfare" effect of these characteristics is to cause the market to fail to meet the information needs of some groups in society. This results because groups express strong preferences for specific types of programming or content. Programming that is targeted at whites is not highly substitutable for programming that is targeted at blacks, from the point of view of blacks. If fixed costs and group preferences are strong, producers must decide at whom to target their content.   Given the profit maximizing incentive to recover the high costs from the larger audience, they target the majority or, in a more fragmented market the plurality. The minorities are less well served.

As articulated and empirically demonstrated by Joel Waldfogel, this might be termed an economic theory of discrimination "because it gives a non-discriminatory reason why markets will deliver fewer products – and, one might infer, lower utility – to 'preference minorities,' small groups of

Democratic Discourse." *Journalism and Mass Communications Quarterly* Spring; Firestone, C. M. and J. M. Schement. *Toward an Information Bill of Rights and Responsibilities*. Washington, DC: Aspen Institute, 1995 Brown, Duncan H. 1994. "The Academy's Response to the Call for a Marketplace Approach to Broadcast Regulation." *Critical Studies in Mass Communications* 11: 254 Benkler, Yochai. 1999. "Free as the Air." *New York University Law Review* 74.

[9] Baker, C. Edwin. *Media, Markets and Democracy*. Cambridge: Cambridge University Press, 2001, p. 42.

[10] Waldfogel, Joel and Lisa George. "Who Benefits Whom in Daily Newspaper Market." *NBER Working Paper 7994*. Cambridge: National Bureau of Economic Research, 2000 (hereafter Waldfogel, Television), p. 1. Other papers in the series of studies of "preference externalities" were made a part of the record in conjunction with Joel *Waldfogel's* appearance at the FCC Roundtable, including, 1999. "Preference Externalities: An Empirical Study of Who Benefits Whom in Differentiated Product Markets." *NBER Working Paper 7391* Cambridge: National Bureau of Economic Research; Siegelman, Peter. "Race and Radio: Preference Externalities, Minority Ownership and the Provision of Programming to Minorities" *Advances in Applied Microeconomics 10*; Oberholzer-Gee, Felix and Joel Waldfogel. Electoral Acceleration: The Effect of Minority Population on Minority Voter Turnout. *NBER Working Paper 8252*. Cambridge, MA: National Bureau of Economic Research, 2001; George, Lisa and Joel Waldfogel. Who Benefits Whom in Daily Newspaper Markets? *NBER Working Paper 7944*. Cambridge, MA: National Bureau of Economic Research, 2000; as well as the statement Federal Communications Commission. *Comments on Consolidation and Localism*. Roundtable on Media Ownership, 29 October 2001 [hereafter, Localism); Oberholzer-Gee, Felix and Joel Waldfogel. "Tiebout Acceleration: Political Participation in Heterogeneous Jurisdictions." *University of Pennsylvania, August 2000* (hereafter Participation).

[11] Baker, 2001, p. 43.

individuals with atypical preferences."[12]   Discrimination results not from biases or psychological factors, but from impersonal economic processes.

> A consumer with atypical tastes will face less product variety than one with common tastes.... The market delivers fewer products – and less associated satisfaction – to these groups simply because they are small. This phenomenon can arise even if radio firms are national and entirely non-discriminatory.

> The fundamental conditions needed to produce compartmentalized preference externalities are large fixed costs and preferences that differ sharply across groups of consumers. These conditions are likely to hold, to greater or lesser extents, in a variety of media markets – newspapers, magazines, television, and movies.[13]

This poses a fundamental challenge to the validity of the assumption that markets allocate resources efficiently.

> Friedman has eloquently argued that markets avoid the tyrannies of the majority endemic to allocation through collective choice. Mounting evidence that minority consumer welfare depends on local minority population in local media markets indicates that, for this industry at least, the difference between market and collective choice allocation is a matter of degree, not kind. It is important to understand the relationship between market demographic composition and the targeting of programming content because related research documents a relationship between the presence of black-targeted media and the tendency for blacks to vote.[14]

UNDER SERVING MINORITY POINTS OF VIEW

Exhibit 1 shows graphically how this tyranny works in media markets. When there are large fixed costs, a limited ability to cover the market and strong differences in preference for programming, profit maximizers serve the core audience and neglect smaller preference minorities. The larger the minority group and the closer its taste to the majority, the more likely it is to be served.

The tyranny of the majority in media markets is linked to the tyranny of the majority in politics because the media are the means of political communication.

> We present evidence that electoral competition leads candidates to propose policies that are supported by proportionately larger groups and that members of these groups are more likely to turn out if they find the proposed policies more appealing. In addition, we show that candidates find it easier to direct campaign efforts at larger groups because many existing media outlets cater to this audience...

---

[12] Waldfogel, 1999, pp. 27-30.
[13] Waldfogel, 1999, pp. 27-30.
[14] Waldfogel, 2001, p. 3; Baker, 2001, p. 80.

Exhibit 1: Conceptualizing the Tyranny of the Majority in Media Markets

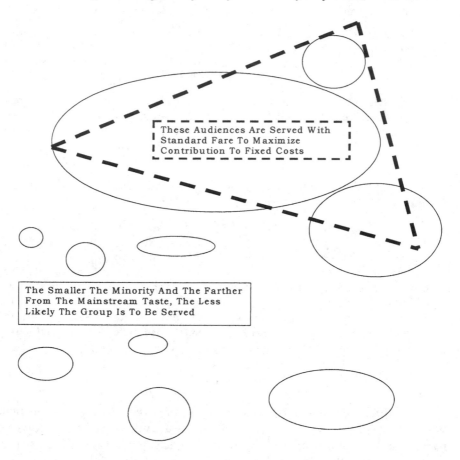

These Audiences Are Served With Standard Fare To Maximize Contribution To Fixed Costs

The Smaller The Minority And The Farther From The Mainstream Taste, The Less Likely The Group Is To Be Served

Channels of communication that are used to disseminate political information rarely exist for the sole purpose of informing potential voters. The number of channels that candidates have at their disposal reflects the cost structure of printing newspapers, establishing radio stations, and founding political groups. To the extent that these activities carry fixed costs, channels that cater to small groups are less likely to exist. The welfare implications – if one views the decision to vote as the decision to "consume" an election — are analogous to those of differentiated markets with fixed costs.[1]

Exhibit 2 demonstrates the strong differences between blacks and whites in their preferences for programming. Similarly, preferences differ sharply across groups defined by

---

[1] Oberholzer-Gee and Waldfogel, 2001b, pp. 36-37.

**Exhibit 2: Most Popular TV Shows Differ Between White
and Black Audiences**

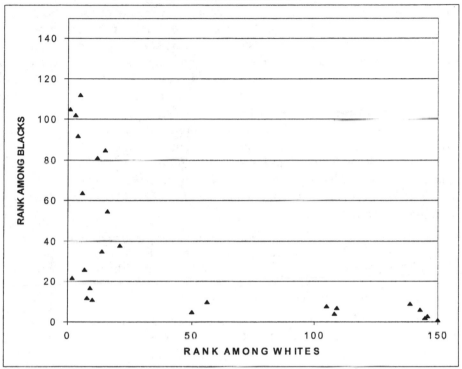

Source: Goldberg, Bernard. Bias. Washington: Regnery, 2002, pp. 150, 155.

gender, age, race and ethnicity (Hispanic). The Figure shows the ranking among whites and blacks of the top ten shows viewed by whites, the top ten shows viewed by blacks, and the six news shows ranked in the top twenty among whites. In all, we have 25 shows, fifteen that are highly ranked among whites and fourteen that are highly ranked among blacks. There is little overlap between the two groups.

The easiest way to appreciate the difference is to note that nine of the top ten ranked shows among blacks do not even rank in the top fifty among whites. The most popular fifteen shows among whites have an average ranking of 57 among blacks. The top ten shows among blacks have an average ranking of 85 among whites. The difference in preference for the popular news shows is similar. The average ranking for the six news shows analyzed among whites was fourteen; among blacks it was 53.

The tendency to under serve minority points of view springs in part from the role of advertising in the media.[2] Advertising as a determinant of

---

[2] Waldfogel, 2001, p. 1.

demand introduces a substantial disconnect between what consumers want and what the market produces.[3] First, to a significant extent, because advertisers account for such a large share of the revenue of the mass media, the market produces what advertisers want as much as, if not more than, what consumers want. Second, because advertising in particular, and the media in general, revolves around influencing people's choices, there is a sense in which the industry creates its own demand.[4] The tendency to avoid controversy and seek a lowest common denominator is augmented by the presence of advertisers, expressing their preferences in the market.

The failure of commercial mass media to meet the needs of citizens is nowhere more evident than in minority communities. Waldfogel has presented strong evidence of a kind of a tyranny of the majority in a number of media markets. These findings have been reinforced by recent findings of other scholars, as a 2002 article in the *Journal of Broadcasting and Electronic Media* makes clear.[5]

> The analyses presented here represent the next step forward in determining the extent to which advertiser valuations of minority audiences affect the viability of minority-owned and minority-targeted media outlets. The results conform to those of previous studies, which found that minority audiences are more difficult to monetize than non-minority audiences...[6]

> Minority-targeted media content suffers from not only the potentially lower valuations of minority audiences but also from the fact that, by definition, it

---

[3] Baker, 2001; Baker, C. Edwin. *Advertising and a Democratic Press*. Princeton: Princeton University Press, 1994. Krotoszynski, Ronald J., Jr. and A. Richard M. Blaiklock, 2000. Enhancing the Spectrum: Media Power, Democracy, and the Marketplace of Ideas. *University of Illinois Law Review*, p. 831: "The larger the audience the station generates, the higher the station's potential advertising revenues. Broadcasters, therefore, attempt to find and air programming that will appeal to the largest possible audience. In doing so, broadcasters necessarily air programming that is likely to appeal to most people within the potential audience – that is they air programming that appeals to the majority culture's viewpoint."

[4] Sunstein, Cass. *Republic.com*. Princeton: Princeton University Press, 2001, pp. 108-109, discusses the implications for democracy.

[5] Napoli, Philip. 2002. "Audience Valuation and Minority Media: An Analysis of the Determinants of the Value of Radio Audiences." *Journal of Broadcasting and Electronic Media* 46: 180-181.

[6] The author notes agreement with Ofori, K. A. 1999. "When Being No. 1 is not Enough: The Impact of Advertising Practices on Minority-Owned and Minority-Targeted Broadcast Stations." *Civil Rights Forum on Communications Policy*, Washington D.C; Webster, James G. and Patricia F. Phalen. *The Mass Audience: Rediscovering the Dominant Model*. New Jersey: Erlbaum, 1997; Baker, C. Edwin. *Advertising and a Democratic Press*. Princeton: Princeton University Press, 1994.

appeals to a small audience. Smaller audiences mean small revenues, particularly when the audience is not highly valued by advertisers...[7]

Moreover, lower levels of audience size and value both exert downward pressures on the production budgets of minority content, which further undermines the ability of such content to compete and remain viable... The differential in production budgets may be enough for some minority audience members to find the majority content more appealing than the content targeted at their particular interest and concerns. Such defections further undermine the viability of minority-targeted content... The end result is lower levels of availability of minority-targeted content.[8]

A long tradition of more qualitative research also supports the conclusion that minority market segments are less well served.[9] Greater concentration results in less diversity of ownership. Diversity of ownership – across geographic, ethnic and gender lines – is correlated with diversity of programming.[10] Simply, minority owners are more likely to present

---

[7] The author cites Owen, Bruce and Steven Wildman. *Video Economics.* Cambridge: Harvard University Press, 1992; Waldfogel, 1999.

[8] Naplio, 2002, p. xx.

[9] Hamilton, James T. *Channeling Violence: The Economic Market for Violent Television Programming.* Princeton: Princeton University Press, 1998; Wildman, Steven. 1994. "One-way Flows and the Economics of Audience Making." in James Entema and D. Charles Whitney (eds.), *Audiencemaking: How the Media Create the Audience.* Thousand Oaks, CA: Sage Publications, 1994; Wildman, Steven and Theomary Karamanis. "The Economics of Minority Programming." In Amy Garner (eds.), *Investing in Diversity: Advancing Opportunities for Minorities in Media.* Washington: Aspen Institute, 1998; and Owen and Wildman, 1992.

[10] Fife, Marilyn D. *The Impact of Minority Ownership on Broadcast Program Content: A Case Study of WGPR-TV's Local News Content.* Washington: National Association of Broadcasters, 1979; Fife, Marilyn D. *The Impact of Minority Ownership on Broadcast Program Content: A Multi-Market Study.* Washington: National Association of Broadcasters, 1986; Congressional Research Service. *Minority Broadcast Station Ownership and Broadcast Programming: Is There a Nexus?* Washington: Library of Congress, 1988; Hart, Jr., T. A. 1988. "The Case for Minority Broadcast Ownership." *Gannett Center Journal*; Wimmer, K. A. 1988. "Deregulation and the Future of Pluralism in the Mass Media: The Prospects for Positive Policy Reform." *Mass Communications Review*; Gauger, Timothy G. 1989. "The Constitutionality of the FCC's Use of Race and Sex in Granting Broadcast Licenses." *Northwestern Law Review*; Klieman, Howard. 1991. "Content Diversity and the FCC's Minority and Gender Licensing Policies." *Journal of Broadcasting and Electronic Media* 35: 411-429; Collins-Jarvis, Lori A. 1993. "Gender Representation in an Electronic City Hall: Female Adoption of Santa Monica's PEN System." *Journal of Broadcasting and Electronic Media* 37:1: 49-65; Lacy, Stephen, Mary Alice Shaver and Charles St. Cyr. 1996. The Effects of Public Ownership and Newspaper Competition on the Financial Performance of Newspaper Corporation: A Replication and Extension. *Journalism and Mass Communications Quarterly* Summer.

minority-centric points of view[11] just as females are more likely to present female-centric points of view[12] in the speakers, formats and content they put forward. Study 12 documents the vast under-serving of minority audiences from the supply side and the link between a lack of minority ownership and concentration.

THE IMPACT OF MARKET FAILURE ON CIVIC DISCOURSE

The impact of the market structure of contemporary media markets and their failures is felt across the forum for democratic discourse. In particular, it results in owner influence, erosion of checks, balances and other positive externalities of vigorous civic discourse and loss of local perspective.

Baker presents a lengthy discussion of the political implications of the monopolistic media market. The first point is that it results in market power, traditionally measured as excess profits.[13] For media markets, however,

---

[11] Empirical studies demonstrating the link between minority presence in the media and minority-oriented programming include Fife, 1979; Fife, 1986; Congressional Research Service, 1988 ; Hart, 1988; Wimmer, 1988; Evans, Akousa Barthewell. 1990. "Are Minority Preferences Necessary? Another Look at the Radio Broadcasting Industry." *Yale Law and Policy Review* 8; Dubin, Jeff and Matthew L. Spitzer. 1995. Testing Minority Preferences in Broadcasting. *Southern California Law Review* 68; Bachen, Christine, Allen Hammond, Laurie Mason and Stephanie Craft. *Diversity of Programming in the Broadcast Spectrum: Is there a Link Between Owner Race or Ethnicity and News and Public Affairs Programming?* Santa Clara: Santa Clara University Press, 1999; Mason, Laurie, Christine M. Bachen and Stephanie L. Craft. 2001. Support for FCC Minority Ownership Policy: How Broadcast Station Owner Race or Ethnicity Affects News and Public Affairs Programming Diversity. *Communication Law & Policy* 6.

[12] A similar line of empirical research dealing with gender exists. See Lacy, Shaver and St. Cyr, 1996; Gauger, 1989; Klieman, 1991; Collins-Jarvis, 1993; Lauzen, Martha M. and David Dozier. 1999. Making a Difference in Prime Time: Women on Screen and Behind the Scenes in 1995-1996 Television Season. *Journal of Broadcasting and Electronic Media* Winter; O'Sullivan, Patrick B. *The Nexus Between Broadcast Licensing Gender Preferences and Programming Diversity: What Does the Social Scientific Evidence Say?* Santa Barbara: Department of Communication, U.C. Santa Barbara, CA, 2000.

[13] Baker, 2001, pp. 43-44: "Monopolistic competition theory applies to media goods. They... characteristically manifest the 'public good' attribute of having declining average costs over the relevant range of their supply curves due to a significant portion of the product's cost being its 'first copy cost,' with additional copies having a low to zero cost. There are a number of important attributes of monopolistic competition that are relevant for policy analysis and that distinguish it from the standard model of so-called pure competition, the standard model that underwrites the belief that a properly working market leads inexorably to the best result (given the market's givens of existing market expressed preferences and the existing distribution of wealth). The first feature to note here is that in monopolistic competition often products prevail that do not have close, certainly not identical, substitutes. Second,

economic profits can be used (dissipated) in another important way. Media owners can use their market power to influence content or policy directly.

The weak competition allows owners to earn monopoly profits and to use monopoly rents to pursue their personal agendas. The claim that ownership of the media does not matter to the selection and presentation of content is not plausible.[14] Whatever their political preferences, media owners are in a uniquely powerful position to influence civic discourse. They can use both the economic resources made available by their market power (as can monopolists in any industry) and the unique role of the media to pursue those preferences.[15]

One set of behaviors that is particularly problematic involves undemocratic uses of media market power in pursuit of the private interests of owners through manipulation, co-optation and censorious behaviors.[16] This can undermine the watchdog role of the press or distort coverage of events, when it suits their interests. The chilling effect need not be conscious or overt. Powerful media owners tend to be very visible figures in their political and policy preferences. Employees and institutions instinctively toe the line and self-censor out of an instinct for self-preservation, which dampens antagonism in the media.[17] It need not be continuous to be effective, but can be exercised at critical moments – elections, policy votes in legislatures.

Even though this is not Waldfogel's central concern, when he looks at the question of ownership, he finds support for the view that ownership

---

this non-substitutability of the prevailing monopolistic product will allow reaping of potentially significant monopoly profits."

[14] Krotoszynski and Blaiklock, 2000, pp. 832...833: "The owners of a television or radio station possess a unique ability to influence the direction of public affairs through selective coverage of contemporary events and candidates for public office.... "To be sure, concentrations of political power present a more direct kind of threat to democracy than do concentrations of media power. That said it is possible to use media power as a means of channeling, if not controlling the flow of political power. The owners of a television or radio station have a unique opportunity to influence the outcomes of electoral contests – both by reporting on candidates favorably and unfavorably and through benign (or malign) neglect. Media exposure is like oxygen to candidates for political office, particularly at the federal level. If a television station pretends that a candidate does not exist, her chances of election are considerably reduced."

[15] Baker, 2002, p. 43. Krotoszynski and Blaiklock, 2000, p. 875, put it as follows: "There is simply no reason to believe that someone like Ted Turner or Rupert Murdock will consistently seek to maximize economic returns rather than use media power to influence political events in ways he deems desirable."

[16] Baker, 2002, p. 73.

[17] Krotoszynski and Blaiklock, 2000, p. 867: "Employees are unlikely to criticize their employers, and this truism holds true for the fourth Estate."

matters beyond "simple" economics. Waldfogel finds in his study of radio markets that "black owners enter in situations that white owners avoid."[18] He continues to consider possible explanations for this behavior and offers a hypothesis that relies on owner preferences,

> A second possibility is that black owners enter for "ideological" reasons, which means they are willing to forego some profits in order to provide a particular sort of programming. This hypothesis would rationalize the observation that black-owned and targeted stations have fewer listeners, on average, than [sic] their white-owned counterparts (in markets with both white and black-owned, black-targeted stations). Black owners' willingness to accept smaller returns could explain why greater black ownership increases black-targeted programming: additional black owners are willing to enter low-profitability market niches (programming to small black audiences) that whites would not enter.[19]

Perhaps Waldfogel puts the word "ideology" in quotes to blunt its negative connotation. Baker presents the policy implications in terms that are familiar and relevant to the arena of diversity policy in civic discourse.

> Choice, not merely market forces, influences quality. Choice explains the variation both within and between ownership categories. Moreover, quality may provide some efficiencies and management qualities that sometimes increase the enterprise's potential for profits or quality. However, the incentives for executives (editors and publishers) in chain firms as well as the added pressures of public ownership are likely to be directed toward focusing on increasing profits. Possibly due to price of membership or involvement within a community that leads to dedication or desires to form status in that community, local ownership might be sociologically predicted to lead to greater commitment to and greater choice to serve values other than the bottom line.[20]

Baker argues that the experiences of civic discourse for minorities and the public at large are deeply affected by ownership. Large, monopolistic structures make it more difficult for opinion leaders within minority or niche communities to gain experience in the industry.[21] Baker links the need to have policies that promote viewpoint diversity to the tendency of the commercial media to under serve the less powerful in society.[22] In order for

---

[18] Siegelman, Peter, Joel Waldfogel. 2001. "Race and Radio: Preference Externalities, Minority Ownership and the Provision of Programming to Minorities" *Advances in Applied Microeconomics* 10, p. 23.

[19] Id., p. 25.

[20] Baker, 2002, p. 47.

[21] Id., pp. 67-68.

[22] Baker, 2001, pp. 96-97: "Thus, from the perspective of providing people what they want, media markets are subject to the following criticisms. They provide much too much "bad" quality content – bad meaning content that has negative externalities.

the media to meet the needs of these groups, it must inform and mobilize them.[23]

The empirical evidence available in the academic and trade literatures overwhelmingly supports the concerns expressed about the emergence of a hyper-commercialized, concentrated mass media. Commercialism can easily overwhelm public interest and diverse content.[24] Concentration drains resources from journalistic enterprises.[25] Empirical evidence clearly suggests that concentration in media markets– fewer independent owners — has a negative effect on diversity.[26]   The evidence to support this conclusion

---

Media markets also may produce a wasteful abundance of content responding to mainstream taste. Otherwise, the main problem is underproduction. Markets predictably provide inadequate amounts and inadequate diversity of media content. Especially inadequate is their production of "quality" content – quality meaning content that has positive externalities. Production of civically, educationally, and maybe culturally significant content preferred by the poor is predictably inadequate. Smaller groups will often be served inadequately, either in relation to democracy's commitment to equally value their preferences or due to the consequences of monopolistic competition."

[23] Baker, 2002, p. 16.

[24] Rifkin, Jeremy. *The Age of Access*. New York: Jeremy P. Tarcher/Putnam, 2000, pp. 7-9.

[25] Layton, Charles, 1999. "What do Readers Really Want?" *American Journalism Review* March. reprinted in Gene Roberts and Thomas Kunkel, *Breach of Faith: A Crisis of Coverage in the Age of Corporate Newspapering*. Fayetteville: University of Arkansas Press, 2002; McConnell, Bill and Susanne Ault. 2001. "Fox TV's Strategy: Two by Two, Duopolies are Key to the Company's Goal of Becoming a Major Local Presence." *Broadcasting and Cable*, 30 July 2001 Trigoboff, Dan. "Chri-Craft, Fox Moves In: The Duopoly Marriage in Three Markets Comes with Some Consolidation." *Broadcasting and Cable*, 6 August 2001; Trigoboff, Dan. 2002. "Rios Heads KCOP News." *Broadcasting and Cable*, 14 October 2002; Beam, Randal A. 1995. "What it Means to Be a Market-Oriented Newspaper." *Newspaper Research Journal* 16; 2002. "Size of Corporate Parent Drives Market Orientation." *Newspaper·Research Journal* 23;Vane, Sharyn. 2002. "Taking Care of Business." *American Journalism Review* March; Neiman Reports. 1999. *The Business of News, the News About Business*, Summer.

[40] Levin, Harvey J. 1971. "Program Duplication, Diversity, and Effective Viewer Choices: Some Empirical Findings." *American Economic Review* 61:2: 81-88 Lacy, Stephen. 1989. "A Model of Demand for News: Impact of Competition on Newspaper Content." *Journalism Quarterly* 66; Johnson, Thomas J. and Wayne Wanta. 1993. Newspaper Competition and Message Diversity in an Urban Market. *Mass Communications Review* 20: 45; Davie, William R. and Jung-Sook Lee. 1993. Television News Technology: Do More Sources Mean Less Diversity? *Journal of Broadcasting and Electronic Media* 37, Fall: 453-464 Wanta, Wayne and Thomas J. Johnson. 1994. "Content Changes in the St. Louis Post-Dispatch During Different Market Situations." *Journal of Media Economics* 7; Coulson, David C. 1994. "Impact of Ownership on Newspaper Quality." *Journalism Quarterly*, 1994.; Coulson, David C. and Anne Hansen. 1995. The Louisville Courier-Journal's News Content After Purchase by Gannett. *Journalism and*

includes both anecdotal examples and statistical studies.   The economic interests of media owners influence their advertising, programming choices, and how they provide access to political information.[27]

Conglomerates are driven by advertisers, who exercise influence over content.[28]   Dangerous abuse of this influence ranges from favorable newspaper reviews of a broadcaster's programming[29] or loss of coverage,[30] to positive editorials/opinion articles about the business interests of a broadcaster or politician.[31] Such favoritism would be more difficult to prevent if cross-ownership were broadly permitted.[32] When the two largest sources of

---

Mass Communications Quarterly 72:1: 205-215; Iosifides, Petros. 1999. "Diversity versus Concentration in the Deregulated Mass Media." *Journalism and Mass Communications Quarterly* Spring; Lacy, Stephen and Todd F. Simon. "Competition in the Newspaper Industry." in Stephen Lacy and Todd F. Simon (eds.), *The Economics and Regulation of United States Newspapers*. Norwood, NJ: Ablex, 1993.

[27] Soloski, John. 1979. "Economics and Management: The Real Influence of Newspaper Groups." *Newspaper Research Journal* 1; Bennett, W. Lance. *News: The Politics of Illusion*. New York: Longmans, 1988; Busterna, John C. 1988. "Television Station Ownership Effects on Programming and Idea Diversity: Baseline Data." *Journal of Media Economics* 2:3: 63-74; Herman, Edward and Noam Chomsky. *Manufacturing Consent*. New York: Pantheon Books, 2002; Glasser, Theodore L., David S. Allen and S. Elizabeth Banks. 1989. The Influence of Chain Ownership on News Play: A Case Study. *Journalism Quarterly* 66; Katz, J. 1990. "Memo to Local News Directors." *Columbia Journalism Review* May/June: 40-45 McManus, J. 1990. "Local News: Not a Pretty Picture." *Columbia Journalism Review* 28; Price, Monroe E. 1999. "Public Broadcasting and the Crisis of Corporate Governance." *Cardozo Arts & Entertainment* 17.

[28] Just, Marion, Rosalind Levine and Kathleen Regan. 2001. "News for Sale: Half of Stations Report Sponsor Pressure on News Decision." *Columbia Journalism Review-Project for Excellence in Journalism* November/December, p. 2.

[29] Strupp, Joe. "Three Point Play." *Editor and Publisher*, 21 August 2000, p. 23; Moses, Lucia. "TV or not TV? Few Newspapers are Camera Shy, But Sometimes Two Into One Just Doesn't Go." *Editor and Publisher*, 21 August 2000, p. 22; Roberts, Gene, Thomas Kunkel, and Charles Clayton. "Leaving Readers Behind." In Roberts, Gene, Thomas Kunkel, and Charles Clayton (eds.), *Leaving Readers Behind*. Fayetteville: University of Arkansas Press, 2001, 10.

[30] Belo. 2003. Comments of Belo Corp., *In the Matter of 2002 Biennial Regulatory Review – Review of the Commission's Broadcast Ownership Rules and Other Rules Adopted Pursuant to Section 202 of the Telecommunications Act of 1996, Cross Ownership of Broadcast Stations and Newspapers, Rules and Policies Concerning Multiple Ownership of Radio Broadcast Stations in Local Markets, Definition of Radio Markets*, MB Docket No. 02-277, MM Dockets 02-235, 01-317, 00-244, pp. 8-9; Karr, Albert. "Television News Tunes Out Airwaves Auction Battle." *Wall Street Journal*, 1 May 1996, p. B1.

[31] See Quincy Illinois Visitors Guide, 2001 edition; McConnell, Bill. "The National Acquirers: Whether Better for News or Fatter Profits, Media Companies Want in on TV/Newspaper Cross-Ownership." *Broadcasting and Cable*, 10 December 2001.

[32] Kunkel, Thomas and Gene Roberts. 2001. "The Age of Corporate Newspapering, Leaving Readers Behind." *American Journalism Review* May. On coverage of the 1996

news and information – television and newspaper – come under the same ownership roof, there is special cause for concern about business pressures that could undermine the forum for democratic discourse.[33]

Left unrestrained, the marketplace will produce fewer watchdog activities conducted by less rigorous institutions. The public at large benefits from the watchdog function beyond the value that individual media firms can capture in their market transactions (advertising revenue and viewer payments). Baker uses investigative journalism as an example. Abuses are less likely to be uncovered and more likely to occur because the deterrent of the threat of exposure will be diminished.[34]

> One item both news entities "sell" is expose's on the content of investigative journalism. Not just the readers or listeners but all members of the community benefit from whatever reform or better government or improved corporate behavior that occurs due to these stories. This journalism can create huge positive externalities. The paper's limited number of purchasers cannot be expected to pay the full value of this benefit - they have no reason to pay for the value received by non-readers. Even more (economically) troubling, a major benefit of the existence of news organizations that engage in relatively effective investigative journalism is that this journalism deters wrong doing by governmental or corporate actors - but deterred behavior produces no story for the journalism to report and hence for the media entity to sell. The paper has no opportunity to internalize these benefits of its journalism - an economic explanation for there being less of this type of journalism than a straight welfare economics analysis justifies.[35]

The positive externalities that Baker identifies with respect to the watchdog and experiential functions are part of a larger category of

---

Telecommunications Act see Gilens, Martin and Craig Hertzman. 1997. "Corporate Ownership and News Bias: Newspaper Coverage of the 1996 Telecommunications Act." Paper delivered at *the Annual Meeting of the American Political Science Association*, August, p. 8.

[33] Davis, Charles and Stephanie Craft. 2000. New Media Synergy: Emergence of Institutional Conflict of Interest. *Journal of Mass Media Ethics* 15, pp. 222-223.

[34] Baker, 2002, Id., p. 64: "Consider the merger of two entities that supply local news within one community – possibly the newspaper and radio station... Presumably the merged entity would still have an incentive to engage in at least a profit maximizing amount of investigative journalism. But how much is that? The amount spent in the pre-merger situation may have reflected merely an amount that the media entity's audience wanted and would pay for (either directly or indirectly through being "sold" to advertisers). Alternatively, the pre-merger profit maximizing level for each independent entity may have reflected a competitive need to compare adequately to a product offered by its competitor. In this second scenario, competition may have induced increased but still inefficiently small expenditures on investigative journalism.

[35] Baker, 2002, p. 64.

externalities associated with information products, particularly civic discourse content. Information products, to a significant degree, are seen as possessing attributes of public goods,[36] which markets fail to provide in adequate quantity or quality.

---

[36] Sunstein, Cass. 2000. "Television and the Public Interest." *California Law Review* 8, p. 517.

STUDY 18:
THE CONTEMPORARY TERRAIN OF MEDIA AND POLITICS DEMANDS MORE CONCERN ABOUT CONCENTRATION OF THE MASS MEDIA

MARK COOPER

OLD THEORIES THAT NO LONGER APPLY MUST BE DISCARDED

The previous studies show that the empirical evidence compiled in the last decade supports traditional explanations of media market behavior in certain areas and rejects them in other areas. The rejection of some of the old saws is not necessarily a function of the fact that the explanations and theories were wrong in the past; rather changes in the social, economic and political structure may have rendered them obsolete. The assumptions about conditions in the market and behavior of media owners that made them good predictors of market structures and output in the past, no longer apply.

The essential point of the Court ruling in *Prometheus* is that public policy choices must reflect social reality. Thus, it is important to give up the old theories that no longer explain reality and adopt new ones. The most obvious first step is to recognize that, left to its own devices, the economic processes in media markets will not produce a vibrantly competitive media marketplace that serves the public interest. Consolidation and conglomeration diminish diversity and create powerful media voices that have excessive influence.

The FCC relied on two theories to claim that concentration of the media is good for consumers: Peter Steiner's[1] argument that concentrated media companies provide greater diversity and Joseph Schumpeter's[2] theory

---

[1] Federal Communications Commission, Initial Notice.

[2] Notice, p. 32, provides the innovation discussion. "Further Notice of Proposed Rulemaking." *In the Matter of Implementation of Section 11 of the Cable Television Consumer Protection and Competition Act of 1992, Implementation of Cable Act Reform Provisions of the Telecommunications Act of 1996, The Commission's Cable Horizontal and Vertical Ownership Limits and Attribution Rules, Review of the Commission's Regulations Governing Attribution Of Broadcast and Cable/MDS Interests, Review of the Commission's Regulations and Policies Affecting Investment In the Broadcast Industry, Reexamination of the Commission's Cross-Interest Policy,* CS Docket No. 98-82, CS Docket No. 96-85, MM Docket No. 92-264, MM Docket No. 94-150, MM Docket No. 92-51, MM Docket No. 87-154, 13 September 2001, Para 36, issued on the same day as the original notice in the media ownership proceedings makes reference to Schumpeter in this discussion. The Chairman had made similar references to monopoly and innovation in his Broadband

that monopolists produce more innovation. The Commission and industry comments that restate these theories present no economic evidence in support of the arguments. The FCC either misrepresents the original idea, or fails to recognize that the assumptions underlying the theories do not fit the media market reality.[3]

The Steiner hypothesis has always been controversial as a proposition about diversity. "Overall, explicit tests of the Steiner model have provided mixed results in studies dealing with program choices. For the most part, studies dealing with television have rejected the Steiner theory on the basis of audience preference and the mechanics of the television broadcast industry." [4]

Many of the studies of the hypothesis conflate variety of formats with diversity of viewpoints. It is about entertainment, not news and information. Even in the narrow realm of variety, support has been mixed.

The critical assumption underlying Steiner's theory is a relative homogeneity of taste. The theory may have been true when it was first offered fifty years ago, given the make-up of the population and the demographic characteristics of the audience at whom the media were targeted. The empirical evidence of the past decade shows that strong differences in taste result in preference minorities that are underserved and undervalued by the commercial mass media. Moreover, as the population becomes increasingly complex, the role of differences in information needs grows. Even where it can be shown that mergers allow a beat to be added, we find that upscale entertainment is the focus (mining the favored audience) at the expense of news and information. It is time for the Commission to abandon the theory supporting increased concentration in media markets. It no longer fits the reality of the conditions of civic discourse in America, if indeed, it ever did.

The Commission relies upon the Schumpeterian argument on transitory monopoly power to suggest it should allow or promote concentrated media markets to provide resources for investment. The

---

Migration speech and the argument appears word for word in the FCC's draft strategic plan (October 1, 2002).

[3] Information Policy Institute. "Comments of the Information Policy Institute." *In the Matter of 2002 Biennial Regulatory Review – Review of the Commission's Broadcast Ownership Rules and Other Rules Adopted Pursuant to Section 202 of the Telecommunications Act of 1996, Cross Ownership of Broadcast Stations and Newspapers, Rules and Policies Concerning Multiple Ownership of Radio Broadcast Stations in Local Markets, Definition of Radio Markets*, MB Docket No. 02-277, MM Dockets 02-235, 01-317, 00-244, January 2, 2003 (hereafter, Information Policy Institute), pp. 53-59.

[4] Chambers, Todd and Herbert H. Howard. 2006. "The Economics of Media Consolidation," in Alan B. Albarran, Sylvia N. Chan Olmstead and Michael O. wirth, *Handbook of Media Management and Economics* (Mahwah: Lawrence Erlbaum), p. 177.

Commission has misinterpreted or misapplied Schumpeter's argument.[5] The FCC seeks to justify market concentration, whereas Schumpeter focused on firm size. There is no doubt that the dominant commercial mass media firms are already large enough to possess economies of scale. Concentration that increases market power may undermine Schumpeterian processes because it dulls competition, which was central to his argument.

The monopoly rents earned by the innovative entrepreneur in the Schumpeterian argument must be transitory, lest they degenerate into plain old antisocial monopoly rents. Media industry moguls look and behave much more like traditional anti-competitive monopolists than innovative Schumpeterian entrepreneurs.[6] The underlying technologies have been relatively stable for decades. Strengthening the hand of entrenched incumbents using off-the-shelf technologies hardly seems the way to promote innovation and creative destruction. The Commission's policies are having the opposite effect.[7] Here, as in the case of the Steiner hypothesis, the Commission has simply failed to accept the empirical facts.

Based upon the empirical evidence, the Commission must abandon the Steiner/Schumpeter justification for concentration and monopoly power in media markets. Whether these two arguments articulated over fifty years ago ever made sense for media markets is debatable, but it is overwhelmingly clear they do not fit the facts of 21st century America.

More importantly, the Commission must fully appreciate the critical role that competition plays in the current environment.

THEORY OF A DIVERSE, HETEROGENEOUS MEDIA ENVIRONMENT WITH STRONG PREFERENCES AND POLITICAL ENTREPRENEURS

Waldfogel's analysis described in Study 18 focuses tightly on media market structure and its political impact[8] and falls within a broader field that applies economic analytic techniques to the study of politics and the media.[9]

---

[5] Information Policy Institute, 2003, pp. 46-52.

[6] Consumers Union, et al. "Initial Comments of Consumer Federation," et al., *Cross Ownership of Broadcast Stations and Newspapers*, MM Docket No. 01-235, December 4, 2001.

[7] Cooper, Mark. *Cable Mergers and Monopolies: Market Power Digital Media and Communications Networks*. Washington, DC: Economic Policy Institute, 2002.

[8] Waldfogel, 2001a. Other papers in the series of studies of "preference externalities" include Waldfogel, 1999, at Siegelman and Waldfogel, 2001, Waldfogel and Oberholzer-Gee, 2001b, George and Waldfogel, 2000, as well as Waldfogel, 2001b; and Oberholzer-Gee and Waldfogel, 2001a.

[9] Glaeser, Edward L., Giacomo A. M. Ponzetto and Jesse M. Shapiro. 2004. "Strategic Extremism: Why Republicans and Democrats Divide on Religious Values." *Harvard Institute of Economic Research Discussion Paper Number 2044*, October; Glaeser, Edward.

In these theories, information dissemination and communications play critical roles, and link directly to a growing literature that concludes that the economics of the commercial mass media ultimately set the conditions for a tyranny of the majority in media markets.   These literatures share fundamental assumptions, in particular an assumption of strong preferences unevenly distributed in a heterogeneous population.   The literatures link media behavior directly to political processes, recognizing that the cost of information dissemination and voting play a key role in the political process.

These theories challenge major tenets of the perceived academic wisdom of the 1950s and 1960s that saw a rush to the middle and the search for the modal voter, which were predicted by an earlier generation of economists studying politics.   These claims have been undermined by the strategic actions of political entrepreneurs in a context of social change.[10]   The claim that the media passively meet consumer needs when they express their desires to advertisers has been undercut by media markets that actively pursue profit maximization by slanting output to serve highly segmented pluralities, especially when and where there are media monopolies.[11]

This realignment of the operation of commercial media markets with respect to the thrust of political activity is part of a broader shift in economic thinking.   The assumption that rational actors, maneuvering freely in markets, can create and sustain efficient, stable economic equilibriums has been challenged.   The stock market crash of 1987 and the bursting of the dot.com bubble in 2000[12] squarely refuted the efficiency and stability of the rational actor theory in the fortress domain of rational market theory – financial markets.   The suspicion spread rapidly to other economic and social sciences.

At a broader level, this paper contributes to one of the central issues in economics, namely whether the presence of rational arbitrageurs keep financial markets "efficient."   In the context of financial markets, Friedman (1953) argued long ago that it does.   Subsequent research, however, has proved him wrong, both theoretically and empirically.   One finding of this research is that, in some situations, such as stock market bubbles, it may pay profit-maximizing firms to pump up the tulips, rather than eliminate irrationality.   Subsequent research has considered the interaction between biased individuals and rational entrepreneurs in other contexts, such as the incitement of hatred, political competition, and product design.   Here we ask a closely related question for the market for news: does competition among profit-maximizing

---

"The Political Economy of Hatred." NBER Working Paper 9171. Cambridge, MA: National Bureau of Economic Research, 26 October 2004; Mullainathan, Sendhil and Andrei Shleifer. 2004. The Market for News. American Economic Review 95.

[10] Downs, Anthony. An Economic Theory of Democracy. New York: Harper, 1957;

[11] As argued by Steiner, Peter O. 1952. "Program Patterns and the Workability of Competition in Radio Broadcasting." Quarterly Journal of Economics 66.

[12] Shiller, Robert J. 2003. "From Efficient Markets Theory to Behavioral Finance." Journal of Economic Perspectives 17:1.

news providers eliminate media bias? We find that the answer, as in both financial and political markets, is no. Powerful forces motivate news providers to slant and increase bias rather than clear up confusion.[13]

As oversimplified economic efficiency explanations falter, sociological explanations fill the gap. Psychology re-enters political analysis and sociology informs the vast analyses of the media's role in society. The key social change that has upended the old theories and gives credence to the economic theory of media discrimination is the increasing heterogeneity of the population.

HETEROGENEITY, EXTREMISM AND POLITICAL ENTREPRENEURSHIP

The terrain of media and discourse is driven by differentiation in a heterogeneous population with an active involvement of politically motivated actors seeking to influence the presentation of news and information in the media. Waldfogel's story in the media is writ large across a number of fields.

Differentiation around salient values is the fundamental concept that links the social science discussions. The fundamental observation that underlies this analysis is that firms or political organizations seek to differentiate themselves along a product dimension. Economists assume salience of values (or the lack thereof) and study its implications for firm behavior. A primary area of sociological inquiry is the analysis of the nature and quality of salience itself. Political science studies how to create salience through priming and agenda setting.[14]

In the economy, firms want to distinguish themselves according to the value that is more meaningful to the consumer. "Firms choose to maximize differentiation in the dominant characteristic and to minimize differentiation in the others when the salience of the former is sufficiently large."[15] Differentiation in the mind of the consumer eases competitive pressures and allows profit maximization. If a single dimension is sufficiently salient, it will become the primary axis of differentiation while other product dimensions will be downplayed.

---

[13] Mullainathan and Schleier, 2004, pp. 5-6. Friedman, Milton. 1953. "The Case for Flexible Exchange Rates." *Essays in Positive Economics*. Chicago: University of Chicago Press, 1953.

[14] Lohmann, 1998, p. 948, "We can expect political competition to work well in preventing an incumbent from acting against the interests of constituents only if an issue is salient in the public mind – or if it can be made salient in a future election by an interest group or a challenger."

[15] Irmen and Thisse, 1998, p. 5; Neven and Thisse, 1990; Tabuchi, 1994; Tirole, 1988. Interestingly, the example chosen involved U.S. Weekly magazines that try to differentiate themselves by cover stories (Irmen and Thisse, 1998).

The sociological literature finds that heterogeneity is the key to group differentiation and negative intergroup perceptions. "Negative perceptions of out-groups are higher for those who live in neighborhoods with more of their own racial group. It is important to bear in mind that, these differences are also relative to the racial composition of the metropolitan area. The effects of neighborhood racial isolation are greatest for people in more diverse metropolitan areas."[16] In other words, as the environment becomes more heterogeneous, the threat from outgroups grows and differentiation becomes more salient.

The social distribution of populations and the psychological perception of groups interact to influence policy preferences. For example, with respect to the key economic issue such as redistribution, the sociological observation parallels the economics described by Waldfogel in Study 18.

> Demographic fragmentation affects redistribution because it influences how the political process aggregates individual preferences. Interpersonal preferences provide a complementary explanation. If individuals prefer to redistribute to their own racial, ethnic or religious group, they prefer less distribution when members of their own group constitute a smaller share of beneficiaries. As demographic heterogeneity increases, on average, the share of beneficiaries belonging to one's own group declines. Thus average support for redistribution declines as heterogeneity increases.[17],[18]

The political science literature offers a conclusion similar to that of the economic literature with respect to differentiation. "At any time, politics will appear largely one-dimensional because the existing party activist equilibrium will define party differences along the dimension that distinguishes them. One-dimensional models will successfully predict most of the variation in legislative voting platforms."[19]

Similar to the sociological literature, the political science literature offers the observation that "[e]xtremism rises with the heterogeneity of voters' preferences. As there is a greater range of preferences in the population, party platforms will get more extreme."[20] But the political science literature goes one step further. Entrepreneurial political leaders and activists tend to be more extreme than the mass of voters and to exploit shifting preferences to drive differentiation.

The political entrepreneur wants to raise the perceived benefit among supporters by lowering the perceived cost of voting, while achieving the opposite among non-supporters. The cost to politicians of reaching voters becomes a critical issue in election campaigns. The cost to consumers of

---

[16] Oliver and Wong, 2003, p. 380.

[17] Luttmer, 2001, p. 519.

[18] Hecter, 2004, p. 400.

[19] Miller and Schofield, 2003, p. 249; Koford, 1999; Karol, 1999.

[20] Glaeser, Ponzetto and Shapiro, 2004, p. 13.

learning the facts is a key determinant to the effectiveness of political entrepreneurs at tailoring and managing the messages they seek to deliver. The political entrepreneur uses media and communications to mobilize voters by influencing individuals – increasing the benefits and lowering the cost of action.

Psychological fundamentals dictate the avenues through which this influence flows. Individuals are considered to have strict core values while remaining flexible (or persuadable) to a greater or lesser degree on other values. The salience of any set of values (even core values) at any moment is neither predetermined nor nearly determinable."

The political activity of targeting exploits the fact that individuals "prefer to hear or read news that [is] more consistent with their beliefs," and that they especially "appreciate, find credible, enjoy, and remember stories that are consistent with their beliefs." Contrarily, individuals "tend to ignore category-inconsistent information unless it is large enough to induce category change."[22] Psychologically, individuals prefer consistency and reinforcement of their views and preferences, but they remain susceptible to influence by their networks, particularly its leaders, and the media.

The effectiveness of the message flows from the "ease with which it comes to mind,"[23] the target's capacity to understand,[24] and the target's willingness to think about the message.[25] Effectiveness may also hinge on whether or not a targeted group considers itself directly and personally affected by the message,[26] especially "where the message is central to the group identity."[27] These characteristics induce elaboration on the message.[28]

We would expect the importance of ideology as a motivation for political participation to vary over time; however, depending on salience and clarity of ideological cues provided. The more extreme the position taken by a party's leaders and the more those leaders emphasize ideological appeals, the more likely that party will be to attract ideologically motivated activists. Identifying one's group as affected and hearing messages that appear to put the groups interests in play catches the listeners attention. The drift to the extreme will be accelerated if the group is moderately large (close to half the population) and can be readily sorted. If this is the case, members of the

---

[21] Murphy, Kevin M. and Andrei Shleifer. 2004. Persuasion in Politics. American Economic Review 94, p. 1.

[22] Mullainathan and Shleifer, 2004, p. 3.

[23] Sengupta and Fitzsimmons, 2000.

[24] Eagly, 1974.

[25] Fabrigar, et al., 1998; Albararacin and Wyer, 2001; Jacks and Devine, 2000.

[26] Petty, Ostrom and Brock, 1981.

[27] Niven, 2004, pp. 878-9; Platow, Mills and Morrison, 2000; Armitage and Conner, 2000.

[28] Nienhuis, Manstead and Spears, 2001; McLeod and Becker, 1974; Scheufele, 2004.

organization are connected to each other but separate from others outside the organization.[29]

THE ROLE OF THE MEDIA AND MESSAGING

We should not be surprised to find that the media play a large part in this process. We have described the impact of the press and the tendency for the press to become politicized earlier, as well as the recent economic analysis of media markets that reach a conclusion on differentiation that is similar to the other social science conclusions.[30] Because the media are the primary means of political communication, especially during elections, the resulting political discourse is skewed against minority viewpoints.

The media play a crucial role because media influence opinions and motivate action. The more aware voters are, the more likely they are to vote. Successful mobilization hinges on lowering the costs of voting for citizens, while facilitating the mobilizing process for parties and organizations. The objective of political entrepreneurs, though, is a differential voter turnout between supporters and non-supporters. This is achieved by moving their platforms away from the center and toward the ideology of the core constituency. The process is stimulated and accelerated by information management, which is effective because differential awareness of a politician's positions increases turnout among supporters more than the opponent's supporters.

Partisan media and channels of communication become extremely important, since they can help to target messages. "Extremism occurs whenever there is some ability to target information to a group whose preferences differ from the preferences of the nation as a whole."[31] Particularly powerful is negative campaigning, which depresses voter turnout among those with the least interest and information about the campaign,[32] but does not have that effect on one's own supporters.

Targeting is aided by ideological, geographical and institutional segregation. "Party affiliation means differential access to information about the party platforms. One way in which parties may gain the ability to broadcast messages is to have access to a selected subgroup of the population,

---

[29] Murphy and Shleifer, 2004, p. 3.

[30] Waldfogel, Joel. 1999. "Preference Externalities: An Empirical Study of Who Benefits Whom in Differentiated Product Markets." *NBER Working Paper 7391* Cambridge: National Bureau of Economic Research , p. 30, had already proven the proposition for radio. Other studies in this line of research demonstrated it for newspapers and television.

[31] Glaeser, Ponzetto and Shapiro, 2004.

[32] Ansolabehere and Iyenger, 1997; Kahn and Kenney, 1999.

such as a Church or a Union."[33] Such organizations facilitate recruitment since "Political mobilizers are most likely to turn to people they know when seeking recruits."[34] People are more likely to be influenced by people they know.

Using organizations and the media, political entrepreneurs seek to energize their supporters, without energizing the supporters of their opponents. Political entrepreneurs target and tailor their messages to activate and unify their supporters while confusing and dividing adversaries. They prevent alienation among their own supporters while promoting indifference among the opponent's supporters. Well-recognized strategies include staging events, spinning, and slanting.

"With access to a social group, a party will shift its policies... towards the preferences of the members of the organization. If the opposing party is prevented from also gaining access to the organization, this shift yields an increase in the margin of victory."[35] Management of preferences across a range of issues is grounded in the core preferences of the group, which are framed by slanting and spin. Sorting and separation enhance the political value of the network, but the location of the groups are not predetermined or given, they are the result of strategic choices and action.

People in different networks are too far apart in their beliefs to persuade each other. Such separation is essential for the leaders of the networks: if a network comes too close to others, its members might come under foreign influence, and as a consequence the ideological coherence of the network is endangered.[36]

Activists have a pivotal function in both the sociology of organizations and the political dynamics of parties and elections. Sociologically, they have key characteristics of influential communicators – commanding respect and sharing characteristics with the broader group of members.[37] Politically, activists are the central agents in the recruitment and motivation process and have the greatest influence over political candidates.[38] Ideological clues make it easier to attract activists.[39]

The battle for the middle requires a campaign to pull voters out of the middle as opposed to repositioning the candidate more firmly on middle ground.[40] Political entrepreneurs want to stimulate activists (interested,

---

[33] Glaeser, Ponzetto and Shapiro, 2004, p. 17.
[34] Campbell, 2004, p. 160; Brady, Schlozman, and Verba, 1999.
[35] Glaeser, Ponzetto and Shapiro, 2004, pp. 18-19.
[36] Murphy and Shleifer, 2004, p. 5.
[37] Nivens, 2004.
[38] Saunders and Abramovits, 2004; West, 1998.
[39] Abramovitz and Saunders, 1998.
[40] Gulati, Girish. 2004. "Revisiting the Link Between Electoral Competition and Policy Extremism in the U.S. Congress." *American Political Science Review* 32:5, rejects the

strong supporters) and motivate more passive supporters. They particularly want to get their activists interacting with passive supporters and interested independents. They want to persuade the interested middle. They want to demobilize the less interested among their opponent's supporters and dishearten the more interested.

Negative campaigning helps among the less interested and less committed. Negative advertising and fear campaigning are inevitable parts of mass media politics as well. They make up a small part of the total expenditure and ideological platform and they drive the important wedges, but they must be used carefully or they can backfire.

The intersection of audiences and messages is complex and makes moving the electorate difficult. Management of messages is made feasible by geographic dispersion and institutional separation of the audiences.

MEDIA BIAS AND POLITICAL ENTREPRENEURS

It should also be noted that the media is not just a tool that political entrepreneurs manipulate to achieve short-term goals like getting elected. One of the most important classes of political entrepreneurs is made up of media owners. Media owners have discretionary resources and the means of influencing public opinion as a result of their market power. Oligopolistic competition gives owners resources and drives them toward extremism. Politically motivated media owners have the same interest in creating and controlling more outlets to give their ideas a greater advantage in finding audiences. The maldistribution of "deep enough pockets," creates a maldistribution of media outlets.

But the politicization of the media goes far beyond the traditional concern about media owners as political entrepreneurs. Just as long-term, underlying social and economic changes may profoundly affect the terrain on which the political battle is fought, so too fundamental changes in media technology can alter the landscape of politics.

The fundamental economic characteristics of media production in the electronic age create forces for oligopolistic, or monopolistic, competition that supports the political role of the media in two ways.

First, the media tend to serve subsets of the population to maximize profits, where preferences are diverse. They value larger groups and target wealthier audiences who provide the bulk of the returns for advertisers.

---

moderation hypothesis and confirms an alternative, mobilization hypothesis, noting that "It seems as if marginal incumbents are concerned that appealing to voters in the center will alienate more of their core supporters than they would gain from new voters in the center (p. 510)." They link this behavior to the role of "their prime constituency... most of whom are well outside the ideological mainstream of the district."

Sensationalism sells, as long as it does not upset the target audience, a technique that weighs particularly heavily on those that can be easily influenced, potentially distorting their view of 'what is really going on' or 'what is really important.'

To differentiate themselves, media outlets tend to be more extreme than the audiences they target. The economic characteristics of media outlets reduce the number of sources available in the major media, especially at the local level. This creates a high rate of profit and reduces competition. Differentiation along major lines of division becomes manageable.

The model of the market for news offers additional insights into the behavior and distribution of news sources. Media outlets do not just reflect the market. To maximize profits, media outlets will slant news to cater to reader bias. Competition does not solve the problem. "With heterogeneous readers, competition by itself polarizes readership and if anything raises the average reader bias. News sources can be even more extreme than their most biased readers. One cannot therefore infer reader beliefs directly from media bias."[41]

News sources taking more extreme positions to differentiate themselves is not the only reason that the distribution of news sources might not simply reflect the underlying distribution of preferences. "[S]uch differences are reinforced by political entrepreneurs, who have an incentive to create particular beliefs that would bring them support... Newspapers would then follow these entrepreneurs in mirroring and reinforcing the beliefs of their supporters."[42]

The political process creates a strong incentive to spin the news, and political entrepreneurs have an interest in managing it.

> Suppose that a politician, or some other figure of authority, has a first mover advantage, i.e. can choose which data... gets presented to the media first... The papers slant these data toward reader beliefs, but... will have significant influence on what they report as compared to their getting data from an unbiased source... This effect becomes even more powerful in a more general model of sequential reporting. In this case, the initial spin may shape reader priors which future papers face and consequently slant news towards. The initial spin would then be reinforced even by ideologically neutral papers.[43]

> Political competition is only one source of underlying reader diversity. We can also imagine entrepreneurs starting newspapers on their own, so long as they have deep enough pockets, creating enough demand for unorthodox views to broaden the range of opinions (and slants) that are being covered. Ideological

---

[41] Glaeser, Ponzetto and Shapiro, 2004, p. 15.
[42] Glaeser, Ponzetto and Shapiro, 2004, p. 20.
[43] Mullainathan and Shleifer, 2004, p. 12.

diversity of entrepreneurs themselves may be the source of diversity of media coverage.[44]

The strategy for slanting and spinning leads back to the initial discussion of the goal of differential mobilization of supporters and opponents. The best issues "bind the networks that support you, and divide those of your opponent."[45]

The role of political entrepreneurs and the political role of media owners add the final link in the analysis. Groups formed around core values become the vehicles for mobilizing voters through asymmetrical informational awareness and are reinforced by slanting and spin. Political entrepreneurs can rent them out on issues that are not at their core.

In this framework, political competition does not lead to convergence of party platforms to the views of the median voter. Rather, parties separate their messages and try to isolate their members to prevent personal influence from those in the opposition.[46]

The battle over bias in the media is an essential outgrowth of the underlying political process discussed above. Discrediting sources of information that the political entrepreneur does not control or are hostile towards serves the purpose of explaining and dismissing inconsistencies that threaten to shake the faith of one's supporters. It diminishes the extent to which channels of uncontrolled media can heighten awareness of one's intentions, which threatens to mobilize opponents. It raises doubts among the supporters of one's opponents and makes it harder for the conscientious citizen to ascertain the facts. The actual behavior of the media need not have changed for the battle over bias to be ignited; nor does the bias actually have to be true for charges of bias to be repeated. The claim serves a political purpose.

A particularly clear example of this from the 2004 Presidential election campaign was a *New York Times* story that reported a private meeting with important supporters at which President Bush was said to have promised to move quickly on privatization of social security (pumping up the base). The Bush campaign adamantly denied the account (attempting to reduce the message to opponents of a threat to one of their core values), claiming the erroneous story was a result of the ongoing bias of *The Times*. Yet, the president's highest domestic agenda priority after the election was privatizing social security, even though exit polls showed that very few mentioned it (less than 5 percent).

If we recount a series of "fact checking" exercises from the 2004 presidential campaign we can see the ambiguity in the outcomes that makes a

---

[44] Glaeser, Ponzetto and Shapiro, 2004, p. 21.
[45] Murphy and Shleifer, 2004, p. 8.
[46] Murphy and Shleifer, 2004, p. i.

simple correlation between reporting and bias difficult to determine.   Abu Ghraib, a scoop that was held up for two weeks at the behest of the Pentagon, proved to be a "true" statement of facts, although its implications and meaning were subject to considerable debate.   The missing 380 tons of high explosives was a scoop that got out sooner than the initial source had intended.   The facts were disputed and remained in dispute until the election, when the relevance of the issue was eliminated and reporting stopped (although the final word seems to indicate the scoop was correct).   The Bush National Guard memo proved to be a fraud.   All three incidents involved one network.   Does the scoop offset the scandal?   Should the network lose its anchor for the journalistic lapse, or get a Pulitzer for its investigative excellence?

The critique of the commercial mass media and the discussion of the impact of message management and the television news cycle on the process of political discourse are structural arguments, not indictments of the citizenry.   Our concern is with the tendency of the institutions to make certain types of content available and ubiquitous, which distorts the pattern of discourse.

THE IMPORTANCE OF COMPETITION

This analysis of the market for news and its impact on the political process does have a potential bright spot.   We can assume that by creating divergent, biased views, competition expands the range of news sources available.   "Market segmentation benefits a conscientious reader, who can then aggregate the news from different sources to synthesize a more accurate picture of reality."[47]   Thus, conscientious readers have a broader range of information to sample in their search for the truth, even though the desire for truth cannot drive out bias.

A different assumption about reader behavior predicts that competition alone will reduce the bias of news outlets.[48]   If readers prefer truth and reputations suffer when errors in reporting are discovered, then competition drives outlets toward less biased reporting.

Under both sets of assumptions, heterogeneity is crucial to reducing the impact of bias.   In the former, it occurs at the level of the reader, who can ferret out the truth by cross-checking, if interested.   Unfortunately, the political process raises the cost of finding sources, particularly where the distribution of sources is skewed.   Moreover, political processes and the informational process of 'spinning' strive to diminish the number of conscientious readers.   The conscientious reader is not part of the constituency sought out by the political entrepreneurs.   In this way, media

---

[47] Mullainathan and Shleifer, 2004, pp. 19-20.
[48] Gentzkow and Shapiro, 2004.

driven political entrepreneurship distorts the production of news and information.

Under the second assumption, bias is reduced at the level of the outlets, which fear loss of readers. Unfortunately, this outcome requires the proportion of conscientious readers to be sufficiently large and their ability to divine the truth sufficiently well developed to impose economic pain on disreputable outlets.

The two conflicting interpretations of the effect of competition lead us back to Baker's formulation of complex democracy.[49] Partisan outlets are probably an inevitable part of the political process and should be recognized as such (so readers can better evaluate bias). Competition, within and between partisan camps, may help to eliminate the most egregious biases. Competition between outlets may prevent them from moving too far to the extremes, but we should not expect them to end up in the middle, consistent with the underlying assumption about differentiation from which this analysis was launched.

In both approaches, competition is to be encouraged. Looking at the level of the behavior of news outlets, Gentzow and Shapiro conclude:

> An advantage of our model is that it generates sharp predictions about where bias will arise and when it will be most severe... In the current debate over FCC ownership regulation in the U.S., the main argument in favor of limits on consolidation has been the importance of "independent voices" in news markets. [Our model] offers a new way to understand the dangers of consolidation: independently owned outlets can provide a check on each others' coverage and thereby limit equilibrium bias, an effect that is absent if the outlets are jointly owned.[50]

Ellmen and Germano argue that one of the avenues competition may reduce bias in news, where readers want accurate reporting, is to weaken the effects of advertising.

> We model the market for news as a two-sided market where newspapers sell news to readers who value accuracy and well space to advertisers who value advert-receptive readers. We show that monopolistic newspapers under-report or bias news that sufficiently reducers advertisers profits. Newspaper competition generally reduces the impact of advertising. In fact, as the size of advertising grows, newspapers may paradoxically reduce advertiser bias, due to increasing competition for readers.[51]

---

[49] Baker, C. Edwin. *Media, Markets and Democracy*. Cambridge: Cambridge University Press, 2001.

[50] Gentzkow and Shapiro, 2004, p. 33.

[51] Ellman, Mathew and Fabrizio Germano. 2004. What Do Papers Sell? *UPF Economics and Business Working Paper No. 800*, p. 1.

Analyzing the behavior of individuals in seeking news sources – a direct test of the conscientious reader hypothesis[52] – Garrett reaches a similar conclusion:

> The data show that though online sources are an important source of news for a large and growing number of individual, major news organizations continue to dominate the news landscape, online and off. Furthermore, when these sources are used, they are used to supplement mainstream sources. Online outlets are not at this point a serious competitive threat to the mainstream players....

> The results confirm that in their search for political news people are unlikely to reject biased news sources... In the absence of unbiased mainstream news sources, however, most people will choose an outlet that consistently supports their own viewpoint over one that is a consistent source of challenge....

> The findings regarding preferences underscore the importance of a news market that contains balanced news outlets, while the data on contemporary uses of Internet news cannot yet look to online news to ensure that such a market exists.[53]

In the heterogeneous, politicized media environment, the only way to promote balance is to promote competition between, not consolidation of media outlets. The theories that touted benefits of concentration do not fit the contemporary media landscape. Competition between mass media is more important than ever.

HETEROGENEITY OF NEEDS AND DIVERSITY OF SOURCES

There is a second strand of the literature that argues for policies that promote diversity that flow from the discussion of the conscientious voter. Heterogeneity of individual characteristics and involvement in the public sphere gives rise to heterogeneity of needs for different types of information. There is a stream of thought about voter behavior that runs through the social science literature that underscores the difference between voter orientations.

---

[52] Tsfati, Yariv and Joseph N. Cappella. 2005. Why Do People Watch News They Do Not Trust? The Need for Cognition as a Moderator in the Association between New Media Skepticism and Exposure. *Media Psychology* 7, demonstrates that the need for cognition, "a need to structure relevant situations in meaningful, integrated ways" (p. 254), is one critical dimension that affects information search strategies. Those with high needs for cognition are good candidates for the role of conscientious voters. "Because those high on NFC enjoy thinking in general, the cognitive need made them process the message regardless of their mistrust of the source. For those low on NFC, message processing was influenced by the source trustworthiness manipulation." (P. 266).

[53] Garrett, R. Kelly. "Media Deregulation and the Online News Market." *Telecommunications Policy Research Conference* September 2005, pp. 26-27.

It is a mistake to assume that voters need to be constantly mobilized and informed.[54]   According to this argument, for average citizens, passive monitoring and intermittent mobilization is all that can be hoped for, or necessary, for democracy to function. Involved, knowledgeable member of the public are best served by more substantive sources.[55] They seek out different types and quantities of information (news v. television) from different types of sources (noncommercial v. commercial).[56] Passive monitors in the public desire simpler presentation and are reached by different types of media.[57]

> Learning about political candidates before voting can be a cognitively taxing task, given that the information environment of a campaign may be chaotic and complicated... Different voters adopt different strategies, with the choice of strategy dependent on the campaign environment and individual voter characteristics.[58]

This is a challenging environment that taps the best of the Supreme Court First Amendment jurisprudence in contemporary society. As Benkler notes,

> *Red Lion*, however, is about a realization that free speech is not an anti-government concept, but rather a commitment to sustain an information environment in which a society's constituents can be both collectively self-governing and individually autonomous.... *Red Lion* continues to be living precedent for the proposition that the value of free speech itself requires government to secure a diverse, open information environment as free of private monopolization as it is of governmental control. It continues to be living precedent for the understanding that free speech is a value respected in the real world, on the background of the technological and economic conditions that make our information environment more or less concentrated, more or less open to public discourse and individual expression. The free

---

[54] Graber, 2003; Baum, 2003; Zaller, 2003; Hibbing, J. and Theiss-Morse, E. *Stealth Democracy: Americans' Beliefs About How Government Should Work*. Cambridge: Cambridge University Press, 2002; Schudson, 1998.
[55] Lipsitz, Keena, et al. 2005.   What Voters Want From Political Campaign Communications. *Political Communications* 22.
[56] Aarts, Kees and Holli A. Semetko. 2003. "The Divided Electorate: Media Use and Political Involvement." *Journal of Politics* 65:3, Newton, Kenneth. 1999. "Mass Media Effects: Mobilization or Media Malaise." *British Journal of Political Science* 29; Druckman, James N. 2005. Media Matter: How Newspapers and Television News Cover Campaigns and Influence Voters. *Political Communication* 22.
[57] Lipsitz, et. al., 2005.
Redlawsk, David P. 2004. "What Voters Do: Information Search During Election Campaigns." *Political Psychology* 25:4, p. 595.

speech value requires government to husband the information environment well. [59]

CONCLUSION

Although theory formation around this new view of media markets and their impact on political processes is in the early stages, it is already affecting the framing of research questions. For example, a study by the FCC,[60] which was suppressed, cites the Mullainathan and Schliefer,[61] George and Waldfogel,[62] and Stromberg studies[63] as part of the animus to analyzing the link between media market structure and production of local news.

We suggest that divergent ownership patterns induce different cost structures, advertising access, and agency problems, each of which, separately and interactively, produce different levels of local news among the firms...

As we suggest in this paper, the FCC media ownership rule-making and subsequent Congressional action may affect the composition of local news broadcasts. This may be important, given the world of Stromberg, and George and Waldfogel that suggest information consumed at the local level has substantial political-economic distributional consequences.[64]

The second line of argument, embodied in the Gentzkow and Shapiro[65] analysis, has been cited as the framework for analyzing the sources on which citizens rely.[66]

First, scholars have noted that media owners are self-interested with political intentions. To the extent that media owners are interested in using their properties to influence public opinion, mergers will often (though not always) reduce ideological diversity.

Gentzkow and Shapiro suggest that a second mechanism linking consolidation with biased coverage is the importance of reputation in the news market paired with news consumers' tendency to perceive viewpoint consistent sources as more reliable....

The findings regarding news preferences underscore the importance of a news market that contains balanced news outlets, while the data on contemporary

---

[59] Benkler, Yochai. 2000. "Review."   *International Journal of Law and Information Technology* 8:2, p. 214.

[60] Anonymous, 2004.

[61] 2004.

[62] 2000

[63] Stromberg, David. 2004. "Mass Media Competition, Political Competition and Public Policy," *Review of Economic Studies*, (71 (2004).

[64] Anonymous, 2004, p. 16.

[65] 2005.

[66] Garrett, 2005

uses of Internet news suggest we cannot yet look to online news to ensure that such a market exists. [67]

---

[67] Garrett, 2005, pp. 5... 27.

PART VIII:
MEASURING MARKET CONCENTRATION

STUDY 19:
THE CRITIQUE OF THE FCC APPROACH TO MEASURING MARKET CONCENTRATION

MARK COOPER

RULERS V. RULES

In discussing the approach taken to market structure analysis, Ken Ferree, head of the Media Bureau, would emphasize that people must not confuse the ruler with the rules. As an example, he recounted a story about his life-long desire to be a fighter pilot. The problem was, he grew to be 6 feet 6 inches. He got too tall to comfortably fit in a cockpit and the military had a height limit. The ruler was not the problem, the rule was.

Market structure analysis is a ruler, not a rule. Whatever rule that is proposed, can be assessed with the ruler. The *Prometheus* Court[1] found that the FCC had bungled both jobs, crafting the ruler (the Diversity Index) and writing the rule (cross-media limits).

The fact that the FCC did such a bad job does not mean it can simply quit. It still must find a way to measure diversity and competition in local media markets and write rules that promote the goal of "the widest dissemination of information from diverse and antagonistic sources." Three Courts have now told the FCC to carefully count voices.[2] Perhaps because it was the FCC's third try, the *Prometheus* Court gave the Commission a detailed road map.

The legal standard for reviewing rules is important because it establishes the quality of the analysis that must be conducted in support of a rule. At the most basic level, Congressional intent is important and a Court "may find an agency rule is arbitrary and capricious where the agency has relied on factors which Congress has not intended it to consider." This can be termed "an abuse of discretion, or otherwise not in accordance with the law."[3] The Court asks whether "the agency examined the relevant data and articulated a satisfactory explanation for its action, including a 'rational' connection between the facts found and the choice made." If not, it can be concluded that "the agency made a clear error in judgment."[4]

---

[1] *Prometheus Radio Project, et al. v. FCC* 373 F.Supp 372(2004) (*Prometheus*).;

[2] *Fox Television Stations, Inc., v. FCC*, 280 F.3d 1027 (D.C. Circ. 2002) (*Fox*); *Sinclair Broadcasting, Inc. v. FCC*, 284 F.3d 148 (D.C. Circ. 2002) (*Sinclair*).

[3] *Prometheus*, 373 F.Supp. at 390.

[4] *Id.* at 389..

Although an expert agency like the FCC is given discretion in writing rules, at a more complex level the Courts will overturn rules if the agency "entirely failed to consider an important aspect of the problem, offered an explanation for its decisions that runs counter to the evidence before the agency, or is so implausible that it could not be ascribed to a difference in view or the product of agency expertise."[5]   In the case of an exercise such as identifying thresholds for merger review under the Administrative Procedures Act (APA),

> the traditional APA standard of review is even more deferential "where the issues involve 'elusive' and 'not easily defined,' areas such as program diversity in broadcasting." Yet... a "rationality" standard is appropriate... when an agency has engaged in line-drawing determinations... its decisions may not be "patently unreasonable" or run counter to the evidence before the agency.[6]

Thus, legal practice does not demand (and social science cannot provide) perfection or even great precision in the analysis.   It demands substantial evidence, consistent reasoning, choices that are reasonable and results that are rational.

ANALYTIC AND METHODOLOGICAL FLAWS IN THE FCC'S RULER

In *Sinclair*, the D.C. Circuit Court had criticized the FCC's rule limiting the ownership of multiple TV stations within a single market (the duopoly rule) because it had counted media "voices" in the same market differently for each of its rules.[7]   The *Sinclair* court wanted consistency between rules. As a result of the *Sinclair* decision, when later reviewing the rule that prevents the holder of a television station license from owning a newspaper in the same market in its biennial review, the FCC had to confront the task of treating different media consistently head on. It had to deal with the challenge of combining media in one framework. Thus, the central issue in the 2003 cross-ownership proceeding – how to count different media within the same market – is the very issue that led the *Sinclair* court to reject FCC's television station duopoly rules.

In 2003, FCC responded to *Sinclair* by modifying a standard antitrust approach to create a consistent empirical framework for evaluating media outlets in a local area. Where different *types* of media had to be considered together (e.g. in the question of mergers between newspapers and television stations) the FCC attempted to create a single "Diversity Index."

---

[5] *Id.*, at 390.

[6] *Id.*

[7] *Sinclair*, 284 F.3d at 162-65.

The *Prometheus* court accepted the general antitrust framework and even the idea that a single index *could* be created, but found the FCC's implementation to be faulty. "But for all of its efforts, the Commission's Cross-Media Limits employ several irrational assumptions and inconsistencies."[8] The Court identified three primary problems in the implementation of the Diversity Index.

The FCC refused to analyze the actual audience of a media outlet, assuming instead that all outlets within a media type are equal. Its weights for combining each type of media were inconsistent and not based on sound empirical measures.[9] The link between the index and the merger approval was tenuous at best.[10]

The Court found that the FCC had not properly weighted the various media. "In converting the HHI to a measure for diversity in local markets, however, the Commission gave too much weight to the Internet as a media outlet."[11] The Court focused on the handling of the Internet, in part, because of the extensive arguments presented by media owners to the Commission that the Internet had dramatically changed the media landscape. In fact, the mishandling of radio actually has a larger impact. However, viewing the issue through the portal of the Internet provided the Court with the opportunity to present a richly nuanced discussion of the media's output and function. By assigning a substantial weight to the Internet, the FCC has failed to note that there is very little independent local news and information produced by many of the websites the FCC pointed to.[12]

The reach of the outlet is also important. The Court made this clear in the discussion of the way the FCC treated cable and the Internet. The Court said it chose to "affirm the Commission's reasoned decision to discount cable . . . [b]ut we think that the same rationale also applies to the Internet."[13] The FCC had excluded cable from the local news and information market, since it found that there was little local news available and few such channels reach the public. For example, the FCC found that for many who said they watched cable for news, "cable news channels were probably confused with broadcast network news."[14] Moreover, only 10 to 15% of cable systems include channels that provide local and public affairs programming."[15]

A close look at the data showed the *Prometheus* Court that the Internet exhibits characteristics that are similar to cable. For example, "62% of Internet

---

[8] *Prometheus*, 373 F.Supp at 402..
[9] *Id.*, at 404-09.
[10] *Id.*, 409-11.
[11] *Id.*, at 403.
[12] *Id.*, at 406.
[13] *Id.*, at 405..
[14] *Id.*
[15] *Id.*

users get local news from newspaper websites, 39% visit television web sites."[16] The FCC's claim that "the Internet is available everywhere," was challenged by the fact that "almost 30% of Americans do not have Internet access."[17] The Court concluded that "on remand the Commission must either exclude the Internet from the media selected for inclusion in the Diversity Index or provide a better explanation for why it is included in light of the exclusion of cable."[18]

As discussed in the analysis of media usage, part of the FCC's problem was caused by weak methodology. The FCC recognized the importance of evaluating the use of the media.[19] In order to address the issue, it commissioned a survey. Yet, the FCC failed to ask the right questions and proceeded to make rules with admittedly faulty data. *"Unfortunately, we do not have data on this question specifically with regard to local news* and current affairs. The available 'primary source' data address local and national news together and do not show that different media have different importance, in the sense that primary usage differs across media."[20]

THE FCC'S INCONSISTENT RULE

Having declared its intention to use the Diversity Index to describe markets, the FCC then wrote a rule that seemed to bear only a tangential relationship to the ruler. The Court remanded the cross media limit for a very precise reason.

Although the Commission is entitled to deference in deciding where to draw the line between acceptable and unacceptable increases in markets' diversity scores, we do not affirm the seemingly inconsistent manner in which the line was drawn. As the chart above illustrates, the Cross-Media Limits allow some combinations where the increases in Diversity Index scores were generally higher than for other combinations that were not allowed.[21]

The Court chose as an example to look at mid-size markets to demonstrate the inconsistency in the Commission's line drawing. Exhibit 1 contains the FCC's chart to which this discussion applies.

The court noted:

---

[16] *Id.,* at 406.

[17] *Id.,* at 407.

[18] *Id.,* at 408..

[19] *FCC Ownership Rules Order,* at ¶¶ 410 (emphasis added). ("If media differ in importance systematically across respondents [e.g. if television were most important to everyone, and everyone made only minor use of radio to acquire news and current affairs information], *then it would be misleading to weight all responses equally.*")

[20] *FCC Ownership Rules Order,* at ¶¶ 410-411 (emphasis added).

[21] *Prometheus,* at 411.

Consider the mid-sized markets (four to eight stations), where the Commission found that a combination of a newspaper, a television station, and half the radio stations allowed under the local radio rule would increase the average Diversity index scores in those markets by 408 (four stations) 393 (five), 340 (six), 247 (seven) and 314 (eight) points respectively. These permitted increases seem to belong on the other side of the Commission's line. They are considerably higher than the Diversity Index score increases resulting from other combinations that the Commission permitted, such as the newspaper television combination, 242 (four stations), 223 (five), 200 (six), 121 (seven) and 152 (eight). They are even higher than those resulting from the combination of a newspaper and television duopoly – 376 (five stations), 357 (six), 242 (seven), and 308 (eight) – which the Commission did not permit. The Commission's failure to provide any explanation for this glaring inconsistency is without doubt arbitrary and capricious, and so provides further basis for remand of the Cross-Media limits.[22]

Exhibit 1: FCC Analysis and Approval of Mergers
(Italicized numbers represent mergers that are prohibited; non-italicized numbers represent mergers that are allowed)

Base Case		Average Change in Diversity Index Resulting From Mergers				
TV Stations In Market	Average Diversity Index	Newspaper + Radio	Newspaper + 1 TV	Newspaper, + 1 TV + 1/2 Radio	Newspaper + 2 TV Stations	Newspaper + Radio, 2 TV Stations
1	1707	*271*	*910*	*1321*	----	----
2	1316	*335*	*731*	*1009*	----	----
3	1027	*242*	*331*	*515*	----	----
4	928	*236*	*242*	*408*	----	----
5	911	263	223	393	376	846
6	889	239	200	340	357	688
7	753	171	121	247	242	533
8	885	299	152	314	308	734
9	705	198	86	207	172	473
10	635	107	51	119	101	292
15	595	149	48	145	97	302
20	612	222	40	128	80	350

Source: Federal Communications Commission, "Report and Order," In the Matter of 2002 Biennial Regulatory Review – Review of the Commission's Broadcast Ownership Rules and Other Rules Adopted Pursuant to Section 202 of the Telecommunications Act of 1996, Cross Ownership of Broadcast Stations and Newspapers, Rules and Policies Concerning Multiple Ownership of Radio Broadcast Stations in Local Markets, Definition of Radio Markets," MB Docket No. 02-277, MM Dockets 02-235, 01-317, 00-244 July 2, 2003, Appendix D.

---

[22] Prometheus, p. 75.

CONCLUSION

As the preceding discussion clarifies, in order to appropriately respond to the *Prometheus* court's remand order, the Commission must develop a ruler that accounts for the differing importance and reach of varying media voices in a given market, and weights them accordingly. It must also develop rules that logically relate to that rule and draw lines within its ownership rule that are consistent across different markets and different media combinations. Studies that follow demonstrate a method of achieving that goal that complies with the direction of the *Prometheus* court.

STUDY 20:
BUILDING A REASONABLE MEASURE OF MARKET STRUCTURE

MARK COOPER

THE ANTITRUST APPROACH TO MARKET STRUCTURE ANALYSIS

For the purpose of merger analysis, antitrust officials define markets by the substitutability of products.[1] Products must be good substitutes and be readily available in a given geographic area to be included in the market. Hence, economists talk about product and geographic markets.

After the market is defined, the analyst looks at the size of the firms in the market as a first screen in assessing the likely impact of a merger. When the number of firms in a market is small, or a single firm is very large, a concern arises that market power can be exercised. Prices can be raised or quality reduced to increase profits through coordinated or parallel actions among a small number of firms, or the unilateral acts of a single dominant firm.

The level of concentration is calculated by taking the market share of each firm, squaring it, then summing the result for all firms, and multiplying by 10,000 to clear the fraction.[2] Known as the "Herfindahl-Hirschman Index HHI" or HHI, this index has an easy interpretation of concentration.[3] A market that is made up of 10 equal-sized firms will have an HHI of 1000. Each firm has a 10 percent market share. Squaring the share yields 100 points

---

[1] U.S. Department of Justice and the Federal Trade Commission, *Horizontal Merger Guidelines*, 1997.

[2] William G. Shepherd, *The Economics of Industrial Organization* (Englewood Cliffs, NJ: Prentice Hall, 1985), p. 389, gives the following formula for the Herfindahl-Hirschman Index (HHI):

$$H = \sum_{i=1}^{n} S_i^2 \times 10,000$$

where
n = the number of firms
S_i = the share of the ith firm.

The HHI is calculated based on ratios rather than percentages and the decimals are cleared by multiplying by 10,000. For ease of discussion the Court adopts the convention of describing the calculation in percentages.

[3] The HHI can be converted to equal-sized equivalents as follows:
Equal-sized voice equivalents = (1/HHI)*10,000.

for each firm, times 10 firms (10x10 x 10). A market with 5 five equal-sized firms will have an HHI of 2000 (20x20=400 x 5).

The Department of Justice considers a market with fewer than 10 equal-sized firms to be concentrated (see Exhibit XII-1). It considers a market with fewer than the equivalent of approximately 5.5-equal sized firms (HHI = 1800) to be highly concentrated. Markets with an HHI between 1000 and 1800 are considered moderately concentrated. A highly concentrated market is called a tight oligopoly.[4] A moderately concentrated market is called a loose oligopoly.

WHICH MEDIA? WHICH MARKETS?

In order to conduct market structure analysis, the market must first be defined. This is accomplished by identifying the products being analyzed and the markets in which they are available.   Both sets of definitions, products and geographic areas, proved to be challenging for the FCC in the 2003 media ownership proceeding.

In analyzing a market structure for policy purposes, one of which is to assess the impact of a merger, we must describe which products to include. Products should be included if they are good substitutes for one-another. Economists look at the cross-elasticity of demand. The question is: "If the price of product increases, or its quality declines, are there substitutes to which consumers can readily switch?"

One of the central concerns that the D.C. Court of Appeals raised in remanding the local ownership rule in *Sinclair* was the fact that the FCC had failed to count non-broadcast outlets. The court held "that the Commission had failed to demonstrate that its exclusion of non-broadcast media from the eight voices exception 'is necessary in the public interest'." [5]

For the purposes of evaluating TV-TV mergers, the FCC did the right thing, when it did not include non-broadcast voices. But why didn't the FCC include newspapers and radios in its voice count for the rule that limited the number of markets in which one owner could hold licenses to more than one TV station (the duopoly rule)? The answer it could have given is now clear and supported overwhelmingly by the empirical evidence in the record. TV has a unique impact on politics and policy debates and all TV markets are highly concentrated. For the purposes of the *cross-media* rules, however, the Commission must count all voices.

We have described the critical characteristics of the various media in the prior discussion of media and localism. Broadcast TV and newspapers are the dominant media on which people rely for their news and information. In this analysis, we address the challenge of combining *types* of media and

---

[4] Shepherd, *supra* note 2, at 4.
[5] *Sinclair Broadcasting, Inc. v. FCC,* 284 F.3d 148, 165 (D.C.Cir. 2002).

follow the road map outlined by the *Prometheus* Court.   Product and geographic market definitions are inherently intertwined. For example, two newspapers are generally considered substitutable, as a product, but not if they are unavailable within a given market. We begin with an area where the *Prometheus* Court seemed to accept the FCC decision, as do we – the geographic market.

COMMERCIAL GEOGRAPHIC MARKETS

One of the key steps in analyzing market structure is to define the geographic scope of the market. Defining the market properly is critical because if the market is defined too broadly, producers who are assumed to be in the market, making their output available, will not actually be there.

It is well recognized that different media cover different areas. Radio signals travel smaller distances than television signals. Cable and satellite distribution expands the reach of television beyond what the market reach available was from over-the-air distribution. However, even if a station has the right to ask for carriage in a wide area, it might not do so because it would attract few viewers outside of its area. Hagerstown, Maryland TV stations do not seek carriage on District of Columbia cable systems, even though they are in the same Designated Market Area (DMA).

We also show that while newspapers may be available in a wide area, their circulation tends to be concentrated in a *limited* geographic area. The reason is simple. By focusing on a geographic area, they are able to attract readers and advertisers who are affected by events in a specific area and are likely to shop in that area. Trying to cover very large areas would result in huge newspapers.

If the viewer/listener/reader wants to find out about the local area efficiently, he or she is likely to turn to sources that focus on that area. There is, of course, a trade-off between clutter, which imposes a cost on the consumer, and the desire of commercial entities to expand their base of users and advertisers. As the reach of the media expands, the probability that any fact or commercial establishment will be relevant to any individual user declines.

This methodological issue is an important part of the conceptual analysis. For years media owners who seek relaxation of the rules have argued that the mere *availability* of a source in an area is all that matters. They have complained that counting users for purposes of market structure analysis "penalizes success" or confuses "success with access."   The *Prometheus* Court has suggested this, recognizing that the size of the audience matters a great deal.

Commercial markets are primarily defined as areas in which broadcasters sell advertising. There are two standards generally used: –

Designated Market Areas (DMAs) for television and Arbitron markets for radio. There are 210 DMAs and 296 Arbitron radio markets. However, a large number of radio stations are not included in *any* Arbitron area. These "omitted" stations represent about 39 percent % of the 13,635 stations included in the BIA data base, but about 33 percent of the 1,986 stations we identify as providing news or information.

The DMA as a market is larger than the Arbitron market and also larger than a typical newspaper market. In the last media ownership proceeding, the FCC defined the market as a market somewhere in between DMA and Arbitron markets. The FCC called it the city, but then misallocated media outlets within that defined market.

The BIA database provides Arbitron areas for radio and allocates newspapers to these markets as well. But it does not actually measure *circulation* within the Arbitron area, however. Thus, a precise geographic definition of the market will remain elusive. Using the Arbitron area with papers allocated is a reasonable approach.

Exhibit 1 shows the calculations of newspaper concentration for a dozen markets based on the DMA, the Arbitron area, the city and the county. The city and county data are taken from a series of profiles that *Editor and Publisher* provided in 2001. We generally observe the expected relationship. The DMA is least concentrated, the city next, the Arbitron area next and the county most concentrated. The very large difference between the Arbitron and county calculations and the wider areas supports the notion that newspapers do not circulated that widely even within cities. Thus, the focus on much smaller geographic areas is justified.

Exhibit 2 presents an analysis of the ten markets for which the FCC provided detailed analysis in the support of its 2003 the proposed rules. It shows that the Arbitron area fits the city definition that the FCC used. Thus, we believe that the Arbitron area is a reasonable geographic area for media market analysis.

Exhibit 1: Concentration of Newspaper Circulation in Various Geographic Markets

		Large Markets		Sub-Markets		
	Year	Type	HHI	Type	N	HHI
NEW YORK	2001	City	2505	County	8	4009
	2004	DMA	1678	Arbitron	2	3612
LOS ANGELES	2001	City	2298	County	5	3825
	2004	DMA	2237	Arbitron	2	3098
SAN FRAN	2001	City	3791	County	6	5949
	2004	DMA	2943	Arbitron	3	3758
DALLAS	2001	City	2298	County	5	3825
	2004	DMA	2237	Arbitron	2	3098
SEATTLE	2001	City	3743	County	5	4976
	2004	DMA	1756	Arbitron	1	2317
CLEVELAND	2001	City	4819	County	5	8046
	2004	DMA	5813	Arbitron	2	6969
ORLANDO	2001	City	4143	County	6	8546
	2004	DMA	3046	Arbitron	3	7364
FRESNO	2001	City	5904	County	5	7427
	2004	DMA	5761	Arbitron	2	8714
TAMPA	2001	City	3161	County	7	7201
	2004	DMA	2546	Arbitron	3	5116
ATLANTA	2001	City	8640	County	5	8944
	2004	DMA	4263	Arbitron	1	5250
RICHMOND	2001	City	8682	County	6	9221
	2004	DMA	8429	Arbitron	1	8429
NEW ORLEAN	2001	City	10000	County	6	10000
	2004	DMA	7117	Arbitron	1	9459
NORFOLK	2001	City	5001	County	6	9662
	2004	DMA	5206	Arbitron	1	5693
LAS VEGAS	2001	City	10000	County	6	10000
	2004	DMA	7117	Arbitron	1	9459

Exhibit 2: Comparing FCC Cities and Arbitron-Defined
Newspaper Markets

| City | # Of Dailies | | DMA | Arbitron |
	FCC	CFA	HHI	HHI
New York	12	9	1661	2174
Kansas City	6	6	6693	8239
Birmingham	2	3	3710	8160
Lancaster	1	1	2546	10000
Little Rock	3	3	5750	8545
Burlington	3	3	1666	5349
Myrtle B.	1	1	3643	10000
Terre Haute	3	4	2419	4532
Charlottesville	1	1	10000	10000
Altoona	1	2	1763	9309

Exhibit 3 shows the figures for the counties in the Los Angeles area, which is one of the least concentrated markets in the U.S. We used average daily circulation for newspapers (the Editor and Publisher and Beacon data bases). Again, we observe much higher levels of concentration at the county level.

Los Angeles is used as an example because it is the third least concentrated (for newspapers) DMA in the country and the five counties identified above account for 95 percent of the households in the DMA.

As applied in this analysis, this is a conservative approach that underestimates the level of concentration somewhat for a number of reasons.

- First, we assume all TV stations in the DMA are available in every Arbitron area. That is not the case in reality.

- Second, the calculation of newspaper concentration in the Arbitron area underestimates newspaper concentration, even assuming all circulation of each newspaper is in its primary Arbitron area. The overestimate of circulation is more than offset by the larger size of the Arbitron area.

GEOGRAPHIC POLITICAL MARKETS

There is another reason to examine the issue of market definition. The commercial definition of the market is not the primary focus of this proceeding. We are concerned about the market for news and information – the forum for democratic discourse. In particular, we are concerned about the areas in which local policy decisions are made.

Exhibit 3: Local Papers Dominate Home Counties

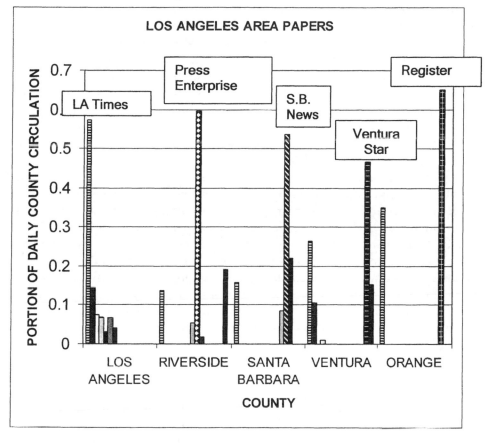

Sources: Eileen Davis Hudson and Mark Fitzgerald, "Capturing Audience Requires a Dragnet," Editor and Publisher, October 22, 2001, p. 20.

One of the most important local policy decisions is the election of representatives to the Congress. How does the political marketplace line up with the commercial marketplace?

Congressional districts are drawn by state legislatures. The typical DMA is much larger than the typical congressional district. The Arbitron market is smaller than the district. This analysis shows that the Arbitron market is a better fit.

The hypothesis is that the decision of a representative about where to locate their district offices is a good indication of where the location of the political marketplace. We identified the location of over 800 district offices. These are the offices of 98 percent of all the districts.

About two-thirds of the district offices are located within a DMA and an Arbitron area (see Exhibit 4). In just over one-third of the observations there is one district office in the Arbitron area. Just over one half of the district offices are located in Arbitron areas with two or fewer offices and two –thirds are in Arbitron areas with three or fewer district offices. For DMAs, there are more district offices within each DMA. About one fifth of the district offices are in DMAs with only one office; 40 percent are in DMAs with two of fewer offices; 50 percent are in DMAs with three or fewer.

Treating the non-Arbitron areas as small markets, makes the difference even more pronounced. Even though these radio stations are not placed within Arbitron areas, representatives know which radio stations serve their district. In sum, Arbitron areas are a much better approximation of political markets than the DMA.

Grand Rapids, Michigan, which ranks just at the limit of the first quintile of Designated Market Areas, provides a good example of the overlap of commercial and political markets (see Exhibit 5). It is made up of 4 Arbitron areas. Each has a leading daily newspaper., with the name of the city in its title (*Grand Rapids Press, Kalamazoo Gazette, The Muskegon Chronicle, Battle Enquire*). Interestingly, one publisher – Advance – owns three of these papers. If there were no geographic specialization, it would make little sense to have separate papers. There is a similar pattern in the radio market, with a leading station in each area and a single owner holding two of the top stations. Each of these cities appears to at the heart of a Congressional District. The location of district offices of members reflects this fact.

PRODUCTS

To build a general model of media markets we have compiled data on the market shares of all TV stations, daily newspapers, weekly newspapers, and radio stations (see Exhibit 6). Following the *Prometheus* court's reasoning, the exercise of estimating the size and make-up of the local news and information market is one of identifying which sources of independent local news respondents use and which sources influences them.

Exhibit 4: Arbitron Areas are a Better Fit for the Political Marketplace than DMAs

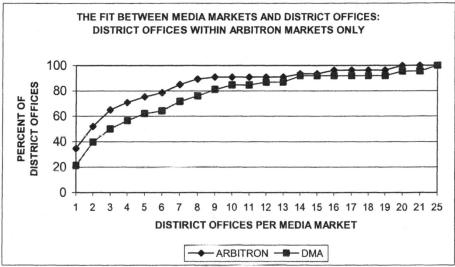

THE FIT BETWEEN MEDIA MARKETS AND DISTRICT OFFICES:
DISTRICT OFFICES WITHIN ARBITRON MARKETS ONLY

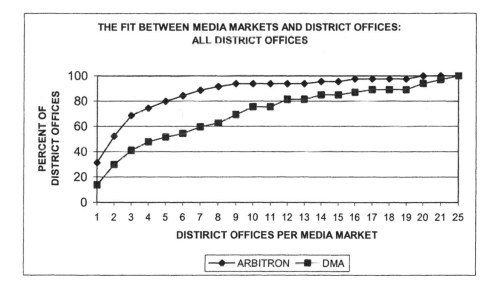

THE FIT BETWEEN MEDIA MARKETS AND DISTRICT OFFICES:
ALL DISTRICT OFFICES

Exhibit 5: Michigan Congressional Districts and Media Markets

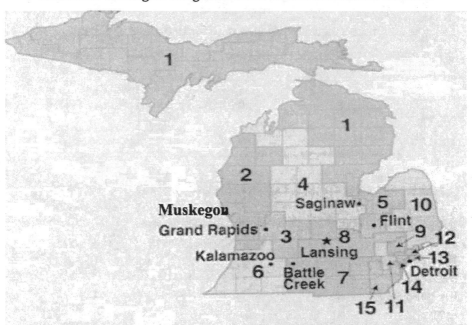

Grand Rapids-Kalamazoo - Battle Creek-Muskegon DMA/Arbitron Areas

Congressional District	Congressional Offices	Number of Dailies	Radio Stations with News Format (non-zero share)	TV Station Commercial Licenses
2nd	Muskegon, Cadillac, Holland	1	1	1
3rd	Grand Rapids	3	2	4
6th	Kalamazoo, St. Josephs	1	1	2
7th	Battle Creek, Lansing, Jackson	1	1	2
Total in DMA		6*	5**	9***

Notes: As of 2003, *Advance owned the top ranked newspaper in 3 of the four Arbitron Areas; **Clear Channel owned three of the radio stations, two of the top ranked radio stations with a news format in different Arbitron areas; ***LIN held 3 of the commercial licenses in is two of the cities and the number one and number five ranked stations. On average, eight of the nine stations are available on cable throughout the DMA.

Sources: Congress At Your Fingertips: 109th Congress, 1st Session 2005 (Capitol Advantage), p. XIV; BIA Database.

Exhibit 6: Constructing the Media Market Measures

Media Weights:
Weighted Average of first and second mentions for influence (Consumer Federation/Consumers Union Survey).

Reach:
Television = All channels in the DMA assumed to reach population in city.
Population reached is households using television (HUT) in early evening and late evening day parts (news day parts) from BIA Financial, *Television Market Reports:* 2003). City population from Arbitron (*Market Ranks: Spring 2004*)
HUT (news day parts) x City Population
Dailies = Average daily circulation (*Editor and Publisher Database: 2003; Beacons Newspapers: 2003*)
Weeklies = Average daily circulation (average weekly circulation divided by seven) (*Beacons Newspapers: 2003*)
Radio = Households using news/information/talk programming (AHQ) (Arbitron, *Radio Today: 2004*) Assumed to be atomistically competitive.
AHQ (News/Info/Talk in the region) x City Population
Internet = Assumed to be atomistically competitive.

Concentration:
Television = Local Commercial share (BIA Financial, *Television Market Reports:* 2003)
Dailies = Average daily circulation (*Editor and Publisher Database: 2003; Beacons Newspapers: 2003*)
Weeklies = Weekly circulation (*Beacons Newspapers: 2003*)
Radio = Revenue market share BIA; Assumed to be atomistically competitive.
Internet: Assumed to be atomistically competitive, 100 equal-sized voices

While we followed the FCC's general approach to geographic market definition, which seems reasonable,[6] unlike the FCC, which ignored the *size* of the audience of each type of product, we focus on estimating the average daily output of relevant news and information for each media firm in the market. In defining the market on an Arbitron area basis, with the household as the unit of analysis, we include the following:

---

[6] 2003 Order, Appendix C.

- Households that use television during news- day parts on an average daily basis.

- Listeners who tune into news/talk and information channels on a routine basis.

- Daily circulation of newspapers.

- Weekly circulation of newspapers (converted to an average daily basis).

Weeklies

Weeklies provide a good example and starting point for how to proceed. We find that weeklies are a moderately influential source of local news. However, weeklies are a very targeted source of information and cover only a small set of the issues covered in dailies in a small geographic area.[7] Indeed, they may be influential precisely because they are so targeted. They deal with the micro- level detail that is directly relevant to the neighborhood or community. Because they are targeted, they are not widely circulated. They are not sold all over a city on newsstands. A city may have a hundred weeklies, but only a few are readily available to the average citizen. Thus, it is important to consider circulation and the geographic reach of the source.[8] We included all the weeklies in the DMA. This overstates the reach of weeklies, since most weeklies are only available in a restricted area. However, the small circulation, particularly when the weekly circulation is converted to daily equivalents to render it comparable to the daily reach of the other media, compensates for this.

For weeklies, we used the average circulation (from the Beacons data base), which is divided by seven to adjust to the daily basis of other media usage. Concentration ratios were calculated based on the total circulation of papers throughout the DMA.

Radio

If weeklies are the most "micro" of the local information sources, radio is likely the next most "micro." In counting radio stations, we have the added problem that the vast majority of radio stations do not do news. Many

---

[7] Lacy, Stephen, David C. Coulson and Hugh J. Martin, "Ownership Barriers to Entry in Non-metropolitan Daily Newspaper Markets," *Journalism & Mass Communications Quarterly* Vol.81, at 331 Summer 2004.. ("Even though weekly and daily newspapers are not perfect substitutes, research indicates that at least some readers may substitute weeklies for dailies and visa versa.")

[8] *Id.* ("Weekly newspaper markets rarely exceed the boundaries of their home county but may be smaller than the county.")

of those that do provide news simply read wire service stories. They are not independent sources of local news as defined by the *Prometheus* court.

To count radio stations in the news and information market, we included all radio stations that list news, information, talk or public service formats as one of the top three formats. We multiplied by the population of the city.

Newspapers

In contrast to radio, which is the least news intensive of the media, daily newspapers are predominantly dedicated to news and cover a wider geographic area, usually a city or county.[9] In an earlier analysis, we found that the daily newspaper circulation in large metropolitan areas tends to be highly differentiated by county. We included all circulation for all newspapers identified by BIA as located in the Arbitron area.

Broadcast Television

Since most households receive their television signals from cable or satellite and because local stations have the right to be carried, they tend to be the most "macro" medium. They are available throughout a wider area, although not all stations are available throughout the Designated Market Area (which is the unit of analysis for the television industry).

However, only about half of all local stations provide news. To compensate for this, we include all TV stations within a designated market area, but based on Nielson ratings as reported in BIA *Television Market Report*, 2003, we used households using television (HUT) in the day parts that are usually devoted to news as the base of viewers. We use the HUT figure as the average of the early evening (e.g. 4:00 pm to 6:00 pm eastern) and late evening (e.g. 11:00 pm to 11:30 pm) news- day parts. Although this implicitly assumes that all local TV stations provide news, which is not the case, in earlier analysis we have shown that the simple count of broadcasters that provide local news is close to the concentration ratio based on the viewer-based HHI. The largest firms that contribute most to the HHI are likely to be represented in each city in the DMA and they provide news.

The news- day part of HUT was multiplied by the city population. The HUT analysis includes noncommercial stations. However, market shares were based on the local commercial audience viewing- share as calculated by BIA Financial. This overestimates concentration slightly, since noncommercial stations are excluded, but their market shares are quite small.

---

[9] Cooper, Mark, *Media Ownership and Democracy in the Digital Information Age* (Center for Internet and Society, Stanford, 2003), pp. 127-130.

Internet

The evidence reviewed in the preceding study of media usage and localism demonstrates that the Internet is not a significant source of local news. The Internet market was assumed to be atomistically competitive, with 100 equal-sized competitors. If ISP market share were used, the number would be closer to 10-equal sized competitors.

DESCRIBING MARKET STRUCTURE

Estimating the Units Sold

In calculating the total media market, we focus on the traditional outlets. We include all media in the denominator of the fraction. We use estimate that the traditional media make account for 91 percent of the total market (see Exhibit 7). Respondents gave the four traditional media as an 87 percent of the market, calculated either as two 2 times first mention, plus a one 1 times second mention. However, several factors should be taken into account in arriving at a final total for the traditional media.

Exhibit 7: Media Usage

| | MENTIONS | | WEIGHTING APPROACH | | | | | |
| | | | (4X1)+2 | | (3X1)+2 | | (2X1)+2 | |
Medium	First	Second	Value	Index	Value	Index	Value	Index
Local TV	33	28	160	0.34	127	0.34	94	0.33
National TV	2	6	14	0.03	12	0.03	10	0.04
Radio	6	15	39	0.08	33	0.09	27	0.1
Internet	3	7	19	0.04	16	0.04	13	0.05
Magazines	0	1	1	0	1	0	1	0
Local Daily	37	20	168	0.35	131	0.35	94	0.33
National Daily	1	2	6	0.01	5	0.01	4	0.01
Local Weekly	12	9	57	0.12	45	0.12	33	0.12
Other	2	2	10	0.02	8	0.02	6	0.02
Sum of Traditional				0.89	378	0.89	282	0.88
Adjustment	Internet			0.91		0.91		0.9
	National Owners			0.92		0.92		0.91

Source: Calculated by author, see text.

First, we should weight first mentions more than second mentions for in evaluating use. Exhibit 7 shows that weighting the first response 2, 3 or 4 times the second adds 1 to 2 percentage points to the total for the traditional media.

Second, about one- fifth of the respondents who said they use the Internet said they go primarily to the web sites of local newspapers. Another fifth said they go to web sites of local TV stations. Since five percent of the respondents mention the Internet, the traditional media total should be increased by about 2 percent.

Third, we should also take account of the fact that the national media, which are cited by about 5 five percent of the respondents as a source of local news, will overlap with the local media in a significant number of cases. The four major networks are allowed to reach 39 percent of the national market. The owners of national newspapers – the New York Times, USA Today and to a lesser extent the Washington Post – own many newspapers and television stations across the country as well. To account for this, we divide the estimate of the traditional local media share by .99. The results show that the traditional media market share of the total media market is about 91 percent.

Calculating the Value of the Units Sold

The audience of each media outlet is one key element of its role in the forum for democratic discourse. This does not tell us how substitutable the different media outlets are. How does listening to a short piece on news radio stack up against reading a long piece in a daily newspaper? In the economic view, this would be the substitutability of the media. For purposes of measuring this characteristic in the forum for democratic discourse, we asked respondents how important each media type was in forming their opinions. This is the weight of the media type, which is one of the factors that in determining its role in the market.

The survey questions address the issue of the "value" of each medium in the question on influence over public opinion (see Exhibit 8). We should weight first and second responses. We also take into account the indirect effect of visiting web sites of traditional outlets. Here however, we must do it for the individual media, rather than for the total market. Based on this analysis we have assigned the following weights to the media.

TV = .33

Dailies = .32

Radio = .11

Weeklies = .10

Exhibit 8: Media Importance as a Source of Local News and Information

Medium	MENTIONS 1st	MENTIONS 2nd	WEIGHTING APPROACH (4X1)+2 Value	(4X1)+2 Index	(3X1)+2 Value	(3X1)+2 Index	(2X1)+2 Value	(2X1)+2 Index	WEIGHT WITH INTERNET/NATIONAL (4X1)+2 Index	(3X1)+2 Index	(2X1)+2 Index
Local TV	30	30	150	0.32	120	0.32	90	0.32	0.33	0.33	0.33
National TV	6	6	30	0.06	24	0.06	18	0.06	0.06	0.06	0.06
Radio	8	15	47	0.1	39	0.1	31	0.11	0.1	0.1	0.11
Internet	4	6	22	0.05	18	0.05	14	0.05	0.05	0.05	0.05
Magazines	1	1	5	0.01	4	0.01	3	0.01	0.01	0.01	0.01
Local Daily	34	17	153	0.32	119	0.31	85	0.3	0.33	0.32	0.3
National Daily	2	2	10	0.02	8	0.02	6	0.02	0.02	0.02	0.02
Local Weekly	10	9	49	0.1	39	0.1	29	0.1	0.1	0.11	0.11
Other	2	2	10	0.02	8	0.02	6	0.02	0.02	0.02	0.02
Sum of Traditional				0.84		0.84		0.83	0.87	0.87	0.86

The remaining 14 percent of the news media market for national TV outlets, Internet, magazines and other is included in the denominator of the HHI calculation, but not in the numerators.

Note that we have taken the non-traditional media into account in both steps of the analysis. First, we calculate the number of units in the media market. The non-traditional media appear in the denominator. Then we weight those units to arrive at a market share for each outlet. Again, the non-traditional media appear in the denominator.

The real world logic is as follows. When someone buys a newspaper, that newspaper is counted in the media market, but a little bit less than when that person turns on the TV during a news- day part. Since weeklies come out once a week, we divide their circulation by 7, but weeklies are given only one-third the weight of TV or dailies. We count radio listeners like TV viewers (i.e. local market share for news- oriented stations), but radio is given one-third the weight of TV stations. The analogy to economic market share analysis is straightforward. We count each unit sold and multiply by the value (price) to calculate the market share.

CONCLUSION

This study lays out a defensible and rational approach to measuring geographic markets and product markets and describing market structure for the purposes of measuring concentration that complies with the Prometheus court's remand order. It turns out, as the next study shows, that the most important factor in arriving at a reasonable picture of the local media market is to count the audience. The media weights described here, are a secondary factor.

STUDY 21:
ESTABLISHING THRESHOLDS FOR MEDIA
MERGER ANALYSIS

MARK COOPER

THE *MERGER GUIDELINES* CATEGORIZATION OF MARKETS

Identifying At Risk Markets

The Department of Justice considers a market with fewer than 10 equal-sized firms to be concentrated (see Exhibit 1). It considers a market with fewer than the equivalent of approximately 5.5-equal sized firms (HHI = 1800) to be highly concentrated. Markets with an HHI between 1000 and 1800 are considered moderately concentrated. A highly concentrated market is called a tight oligopoly.[1] A moderately concentrated market is called a loose oligopoly. Shepherd describes these thresholds in terms of four-firm concentration ratios as follows:[2]

> Tight Oligopoly: The leading four firms combined have 60-100 percent of the market; collusion among them is relatively easy.

> Loose Oligopoly: The leading four firms, combined, have 40 percent or less of the market; collusion among them to fix prices is virtually impossible.

The judicial language on the relationship between ownership and viewpoint diversity and the desire to prevent excessive economic concentration and undue influence is certainly broadly consistent with the vernacular of antitrust. However, the precise analytic link that has developed in the economics literature between the diversity outcomes and the statistical index does not exist for media. So, sufficient qualitative evidence was entered into the prior media ownership proceeding's record to convince the *Prometheus* Court of the link between ownership and diversity, leading to the Court's acceptance of the applications of the antitrust approach to media markets for purposes of diversity analysis.

Economic policy is concerned about market power. The Department of Justice (DOJ) and the Federal Trade Commission (FTC) defines it as follows: "Market power to a seller is the ability to profitably maintain prices above competitive levels for significant period of time... Sellers with market power also may lessen competition on dimensions other than price, such as product quality, service or innovation."

---

[1] Shepherd, p. 4.
[2] Shepherd, p. 4.

In Exhibit 1, the thresholds chosen by the DOJ/FTC are identified.

Exhibit 1: Describing Market Structures

Department Of Justice Merger Guidelines Concentration	Type Of Market	Equivalents In Terms of Equal Sized Firms	Typical HHI	4-Firm In Share Media Markets
	Monopoly	1[a]	5300+	~100
↑	Duopoly	2[b]	3000 - 5000	~100
	Dominant Firm	4<	>2500	
		5	2000	80
High			1800	60
		6	1667	67
	Tight Oligopoly			60
Moderate				
Unconcentrated	Loose Oligopoly	10	1000	40c
↓	Monopolistic Competition			
	Atomistic Competition	50	200	8c

a = Antitrust practice finds monopoly firms with market share in the 65% to 75% range. Thus, HHIs in "monopoly markets can be as low as 4200; b = Duopolies need not be a perfect 50/50 split. Duopolies with a 60/40 split would have a higher HHI.
c = Value falls as the number of firms increases.

Sources: U.S. Department of Justice, Horizontal Merger Guidelines, revised April 8, 1997, for a discussion of the HHI thresholds; See William G. Shepherd, The Economics of Industrial Organization (Englewood Cliffs, NJ: Prentice Hall, 1985), for a discussion of four firm concentration ratios.

A market with an HHI of less than 1,000 – the equivalent of 10 equal-sized firms is considered unconcentrated. This corresponds to a competitive market, although atomistically competitive markets require many more competitors.

The DOJ/FTC consider a market with an HHI between 1,000 and 1,800 to be moderately concentrated.

A market with an HHI above 1,800 – the equivalent of about 5.5-equal sized firms – -- is considered highly concentrated.

Assessing the Impact of Mergers

These thresholds have been chosen based on theory, empirical evidence and experience with the exercise of market power. Mergers between firms that result in markets that are moderately or highly concentrated raise concerns.

> b) <u>Post-Merger HHI Between 1000 and 1800</u>. The Agency regards markets in this region to be moderately concentrated.... Mergers producing an increase in the HHI of more than 100 points in moderately concentrated markets post-merger potentially raise significant competitive concerns depending on the factors set forth in Sections 2-5 of the Guidelines.

> c) <u>Post-Merger HHI Above 1800</u>. The Agency regards markets in this region to be highly concentrated.... Mergers producing an increase in the HHI of more than 50 points in highly concentrated markets post-merger potentially raise significant competitive concerns.... it will be presumed that mergers producing an increase in the HHI of more than 100 points are likely to create or enhance market power or facilitate its exercise.

SETTING STANDARDS FOR MEDIA MARKETS

The Broader Goals of the Communications Act

How does this translate into media policy? In both spheres, competition is deemed important to prevent and discipline these abuses. The legal jurisprudence on media policy uses concepts that are similar to the idea of market power. The goal of the Communications Act is much broader in both what it seeks to promote and prevent. The Supreme Court has repeatedly stated that the First Amendment "rests on the assumption that the widest possible dissemination of information from diverse and antagonistic sources is essential to the welfare of the public."[3] In *Red Lion*, the seminal television case, the Court ruled that "[i]t is the right of the viewers and listeners, not the right of the broadcasters, which is paramount...the right of the public to receive suitable access to social, political, aesthetic, moral and other ideas and experiences...[T]he 'public interest' in broadcasting clearly encompasses the presentation of vigorous debate of controversial issues of importance and concern to the public."[4]

Limits on media ownership are based on the premise that "diversification of mass media ownership serves the public interest by promoting diversity of program and service viewpoints as well as by

---

[3] *Associated Press v. United States*, 326 U.S. 1, 20 (1945).
[4] *Red Lion Broadcasting v. FCC*, 395 US 367, 390 (1969) (hereinafter *Red Lion*).

preventing undue concentration of economic power."[5] Moreover, "the greater the diversity of ownership in a particular area, the less chance there is that a single person or group can have an inordinate effect, in a political, editorial, or similar programming sense, on public opinion at the regional level."[6]

The Communications Act charges the FCC with promoting competition, localism and diversity. Indeed, economic concentration is only one of several dangers that media policy is intended to avoid. Excessive influence over public opinion, diversity and localism are additional goals. In fact, the courts have found that economic efficiency, which is at the core of antitrust policy, is a secondary concern in media ownership policy.

Thus, media ownership limits are concerned about promoting diversity of viewpoint, and preventing undue concentration of economic power and inordinate influence over public opinion. There are other goals of the media policy, as well, such as localism, racial or gender diversity, but this analysis focuses on the concentration issue.

Practical Considerations

The goals of the Communications Act suggest a more rigorous concentration threshold for media mergers is required. This observation is reinforced by several practical factors.

Price increases are relatively easy to see and react to. But slant or bias in reporting or attempt to manipulate the media and influence public opinion are much more difficult to detect.

The episodic nature of important political decisions makes "transitory" abuses a much greater concern. Elections are infrequent and public attention focuses on them for short periods of time. Media entities may behave well for 23 months or 47 months, but it is the brief period before an election that matters most.

Although some have argued that antitrust policy originally had purposes broader than mere economics, and should still, that is not the central concern of antitrust practice. The antitrust laws charge the Department of Justice and Federal Trade Commission with preventing harm to competition in its merger analysis, whereas the Communications Act charges the FCC with promoting the public interest in its merger review.

---

[5] *FCC v. Nat'l Citizens Committee for Broadcasting,* 436 U.S. 775, 780 (1978); Prometheus *Radio Project, et al. v. FCC,* 373 F.3d 372, 383 (3rd Cir. 2004) (citing *Nat'l Citizens Committee for Broadcasting,* 436 U.S. at 780).

[6] *Sinclair Broadcasting Group, Inc. v. FCC,* 284 F.3d 148, 160 (D.C. Cir. 2002) (quoting FCC's 1999 Local Ownership Order, *Review of the Commission's Regulations Governing Television Broadcasting,* Report and Order, FCC 99-209 (rel. Aug. 6, 1999)).

CONCLUSION

Therefore, although we borrow the analytic tools from economics to describe the media market structure, we believe that the thresholds of concern and the targets for concentration as applied to media mergers must be more protective of democratic discourse. Given the greater importance of media diversity, as articulated by the Supreme Court and as embodied in the Communications Act, the larger task that competition must accomplish and the broader set of concerns that media policy must address, the FCC should use a higher standard for media mergers than the antitrust authorities apply for traditional corporate mergers. Mergers should certainly not be allowed in markets that are moderately concentrated because they pose a significant threat to the "widest possible dissemination of information from diverse and antagonistic sources."

PART IX:

VERTICAL INTEGRATION UNDERMINED SOURCE DIVERSITY IN THE VIDEO ENTERTAINMENT INDUSTRY

STUDY 22:
WHY SOURCE DIVERSITY MATTERS:
THE FAULTY READING OF THE RECORD ON
BROADCAST PROGRAM OWNERSHIP RULES

Mark Cooper

The Commission mistakenly relaxed the duopoly rule in part because it failed to treat source diversity as a separate goal or to analyze the role and state of source diversity in detail. It inappropriately and incorrectly failed to examine the ownership of programming and ignored the mountain of evidence in the record that the ownership and control of programming in the television market is concentrated. The Commission arrived at the erroneous decision to triple the number of markets in which multiple stations can be owned by a single entity because it facilely and incorrectly rejected source diversity as a goal of Communications Act.[1] However, whether we consider source diversity as a separate goal of the Act (which the Commission rejected), or as a subcomponent of the broader concept of viewpoint diversity, the underlying flaw is the failure to analyze the ownership of programs and the important role that independent ownership of programs – independent of ownership of outlets – plays in the media market.   The basic problem is easiest to explain if source diversity is treated as a separate goal.

SOURCE DIVERSITY PLAYS AN IMPORTANT ROLE

The FCC concluded that source diversity is not a separate goal of its diversity policy. It reached this erroneous conclusion by conflating program production and program distribution, applying a faulty analysis of the economic/business models of program distributors and ignoring extensive evidence that CFA/CU entered into the record.   Had the Commission conducted a proper analysis of source diversity, it would have concluded that the limit on local duopolies and triopolies should be much more stringent because the concentration of ownership of outlets undermines diversity by reducing the ability of independent programmers to product content.

Considering the fact that the governing constitutional jurisprudence is focused on source diversity – based on the premise that "the widest possible dissemination of information from diverse and antagonistic sources is essential to the public welfare" – it is remarkable that the Order devotes a scant four paragraphs to the issue. Just as remarkable is the number of errors contained in those scant four paragraphs.

---

[1] Order, paras. 42-46, 102-110.

The Order begins its discussion of source diversity in paragraphs 42 by defining it as the "availability of media content from a variety of sources." Paragraph 43 discusses the evidence offered by several commenters about the concentration of production of content that focused primarily on prime time programming, noting that "in 1993, 68% of prime time programming on the largest broadcast networks was independently produced versus 24% today."

With no actual discussion of source diversity, paragraphs 44 and 45 switch from a discussion of source diversity to a discussion of the number of outlets. Paragraph 44 states that "in light of the dramatic change in the television market, including the significant number of channels available to most households today, we find no basis to conclude that government regulation is necessary to promote source diversity." Paragraph 45 goes on to note the increase in channels available to "the vast majority of households" from six in 1979 to an average of 102 channels per home." The Commission claims in paragraph 44 that "Commenters recommending that the Commission adopt source diversity as a goal offer no evidence of the quantity of programming sources across the delivered video programming market (i.e. both broadcast and non-broadcast channels) and why that quantity is deficient."   It concludes in paragraph 45 that "given the explosion of programming channels now available in the vast majority of homes today, and in the absence of evidence to the contrary, we cannot conclude that source diversity should be a policy goal of our broadcast ownership rule." Virtually identical misreading is repeated time and again throughout the order.[2]

Demonstrating that source diversity should be a focal point of public policy to promote diversity and localism in no way detracts from the simultaneous finding, at which the Commission correctly arrives (para. 27), that "outlet ownership can be presumed to affect the viewpoints expressed on that outlet. We continue to believe that broadcast ownership limits are necessary to preserve and promote viewpoint diversity. A larger number of independent owners will tend to generate a wider array of viewpoints in the media than would a comparatively smaller number of owners."   The difference between viewpoint diversity (measured as the independent ownership of outlets) and source diversity (measured as the independent production of content) is easy to maintain and explain as a basis to promote the public interest in localism and diversity, even if the Commission preferred to view independent program sources as a component of viewpoint diversity.[3]

Owners' viewpoints are expressed in the content they choose to deliver to the public through the outlets they control. The outlet owners may

---

[2] Order, paras. 535, 651, 654
[3] CFA/CU, Comments 1, pp. 49-52;

produce their own content or buy it from independent producers. A multiplicity of sources will serve the interests of diversity and localism better by creating competition between sources providing owners a better range of programming from which to choose. More independent source will stimulate greater innovation and creativity and more locally oriented content.[4] Independent programmers can also be expected to produce more vigorous watchdog journalism.[5]

It may also lower the barrier to entry into the media market, since a separate market for independent programming would facilitate entry at one stage of production (programming or distribution) rather than two (vertically integrated production and distribution). The Commission should be well aware of the need to promote source diversity separately from the ownership of outlets, since it accepts higher levels of concentration in mid-size and smaller markets on the basis of a claim about their more demanding economics.[6] Independent ownership of programming could add a significant source of diversity, absent vertical integration.

As demonstrated by CFA/CU in this proceeding, large buyers of programming can exercise monopsony power to the detriment of independent producers and the public, even when they are not vertically integrated, but the problem becomes even more severe when they are vertically integrated, which most of the large program distributors are.[7] Structural limits on concentration of ownership of outlets can help to create an environment that promotes independent production of content.

The FCC also fails to recognize the evidence in the record that demonstrates that this buying power in the national market affects diversity in local markets.[8] CFA/CU worked with Joel Waldfogel in the preparation of an econometric study by Joel Waldfogel, who later was hired by the Commission to conduct one of its task force studies that contradicts this claim.[9] This study is one among many cited in our comments that contradict the FCC claim that consolidation into national chains does not diminish diversity.[10]

---

[4] CFA/CU, Comments 1, pp. 53-57CFA/CU, Comment 2, 58-59, 79-82.
[5] CFA/CU, Comments 2, pp. 26-27, 83-88.
[6] Order, para. 201.
[7] CFA/CU, Comments 2, pp. 186-220.
[8] Order, para. 534, states that "Commenters do not provide evidence that persuades us to alter those views, and we affirm our 1984 conclusion that the national TV ownership rule is not necessary to promote diversity." The Commission provides no discussion whatsoever of the evidence it has rejected.
[9] CFA/CU, Comments 1, Attachment B. The results of this study were summarized in Waldfogel's statement to the Media Ownership Roundtable conducted by the FCC.
[10] CFA/CU, Comments 1, pp. 40-45; Comments 2, pp. 54-59, 250-253

MISREADING THE RECORD

The claim that there is an absence of evidence about concentration in the Delivered Video Programming market could not be farther from the truth. The commenters that the Order identified and several others (who it failed to identify as addressing this issue)[11] provided extensive evidence on precisely the point that the sources of programming are concentrated and therefore lack diversity. It demonstrated this explicitly across "both the broadcast and non-broadcast channels" at both the local and national levels.[12] Perhaps the Commission failed to recognize this evidence because nowhere in the order did it analyze the actual sources of programming. It never did analyze source diversity because it immediately shifted from a discussion of source diversity to a count of outlets, without ever directly analyzing who produces the content that is delivered through those outlets.

In fact, the CFA/CU comments, which the Commission failed to include in its list of commenters who addressed source diversity, presented evidence that directly estimated the lack of source diversity by demonstrating that, at the local level, broadcast and non-broadcast programming is a tight oligopoly (moderately to highly concentrated) across a range of markets.[13]

CFA/CU demonstrated that broadcast network owners who have used their must carry/retransmission rights to gain carriage of their programming on cable systems have recaptured between 50 and 75 percent of the viewers that have shifted to cable.[14] Broadcast and non-broadcast programming was closely analyzed and CFA/CU showed that owners of broadcast networks recapture viewers with their non-broadcast offerings. CFA/CU established the concentration of news programming markets at both the national[15] and local[16] levels.

CFA/CU demonstrated that, at the regional and national levels, in the past decade a handful of cable operators and broadcast network owners completely dominate the launch of new cable networks.[17] Looking at subscribers and writing budgets, CFA/CU and others demonstrated that the programming market is a tight oligopoly as well.[18] CFA/CU showed that joint ventures and cross-ownership among and between the members of this

---

[11] Order, para. 43.

[12] CFA/CU, Comments 1, pp. 104-109; CFA/CU, Comments, 2, pp. 153-159, 203-220, CFA/CU, Replies 2, pp. 12-16.

[13] CFA/CU, Comments 1, pp. 104-109; Comments 2, pp. 153-159;

[14] CFA/CU, Replies, pp. 12-16.

[15] CFA/CU, Comments 2, pp. 104-108 155.

[16] CFA/CU, Ex Parte, pp. 42.

[17] CFA/CU, Comments 2, pp. 218-220.

[18] CFA/CU, Comments 2, pp.156-158.

oligopoly reduce the incentive to compete and creates shared interests in controlling the flow of programming.[19]

The Commission has some vague idea that the dominant broadcasters now commingle broadcast and non-broadcast activities. Para. 523 offers a hypothetical example of program acquisition that shows that the two largest DVP buyers spend over one quarter of their budgets on cable networks. The fact that the Commission resorted to a hypothetical discussion, rather than analyze the data in the record, alone calls its conclusion "we have no evidence that they [television stations owners} exercise market power in the program production market"[20] into doubt.

All this is in addition to the high level of concentration in prime time programming, which CFA/CU and others demonstrated in considerably more detail than the Commission acknowledges.[21]

There can be no mistake about the implication and purpose of this analysis, since CFA/CU clearly explained the important role of source diversity in its initial comments in this long running proceeding.

> Source diversity is also meaningless unless the sources are structurally independent. Source diversity references the same fundamental principle--a distinct entity should be responsible for creating content. The First Amendment is served when independent organizations make decisions about what content will be produced, and thus what content will ultimately reach an audience. Source diversity thus makes no sense without separately *owned* sources and distribution mechanisms. Market power in program and content purchasing will eliminate diversity in program production through the exercise of monopsony power. Sources should not only be separate from each other, but also be separate from outlets to prevent the harms of vertical integration.[22]

Ignoring the extensive evidence of a lack of source diversity across broadcast and non-broadcast, as well as national and local markets has dire consequences for the public interest in diversity and localism. As CFA/CU explained at great length in its comments, allowing dominant firms in the local and national markets to acquire direct control of more outlets will enable them to strengthen their grip on the programming market.[23] As the number of independent owners of outlets shrinks, producers have fewer and fewer opportunities to market their works, especially because the larger program distributors are vertically integrated into program production. As a smaller number of owners controls a larger share of the market they gain greater and

---

[19] CFA/CU, Comments 2, pp. 186-203.
[20] Order, para., 517.
[21] CFA/CU, Comments 2, pp. 200-202.
[22] CFA/CU, Comments 1, pp. 30, footnotes omitted.
[23] CFA/CU, Comments 1, pp. 108-113; CFA/CU, Comments 2, pp. 186-200.

greater leverage in the bargaining with independent producers. Indeed, they can make or break programming.[24]

One of the critical factors that the Order has failed to recognize, in spite of this mountain of evidence provided, is that the owners of the broadcast networks are also substantial owners of non-broadcast programming. Contradicting the claim in the Order that there are two very distinct business model in the television markets, CFA/CU and others have shown that the owners of broadcast networks have monetized their must carry/retransmission rights into carriage on cable systems, which provides them with a substantial stream of subscription revenues.

It is truly ironic that the FCC, which routinely notes that rising programming costs are one of the causes of dramatic increases in cable rates,[25] has failed to notice that the owners of many of the programs most frequently cited as the programming cost culprits are the owners of the dominant broadcast networks.[26] Consider paragraph 61 in which the Commission cites the fact that "in competing with broadcasters, non-broadcast programming networks typically have two income streams to develop or purchase programming. Broadcasters continue to rely overwhelmingly on advertising revenues." The three non-broadcast programming networks it cites as examples, ESPN, CNN, MTV are all owned by entities that also own broadcast networks. In fact, the three owners of these shows own four of the top six national broadcast networks.

The FCC's discussion of non-broadcast programming in its historical overview reconfirms the error in failing to look at ownership of programming. In paragraphs 102 and 109, the cable network mentioned (HBO, TBS, ESPN, CNN, BET, Nickelodeon, MTV) are owned by corporations that also own networks. The owner of USA, Liberty, has a substantial ownership interest in corporations that own networks. The only independent channel in the list is the Weather Channel.

Even the discussion of broadcast networks in paragraph 110 fails to take note of ownership. Two of the three new networks the FCC touts are, owned by corporations that own another network (UPN), or a major cable operator (WB).

The Commission's observation that the top four broadcast networks have an ownership interest in only 25% of the 102 broadcast channels, misses the point that they have guaranteed access to that distribution and close interconnection through stock ownership and joint ventures to the cable

---

[24] CFA/CU, Comments 2, pp. 206-208.
[25] Federal Communications Commission, "Report on Cable Industry Prices." *In the Matter of Implementation of Section 3 of the Cable Television Consumer Protection and Competition Act of 1992, Statistical Report on Average Rates for Basic Service, Cable Programming Service, and Equipment,* various issues.
[26] Order, para. 142.

companies that control the remainder of the channels.[27] The joint activities of this cabal has resulted in a video programming market that is a tight oligopoly by all traditional measures of market structure.[28]

In note 1090, the Commission states that broadcast networks are "organizational units of larger media enterprises," but argues that "corporate management ordinarily expects, however, that each business unit will recover its unit-specific fixed and variable costs, contribute to the cost of shared corporate services and functions, and earn unit-specific profit." The Commission presents no evidence specific to the video industry that this is the case. It does not analyze the obvious fact that such a substantial amount of programming purchased for cable networks is likely to generate substantial revenue not in the traditional broadcast mode, nor does it provide any analysis of the joint assets, like studios, that support both broadcast and non-broadcast programming or the increasing revenue associated with repurposing of programming. The failure to conduct analyses such as these demands that the Commission reconsider its Order in regard to the national cap.

The failure of the FCC to analyze the ownership of programming and to properly understand the economic models being applied in the industry has undermined its analysis of source diversity and led it to incorrectly allow greater concentration of ownership of outlets. For these reasons, the Commission should reconsider the nation cap and restore it the previous level of 35 percent.

EVIDENCE OF BARRIERS TO ENTRY RESULTING FROM VERTICAL INTEGRATION.

The evidence in the record that deals with the impact of vertical integration focuses on the severe difficulty that independent producers have in gaining access to the consumer because of the vertical integration of distributors into content production in three areas, prime time programming, broadcast-cable bundles of programming, and cable self-dealing. In each of the areas the evidence continues to mount that vertical integration is a severe problem for independent content producers.

---

[27] Order, para. 123.
[28] CFA/CU, Comments 2, pp. 203-220.

STUDY 23:
THE IMPACT OF THE VERTICALLY INTEGRATED, TELEVISION-MOVIE STUDIO OLIGOPOLY ON SOURCE DIVERSITY AND INDEPENDENT PRODUCTION

MARK COOPER

INTRODUCTION & OVERVIEW

The Emergence of a Vertically Integrated Oligopoly in Television

This paper examines the impact of three major policy changes in the early and mid- 1990s on the production and distribution of video content, primarily broadcast television programming in America: the repeal of the Financial Interest / Syndication rules and the enactment of both the Cable Act of 1992 and the Telecommunications Act of 1996. It shows that these policy changes led to the formation of a vertically integrated oligopoly in television entertainment and a dramatic shrinkage of the role of independent producers of content. The policy changes and resulting alterations in market structure and behavior were not limited to the broadcast sector, however. They also affected the syndication market, cable television and theatrical movies because prime time programming plays a critical role in the overall video entertainment product space. If not amended, these same policy changes could have a major impact upon the ability of independents to offer product through the Internet and other developing digital platforms, including the rapidly approaching digital multi-cast channels.

Over the course of a decade, the content aired on prime time network television, TV syndication, basic and pay cable channels, and theatrical movies came to be dominated by a handful of vertically integrated entities. Dozens of independent entities that produced video content were replaced by a handful of firms that own major movie studios and television production units, hold multiple broadcast licenses and own the dominant cable networks. The role of independent producers has been squeezed across all distribution platforms.

Effects of the Vertically Integrated Oligopoly on the Television Market

Fifteen years ago, theatrical movie studios and broadcast television were almost entirely separate while cable television was just developing as a primary outlet. In each of these markets, there was a substantial independent sector. Major studios provided about one third of product shown on network prime time television while the networks themselves accounted for just 15%. Non-major studios, known as "independents," supplied nearly one half. One set of independents sold movies to broadcasters. Another set sold series and other programming. A few produced and sold both. Vertical integration has changed that situation.

The vertically integrated major studios and broadcasters now account for over 75% of broadcast prime time television programming while independents account for less than 20%. The few independents that get on prime time television produce reality shows, not scripted programming. As a result, independents have been virtually shut out of the lucrative syndication market, now accounting for just 18% of all first run syndication programming hours and none of the programming hours for shows that have gone into syndication over the last two years.

The economic terrain of cable television has also changed for independents. The vertically integrated media companies own 24 of the top 25 cable channels. The independents' share of pay cable programming also continues to decline as a percentage of programming, dropping by some 15% since the late nineties. Independent product was also squeezed out of syndication. Independent product is increasingly consigned to the far less visible and less financially rewarding basic cable channels where license fees are much lower and in many cases inadequate to cover production costs. Additionally, product placed on basic cable does not have the same potential to realize foreign sales that pay cable product enjoys.

The business practices used to accomplish this dramatic shift in the flow of content in the video product space exhibit characteristics that clearly fit the pattern of abuse of market. By controlling distribution and vertically integrating into production, five of the dominant broadcasters have become gatekeepers who favor their affiliated content, restrict access of independents to the market, and impose onerous terms and conditions on independent producers that have further shrunk the sector.

The key elements of the video entertainment product space fit a pattern that the literature on industrial organization describes as the exercise and abuse of market power. These elements include market structures and vertical integration that are conducing to and conduct that is indicative of the exercise of market power as sellers and buyers of video content.

Policy Implications of Consolidation and Integration

The swift and massive horizontal consolidation and vertical integration in the industry raises a number of concerns. The analysis of the economic impact of horizontal concentration and vertical integration can be found across many areas of economic activity, but the unique nature and role of video entertainment raises additional, perhaps even greater concerns in non-economic areas. Television and movies, the former in particular, are fundamental to democratic discourse. Television is the dominant medium in terms of time spent on entertainment and news and information gathering.[1] It is overwhelmingly the choice for national campaign advertising. Entertainment on television can be cultural, educational or political. Theatrical releases have a prominent role in the public discourse as well, which films such as *Crash* and *The Passion of the Christ* have demonstrated in recent years.

Television and movies play an important part in the marketplace of ideas. A nation that prides itself on freedom of speech and diversity while simultaneously issuing exclusive licenses to private firms to broadcast content faces a dilemma. The issuance of a handful of broadcast licenses in each market in America creates a privileged class of speakers through government action. Local governments issue franchises to cable TV operators, which are even more scarce than broadcast licenses on a city-by-city, county-by-county basis.

How one promotes diversity with such a small number of electronic voices, without dictating what content broadcasters should air, becomes a major source of concern. If those very valuable and powerful government-granted platforms for reaching the public become the core of a tight oligopoly that dominates other areas of expression, the concern is compounded.

If dictating content is ruled out by First Amendment free speech concerns, but policy makers continue to strive for diversity, then the primary option is to build media market structures that disperse the opportunity to speak as much as possible within the confines of the granting of licenses and franchises. The principle on which this approach stands is simple. By ensuring a wider opportunity to put content before the public, diversity and discourse are stimulated without dictating the substance of the content supplied.

Policies to Promote Diversity

For much of the twentieth century, the Congress and the Federal Communications Commission pursued this goal of diversity by simultaneously dispersing ownership of production, and distribution of content. The number of media outlets that could be owned by a single entity was restricted both within a market (the local television multiple ownership rule)[2] and across the nation (a national cap) by the national television multiple

---

[1] Cooper Mark, *Media Ownership and Democracy in the Digital Information Age* (Palo Alto: Stanford Law School Center for Internet and Society, 2003).

[2] 47 C.F. R. 73.355(b), the duopoly rule, lifted the ban on multiple station ownership, but 47 C.F.R. 73.658(g), the dual network rule, restricted the combinations of television

ownership rule.[3] The amount of content aired in prime time that any given network could own was limited as well by the Financial Interest and Syndication Rules (Fin-Syn) and the Prime Time Access Rules.[4] Similarly, consent decrees in cases brought by the Department of Justice mirrored the Fin-Syn rules.[5] Other FCC rules prevented Broadcast license holders from owning other types of media outlets – e.g. newspapers and cable TV systems (cross-ownership limits)[6] -- and restricted their ability to engage in cross-media ownership (e.g. radio).[7] The result was a substantial dispersion of ownership of content.

In the 1990s, the two primary policies to promote diversity of ownership of content in broadcasting were eliminated or cut back. The Financial Interest and Syndication Rules (Fin-Syn) that governed prime time programming were allowed to expire and the consent decree was also vacated – allowing broadcasters to own as much programming as they wanted. The limits on multiple station ownership were relaxed – allowing them to own two stations in the nation's largest and most important markets. A third policy also gave broadcasters the right to carriage on cable systems (must-carry/retransmission).[8] The terrain of the American media landscape was dramatically altered by these policy changes as the broadcasters moved quickly to use these three new sources of leverage in the video market.

Whether or not Congress anticipated the powerful effect that the policy changes of the 1990s would have on diversity of ownership of programming is unclear. Although the FCC has created records on these

---

stations, to disallow dual or multiple network ownership that involves a combination between ABC, CBS, Fox, or NBC. Citations to the rules are currently being reviewed, which generally relaxed the restrictions on cross ownership in the 1990s and are the latest in the evolving regulatory structure.

[3] 47 C.F. R. s 73.3555(e)

[4] The two rules have always been closely linked see Amendment of Part 73 of the Commission's Rules and Regulations with Respect to Competition and Responsibility in Network Television Broadcasting, 23, FCC 2d 282 (1970). Amendment of Part 73 of the Commission's Syndication and Financial Interest Rule, 47 FR 32959 (1982), as they were in the court case that led to their ultimate expiration, see Shurz Communication Inc. v. FCC 982 F. 2d 1043, 1049 (7th Cir. 1992).

[5] Identical consent decrees were entered against the three major networks, which followed the Fin-Syn rules closely. These were vacated when in the early 1990s, as the Fin-Syn rules were allowed to expire...

[6] 47 C.F. R. s 73.3555(d), cross-ownership of broadcast states and newspapers, prohibits the common ownership of a daily newspaper and a broadcast station in the same market.

[7] 47 C.F.R. 73.3555(c), the radio-television cross –ownership rule, limits the number of TV and radio licenses that can be held within a market.

[8] Cable Television Consumer Protection and Competition Act of 1992, Pub. L. No. 102-385, 106 Stat. 1460 (1992).

issues in its proceedings subsequent to the changes in policy, the courts have remanded several of its rules,[9] leaving their regulatory status in flux and Congress has included a provision that requires frequent review of the rules.[10]

The FCC continues to have the authority to implement restrictions on media ownership to accomplish the goals that Congress has set in legislating media policy,[11] with the exception of the national multiple ownership rule. To the extent that Congress continues to embrace the goal of diversity, the current situation and how the policy changes of the 1990s created it are what matters now. Moreover, since Congress ordered the FCC in the Telecommunications Act of 1996 to periodically review its rules, the FCC could conclude that the rule changes it has implemented with agency discretion have harmed diversity, a goal that Congress continues to embrace. The FCC could re-institute those policies that successfully promoted source diversity in the past or it could seek new policies that will promote source diversity in the future.

This paper shows that the current policies are not promoting independent production of video content on the major television platforms. Understanding the impact of past rule changes is the first step in the process of re-examining the decline of sources diversity on television. That is the subject of this paper. While the purpose of this paper is not to recommend specific policy changes, it is clear that if policymakers still believe in source diversity, then a change in policy that directly alters the structure and conduct of the vertically integrated oligopoly is necessary.

DEFINING THE PRODUCT SPACE AND ANALYTIC APPROACH

The Object of Study

This is a study of the industrial organization of the video entertainment sector – theatrical movies, all forms of television and the sale and rental of tapes and DVDs – in the United States. Because the sector is complex, I adopt the following definitions. The sector consists of six primary channels for the distribution of content:

---

[9] Indeed, all of the major structural rules written in the late 1990s have been remanded by the court (broadcast multiple station limits, cable horizontal limits, newspaper cross ownership) or overridden by Congress (national cap).

[10] The 1996 Act provided for a biennial review (*Telecommunications Act of 1996*, Pub. L. No. 104-104, 110 Stat. 56 (1996). This was later extended to four years (*FY2004 Consolidated Appropriations Act* (Public Law 108-109, 118 Stat. 3 et seq. Section 629) and prohibited the FCC from further reviewing the national cap.

[11] As with the other rules overturned by the courts, in the case of the Fin-Syn rules, while the courts rejected the specific FCC rule (*Schurz Communications Inc. v. FCC* 982 F. 2d 1043 (7th Cir. 1992), it did not preclude the writing of an alternative rule. To date, the FCC has elected not to do so.

- **theatrical movie** releases,

- **prime time** airing of movies and series on broadcast television,

- **syndication** on broadcast television in non-prime time slots of both movies and series,

- movies and series aired on **pay cable**,

- movies and series aired on **basic cable** networks,

- **Home Video** – i.e. sale/rental of video for viewing on VCR and DVD players.

I refer to the overall sector made up of the six distribution channels as the **video entertainment product space.** The Internet has just begun to be used as a means of redistributing video product that was originally released through one of the other six outlets. While there are clear indications that it will change the current terrain of the video entertainment product space in the long run, there are also clear indications that it will not deconcentrate the sector.   Already, the networks are multicasting current primetime programming through their websites and Internet protocol television (IPTV) channels are coming on line. Internet video on demand services (VOD), such as Cinema Now and Movielink, are gaining visibility and subscribers as broadband service penetrates deeper into the consumer market, but the same content producers dominate.   Broadcasters are poised to receive a substantial increase in their ability to distribute content with the transition to digital multicasting. The current single channel with be expanded by the granting of rights to use spectrum to broadcast up to six channels digitally. As such, there is growing concern that the same entities that dominate the traditional channels of physical distribution of video entertainment product will extend their dominance to the new Internet and digital distribution channels.

The nature and relationship between these channels has changed over time. Terms of art once applied have stuck, even though they may no longer technically describe the distribution channel.

Theatrical distribution of movies has been around the longest, with the commercial industry stretching back to the early part of the 20th century. Television emerged in the 1950s and 1960s. Cable arrived in the 1970s and 1980s. Distribution of video tapes began in the 1980s and exploded with the advent of DVDs in the early 2000s.

Traditionally, television was divided between broadcast and cable to reflect the different means of delivery. Broadcasters sent signals over the air from TV transmitters (stations) that were licensed by the FCC. Cable signals were sent from a head end through a wire, the laying of which was franchised by a local entity. Today, although broadcast signals are still available over-the-air, most American households (80% to 90%) get the broadcast product through the cable wire or from satellites.

Prime time on broadcast TV was always a focal point of policy because of the huge audience and resources it commanded. Prime time was controlled by the networks, which also held licenses to operate TV stations in the largest markets. They created national networks by affiliating with independent license holders in markets where they did not hold broadcast licenses directly. The major networks – ABC, NBC and CBS, reach virtually every home in America. Fox is a national network as well, although it may be available in somewhat fewer homes.

Although cable has always been a subscription service, it split into two different distribution channels when pay cable services, like HBO, developed the ability to charge a premium for programming and basic cable became advertiser supported, mimicking broadcast television. Historically, one could draw a clear line between production of content by movie studios and exhibition – the presentation to the public of product – in theaters. The distinction breaks down with live television – the broadcast is simultaneously produced and distributed. Television also changes the nature of the exhibition from a public space to a private space, although it is still shared in the sense that programming is watched simultaneously, but separately, by large numbers of people. The sale/rental of videos (and the recording of programming) for home viewing (referred to as Home Video) extended the change from a public to a private experience by allowing people to choose when to watch.

ANALYTIC APPROACH: STRUCTURE, CONDUCT PERFORMANCE

The paper applies a framework of analysis known as the structure-conduct-performance paradigm (see Exhibit 1), [12] which has been the dominant approach to industrial organization analysis for over three-quarters of a century. The premise is simple.

The analysis seeks to identify the conditions that determine the performance of markets. [13] It starts with basic conditions. [14] On the supply-side these include factors such as technology, product durability, business attitudes and the legal framework. On the demand side factors such as price elasticity, cyclical/seasonal patterns, and purchasing methods are

---

[12] Scherer, F. M. and David Ross, Industrial *Market Structure and Economic Performance* (Boston, Houghton Mifflin: 1990); Shepherd, William, G., *The Economics of Industrial Organization* (Prentice Hall, Engelwood Cliffs, N.J., 1985).

[13] Id., p. 4.; Shepherd, William, G., *The Economics of Industrial Organization* (Prentice Hall, Engelwood Cliffs, N.J., 1985), p. 5, presents a similar view.

[14] Scherer and Ross, p. 5.

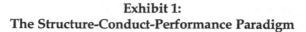

Exhibit 1:
The Structure-Conduct-Performance Paradigm

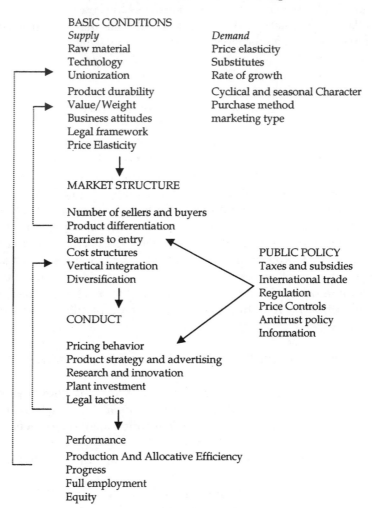

SOURCE: Scherer and Ross, F. M., and David Ross, Industrial Market Structure and Economic Performance (Houghton Mifflin Company: Boston, 1990), p. 5.

included. These interact with characteristics of the market structure, [15] such as the number and the size of sellers and buyers, product differentiation, cost structures and vertical integration (the relationship of production and distribution), to determine the conduct of the market participants. The key types of conduct include pricing behavior, product strategy and advertising, and legal tactics. [16]   Conduct determines performance, traditionally measured in terms of pricing and profits, but increasingly viewed as quality and the nature and speed of innovation.

One of the key features of the structure-conduct-performance paradigm is that it recognizes the importance of public policy. Policies, such as antitrust enforcement, regulation, or taxation and subsidization, can directly affect structure and conduct, thereby altering performance.

HORIZONTAL MARKET POWER

The characteristic of market structures that received most public policy attention is horizontal market power. The concern is that if markets become concentrated – i.e. where a few players have a large market share – competition is dulled. Rather than compete to produce the best product at the lowest price, one large entity may be able to set prices up or otherwise affect output, without a sufficient response from others to discipline such behavior. With small numbers of competitors, they may accomplish the same thing by consciously paralleling each other's behavior. Thus, the Department of Justice defines market power as "the ability profitably to maintain prices above competitive levels for a significant period of time... Sellers with market power also may lessen competition on dimensions other than price, such as product quality, service or innovation." [17]

Pure and perfect competition is rare, but the competitive goal is important. [18] Therefore, public policy pays a great deal of attention to the relative competitiveness of markets as well as the conditions that make markets more competitive or workably competitive. Knowing exactly when a market is "too" concentrated is a complex question. The Department of Justice calculates an index called the Herfindahl-Hirschman Index (HHI) to categorize markets. This index takes the market share of each firm, squares it and sums it. It considers a market with an HHI above 1000 to be concentrated. This is the equivalent of a market with fewer than the equivalent of 10-equal sized firms. It considers a market with fewer than the

---

[15] Scherer and Ross, p. 5.

[16] Scherer and Ross, p. 4.

[17] Department of Justice/Federal Trade Commission, *Merger Guidelines* (1997).

[18] Scherer and Ross, p. 16-17.

equivalent of approximately 5.5-equal sized firms (HHI = 1800) to be highly concentrated. Markets with an HHI between 1000 and 1800 are considered moderately concentrated.

MONOPSONY POWER

A second economic concept that plays an important part in the video entertainment product space is that of monopsony power. Monopsony power is the flip side of monopoly power. Monopoly power is the power of a seller to dictate prices, terms and conditions as a seller of goods and services to the public. Monopsony power is the power of downstream buyers of inputs to create products to sell to the public and to dictate the prices, terms and conditions on which they buy those inputs. If the upstream suppliers lack alternatives, they may be forced to accept terms that under compensate them or force them to bear extra risk.

The downstream buyers have market power over the upstream sellers of the product. This can result in the production of fewer or inferior products for sale downstream.

Many economists describe markets in terms of the market share of the top four firms. Shepherd describes these thresholds in terms of four-firm concentration ratios as follows:[19]

Tight Oligopoly: The leading four firms combined have 60-100 percent of the market; collusion among them is relatively easy.

Loose Oligopoly: The leading four firms, combined, have 40 percent or less of the market; collusion among them to fix prices is virtually impossible.

Although the overlap is not perfect, there is a close correspondence between these two approaches. A highly concentrated market is called a tight oligopoly.[20] A moderately concentrated market is called a loose oligopoly.

Although monopsony has not been the focal point of much antitrust action, it is more likely in precisely the type of sector like the video entertainment product space, where inputs are specialized

Monopsony is thought to be more likely when there are buyers of specialized products or services. For example, a sports league may exercise monopsony (or oligopsony) power in purchasing the services of professional athletes. An owner of a chain of movie theaters, some of which are the sole theaters in small towns, may have monopsony power in the purchase or lease of movies. Cable

---

[19] Shepherd, p. 4.
[20] Shepherd, p. 4.

TV franchises may exercise monopsony power in purchasing television channels that will be offered to their subscribers.[21]

VERTICAL INTEGRATION AND LEVERAGE

A third key characteristic of many industries is the extent of vertical integration. In many industries the act of producing a product can be readily separated from its distribution and sale. Production is referred to as the upstream, distribution and sale are referred to as the downstream. Vertical integration occurs when both activities are conducted by one entity. Because vertical integration involves the elimination of a (presumably market-based) transaction between two entities it has been the focal point of a great deal of analysis. Economic efficiencies are frequently claimed for vertical integration due to the elimination of transaction costs. Others fear inefficiency and potential abuse of the ability to leverage vertical market power that can result from excessive or unjustified vertical integration.

The classic concern is that distributors of content, who are also producers, favor their own content at the expense of the content of unaffiliated producers. Vertical integration may become the norm in the industry, making it difficult for unintegrated producers to survive. Vertically integrated entities may capture the market for inputs, making it difficult for independent entities to obtain the factors of production necessary to produce product. Also, with vertically integrated entities dominating a sector, reciprocity and forbearance rather than competition may become the norm.

CONCLUSION

The remainder of this part documents the emergence of a vertically integrated, tight oligopoly in the video entertainment product space. It shows that when public policies that prevented the exercise of market power were relaxed or eliminated, the conditions for the exercise of market power were quickly created by mergers and acquisitions and changes in behavior. The industry became a vertically integrated, tight oligopoly. Vertical leverage was used to eliminate independent production of prime time content. Monopsony power was exercised to squeeze independent film production into a very narrow, niche space on basic cable channels.

---

[21] Sullivan, Lawrence and Warren S. Grimes. *The Law of Antitrust: An Integrated Handbook*, Hornbook Series. West Group, St. Paul, 2000, p. 138.

PUBLIC POLICY AND THE EMERGENCE OF A VERTICALLY INTEGRATED OLIGOPOLY IN VIDEO ENTERTAINMENT

The Repeal of Financial and Syndication Rules Triggers Horizontal Concentration and Vertical Integration

At the end of the 1980s, policies to disperse ownership in broadcast television were in place. Though they had been debated intensely throughout the 1980s, the policies remained to limit holders of broadcast licenses to one to a market. These stations were known as O&Os (owned and operated). Holders of broadcast licenses could have O & O stations that reached no more than 25% of the nation's television households. The national broadcast networks were restricted in the amount of content that aired in prime time they could own and their participation in the syndication of non-prime time programming (the Financial and Syndication Rule). The broadcast networks filled out their national networks by entering into affiliation agreements with stations they did not own or operate. There were extensive rules that governed the relationships between the affiliated stations and the networks.

Exhibit 2 identifies the key policy changes (ovals) and the structural and conduct changes that followed (rectangles) in the 1990s. The primary policy that triggered the vertical integration in the industry was the decision of the FCC to allow the Financial and Syndication Rules to lapse, rather than write rules that would pass court scrutiny (see Exhibit 2). In retrospect, it is quite clear that the Financial and Syndication rules, which restricted the amount of broadcaster-owned programming in prime time, had a major effect on the diversity of not only the broadcast television market, but television in general. When the rules were eliminated in the mid-1990s, broadcasters moved to replace the lion's share of independent programming with content they produced. Self-dealing became the predominant mode of operation.

Ironically, the impact was more profound than the direct effect on prime time. At the time that the Fin-Syn rules were relaxed, restrictions on vertical integration in the cable industry were implemented. Cable operators were restricted in the percentage of Ironically, the impact was more profound than the direct effect on prime time. At the time that the Fin-Syn rules were relaxed, restrictions on vertical integration in the cable industry were implemented. Cable operators were restricted in the percentage of capacity on their systems they could fill with programming they owned. In the Cable Consumer Protection Act of 1992 they were also required to make their own programming available to competing delivery systems (the program access rules).

Exhibit 2: The Impact of Policy Changes on Independents in the Television Market

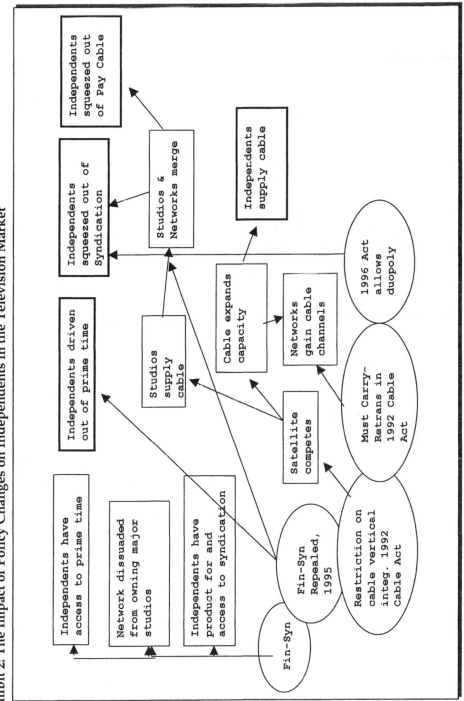

As a result of the improved access to programming, satellite competition, which had been anticipated in the 1984 Cable Act, finally increased its market share. Satellite was a digital technology with greater capacity than cable. The cable industry responded by deploying its own digital capacity. Thus, just as the broadcast space was closing, the cable space opened for the majors and independents. The studios, which had been prevented from integrating with broadcasters, funded and supplied programming for cable channels. Given their structure, they could not provide nearly all the programming that a 24/7 channel required. A substantial market for independent movie production opened up.

Majors and independents were not the only beneficiaries of the 1992 Cable Act. The Act also gave the broadcasters a wedge into the cable platform, with the must carry/retransmission rules. Cable operators needed to carry the major broadcast networks to make their basic subscription packages attractive to the public. The Cable Act of 1992 gave the broadcasters bargaining power over the cable operators. They could insist on a high fee for their national networks or they could negotiate for carriage of other programming. Must-carry and retransmission were government granted rights of carriage, means of ensuring access to audiences. The broadcasters chose to bargain for more channels on cable systems, rather than charge for their broadcast networks.

The 1996 Telecommunications Act reinforced this process. The Act allowed the FCC to lift the ban on horizontal concentration in the television industry. Broadcast licenses had been limited to one per entity in each market. The 1996 Act allowed the FCC to award more than one license per market after it had considered its impact on the industry. The FCC chose to allow duopolies in markets in which there would be at least eight "voices" in the market after the merger of two stations. Generally, the largest markets were opened to duopolies under the reasoning that diversity would be preserved in those markets.

For independents that sold product into TV syndication, this change had the opposite effect. By allowing the broadcast networks to own two stations in the most important markets, especially New York, Chicago and Los Angeles – a second major outlet was pulled into the tightening, vertically integrated core. The new owners of the second station now had a great deal of content of their own since, over the course of a decade, every major network acquired one of the major studios. Vertical integration became complete. Syndication was more difficult because access to the most important markets became much more difficult.

STRATEGIC MOVES

These changes did not take place instantaneously, but unfolded over a number of years for several reasons. When a policy change takes place, it frequently takes a period of time for regulators to implement legislated requirements. Parties will frequently litigate such changes and move slowly until the legal terrain is clear. Further, existing business relations must unwind. Contracts run their course and new models are developed. Finally, because many of these policies are highly visible political decisions, market participants try to avoid triggering a political reaction with extreme moves.

The 1990s policy changes triggered a series of acquisitions and product developments over the course of the decade that created a vertically integrated oligopoly in the television industry (see Exhibit 3).

Most directly, the networks could monopolize access to audiences in prime time broadcast television, foreclosing the streams of revenue that sustain production of all forms of content. Within a decade, the amount of programming on prime time owned by the networks increased dramatically, from 15% to around 75%. First the independents were excluded from prime time, and then the major studios were absorbed.

Each of the big three networks merged with a major studio and acquired cable programming over the course of the 1990s. Fox had taken a different path to vertical integration. After being rebuffed in an effort to acquire Warner studio, News Corp. acquired Twentieth Century Fox and a number of television stations in major markets, both in 1985.

Each of the five also has substantial cable offerings. Indeed 24 of the top 25 cable channels, as measured by homes passed, are owned by these five entities. In terms of actual viewers, as opposed to homes where programming is available, these five entities account for the vast majority – as much as 85 percent -- of prime time viewing.

Since the late 1970s, Twentieth Century Fox had been one of the least active of the major studios in providing television programming. Fox's focus through the 1990s would not be on original programming as traditionally defined for prime time. It would focus on sports in programming and broadcast duopolies.

Interestingly, Fox was vertically integrated but remained below the threshold for being subject to the Fin-Syn rules. For the big three networks who were subject to the rules, the repeal of Fin-Syn made mergers between networks and studios profitable, as self-supply was now allowed.

Exhibit 3: Major 1990s Acquisitions and Launches Create the Vertically Integrated Video Entertainment Oligopoly

Year	Disney/ABC	Time Warner	Viacom/CBS	G.E-NBC	Fox
1993		Turner acquires Castle Rock & New Line			Fox acquires NFL rights
1994			Viacom acquires Paramount		
1995		Time Warner launchesWB	CBS launches UPN		
1996	Disney acquiresABC	Time Warner acquires Turner			
1999			CBS acquires King World Viacom acquires CBS	NBC acquires 30% of Paxson	
2001					Fox duopolies LA, Minn. DC Houston
2002				NBCacquires Telemundo NBC duopolies result	Fox duopolies Chic. Orl.
2003				GE acquires Universal	

Source: Columbia Journalism Review, Who Owns What, August 22, 2006.

THE CURRENT STATE OF THE VIDEO PRODUCT ENTERTAINMENT SPACE

Vertical Integration

Within less than a decade after repeal of Fin-Syn and the passage of the 1996 Telecommunications Act, the process of vertical integration and horizontal consolidation was complete. This paper defines vertically integrated entities at the core of domestic video entertainment as the five firms that, in the past decade, have come to own major studios, broadcast networks and cable TV channels while holding television station licenses as well (see Exhibit 4). The names are familiar to all, in both the television and the theatrical movie space. All of the entities have a presence in each of the major video entertainment areas – network television, cable television and movie production. These firms account for five of the seven studios that produce motion pictures – known as the majors.

Exhibit 4: The Vertically Integrated, Video Entertainment Oligopoly

Parent	TelevisionProperty	Cable/Satellite	FilmProduction
News Corp.	35 TV Stations reach 39% of U.S. Households	Fox News, Fox Movie FX, FUEL, Nat. Geog. Speed, Fox Sports,	20th Century Fox, Fox Searchlight, Fox Television Studios,
	9 duopolies – NY, LA, Chic. Minn., DC, Dallas, Phoenix Orlando, Houston	Regional Sports, College, Soccer	Blue Sky Studios
		DirecTV	
	Fox Network		
General Electric	28 TV stations reaching 34% of U.S. households	CNBC, MSNBC, Bravo Sci-Fi, Trio, USA	Universal
	6 duopolies through Telemudo – NY, LA, Chic., SF, Dallas, Miami		
	NBC Network 30% of Paxson		
Disney	10 TV stations reaching 24% of U.S. households	ESPN, ABCFamily, Disney Channel, Toon Disney	Walt Disney Touchstone Hollywood
	ABC Network	Soapnet, Lifetime A&E	Buenavista Pixar Miramax
CBS/Viacom	17 TV stations reaching 39% of U.S. households CBS Network	Showtime MTV, Nickelodeon BET, Nick at Night TV Land, Noggin	Paramount Paramount Home
	CW	Spike TV, CMT Comedy Central, Flix	
	King World	The Movie Channel Sundance	
Time Warner	CW Network	HBO, CNN, CourtTV,	Warner Bros. Studios Home Video
		Road Runner New York News 1	Domestic Pay-TV Telepictures, Hanna-Barbera
		Time Warner Cable 14.5 million subscribers	Witt-Thomas

Source: Columbia Journalism Review, Who Owns What, August 22, 2006.

The depiction and data in Exhibit 5 are for the early 2000s. While there have been some changes in the direction of deintegration that movement is not complete and its implications are not yet clear. CBS and Viacom have become partially separated. They still share the same Chairman (Sumner Redstone). Each of the two potential entities is vertically integrated on its own, with distinct production and distribution facilities. Similarly, Fox and Liberty remain precariously intertwined by substantial ownership of shares, although an exchange and separation of ownership in Fox and DirecTV may be in the offing. These evolving situations may change the landscape somewhat, but the distribution arrangement made by the separate entities would still reflect the legacy of vertical integration. Thus, we may see these entities unwind toward truer deintegration and independence, although the history of Liberty teaches that spin-offs and pull-backs are entirely possible. Moreover, whether these developments will constitute a true opening of the field to independents, or whether these entities will simply substitute contractual relationships to duplicate the integrated flow of content, also remains to be seen. Nor is it clear that the parts that have been broken up will not use their remaining partially integrated assets (production and distribution) to reintegrate across the entire space.[784] The effects of any real de-integration, if it comes about, will play out over time.

Note that each of the entities has a presence in all of the key areas of video production and distribution. Each owns studios that produce video product for both television and theatrical release. Each has substantial ownership of television distribution. The four national broadcast networks are represented here. The broadcasters have substantial ownership of TV stations. The fifth entity, Time Warner, is a major cable operator. As a result of the recent Adelphia acquisition and exchange of cable systems with Comcast, Time Warner dominates the two entertainment centers in the U.S., New York and Los Angeles. It also has a share in the new broadcast network, CW, to which its production operations are providing content.

Horizontal Concentration

Reflecting this concentration of subscribers, viewers and facilities, these five, vertically integrated entities have come to dominate the domestic U.S. video entertainment product space (see Exhibit 5). They accounted for about three quarters to four-fifths of the output of the video product in terms of writing budgets, programming expenditures, hours of prime time content, and domestic theatrical box office or video sales/rentals.

---

[784] Grove, Martin A., "CBS' Moonves Smart to Eye Movies," *Hollywood Reporter.com*, July 7, 2006.

Exhibit 5: Vertically Integrated Video Oligopoly Domination of Television and Movie Production and Distribution (Circa 2001-2003)

	Television						Movies/DVD (U.S. Rev)	
	Subscribers*		Writing Budgets		Programming Expenditures		Prime Time Share	Box Office	Video
	# (million)	%	$ (million)	%	$ (million)	%	%	%	%
Fxox/Liberty	1250	21	236	19	3803	9	3	11	10
Time Warner	925	15	206	17	7627	18	10	22	20
CBS/Viacom	910	15	45	12	9555	22	28	8	7
ABC/Disney	705	12	132	11	6704	16	21	20	22
NBC/Universal**	720	12	159	13	3879	9	21	12	15
Subtotal	4315	75	772	72	31568	74	83	73	74
Total	6000	100	1225	100	43212	100	100	100	100
HHI		1179		1084		1226	1775	1213	1258
Four Firm CR		63		61		65	70	65	67

Notes and sources: * Subscribers includes broadcast and cable homes passed. ** Universal added to NBC to project post-merger market. Federal Communications Commission, In the Matter of Annual Assessment of the Status of Competition in Markets for the Delivery of Video Programming, CC Docket No. 00-132, Seventh Report, Tables D-1, D-2, D-3, D-6, D-7; Television Market Report: 2001 (Washington, D.C.: BIA Financial Network, 2001); Comments of the Writers Guild of America Regarding Harmful Vertical and Horizontal Integration in the Television Industry, Appendix A. Federal Communications Commission, In the Matter of Implementation of Section 11 of the Cable Television Consumer Protection and Competition Act of 1992; Implementation of Cable Act Reform Provisions of the Telecommunications Act of 1996 The Commission's Cable Horizontal and Vertical Ownership Limits and Attribution Rules Review of the Commission's Regulations Governing Attribution Of Broadcast and Cable/MDS Interests Review of the Commission's Regulations and Policies Affecting Investment In the Broadcast Industry, Reexamination of the Commission's Cross-Interest Policy, CS Docket No. 98-82, CS Docket No. 96-85, MM Docket No. 92-264, MM Docket No. 94-150, MM Docket No. 92-51, MM Docket No. 87-154, January 4, 2002; Bruce M. Owen and Michael G. Baumann, "Economic Study E, Concentration Among National Purchasers of Video Entertainment Programming," Comments of Fox Entertainment Group and Fox Television Stations, Inc., National Broadcasting Company, Inc. and Telemundo Group, Inc., and Viacom, In the Matter of 2002 Biennial Regulatory Review – Review of the Commission's Broadcast Ownership Rules and Other Rules Adopted Pursuant to Section 202 of the Telecommunications Act of 1996, Cross Ownership of Broadcast Stations and Newspapers, Rules and Policies Concerning Multiple Ownership of Radio Broadcast Stations in Local Markets, Definition of Radio Markets, MB Docket No. 02-277, MM Dockets 02-235, 01=317, 00-244, January 2, 2003; Federal Communications Commission, Program Diversity and the Program Selection Process on Broadcast Network Television, Mara Epstein, Media Ownership Working Group Study 5, September 2002, pp. 26; David Waterman, Hollywood's Road to Riches (Cambridge: Harvard University Press, 2005), pp. 21, 25.

In each case, the HHI is in the concentrated range and the four firm concentration ratio is in the tight oligopoly range. The two potential changes in the sector noted above would not change this basic finding. Each of the measures of concentration would likely remain in the concentrated tight oligopoly range, but the identity of the leading firms might change a bit.

The broadcast space at the core of the vertically integrated oligopoly is extremely important to the overall market for video product (see Exhibit 6). Where a program or film is placed in television space strongly affects not only its domestic revenues, but has a large impact on where it will be placed and what revenues it can earn in the international arena. By foreclosing the broadcast space, for both movies and series, the oligopoly core cripples independent producers and forces them into the cable arena, insofar as the independents desire to distribute over the television platform. The cable space, though, is a hostile environment as well, wherein the very same entities own the most attractive distribution channels in the space. Independents are forced into the least attractive cable channels on the least favorable terms.

THE CONDITIONS FOR THE EXERCISE OF MARKET POWER

Thus, the basic conditions for public policy concern about the potential exercise of market power are present. The empirical analysis demonstrates key economic characteristics of the video entertainment product space. It is a moderately to highly concentrated, tight oligopoly that is vertically integrated in production and distribution and exercises monopsony power – control and market power over the purchase of programming from independents. The next study presents evidence that market power has been exercised. In the process of creating the vertically integrated oligopoly, these entities behaved in a manner that created their market power through mergers, acquisitions and product development and exploited their market power through self-dealing, foreclosure of markets and imposition of onerous terms and conditions on suppliers.   The key elements of the video entertainment product space include:

Market structure and market power
- Market shares that have risen to the level traditionally defined as a source of concern about concentration setting the stage for the abuse of market power.
- Substantial barriers to entry in the industry.
- A history of anticompetitive practices.

Vertical Integration
- Barriers to entry increased by vertical integration.
- The foreclosure of markets to unaffiliated producers through favoritism of affiliated upstream production and the subsequent exit of upstream, unaffiliated product suppliers from the market.
- Parallelism and reciprocity among the dominant firms in the oligopoly.
- A rush to integrate and concentrate across the sector.

Exhibit 6: Location in the Domestic Exhibition Space Strongly Influences Prospects in Foreign Markets

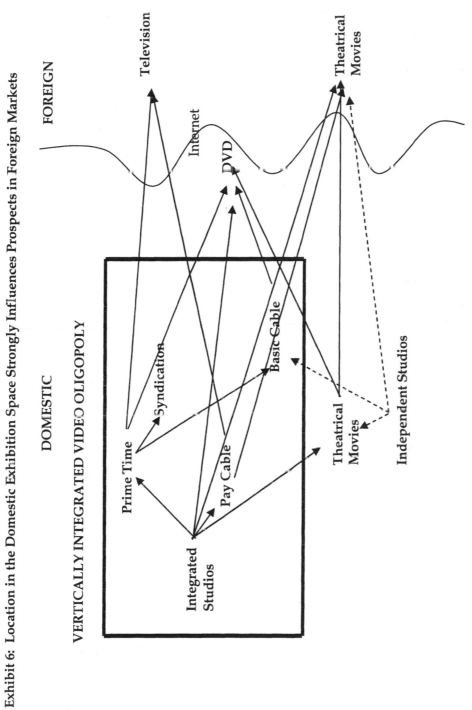

Monopsony Power
- The imposition of prices that squeeze unaffiliated producers and terms that shift risk onto those producers.
- Indications of a decline of quality in product attendant on the abuse of monopsony power.
- Flooding of downstream outlets with integrated product.

STUDY 24
DOMINATION OF THE VIDEO PRODUCT SPACE

MARK COOPER

The paper considers how the production and distribution of movie programming for cable and theatrical release were affected. By two widely accepted economic measures of market concentration, the Herfindahl-Hirschman Index (HHI) and the market share of the top four firms (the 4 Firm Concentration Ration or CR-4), the video market has become a concentrated, vertically integrated, tight oligopoly. As a result, this oligopoly engages in a number of predatory business practices that both limit competition from independents and deprive the public of new, fresh voices. They foreclose the market to independents by leveraging their vertical market power and by self-supplying product. They exercise their market power as buyers of content (monopsony power) with two practices that are especially damaging to competition from independent producers. The first is that networks often demand that they be given an equity participation in an independently developed television series in order for it to be placed on the primetime schedule. The second is that basic cable channels owned by members of the oligopoly will not pay license fees that are commensurate with the production values and the scope of licensed rights they demand in independently produced TV movies.

While it is extremely difficult to assess the impact of the changes in the industry on quality, there is no doubt that the independent sector was a consistent source of innovative and high quality content in both the TV series and movies categories prior to the changes in policy. Measured by both popularity and awards, the independents more than hold their own when given a chance to reach the public. This quantitative evidence reinforces the celebrated anecdotal evidence – shows like *All in the Family* and *Cosby* – frequently offered about the importance of independent production. It is quite clear that the elimination of independents from the high value TV product spaces – prime time and premium cable – cannot be attributed to poor quality of product. It is more readily attributed to changes in the structure of the industry and the business practices of the dominant, vertically integrated oligopoly.

PRIME TIME ON BROADCAST/NETWORK TELEVISION

The central empirical fact at the core of the narrative of the 1990s is the dramatic and swift change in the ownership of prime time programming after the repeal of the Fin-Syn rules (see Exhibit 1). Studies of prime time programming just prior to the repeal of the Fin-Syn rules find that the networks owned around 15 percent of shows aired in prime time. Major studios owned about one-third and independents accounted for about a half. Within five years, the role of the independents had been dramatically reduced – to less than one-fifth of the programming. Networks had grown to almost 40 percent. The major studios still accounted for around 40 percent. The mergers of the networks and studios followed and the vertically integrated entities came to dominate prime time, accounting for over three quarters of the programs. In 1989, fifteen entities produced 2 percent or more of the programming on prime time. By 2002, that number had shrunk to five. The programming produced by independents in 2006 was largely reality shows, not scripted programming, as had been the case in the recent past.

Exhibit 1: Prime Time Market Shares

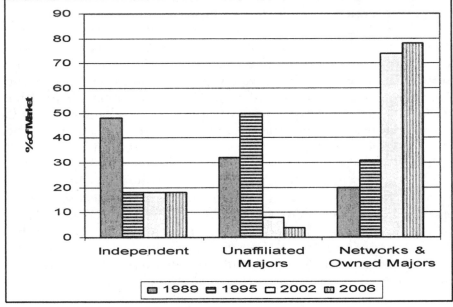

Source: 1989-2002 calculated from Mara Einstein, Media Diversity: Economics, Ownership and the FCC (Mahwah: Lawrence Erlbaum, 2004), p. 169; 2006 based on Baseline Research, Fall Television Schedule: 2006-2007 Season.

Traditional measures of market concentration used in economic analysis reinforce this observation. As Exhibit 2 shows, the prime time market moved very quickly from an unconcentrated competitive market (CR4=34%; HHI=541) to a tight oligopoly (CR4=74%) well up into the moderately concentrated range (HHI=1596). If the calculations are based only on series, i.e. excluding movies, the concentration is even greater. Within a decade after the repeal of Fin-Syn, the market was a highly concentrated (HHI=2070) tight oligopoly (CR4=84).

Exhibit 2: Concentration of Prime Time Programming

Year	All Prime Time Hours		Series Only	
	Four Firm Concentration	HHI	Four Firm Concentration	HHI
1989	35	541	40	703
1995	47	776	57	1165
2002	74	1596	84	2070

Source: Calculated from Mara Einstein, Media Diversity: Economics, Ownership and the FCC (Mahwah: Lawrence Erlbaum, 2004), p. 169.

NEW SHOWS AND PILOTS

Exhibit 3 shows the pattern of ownership by the networks of prime time programming, new shows and pilots. We observe a modest increase in network ownership in the early 1990s, as the Fin-Syn rules were partially repealed, debated and litigated. With final repeal of the rules in 1995, we see a rapid and steady increase in network ownership.

The pattern has persisted, as an analysis of the 2006-2007 season shows (see Exhibit 4). The networks get over half of their programming internally. The four major networks also buy programming from one another. Overall, independents account for less than one-fifth of prime time programming. On the four major networks, the independents account for about one-seventh. The independent programming is generally reality shows, not scripted programming.

The pattern has persisted, as an analysis of the 2006-2007 season shows (see Exhibit 4). The networks get over half of their programming internally. The four major networks also buy programming from one another. Overall, independents account for less than one-fifth of prime time programming. On the four major networks, the independents account for about one-seventh. The independent programming is generally reality shows, not scripted programming.

Exhibit 3: Network Ownership of Prime-Time Programming 1990-2002

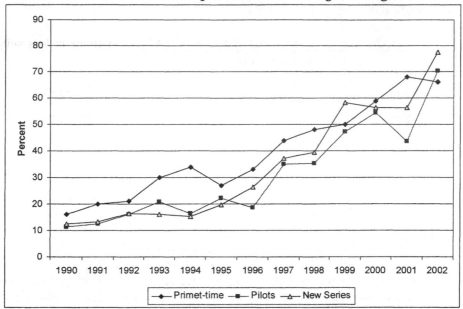

Source: Calculated from Mara Einstein, Media Diversity: Economics, Ownership and the FCC (Mahwah: Lawrence Erbium, 2004), p. 171; William T. Bielby and Denise D. Bielby, "Controlling Prime Time: Organizational Concentration and Network Television Programming Strategies," Journal of Broadcasting & Electronic Media, 47: 4 (2003), p. 588.

Exhibit 4: Primetime 2006-2007 Programming
(Percent of Hours)

	Self-Dealing	Internal Big-5 Dealing	Sony	Independents
ABC-Touchstone	52	20	3	25
CBS-Paramount	57	38	0	5
NBC-Universal	67	14	5	14
FOX-20ᵗʰ Century	52	29	6	13
CW-Warner/Viacom	53	0	7	40
Total	57	21	4	18

Source: Baseline Research, Fall Television Schedule: 2006-2007 Season

SYNDICATION

Syndication has been studied less than prime time, but the available data suggests a similar pattern (see Exhibit 5). Although there is less self-dealing, the five networks dominate the syndication market because of a large amount of internal dealing. Particularly interesting to note is the lack of recent independent shows in syndication. Having been forced out of prime time, independents simply do not have series to place as product in syndication.

Exhibit 5: Self-Dealing and Internal Dealing in First-Run Syndicated Programming (2004)

	Hours	
TYPE OF TRANSACTION	**All Shows**	**Shows Less Than 2 Years Old**
Self-Dealing (Subsidiaries of Big 5 syndicating to themselves)	32%	61%
Internal Dealing (Subsidiaries of Big 5 syndicating to Big 3 station groups)	41%	16%
Independents syndicating to Big 3 Station Groups	18%	0%

Sources and Notes: Calculated from Goro Oba and Sylvia M. Chan-Olmstead, "Self-Dealing or Market Transaction?: An Exploratory Study of Vertical Integration in the U.S. Television Syndication Market," Journal of Media Economics, 19 (2), 2006, p. 113.
Big 3 station groups are CBS/Viacom, Fox and ABC
Big 5 syndicators are King World, Paramount, 20th Century Fox, Buena Vista, WB and Universal. Other Major is Sony (Columbia). Independents are "other."
There are 22.5 hours per week of first-run syndicated programming in the 9am to 8pm day part analyzed (77 hours).

The foreclosure of the broadcast/network television market, particularly for 1st run series, is reinforced by a complete lack of pilots coming from independents. Interviews with independent producers done for this paper reveal that since there is little chance that they will get on the air, they have abandoned this market.

I have noted that the decision to allow broadcasters to hold multiple licenses in a single market contributed to the difficulties of independents gaining access to the syndication market. The network owners would use their internally produced content on the television stations in the largest markets, squeezing the space available to unaffiliated producers. About 75 duopolies were created soon after the ban on holding multiple licenses was lifted. The national networks concentrated their duopoly acquisitions in the top ten markets, even though owning multiple stations within a market did not count against the national cap on how many homes they were allowed to reach (see Exhibit 6). These markets account for about 30 percent of all the TV households in the country and almost 40% of all the TV revenues in the country. The big four network's market share in the top three markets was particularly high. These three markets alone account for about 15 percent of the population and almost 20 percent of TV revenues in the nation.

Exhibit 6: Big 4 Network Duopolies and Market Share in Top 10 Markets

Designated Market Area	Number of Big 4 Duopolies	Market Share of Big 4 Duopolies	Total Market Share of Big 4
New York	2	44	77
Los Angeles	3	62	79
Chicago	2	40	73
Philadelphia	1	25	57
San Francisco	2	37	56
Boston	1	28	42
Dallas	3	59	59
Washington D.C.	1	27	52
Atlanta	0	0	24
Detroit	1	24	42

Source: BIA Financial, Television Market Report, 2003

TV MOVIES, THE ROLE OF CABLE

The history of prime time programming is primarily a story about television series. While a small number of made for TV movies appear in prime time, the overwhelming majority of programming is series. Interestingly, for independents, the growth of cable in the late 1990s was a story about TV movies.

To analyze the changing patterns of TV movies, I examined all films aired in three four-year periods (see Exhibit 7). The first period was before the Fin-Syn rules were in play (1985-1988). The second period was the four years after Fin-Syn was repealed (1995- 1998). The third period was after the networks became integrated with studios (2001-2004). I relied on the baseline database and included only movies that were aired and for which a network and at least one producer was identified. Where a network was listed as a producer, the movie was considered to be produced by the network, even if other (unaffiliated) producers were identified. This is the critical assumption in the sense that I am assuming, implicitly, that the movie would not have been aired on the network, but for the network's interest in the co-production. Of lesser importance is the assumption that where a network and its major movie studio are both listed as producers, the studio was considered to be the producer. While these distinctions could be interpreted in other ways, the basic patterns in the data would not change much. The key findings about independent producers are quite clear (as shown in Exhibit 7).

Exhibit 7: TV Movies Across All Distribution Channels

	Percent of Movies		
	Broadcast	Basic Cable	Premium Cable
1985-1988 (n=47)			
Independent	39	0	2
Network	47	2	2
Majors	9	0	0
1995-1998 (n=206)			
Independent	33	13	16
Network	18	1	5
Majors	11	0	2
2001-2004 (n=634)			
Independent	7	41	9
Network	5	20	7
Majors	5	5	1

Source: Baseline Beta Studio System Database.

In the most recent period, cable movies have become quite prominent. The numbers of movies produced have increased dramatically. In the mid-1990s, independents aired about 120 movies, 95 of them on broadcast and premium cable. In the 2001-2004 period, they produced over 100 movies on broadcast and premium cable, and over 260 on basic cable. The apparent increase in production, however, is less significant than it appears. There are two different sets of reasons that the expansion has not helped independents greatly. One set has to do with the nature of the business and the distribution channels.

First, broadcast and premium movies have much higher budgets and larger audiences. Thus, the 100 movies produced by independents that aired on broadcast and premium cable probably had a substantially larger total budget and a larger audience than the 260 movies that aired on basic cable.

Second, where studios compete for resources to maintain a production base, the relative output is important. Whereas the independents grew by about 6 percent between the mid 1990s and the early 2000s in the high value spaces, the networks and major studios grew by almost 60 percent. As the networks grew larger and larger, they control more resources in the sector.

Third, placement on basic cable makes it more difficult to tap into other revenue streams – DVD sales/rentals and foreign television – which have become vital to maintaining the program's prominence.

The second set of factors that suggest the growth of basic cable as an outlet is less important than it appears, has to do with the market structure.

First, approximately 80 percent of the basic cable movies aired in the 2001-2004 period on networks is now owned by two of the vertically integrated media corporations – ABC/Disney (ABC family, Disney Channel and Lifetime) and NBC (Sci-Fi).

Second, the genres are highly specialized. These cable networks buy three genres, each with a respective dominant buyer. ABC Family/the Disney Channel buy family/children-oriented movies. Lifetime buys romances. Sci-fi buys science fiction films. This is a classic situation for the exercise of monopsony power.

Third, the vertically integrated oligopoly that dominates the other video outlet spaces also thoroughly dominates the TV movie space. The five entities I have identified as the vertically integrated oligopoly account for about three-quarters of the distribution of movies: one-third through broadcast and premium cable, a little over one-third through basic cable, and another handful on general networks (A&E, MTV, ESPN, FX, Spike).

ACCESS TO TELEVISION IS CRUCIAL TO THE HEALTH OF INDEPENDENT PRODUCERS

Thus, I have shown that the independents were largely eliminated from prime time broadcasting and relegated to basic cable movies. This places the independents at a severe disadvantage because television and the broadcast space at the core of the vertically integrated oligopoly remain extremely important to the overall market for video product. Exhibit 8 presents order of magnitude estimates of the revenues, expenditures and audiences for domestic movie producers and the domestic TV sector. It contrasts cable and broadcast revenues with sources of revenue for movie producers that are 'independent' of the domestic TV sector – domestic and foreign theatrical releases and home video sales.

Exhibit 8: The Importance of Television in the Video Product Space (circa 2003-2004)

| | Movies | | | Television | |
	Majors	Independents		Broadcast	Cable/Satell
Revenues (billions)			Ad Revenu Subscriptio	$35	$50
Domestic					
Box Office	$8.0	$1.0			
Home Video	$11.0	$1.3			
Subtotal	$19.0	$2.3			
Foreign					
Box Office	$8.0	$1.0			
Home Video	$8.0	$0.8			
Subtotal	$16.0	$1.8			
Total	$35.0	$4.1		$85	
Programming Budgets (billions	$7.0	$0.4		$40	
Audience (hours per year)					
Theatrical		13	Broadcast	780	
Home Video		80	Basic		830
Total		93	Premium		180

Sources: *U.S. Box Office and Programming budgets are based on MPAA, Theatrical Market Statistical Report, 2005. Programming budgets do not include marketing and assume 120 releases from the majors. Foreign Box Office, home video and TV revenues are from David Waterman, Hollywood's Road to Riches (Cambridge: Harvard University Press, 2005), Table C.1. Independent programming budgets from American Film Marketing Association, The Economic Impact of Independent File Production, April 2003Cable Revenue is from Federal Communications Commission, Twelfth Annual Report in the Matter of Annual Assessment of the Status of Competition in the Market for the Delivery of Video Programming, MB Docket No. 05-255, March 3, 2006, p. 19.*

The revenue from the TV sector is much larger than the domestic revenue sources for the movie industry – about four times as large – even when video sales/rentals are included. Total revenues from these sources are over two times as large. Even if we were to factor in the domestic and foreign TV revenues of movie producers, the domestic TV sector would be almost twice as large.[1] Programming expenditures of the domestic TV sector are on

---

[1] The sources cited in Exhibit IV-8 put this revenue at about $8 billion.

the order of five to six times as large.   The extreme importance of TV in terms of audience is also clear. Broadcast and cable pull almost twenty times the audience of movies, even combining theatrical and home video viewing. Premium cable (arguably similar to movies since it is a pay service) alone has a larger audience.

Although basic cable and broadcast are about equal in audience, prime time broadcast is still the dominant exhibition space on TV.   For example, the advance sales of advertising slots on the four national networks – called the up front sales – equals the total annual Box Office of theatrical releases in the U.S. Advertisers pay a rich premium for this space because the networks still aggregate many more viewers than cable shows. As Mara Einstein, the author of the most comprehensive analysis of the repeal of the Fin-Syn rules noted, the gatekeeper role of the networks is essential since,

> while the networks must decide between best show versus best buy, they remain acutely aware of their ability to provide something that no other media vehicle can, and that is the ability to create a valuable asset because no medium can provide the kind of exposure and promotion that network television does.[2]

The networks are well aware of their advantage. As Les Moonves recently put it, "If you want 30 million people, you can't get that anywhere else."[3] The next section examines how that gatekeeper role impacted access to distribution under the new policies adopted in the 1990s.

THE CRITICAL ROLE OF GATE KEEPING IN THE VIDEO PRODUCT SPACE

At the center of the picture I have painted of vertical integration following the policy decisions of the 1990s stand the broadcasters as gatekeepers of access to audiences. A key role in the process was played by the absorption of the major studios. Interestingly, David Waterman's recent economic history of the major studios is based on the premise that the most important feature of the studios is their role as *distributors,* and we often refer to them by that term.   By controlling distribution, the studios act as gatekeepers: they decide which movies get produced and how they are made, and they also largely determine when and at what price viewers get to see them on which media.[4]

The key gate keeping role of distribution in the video entertainment product space was integrated and consolidated with production in single

---

[2] Einstein, Mara, *Media Diversity: Economics, Ownership and the FCC* (Mahwah: Lawrence Erlbaum, 2004), p. 192.

[3] Fabricant, Geraldine and Bill Carter, "A Tortoise Savors the Lead," *New York Times,* September 12, 2006, p. CC11.

[4] Waterman, David, Hollywood's Road to Riches (Cambridge: Harvard University Press, 2005), p. 16.

entities in the first 50 years of the movie industry. While there is a debate about the factors that shaped the role of the major studios, Waterman pinpoints two critical issues that parallel the core of my analysis of the video product space in the 1990s. One was a policy decision that forced deintegration.

> Fox, MGM, Warner, Paramount, and RKO, known at the time as the five majors, were vertically integrated into production and theater exhibition and had consistently dominated the industry since the mid-1930s. The three others – Universal, Columbia and United Artists, known as "the minors" at the time – owned no theaters... All eight of these studios were brought to trial by the U.S. Justice Department in the 1940s, and an eventual Supreme Court decision in 1948, *United States v. Paramount Pictures, Inc. et al.*, ruled that the eight distributors had violated the Sherman Act and other antitrust laws... The Court ordered the five major distributors to divest their extensive theater holdings... established a number of regulations on contractual relationships between distributors and theaters that were incented to level the playing field for independent companies.[5]

The second factor that shaped the market for theatrical movies was the growth of television.

> After the *Paramount* decision, the prewar stability of industry structure among the eight Paramount defendants began to crumble. Industry positions of the majors and the minors converged, and the extent of independent entry increased. We argue in the following chapter that the almost coincident diffusion of television has more profound long-range effects on the movie industry than did *Paramount*, but it is likely that ascendance of all three of the minor studios into the majors ranks, and perhaps the rise of independents in the 1960s, were related to the Court's intervention.[6]

Thus, the policy of forcing deintegration of production and distribution of theatrically released movies opened the door to entry, while the advent of television created a whole new channel for the distribution of video product. Waterman reckons that the technological factor played a large part in shaping the video entertainment space, although not so much in determining concentration as in altering the types of products the sector produced and the marketing patterns of those products. However, from the point of view of the analysis in this paper, the critical point is that the convergence of the same two factors – integration policy and multiple distribution platforms – that worked to weaken the gatekeeper role of the studios in the 1950s, worked in the opposite direction for the broadcasters in the 1990s. Removing the policy restriction on vertical integration opened the door to reintegration of the production and distribution of video product and the merger of production (studios) and distribution (broadcasting and cable).

---

[5] Waterman, p. 30.
[6] Waterman, p. 23.

The lesson is clear: if given the chance, entities will merge and integrate vertically in order to dominate the sector by controlling distribution.

Mara Einstein, already described above as conducting the most thorough investigation of the Financial Interest and Syndication rules, notes that before and after the policy limiting vertical integration the broadcasters used their control over access to audiences to monopolize ownership of network programming.

Before the Fin-Syn rules were in place, networks asserted ownership over prime-time programming.

> In the 1970s, what led the FCC to institute the financial interest and syndication rules was a concern that the networks were becoming both too powerful and too demanding when it came to the [program] selection process. Too powerful in that they were the gatekeepers of news, information, and entertainment for the American public. This was so because of the limits of radio spectrum... Too demanding, because networks were requiring an equity stake in a program before it would be accepted as part of the prime-time schedule.... [T]he networks had ownership of more than 70% of their prime-time schedule by the mid-1960s, up from only 45% the previous decade. The strong arming of producers was a fundamental reason for the creation of fin-syn.[7]

The timing is informative. TV arrives on the scene in the 1950s and becomes the dominant medium by the early 1960s. In the early days, broadcasters lacked both production capacity and market power to self-supply content. Once television achieved ascendance, the broadcasters used their resources and leverage to assert ownership over prime time programming.

The broadcast networks also had a history of antitrust problems in their role as gatekeepers of access to the television audience. In 1978 they lost an antitrust case that paralleled the *Paramount* case.

> In the *Unites States v. National Broadcasting Co.*, The government specifically accused the National Broadcasting Company (NBC) of restraint of trade as it related to purchasing programs from independent producers and of using its network power to monopolize prime-time programming production of shows broadcast on the network. The Department also claimed that NBC, with CBS and ABC, was trying to develop a monopoly over the television programming market.[8]

After a twenty-year period in which the networks were restrained by the Fin-Syn rules, the broadcasters moved to reassert ownership in prime-time programming once the rules were repealed.

---

[7] Einstein, Mara, *Media Diversity: Economics, Ownership and the FCC* (Mahwah: Lawrence Earlbaum, 2004), p. 179
[8] Einstein, p. 60.

Since the rules were repealed in 1995, the economic structure of the industry changed drastically. The television networks have become vertically integrated institutions with the ability to produce programming through internal business units. Corporate parents put pressure on the networks to purchase programming internally to achieve synergies and, of course, increase profits. Being part of large media conglomerates, there is added pressure on the networks to be profitable so that Wall Street may find the parent company appealing.[9]

The networks each have at least a 50% stake in the programming on the air and some have as high as 70% and even 90%.[10] The networks could never achieve those kinds of ownership numbers without requesting a stake in the programming that appears on their air. It is no secret to anyone that the networks do this.[11]

In the previous section, I have noted the evolving pattern of behavior by the broadcasters in asserting ownership of prime time programming. Bielby and Bielby have argued that network behavior was political, as well as economic, and noted the evolving nature of their rhetoric. At first the broadcasters argued that the independents would not be squeezed out. Later they argued that independents were irrelevant.

The network executives' initial position was that independent producers would thrive in a deregulated industry and that network ownership was not a threat to creativity and program quality. Increasingly, in recent years, network executives and deregulation advocates have taken the position that their opponents' positions are irrelevant, because they are out of touch with the realities of the marketplace. In effect, they are saying, vertical and horizontal integration were necessary for the industry to survive in the face of rising costs and increased competition from new technologies.[12]

As this process unfolded, the impact was felt in more than just access to audiences. The leverage that the vertically integrated core of the industry acquired also dramatically changed the terms of trade between the independents and vertically integrated conglomerates. With a small number of vertically integrated buyers and a large number of much smaller product sellers, the core oligopoly gains monopsony power. They can impose onerous terms on the supplier, appropriating maximum surplus. With all of the major distribution channels under their control, the vertically integrated oligopoly can slash the amount they are willing to pay for independent product.

---

[9] Einstein, pp. 179-180.
[10] Einstein, p. 217, citing Mermigas, 2002,
[11] Einstein, p. 217.
[12] Bielby William T. and Denise D. Bielby, "Controlling Prime Time: Organizational Concentration and Network Television Programming Strategies," *Journal of Broadcasting & Electronic Media,* 47: 4 (2003), p. 585.

MARKET STRUCTURAL IMPACTS OF HORIZONTAL CONCENTRATION AND VERTICAL INTEGRATION

The pattern of behavior and structural changes in the industry should raise red flags for public policy. One major concern about vertical mergers is that the industry undergoes a rush to integration and consolidation. Being a small independent firm at any stage renders a company extremely vulnerable to a variety of attacks.

> Oligopolies often settle down into behavioral patterns in which price competition atrophies, even though some or all sellers suffer from excess capacity. Non-price rivalry then becomes crucial to the distribution of sales. One form of nonprice competition is the acquisition of downstream enterprises, which all else (such as prices) being equal will be purchased from their upstream affiliates. If acquisition of this sort deflects significant amounts of sales, disadvantaged rivals are apt to acquire other potential customers in self-defense, and reciprocal fear of foreclosure precipitates a bandwagon effect in which the remaining independent downstream enterprises are feverishly sought.[13]

> If there are 10 nonintegrated firms and only one of them integrates, then little affect on competition might occur. But if this action induces the other 9 to do the same, the ultimate impact of the first "triggering" move may be large. Any increase in market power is magnified.[14]

A second, related concern about vertical integration that arises from the observed behaviors is that it can create or reinforce barriers to entry into the industry. By integrating across stages of production, incumbents may force potential competitors to enter at both stages, making competition much less likely. "[V]ertical mergers may enhance barriers to entry into the primary industry if entrants must operate at both stages in order to be competitive with existing firms and if entry at both stages is substantially more difficult than entry at one stage".[15]

Capital market hurdles are only one of the barriers to entry that vertical integration and conglomeration can create. Such mergers can also foreclose input markets to competitors.

> When all production at a level of an industry is "in-house," no market at all exists from which independent firms can buy inputs. If they face impediments or delays in setting up a new supplier, competition at their level will be

---

[13] Scherer and Ross, pp. 526-527.

[14] Shepherd, p. 290.

[15] Perry, Martin, "Vertical Integration: Determinants and Effects," in Richard Schmalensee and Robert D. Willig (Eds.) *Handbook of Industrial Organization* (New York: North-Holland, 1989), p. 247.

reduced. The clearest form of this is the rise in capital a new entrant needs to set up at both levels.[16]

The experience in the video product space over the two decades in which the vertically integrated oligopoly emerged suggests that vertical integration increased barriers to entry into the television sector.

[B]ecause the vertically integrated structure creates such a barrier to entry... it is not necessary for these executives to collude.... The complexity has made it almost impossible for new players to enter the market, because they have to do so on so many levels – production, distribution, cable outlets, and so forth.[17]

Compared to recorded music, production costs in television are astronomical, creating substantial barriers to entry to new program suppliers and creating incentives to the networks to demand greater control over costs.... In the increasingly deregulated business environment, the enhanced market power of the corporations that control access to channels of distribution has made it more difficult for independent suppliers of new television series to survive in the industry. Moreover, the high cost of producing episodic television makes it extremely difficult to operate through channels of distribution outside of network television, such as first run syndication or cable (especially when those off-network venues are increasingly controlled by the same corporations).[18]

Favoring Affiliates

The gatekeeper role translates into leverage because "with increased vertical integration, independent producers have less access to audiences, or they must align themselves with studios or networks to get their shows on the air."[19] Einstein concludes that integration favors internally produced product.

Given vertical integration and the combined network/programming departments, all things being equal, an internally produced show is going to get an airing over one in which the network does not have an interest. It is also more likely to get a better time slot and be kept on the air longer. While it is possible that some shows of lesser quality are given preference over those produced by outsiders, this is a situation that is not likely to be sustained.[20]

Producers claim that with the demise of the Fin-Syn Rules, networks have used their enhanced market position in several ways to gain unfair advantage over outside program suppliers. First, they claim that when selecting series for the prime-time schedule and deciding between a series from an outside producer versus one of comparable or even less quality produced in-house by the

---

[16] Shepherd, pp. 289-290.
[17] Einstein, p. 217.
[18] Bielby and Bielby, p. 341.
[19] Einstein, pp. 180-181.
[20] Einstein, p. 194-195.

network or by a network joint venture, the network will favor the series in which it has a financial interest. Moreover, many producers perceive that this kind of favoritism has intensified in recent years.[21]

Exclusive and preferential deals for the use of facilities and products compound the problem.

The first firms to integrate into neighboring stages reduce the number of alternative sources for other firms at either stage. This "thinning" of the market can increase the costs of market or contractual exchange. Subsequent integration by other firms then becomes more likely.[22]

Concerns arise that not only will the dominant firm in the industry gain the leverage to profitably engage in anti-competitive conduct, but also the dynamic processes in the industry will clearly shift toward cooperation and coordination rather than competition. The issue is not simply collusion, although that is clearly a concern.

The *Guidelines* do recognize three major competitive problems of vertical mergers in concentrated industries. First, forward mergers into retailing may facilitate collusion at the manufacturing stage by making it easier to monitor prices or by eliminating a "disruptive buyer." [23]

Beyond collusion, a mutual forbearance and reciprocity occurs as spheres of influence are recognized and honored between and among the small number of interrelated entities in the industry.

Now we consider the big picture, rather than market-by-market effects. Imagine an extreme situation, with five big diversified firms extending into all major sectors. They coexist in parallel, touching one another in hundreds of markets. Whatever their effects on each market might be, they pose a larger problem of spheres of interest, or diplomatic behavior replacing competition …

Reciprocity is an exchange of favors. Reciprocal buying is one form of it. At its simplest, firm A buys from firm B because of some purchase that B makes from A …

Reciprocity: The large conglomerate may have numerous opportunities for reciprocal buying arrangements.

Mutual forbearance: More generally (it is sometimes claimed) large firms treat each other with deference, avoiding competitive confrontation whenever possible.[24]

---

[21] Bielby and Bielby, p. 581.

[22] Perry, p. 247.

[23] Perry, p. 247.

[24] Asch, Peter and Rosalind Senaca, *Government and the Marketplace* (Dryden Press, Chicago: 1985), p. 248.

Einstein and others identify a number of ways in which vertical integration affects the flow of programming. Clearly inferior shows are aired primarily because the vertically integrated media conglomerate owns them, although there is a difference of opinion on how prevalent this outcome is.

There are already many examples of network-produced programs that have failed miserably. Shows that were put on the schedule for no other reason than the network studio produced them.[25]

There is definitely favoritism for internally produced shows over those produced out of house... There are limits to this.... To the extent that they won't put on a bad show that's produced internally over a good show that's not, but certainly if two shows are of equal value the internally produced show will get the nod.[26]

Indeed, according to one producer, a network financial stake in a proposed series "practically guarantees" a slot in the prime-time schedule... "Without question, if I know that I am gonna lose, I just want to know that at the end of the day the shows that beat me out did so because they are better shows and not just because they're co-owned by the network.[27]

More generally, owned-programming gets an inside track and is chosen when there are close calls.

[I]t appears the incentives introduced into the program selection process by the repeal of the Fin-Syn rules have clearly affected the program selection process within broadcast networks. Specifically, the networks have an incentive to select programs produced in-house because of both financial and political reasons.[28]

[I] is important to note here that internally produced programming has the so-called home court advantage when it comes to being selected for the prime-time schedule.... 'If you put the network person in charge of both sides of the fence... It's impossible to ask the network person to have that much objectivity.[29]

Owned programming is given better time slots.

What is less known is that the networks are selling time periods, giving the best time slots on the schedule to those who make the best deal with the network.[30]

Owned programming is kept on the air longer.

Shows are also being maintained on the schedule for longer than they might be if the network did not have an ownership interest in the show.[31]

---

[25] Einstein, p. 194-195.
[26] Einstein, p. 217.
[27] Bielby and Bielby, p. 581.
[28] Einstein, pp. 180-181.
[29] Einstein, p. 187.
[30] Einstein, p. 217.

Owned programming clogs syndication.

A new issue has arisen in the syndication market that is adversely affecting producers to the benefit of the networks and their parent companies. Due to increased vertical integration, more and more companies are selling programs within their own company rather than going out into the marketplace to sell a show. For instance, a network that has its own production company will sell a hit show to its cable network at a below-market rate without opening the show to bidding by other outlets, cable or broadcast. Though this is very lucrative for the company, it is detrimental to the profit participants in the show — the producers, the actors and so forth. If the vertically integrated company sells the show internally, it is at a heavily discounted price, which means that the profit participants are cheated out of their rightfully earned money. By selling internally, the companies have almost created a new form of warehousing. Rather than keeping a show off the market, they are keeping the show off the market to competitors.[32]

The pattern of acquisition of shows and movies discussed in the previous chapter also suggests that when the oligopolists are not self-supplying, they engage in reciprocal dealing, buying shows from one another. Interviews with independent producers conducted in preparing this study indicate that, with the vertical integration of studios into the core of the oligopoly, the problem afflicts the movie segment as well. The field is simply not level.

The interviews with independent movie producers suggest that the problems that afflict independents in syndication are somewhat different for producers of series and movies. The literature on independent producers of series shows that when independents were squeezed out of the prime time series market, they simply did not have product to sell into syndication, since they were literally put out of business. To some extent, producers of movies were similarly affected, since they did not have larger budget movies to sell into syndication, though they managed to remain in the movie business. Their theatrical releases were squeezed in the syndication space as the vertically integrated entities came to dominate syndication. The squeeze was two-pronged: they found it more difficult to get placement and the license fees and other terms deteriorated.

Monopsony Power

The final area of concern identified in the analytic framework is the exercise of monopsony power. The gatekeeper problem is at the core of

---

[31] Einstein, p. 192.
[32] Einstein, pp. 198-199.

monopsony power concerns in the video content industry.[33] The harm in the exercise of monopsony power is the reduction of prices paid to suppliers and therefore a reduction of the quantity or quality of the product supplied.

> By reducing its demand for a product, a monopsonist can force suppliers to sell to it at a lower price than would prevail in a competitive market... If the price is suppressed they will reduce output to a level that once again equals their marginal costs. In any event, both price and output will fall below the competitive level when the buyer is a monopsonist. Some productive assets will be assigned to products that would have been the supplier's second choice in a competitive market. As a result, monopsony allocates resources inefficiently just as monopoly does.[34]

This problem is evident in the TV video space as well. Broadcasters have the leverage to extract equity shares for shows not developed internally.

> [I] in recent years, the networks seem to have refined their strategy even further – recognizing that when series with high potential do appear from outside producers, they can use their market power to extract an ownership stake after the pilot has been produced.

> Secondarily, if the show is not internally produced, then the ability to have equity ownership in an externally produced show is expected for inclusion on the prime-time schedule.[35]

> Even shows in which the networks did not originally have an interest have had their financing restructured to allow the network to become a financial partner for a show to stay on air, particularly in the ever-important fifth year.... "'Shakedown is probably too strong a word, but they should not have the right to insist on ownership just to provide real estate on the airwaves.'"

> Giving a piece of the show to the network has become a normal way of doing business since the repeal of the Fin-Syn rules, because access to the airwaves depends on giving the networks a financial interest in the program. Sometimes these requirements are subtle, like requesting that a producer create their show with their studio's production facilities, and sometimes they are quite blatant – your money or your show.[36]

> Of even greater concern to these producers than the perceived favoritism towards in-house production and joint ventures is an increasingly common practice by the networks of commissioning pilots from independent producers

---

[33] Curtin, John J., Daniel L. Goldberg and Daniel S. Savrin, "The EC's Rejection of the Kesko/Tuko Merger: Leading the Way to the Application of a 'Gatekeeper' Analysis of Retailer Market Power Under U.S. Antitrust Law," 40 B.C. L. Rev. 537 (1999).

[34] Hovenkamp, Herbert, *Federal Antitrust Policy.* Hornbook Series. West Group, St. Paul. 1999,
p. 14.

[35] Einstein, pp. 180-181.

[36] Einstein, p. 192.

then demanding a financial stake as a condition of picking up a series for the prime time schedule.[37]

Networks gain market power to meddle with the content offered by independents.

> The argument being advanced here is that the increase in in-house production following the demise of the Fin-Syn Rules created a conflict of interest as business executives from the networks are placed in a position to meddle in the creative process. Under the Fin-Syn Rules, it is argued that independent producers and those affiliated with the major studios were insulated from this kind of interference.[38]

Interviews with the independent film producers underscore the problem of monopsony power. The pervasive control over distribution channels on TV allows the integrated firms to dictate terms and conditions that squeeze the independents. These include license fees that do not cover the costs, given the quality that is demanded, extremely long license periods, and claims to back end-rights – home video, foreign sales and digital distribution -- that limit the ability of independents to make up for the inadequate license fees. The exercise of this monoposony power has gone so far as to allow the buyers to repurpose content to ""higher" value" distribution channels without additional compensation for the independent producers. By taking a product that was purchased at terms and conditions designed for a lower value outlet and re-using it on a much higher value outlet, the vertically integrated company extracts much greater value (profit), without compensating the producer.

This exercise of monopsony power is akin to a practice that the vertically integrated companies had applied in the series space. In that space, the vertically integrated firms take a high value product and sell it at very low prices to a lower value outlet, in essence under stating the value of the product, to which independent participants might have a claim.

> A new issue has arisen in the syndication market that is adversely affecting producers to the benefit of the networks and their parent companies. Due to increased vertical integration, more and more companies are selling programs within their own company rather than going out into the marketplace to sell a show. For instance, a network that has its own production company will sell a hit show to its cable network at a below market rate without opening the show to bidding by other outlets, cable or broadcast. Though this is very lucrative for the company, it is detrimental to the profit participants in a show – the producers, the actors and so forth.[39]

---

[37] Bielby and Bielby, p. 581.
[38] Beilby and Bielby, p. 580.
[39] Epstein, pp. 198-199.

It should be evident from these examples that the existence of multiple cable outlets does not alter the already restricted television landscape because the networks have captured a substantial hold over the most important cable networks.

> One way that networks are ensuring a faster return on investment is by having a secondary distribution channel usually in the form of a general entertainment cable channel. These channels are used as a secondary outlet through which they can distribute their programs.... Each of these networks present programming on the broadcast network that is then re-presented (or repurposed) on the secondary outlet. This will lead to more redundant programming and less new content through more outlets. Networks are also making their prime time programming available through video-on-demand and DVD collections.[40]

> Another increasingly popular business strategy implemented by the big four and emerging networks also offsets the impact of expanding channels of distribution. "Repurposing" involves exhibiting each episode of a series on an affiliated broadcast or cable network immediately after the initial network broadcast.[41]

THE DEBATE OVER QUALITY

Qualitative Observations

The question of the relationship between vertical integration and declining quality has been hotly debated. The exercise of monopsony power is clearly affecting the structure of the industry. Two effects have been noted.

First, the number of entities engaged in the process has been reduced sharply because the distribution of risk and rewards has been shifted in favor of the networks.

> [T]he statistical patterns summarized above include instances in which the networks have used their enhanced market power to negotiate ownership shares in series pilots brought to them by outside suppliers. In these situations, the program supplier, not the network, absorbs development costs, while the network acquires a share of the back end profits if the series eventually becomes a hit and goes into syndication. From the program suppliers' perspective, the costs of development for new series remain the same, but to reach the prime-time schedule, the supplier has to agree to forgo a share of the future revenues. According to some in the industry, this revenue squeeze on independent program suppliers is the primary reason that a number of them have exited the business of prime-time series development.[42]

---

[40] Einstein, pp. 218-219, on the latter point Einstein cited Adalian, 2002.
[41] Beilby and Bielby, p. 592.
[42] Beilby and Bielby, p. 590.

So far, the most visible impact of deregulation has been a reduction in the number of organizational settings in which those who create television series are employed, and an increase in corporate control over the circumstances under which they practice their craft.[43]

The second effect is to eliminate the creative tension that once existed between the producer and the distributor of product.

Vertical integration is seen as eliminating a valuable step in the development process. First, developing programming is a creative process. When one entity created the programming and another would select it, the two companies could argue and disagree and out of those discussions, the show would often be improved... [T]he process did favor internal shows and eliminated much of the development process altogether. Producers also stated that this process was detrimental to the overall quality of network programming.[44]

One aspect of the debate over quality that is intriguing but little studied is the potential relationship between integration, declining quality and declining ratings. As Bielby and Bielby note:

In 1999, *Advertising Age* editorialized that ABC was "auctioning" its most desirable prime-time time slot to the program supplier willing to give the network a financial stake, part of a trend that is making it "increasingly clear the broadcast networks are more interested in financial deals than putting the best shows they can find on the air." The trade publication warned that the ratings decline experienced by the networks would accelerate if "financial packages rather than program quality determine what gets on the schedule."[45]

The ratings decline certainly did continue, as integrated ownership of programming increased. As is frequently the case in this sector, many other things were changing that could account for the decline in ratings, but the correlation is notable.

Waterman sees some evidence of the latter effect on the studio side of the business.

[E]xcessive movie budgets and an over reliance on sequels or derivative movies have also been associated unfavorably with conglomerate organization and the mentality of the top executive in charge.[46]

Waterman also notes that the claimed efficiency benefits of conglomeration have come into question.

When merger plans are announced, industry analysts often cite efficiencies, such as workforce combinations, or marketing advantages, such as the ability to cross-promote movies using television, magazines or other media assets also

---

[43] Beilby and Bielby, p. 593.
[44] Einstein, p. 194-195.
[45] Bielby and Bielby, p. 581.
[46] Waterman, p. 30.

owned by the conglomerate. Also commonly mentioned are the advantages of vertical integration, such as the ownership of television or cable networks that can serve as guaranteed outlets for movies produced by the conglomerate's studio branch. A related benefit is the ability to consolidate exploitation of a single story idea or character through books, magazines, television shoes, music publishing, Internet web sites, or other media within a single corporation. The economic advantages of such operating efficiencies (often called economies of scope) are plausible. However, real multimedia exploitation within the same conglomerate is apparently infrequent and other efficiency claims have come into recent disrepute – notably in the cases of AOL-Time Warner and the ABC-Disney mergers.[47]

What we may be left with are the market power advantages of a tight oligopoly in the video entertainment space, which do not yield efficiency gains while imposing a heavy price in terms of diversity and quality.

Quantitative Measures of Quality

Claims that programming decisions reflect the efficient choice of the best available product are difficult to support in light of this description of the changes in behavior as well as the patterns in the data. These changes and patterns are more consistent with the argument that the vertically integrated oligopoly favors its own content and prefers to deal within the oligopoly.

Objective measures of quality in product in the entertainment space are notoriously difficult to come by. In the movie space, analysts frequently turn to the annual awards ceremonies. The Oscars and Golden Globe Awards contradict the claim that independents suffered some sort of collapse in the 1990s. In fact, their share of awards has been constant, if not rising (see Exhibits 9, and 10).

Arguably, a second measure of quality is success. For movies, box office is the predominant measure, although success at the box office reflects many things beyond simple quality, such as the advertising budget. For comparative purposes across time and distribution channels, the market shares in Exhibits 11 and 12 make a simple point. Independents held their market share in the Box Office much better than they did in the other distribution channels where vertical leverage was most directly exercised.

---

[47] Waterman, p. 30; Peltier, Stephanie, "Mergers and Acquisitions in the Media Industries: Were Failures Predictable," *Journal of Media Economics*, 17(4), 2004.

Exhibit 9: Major Categories, Golden Globes and Oscars: Majors v. Independents

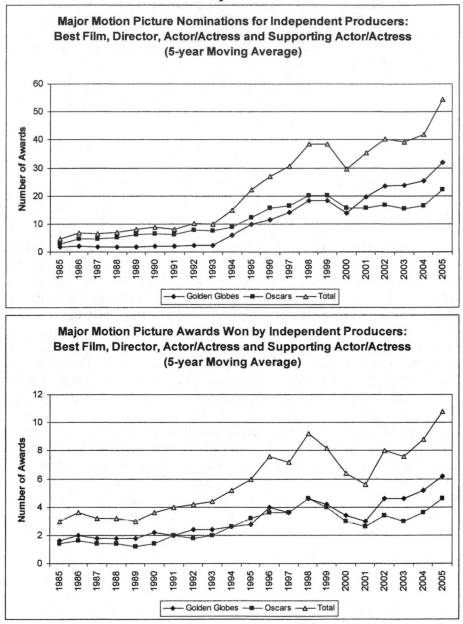

Exhibit 10: Oscar Nominations and Awards 2001-2005: Majors v. Independents

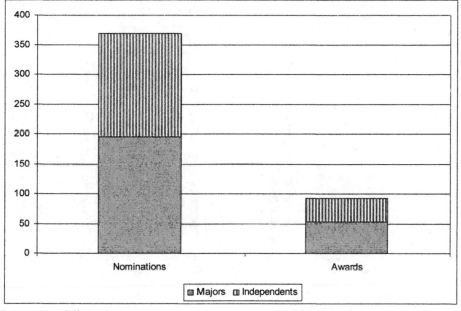

Source: Box Officemojo.com

Exhibit 11: The Shares of Independent Producers in Box Office, Video Revenue and Prime Time Hours Late 1960s to Early 2000s

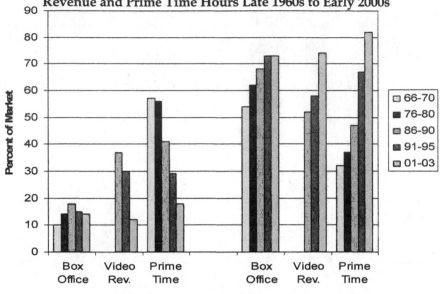

INDEPENDENTS   BIG 5 MAJORS

Sources. Box Office and Video Revenue are five year averages from David Waterman, Hollywood's Road to Riches (Cambridge: Harvard University Press, 2005), pp. 21, 25, 86-90 and 01-03. Big Five Majors are the studios that have been acquired by major TV programmers – Disney/ABC; Fox/20th Century Fox; NBC/Universal; Warner Bros.; CBS/paramount. Other majors (not shown) are MGM/UA and Columbia. Independents are what Waterman calls "the residual." Prime Time is percent of hours in 1989, and 2002 from Mara Einstein, Program diversity and the Program Selection Process on Broadcast Network Television (Washington D.C.: Federal Communications Commission, September 2003), pp. 26. First-run syndication is from C. Puresell and C. Ross, "Vertical Integration and Syndication," Electronic Media, 22(1): 2003, for 1993 and 2002. It includes only vertical integration and not internal dealing among the big 5.

Exhibit 12: Growth of Big 5 Market Share and Vertical Integration in Domestic Markets: Late 1980s to Early 2000s

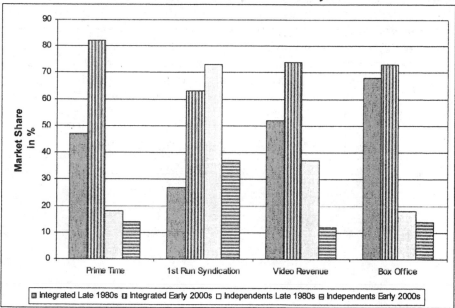

Sources. *Box Office and Video Revenue are five year averages from David Waterman, Hollywood's Road to Riches (Cambridge: Harvard University Press, 2005), pp. 21, 25, 86-90 and 01-03. Big Five Majors are the studios that have been acquired by major TV programmers – Disney/ABC; Fox/20th Century Fox; NBC/Universal; Warner Bros.; CBS/paramount. Other majors (not shown) are MGM/UA and Columbia. Independents are what Waterman calls "the residual." Prime Time is percent of hours in 1989, and 2002 from Mara Einstein, Program diversity and the Program Selection Process on Broadcast Network Television (Washington D.C.: Federal Communications Commission, September 2003), pp. 26. First-run syndication is from C. Puresell and C. Ross, "Vertical Integration and Syndication," Electronic Media, 22(1): 2003, for 1993 and 2002. It includes only vertical integration and not internal dealing among the big 5.*

Television

The quantitative analysis of the quality of television is even more complex. Independents were virtually eliminated from prime time and have little opportunity to bring new product to that space, so before and after comparisons tell us little, other than the fact that they were excluded. Moreover, there is no box office to count. The essential point here is that given the opportunity to appear in the exhibition space, independents held their own.

Exhibit 13 compares the source origin of the top thirty shows for two periods: 1985-1989, which is the base period I have been using for the Fin-Syn era, and 1995 to 2002 for the post Fin-Syn period. Ratings are the closest equivalent to Box Office. I start with the popularity measure because it tells us about the pattern of types of shows. I have included all non-news shows that appeared in the top 30. I have used the same coding approach as in the earlier analysis of all shows on TV. That is, where a major studio is listed in a co-production, it is considered the producer. Where the producer uses both the name of a network and a major studio, it is counted as the major. The details of the counts might change somewhat with a different approach, but the basic patterns would be clear.

Exhibit 13: Producers of Top 30-Rated TV Shows

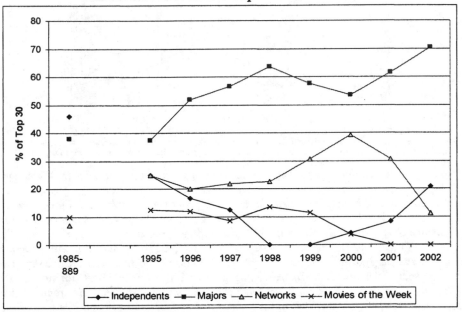

Source: Tim Brooks and Earle Marsh, The Complete Directory to Prime Time Network and Cable TV Shows: 1946 – Present, (New York: Ballantine, 2003), Appendix 3; Beta Study System database.

Prior to the repeal of Fin-Syn, independents and major studios dominated the top shows. The networks did not even pull their weight. They were somewhat underrepresented in these ratings. After the repeal of Fin-Syn, the vertically integrated oligopoly completely dominates the space. There are very few independents and no non-integrated majors in the top 30 shows. When the independents do return to the top 30 in the early 2000s, it is with reality shows, not scripted entertainments.

I have included the category of Movies of the Week, although I do not have the producers for the actual movies for two reasons. First, as we have seen, in the broader market share analysis, these were almost always independents and majors prior to the repeal of Fin-Sin; afterwards, they almost entirely had vertically integrated majors as producers. Second, the nature of prime time movies changed. Movies of the Week were big events with large budgets and appeared in the top 30 shows consistently, accounting for about 10 percent of the total, until the end of the 1990s. They then dropped quickly out of sight. This was the period of the expansion of Basic cable movies.

The pattern of popularity helps to provide background for the analysis of awards - the Emmys. There are a very large number of categories across many different types of shows. The categories also change over time. A separate category for Made for TV Movies was not added until the 1990s, so there is no baseline. For the purposes of this analysis, I focus on the Emmys for Best Comedy and Drama. These are series of scripted shows, for which awards were consistently given, most parallel movies and were available to independents.

Over the course of the 1980s there were 20 such awards given for each genre (see Exhibit 14). The distribution of the awards closely reflected the market share of the different types of producers. The point here is that if these awards represented an independent measure of quality, the independents held their own. The vertical restriction did not cause "inferior" products to be aired. With the repeal of Fin-Syn, independents were banished from these two categories of television entertainment and disappeared from the awards. As I have noted, their presence in prime time is now largely restricted to reality shows. The pattern of awards is similar to the other data we have seen: as Fin-Syn was under attack in the early 1990s the independents declined and were subsequently eliminated after repeal.

Exhibit 14: Emmys for Best Comedy and Drama

Producer	80-84	85-89	90-94	95-99	00-04
Independents	70	40	20	0	0
Networks	20	40	50	100	60
Majors	10	20	30	0	40

Source: Tim Brooks and Earle Marsh, *The Complete Directory to Prime Time Network and Cable TV Shows: 1946 – Present*, (New York: Ballantine, 2003), Appendix 3; Beta Study System database.

The debate over the impact of vertical integration on quality is difficult to resolve, as many factors were affecting the industry. Still, the pattern of declining ratings observed over a twenty year period is consistent with the claim that self-dealing had an impact (see Exhibit 15). The Exhibit shows the average rating of the top 30 shows for each year. There are two shifts downward – one in the early 1990s, as the Fin-Syn rules came under attack; one in the late 1990s and early 2000s as the integration of major studios took place. The correlation with the changing pattern of program acquisition discussed earlier is clear. While the quantitative and qualitative evidence on quality cannot prove that vertical integration was the culprit in the decline of quality, it makes a strong case that independents were eliminated not because of an inability to produce high quality and popular content, but rather as a result of a poorly run marketplace for production.

Exhibit 15: Declining Ratings of the Top 30 TV Shows

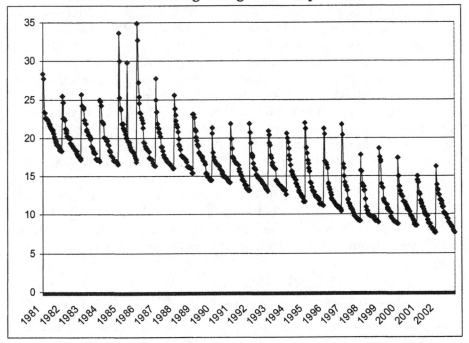

Source: Tim Brooks and Earle Marsh, The Complete Directory to Prime Time Network and Cable TV Shows: 1946 – Present, (New York: Ballantine, 2003), Appendix 3; Beta Study System database.

CONCLUSION: PUBLIC POLICY HAS UNDERMINED SOURCE DIVERSITY, BUT WILL THE INTERNET CHANGE ANYTHING?

Vertical Integration Trumps Technology

This paper has shown that the policies adopted by the FCC and Congress in the 1990s lead to a dramatic decline in source diversity on broadcast television. In the early and mid 1990s, the Broadcast networks were given three huge advantages in the television video product space. First, they were given carriage rights on cable networks (1992). Second, the Financial Interest and Syndication Rules were repealed (1995). Finally, they were allowed to own multiple stations in a single market (1996). They used this leverage to extend their control over the video content product space vertically – by merging with studios – and horizontally – by self-supplying content in broadcast prime time and expanding distribution on cable.

A tight, vertically integrated oligopoly now dominates the broadcast, cable and theatrical space in America. Promises that prime time would not become dominated by the networks, and theories that claimed competition would prevent it, have proven misguided. Hopes that cable and its expanding capacity would create vibrant competition have been dashed as the incumbent broadcaster networks extend their reach over cable's viewers by demanding carriage and extending their brand control into the new space. While the purpose of this paper is to document what happened and why, it is clear that if policymakers still believe in source diversity, then a change in policy to promote it would be in order.

Previous technological changes have not been able to deconcentrate the product space. It has taken policy changes to break the stranglehold on distribution. Whether theaters in the 1940s or broadcasters in the 1970s, gate keeping has long been a powerful force in the industry.

Because of the high cost of producing movies and other video content, the aggregation of audiences remains a critical function. With such a powerful hold on all forms of video distribution, it will be extremely difficult to dislodge the dominant players. They are the established brands and continue to gain momentum in the premium, large audience outlets.

The Internet and Digital Broadcast Platforms

While the history of the video entertainment product space is clear, as is the basis for adopting policies that promote source diversity, there is no doubt that policymakers who contemplate adopting such policies will be bombarded with claims that, even though the policies that affect the traditional video distribution channels have been disastrous, we need not be concerned because 'the Internet changes everything.'

This claim should be viewed with a great deal of skepticism. In fact, the more likely question that policy makers in this area should ask is "Do the Internet and the new digital era change anything?"

The best assessment at present is that "only a few small experiments in altering the movie-release paradigm have been conducted to date."[48] While

---

[48] Thompson, Anne, "Independent Producers and Distributors," *Hollywood Reporter*, August 1, 2006, p. 1.

the role of the Internet is currently unclear, one thing is certain. It is another distribution platform that the vertically integrated conglomerates are moving to dominate.   Whether it will be able to de-concentrate the video exhibition space described in this section remains subject to debate. However, without sufficient regulation that provides equal access to all, the Internet will fall subject to the same fate as broadcast television, premium cable television, and finally basic cable television: domination by the vertically integrated oligopoly created by the regulatory changes of the last decade.

As we have seen, in a world with limited shelf space, placement is everything. If you cannot get on the shelf, the audience cannot find you. In a world of infinite shelf space, placement is _still_ everything. When there is such a cacophony of outlets, the audience cannot find you unless you have prominent placement.   Whether it is simultaneous release on multiple platforms or widespread digital distribution, the key challenge remains "finding a way to brand a movie." In the end, says producer Jim Stark, "Nothing beats five weeks in a theater."[49]

One need only review the critique of the launches of new Internet-based distribution platforms to see the problem in clear relief. The central questions are: what do their libraries look like? What are the majors doing with respect to the platform? If the majors are not there, the platform is deemed to have dim prospects. When the majors and networks are there, they tend to get the best placement and the best deals. Little has changed. They are the most prominent and have the resources to preserve that prominence. This is clearly reflected in the reporting on the announcement of Apple's "video streaming gadget code-named ITV"[50]

> Apple's competition included the movie studios themselves plus many other ambitious firms such as Amazon, which recently unveiled its Unbox download service.

> TV shows are also starting to turn up the online service for Microsoft's Xbox...

> Apple pre-announced its ITV box in a bid to convince potential partners that its ambitions are serious... it hoped to build "momentum" and get movie makers and broadcasters talking about putting content on the Apple service.   For example, Amazon's Unbox offers movie downloads from 20th Century Fox, Paramount, Sony, Universal and Warner Bros. So far, only Disney movies are available from Apple.[51]

The quote from Les Moonves of CBS above, which touted the advantages that broadcasters have, was actually given in response to claims that the Internet was displacing the networks. Responding to the claim that broadcast share would shrink, Moonves said "If you want 30 million people,

---

[49] Thompson, p. 1.
[50] Ward, Mark, "Apple Video Divides Industry," _BBC News,_ September 13, 2006, p. 1.
[51] Ward, p. 2.

you can't get that anywhere else…Television will hold and the Internet will augment what we do."[52]

Dana Walden of 20th Century Fox TV echoes this view. "In the digital space, the extensions seem to come after the fact. We're trying to create brands on the (broadcast) networks that are enhanced by digital opportunities."[53]

While the potential and prospects are unclear, the reaction to a new technology is predictable and the studios and networks will seek to extend their gatekeeper function. Already, as one recent article observed, "studio business affairs executives now were insisting that this exclusivity [in rights to distribute] include the Internet as well."[54]

Thus, the Internet has not done much to break the grip of the vertically integrated oligopoly on the video revenue streams in the video entertainment product space. As the independent producers emphasized in the interviews, these firms control the TV outlets and syndication, have the output deals for domestic and foreign theatrical releases, and have a huge advantage in foreign TV deals. They control the branding process with their access to audiences that is being leveraged into dominance of commercial distribution on the Internet.

Given the history of gate keeping in the industry and these observations on the impact of Internet distribution, the advent of digital TV, which will increase the number of channels the broadcasters control as much as six fold, does not hold much promise to deconcentrate the TV sector. Broadcasters, who have leveraged a series of favorable policies into domination of the video entertainment product space, will now have more resources to strengthen their position, enrich their brands and repurpose their content across another distribution channel. Technological change and an increase in distribution capacity have repeatedly failed to restrict the gate keeping power of vertically integrated entities in this product space.

If policymakers value source diversity, which they should, structural restraints on the market power of the vertically integrated companies will have to be imposed. These structural restraints will have to apply to both the broadcast and cable distribution channels because public policy created the leverage that broadcasters have used to dominate the cable distribution platform. The restraints should also apply to the Internet and all other developing distribution technologies.

---

[52] Fabrikant and Carter, p. C11.
[53] "A TV Navigation Guide," *Hollywood Reporter*, September 13, 2006, p. 2.
[54] Hlestand, Jesse, "Profit Anticipation," *Hollywood Reporter*, June 6, 2006, p. 1.

PART X:

THE REALITY OF LOCAL MEDIA MARKET STRUCTURE

STUDY 25:
MEDIA MARKET CONCENTRATION:
THE FCC'S ANALYSIS vs. A REASONABLE
APPROACH

MARK COOPER

This study presents a comparison between the FCC's analysis of media market concentration and a reasonable approach, as outlined by the *Prometheus* court. The rationale for this approach is as follows: Three Courts have told them to count voice consistently. The *Prometheus* court said the FCC must weight the media in a reasonable and consistent manner, and take audience into account in it counting of voices in order to avoid absurd results. The Court told the FCC to focus on news and information. No one fought about the market definition adopted by the FCC. This paper shows that the Court's ruling can be implemented readily and following its reasoning leads to reasonable, realistic results. There were two fundamental flaws in the FCC analysis – improper media weights and a failure to include the audience of outlets in the analysis. It turns out that the latter is far more important.

THE FCC'S UNREALISTICALLY LOW ESTIMATES OF
MEDIA MARKET CONCENTRATION

Exhibit 1 shows the dramatic difference between the FCC measure of market structure and the methodology outlined in the previous study for the ten markets that the FCC studies in detail. In contrast to the FCC's findings that only one market is above the concentrated threshold and none are above the highly concentrated threshold, we find that every market is above the concentrated threshold and eight of the ten are above the highly concentrated threshold. The average HHI in the FCC analysis is just under 760. In our analysis, it is just over 2160, almost three times are high.

The extremely low levels of concentration estimated by the FCC do not reflect reality, and a glance at the details of its rankings show why. Exhibit 2 shows the rankings of the top five outlets/owners in several markets with substantial anomalies. It also shows the market share, since the magnitude of the differences is as important has the ranking.

The example that bothered the Court of "a community college television station mak[ing] a greater contribution to viewpoint diversity than a conglomerate that includes the third-largest newspaper in America" provides a reality check. The New York Times was the 23rd most important media outlet in the market, with a market share of about 1.4 percent. In our

Exhibit 1: FCC V. CFA Base Cases

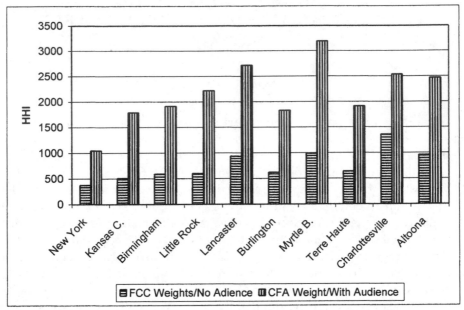

analysis the conglomerate (New York Times) is ranked in a virtual ties for second and accounts for about 13 percent of the New York media market. The community college TV station accounts for barely a speck. The ranking that results from our analysis fits reality.   News Corp. with two TV stations and a major daily is ranked first (19 percent).   Advance with four large northern New Jersey newspapers is ranked second, in a virtual tie with the New York Times, with the leading newspaper and a radio station. NBC/GE is ranked fourth with two TV stations. ABC with a TV station and four radio stations is ranked fifth.

New York City is not the only place where the FCC methodology produces absurd results. For example, in Little Rock, Arkansas Educational Television, with three channels, but less than one percent of news day part viewers is ranked number three, with a market share of 7.2 percent, ahead of several TV duopolies that have between 50 and 100 times the audience. The *Log Cabin Daily*, with a circulation of under 50,000 ties for second most important with the *Arkansas Democrat Gazette*, with a circulation almost three times as large. Both papers are given a market share of 6.7 percent. The highest ranked owner in Little Rock does not provide local news broadcast on its TV station or list news or information as one of its top three formats on its radio station.

Exhibit 2: Absurd Rankings in Individual Cities

FCC RESULTS			CFA RESULTS		
Rank	Owner	Market Share	Rank	Owner	Market Share
NEW YORK			**NEW YORK**		
1	Gannett	5.8	1	News Corp	19.3
2	Univision	5.2	2	Advance	13.6
3	Viacom	4	3	New York Times	13.1
4	Advance	3.9	4	NBC	10.6
5	News Corp	3.9	5	ABC	9.6
14 (tie)	Dutchess County Public TV	1.5		Dutchess County Public TV	~0
27	New York Times	1.4			
LITTLE ROCK AR			**LITTLE ROCK AR**		
1	Equity	5.8	1	Arkansas Democrat	39.2
2	Morris	7.7	2	Albritton	19.5
3	Arkansas Ed. TV	7.2	3	Gannett TV	12.2
4 (tie)	Arkansas Democrat	6.7	4	Nextstar (TV)	10.5
4 (tie)	Denton Caourier	6.7	7	Log Cabin Dem	1.4
4 (tie)	Log Cabin Dem.	6.7	8	Arkansas Ed. TV	0.2
				Equity	~0
BURLINGTON VT.			**BURLINGTON VT.**		
1	Vermont Public TV	13.2	1	Burlington Free Press	34.3
2	Burlington Free Press	6.7	2	Mount Mansfield TV	16.7
3	Press Republican	6.7	3	Press Republican	14.2
4	St Albans Messenger	6.7	4	Heart Argyle TV	9.6
			7	Vermont Public TV	2.7
			8	St. Albans Register	2.3

In our analysis, the *Arkansas Democrat Gazette*, is ranked first with a market share of 39 percent. It is followed by the three commercial TV broadcasters that provide local news. With market shares of 5 to 20 percent. The *Log Cabin Democrat* ranks seventh with a 1.4 percent market share. The Arkansas Educational TV stations ranks eighth, with a combined market share of 0.2 percent.

We find a similar anomaly in Burlington Vermont, where public television towers over the market with a 13.5 percent market share, twice the size of the three daily newspapers, each of which has a market share of 6.7 percent. Here too, we find the anomaly within the newspaper segment, where the St. Albans Messenger is ranked equal to the *Burlington Free Press*, even though it has one-fifteenth the circulation. The highest ranked commercial TV station comes in at 8th, with a 3.4 market share. In our analysis, the *Burlington Free Press* ranks first with a market share of 34.3 percent. The leading TV station comes in second, with a share of 16.7 percent. The *Press Republican* ranks third, with a share are 14.2 percent, followed by three other TV stations with shares ranging from 5 to 9 percent. Vermont Public Television ranks seventh, with a market share of 2.7 percent.

UNDERSTANDING WHY THE FCC WENT SO FAR ASTRAY

Because the FCC must analyze the market structure – count voices – it is important to understand why it went so far astray. This section isolates the problem by systematically varying the assumptions. We show that the primary flaw, the one on which the Court rightly focused, is the failure to take the audience into account.

Exhibit 3 contrasts our media weight with those used by the FCC. In one respect, there is a strong similarity. The FCC weighted the traditional media (TV, dailies, weeklies and radio) at 0.885. We ranked these four media at 0.91. However, the weights are very different across the traditional media. The FCC gave radio a weight of 0.249. We gave it a weight of 0.11. The FCC gave dailies a weight of 0.202, we gave them a weight of 0.32. The FCC gave much more importance to the Internet that we do (0.125 versus 0.03). However, as we show below, the FCC actually got the Internet exactly backwards, assuming it made a major contribution to the concentration of media markets.

Exhibit 4 shows the critical analysis. We apply the FCC's media weights to our audience analysis, keeping all else constant (i.e. our calculation of the "eyeballs" and our treatment of the Internet). It is readily apparent that the audience is the key. Instead of an average HHI of just under 760, the HHI with audience counted and FCC weights is over 1800. This is much closer to our estimate of just over 2160. In fact, audience accounts for about three

Exhibit 3: Media Weights

Medium	FCC	CFA
TV	33.8	33
Dailies	20.2	32
Weeklies	8.5	10
Radio	24.9	11
Traditional Subtotal	88.5	86
Internet	12.5	3
Other	N/A	11

Exhibit 4: FCC V. CFA with Audience in Both

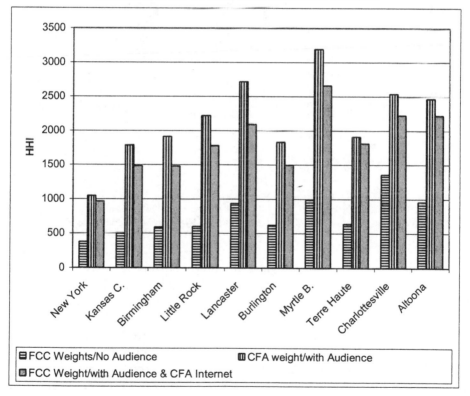

quarters of the difference between our estimate and that of the FCC. Including the audience also results in categorizing the markets similarly. Seven of the eight markets we categorized as highly concentrated are categorized as such including audience and the FCC weights. New York, which we categorized as just above the concentrated threshold (50 points above), is categorized as just below it (32 points below).

In fact, however, if the FCC had analyzed audience market shares and treated the Internet as it did, it would have come even closer to our analysis (see Exhibit 5). This is because the FCC treated the Internet in a ridiculous fashion.

Exhibit 5: FCC v. CFA with Audience in Both and FCC Internet

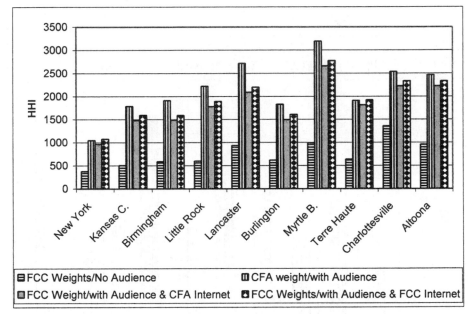

First, as noted above, it gave the Internet a very high weight. Second, it then assumed that the Internet was highly concentrated – a duopoly of cable and telephone companies. Thus, it rejected the notion that people could search the web for news and information. It assumed the Internet added 110 points to the HHI in every market. As a result, in New York City, for example, the Internet accounted for over one-quarter of the total HHI. In five of the cities it accounted for one-fifth to one-sixth of the total HHI. In four it accounted for about one-tenth. We took the opposite approach. Based on survey evidence (that focuses on local news and asked people which web sites they go to), we gave the Internet a much lower weight (about a quarter of the FCC's). We also assumed that the Internet is atomistically competitive. It made no contribution to the HHI. Rather, it deconcentrates the market.

Thus, it was not included in the numerator of the fraction, but was included in the denominator.

Combining FCC weights, FCC treatment of the Internet and our audience analysis moves the estimated HHI closer together. The average HHI is over 1930, compared to our estimate of just over 2160. New York is classified as above the concentrate threshold, so nine of the ten markets are categorized similarly.

The court suggested that, following the reasoning on cable, the FCC might exclude the Internet altogether because there is little local news and information and its penetration rate is similar to that of cable. Exhibit 6 considers this possibility. It adds in two calculations – CFA weights with audience and no Internet, and FCC weights with audience and no Internet. Taking out the Internet from the denominator of the HHI has the effect of increasing the estimated concentration. In the case of the FCC, this effect is larger than the assumption that the Internet was concentrated. We end up with perfect agreement, as the HHIs are both just above 2300. Every market is categorized similarly. We believe that the Internet should be included, but that it should be given its proper weight and assumed to deconcentrate markets.

CONCLUSION

Exhibit 6 also underscores the critical finding of this analysis. Measuring the audience is the key to a realistic assessment of media market structure. This should not be surprising, as market share has been at the core of the analysis of market structure. The *Prometheus* Court used very harsh words to describe the FCC's approach and deservedly so. For the FCC to claim to be measuring media market concentration or analyzing media market structure led to results that were, in the *Prometheus* court's words absurd, illogical and unrealistic.

Exhibit 6: FCC v. CFA with Audience in Both, Internet Excluded

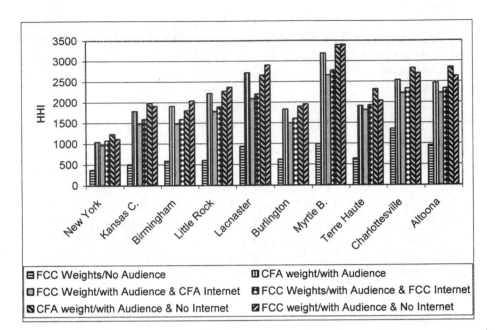

STUDY 26:
THE IMPACT OF LIFTING
THE NEWSPAPER-TV CROSS-OWNERSHIP BAN

MARK COOPER

GOALS

We start from the goals of antitrust merger policy and media policy to answer these questions. Specifying goals is essential to evaluate the impact of any changes in policy. Antitrust merger policy is a useful starting point because it is the pre-eminent area of public policy analysis of market structure and merger impacts. However, while antitrust merger policy provides the analytic tool, the Communications Act and First Amendment jurisprudence set the ultimate goals for policy to set ownership limits on media because the media involve much more than merely commercial activities; they deeply affect the nature and quality of democratic discourse in our society.

What are the goals of antitrust analysis? The goal of the antitrust laws is to protect competition. In a merger review, the Department of Justice and Federal Trade Commission (DOJ/FTC) try to prevent the creation or exercise of market power, which "is the ability profitably to maintain prices above competitive levels for a significant period of time... Sellers with market power also may lessen competition on dimensions other than price, such as product quality, service or innovation market power,"[1]

What are the goals of media policy? The goal of the Communications Act is much broader in both what it seeks to promote and prevent. The Supreme Court has repeatedly ruled that the Communications Act "rests on the assumption that the widest possible dissemination of information from diverse and antagonistic sources is essential to the welfare of the public."[2] In *Red Lion*, the seminal television case, the Court ruled that "[i]t is the right of the viewers and listeners, not the right of the broadcasters, which is paramount...the right of the public to receive suitable access to social, political, aesthetic, moral and other ideas and experiences...[T]he 'public interest' in broadcasting clearly encompasses the presentation of vigorous debate of controversial issues of importance and concern to the public."[3]

Limits on media ownership are based on the premise that "diversification of mass media ownership serves the public interest by promoting diversity of program and service viewpoints as well as by

---

[1] Department of Justice/Federal Trade Commission, *Merger Guidelines* (1997).

[2] *Associated Press v. United States*, 326 U.S. 1, 20 (1945).

[3] *Red Lion Broadcasting v. FCC*, 395 US 367, 390 (1969) (hereinafter *Red Lion*).

preventing undue concentration of economic power."[4] Moreover, "the greater the diversity of ownership in a particular area, the less chance there is that a single person or group can have an inordinate effect, in a political, editorial, or similar programming sense, on public opinion at the regional level."[5]

Thus, media ownership limits are concerned about promoting diversity of viewpoint, and preventing undue concentration of economic power and inordinate influence over public opinion. There are other goals of the media policy, as well, such as localism, racial or gender diversity, but this analysis focuses on the concentration issue.

STANDARDS

What is a concentrated market? The Department of Justice and Federal Trade Commission analyze markets on the basis of the market share of the firms that sell products in the market. They use the Herfindahl-Hirschmann Index (HHI) to analyze markets on the basis of the market shares of firms. When there are fewer than the equivalent of 10 equal sized competitors (an HHI of 1000), the market is considered concentrated. For the DOJ, mergers that increase concentration in these markets by as little as 10 percent (100 points) "raise significant competitive concerns." At this level of concentration, markets are considered oligopolies. Markets with the equivalent of 5.5-equal sized firms (HHI of 1800) are considered highly concentrated and mergers that increase concentration by as little as 3 percent (50 points) are deemed to be "likely to create or enhance market power."

Market structure is also frequently described in terms of the combined market share of the top four firms in the market. When the top four firms have more than 40 percent of the market, the market is considered to be an oligopoly.[6] When the top four firms have more than 60 percent of the market, it is considered a tight oligopoly.

For the purpose of this analysis, we focus on market structure.[7] We describe media markets in terms of the basic antitrust thresholds – whether they are concentrated or oligopolies and whether mergers would increase concentration in excess of the *Merger Guideline* standard. Of course, many

---

[4] *FCC v. Nat'l Citizens Committee for Broadcasting*, 436 U.S. 775, 780 (1978); Prometheus *Radio Project, et al. v. FCC*, 373 F.3d 372, 383 (3rd Cir. 2004) (citing *Nat'l Citizens Committee for Broadcasting*, 436 U.S. at 780).
[5] *Sinclair Broadcast Group, Inc. v. FCC*, 284 F.3d 148, 160 (D.C. Cir. 2002) (quoting FCC's 1999 Local Ownership Order, *Review of the Commission's Regulations Governing Television Broadcasting*, Report and Order, FCC 99-209 (rel. Aug. 6, 1999)).
[6] William G. Shepherd, *The Economics of Industrial Organization* (Englewood Cliffs, NJ: Prentice Hall, 1985), p. 4.
[7] See Mark Cooper, *Building a Reasonable Measure of Media Market Structure* (McGannon Communications Research Center, Fordham University, 2006).

believe that because media ownership affects democratic discourse so profoundly, the standard should be even higher.   Moreover, there is no guarantee that competitive markets achieve the other goals of the Communications Act, such as localism, or ensuring minority ownership.

METHOD

To analyze whether local news and information sources are concentrated, we first calculate the market share of the firms in a particular market.   For daily newspapers, we count the circulation of all the daily newspapers sold in the area and calculate what percentage of the total each paper gets.   We do the same for weeklies and calculate an average daily circulation. For TV, things are slightly more complicated, since news is only a small part of what they do.   Here we look at the ratings of each TV station during the news day parts. For radio, we count only those stations that list news, information, public affairs or talk as one of their top three formats.

What is the market we are talking about? TV broadcast signals can cover a large area, especially when they are distributed over cable systems. Radios cover a much smaller area. Newspapers tend to have circulation concentrated within a small area, which is why they have the name of a city or county in their title.   Weeklies generally serve even smaller areas. Economists refer to this as defining the geographic market. This analysis uses the radio market (Arbitron), which is generally associated with cities, as the basic market. It includes the daily and weekly newspapers that are based in that market and all the TV stations available in the area (Designated Market Area). Other types of media such as the Internet and magazines are included as well, but the merger analysis focuses on newspapers and TV.

How do we compare and combine different media in a market to determine market concentration?   How does the daily circulation of the newspaper compare to the average daily viewership of news shows?   Do people substitute one for the other? Even if they do, does a short spot on the TV morning news have the same impact as a long piece in the morning paper? Weights in this study are based on survey evidence about which media influence public opinion. The evidence shows that the most important sources for local news and information are local TV stations and local daily newspapers, followed by radio and weeklies. The survey reveals the relative importance,[8] or "weight," that the public places on these local news sources, as follows: Television = .33, Newspapers = .32, Radio = .11, Weeklies = .10.

Market shares for the purpose of estimating market concentration are then measured as follows:

---

[8] See Mark Cooper, *Media Usage: Traditional Outlets Still Dominate Local News and Information* (Washington, D.C.: Media and Democracy Coalition, 2006).

WITHIN MEDIA = AUDIENCE

ACROSS MEDIA = AUDIENCE X WEIGHT.

Which Cities are analyzed? This study focuses on the ten sample cities that the FCC chose to be representative of the nation. The subsequent studies focus on states. To assess the current status of local media markets and the potential impact of lifting the cross media ban, we have analyzed three cities in the state to cover the range of possibilities: the largest city in the state; the smallest city in the state in which cross-ownership would be allowed under the FCC rules, and the state capitol, which plays a special roll in policymaking in the state.

What potential mergers were analyzed? We focus on newspaper-TV mergers. The FCC's rules that were remanded gave "no questions asked" approval to all mergers in all markets where minimal safe harbor conditions held. Under these circumstances and given market pressures, we would expect each of the major firms to try to build the biggest conglomerate possible.

To model the potential impact of the green-lighted merger, we consider two scenarios. In the 1st + 1st scenario, the largest firm merges with the largest available cross media firm. The 2nd largest unmerged firm merges with the second largest cross media firm etc. In the 1st + 2nd scenario the mergers are flipped. The largest firm is assumed to merge with the second largest cross media firm available, while the second largest firm mergers with the largest cross media firm available. In both cases, where the largest firm already owns a newspaper and a TV station, we assume it buys a second or third TV station. We assume mergers take place until all significant daily newspapers have merged with TV stations (papers with more than 5 percent of the total market).[9] Under a "no questions asked" approach, there is nothing the agency could do to stop the merger wave. We do not consider additional TV-TV mergers, which also would have been allowed by the FCC's remanded rules and would concentrate markets even more.

Why do you analyze mergers that could happen? There are several reasons. First, when a major change in ownership rules is proposed that could fundamentally alter market structure, it is irresponsible to not examine what could happen.

Second, the experience over the last decade with similar changes suggests substantial merger activity will take place.[10] In less than a decade after the repeal of the Financial and Syndication Rules, the broadcasters went

---

[9] We assume that the largest merger in each scenario takes place first and only the top two mergers are flipped in the second scenario.

[10] These trends are analyzed in Mark Cooper, *Media Ownership and Democracy in the Digital Information Age* (Palo Alto, Stanford Law School Center for Internet and Society, 2003) Chapter VI.

from owning about one-fifth of the shows in prime time to four-fifths. In less than a decade after the lifting of the national cap on radio, the top four firms went form owning about 160 stations to owning over 2,000. In less than a decade after the relaxation of the duopoly rule, over 75 duopolies were created.

Third, in looking at media outlets, it is clear that many properties would be in play. The TV stations that are not owned and operated by the major networks would certainly be targets. Properties owned by Tribune, Belo, Hearst, Media General and Fox would be in play, since all of the parent corporations are already in both the TV and the newspaper business. Only the network-owned and operated stations (O&O's) in the largest markets might be more difficult acquisition targets.   However, with increased pressure from a wave of combinations, these stations too might find it hard to resist assimilation into a cross-owned enterprise.

Fourth, many of the mergers could take place by swapping properties, rather than with buyouts. This would diminish the amount of cash that would be needed to make the deals.

Finally, the issue of mergers and major structural changes in media markets that they could cause is a long-term concern. The question is not which mergers will take place the week, month or year after the policy change, but how it will evolve over a period of years.

In summary, the possibility that a substantial amount of merger activity would take place is high. It is incumbent upon policymakers and the public to understand what could happen in these very important markets.

RESULTS: FCC SAMPLE CITIES

This section describes the impact of the merger scenarios on the cities that the FCC studied in detail in its Media Ownership Order. Exhibit 1 shows the current status of the media markets in terms of the HHI and four firm concentration ratios. Exhibit 2 shows the impact of the mergers on media markets in terms of the increase in the Department of Justice/Federal Trade Commission (DOJ/FTC) market-wide concentration index (HHI) and the market shares of the dominant firms, i.e. how the merger increases the market share controlled by one company in a single city. Exhibit 2 also summarizes the effects of both merger scenarios in terms of the *Merger Guidelines* and leading firm market shares.

Exhibit 1: Current Status of Media Markets

CITY	DOJ/FTC HHI				FOUR FIRM CONCENTRATION			
	Papers	TV	Radio	Combined	Papers	TV	Radio	Combined
New York	1937	1786	3053	1050	83%	77%	95%	54%
Kansas City	7121	2440	5709	1790	90%	95%	100%	75%
Birmingham	7989	1897	3639	1914	99%	80%	100%	70%
Little Rock	7988	2951	10000	2221	99%	100%	100%	82%
Lancaster	9506	3335	3141	2717	100%	89%	100%	84%
Burlington	5070	2792	10000	1831	99%	98%	100%	75%
Myrtle Beach	9120	5103	10000	3192	100%	100%	100%	87%
Terre Haute	4532	4356	1000	1912	99%	100%	100%	81%
Charlottesville	9983	3967	5458	2538	100%	98%	100%	87%
Altoona	1000	3883	8384	2466	100%	100%	100%	91%

Exhibit 2: Impact of Newspaper/TV Mergers

City	Scenario	Market HHI		Post Merger Status	Merger Guidelines Threshold		Leading Firm Market Share			
		Before	After		1st Merger	2nd Merger	Four-Firm CR		Top Firm	
							Before	After	Before	After
New York	1 + 1 Scenario:	979	1923	Highly Conc.	Violated	Violated	57%	80%	19%	29%
	1 + 2 Scenario:	979	1911	Highly Conc.	Violated	Violated	57%	80%	19%	29%
Kansas City	1 + 1 Scenario:	1791	3022	Highly Conc.	Violated	Violated	75%	85%	33%	51%
	1 + 2 Scenario:	1791	2765	Highly Conc.	Violated	Violated	75%	85%	33%	47%
Birmingham	1 + 1 Scenario:	1914	2887	Highly Conc.	Violated	Violated	70%	80%	38%	50%
	1 + 2 Scenario:	1914	2847	Highly Conc.	Violated	Violated	70%	80%	38%	50%
Little Rock	1 + 1 Scenario:	2221	3266	Highly Conc.	Violated	Violated	82%	89%	39%	59%
	1 + 2 Scenario:	2221	3810	Highly Conc.	Violated	Violated	82%	89%	39%	51%
Lancaster	1 + 1 Scenario:	2717	4723	Highly Conc.	Violated	Violated	84%	89%	45%	68%
	1 + 2 Scenario:	2717	3635	Highly Conc.	Violated	Violated	84%	89%	45%	56%
Burlington	1 + 1 Scenario:	1831	3260	Highly Conc.	Violated	Violated	75%	85%	34%	51%
	1 + 2 Scenario:	1831	2971	Highly Conc.	Violated	Violated	75%	85%	34%	44%
Myrtle Beach	1 + 1 Scenario:	3192	5869	Highly Conc.	Violated	Violated	90%	90%	48%	76%
	1 + 2 Scenario:	3192	4274	Highly Conc.	Violated	Violated	90%	90%	48%	59%
Terre Haute	1 + 1 Scenario:	1912	3623	Highly Conc.	Violated	Violated	81%	89%	32%	53%
	1 + 2 Scenario:	1912	3466	Highly Conc.	Violated	Violated	81%	89%	32%	49%
Charlottesville	1 + 1 Scenario:	2538	4794	Highly Conc.	Violated	NA (one daily)	87%	90%	37%	68%
	1 + 2 Scenario:	2538	3559	Highly Conc.	Violated	NA (one daily)	87%	90%	37%	51%
Altoona	1 + 1 Scenario:	2466	4305	Highly Conc.	Violated	NA (one daily)	91%	91%	36%	62%
	1 + 2 Scenario:	2466	4068	Highly Conc.	Violated	NA (one daily)	91%	91%	36%	57%

New York City

Current Status: As shown in Exhibit 1, in New York the HHI for newspapers and radio is well into the highly concentrated range. TV is concentrated. The overall market is just below the concentrated threshold. The largest four firms in each of the individual media have a market share of 75 percent to over 90 percent, making them all tight oligopolies. For the overall media market, the four firm concentration ratio is below 60 percent. Thus, when we combine all of the media outlets into a combined media market, we find that the overall market is right at the edge of the danger zone of concentration and tight oligopoly...

Impact of Mergers: Even in New York, the largest market in the country and one of the least concentrated, any cross media merger involving the top newspaper and TV firms would increase concentration in excess of the DOJ/FTC *Merger Guidelines*. As shown in Exhibit 2, under both of the scenarios considered, New York would become a concentrated, tight oligopoly, with the HHI rising from just over 1000 to just over 1900. The four firm concentration ratio would increase from under 60 percent to 80 percent.

The change in the New York Market that would result from a wave of newspaper-TV mergers is extremely troubling. In the current situation we find a leading firm and a handful of smaller, but closely matched competitors. Cross-media mergers would allow a small group of firms to dominate. The top three firms could increase their market share from just under one-third of the market to over two-thirds. The remaining firms in the market would be much smaller. If the dominant firms added more TV stations to their holdings, which would be allowed under the FCC approach, the situation would become even more dangerous.

Kansas City

Current Status: As shown in Exhibit 1, in Kansas City the HHI for all the media is well into the highly concentrated range. The overall market is just below the highly concentrated threshold. The largest four firms have in each of the individual media has a market share of 90 to 100 percent, making them all tight oligopolies. For the overall media market, the four firm concentration ratio is just below 75 percent. Thus, when we combine all of the media outlets into a combined media market, we find a tight oligopoly, close to the highly concentrated threshold.

Impact of Mergers: Any cross media merger involving the top newspaper and TV firms would increase concentration in excess of the DOJ/FTC *Merger Guidelines*. As shown in Exhibit 2, under both of the scenarios considered, Kansas City would become a highly concentrated, tight oligopoly, with the HHI rising from just under 1800 to over 2500. The four firm concentration ratio would increase from 75 percent to 85 percent.

The leading firm would increase its market share from one-third of the market to about one-half. The number two firm would be about one-third the size of the dominant firm. If the dominant firms added more TV stations to their holdings, which would be allowed under the FCC approach, the situation would become even more dangerous.

Birmingham

Current Status: As shown in Exhibit 1, in Birmingham the HHI for newspapers and radio is well into the highly concentrated range. TV and the overall market are highly concentrated, as well, although closer to the threshold. The largest four firms in each of the individual media have a market share of 80 percent to 100 percent, making them all tight oligopolies. For the overall media market, the four firm concentration ratio is 70 percent, making it a tight oligopoly as well.

Impact of Mergers: Any cross media merger involving the top newspaper and TV firms would increase concentration in excess of the DOJ/FTC *Merger Guidelines*. As shown in Exhibit 2, under both of the scenarios considered, Birmingham suffers a major increase in concentration, with the HHI rising from just over 1900 to just almost 2900. The four firm concentration ratio increases from 70 to 80 percent. The leading firm grows from 38 percent to 50 percent. The second ranked firm would be less than one half the size. If the dominant firms added more TV stations to their holdings, which would be allowed under the FCC approach, the situation would become even more dangerous.

Little Rock

Current Status: As shown in Exhibit 1, the HHI for each individual media outlet indicates a highly concentrated market. The combined media market is highly concentrated as well. Exhibit 2 shows the largest four firms have a combined market share of 90 percent to 100 percent, making them all tight oligopolies. When we combine all of the media outlets into a combined media market, we find that the overall market is highly concentrated and a tight oligopoly.

Impact of Mergers: As shown in Exhibit 2, under both of the scenarios considered, allowing cross-ownership in this market would have a large impact, with the HHI rising from about 2200 to a range of 3200 to 3800, an increase of 1000 - 1600 points.

The four firm concentration ratio increases from 82 to 89 percent. The leading firm's market share would rise from just under 40 percent to almost over 50 percent if cross-ownership were allowed. The second ranked firm in the market would be much smaller, with a market share of about 15 percent. Together, the top two firms would have almost three quarters of the market. If the dominant firms added more TV stations to their holdings, which would be allowed under the FCC approach, the situation would become even more dangerous.

Lancaster

Current Status: As shown in Exhibit 1, the HHI for each individual media outlet indicates a highly concentrated market. The combined media market is highly concentrated as well. Exhibit 2 shows the largest four firms have a combined market share of 90 percent to 100 percent, making them all tight oligopolies. When we combine all of the media outlets into a combined media market, we find that the overall market is highly concentrated and a tight oligopoly.

Impact of Mergers: As shown in Exhibit 3, under both of the scenarios considered, allowing cross-ownership in this market would have a large impact, with the HHI rising from about 2700 to a range of 3600 to 4700, an increase of 1000 - 2000 points.

The four firm concentration ratio increases from 84 to 89 percent. The leading firm's market share would rise from just under 45 percent to 56 - 68 percent if cross-ownership were allowed. The second ranked firm in the market would be much smaller, with a market share of about 10 to 20 percent. Together, the top two firms would have almost three quarters of the market. If the dominant firms added more TV stations to their holdings, which would be allowed under the FCC approach, the situation would become even more dangerous.

Burlington

Current Status: As shown in Exhibit 1, the HHI for each individual media outlet indicates a highly concentrated market. The combined media market is highly concentrated as well. Exhibit 2 shows the largest four firms have a combined market share of 90 percent to 100 percent, making them all tight oligopolies. When we combine all of the media outlets into a combined media market, we find that the overall market is highly concentrated and a tight oligopoly.

Impact of Mergers: As shown in Exhibit 3, under both of the scenarios considered, allowing cross-ownership in this market would have a large impact, with the HHI rising from about 1800 to about 3000, an increase of 1000 points.

The four firm concentration ratio increases from 75 to 85 percent. The leading firm's market share would rise from just under 34 percent to 45 - 50 percent if cross-ownership were allowed. The second ranked firm in the market would be much smaller, with a market share of about 25 to 30 percent. Together, the top two firms would have almost three quarters of the market. If the dominant firms added more TV stations to their holdings, which would be allowed under the FCC approach, the situation would become even more dangerous.

Myrtle Beach

Current Status: As shown in Exhibit 1, the HHI for each individual media outlet indicates a highly concentrated market. The combined media market is highly concentrated as well. Exhibit 2 shows the largest four firms have a combined market share of 90 percent to 100 percent, making them all tight oligopolies. When we combine all of the media outlets into a combined media market, we find that the overall market is highly concentrated and a tight oligopoly.

Impact of Mergers: As shown in Exhibit 2, under both of the scenarios considered, allowing cross-ownership in this market would have a large impact, with the HHI rising from about 3200 to a range of 4200 to 5800, an increase of 1000 - 2600 points.

The four firm concentration ratio is and would remain about 90 percent. The leading firm's market share would rise from just under half the market to 59 – 76 percent if cross-ownership were allowed. The second ranked firm in the market would be much smaller, with a market share less than half the size of the dominant firm. Together, the top two firms would have almost over four-fifths of the market.

Terre Haute

Current Status: As shown in Exhibit 1, the HHI for each individual media outlet indicates a highly concentrated market. The combined media market is highly concentrated as well. Exhibit 2 shows the largest four firms have a combined market share of 99 percent to 100 percent, making them all tight oligopolies. When we combine all of the media outlets into a combined media market, we find that the overall market is highly concentrated and a tight oligopoly.

Impact of Mergers: As shown in Exhibit 2, under both of the scenarios considered, allowing cross-ownership in this market would have a large impact, with the HHI rising from about 1900 to around 3500, an increase of 1600 points.

The four firm concentration ratio would rise from about 80 percent to about 90 percent. The leading firm's market share would rise just over 30 percent to around 50 percent, if cross-ownership were allowed. The second ranked firm in the market would be much smaller, with a market share less than half the size of the dominant firm. Together, the top two firms would have almost over three-quarters of the market.

Charlottesville

Current Status: As shown in Exhibit 1, the HHI for each individual media outlet indicates a highly concentrated market. The combined media market is highly concentrated as well. Exhibit 2 shows the largest four firms have a combined market share of 98 percent to 100 percent, making them all tight oligopolies. When we combine all of the media outlets into a combined media market, we find that the overall market is highly concentrated and a tight oligopoly.

Impact of Mergers: Cross-ownership mergers would not be allowed.

Altoona

Current Status: As shown in Exhibits 1 and 2, Altoona is highly concentrated in each of the individual media and across the entire media market. Four firm concentration ratios are 100 percent for each medium and the overall market is over 90 percent. A single firm dominates the newspaper market.

Impact of Mergers: Because of the dominant position of the newspaper and two dominant television stations, any single merger violates the *Guidelines* by a wide margin. In both merger scenarios, the single combination of the dominant newspaper with a TV station yields an increase in the HHI of over 1500 points. Mergers would result in a market that would be dominated by a single entity with a market share greater than 50 percent. The number two firm would be half the size of the leading newspaper-TV combination.

RESULTS: OTHER CITIES

Our study of the small number of sample cities examined by the FCC suggests that that middle and smaller markets are highly concentrated and would be affected severely by newspaper-TV mergers. The larger markets are much less concentrated, but would also be adversely affected by these mergers. Ten of the top twenty markets were included in the FCC sample cities and the states studied. To explore these market, where there might be some uncertainty about the impact of newspaper-TV merger, this study presents the results of the merger analysis for all of the top twenty markets. This set of markets was also identified in our earlier analysis as demanding closer scrutiny in deciding how to set merger policy.

LARGE MARKETS

Exhibit 3 presents the HHIs and four firm concentration ratios for each of the media as well as the combined media in all 20 markets. Newspapers and radio are highly concentrated, tight oligopolies even in these large markets. The TV market tends to be concentrated, tight oligopoly. Three of the combined markets are just below the threshold for a concentrated market. Three of the markets are well above the threshold for a highly concentrated market (above 2000). The remainder are in the concentrated range. For the four firm concentration ratios we find five markets in the fifties, nine in the sixties, six above seventy.

Exhibit 3: Current Status of Media Markets

City	DOJ/FTC HHI				Four Firm Concentration			
	Papers	TV	Radio	Combined	Papers	TV	Radio	Combined
New York	1937	1786	3053	979	83	77	95	53
Los Angeles	2827	1681	2448	980	88	74	77	54
Chicago	2850	1656	2751	1041	90	71	92	58
Philadelphia	4142	2203	4879	1245	97	87	100	62
San Francisco	3229	1684	3543	1156	97	76	100	59
Boston	3257	2166	5376	1165	91	84	100	61
Dallas	4361	1652	3944	1590	94	77	100	64
Washington D.C.	2712	1947	2174	2068	99	76	100	67
Atlanta	2172	1960	5996	2227	92	73	100	68
Detroit	2959	2497	8694	1183	99	88	100	63
Houston	9199	1569	6859	1519	82	88	100	60
Seattle	2066	2762	5139	934	81	88	100	51
Tampa-St. Pete	2609	1774	6527	1794	69	75	100	73
Minneapolis	4612	2066	8970	1636	95	89	100	72
Cleveland	6251	2006	8970	1636	98	88	100	74
Phoenix	6753	1772	3839	1511	99	76	100	71
Miami	5207	1621	4224	1229	99	73	100	64
Denver	4250	1745	6183	1481	97	76	100	69
Sacramento	6915	2531	3793	1799	95	91	94	83
Orlando	9175	2525	9999	2297	97	91	100	82

There is also a tendency even within the top twenty for the smaller markets to be more concentrated. Thus, the top five market have an average HHI of just under 1100. The bottom five markets have an average HHI over 1600. The average four firm concentration ratio among the top five markets is 57 percent. The average among the bottom five is 72 percent. The earlier findings that concentration levels were much higher in the middle ranked cities (state capitols and FCC sample cities) is consistent with this finding.

Exhibit 4 presents the results of the merger scenario analysis as described in Study 23. With the exception of Los Angeles and Seattle, all of the post-merger markets are highly concentrated. In Los Angeles, the post-merger markets are close to the highly concentrated threshold. In Seattle, the post-merger markets are well into the concentrated range. In all cases, the individual mergers violate the *Merger Guidelines*. Except where the four firm concentration ratios are already above 70 percent, we observe large increases as a result of the modeled mergers, 15 to 25 percentage points. Post-merger, the leading firm tends to have between one-third and one-half of the market, with the increase generally falling in the 10 to 20 percent range.

Exhibit 5 presents the results of analyses of a number of cities of various sizes across the nation. A dozen states were chosen and three cities in each state were analyzed – the largest city in the state, the state capitol and the smallest city that would have been impacted by newspaper-TV cross ownership mergers. Every merger modeled violates the guidelines. With the exception of the very largest cities, discussed above, markets are concentrated or highly concentrated. The smaller markets and many of the state capitols are very highly concentrated. The largest firm in most of the markets would have a dominant position, with a post merger market share of around 50% or higher. The four firm concentration ratios are well up into the tight oligopoly range.

CONCLUSION

Mergers between newspapers and TV stations in the same market are front and center in the ongoing media ownership proceeding at the Federal Communications Commission for several reasons.

- Television and newspapers are the two most important sources of local news and information by far.

- The ban on such mergers was the longest standing of the rules that the Commission is considering.

- The Commission proposed the most radical change in this rule – allowing newspaper-TV combinations in virtually every city in America.

- In rejecting the Commission's cross-media limits, the Court devoted a great deal of attention to the Commission's faulty reasoning and flawed analysis of media markets.

This paper has shown that mergers between newspapers and TV stations in the same market pose a grave threat to democratic discourse.

- In antitrust terms, these mergers result in increases in market concentration that raise significant competitive concerns and are likely to create or enhance market power.

- In terms of the Communications Act and First Amendment jurisprudence, the newspaper-TV combinations that result dominate the local market raising concerns about undue economic concentration and inordinate influence over public opinion.

Historical evidence and logic suggest that many of the mergers analyzed in scenarios considered would take place. Policymakers and the public need to be aware of these dire consequences should the ban on newspaper-TV combinations be lifted.

Exhibit 4: Impact of Newspaper/TV Mergers: Large Markets

| City/Scenario | Market HHI | | Post Merger Status | Merger Guideline Threshold | | Leading Firm Share | | | |
| | Before | After | | 1st Merger | 2nd Merger | 4 Firm Concentration | | Top Firm | |
						Before	After	Before	After
NEW YORK									
1 + 1 Scenario:	979	1821	Highly Conc.	Violated	Violated	53%	79%	19%	29%
1 + 2 Scenario:	979	1675	Highly Conc.	Violated	Violated	53%	79%	19%	23%
LOS ANGELES									
1 + 1 Scenario:	980	1788	Concentrated	Violated	Violated	54%	80%	16%	26%
1 + 2 Scenario:	980	1756	Concentrated	Violated	Violated	54%	80%	16%	24%
CHICAGO									
1 + 1 Scenario:	1041	2090	Highly Conc.	Violated	Violated	58%	75%	18%	33%
1 + 2 Scenario:	1041	1886	Highly Conc.	Violated	Violated	58%	75%	18%	29%
PHILADELPHIA									
1 + 1 Scenario:	1245	2297	Highly Conc.	Violated	Violated	62%	79%	25%	41%
1 + 2 Scenario:	1245	2082	Highly Conc.	Violated	Violated	62%	75%	25%	34%
SAN FRANCISCO									
1 + 1 Scenario:	1156	1926	Highly Conc.	Violated	Violated	59%	83%	23%	30%
1 + 2 Scenario:	1156	1924	Highly Conc.	Violated	Violated	59%	83%	23%	30%
BOSTON									
1 + 1 Scenario:	1165	2108	Highly Conc.	Violated	Violated	61%	77%	24%	38%
1 + 2 Scenario:	1165	2005	Highly Conc.	Violated	Violated	61%	74%	24%	34%
DALLAS									
1 + 1 Scenario:	1590	2525	Highly Conc.	Violated	Violated	64%	85%	34%	43%
1 + 2 Scenario:	1590	2020	Highly Conc.	Violated	Violated	64%	73%	34%	39%
WASH. D. C.									
1 + 1 Scenario:	2068	3054	Highly Conc.	Violated	Violated	72%	84%	47%	52%
1 + 2 Scenario:	2068	3022	Highly Conc.	Violated	Violated	70%	84%	47%	51%
ATLANTA									
1 + 1 Scenario:	2277	2683	Highly Conc.	Violated	Violated	67%	83%	44%	49%
1 + 2 Scenario:	2277	2664	Highly Conc.	Violated	Violated	67%	76%	44%	49%
DETROIT									
1 + 1 Scenario:	1183	2307	Highly Conc.	Violated	Violated	62%	85%	17%	34%
1 + 2 Scenario:	1183	2295	Highly Conc.	Violated	Violated	63%	85%	17%	24%

EXHIBIT 4 (continued): Impact of Newspaper/TV Mergers: Large Markets

City/Scenario	Market HHI		Post Merger Status	Merger Guideline Threshold		Leading Firm Share			
						4 Firm Concentration		Top Firm	
	Before	After		1st Merger	2nd Merger	Before	After	Before	After
HOUSTON									
1 + 1 Scenario:	1519	2262	Highly Conc.	Violated	Violated	63%	83%	32%	44%
1 + 2 Scenario:	1519	2163	Highly Conc.	Violated	Violated	63%	79%	32%	42%
SEATTLE									
1 + 1 Scenario:	934	1774	Concentrated	Violated	Violated	51%	75%	17%	32%
1 + 2 Scenario:	934	1682	Concentrated	Violated	Violated	51%	75%	17%	26%
TAMPA-ST. PETE									
1 + 1 Scenario:	1794	3381	Highly Conc.	Violated	Violated	73%	84%	31%	56%
1 + 2 Scenario:	1794	2581	Highly Conc.	Violated	Violated	73%	84%	31%	34%
MINNEAPOLIS									
1 + 1 Scenario:	1665	2890	Highly Conc.	Violated	Violated	72%	98%	23%	37%
1 + 2 Scenario:	1665	2889	Highly Conc.	Violated	Violated	72%	94%	23%	35%
CLEVELAND									
1 + 1 Scenario:	1636	2585	Highly Conc.	Violated	Violated	68%	83%	34%	45%
1 + 2 Scenario:	1636	2570	Highly Conc.	Violated	Violated	68%	83%	34%	45%
PHOENIX									
1 + 1 Scenario:	1511	2750	Highly Conc.	Violated	Violated	71%	87%	28%	44%
1 + 2 Scenario:	1511	2629	Highly Conc.	Violated	Violated	71%	82%	28%	40%
MIAMI									
1 + 1 Scenario:	1229	1981	Highly Conc.	Violated	Violated	63%	81%	21%	34%
1 + 2 Scenario:	1229	1977	Highly Conc.	Violated	Violated	63%	79%	21%	34%
DENVER									
1 + 1 Scenario:	1481	2484	Highly Conc.	Violated	Violated	69%	85%	25%	37%
1 + 2 Scenario:	1481	2472	Highly Conc.	Violated	Violated	69%	81%	25%	34%
SACRAMENTO									
1 + 1 Scenario:	1799	3157	Highly Conc.	Violated	Violated	75%	82%	33%	53%
1 + 2 Scenario:	1799	2797	Highly Conc.	Violated	Violated	75%	82%	33%	47%
ORLANDO									
1 + 1 Scenario:	2297	3769	Highly Conc.	Violated	Violated	82%	89%	41%	59%
1 + 2 Scenario:	2297	3132	Highly Conc.	Violated	Violated	82%	88%	41%	51%

Exhibit 5: Summary of Impact of Newspaper/TV Mergers

State/City/Scenario	Market HHI		Final Post Merger Market Status	Merger Guideline Threshold		4 Firm Concentration		Leading Firm Share Top Firm	
	Before	After		1st Merger	2nd Merger	Before	After	Before	After
ALASKA									
1 + 1 Scenario:									
Anchorage	2412	4508	Highly Conc.	Violated	NA (one daily)	81%	85%	39%	66%
Juneau	1976	3853	Highly Conc.	Violated	Violated	79%	88%	30%	58%
Fairbanks	3221	5011	Highly Conc.	Violated	NA (one daily)	83%	87%	54%	70%
1 + 2 Scenario:									
Anchorage	2412	3273	Highly Conc.	Violated	NA (one daily)	81%	85%	39%	50%
Juneau	1976	3162	Highly Conc.	Violated	Violated	79%	88%	30%	37%
Fairbanks	3221	4006	Highly Conc.	Violated	NA (one daily)	83%	87%	54%	61%
ARKANSAS									
1 + 1 Scenario:									
Little Rock	2221	3810	Highly Conc.	Violated	Violated	82%	89%	39%	59%
Fayetteville	1294	2357	Highly Conc.	Violated	NA (one daily)	66%	89%	18%	36%
Fort Smith	1724	2887	Highly Conc.	Violated	Violated	78%	90%	28%	56%
1 + 2 Scenario:									
Little Rock	2221	3263	Highly Conc.	Violated	Violated	82%	89%	39%	51%
Fayetteville	1294	2350	Highly Conc.	Violated	NA (one daily)	66%	89%	18%	25%
Fort Smith	1724	2816	Highly Conc.	Violated	Violated	78%	88%	28%	47%
CALIFORNIA									
1 + 1 Scenario:									
Los Angeles	980	1788	Concentrated	Violated	Violated	54%	80%	16%	26%
Sacramento	1799	3157	Highly Conc.	Violated	Violated	75%	82%	33%	53%
Palm Springs	2401	3762	Highly Conc.	Violated	Violated	75%	84%	44%	59%
1 + 2 Scenario:									
Los Angeles	980	1756	Concentrated	Violated	Violated	54%	80%	16%	24%
Sacramento	1799	2797	Highly Conc.	Violated	Violated	75%	82%	33%	47%
Palm Springs	2401	3279	Highly Conc.	Violated	Violated	75%	84%	44%	53%

Exhibit 5 (continued): Summary of Impact of Newspaper/TV Mergers

State/City/Scenario	Market HHI		Final Post Merger Market Status	Merger Guideline Threshold		Leading Firm Share			
						4 Firm Concentration		Top Firm	
	Before	After		1st Merger	2nd Merger	Before	After	Before	After
FLORIDA									
1 + 1 Scenario:									
Miami	1229	1981	Highly Conc.	Violated	Violated	63%	81%	21%	34%
Tallahassee	2703	5081	Highly Conc.	Violated	NA (one daily)	81%	84%	43%	71%
Panama City	2894	4937	Highly Conc.	Violated	NA (one daily)	91%	91%	44%	67%
1 + 2 Scenario:									
Miami	1221	1977	Highly Conc.	Violated	Violated	58%	79%	21%	34%
Tallahassee	2703	3174	Highly Conc.	Violated	NA (one daily)	81%	86%	43%	49%
Panama City	2894	4732	Highly Conc.	Violated	NA (one daily)	91%	91%	44%	65%
MAINE									
1 + 1 Scenario:									
Portland	2796	4292	Highly Conc.	Violated	NA (one daily)	86%	88%	47%	63%
Augusta	2416	3885	Highly Conc.	Violated	Violated	82%	88%	43%	59%
Bangor	2580	4546	Highly Conc.	Violated	NA (one daily)	88%	89%	42%	65%
1 + 2 Scenario:									
Portland	2796	4039	Highly Conc.	Violated	NA (one daily)	86%	88%	47%	61%
Augusta	2416	3674	Highly Conc.	Violated	Violated	82%	89%	43%	56%
Bangor	2580	3778	Highly Conc.	Violated	NA (one daily)	88%	89%	42%	56%
MICHIGAN									
1 + 1 Scenario:									
Detroit	1183	2307	Highly Conc.	Violated	Violated	62%	85%	17%	34%
Lansing	2401	3863	Highly Conc.	Violated	NA (one daily)	81%	85%	42%	59%
Battle Creek	2371	3847	Highly Conc.	Violated	NA (one daily)	85%	90%	41%	59%
1 + 2 Scenario:									
Detroit	1183	2295	Highly Conc.	Violated	Violated	63%	85%	17%	24%
Lansing	2401	3817	Highly Conc.	Violated	NA (one daily)	85%	90%	42%	59%
Battle Creek	2371	3654	Highly Conc.	Violated	NA (one daily)	85%	92%	41%	57%

Exhibit 5 (continued): Summary of Impact of Newspaper/TV Mergers

State/City/Scenario	Market HHI		Final Post Merger Market Status	Merger Guideline Threshold		Leading Firm Share			
						4 Firm Concentration		Top Firm	
	Before	After		1st Merger	2nd Merger	Before	After	Before	After
MONTANA									
1 + 1 Scenario:									
Billings	2963	5559	Highly Conc.	Violated	NA (one daily)	91%	91%	44%	74%
Helena	3292	5693	Highly Conc.	Violated	NA (one daily)	90%	90%	51%	74%
Great Falls	2900	5448	Highly Conc.	Violated	NA (one daily)	87%	91%	44%	73%
1 + 2 Scenario:									
Billings	2963	4024	Highly Conc.	Violated	NA (one daily)	91%	91%	44%	56%
Helena	3292	4586	Highly Conc.	Violated	NA (one daily)	90%	90%	51%	63%
Great Falls	2900	3688	Highly Conc.	Violated	NA (one daily)	87%	91%	44%	53%
OHIO									
1+1 Scenario									
Cleveland	1636	2585	Highly Conc.	Violated	Violated	68%	83%	34%	53%
Columbus	2622	3260	Highly Conc.	Violated	Violated	75%	89%	48%	52%
Toledo	2474	4482	Highly Conc.	Violated	Violated	83%	89%	42%	65%
1 + 2 Scenario:									
Cleveland	1636	2570	Highly Conc.	Violated	Violated	68%	83%	34%	45%
Columbus	2622	2975	Highly Conc.	Violated	Violated	75%	78%	48%	51%
Toledo	2474	3632	Highly Conc.	Violated	Violated	83%	89%	42%	53%
OREGON									
1 + 1 Scenario:									
Portland	1531	2572	Highly Conc.	Violated	Violated	64%	83%	32%	45%
Eugene	1446	2463	Highly Conc.	Violated	NA (one daily)	64%	71%	30%	47%
Medford	2849	4936	Highly Conc.	Violated	NA (one daily)	85%	89%	47%	69%
1 + 2 Scenario:									
Portland	1531	2374	Highly Conc.	Violated	Violated	64%	83%	32%	42%
Eugene	1446	2006	Highly Conc.	Violated	NA (one daily)	64%	71%	30%	39%
Medford	2849	3672	Highly Conc.	Violated	NA (one daily)	85%	89%	47%	55%

Exhibit 5 (continued): Summary of Impact of Newspaper/TV Mergers

State/City/Scenario	Market HHI		Final Post Merger Market Status	Merger Guideline Threshold		Leading Firm Share			
						4 Firm Concentration		Top Firm	
	Before	After		1st Merger	2nd Merger	Before	After	Before	After
PENNSYLVANIA									
1 + 1 Scenario:									
Philadelphia	1245	2297	Highly Conc.	Violated	Violated	62%	79%	25%	41%
Harrisburg	2357	4246	Highly Conc.	Violated	Violated	79%	89%	39%	62%
Erie	2362	3743	Highly Conc.	Violated	NA (One Daily)	85%	89%	36%	62%
1 + 2 Scenario:									
Philadelphia	1245	2082	Highly Conc.	Violated	Violated	62%	75%	25%	34%
Harrisburg	2357	3434	Highly Conc.	Violated	Violated	79%	89%	39%	50%
Erie	2362	3693	Highly Conc.	Violated	NA (One Daily)	85%	89%	36%	57%
TEXAS									
1+1 Scenario									
Dallas	1590	2525	Highly Conc.	Violated	Violated	64%	85%	34%	43%
Austin	2329	4081	Highly Conc.	Violated	NA (one daily)	83%	88%	40%	62%
Abilene	2728	4988	Highly Conc.	Violated	NA (one daily)	88%	90%	45%	65%
1 + 2 Scenario:									
Dallas	1590	2020	Highly Conc.	Violated	Violated	64%	73%	34%	39%
Austin	2329	3354	Highly Conc.	Violated	NA (one daily)	83%	87%	40%	53%
Abilene	2728	4026	Highly Conc.	Violated	NA (one daily)	88%	90%	45%	60%
VIRGINIA									
1 + 1 Scenario:									
Northern VA/DC	2068	3054	Concentrated	Violated	Violated	72%	84%	47%	52%
Richmond	2200	3563	Highly Conc.	Violated	Violated	77%	84%	41%	57%
Norfolk	1541	2721	Highly Conc.	Violated	NA (one daily)	70%	84%	30%	44%
1 + 2 Scenario:									
Northern VA/DC	2068	3022	Concentrated	Violated	Violated	70%	84%	47%	51%
Richmond	2068	3054	Highly Conc.	Violated	Na (one daily)	77%	84%	41%	52%
Norfolk	1541	2660	Highly Conc.	Violated	NA (one daily)	70%	84%	30%	42%
WASHINGTON									
1 + 1 Scenario:									
Seattle	934	1774	Concentrated	Violated	Violated	51%	75%	17%	32%
Spokane	3214	4251	Highly Conc.	Violated	Violated	85%	90%	53%	61%
Yakima	2088	3357	Highly Conc.	Violated	NA (one daily)	75%	79%	40%	56%
1 + 2 Scenario:									
Seattle	934	1682	Concentrated	Violated	Violated	51%	75%	17%	26%
Spokane	3214	4251	Highly Conc.	Violated	Violated	85%	90%	53%	61%
Yakima	2088	2984	Highly Conc.	Violated	NA (one daily)	75%	79%	45%	51%

STUDY 27:
THE IMPACT OF EASING MULTIPLE STATION OWNERSHIP LIMITS ON MEDIA MARKETS

MARK COOPER

INTRODUCTION

The previous analyses have included only newspaper-television cross ownership mergers. The FCC also relaxed the limitation on TV-TV mergers. Its order would have allowed a single owner to hold three licenses in large markets and it expanded the number of markets in which owners would be allowed to hold two licenses. However, at the same time, it continued to ban mergers between two stations ranked in the top four, based on audience shares.

It is also not clear how the Commission should define the market for purposes of evaluating the effects of TV-TV mergers. Although the *Sinclair* court criticized the FCC's decision for not treating voices consistently, it did not say the FCC could not make the case that TV-TV mergers should be considered in the context of the television market only.

As a result, the analysis of the impact of TV-TV mergers becomes quite complex, depending on what one assumes about the policies that will govern the mergers and the market context in which it is viewed. There are three variables – the status of newspaper-TV cross-ownership, the status of the top 4 exclusion, and the market perspective.

Exhibit 1 shows this complex analysis for the top ten markets and four middle sized markets whose Designated Market Areas rank between roughly 40 and 100 (out of a total of 210), which were analyzed in detail in the discussion of newspaper-TV cross-ownership. It includes two TV merger scenarios that parallel the newspaper-TV scenarios – 1+1 and 1+2. In the 1+1 scenario, the top TV station is assumed to merge with the largest available TV station. In the case where top-4 mergers are banned, this would be the fifth ranked TV station. In the case where there is no ban on top-4 mergers, this would be the second ranked TV station. The next largest, unmerged TV station is assumed to merge with the second largest available TV station. In the case where top-4 mergers are banned, this would be a merger between the second and sixth ranked TV stations. In the case of where there is no top-4 exclusion, this would be a merger between the number three and number four stations. Note that in half the FCC sample cities the top-4 exclusion means no mergers would be permitted. In these markets, which are extremely concentrated, if the top-4 exclusion were lifted the impact of the mergers would be severe.

Exhibit 1: Status of TV-TV Mergers

City/Scenario	COMBINED MARKET Top 4 Exclusion								TELEVISION MARKET Top 4 Exclusion			
	With Newspaper-TV				Without Newspaper-TV				With		Without	
	With more		Without more		With more		Without more					
	1st	2nd	1st	2nd	1st	2nd	1st	2nd	1st	2nd	1st	2nd
New York*												
1+1 Scenario	V	V	V	NV	V	V	V	V	V	V	V	V
1+2 Scenario	V	V	V	V	V	V	V	V	V	V	V	V
Los Angeles*												
1+1 Scenario	V	V	V	NV	V	V	V	V	V	V	V	V
1+2 Scenario	V	V	V	V	V	V	V	V	V	V	V	V
Chicago*												
1+1 Scenario	V	V	V	V	V	V	V	V	V	V	V	V
1+2 Scenario	V	V	V	V	V	V	V	V	V	V	V	V
Philadelphia												
1+1 Scenario	V	V	V	NV	V	V	V	V	V	V	V	V
1+2 Scenario	V	V	V	NV	V	V	V	V	V	V	V	V
San Francisco												
1+1 Scenario	V	V	NV	NV	V	V	V	V	V	V	V	V
1+2 Scenario	V	V	NV	NV	V	V	V	V	V	V	V	V
Boston												
1+1 Scenario	V	V	NV	NV	V	V	V	V	V	V	V	V
1+2 Scenario	V	V	NV	NV	V	V	V	V	V	V	V	V
Kansas City												
1+1 Scenario	V	NV	V	NV	V	V	V	V	V	V	V	V
1+2 Scenario	NV	V	NV	V	V	V	V	V	V	V	V	V
Birmingham												
1+1 Scenario	V	NV	V	NV	V	V	V	V	V	V	V	V
1+2 Scenario	NV	V	NV	V	V	V	V	V	V	V	V	V
Norfolk												
1+1 Scenario	V	NV	NV	NV	NV	NV	V	V	V	V	V	V
1+2 Scenario	NV	V	NV	NV	NV	NV	V	V	V	V	V	V
Burlington												
1+1 Scenario	V	NV	V	NV	V	V	V	V	V	V	V	V
1+2 Scenario	V	NV	V	NV	V	V	V	V	V	V	V	V
Dallas*												
1+1 Scenario	V	V	V	NV	V	V	V	V	V	V	V	V
1+2 Scenario	V	V	V	NV	V	V	V	V	V	V	V	V
Washington D.C.												
1+1 Scenario	V	V	NV	NV	V	V	V	V	V	V	V	V
1+2 Scenario	V	V	NV	NV	V	V	V	V	V	V	V	V
Atlanta*												
1+1 Scenario	V	V	V	NV	V	V	V	V	V	V	V	V
1+2 Scenario	V	V	V	NV	V	V	V	V	V	V	V	V
Detroit												
1+1 Scenario	V	V	NV	NV	V	V	V	V	V	V	V	V
1+2 Scenario	V	V	NV	NV	V	V	V	V	V	V	V	V

V= Violates *Merger Guidelines* NV= Does not violate *Merger Guidelines* *= Existing newspaper-TV combination

RESULTS

The results are complex, but broad conclusions can be drawn. If the TV market view is taken, these mergers uniformly violate the *Merger Guidelines*. If cross-ownership mergers take place and then these mergers take place, they overwhelmingly violate the *Merger Guidelines*. The top-4 exclusion prevents many mergers that would violate the *Merger Guidelines*. This is particularly the case for the smaller markets. As markets become smaller, the number of TV stations declines and the markets become much more concentrated. Under the top-4 exclusion the available TV stations have very small market shares.

Exhibit 2 shows three examples of the magnitude of the impact under various scenarios. We have chosen two from the top ten DMAs and two from DMAs 90-100. We have included one of the FCC sample cities in each. In the top ten, we have analyzed Boston since it currently has no cross-ownership situation and exhibited the smallest effects of TV-TV mergers under some scenarios. The ban on cross-ownership and the ban on top-4 mergers keeps the combined market effects relatively small. In the TV market, however, even the top-4 Exclusion fails to prevent a significant increase in concentration. Newspaper-TV mergers have a much larger impact on concentration. Within the TV market, the effects are larger.

In the larger markets, with a ban on cross-ownership and a ban on top-4 TV mergers, the concentration ratios the combined market HHIs remain in the lower part of the concentrated range. However, the TV market becomes highly concentrated in both cases.

This analysis reinforces the case against relaxing the cross-ownership ban and urges extreme caution when it comes to relaxing the limits on multiple station ownership.

Exhibit 2: The Effects of TV-TV Mergers

| City | | | COMBINED MARKET TV POLICY SCENARIOS | | | | TELEVISION MARKET TV POLICY SCENARIOS | | |
| Merger Scenarios | | | | XO | XO+ | XO+ | | TV w/ | TV w/o |
TV	News-TV	Effect	Before	Merger Only	TV w/ top 4 X	TV w/o top 4 X	Before	top 4 X	top 4 X
New York									
1+1	1+1	HHI	979	1793	2601	3266			
		4 Firm CR	53	80	87	83			
1+2	1+2	HHI	979	1788	2371	3210			
		4 Firm CR	53	80	83	83			
1+1	NO XO	HHI	979	Ban	1202	1491	1786	2676	3558
		4 Firm CR	53	Ban	61	68	77	95	95
1+2	NO XO	HHI	979	Ban	1189	1390	1786	2674	3162
		4 Firm CR	53	Ban	60	68	77	95	95
Boston									
1+1	1+1	HHI	1165	2108	2227	2982			
		4 Firm CR	61	74	78	81			
1+2	1+2	HHI	1165	2005	2392	2827			
		4 Firm CR	61	74	78	81			
1+1	NO XO	HHI	1165	Ban	1282	1550	2166	2604	4934
		4 Firm CR	61	Ban	65	73	77	84	95
1+2	NO XO	HHI	1165	Ban	1296	1517	2166	2321	4816
		4 Firm CR	61	Ban	65	73	77	84	94
Birmingham									
1+1	XO	HHI	1991	2887	3586	4423			
		4 Firm CR	70	80	90	90			
1+2	XO	HHI	1991	2847	3127	3912			
		4 Firm CR	70	80	88	88			
1+1	NO XO	HHI	1913	Ban	2103	2310	1897	2703	3586
		4 Firm CR	70	Ban	77	84	80	97	97
1+2	NO XO	HHI	1913	Ban	2097	2282	1897	2703	3540
		4 Firm CR	75	Ban	77	84	80	97	97
Burlington									
1+1	XO	HHI	1831	3260	3919	5777			
		4 Firm CR	75	85	91	93			
1+2	XO	HHI	1831	2971	3531	3748			
		4 Firm CR	75	85	91	93			
1+1	NO XO	HHI	1831	Ban	1921	2153	2792	3376	4864
		4 Firm CR	75	Ban	78	80	78	84	100
1+2	NO XO	HHI	1831	Ban	1878	2004	2792	3127	3901
		4 Firm CR	75	Ban	78	80	78	84	100

BIBLIOGRAPHY

Aarts, Kees and Holli A. Semetko.   2003. "The Divided Electorate: Media Use and Political Involvement." *Journal of Politics* 65:3.

Abramowitz, Alan I. and Kyle L. Saunders. 1998. "Ideological Realignment in the US Electorate." *Journal of Politics* 60:3.

Ahrens, Frank. 2006. "As FCC Digs Into Ownership, Big Media No Longer Cares." *Washington Post*, 29 June.

Ahrens, Frank. 2006. "A Push Toward Private Control of Newspapers." *Washington Post* 17 June.

Ahrens, Frank. 2006.   "Tribune Empire Could Crumble." *Washington Post*, 26 September.

Albarracin, Dolores and Robert S. Wyer. 2001. "Elaborative and Non-elaborative Processing of a Behavior-Related Communication." *Personality and Social Psychology Bulletin* 27.

Albarran, Alan B. and John W. Dimmick. 1993. An Assessment of Utility and Competitive Superiority in the Video Entertainment Industries. *Journal of Media Economics* 6.

Alexander, Peter J. and Brendan M. Cunningham. 2004. *Same Story, Different Channel: Broadcast News and Information* October 4.

Alexander, Peter J. and Brendan M/Cunningham. 2004.   "Diversity in Broadcast Television: An Empirical Study of Local News." *International Journal of Media Management* 6:177.

Alger, Dean. MEGAMEDIA: 1998.   How Giant Corporations Dominate Mass Media, Distort Competition and Endanger Democracy. Lanham, MD: Rowan and Littlefield, 1998.

Alliance for Better Campaigns et al. 2004. in *Digital Audio Broadcasting Systems*, MM Docket No. 99-325 16 June.

Alterman, Eric. 2003. What Liberal Media? The Truth About Bias and the News. New York: Basic

Amar, Ahkil Reed. 1998. *The Bill of Rights*. New Haven: Yale University Press.

American Film Marketing Association 2003. *The Economic Impact of Independent File Production, April*.

An, Soontae, Hyun Seung Jin and Todd Simon. 2006. Ownership Structure of Public Traded Newspaper Companies and Their Financial Performance. *Journal of Media Economics* 19:2.

Anonymous, 2004. Do Local Owners Deliver More Localism? Some Evidence from Local Broadcast News Federal Communication Commission, draft dated June 17.

Anonymous, 2006. "WKBW-TV Owner Says it May Seek Bankruptcy." *Buffalo News*, 6 July

Anonymous. 2006. "A TV Navigation Guide." *Hollywood Reporter*, September 13.

Ansolabehere, Stephen and Shanto Iyengar. 1994. Riding the Wave and Claiming Ownership Over Issues: The Joint Effect of Advertising and News Coverage in Campaigns. *Public Opinion Quarterly* 58.

Ansolabehere, Stephen and Shanto Iyengar.1987.   Going Negative: How Political Advertisements Shrink and Polarize the Electorate. New York: Free Press

Ansolabehere, Stephen, Erik C. Snowberg, and James M. Snyder, Jr. 2005. Unrepresentative Information: The Case of Newspaper Reporting on Campaign Finance Reform. *Public Opinion Quarterly* 69: 2.

Arbitron, Radio Today: 2004.

Armitage, C.J. and M. Conner. 2000. Social cognition models and health behavior: A structured review. *Psychology & Health* 15:2: 173-189.

Asch, Peter and Rosalind Senaca. 1985. *Government and the Marketplace*. Dryden Press, Chicago.

Associated Press v. United States, 326 U.S. 1, 20 (1945)

Aufderheide, P. 1990. "After the Fairness Doctrine: Controversial Broadcast Programming and the Public Interest." *Journal of Communication*, 40.

Auletta, Ken. 1998. "The State of the American Newspaper." *American Journalism Review* June.

Bachen, Christine, Allen Hammond, Laurie Mason and Stephanie Craft. 1999. Diversity of Programming in the Broadcast Spectrum: Is there a Link Between Owner Race or Ethnicity and News and Public Affairs Programming? Santa Clara: Santa Clara University Press.

Bachman, Kathy. 2001. "Music Outlets Tune in More News Reports." *MediaWeek*, 29 October.

Bagdikian, Ben. 2000. *The Media Monopoly*. Boston: Beacon Press.

Baker, C. Edwin. 1994. *Advertising and a Democratic Press*. Princeton: Princeton University Press.

Baker, C. Edwin. 2001. *Media, Markets and Democracy*. Cambridge: Cambridge University Press.

Baker, Dean. 2002. Democracy Unhinged: More Media Concentration Means Less Public Discourse, A Critique of the FCC Studies on Media Ownership. Washington DC: Department of Professional Employees, AFL-CIO, December.

Balan, David J., Patrick DeGraba, and Abraham L. Widkelgren. 2003. Media Merges and the Ideological Content of Programming. *Bureau of Economics FTC*.

Barker, David, C. and Adam B. Lawrence. 2006. Media Favoritism and Presidential Nominations: Reviving the Direct Effects Model. *Political Communications* 23.

Barker, David, C. *Rushed to Judgment*. New York: Columbia University Press, 2002.

Barnes, Brooks. 2006. "Local TV Stations Struggle to Adapt as Web Grabs Viewers, Revenue." *Wall Street Journal*, 12 June.

Barnhurst, Kevin and John Nerone. 2001. *The Form of News: A History* New York: Guilford Press

Baron, David, P. 2005. Persistent Media Bias. Research Paper Series Stanford Graduate School of Business No. 1845R.

Barron, Jerome A. 1967. "Access to the Press--a New First Amendment Right." *Harvard Law Review* 80:8.

Bass, Jack. 2001. "Newspaper Monopoly" in Gene Roberts, Thomas Kunkel, and Charles Clayton (eds.), *Leaving Readers Behind*. Fayetteville: University of Arkansas Press.

Bates, B. J. 1993. "Station Trafficking in Radio: The Impact of Deregulation." *Journal of Broadcasting and Electronic Media* 37:1: 21-30.

Baseline Beta Studio System Database.

Beam, Randal A. 1995. "What it Means to Be a Market-Oriented Newspaper."
    Newspaper Research Journal 16.

Beam, Randall A. 2002. "Size of Corporate Parent Drives Market Orientation."
    Newspaper Research Journal 23.

Becker, Gary. 1958. "Competition and Democracy." *Journal of Law and Economics* 1.

Becker, S. and H. C. Choi. 1987. Media Use, Issue/Image Discrimination.
    Communications Research 14: 267-290.

Belo Interactive. 2004. *Online Credibility Survey.* 9-19 July

Belo. 2003. Comments of Belo Corp., In the Matter of 2002 Biennial Regulatory Review
    – Review of the Commission's Broadcast Ownership Rules and Other Rules
    Adopted Pursuant to Section 202 of the Telecommunications Act of 1996,
    Cross Ownership of Broadcast Stations and Newspapers, Rules and Policies
    Concerning Multiple Ownership of Radio Broadcast Stations in Local
    Markets, Definition of Radio Markets, MB Docket No. 02-277, MM Dockets
    02-235, 01-317, 00-244.

Benkler, Yochai. 1999. "Free as the Air." *New York University Law Review* 74.

Benkler, Yochai. 2000. "Review." International Journal of Law and Information
    Technology 8:2.

Bennett, W. Lance and Regina G. Lawrence. 1995. News Icons and the Mainstreaming
    of Social Change. *Journal of Communications* 45.

Bennett, W. Lance.1988. *News: The Politics of Illusion.* New York: Longmans

Benoit, William L. and Glenn Hansen. 2002. Issue Adaptation of Presidential
    Television Spots and Debates to Primary and General Audiences.
    Communications Research Reports 19.

Berkowitz, D., and D. Pritchard. 1989. Political Knowledge and Communication
    Resources. *Journalism Quarterly* 66.

Bernstein, J. M. and S. Lacy. 1992. Contextual Coverage of Government by Local
    Television News. *Journalism Quarterly* 69:2: 329-341.

Berry, Steven T. and Joel Waldfogel. 1999. Public Radio in the United States: Does it
    Correct Market Failure or Cannibalize Commercial Stations? *Journal of Public
    Economics* 71.

BIA Financial Networks. 2004. "Changing Hands." *Broadcasting and Cable,* 30 August

BIA Financial. 2003. "Investing in Television Market Report." *BIA.*

Bielby, William T. and Denise D. Bielby. 2003. "Controlling Prime Time:
    Organizational Concentration and Network Television Programming
    Strategies," *Journal of Broadcasting & Electronic Media,* 47: 4.

Bishop, Ronald and Ernest A. Hakanen. 2002. In the Public Interest? The State of Local
    Television Programming Fifteen Years After Deregulation. *Journal of
    Communications Inquiry* 26.

Bissinger, Buzz .2001. "The End of Innocence." in Roberts, Gene, Thomas Kunkel and
    Charles Layton (eds.), *Leaving Readers Behind.* Fayetteville: University of
    Arkansas Press.

Bollinger, Lee C. 1991 *Images of a Free Press.* Chicago: University of Chicago Press

Borjesson, Kristina. 2002. *Into the BUZZSAW.* Amherst, New York: Prometheus Books

Boston Globe. 2004. Sinclair's Slander, October 15.

Botein, Stephen. 1980. "Printers and the American Revolution." In Bernard Bailyn and
    John B. Hench, (eds.), *The Press & the American Revolution.* Worcester:
    American Antiquarian Society.

Botein, Stephen. 1975. "Meer Mechanicks' and an Open Press: The Business and Political Strategies of Colonial Printers." *Perspectives in American History* IX.

Box Office Mojo.

Brady, Henry E., Kay Lehman Schlozman, and Sidney Verba. 1999. Prospecting for Participants: Rational Expectations and the Recruitment of Political Activists. *Political Science Review 93*.

Brazeal, LeAnn M, and William L. Benoit. 2001. A Functional Analysis of Congressional Television Spots. *Communications Quarterly* 49.

Brehm, John and Wendy Rahn. 1997. Individual Level Evidence for the Causes and Consequences of Social Capital. *American Journal of Political Science* July.

Brians, C. L. and M. P. Wattenberg. 1996. Campaigns Issue Knowledge and Salience: Comparing Reception for TV Commercials, TV News, and Newspapers. *American Journal of Political* Science 40.

Brooks, Tim and Earle Marsh. 2003. *The Complete Directory to Prime Time Network and Cable TV Shows: 1946 – Present.* New York: Ballantine.

Brown, Duncan H. 1994. "The Academy's Response to the Call for a Marketplace Approach to Broadcast Regulation." *Critical Studies in Mass Communications* 257.

Bruce N. Owen. 2002. "Statement on Media Ownership Rules." Attachment to Comments of Fox Entertainment Group and Fox Television Stations, Inc., National Broadcasting Company, Inc. and Telemundo Group, Inc., and Viacom, In the Matter of 2002 Biennial Regulatory Review – Review of the Commission's Broadcast Ownership Rules and Other Rules Adopted Pursuant to Section 202 of the Telecommunications Act of 1996, Cross Ownership of Broadcast Stations and Newspapers, Rules and Policies Concerning Multiple Ownership of Radio Broadcast Stations in Local Markets, Definition of Radio Markets, MB Docket No. 02-277, MM Dockets 02-235, 01-317, 00-244. 2 January 2003.

Bruns, Alex. 2005. *Gatewatching.* New York: Peter Lang Publishing.

Buhr, T. 2001. "What Voters Know About Candidates and How they Learn It: The 1996 New Hampshire Republican Primary as a Case Study in W.G. Mayer (Eds.), *In Pursuit of the White House 2000: How We Choose Our Presidential Nominees,* Chatham: NJ, Chatham House.

Busterna, John C. 1988. "Television Station Ownership Effects on Programming and Idea Diversity: Baseline Data." *Journal of Media Economics* 2:3: 63-74.

Byerly, Carolyn M. 2006. "Questioning Media Access: Analysis of FCC Women and Minority Ownership Data." Department of Journalism, Howard University.

Campbell, David. 2004. "ACTS OF FAITH: Churches and Political Engagement." *Political Behavior* 26:2.

Carroll, Raymond L. 1989. "Market Size and TV News Values." *Journalism Quarterly 66: 49-56*; Scott, D. K. and R. H. Gopbetz. 1992. Hard News/Soft News Content of the National Broadcast Networks: 1972-1987. *Journalism Quarterly* 69:2: 406-412.

Carroll, Raymond L. and C.A. Tuggle. 1997. "The World Outside: Local TV News Treatment of Imported News." *Journalism and Mass Communications Quarterly* 74:123-33.

Carter, Sue, Frederick Fico, and Joycelyn A. McCabe. 2002. Partisan and Structural Balance in Local Television Election Coverage. *Journalism and Mass Communications Quarterly* 79.

Chafee, Zechariah.   1941. *Free Speech in the United States* Cambridge: Harvard University Press.

Chaffee, Steven and Stacy Frank. 1996. How Americans Get Their Political Information: Print versus Broadcast News. *The Annals of the American Academy of Political and Social Science* 546.

Chaffee, Steven H. Xinshu Zhao and Glenn Leshner. 1994. Political Knowledge and the Campaign Media of 1992. *Communications Research* 21, Spring.

Chaffee, Steven, X. Zhao and G. Leshner. 1994. Political Knowledge and the Campaign Media of 1992. *Communications Research* 21.

Chambers, Todd and Herbert H. Howard. 2006. "The Economics of Media Consolidationn," in Alan B. Albarran, Sylvia N. Chan Olmstead and Michael O. wirth, *Handbook of Media Management and Economics*. Mahwah: Lawrence Erlbaum.

Chen, Rene, Esther Thorson and Stephen Lacy. 2005. The Impact of Newsroom Investment on Newspaper Revenues and Profits: Small and Medium Newspapers, 1998-2002. *Journalism and Mass Communications Quarterly* 82:3: Autumn.

Choo, Sooyoung, Esther Thorson and Stephen Lacy. 2004. The Relationship Between Newspaper Newsroom Investment and Circulation: A study of 27 'Quality' Dailies. *Newspaper Research Journal* 25, Fall.

Clark, Charles E. 1994. The Public Prints: The Newspaper in Anglo-American Culture, 1665-1740. New York: Oxford University Press.

Clarke, Pere and Eric Fredin. 1978. Newspapers, Television and Political Reasoning. *Public Opinion Quarterly* Summer.

Collins-Jarvis, Lori A. 1993.   "Gender Representation in an Electronic City Hall: Female Adoption of Santa Monica's PEN System." *Journal of Broadcasting and Electronic Media* 37:1: 49-65.

Colon, Aly. 2000. "The Multimedia Newsroom." *Columbia Journalism Review*, June.

Coltrane, Scott and Melinda Messineo. 1990. The Perpetuation of Subtle Prejudice: Race and Gender Imagery in the 1990's Television Advertising. *Sex Roles* 42.

Columbia Journalism Review. 2006. *Who Owns What*, August 22.

Congressional Research Service. 1998. Minority Broadcast Station Ownership and Broadcast Programming: Is There a Nexus? Washington: Library of Congress.

Consumer Federation of America, Consumers Unions, Center for Media Education and the Media Access Project. 2003. "Initial Comments." *In the Matter of 2002 Biennial Regulatory Review – Review of the Commission's Broadcast Ownership Rules and Other Rules Adopted Pursuant to Section 202 of the Telecommunications Act of 1996, Cross Ownership of Broadcast Stations and Newspapers, Rules and Policies Concerning Multiple Ownership of Radio Broadcast Stations in Local Markets, Definition of Radio Markets*, MB Docket No. 02-277, MM Dockets 02-235, 01-317, 00-244. January 2.

Consumer Federation of America/Consumers Union Poll. January 2004.

Consumer Group Survey. August 2006.

Consumers Union, et al. 2003. "Reply Comments of Consumers Union, Consumer Federation of America, Media Access Project and Center For Digital

Democracy." *In the Matter of Cross-Ownership of Broadcast Stations and Newspaper Newspaper/Radio Cross-Ownership Waiver Policy*, MM Dockets No. 01-235, 96-197, February 15.

Cook, Timothy E. 1998. Governing with the New: The News Media as a Political Institution. Chicago: University of Chicago Press.

Cooper, Mark N. 2001. "Antitrust as Consumer Protection in the New Economy: Lessons from the Microsoft Case." *Hasting Law Journal* 52, April.

Cooper, Mark N. 2003. *Media Ownership and Democracy in the Digital Information Age*. Palo Alto: Center for Internet and Society.

Cooper, Mark. 2003. Abracadabra! Hocus Pocus! Making Media Market Power Disappear with the FCC's Diversity Index. Washington, D.C.: Consumer Federation of America, Consumers Union.

Copps, Michael. 2003. Dissenting statement on the 2004 Section 257 Report.

Cornell, Saul. 1999. *The Other Founders*. Chapel Hill: University of North Carolina Press.

Coulson, David C. 1994. "Impact of Ownership on Newspaper Quality." *Journalism Quarterly*.

Coulson, David C. and Anne Hansen. 1995. The Louisville Courier-Journal's News Content After Purchase by Gannett. *Journalism and Mass Communications Quarterly* 72:1: 205-215.

Coulter, Ann. 2003. *Slander: Liberal Lies about the American Right*. New York: Three Rivers Press.

Cranberg, Gilbert, Randall Bezanson, and John Soloski. 2001. *Taking Stock: Journalism and the Publicly Traded Newspaper Company*. Ames: Iowa State Press.

Crandall, Robert W. 2003. The Economic Impact of Providing Service to Multiple Local Braodcast Stations Within a Single Geographic Market," attached to Comments of Sinclair Inc. In the Matter of 2002 Biennial Regulatory Review – Review of the Commission's Broadcast Ownership Rules and Other Rules Adopted Pursuant to Section 202 of the Telecommunications Act of 1996, Cross Ownership of Broadcast Stations and Newspapers, Rules and Policies Concerning Multiple Ownership of Radio Broadcast Stations in Local Markets, Definition of Radio Markets, MB Docket No. 02-277, MM Dockets 02-235, 01-317, 00-244. 2 January.

Credit and Guaranty Agreement Among Granite Broadcasting Corporation. 2006.The Subsidiaries of Granite Broadcasting Corporation as Guarantors, Various Lenders, and Silver Point Finance LLC as Administrative Agent." 5 July 2006. Accessed from http://secinfo.com.

Cundy, D. T. 1986. "Political Commercials and Candidate Image." in Lynda Lee Kaid (eds.), *New Perspectives in Political Advertising*. Carbondale, IL: Southern Illinois University Press.

Curran, James. 2002. *Media and Power*. London: Routledge.

Curtin, John J., Daniel L. Goldberg and Daniel S. Savrin. 1999. "The EC's Rejection of the Kesko/Tuko Merger: Leading the Way to the Application of a 'Gatekeeper' Analysis of Retailer Market Power Under U.S. Antitrust Law." 40 B.C. L. Rev. 537.

Dailey, Larry, Lori Demo and Mary Spillman. 2003. The Convergence Continuum: A Model for Studying Collaboration Between Media Newsrooms. *Association for Education in Journalism and Mass Communications* July-August.

Dailey, Larry, Lori Demo and Mary Spillman. 2005. Most TV/Newspapers Partners At Cross-Promotion Stage. *Newspaper Research Journal* 26, Fall.

Damore, David. 2003. "The Dynamics of Issue Ownership I Presidential Campaigns." *Political Research Quarterly*, 57: 391-397.

Davie, William R. and Jung-Sook Lee. 1993. Television News Technology: Do More Sources Mean Less Diversity? *Journal of Broadcasting and Electronic Media 37*, Fall: 453-464.

Davis, Charles and Stephanie Craft. 2000. New Media Synergy: Emergence of Institutional Conflict of Interest. *Journal of Mass Media Ethics* 15.

Della Vigna, Stefan and Ethan Kaplan. 2006."The Fox News Effect: Media Bias and Voting." *NBER Working Paper 12169.* Cambridge, MA: National Bureau of Economic Research.

Dewey, John. 1954. *The Public and its Problems.* Athens, Ohio: Swallow Press.

Dijksterhuis, A., and Van Knippenberg, A. 1999. On the parameters of associative strength: Central tendency and variability as determinants of stereotype accessibility. *Personality and Social Psychology Bulletin* 25: 527-536.

Dimmick, John B. 1997. "The Theory of the Niche and Spending on Mass Media: The Case of the Video Revolution." *Journal of Media Economics* 10.

Dirks, Van Essent & Murray. 2006. "McClatchy will be #2 – Acquisition is Largest in Total Circulation." 1st Quarter Update. 31 March.

Dixon, Travis, L. and Daniel Linz. 2000. Overrepresentation and Underrepresentation of African Americans and Latinos as Lawbreakers on Television News. *Communications Research 50.*

Domke, David, David Perlmutter and Meg Spratt. 2002. The Primes of Our Times? An Examination of the 'Power' of Visual Images. *Journalism 3.*

Dorner, A. 2001. *Politainment.* Frankfurt/Main: Surhkamp.

Downie Jr., Leonard and Robert G. Kaiser. 2002. *The News About the News.* New York: Alfred A. Knopf.

Downs, Anthony. 1957. *An Economic Theory of Democracy.* New York: Harper.

Drew, Dan and David Weaver. 1991. Voter Learning in the 1988 Presidential Election: Did the Media Matter? *Journalism Quarterly* 68.

Drew, Dan and David Weaver. 2006. Voter Learning in the 2004 Presidential Election: Did the Media Matter? *Journalism and Mass Communications Quarterly* 83:1.

Druckman, James N. 2005. Media Matter: How Newspapers and Television News Cover Campaigns and Influence Voters. *Political Communication 22.*

Druckman, James N. and Michael Parkin. 2005. The Impact of Media Bias: How Editorial Slant Affects Voters. *Journal of Politics, 67:4.*

Dubin, Jeff and Matthew L. Spitzer. 1995. Testing Minority Preferences in Broadcasting. *Southern California Law Review 68.*

Dueze, Mark. 2004. "What is Multimedia Journalism." *Journalism Studies* 3:2.

Dugger, Ronald. 2000. "The Corporate Domination of Journalism." in William Serrin (ed.), *The Business of Journalism.* New York: New Press.

Dunbar, John. 2006. "Lawyer Says FCC Ordered Study Destroyed." *Associated Press,* 14 September.

Dupagne, Michel and Bruce Garrison. 2006. The Meaning and Influence of Convergence: A Qualitative Case Study of Newsroom Work at the Tampa News Center. *Journalism Studies 7:2.*

Dyck, Alexander and Luigi Zingales. 2003. The Media and Asset Prices. *University of Chicago, NBER & CEPR.*

Eagly, A. H. 1974. Comprehensibility of persuasive arguments as a determinant of opinion change. *Journal of Personality and Social Psychology 29*: 758-773.

Economists Inc. 2003. Reply Comment, "Economists Inc.'s 'Critique' of the Recent Study on Media Ownership: A Response by the Project for Excellence in Journalism," Federal Communications Commission, *2002 Biennial Regulatory Review – Review of the Commission's Broadcast Ownership Rules and Other Rules Adopted Pursuant to Section 202 of the Telecommunications Act of 1996,* March 18.

Edsall, Thomas B. and Mary D. and Edsall. 1991. Chain Reaction: The Impact of Race, Rights and Taxes on American Politics. New York: Norton.

Einstein, Mara. 2004. *Media Diversity: Economics, Ownership and the FCC.* Mahwah: Lawrence Erlbaum.

Ellman, Mathew and Fabrizio Germano. 2004. What Do Papers Sell? *UPF Economics and Business Working Paper No. 800.*

ELRA Group Inc. 1982. *Female Ownership of Broadcast Stations.* prepared for the Federal Communications Commission, May.

Entman, Robert M., and Andrew Rojecki. 2000. *The Black Image in the White Mind: Media and Race in America.* Chicago: University of Chicago Press.

Evans, Akousa Barthewell. 1990. "Are Minority Preferences Necessary? Another Look at the Radio Broadcasting Industry." *Yale Law and Policy Review* 8.

Fabrigar, L.R. et al. 1998. The impact of attitude accessibility on elaboration of persuasive messages. *Personality and Social Psychology Bulletin* 24: 339-352.

Fabrikant, Geraldine. 2006. "Successful Scripps Seeks Next Food Network." *New York Times,* 14 August.

Fabricant, Geraldine and Bill Carter. 2006. "A Tortoise Savors the Lead," *New York Times,* September 12.

Fairchild, Charles. 1999. "Deterritorializing Radio: Deregulation and the Continuing Triumph of the Corporatist Perspective in the USA." *Media, Culture & Society* 21:4.

Farnsworth, Stephen J. and S. Robert Lichter. 1999. No Small Town Poll: Network Coverage of the 1992 New Hampshire Primary. *Harvard International Journal of Press/Politics,* 4.

Farnsworth, Stephen J. and S. Robert Lichter. 2002. The 1996 New Hampshire Republican Primary and Network News. *Politics and Policy* 30.

Farnsworth, Stephen J. and S. Robert Lichter. 2003. The 2000 New Hampshire Democratic Primary and Network News. *American Behavioral Scientist* 46:5.

FCC 98-281. 1998. Report and Order: In the Matter of 1998 Biennial Regulatory Review -- Streamlining of Mass Media Applications Rules, and Processes -- Policies and Rules Regarding Minority and Female Ownership of Mass Media Facilities, MM Docket No. 98-43, November 25.

FCC v. National Citizens Committee for Broadcasting, 436 U.S. 775 (1978).

Federal Communications Commission. 1978. Statement of Policy on Minority Ownership of Broadcasting Facilities, 68 FCC 2d, 979, 980 n. 8.

Federal Communications Commission. 1998. Report and Order, In the Matter of 1998 Biennial Regulatory Review Streamlining of Mass Media Applications, Rules, and Processes Policies and Rules Regarding Minority and Female Ownership of Mass Media Facilities, MM Docket Nos. 98-43; 94-149, FCC 98-281.

Federal Communications Commission. 2001. "Further Notice of Proposed Rulemaking." In the Matter of Implementation of Section 11 of the Cable Television Consumer Protection and Competition Act of 1992, Implementation of Cable Act Reform Provisions of the Telecommunications Act of 1996, The Commission's Cable Horizontal and Vertical Ownership Limits and Attribution Rules, Review of the Commission's Regulations Governing Attribution Of Broadcast and Cable/MDS Interests, Review of the Commission's Regulations and Policies Affecting Investment In the Broadcast Industry, Reexamination of the Commission's Cross-Interest Policy, CS Docket No. 98-82, CS Docket No. 96-85, MM Docket No. 92-264, MM Docket No. 94-150, MM Docket No. 92-51, MM Docket No. 87-154, 13 September.

Federal Communications Commission. *Comments on Consolidation and Localism.* 2001. Roundtable on Media Ownership, 29 October.

Federal Communications Commission. 2001 -2006. *In the Matter of Annual Assessment of the Status of Competition in Markets for the Delivery of Video Programming.*

Federal Communications Commission. 2001-2006 "Report on Cable Industry Prices." In the Matter of Implementation of Section 3 of the Cable Television Consumer Protection and Competition Act of 1992, Statistical Report on Average Rates for Basic Service, Cable Programming Service, and Equipment, various issues.

Federal Communications Commission, 2002. *Program Diversity and the Program Selection Process on Broadcast Network Television, Mara Epstein, Media Ownership Working Group Study 5,* September.

Federal Communications Commission. 2002. In the Matter of 2002 Biennial Regulatory Review – Review of the Commission's Broadcast Ownership Rules and Other Rules Adopted Pursuant to Section 202 of the Telecommunications Act of 1996, Cross Ownership of Broadcast Stations and Newspapers, Rules and Policies Concerning Multiple Ownership of Radio Broadcast Stations in Local Markets, Definition of Radio Markets, MB Docket No. 02-277, MM Dockets 02-235, 01-317, 00-244, 23 September.

Federal Communications Commission. 2003. "2002 Biennial Regulatory Review." *Report and Order and Notice of Proposed Rulemaking,* 18 FCC Rcd. 13620.

Federal Communications Commission. 2003. 2002 Biennial Regulatory Review – Review of the Commission's Broadcast Ownership Rules and Other Rules Adopted Pursuant to Section 202 of the Telecommunications Act of 1996, 18 FCC Rcd 13620, 13711-47.

Federal Communication Commission. 2003. In the Matter of 2002 Biennial Regulatory Review – Review of the Commission's Broadcast Ownership Rules and Other Rules Adopted Pursuant to Section 202 of the Telecommunications Act of 1996; Cross-Ownership of Broadcast Stations and Newspapers; Rules and Policies Concerning Multiple Ownership of Radio Broadcast Stations in Local Markets; Definition of Radio Markets; Definition of Radio Markets for Areas Not Located in an Arbitron Survey, MB Docket Nos. 02-277. 01-235, 01-317, 00-244, 03-130, FCC 03-127.

Federal Communication Commission. 2004. *Minority Ownership Summary Report.* Available from http://www.fcc.gov/ownership/ownminor.pdf and http://www.fcc.gov/ownership/ownfemal.pdf.

Federal Communication Commission. 2005. *Minority Ownership Summary Report*. Available from http://www.fcc.gov/ownership/owner_minor_2003.pdf and http://www.fcc.gov/ownership/owner_female_2003.pdf.

Federal Communication Commission. 2006. *Minority Ownership Summary Report*. Available from http://www.fcc.gov/ownership/owner_minor_2004-2005.pdf and http://www.fcc.gov/ownership/owner_female_2004-2005.pdf.

Federal Communications Commission. 2006. Further Notice of Proposed Rulemaking, in the Matter of 2006 Quadrennial Regulatory Review – Review of the Commission's Broadcast Ownership Rules and Other Rules Adopted Pursuant to Section 202 of the Telecommunications Act of 1996; 2002 Biennial Regulatory Review – Review of the Commission's Broadcast Ownership Rules and Other Rules Adopted Pursuant to Section 202 of the Telecommunications Act of 1996; Cross-Ownership of Broadcast Stations and Newspapers; Rules and Policies Concerning Multiple Ownership of Radio Broadcast Stations in Local Markets; Definition of Radio Markets, MB Docket Nos. 06-121; 02-277 ; 01-235; 01-317; 00-244, FCC-06-93.

Federal Communications Commission. 2006. "Further notice of proposed rulemaking." 17 September. Available from http://hraunfoss.fcc.gov/edocs_public/attachmatch/FCC-06-93A1.pdf.

Ferrall, V. E. 1992. "The Impact of Television Deregulation on Private and Public Interests" *Journal of Communications* 39:1: 8-38.

Fife, Marilyn D. 1979.The Impact of Minority Ownership on Broadcast Program Content: A Case Study of WGPR-TV's Local News Content. Washington: National Association of Broadcasters.

Fife, Marilyn D. 1986. The Impact of Minority Ownership on Broadcast Program Content: A Multi-Market Study. Washington: National Association of Broadcasters.

Findlay, Prentiss. 2004. "Group Says Stations Not Independent." *Charleston Post and Courier*, 20 December.

Firestone, C. M. and J. M. Schement. 1995. *Toward an Information Bill of Rights and Responsibilities*. Washington, DC: Aspen Institute.

Fiss, Owen M. 1987. "Why the State?" *Harvard Law Review* 100:4.

Fitzgerald, Mark and Lucia Moses. "At the Crossroads." *Editor and Publisher*, 23 June.

Fitzgerald, Mark and Todd Shields. 2003. "After June 2, Papers May Make Broadcast News." *Editor and Publisher*, 27 May.

Fournier, Patrick, Richard Nadeau, Anre Blais, Elisabeth Gidengil and Neil Nevitte. 2004. Time-of-voting Decision and Susceptibility to Campaign Effects. *Electoral Studies* 23:4.

Fox Television Stations, Inc., v. FCC, 280 F.3d 1027 (D.C. Circ. 2002)

Franken, Al. 2003. Lies and the Lying Liars Who Tell Them: A Fair and Balanced Look at the Right. New York: EP Dutton.

Friedland, Lewis. "Statement" Attached to "Reply Comments of Consumer Federation, et al." 2002. *Cross Ownership of Broadcast Stations and Newspapers*, MM Docket No. 01-235, 15 February.

Friedman, Milton. 1953. "The Case for Flexible Exchange Rates." *Essays in Positive Economics*. Chicago: University of Chicago Press.

Future of Music Coalition. 2002. (eds.), "Radio Deregulation: Has It Served Citizens and Musicians?" *Ric Dube and Gillian Thomson*, 18 Nov.

Gandy, Oscar. 2006. "Thinking About Race, Ideology and Structure in the Presentation of Disastrous Events: The Case of Katrina." *Rethinking the Discourse on Race.* St. John's University School of Law, 28 April.

Gans, Herbert J. 2003. *Democracy and the News.* Oxford: Oxford University Press.

Garrett, R. Kelly. 2005. "Media Deregulation and the Online News Market." *Telecommunications Policy Research Conference* September.

Gauger, Timothy G. 1989. "The Constitutionality of the FCC's Use of Race and Sex in Granting Broadcast Licenses." *Northwestern Law Review.*

Gentzkow, Matthew and Jesse M. Shapiro. 2005. "Media Bias and Reputation." University of Chicago, Graduate School of Business and NBER, 14 September.

Gentzkow, Matthew and Jesse M. Shapiro. 2006. Does Television Rot Your Brain? New Evidence From the Coleman Study. *NBER Working Paper 12021,* February.

Gentzkow, Matthew. 2005. "Television and Voter Turnout." University of Chicago Graduate School of Business, 28 October.

George, Lisa and Joel Waldfogel. 2000. Who Benefits Whom in Daily Newspaper Markets? *NBER Working Paper 7944.* Cambridge, MA: National Bureau of Economic Research.

Gilens, Martin and Craig Hertzman. 1997. "Corporate Ownership and News Bias: Newspaper Coverage of the 1996 Telecommunications Act." Paper delivered at *the Annual Meeting of the American Political Science Association,* August.

Gilens, Martin. 1996. "Race Coding and White Opposition to Welfare," *American Political Science Review* 90.

Gilliam, Franklin D. Jr. and Shanto Iyengar. 2000. "Prime Suspects: The Influence of Local Television News on the Viewing Public." *American Journal of Political Science* 44.

Gish, Pat and Tom Gish. 2000. "We Still Scream: The Perils and Pleasures of Running a Small-Town Newspaper." and Shipp, E. R. "Excuses, Excuses: How Editors and Reporters Justify Ignoring Stories." in William Serrin (eds.), *The Business of Journalism* New York: New Press.

Gitlin, T. 1991. "Bits and Blips: Chunk News, Savvy Talk and the Bifurcation of American Politics." in P. Dahlgren and C. Sparks (eds.), *Communications and Citizenship: Journalism and the Public Sphere.* London: Routledge.

Glaeser, Edward L., Giacomo A. M. Ponzetto and Jesse M. Shapiro. 2004. "Strategic Extremism: Why Republicans and Democrats Divide on Religious Values." *Harvard Institute of Economic Research Discussion Paper Number 2044,* October.

Glaeser, Edward. 2004. "The Political Economy of Hatred." *NBER Working Paper 9171.* Cambridge, MA: National Bureau of Economic Research, 26 October.

Glasser, Mark. 2005. "Business Side of Convergence Has Myths, Some Real Benefits." *USC Annenberg Online Journalism Review,* 19 May.

Glasser, Theodore L., David S. Allen and S. Elizabeth Banks. 1989. The Influence of Chain Ownership on News Play: A Case Study. *Journalism Quarterly* 66.

Goldberg, Bernard. 2002. *Bias.* Washington: Regnery.

Gordon, Richard. 2003. "Convergence Defined." *USC Annenberg Online Journalism Review* posted Nov. 13.

Goro, Oba and Sylvia M. Chan-Olmstead, 2006. "Self-Dealing or Market Transaction?: An Exploratory Study of Vertical Integration in the U.S. Television Syndication Market," *Journal of Media Economics,* 19 (2).

Graber, Doris A. 2003. "The Rocky Road to New Paradigms: Modernizing News and Citizenship Standards." *Political Communication 20.*

Graber, Doris. 1997. *Mass Media and American Politics.* Washington, DC: Congressional Quarterly.

Graber, Doris. 2001. *Processing Politics.* Chicago: University of Chicago Press.

Granato, Jim and M.C. Sunny Wong. 2004. Political Campaign Advertising Dynamics. *Political Research Quarterly 57.*

Gray, Herman. 1995. *Watching Race Television and the Struggle for Blackness.* Chicago: University of Chicago Press.

Green, Donald P. and Alan S. Gerber. 2001. The Effect of a Nonpartisan Get Out the Vote Drive: An Experimental Study of Leafleting. *Journal of Politics 62:3.*

Green, Donald P. and Alan S. Gerber. 2000. *Getting Out the Vote in Youth Vote: Results for Randomized Field Experiments.* New Haven: Institution for Social and Policy Studies, Yale University.

Groeling, Tim and Samuel Kernell. 2005. Is Network News Coverage of the President Biased? *Journal of Politics 60:4.*

Groseclose, Timothy and Jeff Milyo. 2005. A Measure of Media Bias. *Quarterly Journal of Economics 120.*

Grove, Martin A. 2006. "CBS' Moonves Smart to Eye Movies." *Hollywood Reporter.com,* July 7.

Gulati, Girish. 2004. "Revisiting the Link Between Electoral Competition and Policy Extremism in the U.S. Congress." *American Political Science Review 32:5.*

Gwiasda, Gregory W. 2001. "Network News Coverage of Campaign Advertisements: Media's Ability to Reinforce Campaign Messages." *American Politics Research 29.*

Hallock, Steve. 2005. "Acquisition by Gannett Changes Paper's Editorials." *Newspaper Research Journal 25:* 2.

Hamilton, James T. 2003. *All the News That's Fit to Sell.* Princeton: Princeton University Press.

Hamilton, James T. 1998. Channeling Violence: The Economic Market for Violent Television Programming. Princeton: Princeton University Press.

Hansen, Glenn J. and William Benoit. 2002. Presidential Television Advertising and Public Policy Priorities, 1952 –2002. *Communications Studies 53.*

Hanson, John Mark. 2003. "The Majoritarian Impulse and the Declining Significance of Place." in Gerald M. Pomper and Marc D. Weiner, (eds.), *The Future of American Democratic Politics.* New Brunswick: Rutgers University Press.

Hart, Jr., T. A. 1988. "The Case for Minority Broadcast Ownership." *Gannett Center Journal.*

Hechter, Michael. 2004. "From Class to Culture." *American Journal of Sociology 110:2.*

Herman, Edward and Noam Chomsky. 2002. *Manufacturing Consent.* New York: Pantheon Books.

Herrson, Paul, S. and Kelly D. Patterson. 2000. "Agenda Setting and Campaign Advertising in Congressional Elections." in James A. Thurber, Candace Nelson (eds.), *Crowded Airwaves: Campaign Advertising in Elections.* Washington D.C.: Brookings.

Hibbing, J. and Theiss-Morse, E. 2002. *Stealth Democracy: Americans' Beliefs About How Government Should Work.* Cambridge: Cambridge University Press.

Higgins, John M. 2006. "Nice Price: Despite Recent Deal Snags, the Station Market is Still Relatively Strong." *Broadcasting and Cable,* 20 February.

Hlestand, Jesse. 2006. "Profit Anticipation," *Hollywood Reporter,* June 6.

Hocking, William Ernest. 1947. *Freedom of the Press.* Chicago: University of Chicago Press.

Holian, David B. 2004. "He's Stealing My Issues! Clinton's Crime Rhetoric and the Dynamics of Issue Ownership." *Political Behavior* 26:2.

Holson, Laura M. 2006. "Yearning to Put Papers Back in Local Hands: In Several Cities, a Push for Dailies Free of Absentee Corporate Owners." *New York Times,* 1 July.

Hopkins, Wat W. 1996. "The Supreme Court Defines the Forum for Democratic Discourse." *Journalism and Mass Communications Quarterly* Spring.

Horrigan, John B. "For Many Home Broadband Users, the Internet is a Primary News Source." *Pew Internet and American Life Project,* 22 March 2006.

Hovenkamp, Herbert. 1999. *Federal Antitrust Policy.* Hornbook Series. West Group, St. Paul.

Huckefldt, Robert and John Sprague. 1995. Citizens, Politics, and Social Communication: Information Influence in an Election Campaign. New York: Cambridge University Press.

Huckfeldt, R., Johnson E. and J. Sprague. 2002. Political Environments, Political Dynamics and the Survival of Disagreement. *Journal of Politics* 62.

Hudson, Eileen Davis and Fitzgerald, Mark. 2001. "Capturing Audience Requires a Dragnet." *Editor and Publisher,* 22 October.

Hutchins, Robert M. 1947. *A Free and Responsible Press.* Chicago: University of Chicago Press.

Information Policy Institute. 2003. "Comments of the Information Policy Institute." In the Matter of 2002 Biennial Regulatory Review – Review of the Commission's Broadcast Ownership Rules and Other Rules Adopted Pursuant to Section 202 of the Telecommunications Act of 1996, Cross Ownership of Broadcast Stations and Newspapers, Rules and Policies Concerning Multiple Ownership of Radio Broadcast Stations in Local Markets, Definition of Radio Markets, MB Docket No. 02-277, MM Dockets 02-235, 01-317, 00-244, January 2.

Interim Report. 2004. Local TV News Ignores Local and State Campaigns. *Lear Center Local News Archive,* 21 Oct, Available from http://www.learcenter.org/pdf/LCLNAInterim2004.pdf.

Iosifides, Petros. 1999. "Diversity versus Concentration in the Deregulated Mass Media." *Journalism and Mass Communications Quarterly* Spring.

Irmen, Andreas and Jacques-Francois Thisse. 1998. Competition in Multi-characteristic Spaces: Hotelling was Almost Right. *Economic Theory 78.*

Iyengar, S. 1991. *Is Anyone Responsible.* Chicago: University of Chicago Press.

Iyengar, Shanto and Donald R. Kinder. 1987. *News That Matters: Television and American Opinion.* Chicago: University of Chicago Press.

Jacks, J. Z., & Devine, P. G. 2000. Attitude importance, forewarning of message content, and resistance to persuasion. *Basic and Applied Social Psychology* 22: 19-29.

Jamieson, Kathleen Hall. 1992. *Dirty Politics: Deception, Distraction and Democracy.* New York: Oxford University Press.

Jason, L.A. 1983. Self-monitoring in reducing children's excessive television viewing. *Psychological Reports* 53:1280.

John, Richard R. 1995. *Spreading the News*. Cambridge: Harvard University Press.

Johnson, Thomas J. and Wayne Wanta. 1993. Newspaper Competition and Message Diversity in an Urban Market. *Mass Communications Review* 20: 45.

Johnson, Thomas J., Mahmoud A. M. Braima, and Jayanthi Sothirajah. 1999. Doing the Traditional Media Sidestep: Comparing Effects of the Internet and Other Nontraditional Media with Traditional Media in the 1996 Presidential Campaign. *Journalism & Mass Communication Quarterly* 76.

Johnson, Thomas J., Mahmoud A. M. Braima, Jayanthi Sothirajah. 2000. Measure for Measure: The Relationship Between Different Broadcast Types, Formats, Measures and Political Behaviors and Cognitions. *Journal of Broadcasting & Electronic Media* 44.

Jones, Nicholas. 1995. Soundbites and Spindoctors: How Politicians Manipulate the Media – and Visa Versa. London: Cassel.

Jordan, Miriam, Dennis K. Berman and John Lyons. 2006. "Investor Group Snags Univision: Televisa Fumes." *Wall Street Journal,* 28 June.

Joslyn, M. and S. Cecolli. 1996. "Attentiveness to Television News and Opinion Change in the Fall of 1992 Election Campaign." *Political Behavior* 18.

Joslyn, R. 1981. "The Impact of Campaign Spot Advertising Ads." *Journalism Quarterly* 7.

Jun, Son Youn and Kim, Sung Tae. 1995. "Do the Media Matter to voters? Analysis of Presidential Campaigns, 1984-1996." Paper presented to the *Political Communication Division of the International Communication Association,* Washington, D.C.

Just, M. R., A. N. Crigler and W. R. Neuman. 1996. "Cognitive and Affective Dimensions of Political Conceptualization." in A. N. Crigler (eds.), *The Psychology of Political Communications.* Ann Arbor: University of Michigan Press.

Just, Marion, R., Ann N. Crigler, Dean F. Alger, Timothy E. Cook, Montague Kern, and Darrell M. West. 1996. *Crosstalk: Citizens, Candidates and the Media in a Presidential Campaign.* Chicago: University of Chicago Press.

Just, Marion, Rosalind Levine and Kathleen Regan. 2001. "News for Sale: Half of Stations Report Sponsor Pressure on News Decision." *Columbia Journalism Review-Project for Excellence in Journalism* November/December.

Kahn, Kim F. and Patrick J. Kenney. 1999. *The Spectacle of U.S. Senate Campaign.* Chicago: University of Chicago Press.

Kahn, Kim Fridkin and Patrick J. Kenney. 1999. Do Negative Campaigns Mobilize or Suppress Turnout? Clarifying the Relationship between Negativity and Participation. *American Political Science Review* 93: 877.

Kahn, Kim Fridkin and Patrick J. Kenny. 2002. The Slant of News: How Editorial Endorsements Influence Campaign Coverage and Citizens' Views of Candidates. *American Political Science Review* 96.

Kaid, L. L., et al. 1993. Television News and Presidential Campaigns: The Legitimation of Televised Political Advertising. *Social Science Quarterly* 74.

Kaplan, Martin. 2004. Testimony. FCC Broadcast Localism Hearing. Monterey, CA. 21 July, www.localnewsarchive.org.

Karol, David. "Realignment without Replacement: Issue Evolution and Ideological Change Among Members of Congress." *Midwest Political Science Association,* Chicago, IL, April 1999.

Karr, Albert. 1996. "Television News Tunes Out Airwaves Auction Battle." *Wall Street Journal,* 1 May, p. B1.

Katz, J. 1990. "Memo to Local News Directors." *Columbia Journalism Review* May/June: 40-45.

Kern, M. 1988. 30 Second Politics: Political Advertising in the Eighties. New York: Praeger.

Ketterer, Stan, Tom Weir, J. Stevens Smethers and James Back. 2004. Case Study Shows Limited Benefits of Convergence. *Newspaper Research Journal* 25, Summer.

Keyssar, Alexander. 2000. *The Right to Vote.* New York: Basic Books.

Kilgard, Susan. 1999. "Identification and Formal Organizational Communication: Exploring Links Between Messages and Membership." Ph.D. dissertation, Arizona State University.

Kim, Sei-Hill, Dietram A. Scheufele and James Shanahan. 2002. Think About It This Way: Attribute Agenda Setting Function of the Press and the Public's Evaluation of a Local Issue. *Journalism and Mass Communications Quarterly* 79.

Klieman, Howard. 1991. "Content Diversity and the FCC's Minority and Gender Licensing Policies." *Journal of Broadcasting and Electronic Media.*

Knoke, David. 1990. "Networks of Political Action: Toward Theory Construction." *Social Forces 68.*

Knoke, David. 1990. Organizing for Collective Action: The Political Economies of Associations. New York: Aldine de Gruyter.

Koch, Adrienne and William Peden. 1944. (eds.), *The Life and Selected Writings of Thomas Jefferson.* New York: Modern Library.

Koford, Kenneth. 1989. "Dimensions in Congressional Voting." *American Political Science Review 83.*

Kohut, Andrew, et. al. 2006. "Maturing Internet New Audience – Broader than Deep." The Pew Research Center for the People & the Press, 20 July.

Kovach, Bill and Tom Rosenstiel. 1999. *Warp Speed: America in the Age of Mixed Media.* New York: The Century Foundation Press.

Krosnick, J. A. and D. R. Kinder. 1990. Altering the Foundation of Support for the President Through Priming. *American Political Science Review* 84.

Krotoszynski, Ronald J., Jr. and A. Richard M. Blaiklock, 2000. Enhancing the Spectrum: Media Power, Democracy, and the Marketplace of Ideas. *University of Illinois Law Review.*

Krugman, Paul. 2002. "In Media Res." *New York Times,* 29 November, p. A39.

Kunkel, Thomas and Gene Roberts. 2001. "The Age of Corporate Newspapering, Leaving Readers Behind." *American Journalism Review* May.

Kurtz, Howard. 2006. "Tribune Co. Ousts Publisher at L.A. Times: Jeffrey Johnson Had Fought Budget Cuts." *Washington Post,* 6 October.

Lacy Stephen and Hugh J. Martin. 2004. Competition, Circulation and Advertising. *Newspaper Research Journal* 25, Winter.

Lacy, Stephan and Hugh J. Martin. 1998. Profits Up, Circulation Down for Thomson Papers in the 80s. *Newspaper Research Journal* 19, Fall.

Lacy, Stephen and Todd F. Simon. 1993. "Competition in the Newspaper Industry." in Stephen Lacy and Todd F. Simon (eds.), *The Economics and Regulation of United States Newspapers*. Norwood, NJ: Ablex.

Lacy, Stephen, David C. Coulson and Hugh J. Martin. 2004. Ownership Barriers to Entry in Non-metropolitan Daily Newspaper Markets. *Journalism & Mass Communications Quarterly* 81, Summer.

Lacy, Stephen, Mary Alice Shaver and Charles St. Cyr. 1996. The Effects of Public Ownership and Newspaper Competition on the Financial Performance of Newspaper Corporation: A Replication and Extension. *Journalism and Mass Communications Quarterly* Summer.

Lacy, Stephen. 1989. "A Model of Demand for News: Impact of Competition on Newspaper Content." *Journalism Quarterly* 66.

Lacy, Stephen. 1992. "The Financial Commitment Approaches to News Media Competition." *Journal of Media Economics* 5:2: 5-21.

Lauzen, Martha M. and David Dozier. 1999. Making a Difference in Prime Time: Women on Screen and Behind the Scenes in 1995-1996 Television Season. *Journal of Broadcasting and Electronic Media* Winter.

Layton, Charles and Jennifer Dorroh. 2002. Sad State. *American Journalism Review* June.

Layton, Charles, 1999. "What do Readers Really Want?" *American Journalism Review* March. reprinted in Gene Roberts and Thomas Kunkel, *Breach of Faith: A Crisis of Coverage in the Age of Corporate Newspapering*. Fayetteville: University of Arkansas Press, 2002.

Lazaroff, Leon. 2004. "Media Firm Accused of Dodging FCC Rules." *Chicago Tribune* 16 Oct.

Lee, Chul-joo and Oscar H. Gandy. 2006.   Others' Disaster: How American Newspapers covered Hurricane Katrina (Methods, Results and Discussion). *Rethinking the Discourse on Race.* St. John's University School of Law, 28 April.

Lee, Tien-Tsung. 2005. "The Liberal Media Myth Revisited: An Examination of Factors Influencing Perception of Media Bias." *Journal of Broadcasting and Electronic Media* 49:1.

Legg Masson. 2004. "Sinclair Move Risks Backfiring by Complicating Company's (and Industry's) Deregulatory Agenda." *Telecom & Media Insider*. Washington, D.C. October 15.

Lemert, James B. William R. Elliott, and James M. Bernstein. 1991. *News Verdicts, the Debates, and Presidential Campaigns.* New York: Praeger.

Lenart, Silvo. 1994. Shaping Political Attitudes: The Impact of Interpersonal Communication and Mass Media. Thousand Oaks, CA: Sage.

Lenhart, Amanda and Susan Fox. 2006. "Bloggers: A Protrait of the Internet's New Storytellers." Washington, D.C.: Pew Internet & American Life Project, 19 July.

Lessig, Lawrence. 1999. *Code and Other Laws of Cyberspace.* New York: Basic Books.

Levin, Harvey J. 1971. "Program Duplication, Diversity, and Effective Viewer Choices: Some Empirical Findings." *American Economic Review* 61:2: 81-88.

Levine, Peter. 2002. "Can the Internet Rescue Democracy? Toward an On-Line Commons." In Ronald Hayuk and Kevin Mattson (eds.), *Democracy's Moment: Reforming the American Political System for the 21st Century.* Lanham, ME: Rowman and Littlefield, P. 124.

Levingston, Steven and Terence O'Hara. 2006. "McClatchy's Paper Chase: Family Owned Chain to By Knight, Plans to Sell off 12 Dailies." *Washington Post,* 14 March.

Levy, Leonard W. 1985. *Emergence of a Free Press.* New York: Oxford University Press.

Lipsitz, Keena, et al. 2005. What Voters Want From Political Campaign Communications. *Political Communications* 22.

Lohmann, Susanne. 1998. "An Information Rationale for the Power of Special Interests." *American Political Science Review* 92:4.

Lott, John R., and Kevin A. Hassett. 2004. *Is Newspaper Coverage of Economic Events Politically Biased?* Washington, D.C.: American Enterprise Institute.

Lowrey, Wilson. 2005. "Commitment to Newspaper-TV Partnering: A Test of the Impact of Institutional Isomorphism." *Journalism and Mass Communications Quarterly* 82: Autumn.

Luttmer, Erzo F. P. 2001. "Group Loyalty and the Taste for Redistribution." *Journal of Political Economy* 109.

Madde, Mary. 2003. "America's Online Pursuits." *Pew Internet and Life Project* December.

Maguire, Miles. 2003. "Wall Street Made Me Do It: A Preliminary Analysis of the Major Institutional Investors in U.S. Newspaper Companies." *Journal of Media Economics* 16:4.

Maguire, Miles. 2005. "Change in Ownership Affect Quality of Oshkosh Paper." *Newspaper Research Journal* 26: 4.

Mason, Laurie, Christine M. Bachen and Stephanie L. Craft. 2001. Support for FCC Minority Ownership Policy: How Broadcast Station Owner Race or Ethnicity Affects News and Public Affairs Programming Diversity. *Communication Law & Policy* 6.

McChesney, Robert W. and John Nichols. 2002. *Our Media, Not Theirs.* New York: Seven Stories.

McChesney, Robert. 2000. Rich Media, Poor Democracy: Communication Politics in Dubious Times. New York: New Press.

McChesney, Robert. 2004. *The Problem of the Media.* New York: Monthly Review Press.

McCombs, Maxwell E. and Donald Shaw. 1972. The Agenda-Setting Function of the Mass Media. *Public Opinion Quarterly* 36.

McConnell, Bill and Susanne Ault. 2001. "Fox TV's Strategy: Two by Two, Duopolies are Key to the Company's Goal of Becoming a Major Local Presence." *Broadcasting and Cable,* 30 July 2001

McConnell, Bill. 2001. "The National Acquirers: Whether Better for News or Fatter Profits, Media Companies Want in on TV/Newspaper Cross-Ownership." *Broadcasting and Cable,* 10 December.

McKean, M. L. and V. A. Stone. 1991. "Why Stations Don't Do News." *RTNDA Communicator,* June: 22-24.

Mcleaod, J. M., S. Sun, A. Chi, and Z. Pan. 1990. "Metaphor and Media." *Association for Education in Journalism,* August.

McLeod, Douglas M. 1995. "Communicating Deviance: The Effects of Television News Coverage of Social Protests." *Journal of Broadcasting & Electronic Media* 39.

McLeod, J. M., and L. B. Becker. 1974. "Testing the validity of gratification measures through political effects analysis." In J. G. Blumler and E. Katz (eds.), *The Uses of Mass Communications.* Beverly Hills, CA: Sage.

McLeod, Jack M., Dietram A. Scheufele, and Patricia Moy. 1999. Community, Communications, and Participation: The Role of Mass Media and Interpersonal Discussion in Local Political Participation. *Political Communication* 16.

McLeod, Jack M., Dietram A.Scheufele, and Patricia Moy. 1999. "Community, Communication, and Participation: The Role of Mass Media and Interpersonal Discussion in Local Political Participation." *Political Communication* 16:3: 315–36.

McManus, J. 1990. "Local News: Not a Pretty Picture." *Columbia Journalism Review* 28.

McManus, J. 1991. "How Objective is Local Television News?" *Mass Communications Review* 18:3:21-30.

McManus, J. H. 1992. "What Kind of a Commodity is News?" *Communications Research*, 19:6:787-805.

Meiklejohn, Alexander. 1960. *Political Freedom.* New York: Harpers.

Mendelberg, Tali. 1997. "Executing Hortons: Racial Crime in the 1988 Presidential Campaign." *Public Opinion Quarterly* 61.

Mendelberg, Tali. 2001. The Race Card: Campaign Strategy, Implicit Messages and the Norms of Equality. Princeton: Princeton University Press.

Meyer, Philip. 2004. "The Influence Model and Newspaper Business." *Newspaper Research Journal* 25, Winter.

Meyer, Thomas. 2002. *Media Democracy.* Cambridge: Polity Press.

Meyerowitz, J. 1985. No Sense of Place: The Effect of Electronic Media on Social Behavior. New York: Oxford.

Miller, Gary and Norman Schofield. 2003. Activists and Partisan Realignment in the United States. *American Political Science Review* 97:2.

Miller, J. M. and J. A. Krosnick. 1996. "News Media Impact on the Ingredients of Presidential Evaluations: A Program of Research on the Priming Hypothesis." In D.C. Mutz, P.M. Sniderman, and R.A. Brody. *Political Persuasion and Attitude Change.* Ann Arbor: University of Michigan Press.

Miller, Joanne and Jon A. Krosnick. 2000. News Media Impact on the Ingredients of Presidential Evaluations: Politically Knowledgeable Citizens are Guided by Trusted Sources. *American Journal of Political Science* 44:2.

Miller, M.M. and S.D. Reese. 1982. Media Dependency as Interaction: Effects of Exposure and Reliance on Political Activity and Efficacy. *Communications Research* 9.

Mills, C. Wright. 1956. *The Power Elite.* New York: Oxford University Press.

Mills, Kay. 2004. "Changing Channels: The Civil Rights Case That Transformed Television." *Prologue Magazine*, Vol. 36, No. 3, Fall.

Mitchell, Bill. 2000. "Media Collaborations." *Broadcasting and Cable*, 10 April.

Mixon, J. Wilson, Amit Sen, and E. Frank Stephenson. 2004. Are the Networks Baised? 'Calling States in the 2000 Presidential Election. *Public Choice* 118.

Moore, D.W. 1984. "The Death of Politics in New Hampshire." *Public Opinion* 7.

Morton, John. 1995. "When Newspapers Eat their Seed Corn." *American Journalism Review* November.

Moses, Lucia. 2003. "Profiting From Experience." *Editor and Publisher*, 3 February.

Moses, Lucia. 2003. "Radio Reception May Be Fading." *Editor and Publisher*, 23 June.

Moses, Lucia. 2000. "TV or not TV? Few Newspapers are Camera Shy, But Sometimes Two Into One Just Doesn't Go." *Editor and Publisher*, 21 August.

Moy Patricia, Marcos Torres, Keiko Tanaka, and Michael R. McCluskey. 2005. Knowledge or Trust? Investigating Linkages between Media Reliance and Participation. *Communications Research* 32:1.

Moy, Patricia, Michael Pfau, and LeeAnn Kahlor. 1999. Media Use and Public Confidence in Democratic Institutions. *Journal of Broadcasting & Electronic Media* 43.

MPAA. 2005, *Theatrical Market Statistical Repor.*

Mulder, R. 1979. "The Effects of Televised Political Ads in the 1995 Chicago Mayoral Election." *Journalism Quarterly* 56.

Mullainathan, Sendhil and Andrei Shleifer. 2004. The Market for News. *American Economic Review* 95.

Murphy, Kevin M. and Andrei Shleifer. 2004. Persuasion in Politics. *American Economic Review* 94.

Mutz, Diana C. 2002. "Cross-Cutting Social Networks: Testing Democratic Theory in Practice." American *Political Science Review* 96.

Napoli, P. M. and M.Z. Yan. (forthcoming). "Media Ownership Regulations and Local News Programming on Television: An empirical analysis." *Journal of Broadcasting and Electronic Media.*

Napoli, P.M. 2004. "Television station ownership characteristics and local news and public affairs programming: An expanded analysis of FCC data." *The Journal of Policy, Regulation, and Strategy for Telecommunications, Information, and Media* 6:2: 112-121.

Napoli, Philip. 2002. "Audience Valuation and Minority Media: An Analysis of the Determinants of the Value of Radio Audiences." *Journal of Broadcasting and Electronic Media* 46.

Napoli, Philip. 2004. "Television Station Ownership and Local News and Public Affairs Programming: An Expanded Analysis of FCC Data." Paper presented at *Annual Meeting of International Communication Association,* May.

National Broadcasting Co., Inc. et al. v. United States, et. al., 319 U.S. 190 (1943) 70.

National Telecommunications and Information Administration. 2006. Letter from NTIA to Ms. Veronica Villafane, President, National Association of Hispanic Journalists, April 27. Available at http://www.nahj.org/nahjnews/articles/2006/april/NTIAResponseLetter.pdf.

Neiman Reports. 1999. The Business of News, the News About Business, Summer.

Nerone, John. 1989. *The Culture of the Press in the Early Republic.* New York: Garland Publishing.

Nerone, John. 1994. Violence against the Press: Policing the Public Sphere in US History. New York: Oxford University Press.

Network Affiliated Stations Alliance. 2001. "Petition for Inquiry into Network Practices" *Federal Communications Commission,* 8 March.

Neven, Damien and Jacques-Francois Thisse. 1990. "On Quality and Variety Competition." In Jean J. Gabszewicz, Jean Francois Richard and Laurence Wolsey (eds.), *Economic Decision Making: Games, Econometrics, and Optimization. Contributions in the Honour of Jacques H. Dreze.* Amsterdam: North-Holland.

Newton, Kenneth. 1999. "Mass Media Effects: Mobilization or Media Malaise." *British Journal of Political Science* 29.

Nielsen Media Research. 2002. "Consumer Survey On Media Usage." *Media Ownership Working Group Study* No. 8, September.

Nienhuis, Annet E., Antony Manstead and Russell Spears. 2001. Multiple Motives and Persuasive Communication: Creative Elaboration as a Result of Impression Motivation and Accuracy Motivation. *Personality and Social Psychology Bulletin* 27.

Niven, David. 2004. "The Mobilization Solution? Face-to-Face Contact and Voter Turnout in a Municipal Election." *The Journal of Politics* 66.

Norton, Michael I. and George R. Goethais. 2004. Spin (and Pitch) Doctors: Campaign Strategies in Televised Debates. *Political Behavior* 26:3.

Notice of Inquiry. 2004. *In the Matter of Broadcast Localism,* MB Docket No. 04-233, 1 July, para. 9.

O'Keefe, G. J. 1980. "Political Malaise and Reliance on the Media." *Journalism Quarterly* 57:1: 133-128.

O'Sullivan, Patrick B. 2000.   The Nexus Between Broadcast Licensing Gender Preferences and Programming Diversity: What Does the Social Scientific Evidence Say? Santa Barbara: Department of Communication, U.C. Santa Barbara, CA.

Oberholzer-Gee, Felix and Joel Waldfogel. 2000. "Tiebout Acceleration: Political Participation in Heterogeneous Jurisdictions." *University of Pennsylvania,* August.

Oberholzer-Gee, Felix and Joel Waldfogel. 2001. Electoral Acceleration: The Effect of Minority Population on Minority Voter Turnout. *NBER Working Paper 8252.* Cambridge, MA: National Bureau of Economic Research.

Ofori, K. A. 1999. "When Being No. 1 is not Enough: The Impact of Advertising Practices on Minority-Owned and Minority-Targeted Broadcast Stations." *Civil Rights Forum on Communications Policy,* Washington D.C.

Oliver, Eric J. and Janelle Wong. 2003. Intergroup Prejudice in Multiethnic Settings. *American Journal of Political Science 47.*

Olson, Kathryn. 1994. "Exploiting the Tension between the New Media's "Objective" and Adversarial Roles: The Role Imbalance Attach and its Use of the Implied Audience." *Communications Quarterly* 42:1.

Overholser, Geneva. 2004. "Good Journalism and Business: An Industry Perspective." *Newspaper Research Journal* 25, Winter.

Owen, Bruce and Steven Wildman. 1992. *Video Economics.* Cambridge: Harvard University Press.

Owen, Bruce M. and Michael G. Baumann, "Economic Study E, Concentration Among National Purchasers of Video Entertainment Programming,"2002. *Comments of Fox Entertainment Group and Fox Television Stations, Inc., National Broadcasting Company, Inc. and Telemundo Group, Inc., and Viacom, In the Matter of 2002 Biennial Regulatory Review – Review of the Commission's Broadcast Ownership Rules and Other Rules Adopted Pursuant to Section 202 of the Telecommunications Act of 1996, Cross Ownership of Broadcast Stations and Newspapers, Rules and Policies Concerning Multiple Ownership of Radio Broadcast Stations in Local Markets, Definition of Radio Markets,* MB Docket No. 02-277, MM Dockets 02-235, 01-317, 00-244, January 2.

Page, Benjamin I. 1996. *Who Deliberates.* Chicago: University of Chicago Press.

Paletz, D. L. and R. M. Entmen. 1981. *Media, Power, Politics.* New York: Free Press.

Paletz, David L. 1999. The Media in American Politics: Contents and Consequences. New York: Longman.

Pan, Z. and G. M. Kosicki. 1997. Priming and Media Impact on the Evaluation the President's Performance. *Communications Research* 24.

Pasley, Jeffrey L. 2001. The Tyranny of Printers: Newspaper Politics in the Early American Republic. Charlottesville: University Press of Virginia.

Patterson, T. E., and McClure, R. D. 1976. The Unseeing Eye: The Myth of Television Power in National Politics. New York: Putnam Books.

Peffley, Mark, Todd Shields and Bruce Williams. 1996. The Intersection of Race and Television. *Political Communications* 13.

Peltier, Stephanie. 2004. "Mergers and Acquisitions in the Media Industries: Were Failures Predictable." *Journal of Media Economics* 17:4.

Perry, Martin, 1989. "Vertical Integration: Determinants and Effects." in Richard Schmalensee and Robert D. Willig (Eds.) *Handbook of Industrial Organization*. New York: North-Holland.

Petty, Richard E., Thomas M. Ostrom and Timothy C. Brock. 1981. (eds.), *Cognitive Responses in Persuasion*. Hillside, NJ: Erlbaum.

Pew Internet and American Life Project. 2005. RDD Tracking Study, Nov/Dec.

Pew Research Center For The People & The Press. 2003. "Cable and Internet Loom Large in Fragmented Political News Universe." *Pew Research Center*. 11 January.

Pew Research Center Survey. 2004. "Perception of Partisan Bias Seen as Growing— Especially by Democrats." 11 Jan. Available from http://people-press.org/reports/display.php3?ReportID=200.

Pfau, M. 1990. "A Channel Approach to Television Influence." *Journal of Broadcasting and Electronic Media* 34: 17-36.

Pfau, M. and H. C. Kenski. 1990. *Attack Politics*. New York: Praeger.

Philip. 2004. "The Influence Model and Newspaper Business." *Newspaper Research Journal* 25, Winter.

Phillips, Peter and Project Censored. 2003. *Censored 2003*. New York: Seven Stories.

Platow, Michael, Duncan Mills and Dianne Morrison. 2000. The Effects of Social Context, Source Fairness and Perceived Self-Source Similarity on Social Influence: A Self- Characterization Analysis. *European Journal of Social Psychology 30*.

Postman, Neil. 1985. Amusing Ourselves to Death: Public Discourse in the Age of Show Business. New York: Penguin Press.

Price, Monroe E. 1999. "Public Broadcasting and the Crisis of Corporate Governance." *Cardozo Arts & Entertainment* 17.

Pritchard, David. 2002. "Viewpoint Diversity in Cross-Owned Newspapers and Television Stations: A Study of News Coverage of the 2000 Presidential Campaign." *Federal Communications Commission*, September.

Project for Excellence in Journalism. 2003. Economists Inc's "Critique of the Recent Study on Media Ownership" A Response by the Project for Excellence in Journalism, March 18, p.1.

Project on Excellence in Journalism. 2006. "Local TV." *The State of the News Media: 2005*.

Project on Excellence in Journalism. 2006. "Overview." *The State of the News Media: 2005*.

Project on Excellence in Journalism. 2000. "The Last Lap: How the Press Covered the Final Stages of the Campaign." *PEJ*, 31 October.

Prometheus Radio Project, et al. v. F.C.C., 373 F.3d 372 (2004), *stay modified on rehearing*, No. 03-3388 (3d Cir. Sept. 3, 2004), *cert. denied*, 73 U.S.L.W. 3466 (U.S. June 13, 2005).

Puglisi, Ricardo. 2006. "Being the New York Times." Political Economy and Public Policy Series Suntory Centre April

Putnam, Robert D. 1993. *Making Democracy Work: Civic Traditions in Modern Italy*. Princeton: Princeton University Press.

Quincy Illinois Visitors Guide, 2001 edition.

Rabasca, Lisa. 2001. "Benefits, Costs and Convergence." *Presstime* June, p. 3.

Radio-Television News Directors Foundation. 2006. *2006 Future of News Survey*. September.

Ray, W. B. 1990. *FCC: The Ups and Downs of Radio-TV Regulation*. Iowa: Iowa State University Press.

Reams, Margaret, and Ray, Brooks. 1993. The effects of three prompting methods on recycling participation rates: a field study. *Journal of Environmental Systems* 22: 371-379.

Red Lion Broadcasting v. FCC, 395 US 367 (1969).

Redlawsk, David P. 2004. "What Voters Do: Information Search During Election Campaigns." *Political Psychology* 25:4.

Riffe, Dan. 2006. "Frequent Media Users See High Environmental Risks." *Newspaper Research Journal* 27: 1.

Rifkin, Jeremy. 2000. *The Age of Access*. New York: Jeremy P. Tarcher/Putnam.

Roberts, Gene, Thomas Kunkel, and Charles Clayton. 2001. "Leaving Readers Behind." In Roberts, Gene, Thomas Kunkel, and Charles Clayton (eds.), *Leaving Readers Behind*. Fayetteville: University of Arkansas Press.

Roberts, Gene. 1996. "Corporatism vs. Journalism." *The Press-Enterprise Lecture Series* 31, 12 February.

Robins, J. Max. 2005. "News Investment Pays Off." *Broadcasting and Cable*, 12 September.

Robinson, J. P. and D. K. Davis. 1990. Television News and the Informed Public: An Information Process Approach. *Journal of Communication* 40:3: 106-119.

Robinson, John P. and Mark R. Levy. 1996. New Media Use and the Informed Public: A 1990s Update. *Journal of Communications* Spring.

Rogers, Richard. 2004. *Information Politics on the Web*. Cambridge: MIT Press.

Romano, Allison. 2005. "Bring it Online." *Broadcasting and Cable*, 12 December.

Romano, Allison. 2005. "Newspapers and Stations try Cross-Pollination." *Broadcasting and Cable*, 25 July.

Romano, Allison. 2005. "Bring it Online." *Broadcasting and Cable*, 12 December.

Romano, Allison. 2006. "Late News Get Earlier." *Broadcasting and Cable*, 12 June.

Romano, Allison. 2006. "Media General Wraps Sales."*Broadcasting and Cable*, 1 August.

Romano, Allison. 2005. "Sinclair Rethinks News Mission." *Broadcasting and Cable*, 20 March, p. 16.

Romer, Daniel, Kathleen Hall Jamieson, and Sean Aday. 2003. Television News and the Cultivation of Fear of Crime. *Journal of Communications* March.

Rosensteil, Tom and Amy Mitchell. 2004. The Impact of Investing in Newsroom Resources. *Newspaper Research Journal* 25, Winter.

Rosenthal, Phil. 2006. "Singleton Sold on Newspapers." *Chicago Tribune*, 21 June.

Rowse, Arthur E. 2000. *Drive-By Journalism*. Monroe, ME: Common Courage Press.

Rowse, Edward. 1975. Slanted News: A Case Study of the Nixon and Stevenson Fund Stories. Boston: Beacon.

Rubinovitz, R. 1991. "Market Power and Price Increases for Basic Cable Service Since Deregulation." *Economic Analysis Regulatory Group, Department of Justice*, 6 August.

Saba, Jennifer. 2006. "It's Official: McClatchy Sells 5 KR Papers – to 4 Companies." *Editor & Publisher*, 7 June.

Saunders, Kyle L. and Alan I. Abramovits. 2004. Ideological Realignment and Active Partisans in the American Electorate. *American Politics Research* 32:3.

Scherer, F. Michael and David Ross. 1990. *Industrial Market Structure and Economic Performance*. New York: Houghton Mifflin Company.

Scheufele, Dietram A. 2000. "Agenda-setting, Priming and Framing Revisited: Another Look at Cognitive Effects of Political Communications." *Mass Communications & Society* 3.

Scheufele, Dietram A., et al. 2004. Social Structure and Citizenship: Examining the Impacts of Social Setting, Network Heterogeneity, and Informational Variables on Political Participation. *Political Communication* 21.

Scheufele, Dietram A., Matthew C. Nisbet and Dominique Brossard. 2003. "Pathways to Participation? Religion, Communication Contexts and Mass Media." *International Journal of Public Opinion Research* 15.

Scheufele, Dietram A., Matthew C. Nisbet, Dominique Brossard, and Erik C. Nisbet. 2004. "Social Structure and Citizenship: Examining the Impact of Social Setting, Network Heterogeity, and Informational Variables on Political Participation." *Political Communications* 21.

Schmelzer, Paul. 2003. "The Death of Local News." *Alternet*, 23 April.

Schneider, Michael. 1999. "Tribune to Acquire Qwest, Creating Big Easy Duopoly." *Daily Variety*, 10 November.

Schudson, Michael. 1998. The Good Citizen: A History of American Civic Life. New York: Free Press.

Schultz, Don E. and Beth E. Barnes. 1995. *Strategic Advertising Campaigns*. Lincolnwood, IL: NTC Business Books.

Schurz Communications Inc. v. FCC 982 F. 2d 1043 (7th Cir. 1992).

Scott, Ben. 2004. "The Politics and Policy of Media Ownership." *American University Law Review* Vol. 53: 3, February.

Scott, Ester. 2003. "Al Gore and the "Embellishment" Issue: Press Coverage of the Gore Presidential Campaign." Kennedy School of Government Case Program c15-02-1679.0, October.

Seelye, Katherine Q. and Jennifer Steinhaur. 2006. "At Los Angeles Times, A Civil Executive Rebellion." *The New York Times*, 21 September, p. C12.

Sengupta, Jaideep and Gavan J. Fitzsimmons 2000. The Effects of Analyzing Reasons for Brand Preferences: Disruption or Reinforcement. *Journal of Marketing Research* 37.

Shepherd, William G. 1985. *The Economics of Industrial Organization*. Englewood Cliffs, NJ: Prentice Hall.

Shiffer, Adam, J. 2006. "Assesing Partisan Bias in Political News: The Case(s) of Local Senate Election Coverage." *Political Communications* 23.

Shiller, Robert J. 2003. "From Efficient Markets Theory to Behavioral Finance." *Journal of Economic Perspectives* 17:1.

Siegelman, Peter, Joel Waldfogel. 2001. "Race and Radio: Preference Externalities, Minority Ownership and the Provision of Programming to Minorities." *Advances in Applied Microeconomics* 10.

Siklos, Richard and Katharine Q. Seelye. 2006. "Fitfully Blending Papers and TV." *New York Times,* 19 June.

Siklos, Richard and Katherine Q. Seelye. 2006. "At Tribune a Call for a Split." *New York Times,* 15 June.

Siklos, Richard. 2005. "How Did Newspapers Land in This Mess?" *New York Times,* 1 October, p. BU4.

Simon, J., W. J. Primeaux and E. Rice. 1986. "The Price Effects of Monopoly Ownership in Newspapers." *Antitrust Bulletin* Spring.

Sinclair Broadcasting, Inc. v. FCC, 284 F.3d 148 (D.C. Circ. 2002)

Sinclair, Jon R. 1995. "Reforming Television's Role in American Political Campaigns: Rationale for the Elimination of Paid Political Advertisements." *Communications and the Law* March.

Singer, Jane B. 2004. "Strange Bedfellows: The Diffusion of Convergence in Four News Organizations." *Journalism Studies* 5:1.

Sirianni, Carmen and Friedland, Lewis. 2001. Civic Innovation in America: Community Empowerment, Public Policy, and the Movement for Civic Renewal. Berkeley: University of California Press.

Slattery, K. L. and E. A. Hakanen. 1994. Sensationalism Versus Public Affairs Content of Local TV News: Pennsylvania Revisited. *Journal of Broadcasting and Electronic Media* 38:2: 205-216.

Slattery, Karen L., Ernest A. Hakanen and Mark Doremus. 1996. The Expression of Localism: Local TV News Coverage in the New Video Marketplace. *Journal of Broadcasting and Electronic Media* 40.

Smith, Culver. 1977. The press, politics, and patronage: the American government's use of newspapers, 1789-1875. Athens: University of Georgia Press.

Smolkin, Rachel. 2006. "Adapt or Die." *American Journalism Review* June/July.

Snider, James H., and Benjamin I. Page. 1997. "Does Media Ownership Affect Media Stands? The Case of the Telecommunications Act of 1996." Paper delivered at the *Annual Meeting of the Midwest Political Science Association,* April.

Soloski, John. 2005. "Taking Stock Redux: Corporate Ownership and Journalism of Publicly Traded Newspaper Companies." In Robert Picard (eds.), *Corporate Governance of Media Companies* Jonkoping, Sweden: Jonkoping International Business Press.

Soloski, John. 1979. "Economics and Management: The Real Influence of Newspaper Groups." *Newspaper Research Journal* 1.

Sorkin, Andrew Ross. 2006. "Univision Considering Better Bid." *New York Times,* 27 June.

Sotirovic and Jack M. McLeod. 2004. "Knowledge as Understanding: The Information Processing Approach to Political Learning." in Lynda L. Kaid (eds.), *Handbook of Political Communications Research.* Mahwah: NJ, Erlbaum.

Sotirovic, Mira. 2003. "How Individual Explain Social Problems The Influences of Media Use." *Journal of Communications* March.

Sparks, Glenn G., Marianne Pellechia, and Chris Irvine. 1998. Does Television News About UFOs Affect Viewers' UFO Beliefs?: An Experimental Investigation. *Communication Quarterly* 46.

Sparrow, Bartholomew H. 1999. *Uncertain Guardians: The News Media as A Political Institution*. Baltimore: Johns Hopkins University Press.

Spavins, T.C., L. Denison, S. Roberts, J. Frenette. 2002. The Measurement of Local Television News and Public Affairs Programs. Washington, DC: Federal Communications Commission.

St. Cyr, Charles, Stephen Lacy and Susana Guzman-Ortega. 2005. Circulation Increases Follow Investment in Newsrooms. *Newspaper Research Journal* 26, Fall.

Stamm, K., M Johnson and B. Martin. 1997. Differences Among Newspapers, Television and Radio in their Contribution to Knowledge of the Contract with America. *Journalism and Mass Communications Quarterly* 74.

Staples, Brent. 2003. The Trouble with Corporate Radio: The Day the Protest Music Died. *The New York Times*, 20 February, pA30.

Stavitsky, A. G. 1994. "The Changing Conception of Localism in U.S. Public Radio." *Journal of Broadcasting and Electronic Media* 38:1: 19-33.

Steiner, Peter O. 1952. "Program Patterns and the Workability of Competition in Radio Broadcasting." *Quarterly Journal of Economics* 66.

Stepp, Carl Sessions. 2001. "Whatever Happened to Competition." *American Journalism Review* June.

Stern, Paul G. 1990. "A Pluralistic Reading of the First Amendment and Its Relation to Public Discourse." *Yale Law Journal* 99:4.

Stone, V. A. 1987. "Deregulation Felt Mainly in Large-Market Radio and Independent TV." *RTNDA Communicator*, April, p. 12.

Stone, V. A. 1988. "New Staffs Change Little in Radio, Take Cuts in Major Market. TV." *RTNDA Communicator*, March, p.30-32.

Street, John. *Mass Media, Politics and Democracy*. New York: Palgrave, 2001.

Stromberg, David. 2004. "Mass Media Competition, Political Competition and Public Policy," *Review of Economic Studies*, 71.

Strupp, Joe. 2000. "Three Point Play." *Editor and Publisher*, 21 August.

Sullivan, Lawrence and Warren S. Grimes2000. *The Law of Antitrust: An Integrated Handbook*, Hornbook Series. West Group, St. Paul.

Sunstein, Cass. 1999. "Television and the Public Interest." *California Law Review* 8.

Sunstein, Cass. 2001. *Republic.com*. Princeton: Princeton University Press.

Tabuchi, Takatoshi. 1994. "Two-Stage Two-Dimensional Spatial Competition Between Two Firms." *Regional Science and Urban Economics* 24.

Tedesco, John, C. 2005. "Issue and Strategy Agenda Setting in the 2004 Presidential Election: Exploring the Candidate-Journalist Relationship." *Journalism Studies* 6:2: 187-201.

Telecommunications Act of 1996, Pub. L. No. 104-104, 110 Stat. 56 (1996).

Terchek, Ronald J. and Thomas C. Conte. 2001. (eds.), *Theories of Democracy*. Lanham, MD: Rowan & Littlefield.

Thompson, Anne, "Independent Producers and Distributors," *Hollywood Reporter*, August 1, 2006,

Time Warner Entertainment Co., L.P. v. FCC, 240 F.3d 1126 (2001)

Tompkins, Al and Aly Colon. 2000. "NAB 200: The Convergence Marketplace." *Broadcasting and Cable*, 10 April.

Trigoboff, Dan. 2001. "Chri-Craft, Fox Moves In: The Duopoly Marriage in Three Markets Comes with Some Consolidation." *Broadcasting and Cable*, 6 August.

Trigoboff, Dan. 2002. "Rios Heads KCOP News." *Broadcasting and Cable*, 14 October.

Tsfati, Yariv and Joseph N. Cappella. 2005. Why Do People Watch News They Do Not Trust? The Need for Cognition as a Moderator in the Association between New Media Skepticism and Exposure. *Media Psychology* 7.

Turner Broadcasting System, Inc. v. FCC, 512 U.S. 622, 638-39 (1994)

U.S. Census Bureau, Population Division. "Historical Census Statistics on Population Totals by Race, 1790 to 1990." and "Hispanic Origin, 1970 to 1990, for the United States, Regions, Divisions, and States." *Working Paper No. 56* for 1970, *Database* for 2003.

U.S. Census Bureau. 2002. *Statistical Abstract of the United States: 2002.* Washington, D.C.: U.S. Department of Commerce, Tables 414-416, 453.

U.S. Census Bureau. 2005. *Economic Census*, data collected in 2002.

U.S. Department of Justice and the Federal Trade Commission. 1997. Horizontal Merger Guidelines.

Valentino, Nicholas A. 1999. "Crime News and the Priming of Racial Attitudes During the Evaluation of the President." *Public Opinion Quarterly* 63.

Valentino, Nicholas A., Vincent L. Hutchings and Ismail K. White. 2002. Cues that Matter: How Political Ads Prime Racial Issues During Campaigns. *American Political Science Review* 96.

Vane, Sharyn. 2002. "Taking Care of Business." *American Journalism Review* March.

Verba, Sidney, Lehman Schlozman and Henry Brady. 1995. *Voice and Equality: Civic Volunteerism in American Politics.* Cambridge: Harvard University Press.

Viscusi, W. Kip, John M. Vernon, and H\Joseph E. Harrington, Jr. 2001. *Economics of Regulation and Antitrust.* Cambridge: MIT Press.

Voakes, Paul S., Jack Kapfer, David Kurpius, and David Shano-yeon Chern. 1996. Diversity in the News: A Conceptual and Methodological Framework. *Journalism and Mass Communications Quarterly* Autumn.

Vogel, Harold. 2004. Entertainment Industry Economics: A Guide for Financial Analysis, 6th Edition. Cambridge: Cambridge University Press.

von Hoffman, Nicholas. 2005. "Anybody Want to Buy a Newspaper?" *The Nation*, 2 December.

Waldfogel, Joel and Lisa George. 2000. "Who Benefits Whom in Daily Newspaper Market." *NBER Working Paper 7994*. Cambridge: National Bureau of Economic Research.

Waldfogel, Joel. 2001. "Comments on Consolidation and Localism." *Federal Communications Commission, Roundtable on Media Ownership*, 29 October.

Waldfogel, Joel. 1999. "Preference Externalities: An Empirical Study of Who Benefits Whom in Differentiated Product Markets." *NBER Working Paper 7391* Cambridge: National Bureau of Economic Research.

Waldfogel, Joel. 2001. *Who Benefits Whom in Local Television Markets?* Philadelphia: The Wharton School, November.

Walgrave, Stefann and Peter Van Aelst. 2006. The Contingency of the Mass Media's Political Agenda Setting Power: Toward a Preliminary Theory. *Journal of Communications* 56.

Wall Street Journal. 2004. "Sinclair and a Double Standard." October 13.

Wall Street Journal. 2006. "Local TV Stations Struggle to Adapt as Web Grabs Viewers, Revenue." 12 June.

Walma, Julliete H., Tom H. A. Van Der Voort. 2001. The Impact of Television, Print, and Audio on Children's Recall of the News. *Human Communication Research* 26.

Walton, Mary and Charles Layton. 2002. "Missing the Story at the Statehouse." in Roberts, Gene and Thomas Kunkel (eds.), *Breach of Faith: A Crisis of Coverage in the Age of Corporate Newspapering.* Fayetteville: University of Arkansas Press.

Wanta, Wayne and Thomas J. Johnson. 1994. "Content Changes in the St. Louis Post-Dispatch During Different Market Situations." *Journal of Media Economics* 7.

Ward, Mark. 2006. "Apple Video Divides Industry," *BBC News,* September 13.

Wat W. 1996. "The Supreme Court Defines the Forum for Democratic Discourse." *Journalism and Mass Communications Quarterly* Spring.

Waterman, David. 2005. *Hollywood's Road to Riches.* Cambridge: Harvard University Press.

Weaver, David and Dan Drew. 1995. Voter Learning in the 1992 Presidential Election: Did the 'Nontraditional' Media and Debates Matter? *Journalism & Mass Communication Quarterly* 72, Spring.

Webster, James G. and Patricia F. Phalen. 1997. *The Mass Audience: Rediscovering the Dominant Model.* New Jersey: Erlbaum.

Weiss, R. F. and B. Pasamanick. 1964. "Number of Exposures To Persuasive Communication in The Instrumental Conditioning of Attitudes." *Journal of Social Psychology, 63.*

West, Darell M., and Burdett A. Loomis. 1998. *The Sound of Money: How Political Interests Get What They Want.* New York: W. W. Norton.

Wilde Anne Mathews. 2002. "A Giant Radio Chain is Perfecting the Art of Seeming Local." *Wall Street Journal,* 25 February.

Wildman, Steven and Theomary Karamanis. 1998. "The Economics of Minority Programming." In Amy Garner (eds.), *Investing in Diversity: Advancing Opportunities for Minorities in Media.* Washington: Aspen Institute.

Wildman, Steven. 1994. "One-way Flows and the Economics of Audience Making." in James Entema and D. Charles Whitney (eds.), *Audiencemaking: How the Media Create the Audience.* Thousand Oaks, CA: Sage Publications.

Wilkins, Karin Gwinn. 2000. "The Role of Media in Public Disengagement from Political Life." *Journal of Broadcasting & Electronic Media* 44.

Williams, Vanessa. 2000. "Black and White and Red All Over: The Ongoing Struggle to Integrate America's Newsrooms." in William Serrin (eds.), *The Business of Journalism.* New York: New York Press.

Wimmer, K. A. 1988. "Deregulation and the Future of Pluralism in the Mass Media: The Prospects for Positive Policy Reform." *Mass Communications Review.*

Wirth, M. O. 1984. "The Effects of Market Structure on Television News Pricing." *Journal of Broadcasting* 28: 215-24.

Wright, Stephen C., Donald M. Taylor and Fathali M. Moghaddam. 1990. Responding to Membership in a Disadvantaged Group: From Acceptance to Collective Protest. *Journal of Personality and Social Psychology 58.*

Writers Guild of America. 2002. *Comments of the Writers Guild of America Regarding Harmful Vertical and Horizontal Integration in the Television Industry, Appendix A. Federal Communications Commission, In the Matter of Implementation of Section 11 of the Cable Television Consumer Protection and Competition Act of 1992; Implementation of Cable Act Reform Provisions of the Telecommunications Act of 1996 The Commission's Cable Horizontal and Vertical Ownership Limits and Attribution Rules Review of the Commission's Regulations Governing Attribution Of Broadcast and Cable/MDS Interests Review of the Commission's Regulations and Policies Affecting Investment In the Broadcast Industry, Reexamination of the Commission's Cross-Interest Policy,* CS Docket No. 98-82, CS Docket No. 96-85, MM Docket No. 92-264, MM Docket No. 94-150, MM Docket No. 92-51, MM Docket No. 87-154, January 4.

Yan, M. Z. and P. M. Napoli. *(forthcoming).* "Market Structure, Station Ownership, and Local Public Affairs Programming on Broadcast Television." *Journal of Communication.*

Yan, M. Z. and Y. J. Park. 2005. "Duopoly Ownership and Local Informational Programming on Television: An empirical analysis." Paper presented at the *Telecommunications Policy Research Conference:* Arlington, VA, September.

Yan, Michael and Philip Napoli. 2004. "Market Structure, Stations Ownership, and Local Public Affairs Programming on Local Broadcast Television." Paper presented at the *Telecommunications Policy Research Conference,* October.

Yan, Michael Zhaoxu. 2006. "Newspaper/Television Cross-Ownership and Local News and Public Affairs Programming on Television Stations: An Empirical Analysis", A report commissioned by the Donald McGannon Communication Research Center at Fordham University, under a grant from the Benton Foundation, October 3rd.

Zaller, J. 1996. "The Myth of Mass Media Impact Revived: New Support for a Discredited Idea." In D.C. Mutz, P.M. Sniderman, and R.A. Brody, *Political Persuasion and Attitude Change.* Ann Arbor: University of Michigan Press.

Zaller, J. R. 1998. *The Nature and Origins of Mass Opinion.* New York: Cambridge University Press.

Zaller, John. 2003. *A Theory of Media Politics.* Chicago: University of Chicago Press.

Zhao Xinshu and Steven Chaffee. 1995. Campaign Advertisements versus Television as Sources of Political Issue Information. *Public Opinion Quarterly* Spring 59.